WORD
BIBLICAL
COMMENTARY

WORD

BIBLICAL

COMMENTARY

Volume 22

Proverbs

ROLAND E. MURPHY

Publishers Since 1798

THOMAS NELSON PUBLISHERS

Nashville

Word Biblical Commentary
Proverbs
Copyright © 1998 by Thomas Nelson, Inc.

Library of Congress Cataloging-in-Publication Data
Main entry under title:

Word biblical commentary.

    Includes bibliographies.
    1. Bible—Commentaries—Collected works.
BS491.2.W67   22.2 ′7   81–71768
ISBN 0–8499–0221–5 (v. 22) AACR2

Printed in Colombia

The author's own translation of the Scripture text appears in italic type under the heading *Translation* **and as a unit at the beginning of the commentary.**

00 01 02 03 QPV 12 11 10 9 8 7 6 5 4 3

To the memory of
David Allan Hubbard,
scholar and friend,
President Emeritus of
Fuller Theological
Seminary

Contents

Author's Preface

   This commentary is in the tradition of the proverbial neglect of the book of Proverbs. The present writer did almost everything else with wisdom literature except write a commentary on this book. Then at the end of academic life, he has turned to this neglected work and written two interpretations—a short one (NIBCOT 12) and the present volume in the *Word Biblical Commentary*. When the late lamented editor of the WBC, Professor David Allan Hubbard, contacted me about taking up Proverbs in this series, I urged a conflict of interest and suggested names of my former students instead. He went out of his way to resolve the conflict and returned within a week with his request. It was too attractive an invitation to refuse. This may have been the last book he commissioned, since he died within a few months of our conversation. Almost at the same time his own popular and valuable commentary on the book of Proverbs appeared. It has its own style, a combination of Hubbard's erudition and control of Israelite wisdom, along with his pastoral insights. I dedicate this commentary to his memory. While his wise counsel will always be missed, I would like to thank the editorial team of John D. W. Watts and James Watts for suggestions they made to improve the commentary. I am also grateful to the publishers for expediting the appearance of this volume, and especially the roles of Mark Roberts and Robert Lintzenich.

ROLAND E. MURPHY, O. CARM.

Washington, D.C.
January 1998

Editorial Preface

The launching of the *Word Biblical Commentary* brings to fulfillment an enterprise of several years' planning. The publishers and the members of the editorial board met in 1977 to explore the possibility of a new commentary on the books of the Bible that would incorporate several distinctive features. Prospective readers of these volumes are entitled to know what such features were intended to be; whether the aims of the commentary have been fully achieved time alone will tell.

First, we have tried to cast a wide net to include as contributors a number of scholars from around the world who not only share our aims but are in the main engaged in the ministry of teaching in university, college, and seminary. They represent a rich diversity of denominational allegiance. The broad stance of our contributors can rightly be called evangelical, and this term is to be understood in its positive, historic sense of a commitment to Scripture as divine revelation and the truth and power of the Christian gospel.

Then, the commentaries in our series are all commissioned and written for the purpose of inclusion in the *Word Biblical Commentary*. Unlike several of our distinguished counterparts in the field of commentary writing, there are no translated works, originally written in a non-English language. Also, our commentators were asked to prepare their own rendering of the original biblical text and to use those languages as the basis of their own comments and exegesis. What may be claimed as distinctive with this series is that it is based on the biblical languages, yet it seeks to make the technical and scholarly approach to the theological understanding of Scripture understandable by—and useful to—the fledgling student, the working minister, and colleagues in the guild of professional scholars and teachers as well.

Finally, a word must be said about the format of the series. The layout, in clearly defined sections, has been consciously devised to assist readers at different levels. Those wishing to learn about the textual witnesses on which the translation is offered are invited to consult the section headed *Notes*. If the readers' concern is with the state of modern scholarship on any given portion of Scripture, they should turn to the sections on *Bibliography* and *Form/Structure/Setting*. For a clear exposition of the passage's meaning and its relevance to the ongoing biblical revelation, the *Comment* and concluding *Explanation* are designed expressly to meet that need. There is therefore something for everyone who may pick up and use these volumes.

If these aims come anywhere near realization, the intention of the editors will have been met, and the labor of our team of contributors rewarded.

General Editors: *Bruce M. Metzger*
David A. Hubbard†
Glenn W. Barker†
Old Testament: *John D. W. Watts*
New Testament: *Ralph P. Martin*

Abbreviations

EB	Echter Bibel
EBC	Expositor's Biblical Commentary
EHS.T	Europäische Hochschulschriften. Theologie
FAT	Forschungen zum Alten Testament
FOTL	The Forms of the Old Testament Literature
FTS	Freiburger theologische Studien
GKC	*Gesenius' Hebrew Grammar,* ed. E. Kautzsch, tr. A. E. Cowley (Oxford: Clarendon, 1910)
HAT	Handbuch zum Alten Testament
HBC	*Harper's Bible Commentary*
HBD	*Harper's Bible Dictionary*
HBIS	History of Biblical Interpretation Series
HBT	*Horizons in Biblical Theology*
HeyJ	*The Heythrop Journal*
HS	*Hebrew Studies*
HTR	*Harvard Theological Review*
ICC	International Critical Commentary
Int	*Interpretation*
JAAR	*Journal of the American Academy of Religion*
JANESCU	*Journal of the Ancient Near Eastern Society of Columbia University*
JAOS	*Journal of the American Oriental Society*
JBL	*Journal of Biblical Literature*
JNES	*Journal of Near Eastern Studies*
Joüon	P. Joüon, *Grammaire de l'hébreu biblique* (Rome: Pontifical Biblical Institute, 1947)
JSOT	*Journal for the Study of the Old Testament*
JSOTSup	Journal for the Study of the Old Testament Supplementary Series
JTS	*Journal of Theological Studies*
KPG	Knox Preaching Guides
LD	Lectio divina
LUÅ	Lunds universitets årsskrift
NAC	New American Commentary
NBE	Nueva Biblia Española
NCBC	New Century Bible Commentary
NEB	Neue Echter Bibel
NIB	New Interpreters Bible
NIBCOT	New International Bible Commentary Old Testament
NJBC	*The New Jerome Biblical Commentary,* ed. R. E. Brown et al. (Englewood Cliffs, NJ: Prentice Hall, 1990)
OBO	Orbis biblicus et orientalis
OTG	Old Testament Guides
OTL	The Old Testament Library
OTM	Old Testament Message
OTP	The *Old Testament Pseudepigrapha,* ed. J. Charlesworth (NY: Doubleday, 1983–85)
OTSSA	Old Testament Society of South Africa

POT	De Prediking van het Oude Testament
QD	Quaestiones disputatae
RB	*Revue Biblique*
RivB	*Rivista biblica*
SB	Sources Bibliques
SBLDS	Society of Biblical Literature Dissertation Series
SBS	Stuttgarter Bibelstudien
SJT	*Scottish Journal of Theology*
TBC	Torch Bible Commentary
TDOT	*Theological Dictionary of the Old Testament*
TLZ	*Theologische Literaturzeitung*
TOTC	Tyndale Old Testament Commentaries
TynBul	*Tyndale Bulletin*
VT	*Vetus Testamentum*
VTSup	Vetus Testamentum, Supplements
VWGTh	Veröffentlichungen der Wissenschaftlichen Gesellschaft für Theologie
Waltke-O'Connor	B. K. Waltke and M. P. O'Connor, *An Introduction to Biblical Hebrew Syntax* (Winona Lake, IN: Eisenbrauns, 1990)
W&W	*Word & World*
WBC	Word Biblical Commentary
WC	Westminster Commentaries
ZB	Zürcher Bibelkommentare
ZfA	*Zeitschrift für Althebraistik*
ZTK	*Zeitschrift für Theologie und Kirche*

ANCIENT VERSIONS

LXX	Septuagint
MT	Masoretic text
Syr	Syriac Peshitto
Tg	Targum
Vg	Vulgate

MODERN TRANSLATIONS

BJ	La Sainte Bible de Jerusalem (1966)
JPS	Jewish Publication Society: *Tanakh*
KJV	King James Version
NAB	New American Bible
NEB	New English Bible
NIV	New International Version
NRSV	New Revised Standard Version
REB	Revised English Bible
RSV	Revised Standard Version

BIBLICAL AND APOCRYPHAL BOOKS

OLD TESTAMENT

Gen	Genesis	Cant	Canticles,
Exod	Exodus		Song of Solomon
Lev	Leviticus	Isa	Isaiah
Num	Numbers	Jer	Jeremiah
Deut	Deuteronomy	Lam	Lamentations
Josh	Joshua	Ezek	Ezekiel
Judg	Judges	Dan	Daniel
Ruth	Ruth	Hos	Hosea
1–2 Sam	1–2 Samuel	Joel	Joel
1–2 Kgs	1–2 Kings	Amos	Amos
1–2 Chr	1–2 Chronicles	Obad	Obadiah
Ezra	Ezra	Jon	Jonah
Neh	Nehemiah	Mic	Micah
Esth	Esther	Nah	Nahum
Job	Job	Hab	Habakkuk
Ps(s)	Psalm(s)	Zeph	Zephaniah
Prov	Proverbs	Hag	Haggai
Eccl	Ecclesiastes	Zech	Zechariah
		Mal	Malachi

APOCRYPHA

1–4 Kgdms	1–4 Kingdoms	Bar	Baruch
1–2 Esdr	1–2 Esdras	Ep Jer	Epistle of
Tob	Tobit		Jeremiah
Jdt	Judith	S Th Ch	Song of the
Add Esth	Additions to		Three
	Esther		Children (or
4 Ezra	4 Ezra		Young Men)
Wis	Wisdom of	Sus	Susanna
	Solomon	Bel	Bel and the
Sir	Ecclesiasticus		Dragon
	(Wisdom of	Pr Azar	Prayer of
	Jesus the son		Azariah
	of Sirach)	1–4 Macc	1–4 Maccabees

NEW TESTAMENT

Matt	Matthew	Rom	Romans
Mark	Mark	1–2 Cor	1–2
Luke	Luke		Corinthians
John	John	Gal	Galatians
Acts	Acts	Eph	Ephesians

Phil	Philippians	Heb	Hebrews
Col	Colossians	Jas	James
1–2 Thess	1–2 Thessalonians	1–2 Pet	1–2 Peter
		1–2–3 John	1–2–3 John
1–2 Tim	1–2 Timothy	Jude	Jude
Titus	Titus	Rev	Revelation
Philem	Philemon		

MISCELLANEOUS

ca.	circa, of approximately
chap(s).	chapter(s)
cf.	compare
ed(s).	editor(s), edited by; edition
e.g.	for example
esp.	especially
et al.	and others
ET	English translation
FS	Festschrift
i.e.	that is
MS(S)	manuscript(s)
pace	despite the interpretation of
passim	elsewhere
rev.	revised
UP	University Press

Main Bibliography

References to commentaries are by author's name only; pages are given when the reference does not obviously deal with a chapter and verse under discussion. The most complete survey of studies on Proverbs in the twentieth century is provided in **R. N. Whybray,** *The Book of Proverbs: A Survey of Modern Study,* HBIS 1 (Leiden: Brill, 1995). **R. E. Murphy** gives a summary of recent publications in *CR:BS,* 1:119–40 (Sheffield: JSOT, 1993) and in *The Tree of Life,* 2nd rev. ed. (Grand Rapids, MI: Eerdmans, 1996) 15–32, 193–202.

COMMENTARIES

Aitken, K. *Proverbs.* DSB. Philadelphia: Westminster, 1986. **Alonso Schökel, L.** *Proverbios.* NBE. Madrid: Ediciones cristiandad, 1984. **Barucq, A.** *Le livre des Proverbes.* SB. Paris: Gabalda, 1964. **Clifford, R. J.** *Proverbs.* OTL. Philadelphia: Westminster/Knox, forthcoming. **Cohen, A.** *Proverbs.* London: Soncino, 1973. **Collins, J. J.** *Proverbs, Ecclesiastes.* KPG. Atlanta: Knox, 1980. **Cox, D.** *Proverbs.* OTM. Wilmington, DE: Glazier, 1982. **Delitzsch, F.** *The Book of Proverbs.* COT 6. Repr. Grand Rapids, MI: Eerdmans, 1982. **Fontaine, C.** "Proverbs." In *Harper's Bible Commentary.* Ed. J. Mays. San Francisco: Harper & Row, 1988. 495–517. **Fox, M. V.** *Proverbs.* AB. New York: Doubleday, forthcoming. **Garrett, D. A.** *Proverbs, Ecclesiastes, Song of Songs.* NAC 14. Nashville: Broadman, 1993. **Gemser, B.** *Sprüche Salomos.* HAT 16. Tübingen: J. C. B. Mohr (Paul Siebeck), 1963. **Hamp, V.** *Das Buch der Sprüche.* EB 8. Würzburg: Echter, 1949. **Hubbard, D.** *Proverbs.* CC. Dallas: Word, 1989. **Jones, E.** *Proverbs and Ecclesiastes.* TBC. London: SCM, 1961. **Kidner, D.** *The Proverbs.* TOTC. Downers Grove: InterVarsity, 1964. **McCreesh, T.** "Proverbs." In *NJBC.* 453–61. **McKane, W.** *Proverbs.* OTL. Philadelphia: Westminster, 1970. **Meinhold, A.** *Die Sprüche.* ZB. Zürich: Theologischer Verlag, 1991. 2 vols. **Mouser, W.** *Walking in Wisdom: Studying the Proverbs of Solomon.* Downers Grove: InterVarsity, 1983. **Murphy, R. E.** and **Huwiler, E.** *Proverbs, Song of Songs, Ecclesiastes.* NIBCOT 12. Peabody, MA: Hendrickson, 1999. **Oesterley, W. O. E.** *The Book of Proverbs.* WC. London: Methuen, 1929. **Perowne, T.** *The Proverbs.* CBSC. Cambridge: Cambridge UP, 1916. **Ploeg, J. van der.** *Spreuken.* BOT 8/1. Roermond, 1952. **Plöger, O.** *Sprüche Salomos (Proverbia).* BKAT 17. Neukirchen: Neukirchener, 1984. **Ringgren, H.** *Sprüche.* ATD 16/1. Göttingen: Vandenhoeck & Ruprecht, 1962. **Ross, A. P.** "Proverbs." *EBC.* Grand Rapids, MI: Zondervan, 1991. 5:883–1134. **Scott, R. B. Y.** *Proverbs, Ecclesiastes.* AB. New York: Doubleday, 1965. **Toy, C. H.** *The Book of Proverbs.* ICC. Edinburgh: T. & T. Clark, 1899. **Tuinstra, E. W.** *Spreuken* I (1–9). POT. Baarn: Callenbach, 1996. **Vaccari, A.** "I Proverbi." In *La Sacra Bibbia/Libri Poetici V, 1.* Firenze: Salani, 1949. 13–85. **Van Leeuwen, R. C.** "The Book of Proverbs." NIB. Nashville: Abingdon, 1997. 5:19–262. **Wildeboer, G.** *Die Sprüche.* KHC 15. Tübingen, 1897.

SPECIAL STUDIES

(References to these will be made by name, obvious short title, and pages.)

Alter, R. "The Poetry of Wit." In *The Art of Biblical Poetry.* New York: Basic Books, 1985. 163–84. **Barré, M.,** ed. *Wisdom, You Are My Sister.* FS R. E. Murphy. CBQMS 29. Washington: Catholic Biblical Association, 1997. **Baumann, G.** *Die Weisheitsgestalt in Proverbien 1–9.*

Traditionsgeschichtliche und theologische Studien. FAT 16. Tübingen: Mohr (Siebeck), 1966. **Blenkinsopp, J.** *Wisdom and Law in the Old Testament.* New York: Oxford UP, 1994. **Boström, G.** *Proverbiastudien.* Lund: Gleerup, 1935. **Brown, W. P.** *Character in Crisis: A Fresh Approach to the Wisdom Literature of the Old Testament.* Grand Rapids, MI: Eerdmans, 1996. **Bryce, G.** *A Legacy of Wisdom.* Lewisburg: Bucknell, 1979. **Bühlmann, W.** *Vom rechten Reden und Schweigen.* OBO 12. Freiburg: Universitätsverlag, 1976. **Camp, C.** *Wisdom and the Feminine in the Book of Proverbs.* BLS 11. Sheffield: Almond, 1985. **Clifford, R. J.** "Observations on the Text and Versions of Proverbs." In *My Sister.* Ed. M. Barré. 47–61. **Collins, J. J.** *Jewish Wisdom in the Hellenistic Age.* OTL. Louisville: Westminster John Knox, 1997. **Delkurt, H.** *Ethische Einsichten in der alttestamentlichen Spruchweisheit.* Neukirchen: Neukirchener, 1993. **Ernst, A. B.** *Weisheitlich Kultkritik.* BThSt 23. Neukirchen: Neukirchener, 1994. **Fontaine, C.** *Traditional Sayings in the Old Testament.* BLS 5. Sheffield: Almond, 1985. **Fox, M. V.** "The Social Location of the Book of Proverbs." In *Texts, Temples, and Traditions.* FS M. Haran. Winona Lake, IN: Eisenbrauns, 1996. 227–39. ———. "Words for Folly." *ZfA* 10 (1997) 4–15. ———. "What the Book of Proverbs Is About." In *Congress Volume Cambridge 1995.* VTSup 66. Leiden: Brill, 1997. 153–67. **Gammie, J.** and **L. Perdue,** eds. *The Sage in Israel and the Ancient Near East.* Leuven: Leuven UP, 1971. **Gilbert, M.,** ed. *La Sagesse de l'Ancien Testament.* BETL 51. Gembloux: Duculot, 1979. **Harrington, D. J.** *Wisdom Texts from Qumran.* London: Routledge, 1996. **Hausmann, J.** *Studien zum Menschenbild der älteren Weisheit (Spr 10ff.).* FAT 7. Tübingen: J. C. B. Mohr (Paul Siebeck), 1995. **Hermisson, H. J.** *Studien zur israelitischen Spruchweisheit.* WMANT 28. Neukirchen: Neukirchener, 1968. **Hoglund, K.,** ed. *The Listening Heart.* JSOTSup 58. Sheffield: JSOT, 1987. **Huwiler, E.** *Control of Reality in Israelite Wisdom Thought.* Duke University dissertation, 1988. **Kayatz, C.** *Studien zu Proverbien 1–9.* WMANT 22. Neukirchen: Neukirchener, 1966. **Krispenz,** *Spruchkomposition im Buch Proverbia.* EHS.T 23/349. Frankfurt: P. Lang, 1989. **Lambert, W.** *Babylonian Wisdom Literature.* Oxford: Clarendon, 1960. **Lang, B.** *Die weisheitliche Lehrrede.* SBS 54. Stuttgart: KBW, 1972. ———. *Wisdom and the Book of Proverbs.* New York: Pilgrim, 1986. **Lichtheim, M.** *Ancient Egyptian Literature.* 3 vols. Berkeley: University of California Press, 1980. **Lindenberger, J.** *The Aramaic Proverbs of Ahiqar.* Baltimore: Johns Hopkins UP, 1983. **Maier, C.** *Die 'fremde Frau' in Proverbien 1–9.* OBO 144. Freiburg: Universitätsverlag, 1995. **Martin, J. D.** *Proverbs.* OTG. Sheffield: Academic Press, 1995. **McCreesh, T.** *Biblical Sound and Sense: Poetic Sound Patterns in Proverbs 10–29.* JSOTSup 128. Sheffield: Sheffield Academic, 1992. **Murphy, R. E.** *Wisdom Literature.* FOTL 13. Grand Rapids, MI: Eerdmans, 1981. ———. *The Tree of Life.* 2nd rev. ed. Grand Rapids, MI: Eerdmans, 1996. **Nel, P.** *The Structure and Ethos of the Wisdom Admonitions in Proverbs.* BZAW 159. Berlin: de Gruyter, 1982. **O'Connor, M. P.** "The Contours of Biblical Hebrew Verse." In *Hebrew Verse Structure.* Winona Lake, IN: Eisenbrauns, 1998. 631–61. **Perdue, L.** et al., eds. *In Search of Wisdom.* FS J. G. Gammie. Louisville: Westminster/John Knox, 1993. **Preuss, H.** *Einführung in die alttestamentliche Weisheitsliteratur.* Stuttgart: Kohlhammer, 1987. **Pritchard, J.,** ed. *Ancient Near Eastern Texts Relating to the Old Testament.* 3rd ed. Princeton: Princeton UP, 1978. **Rad, G. von.** *Old Testament Theology.* New York: Harper & Row, 1962. 2 vols. ———. *Wisdom in Israel.* Nashville: Abingdon, 1972. **Schmid, H. H.** *Wesen und Geschichte der Weisheit.* BZAW 101. Berlin: Töpelmann, 1966. **Scoralick, R.** *Einzelspruch und Sammlung.* BZAW 232. Berlin: de Gruyter, 1995. **Shupak, N.** *Where Can Wisdom be Found?* OBO 130. Freiburg: Universitätsverlag, 1993. **Skehan, P.** *Studies in Israelite Poetry and Wisdom.* CBQMS. Washington: Catholic Biblical Association, 1971. **Skladny, U.** *Die ältesten Spruchsammlungen in Israel.* Göttingen: Vandenhoeck & Ruprecht, 1962. **Snell, D.** *Twice-Told Proverbs and the Composition of the Book of Proverbs.* Winona Lake, IN: Eisenbrauns, 1993. **Steiert, F.-J.** *Die Weisheit Israels— ein Fremdkörper im Alten Testament?* FTS 143. Freiburg: Herder, 1990. **Tov, E.** "Recensional Differences between the Masoretic Text and the Septuagint of the Book of Proverbs." In *Of Scribes and Scrolls.* FS J. Strugnell, ed. H. W. Attridge. Lanham, MD: University Press, 1990. 43–56. **Trublet, J.,** ed. *La Sagesse biblique de l'Ancien au Nouveau Testament.* LD 160. Paris: Cerf, 1995. **Van Leeuwen, R.** *Context and Meaning in Proverbs 25–27.* SBLDS 96. Atlanta: Scholars

Press, 1988. ———. "In Praise of Proverbs." In *Pledges of Jubilee.* Ed. L. Zuidervaart et al. Grand Rapids: Eerdmans, 1995. 308–27. **Weeks, S.** *Early Israelite Wisdom.* Oxford: Clarendon, 1994. **Wehrle, J.** *Sprichwort und Weisheit.* ATSAT 38. St. Ottilien: EOS, 1993. **Westermann C.** *Roots of Wisdom.* Louisville: Westminster John Knox, 1995. **Whybray, R. N.** *The Composition of the Book of Proverbs.* JSOTSup 168. Sheffield, JSOT, 1994. ———. *Wealth and Poverty in the Book of Proverbs.* JSOTSup 99. Sheffield: JSOT, 1990. **Williams, J.** *Those Who Ponder Proverbs.* BLS 2. Sheffield: Almond, 1981. ———. "The Power of Form: A Study of Biblical Proverbs." In *Gnomic Wisdom.* Ed. J. D. Crossan. Chico, CA: Scholars, 1980. 35–58.

Introduction

The commentaries in the above bibliography are usually prefaced with an introduction, and introductory matter can be found in several of the special studies. Particular attention is called to the volume *The Sage in Israel and in the Ancient Near East* (ed. J. Gammie), to *Proverbs* (J. Martin), to R. N. Whybray, *The Book of Proverbs* (HBIS 1), and to the several studies indicated above by Fox, Fontaine, Perdue and others. Although readers of the WBC series may find some repetition here, a brief introduction to the book of Proverbs seems necessary. Some of this material can be found in the epilogue to the commentary *Ecclesiastes* (WBC 23A, 131–55), which contains a full bibliography, and also in my book *The Tree of Life* (2nd rev. ed.; Grand Rapids, MI: Eerdmans, 1996). However singular the profile of the book of Proverbs may be, it should not be viewed apart from the other books of wisdom—Job, Qoheleth—and from two books outside of the Tanakh—Sirach and the Wisdom of Solomon (see also Brown, *Character,* 151–59, for the journey in the "way" of wisdom). Indeed, Proverbs is the fountainhead of the wisdom movement, providing "old things and new."

What information should an Introduction provide a reader for an intelligent study of the book of Proverbs? As can be seen from inspecting the various works mentioned above, almost every commentary follows a certain ritual in supplying data about authorship, date, and so forth, and these questions will not be neglected here. But the Introduction should also make manifest the assumptions of the commentator, explicit or implicit, whether relatively certain, or reasonable, or even unproven (in the frank and open style of B. Childs, *Introduction to the Old Testament as Scripture* [Philadelphia: Fortress, 1979] 545–59). For example, this commentary is based on the recognition that the book is a collection of collections, as the superscriptions within the text indicate (e.g., 10:1; 25:1), prefaced by an introduction (chaps. 1–9). Refining the structure further yields more tentative conclusions, but there is general agreement that there are two basic parts: Chapters 1–9, which contain long poems, are a kind of "introduction" to chapters 10–31, which contain the collections of short sayings that form the bulk of the work. This structural analysis immediately has a bearing on the question of authorship and dating. The implication is that Solomon is not the "author," and that it is not profitable to pursue the question of authorship further. Is it possible to say something about the origins of the collections? This has no easy answer, and at the present time scholarly opinion is divided between the family and the school (perhaps both should be recognized as channels for various chapters within the work). The distinction between chaps. 1–9 and 10–31 is a helpful one. The first nine chapters are a kind of "introduction" containing instructions, the exhortations of a parent/teacher, and the speeches of personified Wisdom. In contrast, the later collections display a different, distinctive, literary style: mainly a succession of short sayings (achieving a benumbing effect on the unwary reader who may fail to stop and analyze them more closely). With this division goes the unproven but likely assumption about dating: that chaps. 1–9 were written, even if some of the material dates before the exile, in the postexilic period to set the tone for the collections, which are for the most part probably preexilic. We can now proceed in an orderly fashion to provide more details.

Authorship and Date

For centuries Solomon was the putative author of this book, due to the venerable tradition about his wisdom (1 Kgs 3:10; 5:9–14), and the superscription of the work (1:1). There is now almost universal agreement that he cannot be considered the "author." Within the book are several collections, some of them clearly ascribed to "authors" other than Solomon. Moreover, there are no available means to identify any proverbs as "Solomonic." It seems to be the nature of ancient proverbs that they lose their "author" as they become popular and perhaps even improved in the process. While the dating of the book of Proverbs remains uncertain, the most satisfactory division is preexilic and postexilic (respectively, chaps. 10–29 and 1–9).

B. S. Childs has maximized the Solomonic tradition for this book (*Introduction*, 552): "the superscription of Proverbs which connects with 1 Kgs 3 thus serves a different function from the psalm titles which establish a link between David's psalmody and Israel's historical tradition. The title of Proverbs . . . forms a connection only with the sapiential material within Kings . . . Secondly . . . , the superscription ties the proverbs to the period of the early monarchy and thus opposes the attempt to derive them only from the late postexilic period." Moreover the titles, including 30:1 and 31:1, also "offer a canonical warrant for comparison with extra-biblical material which is unusual for the biblical tradition." Childs considers more important than the question of "authorship," the thrust of Prov 30:5–6 (*Introduction*, 556): "the passage is highly significant from a canonical point of view. It registers the point that the proverbs which originally derived from man's reflection on human experience of the world and society had become understood as divine word to man which functioned as sacred scripture along with the rest of Israel's received traditions."

The table of contents for this commentary indicates that the book is a collection of collections. Did these originate in oral tradition or were they composed in the first instance as literary works? Despite the great number of studies, there is no completely satisfactory answer to this question (cf. Whybray, *The Book of Proverbs*, 1–33). It is likely that many individual sayings (Prov 10–29) derived from oral tradition, and that the instructions in chaps. 1–9 betray literary composition from the beginning. But other portions would suggest written origins, e.g., the acrostic character of 31:10–31 about the valiant woman. The unique reflection of Egyptian wisdom (Amenemope) in 22:17–23:11 is a special case in itself that will be considered in an excursus. Clearly distinct are the wisdom poems in chaps. 1–9, which are more didactic in character; wisdom has become a subject to be explored in and for herself (e.g., chap. 8).

Did schools play a role in the composition and transmission of the book of Proverbs? There is no hard-nosed archaeological evidence for what might be called "schools." Scholars infer from the existence of schools in Mesopotamia and Egypt that there must have been a similar institution in Israel. It is judged that Israel would have had to provide training for courtiers, and thus there was a court school in Jerusalem, as suggested also by the reference to the role of the men of King Hezekiah in Prov 25:1. But does proverbial wisdom in itself have to await royal establishment for its beginning? Most of Proverbs lacks a royal flavor, and the general content points in a different direction. Hence others maintain that the origins lie in oral tradition handed down first in the family before being collected (e.g., Westermann, *Roots of Wisdom*). There is no ready solution; perhaps the role of both family and some kind of court school should be recognized in the history of the development of this literature.

Some light has been shed on this question by M. V. Fox ("Social Location," 228–32), who points out the ambiguity of the term "school" that has bedeviled the discussion of the issue. There is little profit in rehearsing the misplaced emphases and arguments in the disputes between H. Hermisson and A. Lemaire on the one hand and F. Golka on the other (references can be found in Fox's article). The debate has been off center since "school" has never been defined, and also because the Egyptian/Mesopotamian models used to *postulate* the existence of a school in Israel are not "wisdom," but scribal, schools in which all manner of literature was cultivated. The resulting picture of the Israelite sage (both male and female; cf. Prov 10:1!) as a "school teacher" is quite misleading. In Egypt the authors of the Instructions with which the book of Proverbs has been compared were not teachers, but men of various avocations who wrote for their real sons, e.g., Ptahhotep and Amenemope, who are singled out by Fox. Similarly the transmission in Proverbs is a father/mother to son channel—a family, not a "school" location. Fox puts this succinctly: "The self-presentation of Wisdom Literature is as paternal teaching" (p. 232). In scholarly literature there is also the debate between folk wisdom and court wisdom, i.e., between the sayings that would have been common currency among the people, and those that would have been fashioned in the more controlled atmosphere of a scribal school associated with the court. It is impossible to settle this question one way or another on the basis of content. In terms of style it has been argued that the artistic sayings are the product of highly skilled writers, and thus would not have originated among ordinary people. To this, one can reasonably reply with the words of the Egyptian sage, Ptahhotep, who wrote centuries before Israel ever existed: "Good speech is more hidden than the emerald, but it may be found with maidservants at the grindstones" (*ANET*, 412; *AEL* 1:63).

In all likelihood, both channels were operative. Hence C. Westermann's emphasis on family and wisdom has to be balanced by a recognition of the activity of King Hezekiah's men (Prov 25:1), by the significance of the "king" proverbs and other factors (e.g., the presence of Agur and Lemuel in chaps. 30–31). Although it is impossible now to determine the criteria according to which the various collections in Proverbs were made, the fact remains that they are the result of a *selective* process, as Fox insists. Indeed, some sayings, even if in slightly variant forms, are repeated within the book. The implication is that they were chosen, and eventually found their way into the various collections. The title of D. Snell's book, *Twice-Told Proverbs*, is a salutary reminder of this. His study contains convenient lists of the many variant forms of sayings strewn through the book (e.g., cf. 14:12 and 16:25; 13:14 and 14:27).

Literary Forms

The format of WBC calls for remarks on form for each unit; hence, only general comments are in place here. See also the glossary of form-critical terms in R. E. Murphy (*Wisdom Literature*) for greater detail. The broadest categories are instruction/teaching and proverb/saying, and they are rather blanket terms that cover specific types. The fluctuation in form-critical terminology is inescapable. The well-known Instructions (*sebayit*) of the Egyptian officials and scribes could have provided models, but it must also be admitted that instruction is a mode of communication that hardly needs a foreign model. It includes the natural means of social intercourse and is expressed in subgenres such as commands and prohibitions that are indigenous to the family and society generally. In a sense, the whole book of Proverbs is instruction, for even an experiential observation (which is best included in the neutral term "saying") is meant to impart some awareness or knowledge. However, it is well to note the appropriateness of "instruction" as an overall designation of the kind of writing evidenced in chaps. 1–9, where the parent/teacher strongly urges "son[s]" to a particular lifestyle. The same is true of the section associated with the Instruction of Amenemope, Prov 22:17–24:35. A simple example would be some kind of command, followed by a motive clause ("do this, because"), as in Prov 3:1–2. But this can be developed at great length, as in Prov 2:1–22. In the context of the book, the instructions of chaps. 1–9 can also be called wisdom poems. The command (or the prohibition) can also be framed as a statement. For example, there is no change of meaning between Prov 16:3 (a command) and 16:20 (a saying), despite the differences in form. The proverb/saying is usually a two-line composition, characterized by literary parallelism, that normally forms a world unto itself: "A wise son gives joy to his father / a foolish son is a sorrow to his mother" (10:1). It is best to understand "saying" as a neutral term that has given rise to specific types.

מָשָׁל (*mašal*) is the most general term of all. It is commonly translated "proverb," as in the title of the book. However, its usage is so far-ranging that it is of little use for classification. Thus, the term is used in Isa 14:4 to indicate the satirical poem about Babylon. While its original meaning is disputed, the root seems to indicate comparison, a meaning that is illustrated, implicitly or explicitly, in very many of the sayings in the book. In English usage there is no single or adequate definition of a "proverb." There is wisdom in the well-known quotation from Archer Taylor, "The definition of a proverb is too difficult to repay the undertaking . . . An incommunicable quality tells us this sentence is proverbial and that is not . . . Let us be content with recognizing that a proverb is a saying current among the folk" (*The Proverb and an Index to the Proverb*, 2nd ed. [Copenhagen and Hatboro: Rosenkilde & Baggers, 1962] 3).

דָּבָר (*dabar*) normally means "word" or "thing," and it is used to refer to the individual sayings, as in "the words of Agur" (30:1; cf. Eccl 12:11). In English usage, "saying" and "aphorism" are practically equivalent to "proverb." It should be noted that sometimes the saying is experiential. It tells it "the way it is." At other times, and very often, the biblical saying goes beyond mere observation, and it urges a course of action, either implicitly or explicitly. Thus we read in Prov 13:12: "Hope deferred sickens the heart / but a wish fulfilled—a tree of life." This simply registers the reality of the various ways humans are affected. Such self-knowledge is helpful in coping with life. But in Prov 12:19 a definite value is intended: "Truthful lips last forever / the lying tongue, but a moment." The saying is scoring a moral point: honesty over lying. Most of the proverbs in the book are so oriented. Even the pure observation receives a certain patina of obligation by the very fact that it is included among, and indeed surrounded by, value judgments that are inculcating a given line of conduct. There is a temptation to see moral lessons everywhere, simply because the sayings are in the Bible, but one should be more sensitive to the depths and perspectives of these proverbs. It is obvious from what has been said that Israelite wisdom is more practical than theoretical. It attempts to persuade, cajole, threaten, or command a particular attitude or course of action. The sayings themselves may be regarded as teachings; that is, the wisdom that has been handed down is to be heeded and put into practice. The emphasis is on praxis. When the sage says "listen," "hear," the meaning is "obey."

The parallelism between the lines of the sayings is a well-known phenomenon in biblical poetry, especially in Proverbs, and is not absent from prose. The traditional threefold distinction between synonymous, antithetic, and synthetic that has come down from the days of Bishop Lowth, has been recently refined, or even transformed, by the studies of M. P. O'Connor, J. Kugel, and A. Berlin. Parallelism is far more than a matter of repetition and especially lexical duplication; it is a matter of syntax as well. The idea expressed in the first line is sharpened, specified, intensified, even explained, by the parallel line(s). One can even claim, "If not A, then B" (or even, "all the more so B"). It would be a mistake to be lulled into thinking that the two lines are really the same (cf. J. Kugel, *The Idea of Biblical Poetry: Parallelism and Its History* [New Haven: Yale UP, 1981]). A significant number of studies of biblical parallelism have emerged in recent times. See A. Berlin, "Introduction to Hebrew Poetry," NIB, 4:301–15; M. O'Connor, *Hebrew Verse Structure*, 2nd ed. (Winona Lake, IN: Eisenbrauns, 1997), especially 631–61.

An important feature that strengthens the phenomenon of parallelism of the sayings is the juxtaposition of nouns and predicates, or nominal sentences. See the *Excursus on Translating Proverbs*. The force of this juxtaposition is lost when a translation inserts the copula "is," or makes a comparison explicit by inserting "like." Thus, a literal translation is the best translation of the saying in 28:3: "Poor oneself, and an oppressor of the poor—a devastating rain and no food." The NRSV and most translations insert the copula "is" between the two half-lines. This may be required in formal English, but it lessens the impact of the saying. One can measure this by comparing for effect the following statements: "Examination flunked, course failed." and "The examination was flunked, and the course registered as failure." The impact of the juxtaposition is lost when words are inserted to make the meaning explicit. Here style and meaning coalesce and should not be separated. Another example, "A golden earring and a necklace of fine gold— one who gives wise reproof to a listening ear" (25:12). Many translations insert "like" at the beginning, thus turning a juxtaposition into a comparison. The juxtaposition can be expressed in chiastic fashion, AB-B'A', as in 16:17: "The path of the just—turning from evil / one who preserves his life—one who keeps his path." Very frequently lines *a* and *b* of a verse are joined by the connective *waw*, correctly rendered by "and," or "but" according to context. But in some cases this conjunction is what grammarians have called the *waw adaequationis,* or the "and of equivalence." Thus, in 25:25, "Cold water on a weary soul, and a good report from a distant land." The "and" here means something like "equals"; it is best left untranslated: "cold water on a weary soul—a good report from a distant land." The equivalent in English can be expressed by a dash or a comma, and there is no need to insert "is" or turn the saying into an explicit comparison by inserting "like." The translation in this commentary will try to adhere as closely as possible, insofar as English grammar permits, to the staccato effect of the Hebrew. The concreteness and earthiness of proverbial language and the Hebrew worldview should not be glossed over in favor of "clean" imagery and "idiomatic" English that often amounts to a paraphrase. In this commentary, as the excursus argues, an effort has been made to give a literal translation. The result may not be to everyone's taste. Since several "poetic" renditions of Proverbs already exist, it seemed wise to challenge the reader with a more literal translation. The juxtapositional style creates unusual sequence, but since a commentary accompanies the translation, there should be no doubt about the meaning.

Attention should also be called to the rendering of various organs of the body, so favored by the sages in their succinct expressions. ‏יד‎ *yad,* "hand," is a metaphor for power; ‏לב‎ *leb,* "heart," frequently connotes "mind." The punch of a saying may be lost if the literal meaning is abandoned. There are limits, however. The frequent phrase "lacking in heart" connotes in English more the idea of weakness and discouragement. In Hebrew it denotes "lacking in understanding," or "senseless." In such cases a paraphrase is inevitable. But in general the translation in this volume is deliberately literal.

The "good" and "better" sayings (‏טוב‎ *tob*) are frequent. The former occurs usually in the phrase "not good" (19:2). The "better" saying is more frequent, and it involves analogical imagination. There is some kind of comparison: "A is better than B." This is the simplest form, "Better a near neighbor than a distant relative" (27:10). But the most frequent form is: "Better A with B than C with D." This form gives a paradoxical twist to reality. Although possession is better than lacking something, the form can be used to indicate the opposite: "Better a little with justice than large income with injustice" (16:8). For more details, see G. Bryce, "'Better'-Proverbs: An Historical and Structural Study," *1972 Proceedings of the Society of Biblical Literature,* 2:343–54. In his study of the "better" sayings, J. Wehrle (*Sprichwort,* 202–17) notes that there are twenty of them in Proverbs, mostly in the early strata (chaps. 10ff.), and he closes his work with a Chinese proverb, "it is better to know well a little, than to know something about everything."

Another literary feature is the use of the Hebrew alphabet, either loosely (an "alphabetizing poem") or in strict acrostic fashion. In these cases the structure is determined by alphabetic considerations. Each line of an acrostic begins with a successive letter of the alphabet (*aleph, beth,* etc.), as in Prov 31:10–31 and in certain psalms. The alphabetizing poem (e.g., Prov 2:1–22 and see the commentary below) is so-called because it consists of twenty-two lines (the number of letters in the Hebrew alphabet) or also twenty-three lines. This style was employed especially by Ben Sira (e.g., Sir 1:11–30; 5:1–6:4; 6:18–37). The phenomenon seems to have been cultivated especially in wisdom writings. And other tricks with style could be employed, as the following pattern, detected by P. Skehan (cf. *Studies,* 74), indicates. In Pss 25 and 34 there is a play on *aleph* (the first letter of the Hebrew alphabet): "the use of the letter *pe* is given an allegorical turn, inasmuch as both times it is used in the same verb (*pedeh, podeh*) of 'redemption.' However, a reason that may be called mechanical underlies this device, and presumably antedates any verbal associations of the kind. In the word *aleph* are contained three consonants: the first in the alphabet, the twelfth, *lamed*, which in the twenty-two-letter sequence begins the second half of the alphabet; and the 'extra' letter, *pe*. By going from *aleph* to *taw* and then adding *pe*, one makes *lamed* the exact middle of the series and sums up the whole alphabet in the name of its first letter." The root of the letter *aleph* is *ʾlp*; the verb is an Aramaism in biblical Hebrew, but it means "teach" in the factitive or piel form. This use of the alphabet may imply that everything, from A to Z, is present; a certain perfection seems to be indicated.

The numerical saying takes various forms, but the most common is *x* and *x* plus 1 (e.g., 3/4 and 6/7). Usually the emphasis is on the final item or number (Prov 30:18–19; this chapter contains several examples; see the *Comment* on these verses). Another style popular with the sages is the "blessed" saying (אשרי *ʾašrê*) as in 28:14, "Happy the person who is ever cautious, but the one who hardens his heart falls into evil." Both the numerical and the "blessed" sayings are found also in Psalms and Amos.

Limitations of Proverbial Sayings

The confidence that the Israelite sages had in their teachings is rather disarming. Peace, prosperity, success—every blessing, in short—seem to flow from the observance of the proverbs that were handed down. The recognition of the paternal discipline inflicted by the Lord is somewhat paradoxical (Prov 3:11–12). It seems to be a way of incorporating adversity into life in a "constructive" way, so as to avoid the kind of complaint that is registered in many laments of the Psalter, and especially in the book of Job. Sooner or later, the student of Proverbs is forced to question the serenity and optimism of the book. In fact, the development in the rest of the wisdom literature (Job, Qoheleth) forces the question. A fuller consideration is in order (see also the *Excursus on Retribution*). First of all, there is an underlying realization of the mystery that surrounds all human action: not only self-knowledge, but knowledge of the mysterious role of God. Proverbs 16:9 states that humans may work out their way, but it is the Lord who directs the steps (cf. Jer 10:23). More explicitly, there is the open recognition in Prov 21:30 that wisdom and knowledge ultimately avail nothing against the mystery of the Lord. The incorporation of Agur's admission of ignorance in 30:2–3 serves as a backdrop to the (un)certainties of the proverbs. Moreover, the sayings themselves are fond of pointing out ambiguities in life, so much so that one gets the impression that a large part of wisdom consists in recognizing these ambiguities. Even the ideals of silence and careful speech deserve a hard look, as 17:27–28 suggests: Is a person silent because of nothing to say, or because of care in formulating good sense? And again, should one answer a fool (26:4–5)?

J. Williams (*Gnomic Wisdom*, 35–58) has described how the lapidary and piercing style of a proverb bestows on it a certain power. Many proverbs look innocent and a priori, yet they are highly assertive. But they may not be final; rather they act as a goad, a prod to further thought, as explicitly stated in Eccl 12:11. The proverb's declaratory nature catches our attention, but it also conceals, for it achieves only a slice of reality. That is the nature of a saying: The one who hesitates is lost / Look before you leap. The truth of a saying—call it a partial truth—usually needs another saying to counterbalance it.

Text and Versions

The first striking fact about the transmission of the biblical text is the difference between the Greek and the Hebrew in the order of the material. Thus the LXX order reflects the following sequence of passages numbered according to the Hebrew: 30:1–14; 24:23–34; 30:15–33; 31:1–9; chaps. 25–29; 31:10–31. It is difficult to account for this sequence and its differences from the traditional Masoretic text (MT), which is taken as the basic text in this commentary and in most translations. While not without its difficulties and outright mistakes, there is no other possible basis than the MT. At times the solution of the Septuagint Greek version (LXX) will be given preference. But it must be admitted that our use of the LXX is marred by the fact that a critical text of Greek Proverbs has never been achieved. Hence any study of the translation manner and style of the book is on shaky ground. Pioneer efforts have been attempted by G. Gerlemann (*Studies in the Septuagint III: Proverbs*, LUÅ, n.s. [Lund: Gleerup, 1956] 1:52, n. 3), but the situation is fluid. The Greek has well over 100 extra lines (as well as many omissions). As R. Clifford describes it ("Text and Versions," 61), "There are about twenty-five verses in MT that are not in LXX but there is no general way of knowing if MT added them. LXX, on the other hand, surely added many in the long course of its transmission, most visibly in its doublets and in chaps. 6 and 9." It is not really fair to select a LXX reading simply because it might make better sense than the current MT reading. Gerlemann emphasized the influence of Hellenism on the LXX translation of Proverbs—at first sight a reasonable conclusion. A recent general study of the text by E. Tov distinguishes between inner-translational factors (or "translational exegesis") and those changes which derive from a *Vorlage*, different from the MT, used by the translator. The evidence for the first is the occurrence of the scores of doublets, which are translational, and not Greek translations of Hebrew doublets. The evidence for the different *Vorlage* comes from the transpositions of verses and groups of verses, especially the end of chap. 15 and the beginning of chap. 16, and from the differences in sequence between certain segments of the book in chaps. 24–31. His conclusion is that the Greek translator "used a Hebrew book of Proverbs which differed recensionally from that of the MT" ("Recensional Differences," 56). Despite the valiant efforts of modern scholars such as M. Dahood, W. van der Weiden, G. R. Driver, J. A. Emerton, and M. Black, the outstanding text-critical difficulties in Proverbs remain unsolved. It seems otiose to give further life to hypothetical emendations that have not won any general consensus. See the summary of the situation by R. Whybray, *The Book of Proverbs*, 158–64, esp. 161. R. Clifford ("Text and Versions," 60–61) rightly stresses that each translator intended to translate the Hebrew *verbum e verbo*. At the same time, they relied on other versions. The Syriac used LXX and the Targum used the Syriac. For the Vulgate Jerome was able to draw on the LXX in its several forms and to utilize the Hexapla (esp. Symmachus), Old Latin, Syriac, and various floating interpretive traditions. Besides, he had a sense of the style of the epigram.

The fragments of Proverbs from among the Dead Sea Scrolls were not extensive, and do not really challenge the MT readings. The co-editor, D. J. Harrington (*Wisdom Texts from Qumran*, 15–16), describes their extent: "The manuscripts designated 4Q102 and 4Q103 contain Hebrew fragments of the book of Proverbs. The column that constitutes 4Q102 supplies Hebrew texts from Proverbs 1:27–2:1. 4Q103 contains fragments of Proverbs 14:31–15:8 and 15:19b–31 in two columns, as well as fragments of 13:6b–9b; 14:6–10 and 14:12b, 13b. In both cases the texts are written in 'stichs,' that is, in sense lines with the two parallel clauses of the verse on the same line."

Egyptian and Mesopotamian Influence

More detailed discussion of the wisdom literature of Israel and its neighbors can be found in the appendix to R. E. Murphy, *The Tree of Life*, 151–71, which also contains full bibliographical data of the pertinent primary and secondary sources. See also R. J. Williams in *ABD*, 2:395–99, and J. L. Foster, *Hymns, Prayers and Songs: An Anthology of Ancient Egyptian Lyric Poetry* (Atlanta: Scholars, 1995), with bibliography, 178–83. For the important demotic texts, Ankhsheshonq and Papyrus Insinger, the best source is the translation and notes in M. Lichtheim, *AEL*, 3:159–217. See the *Excursus on International Wisdom*.

The general influence of the wisdom of neighboring cultures on the book of Proverbs is universally acknowledged. The Bible itself boasted that Solomon's wisdom was greater than that of the peoples to the East and specifically to that of Egypt (1 Kgs 5:9 [4:30]). Today, no one denies the remarkable contacts between the teaching of Amenemope and Prov 22:17–23:11; for details, see the *Excursus on the Book of Proverbs and Amenemope*. The opposition between the "silent" man and the "heated" man in Egyptian works (cf. M. Lichtheim, *AEL*, 2:147) seems to be reflected in the patterns of the wise/foolish in Israel. The problematic issue is the determination of the manner of this influence: common cultural ideals? literary dependence? The initial discoveries in the nineteenth century of Egyptian wisdom texts brought on exaggerated claims of Israelite dependence; this has been called a "ma'atizing" of biblical wisdom in general (R. E. Murphy in *Ancient Israelite Religion*, FS F. Cross [Philadelphia: Fortress, 1987] 449). The reference is to *ma'at*, which is both the word for the Egyptian ideal of righteousness and truth and the name of a goddess. The relationship of *ma'at* to the world order postulated for Israelite wisdom has been rightly termed a "crooked parallel" (M. V. Fox, "World Order and Ma'at: A Crooked Parallel," *JANESCU* 23 [1995] 37–48). There is no need to deny Egyptian influence, or a common sharing of worldview, but the result in some quarters has been harmful to a balanced appreciation of Israelite wisdom (e.g., H. D. Preuss, *Einführung*, 20–23, and the description of "older wisdom," 50–60). Hypothetical views on the origins, growth, and nature of Israelite wisdom abound, to the neglect of sober analysis of what the biblical wisdom books intend to say. In a sense the Egyptian connection, which is not to be denied, has been a mixed blessing. On the one hand, it called forth a profitable surge of interest in biblical wisdom, as the study of N. Shupak has proved, but on the other hand, it also often skewed the real message of Israelite wisdom, especially for the book of Proverbs. For a balanced and clear view, see M. V. Fox, "What Proverbs is About."

It is also true that Sumerian and Babylonian wisdom has surfaced (cf. W. Lambert, *BWL*). But proverbial sayings appear in all cultures, ancient and modern, and the biblical ties with Mesopotamian literature are much less evident for Proverbs, than, say, for Gen 1–11. Worthy of specific mention here are the sayings of Ahiqar that seem to have a Mesopotamian origin; cf. J. Pritchard, *ANET*, 427–30, and J. L. Lindenberger, *Proverbs of Ahiqar.* Some of the alleged parallels between these works and the book of Proverbs will be pointed out in the commentary below, and see the *Excursus on the Book of Proverbs and Amenemope* and the *Excursus on International Wisdom.*

History of Interpretation

There is no adequate survey of the history of the interpretation of this work. One can only point to the brief summaries. A bibliography of the primary sources is provided by A. Barucq in "Proverbes (livre de)," *DBSup* 8:1472–73, by L. Bigot, *DTC* 13:932–33, and by B. Smalley, *The Study of the Bible in the Middle Ages* (Oxford: Blackwell, 1984). For a more detailed analysis of medieval views, see *Medieval Exegesis of Wisdom Literature: Essays by Beryl Smalley*, ed. R. E. Murphy (Atlanta: Scholars Press, 1986); and also C. Spicq, *Esquisse d'une histoire de l'exégèse latine au moyen âge* (Paris: J. Vrin, 1944). B. Lang in his *Die weisheitliche Lehrrede*, 13–36, provides a brief sketch from Nicholas of Lyra on up to recent times.

Despite the inescapable lacunae in the history of the interpretation of this book, one presupposition holds steady over many centuries. Origen is the source of the patristic view about "the books of Solomon." Solomon wrote three books, Proverbs, Ecclesiastes, and the Canticle, so that humankind would be instructed in three stages of the spiritual life. Proverbs dealt with the first stage and was meant for beginners, teaching them to live virtuously in the world; cf. B. Smalley, *Medieval Exegesis*, 40–41. Another significant datum to be remembered is that the early Christian interpreters did not comment on the book of Proverbs as a whole. What has come down to us are scattered comments on various proverbs, and much of this, especially from the Greek tradition, can be found in the *Catenae* ("chains," or excerpts from patristic and early writings strung together like a chain, and forming a continuous commentary on a passage of Scripture). Some chapters were preferred above others, especially 31:10–31; under the title of the Latin version, *mulier fortis*, it caught the attention of Bede, and also of Albert the Great.

The Shape of the Commentary

The usual format of WBC is followed, but the nature of the book of Proverbs suggests modifications. This Introduction is supplemented by several excurses, and within the commentary cross-references are made to these. The commentary is divided according to the collections that can be detected within the book. The division into chapters and numbering of chapter/verse is merely for the convenience of finding particular sayings, and is therefore secondary to the natural structure that the collections provide. Each chapter presents a *Bibliography* of more recent studies, a *Translation* of the text, the textual *Notes* dealing with technical matters that undergird the translation, the considerations on *Form/Structure/Setting*, the *Comment*, and finally the *Explanation*.

A new feature is the continuous translation of the entire book of Proverbs (immediately preceding the main body of the commentary) to facilitate reference to a given text. The translation is as literal as possible, while still being intelligible. This means that "Bible English," which many deprecate, appears. But this is not a disadvantage. To the one who knows Hebrew in some measure, this will suggest the Hebrew flavor of words and phrases. In this way the impact and pungency of a proverb can be communicated more effectively. An example of this is the attempt to translate the organs of speech concretely (lips, tongue, mouth, ears) rather than abstractly (words, hearing, etc.). An effort is made to highlight the juxtaposition which is such a steady feature of Hebrew proverbs. Therefore, there is an increased use of commas and dashes, instead of the more usual copula. This should not be a hardship, since the translation is accompanied by a commentary; see the *Excursus on Translating Proverbs*. The translation is relatively conservative and attempts to adhere closely to the MT, while pointing out translation difficulties and uncertainties in the accompanying *Notes*.

For the general reader, the remarks on *Form/Structure/Setting* are helpful. But the reader must constantly bear in mind the ambiguity of the word "setting." To recover the original setting of a proverb, its point of origin, as it were, is practically impossible. There are simply too many possibilities: rural, where the oral form would presumably be the favored mode of expression; or the court, where the literary expression would more likely have been cultivated. These two "settings" are too broad to be of much help. Neither does the choice of subject help. One cannot prohibit country folk from cultivating "king" proverbs, or upper class individuals from reflecting on rural and farming concerns. While this uncertainty may be lamented, the loss is not so very great. For the implicit setting of most proverbs is human experience, an aspect that is always present, even if the specific setting in life cannot be determined. Experience ensures that the proverb, like the proverbial cat, may have nine lives or more. By its very nature, the proverb is open to many more settings. Proverbs are constantly being applied to new situations. For example, "you can lead a horse to water, but you cannot make him drink." *If* that was born of an experience at a watering trough, it has been expanded to all kinds of settings of human obstinacy, disobedience, etc. The various social groups that contributed to the wisdom movement span many settings and centuries. Moreover, as will appear in the treatment of chaps. 10ff., a new issue emerges: what is the setting of a given proverb in the collection, or chapter, in which it is found? In other words, what is its setting in the book? This angle has been assiduously pursued in recent research in the psalms, and it is also being reflected in the recent studies of biblical proverbs. At times it is obvious that topical concerns are behind the collocation of several sayings (e.g., "fools" in Prov 26:1–12); at other times the connection with a neighboring saying may be due to the appearance of a catch word as a bond of union. But one should avoid "creating" unity where it does not truly exist.

In the light of these considerations, the section on *Form/Structure/Setting* has to adapt itself to the nature of this book. Reflections on form will depend upon whether we are dealing with wisdom poems and speeches (chaps. 1–9), or individual sayings (chaps. 10–29). In most cases, the only setting that can be reasonably described is the setting in the chapter and book, the literary setting, because the original setting is beyond our reach. "Probable" settings can be suggested. Hypothetical reconstruction is so uncertain as to be almost unreliable, despite its often stimulating suggestions. In chaps. 1–9 the instructions/poems of the parent/teacher and the speeches of Wisdom do have structures that can be generally indicated. As regards the collections of sayings, the question of structure is twofold: the structure of the individual proverb (parallelism, alliteration, and so forth), and the associations it may have with surrounding proverbs by means of catch words or content. These are necessarily detailed observations and are more suitable for individual comment than for general description. It will become clear that the collections of these sayings were not haphazard, even if they were not generally unified.

The style of the *Comment* on the text will follow, more or less, the verse(s)-by-verse(s) sequence. But very frequently verses will be taken as a group, if the sense or the style calls for it. The *Explanation* will try to capture a theological edge in a chapter, whether pursuing a single verse, a theme, or whatever the chapter provides.

Proverbs

TITLE AND PURPOSE (1:1–7)

Proverbs 1

1:1   The Proverbs of Solomon, Son of David, King of Israel:
2   To know wisdom and instruction,
          to understand intelligent words;
3   To take in insightful instruction:
          justice and judgment and right;
4   To give cleverness to the simple,
          knowledge and thoughtfulness to youth;
5   That the wise may hear and add to what they take in,
          and the intelligent acquire direction;
6   To understand proverb and riddle,
          words of the wise and their puzzles.

7   The fear of the Lord: the beginning of knowledge;
          wisdom and instruction fools despise.

INTRODUCTORY INSTRUCTIONS (1:8–9:18)

1:8   My son, listen to the instruction of your father,
          do not abandon the teaching of your mother,
9   For a gracious wreath on your head, they;
          a necklace for your throat.
10   My son, if sinners entice you,
          do not go along!
11   If they say, "Come with us,
          let us lie in wait for blood!
          For no reason, we will ambush the innocent!
12   We will swallow them alive like Sheol—
          whole, like those who go down to the pit.
13   We will get all kinds of precious things;
          We will fill our homes with loot.
14   Throw in your lot with us;
          We shall all have one purse!"
15   My son, do not walk in the way with them;
          keep back your feet from their path,
16   For their feet run to evil,
          and they hasten to shed blood—

17 In vain a net baited
        before the eyes of any bird—
18 But they lie in wait for their own blood;
        they ambush themselves.
19 Such the ways of all who are bent on gain;
        it takes the lives of its owners.

20 Wisdom cries out in the streets,
        raises her voice in the squares;
21 At a corner of bustling streets she calls;
        at the city gates she speaks her words:
22 "How long, simple ones, will you love being simple,
        and the arrogant delight in their arrogance,
        and the fools hate knowledge,
23 Turning away at my reproof?
        Now I will pour out my spirit to you;
        I will make known my words to you:
24 Because I called and you refused;
        I put forth my hand, but no one gave heed.
25 You disregarded all my counsel,
        and did not accept my reproof;
26 Now I will laugh at your calamity;
        I will mock when your terror comes,
27 When your terror comes like a storm,
        and your calamity arrives like a whirlwind,
        and distress and anguish come upon you.
28 Then they will call to me, but I will not answer;
        they will seek me, but they will not find me,
29 Because they hated knowledge,
        and the fear of the Lord they did not choose;
30 They were not open to my advice;
        they rejected my every reproof.
31 So they shall eat the fruit of their own way,
        and they shall have their fill of their own plans.
32 For the defection of the simple kills them,
        and the complacency of fools destroys them;
33 But whoever listens to me will live in safety,
        peacefully, with no terror to fear."

Proverbs 2

2:1 My son, if you take in my words
        and make my commands your treasure,
2   Giving your ear to wisdom,
        inclining your heart to understanding;
3   If you call out for perception
        and summon understanding;

4   If you seek for her like silver
      and search for her like hidden treasure;

5   Then you will understand the fear of the Lord,
      and acquire knowledge of God,

6   For the Lord gives wisdom,
      from his mouth come knowledge and understanding;

7   He stores up success for the upright—
      a shield for those who proceed with integrity,

8   Protecting the paths of justice,
      guarding the way of the faithful ones;

9   Then you will understand justice and judgment and right,
      everything that leads to good.

10   When wisdom comes into your heart
      and knowledge nestles in your soul,

11   Prudence will keep guard over you;
      intelligence will protect you,

12   To save you from the way of evil,
      from those who speak perversely,

13   Those who abandon straight paths
      to walk in the ways of darkness,

14   Who rejoice in doing evil,
      who delight in evil perversity,

15   Whose paths are twisted,
      whose tracks are devious;

16   To save you from the woman who is a stranger,
      from the outsider whose words are smooth,

17   Who has abandoned the companion of her youth,
      and forgotten the covenant of her God;

18   Her house sinks down to death,
      her tracks, to the shades;

19   No one who enters there ever returns;
      they never reach the paths of life;

20   In order that you may go in the way of the good,
      and observe the paths of the just,

21   Because the upright will dwell in the land,
      and the blameless will remain in it;

22   But the wicked will be cut off from the land,
      and the faithless will be uprooted from it.

Proverbs 3

3:1   My son, do not forget my teaching,
      and let your heart keep my commands,

2   For length of days and years of life
      and peace will they bring you.

3   Do not let kindness and fidelity leave you;

bind them on your neck;
write them on the tablet of your heart,
4 And so find favor and good esteem
in the eyes of God and humans.

5 Trust in the Lord wholeheartedly
and do not rely on your own intelligence;
6 In all your ways acknowledge him,
and he will keep your paths straight.

7 Do not be wise in your own eyes,
fear the Lord and turn from evil.
8 It will be healing for your body
and refreshment for your bones.

9 Give honor to the Lord from your riches
and from the firstfruits of all your income;
10 Then your barns will be filled with plenty,
and your vats will flow with new wine.

11 My son, do not reject the discipline of the Lord,
and do not spurn his reproof,
12 For the Lord loves the one he reproves,
as a father, the child in whom he delights.

13 Happy the one finds wisdom,
the one who acquires understanding!
14 For her profit, greater than gold,
her income, greater than silver.
15 More precious than rubies—
no treasures can compare with her.
16 Length of days in her right hand,
and in her left, riches and glory.
17 Her ways, pleasant ways,
and all her paths, peace!
18 She, a tree of life to all who grasp her;
happy those who take hold of her!

19 The Lord founded the world with wisdom,
establishing the heavens with intelligence.
20 By his knowledge the depths were split,
and the clouds drop down dew.

21 My son, do not let them slip from your eyes:
hold on to discretion and prudence,
22 So that they will be life to your soul
and adornment for your neck.

23   Then you will go on your way securely,
      and your foot will not stumble.

24   When you lie down, you have nothing to be afraid of;
      you will lie down, and your sleep will be sweet.

25   Do not fear a sudden terror,
      or the ruin that comes to the wicked,

26   For the Lord will be your confidence;
      he will keep your foot from being caught.

27   Do not refuse anyone the good that is his,
      when it is your power to act.

28   Do not tell your neighbor, "Go, but come back again,
      and tomorrow I will give," although you can do it now.

29   Do not plot evil against your neighbor
      who lives trustfully beside you.

30   Do not contend with any one for no cause
      when they have done you no evil.

31   Do not envy the violent,
      and do not choose any of their ways,

32   For the devious are an abomination to the Lord,
      but the upright are in his confidence.

33   The curse of the Lord is on the house of the wicked,
      but he blesses the dwelling of the just.

34   The scoffers he scoffs at;
      the humble he favors.

35   Glory, the wise inherit—
      but fools, disgrace.

Proverbs 4

4:1   Hear, children, a father's instruction;
      pay attention and know what understanding is.

2   For I give you sound doctrine;
      do not abandon my teaching.

3   Indeed, a son to my father was I,
      tender, and my mother's only one.

4   He taught me and said to me:
      "Let your heart hold fast my words;
      keep my commands and live!

5   Get wisdom, get understanding!
      Do not forget; do not turn aside from the words of my mouth!

6   If you do not forsake her, she will guard you;
      love her, and she will preserve you.

7 The beginning of wisdom: Get wisdom!
  Above all else that you get, get wisdom!
8 Extol her, and she will exalt you;
  embrace her, and she will honor you.
9 She will place a gracious wreath on your head,
  bestow on you a glorious crown."

10 Hear, my son, and take in my words,
   and the years of your life will be many.
11 I have taught you in the way of wisdom;
   I have put you on a way of straight paths.
12 As you go, your step will not be shortened,
   and when you run, you will not stumble.
13 Hold instruction firmly; do not let go!
   Keep her: your life!
14 Do not go in the path of the wicked,
   and do not walk in the way of the evil.
15 Avoid it; do not go near it;
   turn aside from it and keep going!
16 They cannot sleep without doing evil;
   they lose sleep if they have not caused some to stumble.
17 They feed on the bread of wickedness
   and drink the wine of violence.
18 But the path of the just, like a dawning light
   that keeps shining unto the full day.
19 The way of the wicked, like darkness;
   they do not know what they are stumbling over.

20 My son, pay attention to my words;
   turn your ear to my sayings.
21 Do not let them slip from your eyes;
   keep them in your heart,
22 For they are life to those who find them,
   and a healing to the whole person.
23 More than all else you guard, watch your heart,
   for out of it, the surges of life.
24 Turn aside from your mouth any crookedness;
   put away from your lips any deceit.
25 Let your eyes keep looking forward,
   your eyelids straight ahead of you.
26 Level a path for your feet,
   and let all your ways be firm.
27 Do not turn to right or left;
   keep your foot from evil.

Proverbs 5

^{5:1} My son, pay attention to my wisdom,
  give ear to my understanding,
² That you may keep discernment,
  and your lips may guard knowledge.
³ The lips of the "stranger"-woman drip honey;
  smoother than oil, her mouth.
⁴ But her end, bitter as wormwood,
  sharp as a two-edged sword.
⁵ Her feet go down to death;
  her steps take hold of Sheol.
⁶ Lest you observe the path of life,
  her tracks wander—but you do not know it.

⁷ And now, sons, listen to me,
  and do not turn aside from the words of my mouth.
⁸ Keep your way far from her,
  and do not go near the door of her house,
⁹ Lest you yield your power to others,
  and your years to a cruel one;
¹⁰ Lest strangers have their fill of your wealth,
  and your labor, in the house of another.
¹¹ Then you will groan in the end
  when your flesh and body are consumed,
¹² And you will say, "How I hated discipline,
  and how my heart despised reproof!
¹³ I did not listen to what my teachers said;
  I did not give ear to my instructors.
¹⁴ I have all but come to ruin
  in the midst of the assembled community."

¹⁵ Drink water from your own cistern,
  running water from your own well.
¹⁶ Should your springs be scattered abroad,
  and streams of water in the squares?
¹⁷ Let them be yours alone,
  and not shared with strangers!
¹⁸ Let your fountain be blessed,
  and have joy from the wife of your youth,
¹⁹ A lovely hind, a graceful doe;
  drink your fill of her love;
  be always inebriated by her ardor.
²⁰ Why, my son, should you be inebriated by a "stranger"?
  Why embrace the bosom of an outsider?
²¹ The ways of humans are before the eyes of the Lord,
  and all their paths observed.

22   The wicked person will be caught by his own iniquities,
           held fast by the cords of his own sin.
23   He will die for lack of discipline,
           inebriated by his great folly.

Proverbs 6

6:1   My son, if you have gone surety for your neighbor,
            pledging your hand to another,
2   You have been trapped by the words of your lips,
            caught by the words of your mouth.
3   Then do this, my son, and free yourself,
            for you have played into the hand of your neighbor:
            go, throw yourself down, and pressure your neighbor!
4   Give no sleep to your eyes,
            no slumber to your eyelids.
5   Save yourself, like a gazelle from a hand,
            like a bird from the hand of a fowler.

6   Go to the ant, you sluggard,
            look at its ways and become wise!
7   For though it has no leader,
            overseer, or ruler,
8   It acquires its food in the summer,
            stores up its provisions at the harvest.
9   How long will you stay in bed, you sluggard?
            When will you stir out of sleep?
10   "Just a little sleep, a little slumber,
            a little folding of the arms to rest"—
11   Then your poverty will come like a robber,
            and destitution like an armed man.

12   A scoundrel, a villain,
            one who goes about, crooked of mouth,
13   Darting with his eyes, shifting his feet,
            jabbing with his fingers—
14   Heart intent on disturbance,
            plotting evil at every moment,
            he initiates discord.
15   Therefore disaster will come to him unawares;
            suddenly he is broken, and no remedy.

16   Six things the Lord hates,
            seven, abominations to him:
17   Haughty eyes, a lying tongue,
            hands shedding innocent blood,

18 A heart designing wicked plots,
    feet quick to run to evil,
19 A false witness spreading lies,
    initiating discord among kindred.

20 My son, keep the command of your father
    and do not reject the teaching of your mother.
21 Bind them over your heart always,
    tie them about your neck.
22 Wherever you walk, it will lead you;
    wherever you lie down, it will guard you,
    and when you get up, it will speak with you.
23 For command: a lamp, and teaching: a light;
    a way to life: instruction that reproves,
24 Keeping you from an evil woman,
    from the smooth tongue of a stranger.
25 Do not lust in your heart after her beauty,
    and do not let her capture you with her fluttering eyes,
26 Because for a harlot, scarcely a loaf of bread—
    but a precious life the adulteress hunts for.
27 Can a man carry embers in his bosom
    without burning his clothes?
28 Or can a man walk on live coals
    without scorching his feet?
29 So the one who sleeps with his neighbor's wife;
    anyone who touches her will not go unpunished.
30 A thief is not despised for stealing
    in order to satisfy a hungry appetite;
31 But if he is caught, he must pay sevenfold,
    give up all the goods of his house.
32 Whoever commits adultery, lacking in sense;
    a self-destroyer, he does it.
33 He meets with a beating and disgrace,
    and his shame will not be wiped out;
34 Passion—a husband's rage;
    and he will show no pity on the day of revenge.
35 He will not consider any restitution,
    nor be swayed by many bribes.

Proverbs 7

7:1 My son, keep my words
    and make my commands your treasure.
2 Keep my commands and live,
    and my teaching, like the apple of your eye.
3 Bind them on your fingers,
    write them on the tablet of your heart.

4   Say to Wisdom, "You are my sister";
        Call Understanding, "friend,"
5   To save you from the stranger,
        from the outsider whose words are smooth.
6   At the window of my house
        I looked through the lattices;
7   I saw among the simple ones,
        among the youths, I noticed one who lacked sense,
8   Crossing the street near her corner,
        walking along the way to her house,
9   In twilight, at the end of day,
        at the onset of night and darkness.
10   All at once a woman meets him,
        in harlot attire and with guarded heart.
11   Stormy and rebellious, she;
        her feet can not stay in her own house.
12   Now in the street, now in the squares,
        and at every corner she lurks.
13   Then she grabs him and kisses him,
        and with impudent face she says to him:
14   "My due peace offerings,
        my vows, I have fulfilled today.
15   So I have come out to meet you,
        seeking your presence, and I found you!
16   I have covered my couch with coverlets,
        with colorful linens from Egypt.
17   I have perfumed my bed
        with myrrh, aloes, and cinnamon.
18   Come, let us have our fill of love till morning!
        let us enjoy love!
19   My husband—not at home!
        He has gone on a long journey,
20   Clutching a bag of money in his hand,
        and only at the full moon will he return."
21   She seduces him with all her talk,
        deceives him with her smooth lips.
22   He follows her at once,
        like an ox that goes to slaughter,
    Like a stag springing into a trap,
23   till an arrow splits his liver;
    Like a bird hastening to a snare,
        unknowing, at the cost of his life.

24   Now, sons, listen to me;
        pay attention to the words of my mouth.
25   Do not let your heart yield to her ways,
        do not stray in her paths.

26 Many the wounded she has brought down;
    powerful too, all that she has killed.
27 Her house—the ways to Sheol,
    going down to the chambers of Death.

Proverbs 8

8:1 Does not Wisdom call,
    and Understanding raise her voice?
2 At the top of the heights along the way,
    at the crossroads she takes her stand;
3 By the gates at the entrance of the city,
    at the entryways she cries out:

4 "To you, O men, I call out;
    to all humankind, my cry:
5 You simple ones, learn insight!
    You fools, learn understanding!
6 Listen, for I speak noble things;
    the utterance of my lips, what is right,
7 My mouth proclaims truth;
    an abomination to my lips, wickedness!
8 In justice, all the words of my mouth,
    none of them devious or crooked;
9 All of them straightforward to those who understand,
    upright to those who have found knowledge.
10 Take my instruction instead of silver,
    and knowledge rather than choice gold.
11 For, better wisdom than rubies;
    no treasures can compare with her.

12 I, Wisdom, dwell with prudence;
    I have come to know thoughtfulness.
13 Fear of the Lord—hatred of evil;
    pride and arrogance—an evil way,
    and a perverse mouth I hate.
14 Mine: counsel and success;
    mine: power; understanding: I.
15 Through me kings reign,
    and rulers decree justice.
16 Through me princes rule,
    and nobles, all just judges.
17 I love those who love me,
    and those who seek me shall find me.
18 With me riches and honor,
    wealth that lasts, and justice.

19   My fruit, better than gold, pure gold,
         and my produce, than choice silver.
20   In the path of justice I walk,
         down the correct ways,
21   Giving a rich inheritance to those who love me,
         and filling their treasuries.

22   The Lord begot me at the beginning of his ways,
         the first of his works from of old.
23   Ages ago I was set up,
         from the start, before earth began.
24   As yet no deeps—I was brought forth,
         as yet no fountains, springs of water.
25   Before the mountains were set up,
         before the hills, I was brought forth.
26   When he had not yet made the earth and fields,
         nor the first clumps of world's earth,
27   There I,—when he put the heavens in place,
         when he marked out the horizon on the face of the deep,
28   When he made firm the skies above,
         when he strengthened the sources of the deep,
29   When he placed a limit for the sea
         so that the waters would not disobey his command,
         when he marked out the foundations of the earth,
30   There I was with him, as artisan,
         and I was delight day after day,
         playing before him all the time,
31   Playing on the surface of the earth,
         and my delight: human beings.

32   And now, sons, listen to me:
         Happy those who keep my ways.
33   Listen to instruction and be wise;
         do not reject it.
34   Happy those who listen to me,
         waiting at my gates day by day,
         watching at my doorposts.
35   Those who find me find life,
         and win the favor of the Lord.
36   Those who pass me by, destroy themselves;
         all who hate me love death.

Proverbs 9

9:1   Wisdom has built her house;
         she has set up her seven columns.
2   She has prepared her meat, mixed her wine,

and then set the table.
3   She has sent forth her maidservants to call
         from the heights over the city:
4   "Let those who are simple turn in here!"
         To the one who lacks sense she says:
5   "Come, eat my bread,
         and drink of the wine I have mixed.
6   Give up being mindless and live!
         Walk in the path of understanding."

7   Whoever corrects the arrogant—one who gets insult,
         and whoever reproves the wicked—shame.
8   Do not reprove the arrogant—they will hate you;
         reprove the wise—they will love you.
9   Share with the wise and they become wiser;
         teach the just and they go on learning.
10   The beginning of wisdom: the fear of the Lord;
         knowledge of the Holy One: understanding.
11   Through me your days will be many,
         and the years of your life will increase.
12   If you are wise, that wisdom is yours;
         if you are arrogant, you bear it alone.

13   Woman Folly is stormy,
         mindless, and totally ignorant.
14   But she sits at the door of her house,
         enthroned on the heights of the city,
15   Calling on those who pass by,
         who are going onward in their ways:
16   "Let those who are simple turn in here!"
         To the one who lacks sense she says:
17   "Stolen water is sweet,
         and bread taken in secret tastes better."
18   But they do not know that the shades are there—
         in the depths of Sheol, her guests.

THE PROVERBS OF SOLOMON (10:1–22:16)

Proverbs 10

10:1   The Proverbs of Solomon:
         A wise son gives joy to a father,
            and a foolish son, grief to the mother.
2   Treasures obtained by wickedness do not profit,
            but justice delivers from death.
3   The Lord does not allow the just person to hunger,
            but thwarts the desire of the wicked.

4   Whoever works with slack hands becomes poor,
       but the hand of the diligent brings riches.

5   Whoever lays in stores in the summer, a wise son,
       but whoever sleeps during harvest, a shameful son.

6   Blessings on the head of the just,
       but the mouth of the wicked conceals violence.

7   The memory of the just, for a blessing,
       but the name of the wicked rots.

8   The wise at heart takes in commands,
       but the fool by his lips will fall.

9   Whoever walks honestly walks securely,
       but the one whose paths are crooked will be found out.

10   Whoever winks the eye brings trouble,
       but one who reprimands frankly establishes peace.

11   A fountain of life—the mouth of the just,
       but the mouth of the wicked conceals violence.

12   Hatred stirs up strife,
       but over all offenses love covers.

13   Wisdom is found on the lips of the intelligent,
       but the rod for the back of one lacking in sense.

14   The wise store up knowledge,
       but the mouth of the fool, imminent ruin.

15   The wealth of the rich, a strong city;
       the ruin of the poor, their poverty.

16   The earnings of the just, for life;
       the income of the wicked, for sin.

17   A path to life, whoever observes instruction,
       but whoever rejects reprimand goes astray.

18   Whoever conceals hatred, lying lips,
       and whoever spreads slander, a fool.

19   In much talk, iniquity will not be lacking,
       but those who restrain their lips, sensible people.

20   Choice silver, the tongue of the just;
       the heart of the wicked, of little worth.

21   The lips of the just nourish many,
       but fools die for lack of sense.

22   The blessing of the Lord—that brings riches,
       and no toil can add to it.

23   Like a fool's joy: sinful activity,
       but for the intelligent person: wisdom.

24   What the wicked fear—that will come upon them,
       but what the just desire will be granted.

25   With a passing storm, no wicked,
       but the just, a permanent foundation.

26   Like vinegar to the teeth and smoke to the eyes,
       so the sluggard to those who make him a messenger.

27   The fear of the Lord adds on days,
       but the years of the wicked are shortened.

28   The expectation of the just: rejoicing,
        but the hope of the wicked perishes.
29   A refuge for the upright, the way of the Lord,
        but disaster for evildoers.
30   The just will never be moved,
        but the wicked will not dwell in the land.
31   The mouth of the just puts forth wisdom,
        but the perverse tongue will be cut off.
32   The lips of the just know favor,
        but the mouth of the wicked, perversity.

Proverbs 11

11:1   False scales, an abomination to the Lord,
        but a full weight, his pleasure.
2   When pride comes, then comes shame;
        but with the humble, wisdom.
3   The integrity of the upright guides them,
        but deceit destroys the faithless.
4   Wealth is of no profit on the day of wrath,
        but justice delivers from death.
5   The justice of the upright keeps their way straight,
        but the wicked fall because of their wickedness.
6   The justice of the honest delivers them,
        but the faithless are caught by their desire.
7   With the death of the wicked, hope vanishes;
        what strength can expect vanishes.
8   The just are freed from distress,
        and the wicked take their place!
9   By mouth the impious destroy their neighbor,
        but by knowledge the just are saved.
10   When the just prosper, a city is glad,
        and when the wicked perish, rejoicing.
11   By the blessing of the upright a city is exalted,
        but by the mouth of the wicked it is destroyed.
12   One who despises his neighbor, lacking in sense;
        but a man of intelligence keeps quiet.
13   Whoever slanders, a revealer of confidences;
        but the trustworthy, a keeper of secrets.
14   No guidance, a people falls;
        but in many counselors, safety.
15   Whoever goes surety for a stranger suffers,
        but whoever hates giving pledges, secure.
16   A graceful woman holds to honor,
        but strong men hold on to riches.
17   The kind person benefits himself,
        but the cruel one harms himself.

18 The wicked: making empty profits,
    but one sowing justice: sure wages.
19 Justice is directed to life,
    but whoever pursues evil, to death.
20 An abomination to the Lord, those crooked at heart;
    but his pleasure, those upright in their path.
21 Be assured, the evil person will not go unpunished,
    but the descendants of the just will go free.
22 A golden ring in the snout of a pig—
    a woman beautiful but without sense.
23 The desire of the just, only good;
    the hope of the wicked, wrath.
24 There is one scattering, and still the richer,
    and one too sparing, only the poorer.
25 Those who are a blessing to others will prosper,
    and those who refresh others will themselves be refreshed.
26 Whoever holds back grain, the people will curse him,
    but blessings on the head of the one who sells it.
27 Whoever is intent on good, seeks favor,
    but the one on the watch for evil—it will fall on him.
28 Whoever trusts in their riches, that one will fall,
    but the just shall bloom like foliage.
29 Whoever disturbs his household will inherit the wind;
    and a fool—servant to the wise of heart.
30 The fruit of the just, a tree of life;
    but violence takes away souls.
31 The just is recompensed on earth;
    how much more the wicked and the sinner!

Proverbs 12

12:1 A lover of instruction, a lover of knowledge;
    but a hater of reproof, stupid!
2 The good obtain favor from the Lord;
    but the schemer, he condemns.
3 No one can find a solid support in wickedness,
    but the root of the just shall never be moved.
4 A resourceful woman, the crown of her husband,
    but like rot in his bones, a shameful one.
5 The plans of the just, right!
    the guidance of the wicked, deceit!
6 The words of the wicked, a deadly ambush,
    but the mouth of the upright delivers them.
7 Overthrow the wicked, and they disappear,
    but the house of the just will stand.
8 A person is praised according to intelligence;
    but the twisted of heart will be despised.

9   Better the lightly regarded if he has a servant,
        than the one who puts on airs, but lacks sense.

10   The just know the temperament of their livestock,
        but the compassion of the wicked, cruel!

11   The tiller of the soil will have enough food,
        but whoever pursues empty nothings lacks sense.

12   The wicked desire the snare of the evil,
        but the root of the just puts forth.

13   In the transgression of the lips, an evil trap,
        but the just person gets out of trouble.

14   A person is filled with good from the fruit of his mouth,
        and the work of his hands returns upon him.

15   The way of a fool, right in his own eyes,
        but whoever listens to advice, a wise person!

16   The anger of a fool is known immediately,
        but whoever conceals insult, a clever one!

17   The one who tells the truth, proves trustworthy,
        but a lying witness, deceit!

18   There is one who talks on and on, like sword thrusts,
        but the tongue of the wise, healing!

19   Truthful lips endure forever,
        but a mere moment, the lying tongue.

20   In the hearts of those who plan evil, deceit;
        but for those who counsel peace, joy.

21   No disaster befalls the just,
        but the wicked get their fill of evil.

22   An abomination to the Lord, lying lips,
        but those who act truthfully, his pleasure.

23   A clever person conceals his knowledge,
        but the heart of fools proclaims folly.

24   The hand of the diligent rules,
        but slackness subjects one to labor.

25   Anxiety in heart weighs a person down,
        but a good word gives him joy.

26   The just person shows the way to his neighbor,
        but the way of the wicked leads them astray.

27   Slackness will not have a roast to cook,
        but the wealth of a diligent person is precious.

28   In the path of justice, life;
        the way of abomination, to death.

Proverbs 13

13:1   A wise son—discipline by a father,
        but a scoffer does not heed a scolding.

2   A person eats good things from the fruit of the mouth,
        but the desire of the greedy, violence.

3 Whoever guards his mouth, one who preserves his life;
    whoever opens wide the lips, ruin for him.

4 A lazy person has great craving, but nothing else!
    but the desire of the diligent is fulfilled.

5 The just person hates a deceitful word,
    but the wicked causes shame and disgrace.

6 Justice preserves the blameless in his path,
    but wickedness misleads the sinner.

7 There is a person who pretends to riches, but with not a thing;
    who pretends to be poor, but with great wealth!

8 Ransom for the life of a man: his riches,
    but a poor person hears no threat.

9 The light of the just rejoices,
    but the lamp of the wicked goes out.

10 Arrogance yields only quarreling,
    but with those who take advice, wisdom.

11 Wealth in haste counts for little,
    but one who gathers by hand will have much.

12 Hope deferred, sickness of heart;
    but a tree of life, desire fulfilled.

13 One who despises a word, it will go badly for him,
    but one who reveres a command, he will be rewarded.

14 The teaching of the wise, a fountain of life,
    for turning from deadly snares.

15 Good insight brings favor,
    but the way of the faithless is their ruin.

16 Every clever person acts with knowledge,
    but a fool spouts folly.

17 A wicked messenger falls into evil,
    but a trustworthy envoy, healing!

18 Poverty and shame: whoever rejects instruction!
    But whoever heeds reproof will be honored.

19 A desire realized is sweet to a person,
    and an abomination to fools: turning from evil.

20 Walk with the wise and be wise!
    But the companion of fools fares badly.

21 Evil pursues sinners,
    but as for the just, there is a good reward.

22 A good person leaves an inheritance to grandchildren,
    but stored up for the just: the wealth of a sinner.

23 An abundance of food, the tillage of the poor,
    but property is swept away unjustly.

24 Whoever spares the rod, a hater of his son,
    but whoever loves him disciplines him early on.

25 A just person, one who eats and satisfies hunger,
    but the belly of the wicked is empty.

Proverbs 14

14:1	Wisdom has built her house, but Folly tears hers down by her own hands.
2	Whoever walks uprightly: one who fears the Lord, but whoever is devious in his ways: one who despises him.
3	In the mouth of a fool, a shoot of pride, but the lips of the wise preserve them.
4	In the absence of oxen, the crib is empty, but abundant produce, by the strength of an ox.
5	A trustworthy witness will not lie, but a false witness spreads lies.
6	The scoffer seeks wisdom, in vain! but knowledge is easy for the intelligent.
7	Stay away from a foolish person, for you do not find knowledge on those lips!
8	The wisdom of the clever: the understanding of their way, but the folly of fools: deception.
9	Fools scoff at a guilt offering, but among the upright, favor.
10	The heart knows its bitterness of spirit, and in its joy another cannot share.
11	The house of the wicked will be destroyed, but the tent of the upright shall flourish.
12	There is a way that seems right to a person, but its end, ways to death.
13	Even in laughter the heart may be sad, and the end of joy, grief.
14	The unsteady of heart get their fill of their ways, and good people, of their deeds.
15	The simple person believes everything, but the clever one watches his step.
16	The wise person: fearing and turning from evil, but the fool: reckless and overconfident.
17	The quick-tempered commit folly, and the schemer is hated.
18	The simple inherit folly, but the clever are crowned with knowledge.
19	The evil bow before the good, and the wicked, at the gates of the just.
20	The poor are hated even by their neighbor, but those who love the rich, many!
21	Whoever despises his neighbor, a sinner, but happy, whoever is kind to the poor!
22	Do not those who plan evil go astray? But those who plan good, kindness and fidelity.

23   In all work there will be profit,
         but the talk of the lips—only to deprivation!
24   The crown of the wise, their riches;
         the folly of fools, folly!
25   A trusty witness, one who delivers souls,
         but whoever spreads lies, deceit.
26   The fear of the Lord, strength to trust in,
         and one's children will have a refuge.
27   The fear of the Lord, a fountain of life,
         to turn from the snares of death.
28   A large population, a king's glory,
         but without people, a leader's ruin.
29   Slow to anger, great intelligence,
         but the quick-tempered exalts folly.
30   The life of the body, a calm heart,
         but rot in the bones, envy.
31   Whoever oppresses the needy blasphemes his maker,
         but whoever is kind to the poor honors him.
32   The wicked is overthrown by his evil,
         but the just, one who relies on his integrity.
33   Wisdom nestles in the heart of the intelligent,
         but among fools can it come to be known?
34   Justice exalts a nation,
         but sin, a reproach for a people.
35   The favor of a king, for a clever servant,
         but his wrath is for a shameful one.

Proverbs 15

15:1   A soft answer turns back wrath,
         but a sharp word stirs up anger.
2   The tongue of the wise advances knowledge,
         but the mouth of fools pours out folly.
3   In every place, the eyes of the Lord,
         watching the evil and the good.
4   A healing tongue, a tree of life,
         but when perverse, a broken spirit.
5   A fool despises the instruction of his father,
         but whoever heeds reproof is smart.
6   The house of the just, much treasure,
         but in the revenue of the wicked, trouble.
7   The lips of the wise spread knowledge,
         but the heart of fools, not so.
8   The sacrifice of the wicked, an abomination to the Lord,
         but the prayer of the just, his delight.
9   An abomination to the Lord, the way of the wicked,
         but whoever pursues justice, he loves.

10 Discipline is an evil for one who abandons the way;
    whoever hates reproof will die.
11 Sheol and Abaddon before the Lord—
    how much more, human hearts!
12 The scoffer does not like being reproved;
    to the wise he will not go.
13 A joyful heart lights up the face,
    but in a troubled heart, a crushed spirit.
14 An understanding heart seeks out knowledge,
    but the mouth of fools feeds on folly.
15 Every day of the afflicted, evil!
    But the contented in heart, a continual feast.
16 Better a little with fear of the Lord,
    than great treasure and with it trouble.
17 Better a dish of herbs, but with love,
    than a well-fed ox, but with hatred.
18 An angry person stirs up strife,
    but the patient man quiets disputes.
19 The way of the lazy, like a thorn hedge,
    but the path of the upright, a highway.
20 A wise son gives joy to the father,
    but a fool of a man despises his mother.
21 Folly, joy to the one who lacks sense,
    but one who has understanding goes straight ahead.
22 Plans are thwarted in the absence of counsel,
    but with many counselors they will hold.
23 Joy to a man from the answer of his mouth,
    and a timely word, how good!
24 For the prudent, a path of life upward,
    in order to turn from Sheol below.
25 The Lord tears down the house of the proud,
    but he makes firm the widow's landmark.
26 An abomination to the Lord, evil plans,
    but gracious words, pure.
27 A disturber of his own house, one who is greedy for gain,
    but whoever hates a bribe will have life.
28 The heart of the just plans how to answer,
    but the mouth of the wicked pours forth evil.
29 The Lord, far from the wicked,
    but the prayer of the just he hears.
30 The light of the eyes give joy to the heart;
    good news refreshes the bones.
31 The ear that listens to an enlivening reproof
    lodges among the wise.
32 Whoever spurns instruction, one who loathes himself,
    but whoever heeds reproof, one who acquires sense.
33 Fear of the Lord, instruction in wisdom;
    and before glory, humility.

Proverbs 16

16:1 The designs of the heart, for human beings,
　　　but from the Lord the response of the tongue.
2　All the ways of a person, pure in his own eyes,
　　　but the one who weighs the spirits, the Lord.
3　Commit your works to the Lord,
　　　and your plans will be firm.
4　The Lord has made everything for a purpose,
　　　even the wicked for the evil day.
5　An abomination to the Lord, every proud heart;
　　　be assured, they shall not go unpunished.
6　By kindness and fidelity iniquity is atoned for,
　　　and by fear of the Lord, a turning from evil.
7　When a person's ways please the Lord,
　　　he makes even his enemies peaceful toward him.
8　Better a little with justice
　　　than great income with injustice.
9　The heart of a man plans his way,
　　　but the Lord directs his steps.
10　An oracle on the lips of a king:
　　　justice from his mouth never fails.
11　Honest balances and scales—the Lord's;
　　　his concern, all the weights in the bag.
12　Wicked actions, an abomination to kings,
　　　for a throne is made firm by justice.
13　Justice from lips, the delight of kings,
　　　and they love the one who speaks honestly.
14　The wrath of a king, messengers of death;
　　　but a wise person can pacify it.
15　In the light of the king's face, life;
　　　and his favor, like the cloud of rain in spring.
16　How much better to get wisdom than gold,
　　　preferable to silver, to get understanding.
17　The highway of the upright, turning from evil;
　　　whoever watches his way saves his life.
18　Before a collapse, pride,
　　　and before stumbling, haughtiness of spirit.
19　Better humble in spirit with the poor,
　　　than dividing booty with the proud.
20　Whoever ponders a word will find good,
　　　but whoever trusts in the Lord, happiness!
21　The wise of heart will be called intelligent,
　　　and sweetness of lips increases learning.
22　A fountain of life, a possessor of insight,
　　　but folly, the discipline of fools.

23   A wise heart makes a smart mouth,
            and increases learning on the lips.
24   A honeycomb, pleasant words!
            Sweet to taste, and healing for bones.
25   There is a way, straight for a person,
            but its end, ways of death.
26   The desire of a toiler toils for him,
            for his mouth urges him on.
27   A villain, a digger of evil,
            and upon his lips, like a burning fire.
28   A perverse man initiates discord,
            and a gossiper separates friends.
29   A violent person seduces his neighbor,
            and leads him in a way that is not good.
30   Whoever winks the eye, for planning upsets;
            whoever purses the lips accomplishes evil.
31   A crown of glory, gray hair;
            it is found in the way of justice.
32   Better one slow to anger, than a warrior,
            whoever controls his spirit, than one who conquers a city.
33   Into the lap the lot is cast,
            but from the Lord, its entire decision.

Proverbs 17

17:1   Better a dry crust, with quiet,
            than a house full of feasting, with quarrels.
2   A clever servant will rule a shameful son,
            and will inherit along with the heirs.
3   The crucible for silver, the furnace for gold—
            but the tester of hearts: the Lord.
4   An evildoer, one who listens to wicked lips;
            a liar, one with an ear for a destructive tongue.
5   Whoever mocks the poor blasphemes the Maker;
            whoever rejoices at a disaster will not go unpunished.
6   The crown of old men, grandchildren,
            and the glory of children, their fathers.
7   Unbefitting a fool, honest lips;
            the more so, deceitful lips in a noble.
8   A bribe, a charm in the eyes of the one who gives it;
            everywhere he turns he succeeds.
9   One who disregards a fault, one who seeks friendship;
            one who insists on it, one who loses a companion.
10   A rebuke gets to an intelligent person
            better than a hundred lashes on a fool.
11   The evil person seeks out only rebellion,
            but a cruel messenger will be sent to him.

12 Encounter a bear deprived of her cubs—
    but not a fool in his folly!
13 Whoever returns evil for good—
    evil will never depart from that house.
14 Whoever unleashes water, the beginning of strife;
    so before the burst, stop quarreling!
15 One who justifies the wicked or one who condemns the just—
    an abomination to the Lord, both of them.
16 For what purpose the price in the hand of a fool
    to buy wisdom when there is no heart for it?
17 A neighbor, loving at all times—
    and a brother is born for adversity.
18 A person lacking sense, one who pledges his hand,
    going surety in the presence of his neighbor.
19 One who loves iniquity, one who loves strife;
    one who makes his gate high, one who seeks destruction.
20 The crooked of heart cannot find good,
    and one perverse of tongue falls into evil.
21 Whoever begets a fool, his the grief,
    and the father of a stupid person can have no joy.
22 A joyful heart makes for good health,
    but a crushed spirit dries up the bones.
23 The wicked draw upon a pocketed bribe
    to pervert the ways of justice.
24 In front of the perceptive: wisdom,
    but the eyes of a fool: on the ends of the earth.
25 A vexation to his father, a foolish son,
    and bitterness to the woman who bore him.
26 Punishment of the just, surely not good;
    striking honorable people, against justice.
27 Whoever moderates his words, a knowing person,
    and the cool of spirit, an understanding person.
28 Even a fool, keeping silent, can be taken to be wise;
    a tight-lipped person, intelligent.

Proverbs 18

18:1 An alienated person seeks out his own desire;
    he quarrels with any success.
2 A fool takes no pleasure in understanding,
    but rather in revealing what is in his heart.
3 Comes the wicked, comes scorn also,
    and with disgrace, reproach.
4 Deep waters, words from one's mouth;
    a flowing stream, a fountain of wisdom.
5 Not good: showing favor to the wicked
    so as to oppress the just in a judgment.

6   The lips of a fool lead to strife;
           his mouth calls for blows.
7   The mouth of a fool, his destruction,
           and his lips, a snare for his life.
8   The words of a gossiper, like dainty morsels,
           and they go down to one's inmost being.
9   Whoever is slack in his work,
           a brother to the destroyer.
10   The name of the Lord, a strong tower;
           the just run to it and are set on high.
11   The wealth of the rich, a strong city,
           and like a high wall, so he imagines.
12   Before a collapse the heart is proud,
           but before honor, humility.
13   One who answers before listening,
           his the folly and shame.
14   The spirit of a person sustains him when ill,
           but a crushed spirit, who can bear?
15   An understanding heart acquires knowledge,
           and the ears of the wise seek out knowledge.
16   A man's gift creates room for him,
           giving access to important people.
17   The first to plead a case—right!
           then comes his opponent and examines him.
18   The lot settles quarrels,
           and is decisive among the powerful.
19   A brother offended, stronger than a city,
           and disputes, like the bars of a castle.
20   By the fruit of one's mouth the belly is sated;
           by the product of the lips is one sated.
21   Death and life, in the power of the tongue;
           those who love it will eat its fruit.
22   He who finds a wife finds good,
           and obtains favor from the Lord.
23   The poor utter entreaties,
           but the rich reply roughly.
24   Friends—for one to associate with,
           but there is one more loving and closer than a brother.

Proverbs 19

19:1   Better the poor person, walking in integrity,
           than one with perverted lips, and a fool besides!
2   Not good: desire without knowledge;
           one who is hasty in step misses the goal.
3   Folly leads one astray,
           but his heart rages against the Lord.

4   Wealth makes many friends,
        but the poor man—he is deserted by his friends.
5   A false witness will not go unpunished,
        and one who tells lies will not escape.
6   Many curry favor with a noble,
        and all are friends of a giver of gifts.
7   All the relatives of the poor hate them;
        all the more do friends desert them.
    Whoever pursues words, they are not (fruitful?)
8   A keeper of heart, a lover of self;
        a preserver of understanding—for finding happiness.
9   A false witness will not go unpunished,
        and one who tells lies will perish.
10 Unbefitting a fool: luxury;
        all the more so, the rule of a slave over princes.
11 It is the intelligent person who contains anger,
        and it is an honor to overlook an offense.
12 Like a lion's growling, anger of a king,
        but like dew on the grass, his favor.
13 A disaster to his father, a foolish son,
        and a quarrelsome wife, a continual downpour.
14 House and wealth, an inheritance from forebears,
        but a prudent wife, from the Lord.
15 Laziness brings on deep sleep,
        and a slacker's appetite stays hungry.
16 A keeper of a command, a keeper of life;
        a despiser of his ways will die.
17 Showing kindness to the poor: making a loan to the Lord,
        and a reward will be given for it.
18 Discipline your son while there is hope,
        but no death! Don't get overwrought!
19 One of great wrath, a receiver of punishment—
        for if you get (him) free, you must do it again.
20 Listen to advice and take instruction,
        so that finally you become wise.
21 Many are the intentions in one's heart,
        but the plan of the Lord—that will prevail.
22 One's desire, one's disgrace;
        so better poor than a liar.
23 The fear of the Lord—for life,
        and one spends the night satisfied and without harm.
24 A sluggard puts hand into the dish
        without ever lifting it to the mouth.
25 If you beat a scoffer, the naive will be wiser;
        if you reprove the intelligent, they gain in knowledge.
26 Whoever mistreats father, drives mother away,
        a shameful and disgraceful son.

27 Cease, my son, to listen to instruction—
   a wandering from words of knowledge!
28 A malicious witness scoffs at what is right,
   and the mouth of the wicked swallows iniquity.
29 Judgments are directed to scoffers,
   and blows for the backs of fools.

Proverbs 20

20:1 Wine, a scoffer; strong drink, stormy!
   And whoever gets drunk on them is not wise.
2 The wrath of a king, the roar of a lion;
   whoever angers him, a gambler with life.
3 Ceasing from strife, an honor to a person;
   but any fool gets into a quarrel.
4 In winter the sluggard does not plow;
   at harvest he will look—but not a thing!
5 Counsel in the human heart—deep waters;
   but the understanding person draws it up.
6 Many people—each one proclaiming personal loyalty,
   but who can find the one to be trusted?
7 Whoever walks in integrity—a just person;
   happy the descendants after him.
8 A king sitting on his judgment seat,
   one who winnows any evil with his eyes.
9 Who can say, "My heart is pure;
   I am cleansed of my sin?"
10 Alternate stones, alternate measures;
   an abomination to the Lord—all of them!
11 Even by his acts a child is known,
   whether his conduct will be pure and upright.
12 A listening ear, a seeing eye—
   the Lord made them both.
13 Do not love sleep lest you lose your inheritance;
   keep your eyes open, have bread enough!
14 "Bad, bad," says the buyer,
   but he goes off and then boasts!
15 There is gold, also a mass of rubies,
   but a precious jewel—lips of knowledge.
16 Take his garment for he has provided surety for a stranger,
   and if for foreigners, hold him in pledge!
17 Sweet to a person, the bread of deceit,
   but afterward the mouth is filled with gravel.
18 Plans are made firm by advice;
   wage war with wise directions!
19 Whoever slanders, a revealer of secrets;
   so have nothing to do with the open-mouthed.

20 Whoever curses father or mother—
      his lamp will go out in deep darkness.
21 An inheritance at first acquired in haste
      in the end will not be blessed.
22 Do not say: "I will repay evil."
      Wait for the Lord, and he will save you.
23 An abomination to the Lord, alternate stones;
      deceitful weights, not good!
24 From the Lord the steps of a person—
      how can anyone understand the way to go?
25 A trap for a man who claims "holy!"
      and only after vows investigates.
26 A winnower of the wicked, a wise king,
      and he rolls the wheel over them.
27 The lamp of the Lord, the human life-breath,
      searching all the inmost parts!
28 Loyalty and fidelity preserve a king;
      he supports his throne by loyalty.
29 The glory of youth, their strength;
      the adornment of elders, white hair.
30 Wounds and bruises clean away evil,
      and blows, the inmost being.

Proverbs 21

21:1 Waterchannels, the heart of a king in the hand of the Lord;
      wherever he wishes, he turns it.
2 Every way, upright in a person's eyes,
      but the one who weighs hearts, the Lord.
3 The practice of justice and right—
      more preferable to the Lord than sacrifice.
4 Haughty eyes and arrogant heart—
      the tillage of the wicked, sin.
5 The plans of the diligent—only for plenty,
      but everyone in haste—only for penury.
6 Acquiring treasures by a lying tongue—
      driven vapor, snares of death.
7 The violence of the wicked sweeps them off,
      for they refuse to act rightly.
8 Devious the way of a person, and strange,
      but the pure, upright in conduct.
9 Better to dwell in a corner of a roof
      than with a quarrelsome woman and a shared house.
10 The intent of the wicked craves evil;
      no neighbor experiences mercy in his eyes.
11 At the punishment of the scoffer, the naive become wise;
      at the instruction of the wise, they gain knowledge.

12 The Just One attends to the house of the wicked,
    bringing the wicked to disaster.
13 One stopping his ears at the cry of the poor—
    he too will cry, and not be heard.
14 A gift in secret assuages anger,
    and a pocketed present, vehement wrath.
15 Joy for the just, acting rightly;
    but ruin, for evildoers.
16 A person wandering from the way of insight
    will rest in the assembly of the shades.
17 A person in financial straits—a lover of pleasure;
    a lover of wine and oil shall never get rich.
18 The wicked, a ransom for the just,
    and replacing the upright, the faithless.
19 Better to live in a desert land
    than with a quarrelsome woman and strife.
20 Desirable treasure and oil in the house of the wise,
    but a fool of a man will swallow them up.
21 One pursuing justice and kindness
    will find life and honor.
22 A wise man scales the city of warriors
    and brings down the stronghold they trusted in.
23 One guarding mouth and tongue—
    one keeping self from troubles.
24 Proud, arrogant—scoffer the name,
    acting with excessive pride.
25 The desire of the sluggard kills him,
    for he refuses to work with his hands.
26 All day one craves and craves,
    but the just person gives without stint.
27 The sacrifice of the wicked, an abomination;
    all the more so when offered with cunning!
28 A lying witness will perish,
    but one who listens will have the last word.
29 The wicked person presses on,
    but the just, he discerns his course.
30 No wisdom, and no understanding,
    and no counsel against the Lord.
31 The horse prepared for the day of battle—
    but victory, the Lord's!

Proverbs 22

22:1 A name is preferable to great wealth,
    and graciousness better than silver and gold.
2 The rich and the poor meet;
    the Lord the maker of them all.

3 The prudent person perceives an evil and disappears;
the naive plunge forward and pay for it.

4 The result of humility—the fear of the Lord:
riches, honor, and life.

5 Thorns, snares, in the path of the perverse;
one who preserves his life stays distant from them.

6 Train a youth in the way he should go;
even in old age, he will not turn from it.

7 The rich have power over the poor;
and one who borrows, a slave to one who lends.

8 One who sows iniquity reaps calamity,
and the rod of his pride will fail.

9 The generous one, he will be blessed,
for he shares bread with the poor.

10 Get rid of the scoffer and strife disappears,
and quarreling and insult cease.

11 One who loves purity of heart—
gracious his lips, his friend a king.

12 The eyes of the Lord preserve the knowledgeable,
but he overturns the words of the renegade.

13 The sluggard says: "A lion outside!
I'll be killed in the streets!"

14 A deep pit, the mouth of women who are strangers;
one who incurs the Lord's anger will fall into it.

15 Folly is bound up in the heart of a youth;
the rod of discipline will drive it far from him.

16 One oppressing the poor—for his enrichment;
one giving to the rich—only for impoverishment!

THE WORDS OF THE WISE (22:17–24:22)

22:17 Words of the Wise.
Bend your ear and listen to my words,
and apply your heart to my knowledge.

18 For it is well that you keep them in your belly;
let them settle together on your lips.

19 That your trust may be in the Lord,
I make them known to you today—even you.

20 Have I not written to you "Thirty"
of counsels and knowledge?

21 To let you know truth, words that are reliable,
to bring back reliable words to the one who sent you?

22 Do not rob the poor, because they are poor,
and do not crush the needy at the gate.

23 For the Lord will defend their cause,
and despoil those who despoil them of life.

24 Do not be friendly with an irascible person,
    and do not associate with the wrathful,
25 Lest you learn his ways
    and get yourself ensnared.

26 Do not be one of those who pledge hands with another,
    those who go surety for debts.
27 When you have nothing to pay,
    why should he take your bed from under you?

28 Do not remove the ancient boundary mark
    that your ancestors have fixed.

29 Have you seen a person skilled in his work?
    He shall serve kings;
    it will not be shadows that he serves!

Proverbs 23

23:1 When you sit down to eat with a ruler,
    consider carefully the one before you,
2 And put a knife to your throat
    if you have a big appetite.
3 Do not desire his dainties,
    for they are a deceptive food.

4 Do not wear yourself out to acquire wealth;
    have enough sense to stop.
5 Will you let your eyes fix on it?—It is gone!
    For it grows wings for itself
    and flies to the sky like an eagle.

6 Do not eat food with an avaricious person,
    and do not desire his dainties,
7 For it is like a hair in the throat!
    "Eat and drink," he says to you,
    but his heart is not with you.
8 The little you have eaten you will vomit up,
    and waste your pleasant words.

9 Do not speak to the ears of a fool,
    for he will despise the wisdom of your words.

10 Do not move the ancient boundary mark,
    and do not enter the fields of orphans.
11 For their vindicator is strong;
    he will fight for their cause against you.

¹² Apply your heart to instruction,
    and your ears to words of knowledge.
¹³ Do not hold back from disciplining a youth
    because the blows of your rod will not kill him—
¹⁴ If you beat him with a rod,
    you will deliver him from Sheol.
¹⁵ My son, if your heart is wise,
    my heart, too, will be happy.
¹⁶ My kidneys will rejoice
    when your lips speak rightly.
¹⁷ Let not your heart have envy for sinners—
    rather, for the fear of the Lord, the whole day!
¹⁸ For then there is a future,
    and your hope will not be cut off.
¹⁹ You, my son, listen and be wise,
    and walk the way of your heart.
²⁰ Do not be with those who soak up wine,
    who glut themselves on meat,
²¹ For wine addicts and gluttons will be impoverished,
    and stupor clothes with rags.
²² Listen to your father who begot you,
    and do not disdain your mother because she is old.
²³ Get truth, but not for selling it:
    Wisdom and instruction and understanding!
²⁴ The father of the just will greatly exult;
    whoever begets a wise person will rejoice in him.
²⁵ Your father and your mother will rejoice,
    and she who bore you will exult.
²⁶ My son, give me your heart,
    and let your eyes observe my ways,
²⁷ For a deep pit, the harlot,
    and the woman who is a stranger, a narrow well,
²⁸ For like a robber she lies in wait,
    and adds to faithless men.

²⁹ To whom "woes"? To whom "groans"?
    Whose the strife? Whose the troubles?
To whom wounds for no reason?
    To whom glazed eyes?
³⁰ Those last to finish off the wine,
    who gather to taste mixed wine.
³¹ Do not look at wine when it is red,
    when its eye shines in the cup,
    when it goes down smoothly.
³² Its aftereffect: like a snake it bites,
    and like an adder it stings.
³³ Your eyes see strange things,
    and your heart utters incoherencies.

34   And you are like one who lies down in the heart of the sea,
  and like one who lies down at the top of a mast.
35   "They have struck me—I have no pain.
  They have beaten me—I did not know it.
  When shall I wake again?—I'll keep looking for it."

Proverbs 24

24:1   Do not envy the evil,
  and have no desire to be with them,
2   Because their heart plans violence,
  and their lips speak troubles.

3   By wisdom is a house built,
  and by understanding it is established,
4   For by knowledge are the chambers filled
  with all precious and pleasant wealth.

5   A wise person: in strength;
  and one who has knowledge grows in power,
6   Because by cleverness you win battles,
  and with many counselors, victory.

7   Wisdom is too high for a fool;
  he cannot open his mouth in the gate.

8   To whoever plans to do evil
  the name "crafty one" is given.
9   Foolish plans: sin;
  an abomination to a man: the scoffer.

10   If you give up on a day of pressure,
  depressed: your strength.
11   Deliver those dragged off to death!
  Do not hold back from those stumbling to slaughter;
12   If you say, "Well, we did not know this."
  The one who weighs the hearts—does he not understand?
  The one who guards your life—does he not know?
  And will he not render to all according to their deeds?

13   Eat honey, my son, for it is good,
  and the honeycomb sweet to your palate;
14   Know that wisdom is such for you;
  If you find it, then there is a future,
  and your hope will not be cut off.

15 Do not lie in wait at the dwelling of the just;
  do not destroy his home.
16 For the just may fall seven times, but he will rise;
  while the wicked stumble about in misfortune.

17 Do not be happy over the fall of your enemy,
  and let not your heart rejoice when he stumbles,
18 Lest the Lord see it, and it be evil in his eyes;
  then he will turn aside his wrath from him.

19 Do not be angry at evildoers;
  do not envy the wicked;
20 For the evildoer has no future;
  the lamp of the wicked goes out.

21 My son, fear the Lord and the king;
  do not associate with those who rebel against them.
22 For destruction from them will rise suddenly,
  and the ruin from both—who can know?

WORDS OF THE WISE (24:23–34)

24:23 These also by the wise.

  Showing partiality in judgment, not good;
24   whoever says to the wicked: "Just one!"
  peoples shall curse him, nations condemn him.
25 But it will go well for those who make the accusations;
  upon them will come generous blessing.

26 He kisses the lips,
  whoever replies with honest words.

27 Arrange your outside work,
  and get your things ready in the field;
  afterwards build your house.

28 Do not testify against your neighbor without cause,
  or would you deceive with your lips?
29 Do not say, "As he did to me, so I will do to him;
  I will render to him according to his deed."

30 I passed by the field of a sluggard,
  by the vineyard of one who lacks heart.
31 And—all of it overgrown with thistles!
  Nettles covered its surface,
  and the stone wall was broken down.

32 And I gazed—taking it to heart;
    I took a lesson from what I saw.
33 "A little sleep, a little slumber,
    a little folding of the arms to rest—
34 Then your poverty will come like a robber,
    and destitution like an armed man."

PROVERBS OF SOLOMON (25:1–29:27)

Proverbs 25

25:1 The Proverbs of Solomon, which the men of King Hezekiah of
    Judah copied out.
2 The glory of God, to conceal a matter,
    and the glory of kings, to search out a matter.
3 The heaven for height, the earth for depth,
    the hearts of kings: unsearchable.
4 Remove dross from silver,
    and a vessel emerges for a refiner.
5 Remove the wicked from before the king,
    and his throne is made firm by justice.
6 Do not claim honor in the presence of a king,
    and do not take over the place of the great,
7 For it is better to be told "Go up ahead,"
    than to be humiliated before a nobleman.
    Whatever your eyes see,
8   do not be quick to argue for;
    Lest . . . what will you do afterwards
    when your neighbor makes a shame of you?
9 Argue your own case with your neighbor,
    but do not reveal the secret of another,
10 Lest the one who hears it reviles you,
    and your bad reputation never ceases.
11 Apples of gold in silver settings,
    a word spoken at the right time.
12 A gold earring, an ornament of fine gold—
    the sage who reproves a listening ear.
13 Like the cold of snow on a harvest day,
    a faithful messenger for the one who sent him,
    for he restores the spirit of his master.
14 Clouds and wind, but no rain:
    one who boasts of a gift never given.
15 By patience a ruler can be persuaded,
    and a soft tongue can break a bone.
16 If you find honey, eat only what you need,
    lest you have your fill of it and vomit it up.

17   Let your foot be seldom in your neighbor's house,
          lest he have his fill of you and hate you.
18   A club, sword, and sharp arrow:
          one bearing false witness against a neighbor.
19   A bad tooth and an unsteady foot:
          trusting a faithless person in time of trouble.
20   One who takes off clothes on a cold day—
          vinegar on a wound—
          one who sings songs to a sad heart.
21   If your enemy is hungry, give him food to eat;
          or if thirsty, water to drink;
22   For you will heap coals on his head,
          and the Lord will reward you.
23   The north wind brings rain,
          and a backbiting tongue, angry faces.
24   Better to dwell in a corner of a roof
          than with a quarrelsome woman and a shared house.
25   Cold water for a dry throat:
          good news from a far country.
26   A trampled spring, or a polluted fountain—
          a just person who gives way before the wicked.
27   Eating much honey, not good;
          nor to seek honor after honor.
28   A city breached, without a wall—
          a man without self-control.

Proverbs 26

26:1   Like snow in summer, and like rain at harvest,
          so honor is not fitting for a fool.
2   Like a bird for flitting, like a swallow for flying,
          so a curse without reason never arrives.
3   A whip for the horse, a bridle for the donkey:
          and a rod for the back of fools.
4   Do not answer a fool according to his folly,
          lest you too become like him.
5   Answer a fool according to his folly,
          lest he be wise in his own eyes.
6   Cutting off feet, drinking down violence:
          one who sends a message by a fool.
7   Legs dangle from a cripple:
          and a proverb in the mouth of fools.
8   Like tying a stone in a sling,
          so the one who gives honor to a fool.
9   A thorn goes up into the hand of a drunkard:
          and a proverb in the mouth of fools.

10   An archer wounding all who pass by:
        one who hires a fool and drunkard.
11   Like a dog that returns to its vomit,
        a fool repeating his folly.
12   If you see a man wise in his own eyes,
        there is more hope for a fool than for him.
13   The sluggard says: "A lion in the street!
        A lion in the squares!"
14   The door turns on its hinge,
        and the sluggard on his bed.
15   The sluggard buries his hand in the dish,
        too lazy to lift it to his mouth.
16   The sluggard, wiser in his own eyes
        than seven who answer smartly.
17   Whoever grabs a passing dog by the ears:
        one who meddles in another's quarrel.
18   Like a madman slinging firebrands,
        arrows and death,
19   So the one who deceives his neighbor
        and says, "I was only joking."
20   Without wood, a fire goes out,
        and without a gossiper, a quarrel comes to an end.
21   Charcoal for coals, and wood for fire,
        and a quarrelsome person for enkindling strife.
22   The words of a gossiper, like dainty morsels,
        and they go down to one's inmost being.
23   Silver dross laid upon earthenware:
        burning lips and an evil heart.
24   One who hates dissembles with his lips,
        and he keeps deceit within.
25   When his speech is kind, do not believe him,
        for in his heart, seven abominations.
26   Hatred is covered over by deceit;
        his evil is revealed in the assembly.
27   Whoever digs a pit may fall into it;
        and whoever rolls a stone—it can come back upon him.
28   A deceitful tongue hates those it crushes,
        and a smooth mouth works ruin.

Proverbs 27

27:1   Do not boast about tomorrow,
          for you do not know what a day can bring forth.
2   Let another praise you, and not your own mouth;
          a stranger, and not your own lips.

3   Heavy stone and weighty sand—
       but vexation from a fool is heavier than both.
4   Cruel wrath and raging anger—
       but who can stand before jealousy?

5   Better an open rebuke
       than a love that is hidden.
6   Reliable the wounds from one who loves,
       unwelcome the kisses from one who hates.

7   A person who is full tramples on honey,
       but the hungry person—anything bitter, sweet.
8   Like a bird wandering from its nest,
       so one who wanders from his place.

9   Oil and incense make the heart joyful,
       and the sweetness of a friend, more than one's own counsel.
10   Do not abandon your friend and the friend of your father,
       and do not enter your brother's house on the day of your
          misfortune—
       better a near neighbor than a distant brother.

11   Be wise, my son, and give joy to my heart,
       that I may give answer to the one who taunts me.
12   The prudent person perceives an evil—he disappears;
       the naive plunge forward—they pay for it.
13   Take his garment for he has provided surety for a stranger,
       and if for a woman who is a stranger, hold him in pledge!
14   Whoever greets a neighbor with a loud voice in early morning—
       to him it will be counted a curse.

15   A continual downpour on a rainy day
       and a quarrelsome woman are alike.
16   Whoever hides her, hides the wind;
       and his right hand meets oil.

17   Iron is sharpened by iron,
       and a man sharpens the face of his friend.
18   Whoever tends a fig tree eats its fruit,
       and whoever cares for his master shall receive honor.
19   Like water—face to face;
       so the heart of a man to a man.
20   Sheol and Abaddon are never satisfied,
       nor the eyes of human beings ever satisfied.

21   Crucible for silver and furnace for gold,
       and a human being—according to the praise.

22   If you crush a fool in a mortar
            with a pestle among the grains,
            his folly will not depart from him.

23   Know well the state of your flock;
            pay attention to your herds.
24   Because not forever, riches;
            nor a crown, for all generations.
25   The hay is removed, and the new growth appears,
            and the greens from the mountains are gathered in:
26   Lambs for your clothes,
            and goats, the price of a field;
27   Enough goats' milk for your food,
            food for your household,
            and sustenance for your maidens.

Proverbs 28

28:1   The wicked flees, without anyone pursuing,
            but the just has the confidence of a lion.
2   Because of transgression of the land—many its princes;
            but with a person intelligent, knowing—stability will endure.
3   A man poor, but oppressing the lowly—
            a torrential rain and no food.
4   Those who abandon the law praise the wicked,
            but those who observe the law oppose them.
5   Evil people do not understand what is right,
            but those who seek the Lord understand everything.
6   Better the poor, walking in integrity,
            than one with twisted ways, though rich.
7   One who keeps to the teaching, a wise son,
            but a companion of the riotous shames his father.
8   Whoever acquires wealth by interest and overcharging
            gathers it for those who are kind to the poor.
9   Whoever turns aside his ear from hearing the law—
            his very prayer is an abomination.
10   Whoever seduces the upright to an evil way
            will fall into his own pit,
            but the blameless will inherit good.
11   A rich man: wise in his own eyes;
            though poor, an understanding person sees through him.
12   When the just rejoice, great glory;
            but when the wicked arise, people hide.
13   Whoever conceals his transgressions will not prosper,
            but whoever confesses and desists will receive mercy.
14   Happy the person who is ever cautious,
            but the one who hardens his heart falls into evil.

15   A roaring lion or rampant bear—
          a wicked ruler over a poor people.
16   A prince, lacking in revenues, increases oppressions—
          whoever hates unjust gain will prolong his days.
17   A man oppressed by the blood of a person
          is in flight to a pit—let no one support him.
18   Whoever walks blamelessly will be safe,
          but one with twisted ways will fall quickly.
19   Whoever works the soil will get plenty of food,
          but whoever pursues empty goals will get plenty of poverty.
20   A faithful person—greatly blessed;
          but one in haste for riches does not go unpunished.
21   Showing partiality, not good;
          even for a piece of bread people do wrong.
22   An avaricious person is in a hurry to get rich,
          but unaware that loss is coming to him.
23   Whoever rebukes a person finds favor afterwards,
          more than the one who is smooth-tongued.
24   Whoever robs father or mother and then says: "nothing wrong"—
          a companion to a destroyer, he.
25   The greedy person stirs up strife,
          but whoever trusts in the Lord will be refreshed.
26   Whoever trusts in his own heart—a fool!
          but one who walks in wisdom—he will be delivered.
27   Whoever gives to the poor—nothing lacking;
          whoever closes his eyes—many a curse.
28   When the wicked arise, people hide;
          but when they perish, the just are many.

Proverbs 29

29:1   Stiff-necked, a person reprimanded
            will be broken suddenly and without remedy.
2   When the just are many, the people rejoice,
            but when the wicked rules, people groan.
3   A lover of wisdom gives joy to his father,
            but a companion of harlots squanders possessions.
4   By justice a king maintains a country,
            but one who makes demands tears it down.
5   One who deceives his neighbor
            spreads a net for his steps.
6   In the wrongdoing of an evil person, a snare,
            but the just person sings and rejoices.
7   A just person acknowledges the rights of the poor,
            but the wicked does not understand acknowledgment.
8   Scoffers fire up a city,
            but the wise turn away anger.

9 A wise person disputing with a fool—
      anger or laughter, but no peace.
10 Those who shed blood hate the blameless,
      but the upright seeks him out.
11 A fool expresses all his wrath,
      but a wise person keeps it still within.
12 A ruler listening to lies—
      all his ministers, wicked.
13 Poor and oppressor meet—
      the Lord gives light to the eyes of both.
14 A king judging the poor with honesty—
      the throne is forever firm.
15 Rod and reprimand yield wisdom,
      but a youth unrestrained shames the mother.
16 The more wicked, the more wrongdoing,
      but the just shall see their downfall.
17 Discipline your son and he will be a comfort to you,
      and bring delight to your life.
18 Without vision, people have no restraint;
      whoever observes the law, happy!
19 With words a servant is not to be corrected;
      though he understands, no response!
20 You see someone hasty with words?
      There is more hope for a fool than for him.
21 Whoever pampers a servant from childhood—
      the final result is trouble.
22 An angry person stirs up strife;
      a wrathful person—much wrongdoing.
23 Human pride brings one low,
      but a lowly spirit obtains honor.
24 Whoever goes with a thief, a hater of self;
      he hears a curse, but says nothing.
25 Fear of someone provides a snare,
      but one trusting in the Lord is set on high.
26 Many seek the presence of a ruler,
      but from the Lord: judgment of a person.
27 An abomination to the just: an evildoer;
      and an abomination to the wicked: one whose way is upright.

THE WORDS OF AGUR (30:1–14)

Proverbs 30

30:1 The words of Agur, son of Jakeh, the Massaite.
      The oracle of the man: I am not God,
         I am not God, that I should prevail.

2   More brute than human, I;
        not mine, human intelligence.
3   I have not learned wisdom,
        nor do I have knowledge of the Holy One.
4   Who went up to heaven and came down?
        Who gathered the wind in open hands?
    Who tied up the waters in a cloak?
        Who set up all the ends of the earth?
    What is his name, and the name of his son,
        if you know?

5   Tested: every word of Eloah,
        a shield to those who trust in him.
6   Add nothing to his words,
        lest he reprove you and you be proved a liar.

7   Two things I ask of you;
        do not deny them to me before I die:
8   Put falsehood and lying far from me;
        give me neither poverty nor riches;
        feed me with my ration of food,
9   Lest, being full, I become a renegade,
        and say: The Lord—who?
    Or lest, being poor, I steal,
        and blaspheme the name of my God.

10   Do not speak about a servant to his master,
        lest he curse you, and you be held guilty.

11   A generation: they curse their father,
        and their mother they do not bless.
12   A generation: pure in their own eyes,
        but not washed of their filth.
13   A generation: how haughty their eyes;
        how lofty their orbs!
14   A generation: swords their teeth,
        and knives their jaws,
    Devouring the needy from the earth
        and the poor from the people.

NUMERICAL SAYINGS (30:15–33)

30:15   To the leech: two daughters,
        "Give," "Give."

    Three things are never satisfied;
        Four never say, "Enough!":

16 Sheol and a barren womb,
>>> the earth, ever thirsting for water,
>>> and fire, never saying, "Enough!"

17 The eye that mocks a father,
>>> and despises obedience due a mother—
> Let the vultures of the valley pluck it out,
>>> let the brood of eagles consume it.

18 Three things are too wonderful for me,
>>> and four I cannot understand:
19 The way of an eagle in the sky,
>>> the way of a serpent on a rock,
> The way of a ship on the high seas,
>>> and the way of a man with a woman.
20 Such is the way of an adulteress:
>>> she eats and wipes her mouth,
>>> and says, "I have done no wrong."

21 Under three things the earth trembles,
>>> under four it cannot carry on:
22 A slave when he becomes king,
>>> a fool when he has enough to eat,
23 A hateful woman when she is married,
>>> a maidservant when she displaces her mistress.

24 Four things—smallest on earth,
>>> but wiser than the wisest—
25 Ants, a group not strong,
>>> but they prepare their food in the summer.
26 Badgers, a group not powerful,
>>> but have their home in rocky crags.
27 Locusts, without a king,
>>> but they all go forth in order.
28 Lizards—you catch them by hand,
>>> but, in royal palaces!

29 Three things, stately in stride;
>>> four, stately in carriage:
30 The lion, champion among beasts,
>>> and never retreating before anything.
31 The strutting cock, the he-goat,
>>> and the king leading his people.

32 If you have acted foolishly in your pride,
>>> or if you have been plotting,
>>> hand on mouth!

³³   For pressure on milk yields curds;
>>>>>pressure on the nose yields blood;
>>>>>pressure on anger yields strife.

THE WORDS OF LEMUEL (31:1–9)

Proverbs 31

^{31:1}   The words of Lemuel, king of Massa, with which his mother in-
structed him.

²   What, my son?
>>>>>What, son of my womb?
>>>>>What, son of my vows?

³   Do not give your strength to women
>>>>>or your power to those who destroy kings.

⁴   Not for kings, Lemuel,
>>>>>not for kings to drink wine,
>>>>>or strong drink for princes,

⁵   Lest they drink and forget the decrees
>>>>>and violate the rights of all the afflicted.

⁶   Give strong drink to whoever is perishing,
>>>>>and wine to the bitter in spirit.

⁷   Let them drink and forget their poverty;
>>>>>then they will no longer recall their troubles.

⁸   Open your mouth for the mute,
>>>>>in defense of all the dispossessed.

⁹   Open your mouth, give a just sentence,
>>>>>and defend the afflicted and the poor.

THE IDEAL WOMAN (31:10–31)

^{31:10}   A woman of valor, who can find?
>>>>>Her value is beyond rubies.

¹¹   Her husband entrusts his heart to her,
>>>>>and never lacks for profit.

¹²   She brings him good, not evil,
>>>>>all the days of her life.

¹³   She seeks out wool and flax,
>>>>>and works with joyful hands.

¹⁴   She is like a merchant ship;
>>>>>she brings her food from afar.

¹⁵   She rises while it is still night
>>>>>and provides food for her household,
>>>>>a ration for her maidservants.

¹⁶   She surveys a field and takes it over;
>>>>>from what her hands achieve, she plants a vineyard.

17 She girds herself with strength,
and makes her arms sturdy.
18 She senses that her profit is good;
her lamp never turns off at night.
19 She puts her hand to the distaff;
her palms grasp the spindle.
20 Her palms she extends to the poor;
her hands she reaches to the needy.
21 If it snows, she has no fear for her household,
for they are all doubly clothed.
22 She makes covers for herself;
fine linen and purple, her clothing.
23 Her husband is well known at the gates,
presiding with the elders of the land.
24 She makes garments and sells them,
and provides girdles for merchants.
25 Strength and dignity, her clothing,
and she laughs at the days ahead.
26 Her mouth she opens with wisdom,
and kind instruction on her tongue.
27 She watches over the activity of her household,
and does not eat the bread of idleness.
28 Her children rise up and call her "happy!";
her husband, he too praises her:
29 "Many women act with valor,
but you are above them all."
30 Deceptive, grace—and vain, beauty;
Fear of the Lord in a woman, that is to be praised.
31 Celebrate what her hands achieve,
and let her deeds be her praise at the gates.

Proverbs

Title and Purpose

Proverbs 1:1–7

Bibliography

Brown, W. P. *Character in Crisis.* 23–30. **Fox, M. V.** "Words for Folly." *ZfA* 10 (1997) 4–15. ———. "Words for Wisdom." *ZfA* 6 (1993) 149–69. **Renfroe, F.** "The Effect of Redaction on the Structure of Prov. 1:1–6." *ZAW* 101 (1989) 290–93. **Whybray, R. N.** *Composition.* 51–56.

Translation

1:1   *The Proverbs of Solomon, Son of David, King of Israel:*
2   *To know wisdom and instruction,[a]*
       to understand intelligent words;
3   *To take in insightful instruction:*
       justice and judgment and right;
4   *To give cleverness to the simple,[a]*
       knowledge and thoughtfulness to youth;
5   *That[a] the wise may hear and add to what they take in,*
       and the intelligent acquire direction;[b]
6   *To understand proverb and riddle,[a]*
       words of the wise and their puzzles.

7   *The fear of the Lord: the beginning of knowledge;*
       wisdom and instruction fools despise.

Notes

2.a. מוסר means both "instruction" and, more narrowly, "discipline" (including physical, as this forms part of instruction; cf. 12:24; 19:18); cf. v 3a.

4.a. פתאים indicates those who are "simple" in the sense of being naive, untutored, and in need of wisdom. They may or may not be receptive; cf. 2:22.

5.a. The series of infinitives is interrupted by the finite form of the verb, which continues the sense of purpose.

5.b. תחבלות means "steering."

6.a. ליץ is the root of this noun, which is a hapax legomenon, and the root occurs mostly in Proverbs; the meaning is obscure (scoff, be arrogant, boast, mock, ridicule), and the verb is usually used in the hiphil. Fox (*ZfA* 10 [1997] 7) characterizes the noun as "scornful man"; "cynic."

Form/Structure/Setting

These verses are clearly composed as a kind of preface to the book. There is a clever combination: the title is connected immediately to the following verses by means of infinitives which develop the purpose of the "proverbs" mentioned in the title. The interruption in v 5 (a finite form of the verb) does not change matters; the title leads into a single sentence, vv 1–6. One may dispute whether v 7 on the fear of the Lord is part of vv 1–6 or is to be construed as beginning the next section (and thus a kind of inclusion with 9:10, or even 31:31, is formed?). But because fear of the Lord is, as it were, a keystone of wisdom teaching (cf. Prov 9:10; 15:33; and also Ps 111:10; Job 28:28; Sir 1:14), or a kind of motto, v 7 can be associated with the preface. See the *Excursus on Fear of the Lord.*

G. von Rad (*Wisdom,* 13) has pointed out the difficulty in distinguishing among the plethora of terms in vv 2–6; they seem to overlap, and a true translation is difficult to achieve. See, however, the studies on words for wisdom and folly by M. V. Fox, mentioned above. Particularly important is his distinction among words for wisdom (p. 151; see also the summary on p. 165) between the categories of faculty, activity, and knowledge. In any case, the preface suggests that the aim of the work is "something larger" (the entire wisdom program?). W. Brown has recognized a concentric circle: abc (2a, 2b, 3a) and c′ b′ a′ (4–5, 6, 7) with d (v 3b) in the middle position, proclaiming "righteousness, justice and equity" (cf. Prov 2:9). An important signal is the combination of חכמה and מוסר ("wisdom" and "instruction") in vv 2a, 7b, perhaps an inclusion.

As far as the setting is concerned, it is likely that these verses were composed precisely for their present position in the book. The ideas and terminology are not new, for they have antecedents in the wisdom tradition, as chaps. 1–9 especially testify.

Comment

1–2 On Solomonic "authorship," see the remarks in the *Introduction* above. The terminology in v 2 is heavily intellectual in appearance, for although wisdom aims at praxis, it also includes the knowledge component "how to," and it contains "teaching" handed down from the parents. "Instruction" (see *Note* 2.a.) is joined with wisdom, and this combination points forward to v 7; it is also significant that the key concept of fear of the Lord occurs in v 7. The association of wisdom and instruction is frequent in the following chapters (e.g., 23:23b).

3 The verb "take" (לָקַח) has a quite active meaning in sapiential language; the noun derived from it (לֶקַח, occurring in v 5a) indicates a lesson or teaching, what is "taken in." The ideals in v 3b, which are repeated in 2:9, are traditional with sages and prophets alike. "Right" translates a word meaning "straight" or "even."

4 In a special way, naive and innocent youths are in need of the teaching of the sages; they will appear frequently in chaps. 1–9, addressed by parents, by Woman Wisdom, and by Woman Folly. Because folly can take various forms, it must be met with a cleverness and prudence that will be a match for it.

5 See *Note* 5.a. This verse is directed to the wise or those who would become wise; it encourages them to "listen" and sharpen their sense of direction. "Listen" is one of the most frequent verbs in the wisdom vocabulary; it denotes an active listening, an obedience. That attitude is also characteristic of Egyptian wisdom instructions (*Sebayit;* cf. Lichtheim, *AEL,* 1:73–76, for the emphasis on hearing in the epilogue to the Instruction of Ptahhotep). Were the wise person to fail to listen, he might be one who is "wise in his own eyes," the most dangerous of all situations; cf. Prov 26:12. The truly wise, but not the fool, is open to correction, e.g., 12:15; 15:5.

6 This book is characterized by the term "proverb" (מָשָׁל). The riddle (see *Note* 6.a.) and the puzzle, if these are correctly translated, are hardly in evidence in the collections, unless they refer to those sayings that are often paradoxical and hence puzzling. See also the *Comment* on the words of Agur in 30:1–4. The "words of the wise" will appear in 22:17 as a title (emended text) and implicitly in 24:23.

7 The verse enunciates a basic principle, even a motto, of the sages, which was at the same time intrinsic to Israelite faith; cf. Exod 3:6; 19; Deut 5:5. "Knowledge" means "wisdom" here, as 9:10 makes explicit, and see also Ps 111:10; Job 28:28; Sir 1:14. The word for "beginning" could be translated as "essence" or "chief part," but in 9:10 "beginning" is definitely used. See also 15:33. Perhaps von Rad has provided the most perceptive comment on this topic: "To this extent, Israel attributes to the fear of God, to belief in God, a highly important function in respect of human knowledge. She was, in all seriousness, of the opinion that effective knowledge about God is the only thing that puts a man into a right relationship with the objects of his perception . . ." (*Wisdom,* 67–68). See the *Excursus on Fear of the Lord.*

Explanation

This is an imposing preface to the book. It is also quite unusual in that no other biblical work begins with a statement of purpose as clear as this. At the same time, it hides more than it reveals. One need only read the rest of the book and assess the wisdom tradition to appreciate how "proverbs" open up vast issues in every corner of ancient and modern daily life.

One reason for characterizing vv 1–7 as a "preface" is the striking literary style with which its message is announced: a long sentence followed by a motto ("fear of the Lord") that is in a pivotal position. Many scholars are of the opinion that all of chaps. 1–9 serve as an introduction to what follows. As it were, they set the tone or provide the hermeneutical key to the disparate sayings in the following chapters. The editor saw no conflict between early and late wisdom. We have already noted the telling association of wisdom and instruction with "fear of the Lord" that sums up all else; wisdom leads to fear of the Lord; cf. 9:10.

Introductory Instructions   (1:8–9:18)

Proverbs 1:8–33

Bibliography

Aletti, J. "Séduction et parole en Proverbes I–IX." *VT* 27 (1977) 129–44. **Baumann, G.** *Weisheitsgestalt.* 224–27. **Fox, M. V.** "Ideas of Wisdom in Proverbs 1–9." *JBL* 116 (1997) 613–33. ———. "What the Book of Proverbs is About." In VTSup, IOSOT Congress 1995 volume (forthcoming). **Habel, N.** "The Symbolism of Wisdom in Proverbs 1–9." *Int* 26 (1972) 131–57. **Harris, S.** *Proverbs 1–9: A Study of Inner-Biblical Interpretation.* SBLDS 150. Atlanta: Scholars, 1995. **Lang, B.** *Die weisheitliche Lehrrede.* 27–60. **McKinlay, J. E.** *Gendering Wisdom the Host. Biblical Invitations to Eat and Drink.* JSOTSup 216. Sheffield: Academic Press. **Moss, A.** "Wisdom as Parental Teaching in Proverbs 1–9." *HeyJ* 38 (1997) 426–39. **Newsom, C.** "Woman and the Discourse of Patriarchal Wisdom: A Study of Proverbs 1–9." In *Gender and Difference in Ancient Israel.* Ed. P. L. Day. Minneapolis: Fortress, 1989. 142–60. **Robert, A.** "Les attaches littéraires bibliques de Prov. I–IX." *RB* 43 (1934) 42–68, 172–204, 374–84; *RB* 44 (1935) 344–65, 502–25. **Steiert, F.-J.** *Die Weisheit Israels—ein Fremdkörper im Alten Testament?* FTS 143. Freiburg: Herder, 1990. 213–309. **Van Leeuwen, R. C.** "Liminality and Worldview in Proverbs 1–9." In *Paraenesis: Act and Form.* Ed. L. Perdue. Semeia 50. Atlanta: SBL, 1990. **Whybray, R. N.** *The Book of Proverbs.* 62–71.

Prov 1:20–23: **Baumann, G.** *Weisheitsgestalt.* 173–99. **Emerton, J.** "A Note on the Hebrew Text of Proverbs 1,22–33." *JTS* 19 (1968) 609–14. **Gilbert, M.** "Le discours menaçant de Sagesse en Proverbes 1, 20–33." In *Storia e tradizioni di Israele: scritti in onore di J. Alberto Soggin.* Ed. D. Garrone and F. Israel. Brescia: Paideia, 1991. 99–119. **Harris, S.** *Study.* 67–109. **Lang, B.** *Frau Weisheit.* 23–53. **Murphy, R. E.** "Wisdom's Song: Proverbs 1:20–33." *CBQ* 48 (1986) 456–60. **Robert, A.** "Les attaches." *RB* 43 (1934) 172–81. **Trible, P.** "Wisdom Builds a Poem." *JBL* 94 (1975) 509–18. **Whybray, R. N.** *Composition.* 11–15, 32.

Translation

1:8   My son, listen to the instruction of your father,
          do not abandon the teaching of your mother,

9   For a gracious wreath on your head, they;
          a necklace for your throat.

10   My son, if sinners entice you,
          do not go along![a]

11   If they say, "Come with us,
          let us lie in wait for blood!
          For no reason, we will ambush the innocent!

12   We will swallow them alive like Sheol—
          whole, like those who go down to the pit.

13   We will get all kinds of precious things;
          We will fill our homes with loot.

14   Throw in your lot with us;
          We shall all have one purse!"

15 *My son, do not walk in the way with them;*
    keep back your feet from their path,
16 *For their feet run to evil,*
    and they hasten to shed blood [a]—
17 *In vain a net baited* [a]
    before the eyes of any bird [b]—
18 *But they lie in wait for their own blood;*
    they ambush themselves.
19 *Such the ways of all who are bent on gain;*
    it takes the lives of its owners.

20 *Wisdom* [a] *cries out in the streets,*
    raises her voice in the squares;
21 *At a corner of bustling streets* [a] *she calls;*
    at the city gates she speaks her words:
22 *"How long, simple ones, will you love being simple,*
    and the arrogant delight in their arrogance,
    and the fools hate knowledge, [a]
23 *Turning away at* [a] *my reproof?*
    Now I will pour out my spirit to you;
    I will make known my words to you:
24 *Because I called and you refused;*
    I put forth my hand, but no one gave heed.
25 *You disregarded all my counsel,*
    and did not accept my reproof;
26 *Now I will laugh at your calamity;*
    I will mock when your terror comes,
27 *When your terror comes like a storm,*
    and your calamity arrives like a whirlwind,
    and distress and anguish come upon you.
28 *Then they will call to me, but I will not answer;*
    they will seek me, but they will not find me,
29 *Because they hated knowledge,*
    and the fear of the Lord they did not choose;
30 *They were not open to my advice;*
    they rejected my every reproof.
31 *So they shall eat the fruit of their own way,*
    and they shall have their fill of their own plans.
32 *For the defection* [a] *of the simple kills them,*
    and the complacency of fools destroys them;
33 *But whoever listens to me will live in safety,*
    peacefully, with no terror to fear."

Notes

10.a. Many MSS and the versions write תאבה supporting the meaning "be willing." A few MSS have תבוא "go." תבא is an irregular imperfect form (GKC §68h, 75hh) of אבה, "be willing," although it can also be vocalized as from בא, "come." The translation tries to combine both ideas.

16.a. Missing in LXX; see the *Comment* below.

17.a. מזרה is to be understood as the pual participle of זרה meaning "scatter," but this hardly suits "net." It has been interpreted to refer to grain scattered on the net (so Rashi); hence, "baited."

17.b. Literally, "a possessor of wings"; the expression is found also in Eccl 10:20.

20.a. The plural ending (cf. also 9:1; singular in 8:1) on "wisdom" has been explained as a plural of intensity or majesty (Gemser) and also as an abstract ending (GKC §86l), and as a singular form influenced by Phoenician. In any case, wisdom is clearly singular in meaning here, the subject of the verb תרנה, "cries out," from רנן, "cry out," although the cohortative form remains a puzzle.

21.a. Literally, "at the head of noisy (places)."

22.a. The change to the third person is sudden, and may indicate an insertion. It has misled some translations that fail to see that "how long" also governs v 23a.

23.a. See the arguments proposed in *CBQ* 48 (1986) 456–60, favored also by M. Gilbert, "Le discours . . . ," that indicate the connection of this verse with v 22, and reject the translation of "return" or "heed" (NRSV) for תשובו. The conditional translation of the phrase (so NIV, "if you had responded . . ." and several commentators) is also less likely. "Turn away from" finds a kind of inclusio in v 32, משובת, "defection."

32.a. This word translates משובת with the meaning of "turn from"; cf. Jer 2:19; 3:6, and see previous note.

Form/Structure/Setting

There are two units: vv 8–19, an instruction of the father to the son, and vv 20–33, Wisdom's speech. The first, vv 10–19, is composed mainly of a warning against the vividly described temptations posed by the wicked, who will be undone by their wickedness. "Such the ways . . ." (v 19) is a "summary-appraisal formula," typical of wisdom teaching (e.g., Job 8:13; 18:21) and also used in the prophets (e.g., Isa 14:26).

In the second unit Wisdom is personified as a woman who delivers a condemnatory speech in the style of a prophet denouncing the failure of the people; cf. Jer 7 and 20. It is threatening, in contrast to the other speeches of personified Wisdom (chaps. 8 and 9). For the literary structure, see the study of P. Trible. However, the meaning of the whole turns on the interpretation of vv 22–23. The introduction (vv 20–21) places Wisdom in a prominent position for public address (vv 22–33). The prophetic mood shifts into didactic language at the end (vv 30–33), but the grim lesson remains clear. The audience is called "the simple" (i.e., naive) and "fools," who will also be addressed in the other speeches of wisdom (cf. 8:5 and also 9:4, 6). It is possible that the language reflects the threatening language of a teacher, but only in part, since it is not characteristic of wisdom teaching to threaten in such a prophetic style as in 1:24–28. Rather, the lessons of experience and the teaching of parents are the more normal motivation. In 1:20–33, the stance is that of a prophet, not a teacher. The setting for the first unit could well be the family (cf. vv 8–9), and now it forms part of the several addresses to "my son" in this collection. The second unit is clearly condemnatory, and can be understood as strengthening the warning against the sinners in vv 8–19 by its mixture of prophetic (vv 24–29) and wisdom (vv 29–33) motifs.

R. N. Whybray (*Composition*, 12–13) claimed to find in chaps. 1–7 ten instructions, based on the distinct literary type of introduction ("my son," "hear," etc.). He admits it is difficult to determine the length in some instances, and he has recourse to several expansions. But one cannot separate the "original" from the expansion without introducing arbitrary criteria. See the *Comment* below on vv 8–10. Many other scholars (B. Lang, *Lehrrede,* 27–36; A. Meinhold, 43–46; M. Fox, *JBL* 116 [1997] 614–16) follow this lead provided by the introductory appeals, "my son," and adopt the pattern of ten discourses. However, they have recourse to extra "poems," or "interludes," in the case of Wisdom's speech in 1:20–33 and also differ in details. S. Harris (*A Study,* 52–65, 67–109) follows in the steps of the "anthological composition" first applied to Prov 1–9 by A. Robert. He finds an "inner-biblical interpretation" in the use of Gen 37 (the Joseph story) in Prov 1:8–19. Resemblances in vocabulary (pp. 52–54) are not sharp enough to sustain such a thesis. Similarly, he correlates Prov 1:20–33 with Jer 7, as did Robert, and also with Jer 20. The arguments are delicate and uncertain despite the common vocabulary listed by him on pp. 93–94.

Comment

8–9 V 8 presents the typical introduction to an instruction, often repeated in various forms. The principal figures of vv 10–19 are mentioned at once: father, mother, son, and sinners. "My son" suggests parental instruction. *Both* parents are mentioned again in 6:20, and also several times among the separate sayings; see especially 10:1, which is significant because it opens the collection, thus providing continuity with chaps. 1–9. The term "son" is probably stylized here to indicate the recipient of the instructions in all the following chapters. "My son" occurs many times in the first nine chapters: 1:8, 10, 15; 2:1; 3:1, 11, 21; 4:10, 20; 6:1, 3, 20; 7:1. As indicated above, this characteristic is used as a basis for discovering ten instructions. But can this phrase, repeated twice in vv 8–10 and again in v 15, bear all the weight of indicating fundamental divisions within these nine chapters, as Whybray and others claim? **9** As often, the direct address is accompanied by a motive clause. Here the "wreath" anticipates the gift in 4:9. Vv 8–9 give the impression of a deliberate positioning here, before the warning to beware of sinners in v 10.

10–14 The instruction begins with a dramatic description of temptation that youths can expect to face. **10** The parent/teacher issues a command and proceeds to describe the danger coming from "sinners"; they are not called "fools." **11** The quotation of the sinners (vv 11–14) is a creation of the teacher, phrased in a vivid way to highlight the implications of the evil project: blood (a theme repeated in vv 16–18), slaying the innocent, Sheol, a share in the precious booty. The slaying of the innocent appears to be practically mindless, despite the motivation of gain, since it is without reason, totally unprovoked. A similar description of the machinations of the wicked against the just is found in Wis 2:6–20. **12** The wicked speak of Sheol/pit almost as an ally that will aid them. Sheol, which is so often paired with Death, is conceived in biblical thought as a power that pursues its victims, and opens its mouth to swallow them (e.g., Isa 5:14). **14** The use of the word "lot" is almost blasphemous in view of the function of the lot (Prov 16:33), to determine the will of God. It stands here for the common fate and sharing that will come from the evil adventure. Actual temptations would hardly be so blatant; the sage has deliberately created a dramatic scenario. Time after time (e.g., 2:16; 5:3), the youth is warned to beware of the "smooth" words; the teacher is attempting here to paint evil in its true colors, and to make evident its poisonous speech.

15–19 The sage has finished the description of the temptation, and now takes up the earlier admonition and introduces the central theme of the "way" (vv 15, 19). The motivation is developed with a general description of sinners (vv 16–18), and it ends with the summary appraisal in v 19.   **16**   This verse appears to be a gloss or insertion from Isa 59:7a (and see the repetition in Prov 6:17b, 18b). It is quite appropriate, since "feet" is a catch word with v 15, and "blood" connects back with v 11, and looks forward to v 18.   **17**   Obscure in itself (see *Note* 17.a.), this verse has the appearance of a proverb, and it is ambiguous. It is a kind of parenthetical remark in the context of sinners hastening to evil (v 16) and to self-destruction (v 18). The ambiguity of the verse comes from two sources: its very meaning, and the referent of the verse. Two meanings are possible: the trap fails because the bird sees it and avoids it—or the bird sees the net and foolishly plunges into it. In the second case, the folly of the bird seems to be inferred from the folly of the sinners who are being described. Moreover, to whom is the verse addressed? If it is an aside to the "son," it implies that any trap the wicked set for him will fail because of the good advice he receives—or possibly that the son can avoid the trap which is so obvious. If the saying concerns "them," the wicked, it is a comment on the way they foolishly rush to their own destruction. If the saying is applied to the wicked, then the point is that any warning is inefficacious since they go ahead with their project. It can hardly apply to the youth who would not be as stupid as the birds, even though warned. Surely he is wise enough to avoid the trap, thanks to the warning by the sage.   **18**   There is an ironic repetition of key words (blood, ambush) used by the wicked in v 11. But now their designs are turned against them; their own evil brings them down.   **19**   "Way" appears as a key symbol in chaps. 1–9, and need not be changed to "end," as some translators prefer. The "it" refers in a general way to the pursuit of the unjust "gain," which slays its owner. Clearly, the issue is shaping up here to be one of life and death; this note will be sounded frequently in future chapters.

20–21 The torah of the father/mother (v 8) has ended, but Woman Wisdom is now given center stage with a biting speech. She is no shrinking violet. Like the prophets she appears in public where she can address the entire populace; the manner and place of her public appearance are regularly noted; cf. 8:2–3; 9:3.

22–23 See *Notes* 22.a. and 23.a. Wisdom begins her speech (vv 22–32), which is clearly condemnatory in tone. The word "reproof" in vv 23, 25, 30 unifies the poem. She is not inviting the audience to listen (as many translations indicate); she is hurling her condemnation at them.   **22**   The addressees are described as the simple, or naive; the *pětāyîm* are a favorite audience for Woman Wisdom; cf. Prov 8:5; 9:4. V 22 is an overloaded line, and the arrogant and fools are spoken of in the third person, but the text as it stands includes them.   **23**   Her "spirit" is really the anger that is manifest in the threatening "words" that follow.

24–27 The reasons for the coming destruction are given in phraseology known from the prophets, especially vv 24, 28.   **24**   Calling and not receiving an answer is a complaint of the Lord: see Isa 50:2 and 66:4; cf. also 65:1–2; Jer 7:13, 24–27; Zech 7:13. The extending of the (divine) hand echoes Isa 65:2. It is of utmost significance that what the prophets attributed to God is now attributed to Woman Wisdom.   **25**   The failure of the people is described in wisdom terminology; cf. also vv 23a, 30. Reproof is always welcome to the wise person.   **26**   The scornful laughter of Woman Wisdom, a kind of *Schadenfreude* ("joy at another's downfall"), is especially chilling since it recalls the divine laughter of Ps 2:4. **27** The description of the coming calamity uses the word "shoah," which has been appropriated in recent times to indicate the Holocaust under the Nazi regime. The series of terms in v 27 is marked by alliteration and assonance: שׁואה, "terror," סופה, "calamity," צרה, "distress," and צוקה, "anguish." They are used in prophetic and apocalyptic literature to describe a coming doom; cf. A. Robert, "Les attaches," *RB* 43 (1934) 178–79.

28–30 A description of the reaction of the foolish, who are slain by their own rebelliousness (v 32). There is a switch here from direct address to the third person. **28** The talion law is applied: now they call, but receive no answer, because they had failed earlier (v 24) to heed the call of Wisdom. **29-30** Their faults are not described in traditional terms for sin, but in typical sapiential language: failure to respond to fear of the Lord, counsel, reproof. V 30 is almost a total reprise of v 25.

31–33 The closure to the speech continues the sapiential language: the unfaithful will be requited by the evil they have done, in contrast to those who "listen" and will dwell in safety. **31** The image of eating and being sated by fruit is common in this book; cf. 12:10; 13:2; 18:20–21; the fruit will correspond to the conduct. See the *Excursus on Retribution* for a discussion of the deed-consequence understanding of reality. **32** See *Note* 32.a.; the word translated as "defection" is a kind of inclusio to the "turning away" of v 23. **33** The sapiential style continues, but in contrast to what has gone before, on an upbeat note: safety and security for those who listen to Wisdom. It should be emphasized that a similar ending is found at the end of her speech in 8:35. The "terror" (פחד) mentioned here picks up on the same word in v 26.

Explanation

After the imposing introduction (1:1–7) there are two speeches that dominate chap. 1. First is the opening admonition given to the "son," which contains the carefully crafted and seductive speech of sinners. This is followed by Wisdom's speech, a condemnation of those who will not listen to her. Thus the teaching of the mother and father are paired with the words of Wisdom. The association of wisdom with virtue, and folly with wickedness, will appear throughout the book, and many sayings, especially, but not only, in chaps. 10–15, will contrast the just and the wicked. The focus of the book is the moral formation of youth (cf. W. Brown, *Character*, 1–49), and this goal is apparent from the first chapter on. The views of M. Fox (*JBL* 116 [1997] 613-33) are not dissimilar to the emphasis on character formation of W. Brown. He asks, "what is wisdom?" in chaps. 1–9 and points out that it is more than the father's teachings; it is "power." This power is to be manifested in the praxis of the "son," and the father makes use of personal authority, promises, warnings, etc. to achieve this purpose. Fox considers the speeches of wisdom in chaps. 1, 8, and 9, along with 3:13–20 and 6:1–19, as "interludes"—a rather delicate term. But personified Wisdom is to be seen as another authoritative voice, and in fact more than a voice; she is a persona who is to be *loved*, one who loves those who love her (8:17). When Woman Wisdom proclaims "Happy the one who listens to me," she is "first of all telling us to give attention to the proverbs in the subsequent chapters of Proverbs" (Fox, *JBL* 116

[1997] 632), and this can be summed up in *musar,* or the body of ethical and religious instruction.

It should be emphasized that "my son" is not to be taken in a gender exclusive sense. This book is for all Israel, and the observations deal with universal human experience, except in very few cases. An astonishing feature of Wisdom's speeches in chaps. 1–9 is that she speaks like the Lord, no less. The references to the prophetic language given above are an indication of this. What was referred to God is now referred to her. It is she who feels rebuffed, and who threatens those who refuse to listen. She has divine authority, and she hands out reward and punishment. She does not mention the Lord; she does not urge conversion to God, but to herself! One looks forward with a certain wonderment to speeches that will be proclaimed by her. A. Moss (*HeyJ* 38 [1997] 426–39) has also raised the question of the relationship of the parental teaching to that of personified Wisdom. For him they are "equivalent" (p. 426), but as pointed out above, such a characterization fails to attend to the levels of authority, which are significantly different. The tone of 1:20–33 is foreign to the parental exhortations, and both the tone and the description of the messages of Woman Wisdom in chaps. 8–9 are not an "equivalent." Rather, the Wisdom passages point to a deeper, if also mysterious, level of meaning and exhortation that transcends parental instruction. Personified Wisdom adopts quite naturally didactic language in inviting her audience to listen and to follow her, e.g., 1:33; 8:32–34. But she is a lover (8:17) playing on earth and finding delight with human beings. See the *Excursus on Woman Wisdom and Woman Folly.*

Proverbs 2:1–22

Bibliography

Fox, M. V. "The Pedagogy of Proverbs 2." *JBL* 113 (1994) 233–43. **Maier, C.** *'fremde Frau.'* 69–110. **Michel, D.** "Proverbia 2—ein Dokument der Geschichte der Weisheit." In *Alttestamentlicher Glaube und Biblische Theologie: Festschrift für Horst Dietrich Preuss.* Ed. J. Hausmann et al. Stuttgart: Kohlhammer, 1992. 233–43. **Pardee, D.** *Ugaritic and Hebrew Poetic Parallelism: A Trial Cut ('nt I and Proverbs 2).* VTS 39. Leiden: Brill, 1988. **Skehan, P. W.** *Studies.* 1, 9–10, 32.

Translation

2:1 *My son, if you take in my words*
      and make my commands your treasure,

2 *Giving your ear to wisdom,*
      inclining your heart to understanding;

3 *If*[a] *you call out for perception*
      and summon understanding;

4 *If you seek for her like silver*
      and search for her like hidden treasure;

5 *Then you will understand the fear of the Lord,*
   and acquire knowledge of God,

6 *For the Lord gives wisdom,*
   from his mouth[a] *come knowledge and understanding;*

7 *He stores up*[a] *success for the upright—*
   a shield for those who proceed with integrity,

8 *Protecting the paths of justice,*
   guarding the way of the faithful ones;

9 *Then you will understand justice and judgment and right,*[a]
   everything that leads to good.[b]

10 *When wisdom comes into your heart*
   and knowledge nestles in your soul,

11 *Prudence will keep guard over you;*
   intelligence will protect you,

12 *To save you from the way of evil,*
   from those who speak perversely,[a]

13 *Those who abandon straight paths*
   to walk in the ways of darkness,

14 *Who rejoice in doing evil,*
   who delight in evil perversity,

15 *Whose paths are twisted,*
   whose tracks are devious;

16 *To save you from the woman who is a stranger,*
   from the outsider whose words are smooth,[a]

17 *Who has abandoned the companion of her youth,*
   and forgotten the covenant of her God;

18 *Her house sinks down*[a] *to death,*
   her tracks, to the shades;

19 *No one who enters there ever returns;*
   they never reach the paths of life;

20 *In order that you may go in the way of the good,*
   and observe the paths of the just,

21 *Because the upright will dwell in the land,*
   and the blameless will remain in it;

22 *But the wicked will be cut off from the land,*
   and the faithless will be uprooted[a] *from it.*

Notes

3.a. כי functions here as an asseverative; cf. GKC §159ee.

6.a. As *BHS* indicates, LXX would reflect מפניו, "from his face," but the MT can stand; cf. Sir 24:3.

7.a. Read the Qere, as is shown in *BHS*.

9.a. Although the LXX reads a verb (cf. *BHS*), there seems to be a repetition here of Prov 1:3.

9.b. Literally, "all tracks of/to good." מעגל means "track, trace, course" and is used again in vv 15, 18, as the writer seeks synonyms for "path" and "way."

12.a. Literally, "things upside down," from the root הפך, "to turn upside down," hence "perverse"; cf. v 14.

16.a. Translations and understanding of the אשה נכריה, "a foreign woman," and the אשה זרה, "a strange woman," vary considerably. The literal sense of the terms includes: stranger, outsider (outside of what? family, tribe, nation?), foreign, alien, another. A secondary meaning that may be derived from some contexts is adulteress. It is better to keep to the literal meaning wherever possible, and let other levels of meaning, if any, emerge in the course of chaps. 1–9. The reference to "smooth words" is found again in 7:5 and 7:21 (see also 5:3), where the context is that of adultery. See the *Comment* below, and also the *Excursus on Woman Wisdom and Woman Folly.*

18.a. The translation is doubtful; literally the MT reads "she sinks down to death, her house." Even if "house" can be construed as the subject, the picture of a house sinking down to the nether world is unusual. Parallelism suggests reading נתיבה, "road, path," instead of ביתה, "her house."

22.a. The verb is נסח, "uprooted," and is best vocalized as a passive form as indicated in *BHS,* and adopted by commentators (Plöger, Whybray).

Form/Structure/Setting

What catches the eye is not the form (an instruction), but the structure. It is unique in chaps. 1–9: a twenty-two line poem, exactly the number of the letters in the Hebrew alphabet, and it constitutes one continuous (and conditional) sentence. This was first observed by Skehan (*Studies,* 9–10, 16). The verses are marked by the starting letter *aleph,* which opens v 1 (after the frequent "my son") and closes v 4; the same letter also begins vv 5 and 9 (אז, "then," twice). The second half of the Hebrew alphabet begins with *lamed,* and so here at v 12. This letter *l* (*lamed*) begins at key verses: in vv 12, 16, and 20, all indicating purpose. The consecutive nature of the long sentence can be seen thus: "if . . . then . . . then . . . to save you . . . to save you . . . in order that you may walk . . . ." One can even speak of strophes or stanzas since the chapter breaks down into six units of 4, 4, 3; 4, 4, 3 verses. Moreover, the contents agree with the structure. They can be divided at the halfway mark (*lamed*). Vv 1–11 portray the advantages that wisdom brings. Vv 12–22 indicate the dangers that wisdom preserves one from: the wicked men, the "stranger"-woman, and finally there is a contrast between the fate of the just and the wicked in vv 20–22. In form, this is an instruction, but it has the air of a program or paradigm, providing themes that will be developed in the instructions that follow. Thus, as Skehan has pointed out specifically for 2:1–19: (1) In 2:1–8, the seeker after wisdom is promised to be drawn close to the Lord—the relationship to the Lord is taken up again in 3:1–12. (2) The relationship to Wisdom in 2:9–11 is taken up again in 3:13–26 and 4:1–9. (3) The relationship to wicked men in 2:12–15 is taken up again in 4:10–27. (4) The relationship to a woman in 2:16–19 is taken up again in 5:1–23 and 6:20–7:27. This is a remarkable, even singular, example of reprise, and such detail argues to a single author or editor for most of chaps. 2–7. It is also an indication that the function of chap. 2 is to serve as a literary setting for the instructions to follow. The general encouragement and warnings *may* derive ultimately from oral teaching, but chap. 2 seems to be a carefully prepared literary construction, and its setting is precisely for these chapters.

Apparently independently, C. Maier (*'fremde Frau,'* 102) has described a similar development of themes, but the structure of the chapter is disfigured by the needless hypothesis that 2:5–8, 21–22 are later insertions (p. 90). Her table of the semantic spread of key words shows how tightly knit this chapter is (p. 88). In a similar vein, Alonso Schökel (*Proverbios,* 167–71) has analyzed the terminology and structure according to four categories: wisdom, ethics, religious, and existential. The distribution of key words is striking.

There has been no lack of attempts to divide this chapter. Although the study of D. Pardee concentrates on literary features, such as parallelism and chiasmus, etc., he does indicate a division based on a thematic basis (*Parallelism,* 70–71). There is a basic instruction on how a son may acquire wisdom (vv 1–11); a statement of the effects of wisdom (vv 12–19), and a conclusion in form of promise and warning. Further subdivisions follow, but the whole chapter is treated as a unit. Whybray's hypothesis of ten instructions leads to a dislocation in chap. 2; thus he discerns a "Yahweh addition" in 2:5–8, that is "appended to the wisdom addition of vv. 2-4" (*Composition,* 32, 58–59). Similarly, D. Michel, although he recognizes the programmatic structure indicated above, discovers later additions that supposedly reflect the "history" of the development of wisdom. Thus vv 5–8 concerning fear of the Lord are a later insert to bind wisdom and religion together. Vv 16–19 are likewise a later insertion because certain sages perceived the "stranger" as the root of evil (chaps. 5–7) and wanted this to be indicated in chap. 2. Finally, 2:21–22 is an addition growing out of apocalyptic aspirations; this development caused a union of sapiential and apocalyptic thought, but he admits that this aspect of the history of wisdom has not yet been written! Such an analysis is fraught with hazards; it tears apart the clearly unified structure of the text on the basis of later hypothetical views. Such hypotheses are simply not compelling. What is the likelihood of three later hands creating the alphabetic structure, i.e., the *aleph, lamed,* indicated above, that is the framework of the chapter?

Comment

1–4 The teacher promises wisdom as a gift of the Lord, if the "son" truly follows the bidding to seek wisdom above all else, beyond any riches. The intensity of the appeal matches the intensity of the speeches of Moses in Deuteronomy. **1** The "commands" are those of the teacher, not the Torah. Although the technical term (מצות), so frequent in Deuteronomy, is used, and thus may have another level of meaning for later readers, it is generally understood here in its literal historical sense as referring to the commands of the father/teacher. **2** The emphasis on hearing, listening, and attentiveness is characteristic of Israelite and Egyptian wisdom, and these attitudes appear frequently throughout the book. **3–4** The conditions for obtaining wisdom are heightened by the "call" that the youth is to make (answering Wisdom's speech in 1:20–31?), and by a diligent search for her as one would look for a "hidden treasure." Throughout the book the value of wisdom is portrayed as surpassing precious stones, e.g., 3:14–15.

5–8 The apodosis follows upon the protasis and describes the happy results of obedience and searching. **5** The many synonyms for wisdom in vv 1–4 find a climax here: "the fear of the Lord" is parallel to "knowledge of God"; cf. Hos 4:1; 6:6. **6** Most important is the emphasis on wisdom as a gift of God. This is somewhat paradoxical. On the one hand, the teacher speaks as if everything depends upon the listening and obedience of the youth. On the other hand, wisdom is a divine *gift.* Her origin is described as from the mouth (see *Note* 6.a.) of the Lord, an anticipation of Sir 24:3; cf. Prov 8:22–24. As things develop, it will be seen that there is divine mystery lurking behind the security and the certainty of wisdom teaching. One must strive for the goal, but also realize that wisdom remains a divine gift. Ultimately we have a picture of the acquisition of wisdom by means of human industry *and* divine aid and generosity. **7–8** Wisdom is never without an ethical ideal, and this is to be realized by the Lord's sheltering and protection of his loyal followers. When the Lord is a "shield" (Prov 30:5; and many times in the psalms), then "success" will be theirs.

9–11 The emphasis on the Lord's "guarding" (v 8b) leads to the description of Wisdom's standing guard (v 11) over the "heart" that possesses her. Wisdom and the Lord are, as it were, interchangeable, at least in their effects. **9** The three key terms of 1:3b are repeated; to "understand" these virtues is to put them into practice. **10–11** Now wisdom takes the initiative, entering the "heart," the very center of being, of the youth and exercising the protection that was ascribed to the Lord in vv 7–8.

12–15 The key symbol of the "way" reappears, cf. 1:15, 21, and it will be taken up again in 4:10–27 and elsewhere; cf. N. Habel, "Symbolism," 131–56. There is a steady contrast between the two ways of virtue and wickedness running through chaps. 1–9, and a doctrine of the two ways will be continued and developed in Jewish and Christian tradition (cf. Matt 7:13–14; the *Didache,* and the Dead Sea Scrolls). This strophe deals with evil ways (v 13, "darkness"; v 14, "perversity"), and these will be paralleled by the ways to which the "stranger" of vv 16–19 will entice the youth.

16–19 All through the twentieth century several studies of the "woman-stranger/outsider" (אשה זרה / נכריה) appeared. Nevertheless, it has been difficult to pin down her identity, and opinions differ widely; see the survey of research in C. Maier, *'fremde Frau,'* 7–24, and also the *Excursus on Woman Wisdom and Woman Folly.* In these verses one must settle for a relatively narrow identification, a seductive woman, while allowing for the fact that this figure can take on further meaning in later chapters (esp. chap. 9). **16** See *Note* 16.a. It is clear that the woman represents a threat to the youth, and the threat is of a sexual nature. This is indicated by the "smooth" talk which characterizes her; cf. also 6:24; 7:5, 21. But this characteristic is not restricted to women; cf. Prov 26:28. **17** More important is the statement that she has abandoned her lifetime partner, and "forgotten" the covenant of her God. The charge of adultery is made in v 17a, but "the covenant of her God" in v 17b is vague. Even if the "stranger" were to be identified as a non-Israelite, the involvement of her God with marriage remains unknown. It seems best to refer here to Mal 2:14, which speaks of the Lord witnessing "between you [i.e., the husband] and the wife of your youth, to whom you have been faithless, though she is your companion and your wife by covenant" (NRSV). The use of "the covenant of our God" in v 17b refers then to the marriage bond as a sacred covenant, and "the woman" would refer to an adulterous Israelite (so Whybray, Van Leeuwen, and others). Plöger leaves open the question of nationality. As it stands, v 17b does not preclude further refinement, e.g., the symbolism of the covenant between the Lord and Israel. **18–19** The death metaphors attached to the "stranger" suggest another important dimension. There is more than mere sexual activity concerned here. Of itself this could merely mean the harm to the male, even unto physical death, that is indicated in 6:33–35. But the aura of death leaves open other possibilities, such as spiritual death. This aspect need not be taken up here. Suffice it to say that this woman appears also as a metaphor, a figure that is open-ended and capable of expansion. She is described as having a house (v 18; see *Note* 18.a. also), and this is associated with death. Similarly in 9:14, 18, Woman Folly has a house, and her guests are in Sheol! The "shades" of v 18 (cf. 9:18) are to be identified with the inhabitants of Sheol who have no real "life," but only a shadowy existence. In such manner was an "afterlife" imagined. Although the term has Ugaritic connections, these contribute little or nothing to understanding the general meaning of "death" in this verse. Sheol is the place "of no return"; cf. Job 7:9–10; 10:21; 16:22. The imagery of no return is reminiscent of the "Descent of Ishtar to the Nether World" (*ANET*, 107, lines 1–10) and practically duplicated in the Epic of Gilgamesh (*ANET*, 87, "the House of Darkness"). The woman represents a danger that is described in more serious terms than the temptation offered by the wicked in 1:10–19. Moreover, juxtaposition of vv 12–15 with vv 16–19 establishes a deliberate parallel/contrast between the stranger and Wisdom: by means of the main verbs ("to save you from," להציל, in vv 12 and 16) and also the term "abandon" (עזב, in vv 13 and 17). The dangers from evil people (cf. also the "sinners" of 1:10–19) and from the stranger are thus closely associated. The most insidious approach is by way of speech; cf. vv 12b, 16b.

20–22 The significant metaphors of the "path" or "way" occur so frequently that there is danger that their impact can be lost on the reader (v 20; cf. vv 8, 12–15). **21–22** The "land" is a new metaphor to express the security of the wise, but it picks up a theme strongly entrenched in biblical tradition; e.g., Deut 28:1–14; Ps 37. The fate of the wicked continues the metaphor; they shall be cut off from the land.

Explanation

Looking back at this unusual chapter, one must recognize its programmatic character. But it is also a daring vision for the youth to follow: promises of great wisdom and a closeness to God that will enable one to avoid all dangers to the moral life, and attain a secure existence. This vision is really overwhelming. How firmly did the sages and their students adhere to these forthright claims? The adherents of any religion, including Christianity and Judaism, could be asked the same question: Who really accepts the wisdom perspective? If not, why not? Do the books of Job and Ecclesiastes contribute nuances, to say the least, to this chapter?

Even more serious questions are beginning to take shape. Is there another level of meaning in the description of the dangerous "stranger" (cf. chap. 9:13–18)? Is Wisdom personified in chap. 2? G. Baumann (*Weisheitsgestalt*, 227–231) sees rather a personification of the synonyms for wisdom in vv 1–11, namely, perception and understanding (v 3), and prudence and intelligence (v 11). However, she points out that these terms have almost the same meaning as "wisdom," which does occur in vv 2, 6, and 10. She co-relates v 6 with Deut 8:3, "every word that comes forth from the mouth of the Lord." Even though we do not possess the Hebrew original of Sir 24:3, which Baumann notes, there can hardly be any doubt of a reprise in Sirach. In view of the passage in Prov 8:22–31, I would be inclined to say that 2:6 belongs to the same world: Wisdom (personified) comes from the Lord.

Proverbs 3:1–35

Bibliography

Kayatz, C. *Studien.* 104–5. **Markus, R.** "The Tree of Life in Proverbs." *JBL* 62 (1943) 117–20. **Murphy, R. E.** "The Kerygma of the Book of Proverbs." *Int* 20 (1966) 3–14. **Robert, A.** "Les attaches." *RB* 43 (1934) 42–68. **Whybray, R. N.** *Composition.* 18–20, 33, 36–38.

Translation

3:1 *My son, do not forget my teaching,*
    and let your heart keep my commands,
2 *For length of days and years of life*
    and peace will they bring you.

3 *Do not let kindness and fidelity leave you;*
    bind them on your neck;
    write them on the tablet of your heart,[a]
4 *And so find favor and good esteem*
    in the eyes of God and humans.

5 *Trust in the Lord wholeheartedly*
    and do not rely on your own intelligence;
6 *In all your ways acknowledge him,*
    and he will keep your paths straight.

7 *Do not be wise in your own eyes,*
    fear the Lord and turn from evil.
8 *It will be healing for your body*[a]
    and refreshment for your bones.

9 *Give honor to the Lord from your riches*
    and from the firstfruits of all your income;
10 *Then your barns will be filled with plenty,*[a]
    and your vats will flow with new wine.

11 *My son, do not reject the discipline of the Lord,*
    and do not spurn his reproof,
12 *For the Lord loves the one he reproves,*
    as a father, the child in whom he delights.[a]

13 *Happy the one finds wisdom,*
    the one who acquires understanding!
14 *For her profit, greater than gold,*
    her income, greater than silver.
15 *More precious than rubies—*
    no treasures[a] *can compare with her.*

16   *Length of days in her right hand,*
       and in her left, riches and glory.
17   *Her ways, pleasant ways,*
       and all her paths, peace!
18   *She, a tree of life to all who grasp her;*
       happy [a] *those who take hold of her!*

19   *The Lord founded the world with wisdom,*
       establishing the heavens with intelligence.
20   *By his knowledge the depths were split,*
       and the clouds drop down dew.

21   *My son, do not let them* [a] *slip from your eyes:*
       hold on to discretion and prudence,
22   *So that they will be life to your soul* [a]
       and adornment for your neck.
23   *Then you will go on your way securely,*
       and your foot will not stumble.
24   *When you lie down,* [a] *you have nothing to be afraid of;*
       you will lie down, and your sleep will be sweet.
25   *Do not fear a sudden terror,*
       or the ruin that comes to the wicked,
26   *For the Lord will be your confidence;*
       he will keep your foot from being caught.

27   *Do not refuse anyone the good that is his,* [a]
       when it is your power [b] *to act.*

28   *Do not tell your neighbor, "Go, but come back again,*
       and tomorrow I will give," although you can do it now.

29   *Do not plot evil against your neighbor*
       who lives trustfully beside you.
30   *Do not contend with any one for no cause*
       when they have done you no evil.

31   *Do not envy the violent,*
       and do not choose [a] *any of their ways,*
32   *For the devious are an abomination to the Lord,*
       but the upright are in his confidence.

33   *The curse of the Lord is on the house of the wicked,*
       but he blesses the dwelling of the just.
34   *The scoffers he scoffs at;* [a]
       the humble he favors.
35   *Glory, the wise inherit—*
       but fools, disgrace. [a]

Notes

3.a. The third line is suspect, in view of the general style, and it is suggested that since it is lacking in Greek MSS, it might be a gloss from Prov 7:3. But many authors judge that it is the first line that may be dubious (cf. Whybray and Plöger). There is no easy decision.

8.a. שֹׁר means "navel," and may possibly be interpreted as body (part for the whole). But it may also be a mistake for בְּשַׂר, "flesh" (cf. 4:22); cf. *BHS*.

10.a. Instead of "plenty," some read "grain" (שֶׁבֶר for שָׂבָע), which is in contrast to wine. The LXX reads "fullness of grain" (cf. *BHS*).

12.a. Better parallelism is secured by reading יַכְאִב for וּכְאָב, "he chastises the son whom he loves." This is apparently also the interpretation of the LXX, which reads μαστιγοῖ.

15.a. Read the Qere, which has the support of the versions.

18.a. There is no need to change to the plural; cf. GKC §145l.

21.a. The Hebrew is difficult because the identity of the (plural) subject of the verb in v 21a is not clear. The real subjects occur in v 21b, and hence the translation anticipates by inserting "them," referring to these subjects. This solution is preferable to the suggestion in *BHS*.

22.a. "Soul" is a frequent, if inadequate, translation of נֶפֶשׁ, which can also mean "throat," and so provide a better parallel to "neck" in v 22b.

24.a. So the MT; others would prefer to read with the LXX, "sit down," as suggested in *BHS*, and thus avoid the repetition of the same verb in v 24b. However, שָׁכַב also has the nuance of "sleeping with," and it is appropriate also in v 24b.

27.a. The literal translation of the Hebrew would normally be "good from its possessors," but most interpreters take it to mean the possessor who has a right to it. LXX has "the one in need."

27.b. Read the Qere יָדְךָ, "your hand," with LXX, Tg, i.e., "the power of your hand," instead of Ketib יָדֶיךָ, "your hands," with Syr. For the phrase לְאֵל יָד, "for power of a hand = power to act," cf. Gen 31:29.

31.a. For the Hebrew "choose," the LXX has "be envious," which is in line with Prov 24:19 and Ps 37:1. However, the Hebrew reading is better supported by the motivation provided in v 32 (with Plöger and Whybray).

34.a. The Hebrew אִם, "if," is difficult; it should be changed to עִם, "with"; cf. Ps 18:26–27.

35.a. The Hebrew מֵרִים, "lift up?" is the singular (distributive use?) form of the hiphil participle of רוּם, "rise up," or possibly from מוּר, "exchange." But neither of these has been satisfactorily explained; cf. the commentaries of Delitzsch and Whybray. The meaning seems to be that fools will meet with disgrace.

Form/Structure/Setting

This chapter is a rather mixed bag. For the first time, separate couplets, mainly positive in form, appear, six of them in vv 1–12; note the repetition of the sacred name יהוה, "YHWH." They are admonitions with motive clauses. Vv 13–18 are set off by an inclusion ("happy"), and they celebrate personified (?) Wisdom in a hymnic style. This is presumably uttered by the teacher and seems independent of vv 1–12. To it have been associated a couplet about the role of wisdom in creation (vv 19–20). Somewhat parallel in content to vv 13–20 (which in a sense anticipate chap. 8) are vv 21–26, an exhortation to hold to wisdom and thus enjoy security against any terror. The chapter seems disjointed, but there is no easy solution for it. The couplet style reappears in vv 27–32, with prohibitions, and in vv 33–35, with sayings. Perhaps one can divide the chapter thus: vv 1–12, 13–18 (20), 21–26, 27–35. No definitive setting can be determined, except for a father/teacher-son relationship (vv 1, 11, 21).

Comment

1–2 The opening couplet is echoed many times (4:10: 5:1). The promise of a long life and prosperity are characteristic of the benefits of following wise teaching.

Life is to be taken in a qualitative sense, as the good life, indicated by "peace" or "shalom" (cf. also v 16).

3–4 This recommendation intensifies the appeal of the previous verses. It is striking that the teaching is now equated with two words that have a rich history. חסד, "kindness," and אמת, "fidelity," have been rendered in various ways, and they can stand for divine (Exod 34:6) as well as human qualities—relations between God and humans and also between humans. In Prov 16:6 the phrase is parallel to "fear of the Lord." The intensity is indicated by the manner in which the recommendation is expressed: love and fidelity are not to depart from the youth, and they are to be written on the tablet of the heart; cf. Prov 7:3; Deut 30:14; Jer 17:1, and the interiorization in Jer 31:33. The phrase "God and humans" is striking in that יהוה, "YHWH," is not preferred. "God" (אלהים, "Elohim") is seldom used in the book.

5–6 O. Plöger points out that wisdom joins Yahwism (were they ever really separate?) in this command to trust in the Lord, an ideal that is sounded frequently in the Psalter and elsewhere. The contrast between such trust and one's own intelligence or insight is not a put-down of wisdom teaching, because the truly wise person knows of limits. Wisdom is a gift of God (2:6), but whoever claims to be wise is more foolish than the fool (Prov 26:12; cf. also Jer 9:22–23), and the next couplet (vv 7–8) reinforces this idea. The Lord's role in the ways of humans is also indicated in 16:9 and 20:24 (cf. Hos 14:10).

7–8 To be "wise in one's own eyes" is to be in an utterly hopeless situation. According to 26:12 (see *Comment* there), there is more hope for a fool than for such a person! It is surely significant that the sages could modify wisdom in this way. When does wisdom cease to be wisdom? When you think you are wise. Personal wisdom must always be tested, as the sages recognized, and the "tester of hearts" is the Lord (Prov 17:3; cf. 27:21). Avoidance of evil is joined to the fear of the Lord in 16:6 and several times in Job (1:1, 8). But only here and in 24:21 is the direct imperative used (also favored by Qoheleth; cf. Eccl 5:5). The benefit of true wisdom is physical health and vigor (v 8; "refreshment" is literally "drink"). See also *Note* 8.a. The idea is much stronger than the Latin saying *nemo judex in causa sua*, "no one can be a judge in his own case."

9–10 Sacrifices are mentioned in the book (7:14; 15:8; 21:3, 27), but A. Meinhold points out that this is the only time that sacrifice is prescribed. The reference is to the firstfruits; cf. Exod 23:19; Deut 26:1–3. This generosity is to be rewarded by the material blessings for the people (Deut 7:13; 28:8). The "new wine" designates the grape juice before fermentation.

11–12 Only here in Proverbs is the problem of suffering directly touched upon. The application of human discipline (as the sages understood it, quite physical) to the Lord is a bold move. In 13:24 physical beating is seen as a sign of a father's love for his son—a paradox. In the same way, discipline from the Lord is to be understood as a sign of divine paternal love; cf. also Deut 8:5. A similar line of thought appears in Job 5:17–27; 33:15–30, where suffering (of a sinner, however) is seen as medicinal and contributing toward conversion. Heb 12:5–6 takes up this couplet. The book of Proverbs remains resolute in its assurance of material well-being for the wise and virtuous, despite the fact that adversity and suffering bore witness to the contrary. But the sages were aware of problems; see the *Excursus on Retribution* and the *Excursus on Wealth and Poverty*.

13–20 A kind of hymn about wisdom begins here. The word for "happy" (or "blessed"), אַשְׁרֵי, in v 13 "finds" an inclusion in v 18, and "intelligence/understanding," תבונה, appears in vv 13, 19. **13** To "find" (מצא) means also to reach and to possess. Thus one who finds wisdom finds life (Prov 8:35), and one who "finds" a wife (18:22; cf. 31:10) finds a gift from God. But who can "find" wisdom? No one, according to Job 28:12, 20, because it is with God. It is no wonder that the finder is hailed in this verse as "happy." See also 8:32, 34! **14–15** The comparison of wisdom to precious metals is a commonplace (e.g., 2:4; see also 8:10, where 8:11 seems to be a repetition of 3:15; also 8:18–19). The precise nature of פנינים, "rubies" (also translated as "corals"), is unclear, but they are associated with gold also in 20:15. Wisdom is clearly superior to any material gain that precious objects could achieve. This judgment qualifies and even rejects the materialism that is often associated with the promises of wisdom. A further question arises: what is the significance of material riches? The question will be illuminated from many sides in the book of Proverbs. **16** There is a personification here. The description of Wisdom has been illustrated by representations of the Egyptian goddess, Ma'at (and also other divinities), with the sign for life, the *ankh,* in one hand and a scepter, a symbol of riches and honor, in the other; cf. C. Kayatz, *Studien,* 104–5. "Riches and glory" have royal associations; e.g., 1 Chr 29:28; in Prov 8:18 they are attributed to Woman Wisdom. They also appear, in a lesser key, in 11:16; 22:4. **17** The familiar symbol of the "way" (דרך) appears, picking up on v 6, where the Lord directs the ways of human beings. This also anticipates 8:20, 32, where Woman Wisdom speaks of her paths of justice, which are also the ways to be kept by her followers. The "peace" (שלום) arrived at by these paths reflects v 2. **18** The tree of life is a frequent metaphor in the book (11:30; 13:12; 15:4), where it no longer enjoys its original mythological background reflected in Gen 2–3, and in many references in Akkadian and Egyptian literature. In the context of the book, it is a metaphor for the happiness that was associated with the good life in sapiential teaching (see the discussion in W. Bühlmann, *Vom rechten Reden,* 279–283). "Holding on" to the tree of life is illustrated by Kayatz (*Studien,* 106–7) from Egyptian Pyramid texts. The verbs in v 18 reflect the erotic ambience in which Woman Wisdom is described in these chapters (cf. R. E. Murphy, "Wisdom and Eros in Proverbs 1–9," *CBQ* 50 [1988] 600–603).

19–20 The appearance of a cosmological role for Wisdom is sudden. She is now associated with the creative acts of the Lord, who imitates human building (cf. 24:3). In a sense it has been adumbrated in Ps 104:24a and Jer 10:12. **18** It is difficult to be more precise about the meaning of "in/with wisdom." The role of wisdom here seems to be instrumental. But to say that wisdom is merely a divine attribute is to adopt ultimately Greek philosophical language, and it says very little. Moreover, the context speaks of Wisdom's "hands" (v 16), as though she were a person. Did she assist in creation? Her role is described at greater length in Prov 8:22–31, but it still remains mysterious. If one gives full force to the preposition ב, "be," as instrumental, Wisdom does have a role in creation, whereas her role in Prov 8:30 remains uncertain; see *Comment* there. It is important to note that wisdom and intelligence are together again (vv 13, 19) and that they are set forth with knowledge (v 20) as one in the creative activity of God. G. von Rad's interpretation (*Wisdom,* 155) suggests that wisdom is an attribute of the earth, so that God created the world as it were *into* wisdom; this is not likely. **20** This verse picks up the theme of water, above and below, but goes no further with it or with any other aspect of creation; it has the appearance of a misplaced verse from a creation poem. Vv 19–20 are unexpected here and give the appearance of an addition.

21–26 An address to "my son" occupies the rest of the chapter. The opening lines assure the youth about the safety and security that come to the follower of wisdom. **21–22** See *Notes* 21.a. and 22.a. Despite the grammatical difficulty, the message is clear enough and even repetitious. Wisdom will be a protection, providing "life" (cf. vv 2, 16, 18), and the adornment for the neck as in 1:9. **23–24** The metaphors for life's journey appear: walking without mishap (cf. Ps 91:12) and sleeping without any fear. The Lord protects followers when they sleep (Ps 3:6; 4:9), and there is always the threat of the "terror of the night" (Ps 91:5). **25–26** These verses continue the confident tone; the assurance takes the form of a prohibition: Do not fear! Terror is for the wicked, and security lies with the Lord. The "terror" (פַּחַד) or panic (v 26) is left unspecified, but one can think of the ambush prepared by the wicked in 1:11–12. It is against such unexpected attacks that the Lord will protect the one who shows trust.

27–28 The couplet style returns (if not already in vv 25–26) with prohibitions and commands dealing with relationship to neighbors. **27** The presupposition seems to be that a neighbor has some right to consideration (in the LXX translation, a poor person), and that one has the means to help. **28** The admonition to help the neighbor is strengthened by this verse; there is no reason for postponing kind action. Delaying tactics are equivalent to a refusal. Cf. Jas 4:16.

29–30 These are commands to live at peace with one's neighbor, and in particular to avoid unjustified legal disputes (such is the meaning of "contend").

31–32 Those who are apparently virtuous are frequently subject to envy of the wicked who prosper (cf. Pss 37:1; 73:3). Here the prohibition against envy concerns criminals whose prosperity might prove to be a temptation. The "violent" (חָמָס is a particularly expressive word) and the devious are described as an "abomination" to the Lord. Thus they will not belong to the inner circle (Hebrew סוֹד) of the Lord, enjoying the divine confidence; there will be no sharing, for God is intimate only with the upright. "Abomination to the Lord" has cultic associations, and can be found frequently in Proverbs (e.g., 11:1, 20; 15:8, 9, 26), Deuteronomy, and Ezekiel. R. E. Clements ("Abomination in the Book of Proverbs," in *Texts, Temples, and Traditions. A Tribute to Menachem Haran*, M. V. Fox et al., eds. [Winona Lake, IN: Eisenbrauns, 1996] 211–25) has pointed out the nuances of the phrase in the wisdom tradition: "what is wrong is wrong *in itself* and is recognized by the feelings of outrage that it engenders" (p. 222). It appears in cases where legal redress is difficult, and where various antisocial, even criminal, attitudes are the issue. Cf. also the *Comment* on 6:16–19.

33–34 The curse and the blessing are meted out according to the conduct of individuals. One destroys the very residence of the wicked; the other operates for the good of the just. The punishment of the "scoffers" is expressed in an unusual manner; the Lord pays them in kind. The sense is that he "outscoffs" the scoffers (cf. Ps 18:27). V 34 (LXX) is taken up in Jas 4:6 and 1 Pet 5:5.

35 The conclusion equates the moral condition of the just and the wicked with the category of wise and foolish. This is another expression of just = wise, fool = wicked. It is found in a snappy chiasm (despite the uncertainty in v 35b; see *Note* 35.a.).

Explanation

The description by N. Habel ("Symbolism," 144–45) points out that YHWH takes over the role of wisdom, preserving the youth on the way (cf. v 31 and the ensuing blessing/curse): "The way of wisdom becomes the religious way of Yahweh." Thus wisdom and virtue are again combined. Jas 4:6 quotes v 34 in its LXX form, and the sharpness of v 34a disappears; it is now a question of the opposition between the proud (sinners) and the humble (poor), whom God favors with grace.

Apropos of vv 9–10 Whybray remarks that we have here "the most blatant expression in the Old Testament of the principle of *do ut des*—the offering of gifts to God solely in order to elicit material rewards from him," and he is of the opinion that this attitude colors vv 5–8 as well. He invokes this Latin principle, that drips with selfishness and greed, and applies it harshly to the daily tasks of the ancient Israelite. Of course they sought material blessings, but this must be put in the broader context of the covenant relationship with the Lord, which provides such motivations (Deuteronomy!). The prescriptions in 3:1–12 promised the benefits of the good life if the Israelite remained faithful (e.g., Deut 30:9–10). In a deeper sense, one can even speak of a sacramental view of the universe; the goods of this world are a sign of divine pleasure, a sign that the covenant relationship is in good order. They are not "solely" for the sake of reward, nor are they infallible signs. It is always possible to exaggerate and to become legalistic in such matters, but the sages question often enough human motivation (e.g., Prov 21:2!), and should not be categorized so crassly. The careful reader will detect in chaps. 1–9 wave after wave of statements about the beauty and the desirability of Wisdom. There is an idealism, and enthusiasm about wisdom, which correlates easily with the thrust of Israelite religion. Perhaps one sign of this is the manner in which the text will suddenly speak of Wisdom in the style of personification (vv 16–20) and then return to a more distant mood of description. G. Baumann (*Weisheitsgestalt*, 231–38) can find no unambiguous personification of wisdom in v 19. She subjects vv 13–20 to careful analysis and argues that Wisdom is personified only in vv 16–17. The verses that speak of the instrumental role of Wisdom in creation stand outside the unit in vv 13–18, which has an inclusion. It is difficult to draw any certain conclusion about personification when v 19 is separated from the context.

Proverbs 4:1–27

Bibliography

Aletti, J. "Séduction et parole en Proverbes I–IX." *VT* 27 (1977) 131–44. **Habel, N.** "Symbolism." *Int* 26 (1972) 135–42. **Murphy, R. E.** "Wisdom and Eros in Proverbs 1–9." *CBQ* 50 (1988) 600–603. **Whybray, R. N.** *Composition.* 21–22, 30–31, 33–34.

Translation

4:1	*Hear, children, a father's instruction;*
	pay attention and know what understanding is.
2	*For I give you sound doctrine;*
	do not abandon my teaching.
3	*Indeed, a son to my father was I,*
	tender, and my mother's only one.
4	*He taught me and said to me:*
	"Let your heart hold fast my words;
	keep my commands and live! [a]
5	*Get wisdom, get understanding!*
	Do not forget; do not turn aside from the words of my mouth!
6	*If you do not forsake her, she will guard you;*
	love her, and she will preserve you.
7	*The beginning of wisdom: Get wisdom!*
	Above all else that you get, get wisdom! [a]
8	*Extol her, and she will exalt you;*
	embrace her, and she will honor you.
9	*She will place a gracious wreath on your head,*
	bestow on you a glorious crown."
10	*Hear, my son, and take in my words,*
	and the years of your life will be many.
11	*I have taught you in the way of wisdom;*
	I have put you on a way of straight paths.
12	*As you go, your step will not be shortened,*
	and when you run, you will not stumble.
13	*Hold instruction firmly; do not let go!*
	Keep her: your life!
14	*Do not go in the path of the wicked,*
	and do not walk in the way of the evil.
15	*Avoid it; do not go near it;*
	turn aside from it and keep going!
16	*They cannot sleep without doing evil;*
	they lose sleep if they have not caused some to stumble.
17	*They feed on the bread of wickedness*
	and drink the wine of violence.
18	*But the path of the just, like a dawning light*
	that keeps shining unto the full day. [a]
19	*The way of the wicked, like darkness;*
	they do not know what they are stumbling over.
20	*My son, pay attention to my words;*
	turn your ear to my sayings.
21	*Do not let them slip from your eyes;*
	keep them in your heart,

22   *For they are life to those who find them,*
        and a healing to the whole person.
23   *More than all else you guard, watch your heart,*
        for out of it, the surges of life.
24   *Turn aside from your mouth any crookedness;*
        put away from your lips any deceit.
25   *Let your eyes keep looking forward,*
        your eyelids straight ahead of you.
26   *Level a path for your feet,*
        and let all your ways be firm.
27   *Do not turn to right or left;*
        keep your foot from evil.

Notes

4.a. The last phrase of v 4a is repeated in 7:2a; it is lacking in the Greek (which itself is a rather free rendering). Also, v 5 seems to be overloaded. All this may be due to the obvious emotional style of the address, and it seems better not to tamper with the text.

7.a. The MT has literally "with/in your possession (or, property)." But the sense of it is that Wisdom is more precious than any other possession; cf. v 23. The fourfold repetition of the verb קנה, "get," in vv 5, 7 is significant; it is used in Ruth 4:8, 10, where Boaz "acquires" Ruth in marriage. Notice also the verb חבק, "embrace," in v 8, and in v 9 עטרת (a wedding crown, in Cant 3:11).

18.a. The MT reads "until the establishment of the day"; it is probably an indication of noontime when the sun is at its highest.

Form/Structure/Setting

The forms in this chapter are essentially threefold: 1:1–9 constitutes a reminiscence of a father to "sons," relating the advice he received from his father. A relatively independent development of the two ways is found in vv 10–19; because of the opening words ("my son") it should be viewed as an instruction. The remainder of the chapter (vv 20–27) consists of warnings, especially about the use of the organs of the body—again, an instruction for "my son" (v 20). This description of the forms indicates at the same time the structure. One cannot detect any unifying theme, but two emphases may be noted. First there is the love relationship with wisdom—a prominent feature of the teaching that the father receives and transmits (vv 5–9). Second, the admonitions concerning the "ways," positive and negative. One can postulate various settings for the units in this chapter. An original oral setting is fitting for a father who speaks of the lesson transmitted by his father to him. But it is difficult to distinguish between home and school—or between an oral and a literary setting, especially for the instructions in vv 10–27. The well-known theory of W. McKane concerning later Yahwistic reworking makes an exception for this chapter as "probably" (p. 302) unaffected by a later hand. In general his distinction of levels within the book (e.g., for the sentences, cf. pp. 10–11) on the basis of God-language is too hypothetical. Plöger (p. 46) regards the beginning (4:1–9), the report of an experience, as opening a framework extending to chap. 7, which is another report of an experience.

Comment

1–3 The opening address is unique in the collections. The father assures "sons" (the plural also, if the *mem* is not enclitic, in 5:7; 7:24; 8:32) of the solidity of his doctrine, called "torah" in v 2, by relating his own experience in his home. **1–2** The plural "sons" may be explained as a variation of the customary singular address, or perhaps to avoid the impression that the teaching was intended only for the individual and was not universal (so Plöger). **3** The implication of this verse may be that after the early training received from the mother, the father assumed responsibility. So the speaker is ostensibly describing the training that he received and is now going to pass on.

4–9 These verses are to be regarded as a summary in the form of a "quotation" of the grandfather. It is a very intense passage, and its erotic quality has been described by R. E. Murphy (*CBQ* 50 [1988] 600–603). **4** The father was pressured by his father to keep the "commands" (see *Comment* on 2:1) and to pursue wisdom, which stands in parallelism with the "words" from the grandfather's mouth. **5–9** The pursuit is a love engagement: one is to "get," "love," and "embrace" wisdom beyond anything else. The intensity can be seen from the fourfold repetition of "get." See *Note* 7.a. Wisdom will reciprocate, and bestow a "gracious wreath" (in 1:9 a symbol of parental teaching), a "glorious crown" (for a wedding? cf. Cant 3:11). Again, Wisdom is portrayed as a Woman to be loved, one who will exalt her lover when he "embraces" (v 8, חבק) her, and will decorate him with wreath and crown. All these are the actions of a person, so that personification seems undeniable in vv 5–9. The "getting" of wisdom and understanding will appear again in 16:16, another indication of the join between the early and later chapters of the book.

10–19 Now the father/teacher begins his own teaching, and is represented as directly addressing "my son." The subject is the topic of the right way, "the way of wisdom," which is defined by Wisdom herself as "the path of justice" (8:20) in which she walks. **10** Note the emphasis on a long life (cf. v 13, and also 3:2); this is an emphasis of Deuteronomistic theology as well; cf. Deut 30:16, 19. **11–13** The terminology of the "way of wisdom" accords with the symbol: path, step, guide, run, stumble, walk, go, turn, etc. N. Habel describes the metaphor accurately ("Symbolism," 136): "This road, however, is not so much the 'straight and narrow' as the 'straight and clear.' It is an open highway where men may run and not fall (4:12) . . ." There is a vivid contrast between this highway and the stumbling that will be the lot of the wicked (v 19). **13** The firm hold (cf. Cant 3:4) on instruction, or מוסר, harks back to the "embrace" of v 8. The exhortation begins and ends on the note of life (vv 10, 13). **14–15** The "way of wisdom" cannot be described without a warning against the "path of the wicked." The same kind of energetic intensity as witnessed above for the pursuit of wisdom is now poured into the prohibitions against walking down the path of the wicked. **16–17** The path of evil is their continual preoccupation (cf. also 2:12–15). They eat, drink, and sleep wickedness, as indicated by the striking phrases "cannot sleep," "bread of wickedness" (i.e., the livelihood that they secure by their sinful profits), and "the wine of violence" (4:17). Their ways were already graphically described in 1:10–19, especially vv 15, 19. **18–19** The symbols of light and darkness that accompany the journey in these "ways" are fitting conclusions. The way of wisdom is surely not "the road less travelled" of Robert Frost; rather, it is "life" (v 13), and it is a path ever shining as opposed to the darkness that drenches the road of the stumbling wicked. "Stumble" serves as a catch word for this section (vv 12, 16, 19).

20–27 These verses repeat ideas already enunciated in the chapter, but give them a new twist by emphasizing the parts of the body: first the ear, then the eyes, and, most important of all, the heart. Only after these organs are operating correctly will "life" (v 23) be secured. **20–23** The address to "my son" calls for total attention and concentration on the father's words. The connection between heart and way (cf. also 4:26–27) was already indicated in 2:10–13 (cf. also 2:15, 18, 20). In 3:3–6 a wholehearted trust in the Lord is associated with direction in the right paths (cf. 3:23). These symbols are taken up again here. Just as important as the "way" of Wisdom is the "heart" of those who would travel that path. The youth is to take to heart the parental instructions and then to guard the heart above all else. The heart is the central organ of the body in the wisdom literature. It is often paraphrased as "mind," since it does have an intellectual component (cf. the usual, if unfortunate, translation of the "listening heart" of Solomon in 1 Kgs 3:9 as "understanding mind"). But it is also the basic orientation of a person, embracing desires, emotions, and attitude. The description of the deterioration of Solomon's "heart" in 1 Kgs 11:3–4, 9 is more than a picture of mental lapse! If the teacher's words are in the heart, they are life and healing (v 21; cf. 3:8). Hence the need to guard the heart, for it is the source of "the surges of life"—literally, "from it the goings out of life" (v 23). The heart is imaged as a water source from which life erupts. **24–27** Appropriately in this passage the heart carries along several other organs of the body (cf. ear and eyes already in vv 20–21) mentioned frequently in wisdom instruction: mouth, lips, and eyes (parallel to "eyelids" or "orbs" in v 25), mouth, lips, and even the foot and hand. Such organs are affected by what is in the heart, for this gives the direction from which one is never to swerve, either right or left (v 27; cf. Deut 5:29). Two words for "eyes" appear in v 25, the second of which seems to mean the "eyelid" or "eyelash" (עפעפים, probably related to the root עוף, "to fly," and hence indicating the fluttering eyelashes). The youth is to have "tunnel" vision, without any blinking, as described in Prov 17:24: the perceptive person looks straight ahead at wisdom, but the eyes of a fool are on the ends of the earth. The internalization of wisdom teaching (v 21) is matched by the internalization of evil in the heart of the wicked in 6:14, 18. This theme will be abundantly treated in the sayings of chaps. 10–15.

Explanation

A. Meinhold (p. 90) notes that the teaching of the grandfather (4:4b–9) is the only one of the four quotations in chaps. 1–9 that contains no negative content. The other quotations are 5:12–14, the lament of the youth, and a framework that is composed by 1:11–14 (the enticement by the wicked) and 7:14–20 (the seductive pitch of the harlot). The union of heart and hearing occurs in a stirring passage of the Instruction of the Egyptian vizier, Ptahhotep (ca. 2300?): "He who hears is beloved of god, He whom god hates does not hear. The heart makes of its owner a hearer or non-hearer, Man's heart is his life-prosperity-health!" (M. Lichtheim,

AEL, 1:74). Throughout the book there will be constant emphasis on the importance of control over mouth/lips (4:22), from which truth, not falsehood, is to proceed. Control of speech and the inner self is at the core of self-control, the ideal of the sages.

Another important theme makes its appearance in this chapter: the erotic language with which the relationship of the youth to wisdom is described, especially in vv 5–9, 13 (cf. R. E. Murphy, *CBQ* 50 [1988] 600–603). G. Baumann (*Weisheitsgestalt*, 239–42) agrees that Wisdom is personified in vv 5–9. In particular, v 6, with its admonition not to leave but to love Wisdom, is a preparation for the emphasis placed on marital fidelity in the next chapter. If one is faithful to her, one will be faithful to one's married partner. One can go even further: fidelity to Wisdom means fidelity to God. It is remarkable that God is never mentioned in this fervent appeal "to walk the walk." But the tone is as urgent as in the speeches of Moses or the prophets. There is no question but that the figure of God/the Lord lurks behind these chapters. The choice between life and death, good and evil, is no different from the same choice urged in circles that some current scholars may consider more "orthodox," or Yahwistic.

Proverbs 5:1–23

Bibliography

Aletti, J. "Séduction." *VT* 27 (1977) 129–44. **Alter, R.** *The Art of Biblical Poetry.* 179–84. **Goldingay, J.** "Proverbs V and IX." *RB* 84 (1977) 80–93. **Maier, C.** *'fremde Frau.'* 110–39. **Skehan, P.** "Proverbs 5:15–19 and 6:20–24." In *Studies.* 1–8. **Whybray, R. N.** *Composition.* 22–24.

Translation

5:1   *My son, pay attention to my wisdom,*
          give ear to my understanding,
2   *That you may keep discernment,*
          and your lips may guard knowledge.
3   *The lips of the "stranger"-woman* [a] *drip honey;*
          smoother than oil, her mouth.
4   *But her end, bitter as wormwood,*
          sharp as a two-edged sword. [a]
5   *Her feet go down to death;*
          her steps take hold of Sheol.
6   *Lest you observe the path of life,*
          her tracks wander—but you do not know it. [a]

7   *And now, sons, listen to me,*
          and do not turn aside from the words of my mouth.
8   *Keep your way far from her,*

9
and do not go near the door of her house,
Lest you yield your power [a] *to others,*
and your years to a cruel one;

10
Lest strangers have their fill of your wealth, [a]
and your labor, in the house of another.

11
Then you will groan in the end
when your flesh and body are consumed,

12
And you will say, "How I hated discipline,
and how my heart despised reproof!

13
I did not listen to what my teachers said;
I did not give ear to my instructors.

14
I have all but come to ruin
in the midst of the assembled community." [a]

15
Drink water from your own cistern,
running water from your own well.

16
Should your springs be scattered abroad,
and streams of water in the squares? [a]

17
Let them be yours alone,
and not shared with strangers!

18
Let your fountain be blessed,
and have joy from the wife of your youth,

19
A lovely hind, a graceful doe;
drink your fill of her love;
be always inebriated by her ardor. [a]

20
Why, my son, should you be inebriated by a "stranger"?
Why embrace the bosom of an outsider? [a]

21
The ways of humans are before the eyes of the Lord,
and all their paths observed.

22
The wicked person will be caught by his own iniquities,
held fast by the cords of his own sin.

23
He will die for lack of discipline,
inebriated by his great folly.

Notes

3.a. For the translation of זרה, refer to *Note* 2:16.a. and *Comment* on 2:16; the reference to honey occurs also in Cant 4:11, but it indicates the sweetness of the beloved's kisses. "Mouth" is literally "palate" (חך).

4.a. The Hebrew has פיות, perhaps for פיפיות, a reduplicated form meaning "two-edged."

6.a. The text is ambiguous. The two main verbs can be either 2nd person masculine or 3rd person feminine. It is possible to render "she observes . . . she does not know . . ." There are also other difficulties. Some would change פן, "lest," to אל, "not," or בל, "not" or "hardly," but this is not necessary. The meaning of the root פלס is doubtful; it is translated "level" in 4:26, but see 5:21.

9.a. הוד is translated in many ways, and its meaning is guessed at in the context: power, height, etc. The ambiguity is reflected in the ancient versions; cf. *BHS*.

10.a. כח is another word whose meaning is shaded by context; literally it is "strength."

14.a. Other translations would refuse the hendiadys and translate "assembly and congregation," but it is difficult to see here the point of the distinction.

16.a. The text does not have the sign for the question, but neither is it necessary (cf. GKC §150a). As a question, the verse leads nicely into the emphatic v 17.

19.a. שׁגה indicates reeling from intoxicating drink—in this case, drunk with love, but in vv 20, 23, with unlawful love; it serves as a catch word for 19–23. דד can be vocalized in two ways, yielding "breast" or "love"; the latter makes stricter parallelism with אהבה, "love."

20.a. See *Note* 3.a.

Form/Structure/Setting

Structure and *Form* combine rather easily here. The introductory appeal for attention (vv 1–2) is followed immediately by a short statement about the main topic of the chapter, the זרה, or "stranger"-woman. She appeared already in 2:16–19. Now in vv 3–5 she is described as a deadly threat. The formal instruction is an admonition to avoid her, or face a shattering end and self-indictment (vv 7–14). The admonition gathers strength in vv 15–20 by urging the delights of fidelity to one's own wife; true intoxication lies with her, not with a זרה. The instruction ends with the reminder that the Lord sees all and the sinner will receive his comeuppance. There have been several suggestions for rearrangements within the chapter (R. Scott, P. Skehan, J. Goldingay), but these are not compelling. An oral setting could have been appropriate for the quotation in vv 12–15, and the commands of vv 15–20 about fidelity. They are a timely instruction for any man, married or single. There is also the setting within the book—the relationship of this passage to the others concerning the זרה. The preoccupation with this topic is unusual, even striking; it is an encouragement to fidelity, but is it also more than that? What brought about this emphasis, especially in view of the relative absence of the topic of marital fidelity in the rest of the collections? It is surely a topic worthy of discussion, and this may even be one of the reasons for the preservation and transmission of the Song of Songs. But why does it appear almost only in chaps. 1–9? Does this have some kind of link to the marriage with Woman Wisdom and the avoidance of Woman Folly? Like Woman Wisdom, one's wife is a "good" that is "found" as a favor from the Lord (Prov 18:22), but Woman Folly is either unfaithful to marriage, or else considered "ineligible."

Comment

1–2 Although the teacher/parent has referred to "my" words and teachings, etc., this is the only time that "my" wisdom is referred to. Wisdom and understanding, as often, are associated together; cf. 2:2, 6; 3:13, 19. There is to be harmony between lips and knowledge; the lips form a catch word with v 3.

3–6 Van Leeuwen has caught the sensuality in v 3: "Mouth" in v 3b is properly "palate" (חך), which puns on "bosom" (חכך). Moreover, there is a deliberate ambiguity to the honey that drops from the lips of the *zārâ;* it does not mean sweet kisses, as those indicated by the same metaphor in Cant 4:11, but rather the seductive and insincere speech of a harlot (cf. 7:5, 14–21), and "lips" and "mouth" evoke "the liquid delights and organs of love" offered by the stranger. These turn out to be deadly (v 5), an echo of death in 2:18 and an anticipation of 7:27; cf. 9:18. Although the legislation stipulates death for the adulteress (Lev 20:10; Deut 22:22), it is not clear how it was enforced in Old Testament times. In any case, the deadliness here is intended as a message for the youth, whether married, as the context of vv 15–20 suggests, or not.   **4**   The bitter "end" to which she leads is taken up in the "end" mentioned in v 11. As Van Leeuwen remarks, "the imagery here ironically reverses the devouring roles of deadly male sword and female mouths (literal and metaphorical)." Various kinds of wormwood grow in Palestine; it is a plantlike shrub with a bitter taste.   **5–6**   Again the metaphors of feet and path reappear. The ambiguity of v 6 (cf. *Note* 6.a.) allows this to be a forceful warning directed to the youth about the wandering ways of the woman (cf. 4:19), or a continuation of the description of her "steps" (v 5). The "path of life" means escape from the stranger, and hence it leads to the good life, and also "long life" (as in 3:16, which sounds in Hebrew much like "path of life").

   7–14   Although the address is to "sons" (cf. 4:1), the speaker has particularized the audience in v 8 and continues the warning that began in v 3: Stay your distance! The "door" (cf. 9:14) of her "house" (cf. 2:18; 7:8, 11; 9:14!) is an ominous phrase, as the cross-references indicate.   **9–11**   If the (married) man fails to listen, he stands to lose everything: power, years, wealth, and the fruit of hard-earned labor ("in the house of another," v 10). Others, total strangers (who are left undefined; perhaps the "cruel" one is an aggrieved husband who has been cuckolded?), will reap his profits and treat him cruelly, so that his end (vv 4, 11; not the end of life, but the end of the affair) is gruesome. He comes to his senses too late.   **12– 14**   The lament is vividly presented by the rueful admission of the youth that he has failed to follow the instruction of those who taught him. He escapes with his life, but his standing in the community has gone. This is reflected in Sir 23:21 for the adulterer (see Sir 23:22–26 for the adulteress).

   15–20   The sequel in these verses gives advice to one who is married. But the author probably does not have in mind a particular individual. These are lessons for anyone to learn, married or not.   **15**   The man is urged to find his sexual pleasure only in his wife, not in the arms of the זרה/נכריה (v 20). Cisterns provided a repository for a runoff of rainwater, although the water was stagnant in comparison to the freshness of well water, or a spring. The same fresh water sources (vv 15b, 16a) are symbols in the Song of Songs (Cant 4:15) for the woman who provides sexual delight and satisfaction to her partner. Hence the command in v 15 to drink of one's own source.   **16**   See *Note* 16.a. Whether or not this verse is conceived as a (rhetorical) question, the implication is clear: there is to be no unleashing of the springs in the streets. The "springs/streams" have been interpreted to refer to the man straying outside of marriage. But the symbolism of Cant 4:12, 15 is enough to suggest that these terms refer to the woman. Therefore, she is not to be neglected and exposed to seeking consolation elsewhere.   **17**   That point of view is now emphatically urged. It should be noted that the term "strangers" refers to other men (זרים, in contrast to the feminine זרה)   **18**   The water image ("fountain") is used again for the woman, who is called the wife of his youth (cf. Cant 2:17), who will give him the joy that he seeks, for she is "blessed."   **19**   The woman is described in terms ("hind," "doe") that symbolize womanly attractiveness and beauty, as the love language in the Song (Cant 2:7; 3:5) indicates; in the Song the man is called a stag (Cant 2:9, 17; 8:14). Such esthetic appreciation is downplayed in Prov 31:30! The inebriation of love (see *Note* 19.a.) is also featured.   **20**   This rhetorical question taunts the man and leaves open only one possible answer: fidelity. At the same time, there is a certain coloring here: "embrace" (חבק) occurs also in 4:8 to indicate an erotic

7   *For though it has no leader,*
        overseer, or ruler,

8   *It acquires its food in the summer,*
        stores up its provisions at the harvest.

9   *How long will you stay in bed, you sluggard?*
        When will you stir out of sleep?

10   *"Just a little sleep, a little slumber,*
        a little folding of the arms to rest"—

11   *Then your poverty will come like a robber,*[a]
        and destitution like an armed man.[b]

12   *A scoundrel, a villain,*
        one who goes about, crooked of mouth,[a]

13   *Darting with his eyes, shifting his feet,*
        jabbing with his fingers—

14   *Heart intent on disturbance,*[a]
        plotting evil at every moment,
        he initiates discord.[b]

15   *Therefore disaster will come to him unawares;*
        suddenly he is broken, and no remedy.

16   *Six things the Lord hates,*
        seven, abominations [a] *to him:*

17   *Haughty eyes, a lying tongue,*
        hands shedding innocent blood,

18   *A heart designing wicked plots,*
        feet quick to run to evil,

19   *A false witness spreading lies,*
        initiating discord among kindred.

20   *My son, keep the command of your father*
        and do not reject the teaching of your mother.

21   *Bind them over your heart always,*
        tie them about your neck.

22   *Wherever you walk, it will lead you;*
        wherever you lie down, it will guard you,
        and when you get up, it will speak with you.[a]

23   *For command: a lamp, and teaching: a light;*
        a way to life: instruction that reproves,

24   *Keeping you from an evil woman,*[a]
        from the smooth tongue of a stranger.

25   *Do not lust in your heart after her beauty,*
        and do not let her capture you with her fluttering eyes,

26   *Because for a harlot, scarcely a loaf of bread—*
        but a precious life the adulteress hunts for.[a]

27   *Can a man carry embers in his bosom*
        without burning his clothes?

28   *Or can a man walk on live coals*

29   *without scorching his feet?*
So the one who sleeps with his neighbor's wife;
    anyone who touches her will not go unpunished.
30   *A thief is not despised for stealing*
    in order to satisfy a hungry appetite;
31   *But if he is caught, he must pay sevenfold,*
    give up all the goods of his house.
32   *Whoever commits adultery, lacking in sense;*
    *a self-destroyer, he does it.*ᵃ
33   *He meets with a beating and disgrace,*
    and his shame will not be wiped out;
34   *Passion—a husband's rage;*ᵃ
    and he will show no pity on the day of revenge.
35   *He will not consider any restitution,*
    nor be swayed by many bribes.

Notes

1.a. For the grammatical difficulty of construing ערב, "gone surety," with ל, "for," see Harris, *A Study*, 136, n. 48.

1.b. Literally, "striking your palms to/for another"; what is meant is a handshake in agreement over some transaction. The term זר need not indicate a foreigner, but merely a stranger, more or less synonymous with "neighbor" in this context.

2.a. The MT reads "mouth" twice; one should probably read שפתיך, "your lips," in the first case, as *BHS* suggests on the basis of the Syriac.

3.a. The meaning of התרפס, "thrown yourself down," is uncertain, and "pressure" is an interpretation of רהב (storm at? pester?).

5.a. The repetition of יד, "hand," is suspect; the first one perhaps should be מציד, "from a hunter," as suggested in *BHS*.

11.a. "Robber" is an interpretation of the hiphil participle of הלך, "to go"; the hithpael form is used in the same passage in 24:34.

11.b. The "armed man" is the "man of the shield" (איש מגן); other translations have been proposed, without any certainty.

12.a. Literally, "one who goes—crookedness of mouth"; cf. 4:24.

14.a. Literally, "overturnings in his heart."

14.b. In terms of meaning, it makes no difference whether the Qere or the Ketib (which appears in v 19) is followed.

16.a. So the Ketib; the Qere has the singular form, supported by the LXX.

22.a. This verse is troublesome: the subject of the three main verbs is feminine and singular (translated "it" here), but there is no clear antecedent (cf. "them" in v 21). P. Skehan, R. Scott, and NEB (but not REB) concur in transferring the verse after 5:19, where it refers to the "wife of your youth"; cf. Skehan, *Studies*, 1–8, for the arguments. It is gratuitous to suppose that personified wisdom is the subject here (A. Meinhold). The above translation follows O. Plöger in seeing the parental instruction of v 20 referred to here as a singular unit, despite the plural reference in v 21. There is no easy solution.

24.a. LXX interprets רע as "neighbor," instead of "evil." This may well be correct; the woman is the wife of another. The parallel to it in v 24b is the familiar נכריה, "stranger," meaning here simply an "outsider," or "another."

26.a. The MT is obscure. Perhaps literally: "For on behalf of a woman, a harlot, unto a loaf of bread; and the wife of a man hunts a precious soul." One can coax a meaning: either harlotry brings poverty to a person, but adultery means death, or one pays a mere loaf of bread for a harlot compared to the high price (life) exacted by adultery. The ancient versions interpret בעד to mean "price," and some moderns have defended this meaning (G. R. Driver, *VT* 4 [1954] 243–44; cf. also P. Berger, *ZAW* 99 [1987] 98–106). Even so, uncertainty remains: the final line could be translated: "you hunt." Moreover, the loaf of bread could signify the harlot's hire, or the poverty to which the man is reduced.

32.a. The meaning is clear, but the grammar raises questions. The main verb in v 32b has the feminine suffix; does this refer to an indefinite "it" (adultery), or to "life" (נפשׁ)?

34.a. The style is juxtapositional; the rage is that of the injured husband.

Form/Structure/Setting

There is widespread agreement that vv 1–19 are interruptive since vv 20–35 deal with the topic of marital fidelity that was featured in the previous chapter. The ties with 5:21–23 that have been suggested are weak and too general (e.g., folly and wickedness); 5:21–23 has every appearance of a closure. The distinct and distinctive nature of 6:1–19 is supported by the four separate topics in vv 1–5, 6–11, 12–15, 16–19, all of them familiar themes of wisdom teaching: going surety, laziness, characteristics of scoundrels, and a numerical saying about "abominations" to the Lord. The first two are in the form of an instruction, and implicitly, the third also. The numerical proverb (6/7; see the *Introduction*) is a typical sapiential form, and it is featured in chap. 30.

If 6:1–19 is judged disruptive, this does not mean that the four units cannot be associated by catch words or other devices; both Plöger and Meinhold speak of a "heightening." Whybray points to "folly" as the topic of vv 1–11, and "wickedness" unites vv 11–19 (*Composition*, 51). It is difficult, however, to agree with the allusive and elusive arguments of S. Harris. His claim is that vv 1–19 "imply events (i.e., the action) in the Joseph story concerning Judah's role both in the selling of Joseph and in the surety for Benjamin" (*A Study*, 134; see especially pp. 142–56).

Vv 20–35 form an instruction in which the author returns to the theme of adultery. In contrast to the positive tone in 5:15–19, which urges marital fidelity, there is now a clear warning concerning the dire consequences of adultery with a "stranger" (the wife of a neighbor, vv 24, 26, 29–35). In vv 20–24 the theme is introduced as a parental teaching, to be treasured and observed so that the youth will not fall prey to the stranger. The following verses (vv 25–35) prohibit lustful desire for a stranger, and reinforce this by several examples of disaster: playing with fire, vv 27–29; comparison with theft, vv 30–31; self-destructive character, vv 32–33; the danger from the cuckolded husband. The setting is clearly that of parental teaching.

Comment

1–5 The topic is that of going surety, of providing some financial backing for someone who is in debt. **1** The instruction is addressed by the father/teacher to "my son," but without the customary command "listen." A warning is issued: Do not go surety for another person. It is not clear just what procedure is involved, but a handshake seemed to be the outward sign sealing the agreement (v 1b; cf. 17:18). The one who goes surety will pay the debt (or lend some kind of financial aid) of the needy one. It is probable that the "neighbor/stranger" of v 1 is the debtor, although some have argued that the "stranger" is a creditor. The Israelites were forbidden to exact monetary interest from each other (Exod 22:24). There is some legislation concerning the details of taking a pledge (Deut 24:6, 10–11) but no legislation about surety itself. Perhaps later social conditions (cf. 2 Kgs 17:10) rendered the practice necessary, and also precarious. In the other

collections there is frequent and adverse reference to the practice: Prov 11:15;
17:18; 20:16 (= 27:13); 22:26–27. The attitude of Ben Sira is less severe; he is
cautious, but not adamant; cf. Sir 19:1–7, 14–20. The tone of vv 1–5 is particularly
drastic.   **3**   The positive advice is not clear (see *Note* 3.a.); it seems to suggest
treating the debtor severely (some would refer it to the creditor) in order to be
quit of the pledge.   **4–5**   With all speed (no sleep), one is to make every effort
to get out of the trap; note the verbs in v 2 and the hunting metaphors in v 5.

  6–11   Warnings about laziness are to be found frequently in the other
collections, e.g., the series about the lazy person in 26:13–16. Vv 10–11 are taken
up in 24:33–34 to furnish the moral of an "example story" (24:30–31). The ant is
mentioned again in Prov 30:25 as small but wise in taking care of winter stores;
30:25b is a variant of 6:8a.   **6–8**   The point is the diligence and industry of the
ant which needs no supervisor to see to its performance. Animals form part of
the wisdom lore; humans could learn from them (Job 12:7; Prov 30:24–30). There
is a Caananite saying that speaks of the ant biting the hand of anyone who smites
it(cf. Pritchard, *ANET,* 486).   **9–11**   These verses have been variously interpreted.
V 9 is a jab at the attitude of the lazy one. The quotation marks in the above
translation of v 10 suggest that it might be mimicking the words of the sluggard
who, in reply to the taunt in v 9, asks for just a little more sleep (cf. 26:14). V 10
could also be merely the continuation of v 9, as the speaker ridicules the laziness.
The "folding of the arms" is a preparation for sleep; cf. Eccl 4:8. In any case, the
lazybones cannot escape the formidable threat of poverty (even if the metaphors
in v 11 are not certain; see *Notes* 11.a. and 11.b.).

  12–15   The אדם בליעל, "man of Belial," is given a full description. He is a
scoundrel; the phrase means more than "worthless," and less than "devilish." He
is described as evil in 16:27, where he is certainly in bad company (16:27–30),
and in 19:28 he is associated with unjust and false witness.   **12–14**   The
description signals both exterior and interior characteristics. The crooked mouth
(cf. 4:24, the only other occurrence) characterizes him as a liar. The physical
appearance is, as it were, a sign language that supposedly betrays the inner person.
Although the judgment is based on appearances, these are not simply picked out
of the air; see similar characterizations in Prov 10:10; 16:30. They describe the
rascal and serve as a warning about their inner evil. See further comment below
in the *Explanation.*   **15**   For this type of person, the end will be sudden and
definitive, like the destruction of the wicked portrayed in 3:25. V 15b is found
exactly in 29:1b.

  16–19   A numerical saying: x and x plus 1. As in the previous vv 12–15, the
organs of the body (v 19 is an exception) are associated with particular evil actions.
The one who incorporates these vices is "an abomination to the Lord." See the
Comment on 3:22 for this important phrase, which occurs in many other places
(Prov 11:20; 12:22; 15:26; 16:25). A clear moral judgment is rendered.

  20–21   The address to "my son" is an introduction to the final section of the
chapter that deals with adultery. These opening verses (vv 20–21) are similar to
Prov 3:1–3 and also to 7:1–3. Here, too, the youth's attention is called to the
instruction and command of the teacher; they are to be "bound" on the heart,
"tied" on the neck, and also "written on the tablet of the heart" (3:3; 7:3). Such
recommendations seem to be a deliberate recall of Deut 6:6–9 (the "Shema")
and Deut 11:18–21, as pointed out by C. Maier, *'fremde Frau,'* 153–58. The

agreement among these three introductions is significant. One may even draw the conclusion that sapiential and "Yahwistic" teaching do not differ, one from another. The teaching of the parents are on a level with, or better, analogous to the commands of Moses. It would not be surprising to find these prescriptions concretized in amulets and other objects. Their apotropaic character (warding off evil) is also to be presumed; cf. P. Miller, *JNES* 29 (1970) 129–30.

22 See *Note* 22.a.; this verse has three lines instead of the usual two and also a feminine singular, not easily explained. One solution to the difficulty is to claim (with F. Delitzsch, A. Meinhold) that personified Wisdom is the subject; but she is not mentioned anywhere in this area. A grammatical reference back to v 20 is not easily made because the topics there are plural: command and teaching. Plöger thinks that the parental instruction of v 20 is viewed as a unit, despite the plurals in v 21. One might point to Prov 3:23–24 as a kind of parallel to this verse: discretion and prudence will guide one's step and assure one's sleep.

23 The verse picks up the command and torah of v 20, a kind of inclusio. The comparison of the parental teaching to a lamp and light is also striking; cf. Prov 13:9. The comparison to a lamp finds a parallel to the function of the word of the Lord in Ps 119:105. It is the "way to life" (v 23b; cf. the frequent phrase "path[s] of life" in Prov 2:19; 5:6; 10:17; 15:24).

24–35 V 24 begins literally "to keep you from." This can be considered as indicating the purpose of the instruction: a warning against the "evil woman" who is identified as an adulteress in vv 26, 29, 32. One must be on guard against her smooth talk; cf. 2:16b; 5:3b. **25** The emphasis is put on the responsibility of the man. Only too often in these chapters is the woman quickly blamed. Now the teacher stresses the unruly desire of the male. He is to watch over his "heart," as well as refuse to be caught by her eyes (cf. Cant 4:9). **26** The translation of this verse is uncertain; see *Note* 26.a. It seems to warn the youth about the practical (not moral!) difference between harlotry and adultery. The price that one pays for harlotry is as nothing, a mere "loaf of bread"—compared to the price for adultery, one's very "life." **27–29** Further motivation is supplied in these questions; there seems to be a play on אִישׁ, "man," and אֵשׁ, "fire." What does the youth expect if he plays with fire? Fire is the dominant image in these verses, and it fits neatly with sexual passion. **30–32** The contrast with thievery is at first sight unusual because the thief is not as guilty, it is presumed here, as the adulterer. But the comparison brings out the evil of stealing another's wife, lusting after her. There are two appetites here: those of the hungry thief and of the lustful adulterer. A thief steals because of hunger, but must still pay the penalty when caught. "Sevenfold" is not indicated in the law; cf. Exod 21:37; 22:1–3, 8. Perhaps "seven" is used metaphorically to designate everything. Then it is already pointing to the fate of the adulterer who loses everything because he destroys himself (v 32; see *Note* 32.a.). The further punishment of the thief, in v 31b, is that he must give up all the goods of his house; the context suggests that this may be an ironic twist on Cant 8:7, where anyone who would give up his goods to buy love is an object of condemnation! **33–35** These verses make explicit the ruin that the adulterer brings on himself. He will pay a fierce penalty in disgrace. He will also face the physical blows and wrath of the husband who has been betrayed (v 34). There will be no escape by means of bribery.

Explanation

The section on adultery acquires importance because it continues a theme of the previous chapter. There a positive attitude was foremost. Here a warning is delivered, intended to wake up the youth to aspects of loose sexual conduct that he has to keep in mind. In both cases, the point of view is that of the man, not of the woman, who is merely regarded as a siren. But some protection from the rampant desire of a man is thereby afforded. Although she is called נכריה, "stranger," she is also termed the "evil woman" (MT vocalization) or "neighbor's woman" (changing the vocalization; see *Note* 24.a.). She is to be understood here as already married. If in the literal sense the wife of a neighbor is intended, this woman never loses the mysterious aura acquired throughout chaps. 1–9.

Moreover, the tie between the introductory verses (vv 20–24) and Deut 6 and 11 was pointed out. This is an important orientation because now the parental teaching is presented in the same light as the fundamental Yahwistic document of Deuteronomy. The passage "actualizes" the traditional law for the youth. That is to say, it attempts formation of moral character, not moral legislation which presumably is known—hence the vivid style, the rhetorical questions, the threats.

It has already been indicated above in the discussion of structure that there is no satisfying explanation of the presence of the four disparate slices of wisdom teaching in 6:1–19. The description of the "man of Belial" in vv 12–15 is perhaps the most unusual. Although בליעל is not easily translated, his fate (v 15) makes clear that he is a menace to himself and everyone else. But the question arises: what credence was placed in the exterior signs mentioned in v 13 (eyes, feet, fingers)? This kind of body language functions even in the culture of the twentieth century. But it is accompanied also with some skepticism as to its significance. We have noticed before how the Old Testament sages paid very close attention to body signs. V 14 immediately spells out the interior dispositions that are judged to lurk behind an exterior mien that is judged to be threatening.

Proverbs 7:1–27

Bibliography

See the *Excursus on Woman Wisdom and Woman Folly,* and also note the following: **Alter, R.** *The Art of Biblical Poetry.* 54–61. **Garrett, D.** "Votive Prostitution Again: A Comparison of Proverbs 7:13–14 and 21:28–29." *JBL* 190 (1990) 681–82. **Maier, C.** *'fremde Frau.'* 177–214. **Robert, A.** "Attaches littéraires." *RB* 43 (1934) 172–204. **Whybray, R. N.** *Composition.* 25–26, 34–35. **Yee, G.** " 'I have perfumed my bed with myrrh': The Foreign Woman (*'iššâ zārâ*) in Proverbs 1–9." *JSOT* 43 (1989) 53–68.

Translation

7:1   *My son, keep my words*
            and make my commands your treasure.

2 *Keep my commands and live,*
   and my teaching, like the apple of your eye.

3 *Bind them on your fingers,*
   write them on the tablet of your heart.

4 *Say to Wisdom, "You are my sister";*
   Call Understanding, "friend,"

5 *To save you from the stranger,*
   from the outsider whose words are smooth.

6 *At the window of my house*
   I [a] *looked through the lattices;*

7 *I saw among the simple ones,*
   among the youths, I noticed one who lacked sense,

8 *Crossing the street near her corner,* [a]
   walking along the way to her house,

9 *In twilight, at the end of day,*
   at the onset [a] *of night and darkness.*

10 *All at once a woman meets him,*
   in harlot attire and with guarded heart. [a]

11 *Stormy and rebellious, she;*
   her feet can not stay in her own house.

12 *Now in the street, now in the squares,*
   and at every corner she lurks.

13 *Then she grabs him and kisses him,*
   and with impudent face she says to him:

14 *"My due peace offerings,*
   my vows, I have fulfilled today.

15 *So I have come out to meet you,*
   seeking your presence, and I found you!

16 *I have covered my couch with coverlets,*
   with colorful linens from Egypt.

17 *I have perfumed my bed*
   with myrrh, aloes, and cinnamon.

18 *Come, let us have our fill of love till morning!*
   let us enjoy love!

19 *My husband—not at home!*
   He has gone on a long journey,

20 *Clutching a bag of money in his hand,*
   and only at the full moon will he return."

21 *She seduces him with all her talk,*
   deceives him with her smooth lips.

22 *He follows her at once,*
   like an ox that goes to slaughter,

 Like a stag springing into a trap, [a]
23   *till an arrow splits his liver;*

 Like a bird hastening to a snare,
   unknowing, at the cost of his life.

24   *Now, sons, listen to me;*
            pay attention to the words of my mouth.
25   *Do not let your heart yield to her ways,*
            do not stray in her paths.
26   *Many the wounded she has brought down;*
            powerful too, all that she has killed.
27   *Her house* [a]—*the ways to Sheol,*
            going down to the chambers of Death.

Notes

6.a. As a matter of interest, it should be noted that the LXX and Syriac read the woman as subject, and the Greek is παρακύπτουσα, "leaning forward." This reading has given rise to theories about the "woman in the window," a theme found in the ancient Near East, but which has no basis in this verse (*pace* G. Boström). The theory has been effectively dismantled by C. Maier in an excursus in '*fremde Frau,*' 198–208.

8.a. "Corner" is the correct translation, but the form with the suffix in the MT is abnormal; cf. v 12 and follow the suggestion of *BHS*.

9.a. The MT vocalizes the word as in 7:2, "the apple of the eye," but it should be understood as the approach of darkness, with the Ketib reading as in Prov 20:20.

10.a. נצרת can be derived from נצר or צרר, "guarded" or "straitened." It modifies the "woman." Perhaps "guarded" indicates her duplicity, but the meaning is uncertain.

22.a. The text is corrupt; MT seems to have "like an anklet to the discipline of a fool" (JPS: "Like a fool to the stocks for punishment"). Parallelism with the previous line suggests another animal comparison, and this is adopted here, following the suggestion in *BHS*.

27.a. If the juxtaposition of subject and predicate nominative be allowed, there is no reason to emend the text; cf. 2:18.

Form/Structure/Setting

This is the last of the parental instructions, and there is a clear structure: introduction (vv 1–5), body (vv 6–23), and conclusion (vv 25–27). The opening verses reflect the similar instruction in 3:1–3, and vv 4–5 prepare for the extended narrative by introducing the erotic vision of Wisdom/Understanding and also of the "stranger." The episode in vv 6–23 has the (fictive) character of an eyewitness report, and this suggests that it serves as a typical "example story" (as in Prov 24:30–34; cf. Eccl 4:13–16) to bolster the instruction of the teacher. In vv 24–27 the teacher takes up again the style of the introduction and delivers a final admonition; cf. Prov 2:18–19. The story could have been based on a real experience, although it is without doubt embellished in the telling (cf. the mysterious movement of the woman in the city at night in Cant 3:1–5). One wonders if the glimpse through the window ever alighted upon a woman who had to resist a man, or upon a young man who actually resisted the advances.

Comment

1–3   The introduction reflects 3:1–3, and thereby Deut 6:6–9. "Teaching" and "command" are parallel as in 3:1; cf. 4:1–2.   **2**   V 2a is the same as 4:4b; again, the typical wisdom emphasis on life appears.   **3**   The commands are to be bound on the "fingers" (like amulets, or *tephillin*?) and also on the tablet of the heart, a phrase occurring in 3:3; cf. Deut 6:6 and Jer 31:33. It is not certain that a material tablet is meant; so B. Couroyer, *RB* 90 (1983) 416–51. It could be metaphorical, emphasizing the interiorization of the teaching.

4–5 The introduction continues as the father/teacher personifies the Wisdom he is urging. The important term is "sister," and its meaning is colored by the love language exemplified in Cant 4:9–5:1, where "sister" occurs several times, coupled with "bride." The parallel term "friend" indicates a kin relationship (Ruth 2:1; 3:2). This erotic description (cf. Prov 4:5–8) is deliberate and very important in view of what is to follow. See further comment in the *Explanation* below. V 5 introduces the opposite of "sister" Wisdom, the figure of the זרה/נכריה, who is the lady against whom the youth is warned in the following verses. As in 2:16 (cf. 6:24), she is characterized by her smooth talk.

6–9 See *Note* 6.a.; it is the narrator who appears at the window and witnesses the following scene. The dramatic effect of the narrative is achieved by a kind of serious understatement, e.g., vv 7–9, 21–22. There is also an effective use of a creative dialogue, which could hardly have been heard from the window! Note the somber references to the darkness of night, and the telltale path of the youth who is aiming at "her" house; the antecedent is not specified, but "her" must refer back to the woman of v 5. The youth appears to be one of the "simple" or naive ones who are milling around, but he has a surprising sense of direction at this time of night; see *Note* 9.a.

10–13 The tempo of the narrative increases with the appearance of the woman. The speaker takes some time to describe her style (vv 11–12), and suddenly she is kissing the youth (v 14)! **10** See *Note* 10.a. If "guarded of heart" is the correct translation, she seems devious and wily. Why is she dressed in harlot's attire? It seems that harlots did dress distinctively, according to Gen 38:14–15 (cf. Hos 2:4). But the dress plays no role in the story and she seems to need no identification. Perhaps it is merely a symbolic touch, part of the picture, in the speaker's emphasis on the conduct of the woman. It is another detail in the passage that suggests the fictive character of the description. From his window the narrator could not hear the conversation, but his interpretation follows easily. All these traits add to the charm of the narrative. **11–13** She is not only restless, frequenting "every corner" (v 12, another fictive detail) to set up as it were an "ambush." She is also "stormy"—unable to contain herself and on the prowl at night?—a characteristic she shares with Woman Folly (Prov 9:13). C. Maier (*'fremde Frau,'* 187, n. 51) notes that the place of the stranger is at (literally "beside," אצל) every corner, whereas Woman Wisdom's place is "beside" (אצל) the Lord in 8:30. These verses about the slinking stranger are in vivid contrast to the open, universal, style of Wisdom in 8:1–3. Another contrast can be seen in the agonizing but love-driven search for the beloved in Cant 3:1–5. The narrator communicates the bold, almost ugly mood of the stranger by describing her aggressive, almost brutal greeting which follows.

14–20 The encounter, which begins with a kiss, is all talk. But the woman's speech contains some puzzling references. **14** Most obscure is the mention of her fulfilling obligatory vows concerning peace offerings. How is this to be understood? It is not likely that it refers to a festive meal (eating a portion of the peace offerings). It is clear that she wants him for sexual services. Is it perhaps an indication that she needs money (the harlot's salary) for the fulfillment of her vows (cf. K. van der Toorn, *JBL* 108 [1989] 193–205)? Or is the woman a foreigner who worships her own divinity and needs the services of the youth for "devotion's" sake? Such a passing reference is a rather obscure way of enticing the youth, and not easily intelligible in such a story as the narrator has composed. Or is she employing some religious camouflage in case the youth has any scruples? Finally, the combination of sexual intercourse, which would render one ritually impure to say the least, with "peace offerings" is not easy to comprehend in the light of Lev 7:11–18. The implications of this verse escape us. **15–17** The rest of the invitation is fairly clear. She has spared no expense in preparing for a luxurious situation in which they can drink their fill of love: a bed that is provided with imported coverings and perfumed with expensive aromatic scents of myrrh, aloes, and cinnamon (mentioned also in Cant 4:14). **18–20** This all-night stand need not bother the youth since the threat of her husband can be dismissed; cf. Prov 6:32–35. And that is provided; her husband is away, safely and securely. Although he will eventually return, the date is known, so there is nothing to fear.

21–23 The adulteress has finished her speech, and the speaker at the window describes the triumph she has scored by means of her smooth lips. It seems as if the whole affair can be taken as a tissue of lies. **21** With some irony the writer employs a term that is used often and favorably for wisdom teaching, לקח, which is translated above as "talk" since it is parallel to smooth lips. It has already been observed that the woman's main weapon is her words (v 5). **22–23** See *Note* 22.a. Although the text is difficult, it is clear that the youth is described as a dumb animal led to slaughter, e.g., as a bird that loses its life in a snare without realizing it (v 23). The note of death is sounded again in vv 26–27.

24–25 The speaker now addresses "sons" (cf. 4:1; 5:7), but the singular appears in the next verse. In any case he wants to draw the important lesson: Avoid such a woman. Her ways/paths are in total opposition to the ways/paths of wisdom that have been mentioned so often: Prov 2:8–20; 4:11, 25–27.

26–27 As if the vivid story were not enough, concrete reasons are now given; she is described as a warrior who has a host of victims that she has slain! There may be an echo of the famous ancient Near Eastern goddesses that excelled at love and war, such as Ishtar and Anat. That would be a fitting reference. There can be no mistake about the finality of all this: in v 27 Sheol and Death, ever the "enemies" of human existence, are in parallelism. That is where her victims are; cf. 2:18–19. Similar metaphors are used in 22:14; 23:27. These final verses, when interpreted in the light of the "houses" in 9:1-4 and 9:18, suggest another level of meaning. Wisdom and Folly are in conflict, mirrored in this episode of the young man with the "stranger." In other words, the admonition (vv 25–26) and the story are an anticipation of a deeper struggle that dominates chaps. 1–9.

Explanation

This chapter is rather beguiling. It seems like a clear, straightforward description of the way a youth, apparently only too willing, has been duped by an adulteress. The moral is clear: Avoid adultery, which is the realm of death; don't be like a dumb animal and fall for the wiles of such a woman. That much is obvious. Although various theories have been built around the interpretation of the obscure v 14, the advice of the speaker seems to be centered on the lies and specious reasons about which the youth should be warned. Is it just that, a story with a moral to avoid adultery?

The negative tone of the warning stands in tension with the summons in v 4 to call Wisdom "sister" and enter into a particular relationship with her. G. Baumann (*Weisheitsgestalt*, 245–47) admits that Wisdom is personified in v 4, but she discounts the marital implications of "sister" as this appears in Cant 4:9, 10, 12; 5:1, 2, since "bride" does not appear in Proverbs. C. Maier (*'fremde Frau,'* 188) also agrees that "sister" means merely a family or blood relationship. It would be difficult to prove that marriage is the point, but the language is clearly erotic, and that suffices to flesh out the symbolism underlying the passage. In the light of Prov 4:5–9 and also the ending in this chapter, vv 26–27, this seems to be more than just an example story.

The most effective counter-invitation to the deceptive adulteress has already been issued in the recommendation of 5:15–19. Moreover, the tie-in between the introductory verses (vv 1–3) and Deut 6 and 11 has important implications. Now the parental teaching is presented as an analogue to the fundamental Yahwistic document of Deuteronomy. The passage "actualizes" the traditional law for the youth, making it relevant to him. What should be central to his life? Attention has already been called to the fact that sexual delinquency is not a frequent topic in the sayings that follow in chaps. 10–29; the only references are 22:14; 23:27; 29:3. The contrast with the emphasis on adultery and sexual excess in chaps.1–9 is all the more striking. O. Plöger (pp. 81–82) singles out three aspects of this chapter. He suggests that the "stranger" is a kind of collective concept or catch word that embraces all the pertinent texts of chaps. 2–7, without determining whether the woman is a foreigner or simply the wife of another, whether native or not. Thus the concept of "stranger" simply lacks clarity and prevents a specific interpretation. I would infer from this that she is an open-ended character. A second characteristic is the emphasis on the smooth speech of the woman. Although Plöger does not develop this point, one may well wonder if it at least partially suggests the preoccupation of the sages with words. The third note is the sad result of such conduct, described as shame, physical punishment, or especially as death with its ominous overtones. The whole gives the reader an eerie feeling concerning the "stranger."

Proverbs 8:1–36

Bibliography

See the *Excursus on Woman Wisdom and Woman Folly,* and the *Bibliographies* for 1:8–33 and 9:1–18. **Baumann, G.** *Die Weisheitsgestalt in Proverbien 1–9.* 66–173. **Donner, H.** "Die religionsgeschichtlichen Ursprünge von Prov. Sal. 8." *ZAS* 82 (1958) 8–18. **Gilbert, M.** "Le discours de la Sagesse en Proverbes, 8." In *La Sagesse de l'Ancien Testament.* Ed. M. Gilbert. BETL 51. Leuven: University Press, 1979. 202–18. **Kraus, H.-J.** *Die Verkündigung der Weisheit. Eine Auslegung des Kapitels Sprüche 8.* Biblische Studien 2. Giessen, 1951. **Lang, B.** *Frau Weisheit.* Düsseldorf: Patmos, 1975. 57–111. **Stecher, R.** "Die persönliche Weisheit in den Proverbien Kap 8." *ZTK* 75 (1953) 411–51.

Prov 8:22–31: **Aletti, J.** "Proverbes 8,22–31. Etude de structure." *Bib* 57 (1976) 25–37. **Dahood, M.** "Proverbs 8:22–31. Translation and Commentary." *CBQ* 30 (1968) 512–21. **Landes, G.** "Creation Tradition in Proverbs 8,22–31 and Gen 1." In *A Light unto My Path.* FS J. Myers, ed. H. N. Bream et al. Philadelphia: Temple University, 1974. 279–93. **Savignac, J. de.** "Interprétation de Proverbes VIII 22–31." *VTSup* 17 (1969) 196–203. **Yee, G.** "An Analysis of Prov 8 22–31 According to Style and Structure." *ZAW* 94 (1982) 58–66.

Translation

8:1 *Does not Wisdom call,*
   and Understanding raise her voice? [a]

2 *At the top of the heights along the way,*
   at the crossroads she takes her stand;

3 *By the gates at the entrance of the city,*
   at the entryways she cries out:

4 *"To you, O men, I call out;*
   to all humankind, my cry:

5 *You simple ones, learn insight!*
   You fools, learn understanding!

6 *Listen, for I speak noble things;* [a]
   the utterance of my lips, what is right,

7 *My mouth proclaims truth;*
   an abomination to my lips, [a] *wickedness!*

8 *In justice, all the words of my mouth,*
   none of them devious or crooked;

9 *All of them straightforward to those who understand,*
   upright to those who have found knowledge.

10 *Take my instruction instead of silver,*
   and knowledge rather than choice gold.

11 *For, better wisdom than rubies;*
   no treasures can compare with her.

12 *I, Wisdom, dwell with prudence;*
   I have come to know thoughtfulness.

13 *Fear of the Lord—hatred of evil;*
   pride and arrogance—an evil way,
   and a perverse mouth I hate. [a]

14 *Mine: counsel and success;*
   mine: power; understanding: I.

15 *Through me kings reign,*
   and rulers decree justice.

16 *Through me princes rule,*
   and nobles, all just [a] *judges.*

17 *I love those who love me,* [a]
   and those who seek me shall find me.

18 *With me riches and honor,*
   wealth that lasts, and justice.

19   *My fruit, better than gold, pure gold,*
       and my produce, than choice silver.

20   *In the path of justice I walk,*
       down the correct ways,

21   *Giving a rich inheritance to those who love me,*
       and filling their treasuries.

22   *The Lord begot me at the beginning of his ways,*
       the first of his works from of old.[a]

23   *Ages ago I was set up,*
       from the start, before earth began.[a]

24   *As yet no deeps—I was brought forth,*
       as yet no fountains, springs of water.[a]

25   *Before the mountains were set up,*
       before the hills, I was brought forth.

26   *When he had not yet made the earth and fields,*
       nor the first clumps of world's earth,

27   *There I,—when he put the heavens in place,*
       when he marked out the horizon on the face of the deep,

28   *When he made firm the skies above,*
       when he strengthened the sources of the deep,[a]

29   *When he placed a limit for the sea*
       so that the waters would not disobey his command,[a]
       when he marked out the foundations of the earth,

30   *There I was with him, as artisan,*[a]
       and I was delight[b] *day after day,*
       playing before him all the time,

31   *Playing on the surface of the earth,*
       and my delight: human beings.

32   *And now, sons,*[a] *listen to me:*
       Happy those who keep my ways.

33   *Listen to instruction and be wise;*
       do not reject it.

34   *Happy those who listen to me,*
       waiting at my gates day by day,
       watching at my doorposts.

35   *Those who find me find*[a] *life,*
       and win the favor of the Lord.

36   *Those who pass me by, destroy themselves;*
       all who hate me love death.

Notes

1.a. In form this is a question, "Does not wisdom call" (הלא), but it is equivalent to an affirmation.

6.a. The MT has "nobles"; read with *BHS* נגדים, "noble things."

7.a. The LXX has smoothed this out, "an abomination to me, lying lips," as indicated in *BHS*. But the MT should be retained.

13.a. This verse is overloaded although it is represented in the LXX. Lines *b* and *c* appear to be an explanation of the hatred of evil in line *a;* see the *Comment* below.

16.a. See *BHS* for evidence in support of reading "of the earth" instead of "just." But the MT makes sense; the phrase identifies the "nobles."

17.a. It is important to read the Qere "love me," instead of the Ketib "love her." See also the *Comment.*

22.a. Several questions are raised about this verse: (1) the meaning of קָנָנִי: "create," "begot," and "acquired" are all possible. The LXX reads "create" (ἔκτισε), and this caused some turmoil in early christological disputes. In view of the following verb (חוֹלָלְתִּי, "I was brought forth," vv 24–25), "beget" seems preferable (cf. also Gen 4:1), despite the arguments of B. Vawter (*JBL* 99 [1980] 205–16) for "acquired," which was also the understanding of Symmachus, Aquila, and Theodotion. (2) "Beginning" (רֵאשִׁית) is the preferred translation, but it can also be rendered as "first" (born) or "best." The above translation construes it as being in apposition to "me" (a reference back to Gen 1:1?) or as an accusative of time. For a discussion of the various renditions of v 22, see G. Baumann, *Weisheitsgestalt,* 116–20.

23.a. It is possible to derive נִסַּכְתִּי from נסך or סכך, "set up" (cf. Ps 2:6) or "weave" (cf. Ps 139:13), but probably calling for a different vocalization here. The form would be niphal; cf. the lengthy discussion in Baumann, *Weisheitsgestalt,* 120–22; after weighing the possibilities, she argues for "weave."

24.a. MT reads "heavy with water"; read נִכְבַּדֵּי, in view of LXX (τὰς πηγὰς τῶν ὑδάτων) and Job 38:16.

28.a. Literally the MT reads "when the sources of the deep are strong"; either one should read the piel of עזז, or another meaning has to be postulated.

29.a. "Command" is literally "mouth," and the reference is to the Lord's dominion over the waters, so frequently mentioned in the Bible (e.g., Gen 1:2; Ps 33:9). Plöger interprets the Hebrew as "its mouth" and hence referring to the edge or limit of the water (*Rand*).

30.a. אָמוֹן has been variously interpreted: "crafts(wo)man," on the strength of Jer 52:15 (itself doubtful), and upon a slightly different form in Cant 7:2. This meaning is reflected in LXX (ἁρμόζουσα) and in Wis 7:22; 8:6. The common alternative is "nursling" or "child," based on the interpretation of the word as the passive participle, presumably supported by the τιθηνουμένη of Aquila. For various interpretations, see the summary by G. Baumann, *Weisheitsgestalt,* 131–40; H. P. Rüger, "Amon— Pflegekind: Zur Auslegungsgeschichte von Prv 8:30a," in *Uebersetzung und Deutung, A. R. Hulst gewidmet* (Nijkerk, 1977) 154–63. Both of these scholars argue for "child" (*Schosskind*). There is also the argument that the context (the references to birth in vv 22–25; also "delight" and "playing" in vv 30–31) favors this meaning. It is also possible that the meaning is to be related to the Akkadian *umānnu,* "court counselor." Our translation takes a cue from the book of Wisdom (Wis 7:21; 13:1, τεχνῖτις), and favors "crafts(wo)man," and the word refers to Wisdom, not to the Lord. M. V. Fox, "*AMON* AGAIN," *JBL* 115 (1996) 699–702, presents a succinct summary of three principal solutions ("artisan," "constantly," "nursling"), and then proposes his own, borrowing from Jewish tradition. He understands the form as an adverbial complement (infinitive absolute) to the main verb, and he translates: "And I was near him, growing up." Among the reasons for which he rejects "artisan" is 8:30–31, which states that "Wisdom played while God worked" (cf. *JBL* 116 [1997] 628). But is that really so inconceivable—working and playing? Besides, her play blends neatly with her craftsmanship, which is associated with creation of the world where she will find delight in the company of mortals. The solution of C. Z. Rogers, III, "The Meaning and Significance of the Hebrew Word אָמוֹן in Proverbs 8,30," *ZAW* 109 (1997) 208–21, is in favor of the "artisan" meaning; his translation: "I was close to Him who is the master workman, and I was rejoicing daily, delighting before Him all the time." The term is in apposition to the preceding pronominal suffix.

30.b. In many translations "his" is often added to "delight," presumably on the basis of the LXX. But there is no reason to depart from the MT; see the *Comment.* The delight seems to be connected with the "playing" (mentioned twice).

32.a. The rewriting of vv 32–34 in the light of the LXX, which omits vv 32b–33 as signaled by *BHS,* has been proposed by Gemser and adopted by many, but changing the MT is simply unnecessary.

35.a. As in v 17, it is important to read the Qere; cf. *BHS.*

Form/Structure/Setting

The second speech (cf. 1:20–33) of Woman Wisdom is neatly structured: introduction (vv 1–3); the speech, in three main parts (vv 4–11, 12–21, 22–31); and the conclusion of the speech (vv 32–36). Wisdom is described as taking up a public position (cf. 1:20–21) in order to issue her call. The form is best designated as a Wisdom speech. Like 1:22–33, this is *sui generis,* for nowhere else does Wisdom speak about herself in the first person, except in Sir 24. It is not an instruction given by a parent/teacher, in the style of the other poems in chaps. 2–7. In the conclusion, vv 32–36, she assumes the accents of the parent ("my sons," v 32), but she remains speaking until the end. It has been observed that vv 1–11 and 22–31 could be an alphabetizing poem, consisting of twenty-two lines, but this remains hypothetical; the two blocks are separated by ten verses that are dominated by the "I" form אֲנִי in vv 12, 14, 17. In part 1 (vv 4–11), Wisdom speaks directly to humanity in general and points to her high moral integrity: noble things, right, and truth. In part 2 (vv 12–21), she speaks more about herself, as it were losing direct contact with the audience. There is a strong emphasis on her person ("I," "mine," etc.). Two aspects of her work appear: her royal associations (vv 12–16) and the benefits she brings to those who love her (vv 17–21). Finally, part 3 (vv 22–31) indicates her primeval origins from God and also her play and delight with God and human beings. This part has been outlined in various ways by scholars, as can be seen from the treatment in G. Baumann (*Weisheitsgestalt,* 113–16), but the differing outlines are not substantive for interpreting the speech. There is a broad agreement that the speech consists in three parts. The conclusion (vv 32–36) consists of a command and the blessings that are pronounced upon those who listen to her and find her. The only pertinent setting is the present one in the book of Proverbs. Here it occupies a climactic position, coming after description of the "stranger" in previous chapters. There has been considerable discussion of the pre-history of the chapter. For example, vv 22–31 have been taken as a separate composition that was inserted. Moreover, many non-Israelite influences on the figure of Wisdom have been advanced, but none of them has been strong enough alone to establish her pedigree. See the survey of possible origins and identities for Woman Wisdom given by G. Baumann, *Weisheitsgestalt,* 4–41, and by B. Lang, *Frau Weisheit,* 147–76, and also the *Excursus on Woman Wisdom and Woman Folly.*

Comment

1–3 Woman Wisdom is introduced in the third person, presumably presented by the parent/teacher, as in 1:20–21. The setting for the Wisdom speeches is described with unusual detail and emphasis. There are no less than four indications of place, and some confusion results; for example, she seems to be within the city at street corners in 8:2. The most important designation is the "gates" of the city (8:3). These designate the heart of commerce, judicial activity, and social exchange, and here the "heights" would suggest the top of the city walls. There is no indication elsewhere of any prophet occupying such a "pulpit." Here Woman Wisdom could engage a large audience. This public place is in contrast to the "stranger" who operates under the cover of darkness (7:5, 9) to bring her captive youth to her house. It is also in contrast to the setting of the wisdom teacher in chaps. 1–9, who assumes a private one-to-one relationship to the youth that is addressed (only in a couple of instances, "my sons").

4–5 Wisdom designates her audience: everyone, even fools (see also 1:22). It is surprising that no limits are put upon the audience—the address is to any who are ready to listen. These would be especially the simple or naive. Fools and the wicked are presumed to be incorrigible generally (e.g., Prov 27:22). It may be that the harsh view of the fools is formed for pedagogical purposes, to describe sharp alternatives in the matter of wisdom and folly; personally there may have been a more benign and hopeful attitude. Wisdom's first speech (1:22–33) did not extend much hope to anyone. Now, if only the listeners would have a "heart" (as the Hebrew has literally in v 5) to understand! V 5 is a command; the tone of the speech remains imperious throughout; it is not the pleading tone of the parent/teacher. What she has to offer (v 5) is intellectual ("learn!") but preeminently moral, as the following verses make clear. She presents a doctrine that is to be put into practice.

6–11   Wisdom describes the values she stands for.   **6–10**   Wisdom claims nobility, truth, and justice for the instruction she offers. Meinhold remarks that "eight times Wisdom recommends the goodness of her words," i.e., the integrity of what she utters. The emphasis on these virtues (cf. 1:3) matches the smooth talk of evil, both of evil men (1:11–14) and of the stranger (e.g., 5:3). Vv 6–9 have an inclusion, "right " and "upright" (ישרים/מ). As usual, the organs of speech are featured: "mouth," "lips." M. Gilbert ("Le discours," 205) has pointed out that the words of Wisdom in vv 7–8 reflect the description of the Lord in the Song of Moses, Deut 32:4–5. The honesty of her speech needs to be emphasized in view of the abuse of speech on the part of the wicked. Moreover, wickedness is an "abomination" to her lips. This recalls the parallel phrase "abomination to the Lord," which occurs so many times in the collections (e.g., Prov 11:1, 20). V 9 indicates the requisite reaction: Those who have understanding will "find," or acquire knowledge. The comparison to precious objects such as gold and silver is a frequent one (e.g., 2:4; 3:14–15; 16:16), but v 10 is a command, not merely a comparison. Such comparisons may lose their impact and appear to be merely pious sentiments. This would be a mistake, because they are on the verge of paradox. Most would probably settle for silver and gold, and treat wisdom as a side issue.   **11**   This verse, a "better" saying, is a clear comparison, and it resembles 3:15 so closely, that it looks like a gloss that came to be inserted here. It speaks *about* Wisdom in the third person, thus interrupting her direct address.

12–16   In the first "I" passage Wisdom identifies herself with cleverness (v 12, ערמה, as in v 5) or insight, and with what appear to be particularly royal qualities: counsel and power (v 14). Furthermore she claims as her achievement the rule of earthly kings (vv 15–16). This claim resonates with the role of wisdom in the "gift" to Solomon in 1 Kgs 3:9. In view of the alleged courtly associations of the wisdom movement (certainly not to be denied in view of Prov 25:1 and also the background of Prov 25–29), it is striking that only here in chaps. 1–9 are wisdom and royalty intimately associated.   **12**   Literally, Wisdom claims to "inhabit," or to live with, prudence and to have "found" knowledge. Delitzsch captures the spirit of this verse with the comment, "Wisdom describes herself here personally with regard to that which she bestows on men who receive her" (p. 177).   **13**   There are three lines, and the first is suspect. It interrupts the first-person speech in vv 12–14. It is not opposed to wisdom's description of herself, but it is out of line with the style she is utilizing. "Fear of the Lord" suggests the standard teaching of the sage; the rest of the verse reflects earlier ideas (cf. 4:24–27; 6:12), but need not be omitted; they underscore the morality inculcated in the wisdom tradition. **14** This verse is reminiscent of Job 12:13, where three of the attributes are those of God, and also Isa 11:2, where these attributes are among the gifts of the spirit of the Lord, and predicated of the "messianic" king. The phrase in v 14b is particularly strong: literally, "I (am) Understanding." **15–16** These are remarkable statements about Wisdom's worldwide influence over various classes of rulers. Both verses begin the same way ("by me"), and she constitutes, as it were, the "mirror of princes" by which royalty and other leaders are guided. She is the gift given to Solomon in 1 Kgs 3:28.

17–21 The second "I" passage is framed by the word "love," vv 17, 21. **17** See *Note* 17.a. The reciprocal nature of the love between Wisdom and her lovers is proclaimed by Wisdom herself. C. Kayatz (*Studien,* 101–2) has pointed out that the formula of reciprocity is never found in the OT in the mouth of the Lord. It is found several times in Egyptian sources (a god loves those who love him), and thus it may ultimately be a formula going back to an Egyptian model. Be that as it may, it is never found in the mouth of the Egyptian goddess, Ma'at, who is usually co-related with Israelite Wisdom. M. Fox has pointed out ("World Order and Ma'at: A Crooked Parallel," *JANESCU* 23 [1995] 44–47) that the "I-style" is found also in Mesopotamia, but he looks to the Hellenistic Isis aretologies as a more likely connection with Prov 8. But that suggests a later date than one would otherwise suspect for chap. 8. Perhaps the formula was more common than we realize. As it stands, v 17 is another sign of the erotic language (e.g., 4:5; 7:4) used in the pursuit of Woman Wisdom. Elsewhere, however, it is a question of humans loving Wisdom. Now the emphasis is upon Wisdom's affection for those who love her. Another important aspect is the seeking and finding theme (v 17b) which also appears in Cant 3:1–4; 5:6. The key word is "find"—finding a wife, Prov 18:22; 31:10, and also finding wisdom, 3:13; 8:35. Perhaps ironically, "find" is also on the lips of the seductive woman in 7:15b. While any specific vocabulary range has limits, there is a deliberate echoing of key terms throughout these chapters. **18–21** Wisdom describes the gifts that this love bestows, such as justice and riches. Then she immediately boasts that her gifts are more precious than any gold or silver (v 19). This is an echo of 3:14, and like 8:10 it is another "better" saying, but there is no reason to excise it. **20** The very frequent metaphor of the way/path turns up again. In contrast to 1:15; 2:13–15; 4:14–15 which describe paths of the evil, the figure changes slightly; here Wisdom herself, and not the youth, is traveling the path of justice. The association of צדקה and משפט in this verse is particularly important since these are attributes central to the understanding of the Lord (cf. Isa 5:16; Jer 9:23–24). **21** It is not surprising that those who love Wisdom will prosper; she provides more than precious riches (v 19). To this verse the Septuagint adds an extra statement that serves as a remarkable introduction to the next section: "If I tell you about daily happenings, I will now remind you of what happened in ages past" ("from eternity," literally; cf. A. Barucq, 92, who remarks that it may indicate the end of a strophe). A certain intensification in Wisdom's speech can be detected. From the present, which manifests Wisdom's generosity, she now turns to the past, which will highlight her origins from God before creation.

22–31 This striking passage describes, in a mysterious way, the relationship of Woman Wisdom to the Lord. There is a strong emphasis on her origins and age. She was begotten of the Lord, and before anything else in creation. The style is unusual in its constructions: four times the use of the preposition "from" ("of old," etc., in vv 22–23), and five times the implication of "not yet" ("when," "before," in vv 24–26). These constructions underline Wisdom's origins before all else. But where was Wisdom? She was already present with God, at the very least witnessing if not cooperating in the creative acts that were taking place (vv 27–29); in addition to her special relationship with God, she finds delight in human beings (vv 30–31). This description is not only unexpected, but mysterious. **22** The beginning of the Lord's ways would mean that Woman Wisdom is the firstborn, and therefore preexistent to anything else, despite the various translations; see *Note* 22.a. "Way" indicates the divine pattern of creative acts. The text uses a plethora of expressions to designate antiquity, but the meaning is clear: Wisdom was there before anything else. Her preexistence is not only and simply a sign of her dignity. It has everything to do with Wisdom as knowledge. Thus, in Job 15:7–8 Eliphaz taunts Job as though he were claiming to be firstborn, created before the hills, and thus able to listen in on God's council; all this is an indication of possessing the highest wisdom. But only Woman Wisdom is in such a position. **23** The meaning of the main verb is uncertain; see *Note* 23.a. But the temporal indication of preexistence is clear; cf. v 22. **24** The "not yet" style begins; "deeps" and "fountains" are parallel, indicating that the primeval waters, when split (cf. Prov 3:20), yielded these fountains, or sources, that provide water for the earth. **25** After the abyss come the mountains, which are described as being "sunk" (translated as "set up"). The presupposition here is that the mountains/hills have their bases or roots in the water below (cf. Jon 2:7), just as is the case with the pillars of the earth (Job 38:4–6). This has been explained as a kind of "word-axis," which keeps the world stable. But the emphatic point of this verse is the repetition of the verb "born, brought forth" (vv 24–25)—a bold claim, even if metaphorical. **26** There seems to be an ascending order: the depths, then earth, and in v 27 the heavens. The precise distinction of various parts of the earth in v 26, e.g., the earth and the fields, is not clear. The parallelism calls for something like "clods" or "clumps" (the plural of "dust") of earth in v 26b. **27** The "circle" that is drawn on the face of the deep indicates either the flat earth or its horizon; cf. Isa 40:22, "the vault of the earth," and Job 26:10; 22:14. It is difficult to reconstruct the exact understanding of the created world on the basis of the varied references in the Old Testament. Again, the presence of Wisdom is emphasized; she is present before and during this divine activity: "there, I" in v 27. **28** The direction of the divine activity goes down from heaven, from the clouds (cf. Job 37:18), to the deeps, the sources of water. The translation of v 28b is uncertain: Did God strengthen the sources, or simply, were the sources strong? **29** The reference to the "sea" may be a faint echo of the mythical battle between the Lord and Sea which is supposedly featured in other creation narratives. Here Sea is tamed by the word of the Lord. The final line in v 29 portrays the earth on its foundations below; the earth rests on its "pillars"; cf. Job 9:6. **30** See *Note* 30.a. The meaning of this famous verse depends on the translation(s). Even the very beginning is marked twice by a solemn אהיה ("I am"), which recalls the mysterious revelation of Exod 3:14, where "I am Who I am" occurs twice and "I am" once more. However the mysterious aura surrounding these verbs is to be understood, there can be hardly any doubt that v 30 alludes to that passage. This is worthy of note in view of the general tendency in Proverbs to avoid the verb "to be" in favor of juxtaposition or simple comparison. Thus the description of Wisdom's presence at creation contains a deliberate recall of the active presence of the Lord for his people. In any case, there can be no denying Wisdom's presence with the Lord; she is "at his side," or "with" him, once more emphatically stated; cf. also "there, I" in v 27a. The issue is: Just what was she doing? The two dominant interpretations are: (1) She somehow aids the Lord as "crafts(wo)man" (cf. 3:19!), and also she "plays." (2) Or, she is a "child" who plays before him. In any case, she describes herself as "delight," which the LXX, followed by many translations, interpreted as being "his" (God's) delight. This seems to mean that she is of herself sheer delight, and implicitly a delight to God. The notion of playing is emphasized by its repetition in v 31. One can only conjecture what this consisted in. Was it like the joyous singing of the morning stars, when God created, as in Job 38:7? Even more imaginatively, O. Keel (*Die Weisheit spielt vor Gott* [Universitätsverlag Freiburg Schweiz, 1974] 68–74) co-relates this "playing" with figures who are doing cartwheels in the processions of Egyptian divinities, as evidenced in Egyptian iconography.   **31**   If Wisdom plays before God, presumably at his side, she also plays on earth, and there is a "play" on the meaning of "delight." Now her "delight" is with human beings; in v 30a she seemed to be God's delight, or at least, she played daily before him. There is a new twist here: She plays with human beings who live on God's earth. Interestingly, she says nothing more; there is no mention of any admonition or correction. She just plays, almost as if these humans were fitting playmates. Is this a kind of paradise experience? It is hard to imagine a bolder claim: to operate joyfully both before God and before humans. Just who is she, and what is she up to? See the *Excursus on Woman Wisdom and Woman Folly.*

32–36   The vigorous opening phrase calls attention to a new development, an address to "children" by way of a conclusion to the speech. Wisdom has ranged far and wide in her description of her prerogatives and her preexistence, and she has just underscored her "delight" with human beings. Now, like the teacher in the earlier chapters, she returns to her audience of v 4. She concludes, exhorting them to "listen" (twice, vv 32–33), and she gives advice in the form of imperatives and blessings. The tone is quite positive; only at the end (v 36) is penalty indicated for rejecting her, and then somewhat reluctantly, since it is set off neatly against the great promise of v 35.   **32–34**   The repetitions, and the readings of the LXX, have induced commentators (e.g., Gemser, Whybray; cf. also NAB) to eliminate and/or rearrange certain lines. Thus, v 33a reflects 6:6b and 7:24. Admittedly, the appearance of "sons," a plural never before used in Wisdom's speeches, does not fit with the blessing (v 34) upon a single person. But there is sufficient fluctuation between singular and plural to render the various rewritings of the MT unnecessary. There seems to be a deliberate threefold repetition of the catch word "listen" that connects these verses, as well as the twofold blessing or macarism. The conclusion does reflect former introductions by the parent/teacher, but that is not surprising. Both blessings deal with Wisdom's ways (v 32; cf. v 20), and the gates/doors (v 34) of her house which will receive prominent attention in 9:1–4. In v 33 there is the familiar connection of instruction (מוסר) and wisdom, perhaps an echo of 8:10, but also recalling the prologue (1:2) and the association of wisdom and instruction with fear of the Lord in 15:33. When Woman Wisdom makes use of the phrase, it indicates instruction from the elders, but מוסר can also be the discipline from the Lord; cf. 3:11. The scene portrayed in v 34 suggests the daily attendance of an eager lover at the door of the house of the beloved. Although the theme of waiting at the doors is not found elsewhere in Proverbs, it does occur in Sir 14:23; cf. also the description of the lover in Cant 2:8–10. It may also be an anticipation of the "house" of Wisdom in 9:1, although no doors are mentioned. **35** This verse is important for several reasons. First, it repeats the theme of *life* that Wisdom brings to her followers. It is a distant echo of the formula in v 17b; whoever "finds" her, finds life. Again, the verb "find" retains a certain aura. There is the famous question in Job 20:12, "Where is wisdom to be found?" And Prov 18:22 declares that the one who "finds" a wife "finds" a great good. Actually this verb does not suggest mere search or happenstance; it indicates attainment (cf. A. Ceresko, *CBQ* 44 [1982] 551–69). The only other occurrence of "find life" is in Prov 21:21, where it is the result of pursuing justice. But wisdom and life are more closely associated than any other concepts in Proverbs: the goal of wisdom is life, e.g., 4:13, 23; 10:17. Moreover, v 35 associates this life with the favor of the Lord. V 35b is a kind of rewriting of 3:13, replacing "understanding" with the "favor" of the Lord. The favor is not merely a divine attitude; it is described as *from* the Lord, objectified as a gift. See also Sir 4:12. **36** In contrast, those who are "off the mark" or who "sin" (the word חטא has both meanings) destroy themselves. Since sin can be directed only against the Lord, probably "miss the mark" is a better translation. The language is particularly sharp: "love death" does not occur elsewhere. There is a violent contrast between love and hatred. This is a characteristic biblical opposition that normally means choice, without the emotional charge with which we invest these words—hatred of Wisdom means love of, or the choice of death. Once more, one is confronted with that fundamental move: life or death; cf. Deut 30:19; Sir 15:17.

Explanation

Chap. 8 is mind-boggling in view of the claims that Woman Wisdom makes. It is helpful to review these points. First we notice that she addresses all humankind, not just the naive or fools. The personification begins with relatively modest claims, those that are associated with wisdom in earlier chapters: truth, justice, value exceeding gold, etc. But there is an escalation when Wisdom becomes, as it were, a social worker, and is associated with kingship and universal rule, establishing justice and right by which rulers are to operate. The love relationship she has with her followers is a guarantee of prosperity, provided they walk in her ways. Then, in the astounding passage in vv 22–31, she affirms her origins from God, and from of old before creation. The description of creation in vv 25–29 is not really important here; there is no concentration on creation itself, which merely serves to underscore Wisdom's preexistence. The climax comes in vv 30–31 where her relationship to God and to human beings is affirmed. Whether as crafts(wo)man (preferable, in my view), or as child, she brings delight to the Lord, playing before God and finding delight among human beings. That is a tall order, indeed. Perhaps the most famous interpretation of Woman Wisdom has been given by G. von Rad (*Wisdom,* 144–76). Utilizing the texts of Job 28 and Sir 24, he argues that she is the "self-revelation of creation." I would prefer to see her as "the revelation of God, not merely the self-revelation of creation. She is the divine summons issued in and through creation, sounding through the vast realm of the created world and heard on the level of human experience. Thus she carries out her function with human beings (Prov 8:31)" (R. E. Murphy, "Wisdom and Creation," *JBL* 104 [1985] 9–10). By human experience I mean to emphasize that this chapter finds its proper place within the book of Proverbs. Wisdom also points forward to the chapters that follow, since they contain the deposit of the experience of God and humans which flourished in Israel's daily life. See the *Excursus on Theology,* and especially the observations on "natural theology."

No other passage in Proverbs has enjoyed the *Nachleben* that vv 22–31 has had. In the Arian controversy it was particularly prominent, and in favor of Arius, because of the translation of the opening verb: "he created me" (following the Septuagint). This played into the Arian doctrine that held Sophia/Logos/Christ to be a created being, and not eternal. More important today, however, is the role of this chapter, along with Sir 24 and Wis 7–9, in the development of Sophia/Wisdom to Logos/Word, a notion that culminates in the Logos of John's Gospel. There is no need to doubt that other sources also influenced the gospel writer, but there are biblical roots as well. While Logos means "word," the traits of biblical wisdom are carried along in the gospel prologue: creation, light, and life. For a broader perspective on this issue, cf. R. E. Brown, *An Introduction to New Testament Christology* (New York: Paulist, 1994) 519–24; H. Gese, "The Prologue to John's Gospel," in *Essays on Biblical Theology* (Minneapolis: Augsburg, 1981) 167–222; J. E. McKinlay, *Gendering Wisdom the Host,* JSOTSup 216 (Sheffield: Sheffield Academic Press, 1996).

Proverbs 9:1–18

Bibliography

Baumann, G. *Die Weisheitsgestalt.* 199–224. **Clifford, R.** "Woman Wisdom in the Book of Proverbs." In *Biblische Theologie und gesellschaftlicher Wandel.* FS N. Lohfink, ed. G. Braulik et al. Freiburg: Herder, 1993. 61–72. **Fox, M. V.** "Who Can Learn? A Dispute in Ancient Pedagogy." In *My Sister.* Ed. M. Barré. 62–77. **Lichtenstein, M.** "The Banquet Motif in Keret and in Prov 9." *JANESCU* 1 (1968/69) 19–31. **Maier, C.** *'fremde Frau.'* 215–51. **McKinlay, J.** *Gendering Wisdom.* 38–65, 81–99. **Robert, A.** "attaches littéraires." *RB* 43 (1934) 374–84. **Skehan, P.** *Studien.* 16, 27, 35.

Translation

9:1	*Wisdom*[a] *has built her house;*
	she has set up[b] *her seven columns.*
2	*She has prepared her meat, mixed her wine,*
	and then set the table.
3	*She has sent forth her maidservants to call*[a]
	from the heights[b] *over the city:*
4	*"Let those who are simple turn in here!"*
	To the one who lacks sense she[a] *says:*
5	*"Come, eat my bread,*
	and drink of the wine I have mixed.
6	*Give up being mindless*[a] *and live!*
	Walk in the path of understanding."
7	*Whoever corrects the arrogant—one who gets insult,*
	and whoever reproves the wicked—shame.[a]
8	*Do not reprove the arrogant—they will hate you;*
	reprove the wise—they will love you.
9	*Share with the wise and they become wiser;*
	teach the just and they go on learning.
10	*The beginning of wisdom: the fear of the Lord;*
	knowledge of the Holy One: understanding.
11	*Through me your days will be many,*
	and the years of your life will increase.[a]
12	*If you are wise, that wisdom is yours;*
	if you are arrogant, you bear it alone.
13	*Woman Folly*[a] *is stormy,*
	mindless,[b] *and totally ignorant.*[c]
14	*But she sits at the door of her house,*
	enthroned on the heights of the city,
15	*Calling on those who pass by,*
	who are going onward in their ways:
16	*"Let those who are simple turn in here!"*
	To the one who lacks sense she says:[a]
17	*"Stolen water is sweet,*
	and bread taken in secret tastes better."
18	*But they do not know that the shades are there—*
	in the depths of Sheol, her guests.

Notes

1.a. Refer to *Note* 1:20.a. and cf. GKC §l.

1.b. The MT has "hewn" from חצב, but a change in vocalization can derive it from נצב, which also seems the way in which the LXX ("cause to stand," "erect") interpreted it.

3.a. The MT reads the third feminine singular "she calls," and the subject is Woman Wisdom. She is indeed the implied subject, although she obviously sends her maidens through the towns to announce the summons.

3.b. קָן is hapax legomenon, and the meaning is derived from the context, i.e., from the "heights" (cf. 8:2); it must mean something like "on (top of)."

4.a. So the MT. This verse is practically repeated in v 16, where the LXX and Syriac read the first person "and I say." The change is merely a matter of vocalization, and it would mean there is no interruption between v 4a and v 5. No change in meaning is involved.

6.a. "Mindless" renders the unusual plural form of Hebrew פֶּתִי. Cf. v 13b. Others translate "the simple," but the difference is negligible.

7.a. The suffix in מוּמוֹ refers to the one who reproves rather than to the wicked; the word means literally "stain," "blemish."

11.a. There is no need to adopt the emendation proposed by *BHS;* for the grammar, see GKC §144g.

13.a. "Folly" is hapax legomenon, but the meaning is clear. The normal translation of אֵשֶׁת כְּסִילוּת would be simply "foolish woman" (so McKane, jps, and others). In that case, she is not a personification of folly, but would seem to refer back to the wicked woman who is also described as "stormy" in 7:11. However, she seems to be the counterpart to Woman Wisdom in this chapter, and then one understands the construct relationship as explicative or predicative, "Woman Folly."

13.b. פְּתַיּוּת is also hapax legomenon, but it is an abstract, with the meaning of the familiar "simple" ones (or "mindless," "naive") so often addressed by Wisdom. See the note on v 6. Folly is as "mindless" and "ignorant" as the youths she attempts to seduce (cf. v 16).

13.c. For the expression, cf. GKC §137c. There is no need to emend the text, as suggested in *BHS,* כְּלִמָּה, "shame," on the basis of the Greek (Syr) αἰσχύνην.

16.a. See *Note* 4.a.

Form/Structure/Setting

The structure of this chapter is clear, but it leaves a question. The first six verses are given over to Woman Wisdom, and this is balanced by another six verses, vv 13–18, that are given to her counterpart, Woman Folly. But what is to be done with the intervening six verses, vv 7–11? Even the relationship between the two women in the chapter has been disputed. W. McKane has adopted the theory of G. Boström that the description of "Wisdom" (vv 1–6) is secondary in that it is formed on the basis of the אֵשָׁה זָרָה of earlier chapters, especially chap. 7. This may be due to a refusal to recognize the personification in v 13; but it is difficult to prove that one portrait is original and the other secondary. One should recognize that the two portraits are both influenced by previous chapters. The translation above supposes that they are deliberately opposed, and with notable parallelism. In both cases there is the essential positioning of the characters: vv 1, 3; 13–14, and the appeal followed by the invitation to the meal: vv 4–5, 16–17. Both presentations conclude with comment from the composer: vv 6 and 18. The parallelism between the two figures is slanted in favor of the superior call of Woman Wisdom, who has a seven-columned house and a group of maidens. And she is up front with a menu of attractive food, vv 5–6, in contrast to the devious description in v 17. What we have, then, are portraits of two Women who preside at their private "house" (vv 1, 14) and who issue invitations to dinner with a definite (but yet mysterious) menu. The dinner is prominent in the case of Woman Wisdom; it finds its counterpart in the vivid invitation by Folly in vv 16–17. Wisdom's banquet is clearly described in vv 2–3a, 5—itself a suggestion about where one should dine!

Thanks to scholarly research, the banquet motif has been studied in ancient texts. The most significant is the festive meal for "Hurriya" in the Keret epic, where the same sequence of events occurs as in 9:2–3 (cf. Lichtenstein, "Banquet Motif," 19–31). However, this sequence also seems like a logical way of proceeding, and the question of dependence seems otiose. More important is the *fact* of banquets constituting a motif in the ancient world. In connection with 9:1–6 there are inner-biblical parallels, as pointed out below; cf. esp. Isa 55:1–2 and also 65:11–14. For a summary of this research, see G. Baumann, *Weisheitsgestalt,* 214–20.

The invitation of Woman Wisdom is brief; suddenly new topics are introduced. There is no easy explanation for the presence of vv 7–12. Their awkward placement between the two women is reminiscent of a similar (dis)placement in the case of 6:1–19. They seem to have a dubious history, in view of the LXX version which has an addition after v 10: "To know the law is a sign of good understanding" (v 10a in Rahlfs edition). Then after v 12 there is a lengthy addition: "Whoever relies on lies, leads winds to pasture; he is one who would pursue birds in flight" (v 12a). "He abandons the ways of his vine; he departs the paths of his own field" (v 12b); "he passes through a waterless desert and a land that is thirsty, and for the work of his hands he receives no yield" (v 12c). This LXX expansion is surely not a happy insert after v 12.

The particular forms in 9:7–12 of the Hebrew text are relatively simple: a saying (v 7), admonition (vv 8 and 9), a saying that is a variant on 1:7 (v 10), an affirmation (v 11) that fits better after v 6 (so NAB), and an apparently independent conditional sentence (v 12). Significant here is v 10, which takes up the motto about fear of the Lord in 1:7 in a manner that reminds one of an inclusion for the first nine chapters. A. Meinhold's close analysis of these verses suggests that vv 10–11 (notice the first person in v 11!) form the center, and are framed by the arrogant/wise contrast in vv 7–9 and the wise/arrogant contrast in v 12. The whole is marked by several key repetitions: wise, arrogant, take (noun and verb), and reprove. He regards vv 7–11 as giving a small "foretaste" (*Vorgeschmack,* 155) of the collections of proverbs to follow. It remains difficult to determine the purpose of these verses at this particular point. Perhaps v 10 can be said to fit into the contrast between the two women, by its emphasis on wisdom, and thus it could have carried the rest of the verses with it. See also the *Explanation* below.

Comment

1–6 These verses form a clear unit. There is a description of Wisdom's preparation for a banquet, vv 1–3, and her invitation to the guests, vv 4–6. **1** Much theorizing has gone on about the seven columns or pillars of Wisdom's house. These have been described not unfairly by J. Greenfield (*JQR* 76 [1985/86] 13–20): "The seven pillars of wisdom have been variously interpreted: the seven firmaments or heavens, the seven planets, the seven regions or climates, the seven days of creation or the seven books of the law, the seven gifts of the holy ghost, the seven eras of the church, the seven sacraments, the seven liberal arts, and even the first seven chapters of the Book of Proverbs" (p. 13). This did not prevent him from adding his own theory, relating the seven pillars to the seven sages of Mesopotamian myth. A discussion of various theories is like walking through a cemetery; one should leave them all in peace. Yet a commentary calls for some kind of position to be taken. The following has been articulated by G. Baumann in *Weisheitsgestalt,* 207–9. The book of Proverbs is the (only) house of Woman Wisdom. The evidence for this can be drawn from Prov 14:1, however that be translated; see the *Comment* on

14:1: "Wisdom has built her house, but Folly tears hers down by hand." To this may be added the observation in 24:3 that a house is built by wisdom/understanding. Wisdom's columns are the teachings of Prov 1–8 (here the previous studies of P. Skehan are reflected). They are there to be studied and absorbed. But this backward glance does not cut off the rest of the book. As 14:1 and 24:3 suggest, the rest of the collections are part of Wisdom's residence.   **2**   Wisdom needs a house to which her guests can be invited for a meal to which she has given personal attention. The food is briefly indicated: meat and mixed wine. There is a precedent for such an invitation. R. Clifford ("Woman Wisdom," 61–72) has described Ishtar and Anat issuing invitations to various characters, such as to Gilgamesh and to Aqhat. But these meetings with the goddesses turn out to be matters of life and death, and the goddesses are deceiving their prospective lovers. That is not the case here.   **3**   In keeping with the dignity ascribed to her, Wisdom has "maidservants" to convey her invitations. As in 8:2 (cf. 1:21) the summons is issued from on high, presumably at the city gates (cf. 8:3), so as to reach the invited.   **4**   These are the simple or naive, those who lack "heart," as the Hebrew puts it. The meal is a symbol of the rich fare that only Wisdom can offer, similar to the "food" that is offered in Isa 55:1–2. There is even a certain sapiential coloring to the invitation in Isa 55:3: "Incline your ear and come to me; listen, that you may live." There is also an erotic quality to eating and drinking, in view of the command to the lovers in Cant 5:1 ("drink freely of love").   **4**   See *Note* 4.a. The "simple" were already envisioned in 1:4 as people in need of wisdom, but they are not portrayed harshly; cf. 1:22, and the "young man" in 7:7. Now they are the addressees of an invitation issued by Wisdom herself, whose delight is to be with human beings, Prov 8:31.   **5**   There is a deliberate use of the imperative in this verse, which is echoed in the less coercive but subtle invitation issued in practically the same words by Woman Folly in v 16; cf. 4:17. The bread and wine is the counterpart to the (stolen) water and bread of v 17.   **6**   The symbolism of the meal, the union of the diners with their host, is made explicit. Now as if to forestall any misunderstanding the composer explains the significance of the meal. The addressees are told to abandon the "mindless" (or "naiveté," according to the LXX). It was the "naive" that were originally invited (v 4); now they shall no longer be so. The verse hearkens back to the ideas of "way" and "life" that have been featured in earlier chapters. The food is indeed unto "life," for Wisdom is the tree of life; cf. 3:18; 11:30; 13:12; 15:4.

  7   As already indicated, there is an abrupt transition here to standard wisdom instruction. The meaning of the verse seems to be that it is more than futile to issue a correction to certain people, such as the arrogant (or scoffer, Hebrew לץ, parallel to "wicked" here and also in Ps 1). Well-meant advice meets with not just rejection but contumely. As a matter of fact, the sages generally seem to regard fools/wicked as (relatively) incorrigible. Hence there is the frequent injunction to avoid their company. This meaning is also supported by v 8a. The meaning of v 7b is obscure because of the ambiguity of the final phrase "his blemish" (translated above as "shame"). Some understand it as referring back to the one who reproves. This is unlikely since it is not conceivable that he should be stained by the wicked. The blemish must be that of the wicked, meaning something like harm or "insult" in v 7a, with which it is parallel.

8–9 What was enunciated as a saying in the previous verse is now set forth as a prohibition in v 8a. There is a close parallel in the Instruction of Ankhsheshonq: "Do not instruct a fool, lest he hate you. Do not instruct him who will not listen to you" (7, 4–5; Lichtheim, *AEL*, 3:165). The advice given in v 8b is at the heart of the wisdom enterprise: the wise almost by definition are docile; they *listen,* and they are open to reproof; see the *Explanation* below.   **9**   This verse supports the claim of v 8, and significantly equates the wise and the just, or wisdom and justice. This teaching is familiar, and could indicate that the speaker is the parent/teacher. But what was the intention of the editor in positioning verses such as these between the two invitations? Perhaps the answer lies in the central importance of v 10, without which the wisdom enterprise is in vain.

10   This is a strong affirmation about the value of wisdom, after the note of futility that was voiced in v 7. That note was overcome by vv 8–9, and the capstone of wisdom teaching is repeated in v 10. V 10a reflects 1:7; perhaps it forms an inclusio for chaps. 1–9. V 10b is noteworthy: "the Holy One" is literally "the holy ones" (קדשׁים, plural of majesty?), and this appears with the singular meaning in Prov 30:3 and Hos 12:1. The saying has the character of a summary verse concerning the teaching of wisdom, but it may be connected with the following lines of the MT.

11   In context the first-person reference can only be to personified Wisdom, although she seemed to finish her statements in v 6. It is surprising find her speaking here without any introduction. Perhaps v 10, with its reference to fear of the Lord, wisdom, and understanding, can be construed as a kind of introduction. The association of wisdom with life, already expressed in v 6b, has been mentioned frequently; cf. 3:16, 18; 4:13b; 8:35. Hence it seems more reasonable to attribute these words to Wisdom rather than to the parent/teacher who has not appeared in this chapter, although he may be presumed to be speaking in the introduction, vv 1–3. He, too, has promised life as the fruit of wise instruction, Prov 3:2; 4:10. See also the *Comments* on vv 7–9. On the whole, however, it seems more reasonable to understand this verse as spoken by Woman Wisdom, since only she can ensure such a promise of long life.

12   This saying is a kind of no-nonsense statement, pointing out the effects that wisdom/arrogance have for their possessors. It balances vv 7–9, which envision communication of wisdom to others, both the arrogant and the wise, in v 8. Wisdom is a boon that is considered to be something to be communicated, even in the home, from mother and father, and also throughout life. The youth may or may not choose to listen, and will accordingly bear the responsibility with its inevitable results. It is not clear why this emphasis on personal responsibility and profit (life; cf. v 6a) should be stated at this particular point.

13–15 Woman Folly, if that translation be allowed (see *Note* 13.a.), is characterized as "stormy," or "noisy," a term used of the streets in 1:21, and also of the adulteress in 7:11. Her ignorance is far more than intellectual inadequacy; she is infecting all who listen to her with her own folly. Her house seems to be situated on the city walls from whose heights she can address the passersby. This is where her seat, or "throne" is. The description differs from that of the "house" of Woman Wisdom (v 1). She gives the impression of a shrewish person raucously making her pitch, in contrast to the dignified messengers commissioned by Wisdom in v 3.

16–17 The similarity of v 16 to v 4 is deliberate; the two figures issue the same invitation to the same people. But there is an artful difference in the menu. The bread and wine offered by Woman Wisdom is the opposite of the bread and wine of the foolish; cf. 4:17, wickedness and violence. Woman Folly does not offer a menu. In what sounds like a proverb, she throws out a suggestive advertisement that promises, at the same time that it deceives. This is that slippery style, the "smooth talk" employed by the stranger, which the parent so often warns against.

18 The deceit is now ridiculed by a clever statement of the writer: Acceptance of such an invitation is to dine with the shades (2:18) in Sheol (7:27). *Caveat emptor (lector)!*—let the wise person be on the alert about such invitations.

Explanation

This final chapter may be viewed as a kind of either/or: Either Wisdom or Folly. A summons to a decision has been issued to the reader from the beginning, and it is sustained throughout. Now it is dramatized in the depiction of Woman Wisdom and Woman Folly extending dinner invitations to the "simple," or naive. While the interruptive character of vv 7–12 was recognized, it may be also asked if it is a bias on the part of the modern reader to characterize these verses so. If they are an insertion, are they really interruptive? What was the intention behind this? It is a delicate operation to determine the "intention" in such a case. Ultimately we tend to ascribe motives, always based of course on the thrust of these verses, to another hand. Indeed, we may rightly assume that the architect of this final contrast regarded, or would have regarded, the intervening verses as somehow necessary or at least fitting. In that case, can we legitimately conclude that they are an insertion? Could they not have been there from the beginning? Our concept of logic and esthetics is modern and has its own presuppositions. We cannot glibly assume that the ancients operate along the same lines. The importance of 9:10 on "fear of the Lord" may indeed be the pivot of the chapter in ways that the modern interpreter does not fully comprehend. The problems and joys of instruction, highlighted in vv 7–9, are surely the concern of the sage. The theme of personal responsibility in v 12 is congenial to the wisdom enterprise. This is a *final* unit to the variegated but passionate instructions in chaps. 1–9. Should it be chopped up? Plöger (p. 104) describes vv 7–12 as possibly taken from a previous context, but their immediate join with v 6 indicates that the figure of Woman Wisdom in vv 1–5 has stimulated this further comment. Although it does not fit into the invitation scene, vv 7–12 are not to be separated from Wisdom.

M. V. Fox has a penetrating analysis of 9:7–10 in M. Barré, ed., *My Sister,* esp. 63–69. He grants that these verses are a later addition, but asks what points they make. He finds three: (1) some cannot learn; (2) if the method is stringent enough, all can be taught; (3) yet the right approach, such as is laid out in Prov 2, is required. This is a very optimistic view of the teachability of human beings. He is correct in pointing out that even the לֵץ (Prov 1:22) and the כְּסִיל (Prov 1:22; 8:5), who are the truly obdurate, are addressed. Presumably they would also be included in the universal call issued in 8:4. If even the prophets addressed the wicked, why not also the teachers? But there were doubtless degrees of obduracy, and what teacher was so finely tuned to these differences? Moreover exaggeration, as well as caution (stay away from fools!), precluded any single unchangeable stance. Probably one should write off as exaggeration that fierce proverb of Prov 27:22, "Even if you pound the fool in a mortar / With a pestle along with grain, / His folly will not leave him." Fox himself realizes that "some people are beyond redemption." He concludes that the author "does not believe that fools *can* be educated, at least not if their ignorance is rooted in arrogance and vice. The types of fools he refers to are worse than those addressed by Wisdom, as if to say: You might attempt to educate the naive and mindless (though this too is probably a hopeless task), but if you go further and try to straighten out a לֵץ or (even worse) a רָשָׁע—the very ones who most need correction—you will only bring harm upon yourself" (pp. 66–67). See also the *Comment* on 26:4–5 with the *Explanation*, and also on 27:22.

Concluding Reflections on Chapters 1–9. It will be profitable to look back and make an assessment of these chapters which are so unique in the book. The purpose of the following considerations is to raise questions that can lead to a greater appreciation of this instruction. For it *is* an instruction, and that intent must be kept in mind. We take our cue from the "purpose" described in 1:1–6. This can be stated in other words: the instruction is a program in character formation portraying the several values that should be exemplified in the conduct of youths. Although knowledge and learning are stressed because there are "lessons" to be learned, there is a tradition to be followed. One may not stop there. The goal is praxis: how to live (*savoir faire/savoir vivre*). To this end the educators, whom the text identifies as father/mother, lay out a lifestyle that must be followed, if one is to avoid folly (= death). This is education with passion: the tone of the parent/teacher runs a certain gamut: from cajoling to threatening. The pursuit of wisdom breaks down into several goals: self-control, justice, diligence, avoidance of temptation, and so forth. Thus wisdom *becomes* justice or righteousness, and folly becomes sin or wickedness. Undergirding this program is the belief that wisdom leads to true life (prosperity, etc.), while folly destroys. This is obvious from the great emphasis laid on the two ways that confront youth.

Is the program too simplistic? In the *Introduction* above we touched on the "limitations" of wisdom. We examined a few of the sayings in chaps. 10ff. and pointed out that these insights were not to be dismissed as banal or unrealistic. Chaps. 1–9 have a different purpose, and we have to allow for it. They aim to persuade, whereas the sayings aim more at expanding the minds of readers, even if "teaching" is never absent. This is not to deny that many of the sayings have their own slant and leave no choice between wisdom and folly. If the reader has been won over by the teaching of the sage, he or she can appreciate all the more the complexity of the sayings.

However, one may ask if the ideals and promises of chaps. 1–9 are realistic. This introduction is doubtless admirable, but does it go too far in the assurances that it gives to the youth? Modern readers may conclude with some justice that these chapters are over-optimistic, in the sense that they promise too much from life. In fact, one can turn to later works of wisdom literature, such as Job or Ecclesiastes, and point out that these works voice or imply the same criticism. However, Deuteronomy and many other biblical works reflect the premises of the book of Proverbs. Are they not all permeated by the view that good is rewarded and evil is punished? In fact, this basic view is challenged more vigorously in the wisdom literature than elsewhere—even in Psalms, where the problem is surely faced as shown in the contrast of Pss 37 and 73. So one may conclude that we are confronted with a familiar problem: various parts of the Bible are in tension with each other. One must beware of selectivity in Bible reading. Human nature, being as it is, hears an upbeat message more easily than its opposite, and at the same time fails to provide for inevitable contradictions in life. Is there anything in these chapters that prepares one for such contradictions? Relatively little. One can point to the mysterious implications of Prov 3:11–12, but it is practically the sole questioning of the sapiential optimism. Of course, we should realize that it ill behooves a wisdom program to begin with difficult questions, and attempt to give answers to the problem of retribution that the Israelite faithful had to face. This positive, as opposed to a negative, even if realistic, approach is intelligible in the light of the general teaching of the covenant people, who believed ultimately in the truth of the Lord's mercy (Exod 34:6), which is so often recalled. Yet, the mystery of the divine action is the mystery of God, as Israel well knew. And nowhere is the mystery of suffering penetrated. See the *Excursus on Retribution*.

The commentary has pointed out the basic data that have to be considered in the evaluation of Woman Wisdom and Woman Folly. Their relationship, however, is more complex than the data, due to the symbolism that invests both figures. Hence the need of an excursus where these two can be more leisurely examined. R. Clifford ("Woman Wisdom," 27–28) has described appropriately the transition from these chapters to the following collections: "Chapters 1–9 have helped readers re-imagine morality. The chapters teach that wisdom herself is more important than any single wise action. The disciple must first desire her and pursue her over any good. She lies within their grasp. Chapters 8 and 9 have promised that the disciple can live in Wisdom's house. The following chapters will suggest that living with her will be partly through pondering the sayings in chaps. 10–31. We will see that most of the sayings are not immediately obvious, that they challenge the reader to read and think, i.e., to practice discernment. Living in Wisdom's house is as challenging and rewarding as living with one's spouse."

The Proverbs of Solomon   (10:1–22:16)

Bibliography

Prov 10:1–22:16 and 25–29: **Boström, G.** *Paronomasi I den äldere hebreiska maschalliteraturen.* LUÅ 29/8. Lund: Gleerup, 1928. **Bühlmann, W.** *Vom rechten Reden und Schweigen: Studien zu Proverbien 10–31.* OBO 12. Freiburg: Universitätsverlag, 1976. **Goldingay, J.** "The Arrangement of Sayings in Proverbs 10–15." *JSOT* 61 (1994) 75–83. **Hausmann, J.** *Menschenbild,* passim. **Hermisson, H.-J.** *Studien.* 171–83. **Hildebrandt, T.** "Proverbial Pairs: Compositional Units in Proverbs 10–29." *JBL* 107 (1988) 207–24. **Krispenz, J.** *Spruchkomposition im Buch Proverbia.* EHS.T 23/349. Frankfurt: P. Lang, 1989. **McCreesh, T.** *Sound and Sense.* **Murphy, R. E.** *Wisdom Literature.* FOTL 13. Grand Rapids: Eerdmans, 1981. 63–74. **Perry, S. C.** *Structural Patterns in Prov 10:1–22:16. A Study in Hebrew Stylistics.* Ann Arbor, MI, 1987. **Scoralick, R.** *Einzelspruch.* **Skehan, P.** *Studies.* 17–20, 22–23, 35–36. **Snell, D. C.** *Twice-Told Proverbs.* **Whybray, R. N.** *Composition.* 62–131. ———. *Proverbs.* 34–61.

It will become clear that several of the above studies have made important progress in the discernment of units within the book of Proverbs. The insight that a biblical book, even if it is unmistakably a collection, can constitute a certain unity has been applied to the book of Psalms, and perhaps with less success to the book of Proverbs. But in any case it is now recognized that the collections of sayings, especially of chaps. 10–22, and of 25–29, are *not* haphazard. In particular, the analyses of J. Krispenz and R. Scoralick have analyzed several units within these chapters. This research has been guided primarily by such literary features as catch words, paronomasia, etc., supported by analysis of the development of thought. The sound patterns studied by G. Boström and T. McCreesh have contributed to the recognition of units; stylistics do have a bearing on the collocation of proverbs in a group. Using such phenomena as catch words, etc., J. Krispenz analyzes chaps. 10–22 and 25–29 into some nineteen units, although in an appendix (pp. 164–78) she lists the pertinent Hebrew terms that would be the basis for some thirty-six units, as she sees them. In addition to the catch words and other literary tricks, she argues from the flow of meaning (*Gedankengang*) of a unit. This latter evidence is much more difficult to establish; the broad range of topics seldom provides a "logical" sequence of thought in the sayings. So far, this appears to be the Achilles heel of all the efforts to break down these chapters into smaller units or collections. Literary features are not always coordinated with theme. Hence arguments for units that would have had previous independent existence have to be scrutinized carefully. R. Scoralick limits herself to Prov 10–15, and the units are much larger, but here too, the *meaning* or theme of the sayings is not always favorable to the division on the basis of literary features.

The extent of the collection in 10:1–22:16 can be definitively determined by the title that opens 10:1, and the clear beginning of a new collection, of a quite different style, in 22:17 (an emended text in 22:17 also yields a new title). Moreover, the Hebrew letters of the name of Solomon in 10:1 have the numerical value of 375 (300 + 30 + 40 + 5), which is also the number of proverbs in the collection. This can hardly be a mere coincidence. It is also probable that the sayings in 10:1–22:16 could have formed more than one collection before being incorporated into the book. There is reason to speculate about a new collection beginning with chap. 16, since the antithetical parallelism which characterizes almost all of chaps. 10–15 begins to disappear. Moreover, if one examines the list of catch words listed for 10:1–15:33 by R. Scoralick (*Einzelspruch,* 127–29), which is reproduced in the following paragraph, it is hard to deny a certain coherence to chaps. 10–15 as a collection. These were not put together haphazardly. But it is not profitable to hypothesize here about the formation of collections for which we can advance only arguments internal to the text itself. The survey of research on this topic by Scoralick (*Einzelspruch,* 11–52, 111–59) is instructive; it has been very difficult to reach firm conclusions. See the cautions put forth by R. Whybray (*Composition,* 66–76, 79–83), but even his criteria of "pivotal verses" and "Yahweh proverbs" remain quite hypothetical.

This discussion about form and theme can be concretized to a certain extent by listing key Hebrew words. The following list of catch words for chaps. 10–15 is taken from Scoralick, pp. 127–29, with the permission of the publisher. She corrected and improved upon G. Boström's *Paronomasi* of 1928. For a partial indication of catch words in the succeeding chapters, see R. E. Murphy, *Wisdom Literature,* 71–79, and especially the selective tables offered by Krispenz, 164–78. The list compiled by Scoralick makes concrete the connections created between verses by these catch words. The words that are underlined indicate that a catch word connects more than two sayings. The statistics given by her are: 63 couplets (combining two sayings) are connected by catch words. More than one-third of the 184 sayings are connected by a catch word. There are even eight instances of a catch-word association for three verses, and there is one example for four verses (15:29–32, "listen").

10:2	לא רשע צדקה "wicked/just"		27	רשעים "wicked"
3	לא צדיק רשעים "just/wicked"		28	רשעים "wicked"
6	ברכות צדיק רשעים "just/ wicked"		30	צדיק "just"
			31	פי צדיק תהפכות "mouth/just/ perverse"
7	צדיק לברכה רשעים "just/ wicked"		32	צדיק רצון פי תהפכות "just/ pleasure/mouth/ perverse"
11	צדיק רשעים יכסה "just/wicked/ conceals"		11:1	רצונו "his pleasure"
12	תכסה "conceals"		4	צדקה "justice"
13	חכמה "wisdom"		5	צדקת תישר "justice keeps straight"
14	חכמים מחתה "the wise/ruin"		6	צדקת ישרים "justice of the upright"
15	מחתת "ruin"			
16	לחיים "for life"		7	רשע "wicked"
17	לחיים "to life"		8	צדיק נחלץ רשע "just/are freed/ wicked"
18	שפתי "lips"		9	צדיקים יחלצו "the just are saved"
19	שפתיו "his lips"		10	צדיקים קריה רשעים "just/city/ wicked"
20	צדיק לב "just/heart"		11	קרת רשעים "city/wicked"
21	צדיק לב "just/heart"			
24	רשע צדיקים "wicked/just"			
25	רשע צדיק "wicked/just"			

16 אשה "woman"
17 איש "man"

18 צדקה "justice"
19 צדקה "justice"

23 אך "only"
24 אך "only"

25 ברכה "blessing"
26 ברכה "blessing"

29 לחכם "wise"
30 צדיק חכם "just/wise"
31 צדיק "just"

12:2 ירשיע "he condemns"
3 ברשע "in wickedness"
5 רשעים "<u>wicked</u>"
6 רשעים "<u>wicked</u>"
7 רשעים "<u>wicked</u>"
12 רעים צדיקים "evil/just"
13 רע צדיק "evil/just"

15 אויל "fool"
16 אויל "fool"

18 לשון "tongue"
19 לשון "tongue"

20 רע שמחה "evil/joy"
21 רע צדיק "evil/just"

13:2 פי נפש "mouth/<u>desire</u>"
3 פיו נפשו "his mouth/<u>life</u>"
4 נפשו נפש "<u>his</u> desire/desire"

5 צדיק רשע "just/wicked"
6 צדקה רשעה "justice/wickedness"

7 מתעשר מתרושש "pretends to riches/pretends to be poor"
8 עשרו רש "his riches/the poor person"
19 כסילים מרע "from fools/<u>evil</u>"
20 רעה כסילים ידוע "the companion of fools <u>fares badly</u>"
21 חטאים רעה צדיקים טוב "sinner/<u>evil</u>/just/good"

22 טוב לצדיק חוטא "good person/for the just/a sinner"

14:6 דעת "knowledge"
7 כסיל דעת "fool/knowledge"
8 אולת כסילים "the folly of fools"
9 אולים "fools"

11 ישרים "upright"
12 ישר אחריתה "right/its end"
13 לב אחריתה "heart/its end"
14 לב "heart"

17 אולת "folly"
18 אולת "folly"

20 לרעהו "to his neighbor"
21 לרעהו "to his neighbor"

26 ביראת יהוה "in the fear of the Lord"
27 יראת יהוה "the fear of the Lord"

28 ברב "in a large"
29 רב "great"

15:2 תיטיב "makes good (advances)"
3 טובים "the good"

8 רשעים תועבת יהוה "the wicked/an abomination to the Lord"
9 תועבת יהוה רשע "an abomination to the Lord/the wicked"

13 לב פנים לב "<u>heart</u>/face/<u>heart</u>"
14 לב פני "<u>heart</u>/face"
15 טוב לב "contentment <u>of the heart</u>"
16 טוב בו "better/with it"
17 טוב בו "better/with it"

20 ישמח "gives joy"
21 שמחה "joy"

25 יהוה "YHWH"
26 יהוה "YHWH"

28   צדיק רשעים "just/wicked"
29   מרשעים צדיקים <u>ישמע</u> "from the wicked/the just <u>he hears</u>"

30   שמועה "<u>news</u>"
31   שומע תוכחת "<u>listens to</u> reproof"
32   מוסר שומע תוכחת "instruction/ <u>listens to</u> reproof"
33   מוסר "instruction"

The attempts to analyze the prehistory of the Proverbs collections are stimulating in that they have pointed out aspects of these chapters that either went unnoticed or at least were undeveloped. We are far from simply accepting the dictum that a proverb in a collection is dead (perhaps the reader is dead—in imagination and in understanding). First of all, it is clear that the arrangement of sayings at many points shows signs of deliberate placing. Themes, catch words, and various forms of plays on words (alliteration, assonance, etc.) indicate units of varying lengths, whether proverbial pairs or larger groupings. In this sense we can speak of a "context" for proverbial sayings. However, it is worthwhile reiterating a caution that has been mentioned in the *Introduction* above. "Context" is to be understood broadly, not in an interpretive sense. That is to say, a given saying does not lose its independence, its own meaning. A new dimension of *meaning* has not been added in virtue of its place within the collection. It can be balanced, as it were, by being placed in opposition to another saying. But both sayings retain their own meanings; it is simply the nature of a proverb to come up short of total reality, and to be in conflict with other sayings. The examples of this are numerous in our own culture ("one who hesitates is lost," "look before you leap"). No proverb says everything, and that is why the remarkable "contradiction" about answering/not answering a fool (Prov 26:4–5) is even to be expected. Hence "context" has to be properly understood when applied to the sayings. It does not change their meaning; rather, it situates them in a broader world of reality. It can also point up the individual preferences of unknown collectors, for example, the bunching of just/wicked sayings especially in chaps. 10–12. But a synthetic picture of a conceptual nature (e.g., the characteristics of the "just," or the "wise") can be misleading, if it simply totals up the sayings scattered throughout the book. The singularity and individuality of each proverb has to be respected. One must also distinguish between a collection that is not made in a haphazard fashion, and a collection that is intended as a meaningful, more or less logical whole. The transition from stylistics to composition or logical coherence (*Gedankengang*) is not as smooth as some scholars claim.

We will attempt to give a kind of context, based on themes, catch words, and so forth, to the sayings as they appear. Here we wish to alert readers to various observations that scholars have made about the centrality of chaps. 14–16. Certain catch words may form a magnet that attracts similar proverbs. In translation this may not be obvious, but the Hebrew usage (noun, adjective, or verb, as the case may be) makes it clear (cf. T. McCreesh, *Biblical Sound and Sense,* passim). It is widely agreed that antithetical parallelism dominates chaps. 10–15. By Scoralick's count (*Einzelspruch,* 54–55), only fifteen verses do not follow this pattern, and almost half of these occur after 15:9. And there are other important observations, both thematic and formal, that can be made. Thus, there is a preponderance of just/wicked sayings in chaps. 10–12, whereas chaps. 13–15 seem to prefer wisdom terminology (wise/ fool). The combination of "abomination" (תועבה) and "favor/"pleasure" (רצון) occurs only four times in the Hebrew Bible, and all of them in these chapters, 11:1,

20; 12:22; 15:8 (*Einzelspruch*, 76). The parallelism between "instruction/discipline" (מוסר) and "reproof" (תוכחת) appears six times: 10:17; 12:1; 13:18; 15:5, 10, 32. Elsewhere in the book it appears three times in chaps. 1–9 (*Einzelspruch*, 77). Many questions will strike the reader: What is the significance of the unusual cluster of YHWH sayings in 15:33–16:11? Or the group of "king" sayings in 16:10–15? In 15:33 there is a saying about the "fear of the Lord"; is this a closure, picking up 1:7 and 9:10? Could it be that the editor of the book has provided a suture or bonding (Skehan, *Studies*, 18–20, 36; Snell, *Twice-Told Proverbs*, 12–13, 71) between groups of sayings with these clusters in 14:16–16:15?

We have just raised several questions to which we do not have answers, or to which differing answers have been given. These can be seen conveniently in the study by R. N. Whybray (*Composition*, 62–139), along with his own solutions. The study of Scoralick proposed a different solution to chaps. 10–15. Also, the study of J. Krispenz leads to still other conclusions for chaps. 10–22 and 25–29. There is simply no consensus on the subunits that allegedly were put together in the present form of the book. Although no certainty is possible, there is profit in incorporating some of these results for the sake of all who would read and study a series of proverbial sayings—is there any way of interrupting the stream of proverbs, so to speak, in order to ask about their parentage, or about their perceived relationship to one another? The scholarly studies are in themselves stimulating and prompt the reader to ask new questions about many sayings that might at first sight appear innocuous.

The setting of a biblical text is an important part of the format in a WBC commentary which deals explicitly with the "setting in life" (*Sitz im Leben*). We have discussed aspects of "setting" above (see the *Introduction:* The Shape of the Commentary). The original setting of a proverb is beyond recovery, whether it was oral (perhaps more probable for experiential observations) or written (perhaps more probable in the case of the just/wicked sayings). One cannot determine the origins from the topic or the style. But another question can be asked: What is the setting in the book? What difference does this make? For example, 16:1–9 are generally considered to form a unit; eight of them are YHWH sayings, and they deal with the Lord's control over human beings. Vv 1 and 9 form an inclusion, as far as the content is concerned. These are followed by vv 10–15, all but one of which deal with the king and royal power. As Whybray puts it, "the intention of the editor was to link the two topics together" (*Composition*, 88); vv 9 and 10 are considered to be "pivotal" or "linking." Can the intentions of an editor be so easily determined? Perhaps this example is the best that can be offered for such intentional linkage. But is there a real gain? Granting the "intention" of the editor, has a new meaning been reached? I do not think so. There is nothing *new* in acknowledging the difference between divine and human power (or lack thereof). The juxtaposition would not convey a contrast between God and humans that was not already well known. Indeed, if one accepts the deliberate editorial linkage, this was done because of previously accepted belief. But there perhaps lies the advantage of considering the linkage as intentional—"to provoke a consideration of the relationship between Yahweh and kings" (Whybray, *Composition*, 84). Whybray makes the following observations that we may all keep in mind: "With few exceptions, the verses of which these chapters [10:1–22:17 and 25–29] are composed had been in use, before the editorial process began, as independent self-contained proverbs reflecting a largely agricultural society uninfluenced by the interests of a scribal class. Their formation into groups, however, gave many of them a new interpretation: they became 'wisdom literature'" (p. 129). I would understand "new interpretation" here to indicate not new meaning, but rather a new impact, and the possibility of new application, on readership. This is a reasonable way of envisioning the lively interplay in the editorial process behind the greater part of these collections. And it is profitable for a modern readership to look for "pivotal verses," where these can be detected, even if there is a certain subjectivity to the enterprise.

There is an inherent difficulty in analyzing editorial process. A delicate judgment has to be made, and it is fraught with great implications. Thus, for Whybray (*Composition*, 89, 107, 130), the final saying in chap. 15 (15:33) is considered to be a "pivotal verse," joining chaps. 15–16 together. V 33a, which identifies wisdom and fear of the Lord, looks backward, and v 33b on humility and honor can be seen to point to 16:1ff. But for Scoralick (*Einzelspruch*, 79–84), the unit is 10:1–15:32. V 33 is to be excluded. For her, the final unit of the collection of chaps. 10–15 is 15:29–32, which is united by the root שמע, "hear." She grants there is a catch word, מוסר, "instruction," connecting vv 32–33, and also acknowledges that the term YHWH points it forward to the sayings about the Lord in 16:1ff. But it is not sufficiently integrated into the type of YHWH sayings that follow, and 15:33a, with its "fear of the Lord," points back to chaps. 1–9 (cf. 1:7 and 9:10). Such judgments are delicate, indeed.

The reader may well be disappointed to be studying sayings that have no specific context, or only an uncertain "editorial" context. But that is part of the charm of the proverbs; each one can be confronted and applied anew. The commentary will supply as many cross references as possible, while not laying claim to an exhaustive context. Simply to comment on one proverb after another would neglect the various signs that unite them, on however fragile a basis, such as common themes, catch words, repetitions, and so forth. There are enough indications to show that the distribution of the sayings was *not* careless. At the same time, there is no commentator whose grouping of proverbs commands the field. Let the reader be the judge!

Proverbs 10:1–32

Bibliography

Hermisson, H.-J. *Studien.* 171–83. **Hildebrandt, T.** "Proverbial Pairs: Compositional Units in Proverbs 10–29." *JBL* 107 (1988) 207–24. **Krispenz, J.** *Spruchkomposition im Buch Proverbia.* EHS.T 23/349. Frankfurt: P. Lang, 1989. **Krüger, T.** "Komposition und Diskussion in Proverbia 10." *ZTK* 92 (1995) 413–33. **Plöger, O.** "Zur Auslegung der Sentenzensammlung des Proverbienbuches." In *Probleme biblischer Theologie.* FS G. von Rad, ed. H. W. Wolff. Munich: Kaiser, 1971. 402–16. **Scoralick, R.** *Einzelspruch.* **Whybray, R. N.** *Composition.* 93–96.

Translation

10:1   *The Proverbs of Solomon:* [a]
        A wise son gives joy to a father,
            and a foolish son, grief to the mother.

2   *Treasures obtained by wickedness do not profit,*
        but justice delivers from death.

3   *The Lord does not allow the just person to hunger,*
        but thwarts the desire of the wicked.

4   *Whoever works with slack hands becomes poor,*[a]
        but the hand of the diligent brings riches.

5   *Whoever lays in stores in the summer, a wise son,*
        but whoever sleeps during harvest, a shameful son.

6   *Blessings on the head of the just,*
        but the mouth of the wicked conceals violence.[a]

7   *The memory of the just, for a blessing,*
        but the name of the wicked rots.

8   *The wise at heart takes in commands,*
        but the fool by his lips will fall.[a]

9   *Whoever walks honestly walks securely,*
        but the one whose paths are crooked will be found out.

10   *Whoever winks the eye brings trouble,*
        but one who reprimands frankly establishes peace.[a]

11   *A fountain of life—the mouth of the just,*
        but the mouth of the wicked conceals violence.[a]

12   *Hatred stirs up strife,*
        but over all offenses love covers.

13   *Wisdom is found on the lips of the intelligent,*
        but the rod for the back of one lacking in sense.[a]

14   *The wise store up knowledge,*
        but the mouth of the fool, imminent ruin.

15   *The wealth of the rich, a strong city;*
        the ruin of the poor, their poverty.

16   *The earnings of the just, for life;*
        the income of the wicked, for sin.

17   *A path to life, whoever observes instruction,*
        but whoever rejects reprimand goes astray.[a]

18   *Whoever conceals hatred, lying lips,*
        and whoever spreads slander, a fool.[a]

19   *In much talk, iniquity will not be lacking,*
        but those who restrain their lips, sensible people.

20   *Choice silver, the tongue of the just;*
        the heart of the wicked, of little worth.

21   *The lips of the just nourish many,*
        but fools die for lack of sense.

22   *The blessing of the Lord—that brings riches,*
        and no toil can add to it.

23   *Like a fool's joy: sinful activity,*
        but for the intelligent person: wisdom.

24   *What the wicked fear—that will come upon them,*
        but what the just desire will be granted.

25   *With a passing storm, no wicked,*
        but the just, a permanent foundation.

26   *Like vinegar to the teeth and smoke to the eyes,*
         so the sluggard to those who make him a messenger.

27   *The fear of the Lord adds on days,*
         but the years of the wicked are shortened.

28   *The expectation of the just: rejoicing,*
         but the hope of the wicked perishes.

29   *A refuge for the upright, the way of the Lord,*[a]
         but disaster for evildoers.

30   *The just will never be moved,*
         but the wicked will not dwell in the land.

31   *The mouth of the just puts forth wisdom,*
         but the perverse tongue will be cut off.

32   *The lips of the just know favor,*
         but the mouth of the wicked, perversity.

Notes

1.a. One can only speculate on the reason for the absence of the title in the Greek and Syriac; perhaps the superscription in 1:1 was simply considered sufficient.

4.a. The first two words should be revocalized as suggested in *BHS;* the meaning is clear.

6.a. The second part of the verse is suspect. It occurs also in v 11, where it fits, but here the usual parallelism is simply absent, and the connection with the first line is not clear. In fact, it could also be translated "the mouth of the wicked covers violence," but neither is that satisfactory here. The LXX offers little help—"premature sadness closes the mouth of the wicked"—and other ancient versions are inadequate. The text is simply corrupt, and the ingenuity of textual critics has not solved the problems.

8.a. Again there is repetition; v 8b is repeated in v 10b. There is a greater chance that it is original in v 8b, although the parallelism is not obvious.

10.a. The second line is repeated from v 8, and it is difficult to associate the two lines in v 10. W. Bühlmann (*Vom rechten Reden*, 109) and others adopt the LXX reading that is suggested in *BHS* and reflected in the translation above.

11.a. The second line repeats the second line of v 6, but at least there is better parallelism.

13.a. The MT can stand, while the LXX reads: "The one who brings forth wisdom from the lips strikes a senseless person with a rod."

17.a. תעה normally means "to lead astray" in the hiphil; here it may be used intransitively (?), meaning "wander." The suggestion of *BHS* to read the participle of ארח, "path or way," yields better parallelism, but the Masoretes insisted on a more difficult (?) reading.

18.a. The slight harmony between lines *a* and *b* seems to reflect synonymous parallelism, which is exceptional in these early chapters. The one who conceals is the subject, and lying lips (i.e., a liar) is the predicate in the first line. Others would attempt to render it without regard to parallelism; roughly: the concealer of hatred with lying lips and the slanderer are fool(s). In either case, the proverb lacks bite, and the text may be faulty.

29.a. The Hebrew is ambiguous; the Lord can be understood as the subject: "a refuge to integrity of way [or, those whose way is honest], the Lord!" Or else, "the way of the Lord" is the subject, as in the above translation. In any case, "integrity of way" is to be understood as concrete for the abstract, and hence "upright," as the parallel in v 29b suggests ("evildoers"). Some insist on a revocalization of תם to תם, the change suggested by *BHS* on the basis of Greek "holy" and the versions; on this, see also Prov 13:6.

Form/Structure/Setting

The antithetic parallelism is so conspicuous that any deviation makes one suspect the correctness of the text. As far as the grouping of the proverbs is concerned, there are some telling catch words that unite otherwise disparate sayings: such as "ruin" in vv 14–15; "life" in vv 16–17; "heart" in vv 20–21 (translated as "sense" in v 21); "perversity" in vv 31–32. It is almost otiose to point out the frequency of the comparison between the just and the wicked; this dualism rules chaps. 10–15. This theme ties together many sayings (e.g., vv 27–32). The topic of speech also forms a kind of center, in which the corresponding organs (tongue, lips, mouth) of the body are given full play: vv 11–13 and 18–21. Perhaps vv 1–5 form a larger unit, with "son" occurring twice and forming an inclusion (see the analysis in Scoralick, *Einzelspruch*, 170–76, and also in Krüger, "Komposition," 417–22). Scoralick recognizes another unit extending from 10:28 to 11:7 (note the inclusion and cluster of catch words). R. Whybray (*Composition*, 93) lists the divisions of five different authors, and the lack of agreement is evident. It is easy to grant a unity to vv 31–32 because of the catch words and obvious theme, but are these to be associated with the "just" that are featured in vv 28, 30? Such questions are difficult because they involve many judgment calls on what is the course of thought in a given unit, and what is the power of a catch word in linking up various verses. It is not surprising that there is no unanimity among the commentators. See also the detailed treatment of this chapter by T. Krüger, "Komposition," esp. 417–33; he argues for meaningful (and hence intentional) units in vv 1–5, 6–11, 12–18, 19–21, 22–27, 28–32. But this faces the ever-recurring difficulty: how much weight is to be attached to literary repetitions, chiastic framework, and other arguments that are advanced for these intentional units? Nonetheless, the reader is challenged to determine the range of any alleged unit within a chapter, weighing the arguments for similarity of theme, presence of catch words, etc.

Comment

1–5 The marked references to the types of "son" in vv 1, 5 indicate an inclusion, and the verses deal with similar topics: just/wicked in vv 2–3; diligence in vv 4–5. The sacred name, YHWH, in v 3, then dominates the section. **1** See *Note* 1.a. The title appended to the beginning seems intended to cover the material up to 22:17. With the reference to "son" in v 1, this section takes on the appearance of continuing the wisdom advice that was laid out in chaps. 1–9, and of course many of the same emphases will appear. "The wise son" occurs elsewhere at 13:1 and 15:20 (in which 1:1a is repeated), thus at the beginning, middle, and end of chaps. 10–15, a kind of structural signal, as Scoralick interprets it (*Einzelspruch*, 174). See also 17:21, 25; 23:24–25; all of this supports the view that the origin of the wisdom teachings is to be found in the family. For a full treatment of the family in this book, cf. J. Hausmann, *Menschenbild*, 105–22. **2** This saying boldly confronts the dilemma of the pious Israelite; cf. Pss 37; 73; Jer 12:1. Ill-gotten treasures ultimately cannot be profitable; it is honest living, recognized by the Lord (v 3), that preserves one from death. What kind of death is meant? Physical death that may be sudden and sorrowful, for it would certainly separate the dying from their "treasures." And death leads to the nonlife in Sheol. Is this view simply an application of the deed-consequence theory (or *Tat-Ergehen Zusammenhang*), according to which evil deeds automatically beget evil results, and good deeds beget good results? It may very well be that this mentality prevailed in some quarters, but equally if not more emphasized is the view that it is the Lord with whom one must deal, and in the very next v 3 the direct activity of the Lord is described. See the discussion in the *Excursus on Retribution*. One might summarize the spirit of v 2 in an objective manner: "illicit gain does not pay," but such a saying does not deny direct divine activity. In the context of Proverbs deliverance from death has nothing to do with personal immortality beyond death. The phrase v 2b is a pregnant one, taken up again in Prov 11:4. It could have been reinterpreted in a later period, as in Tob 4:10, where almsgiving replaces justice: "almsgiving delivers from death" (and here, is the death of the donor or the recipient meant?). Again, in Wis 1:15 justice is said to be undying, and the context is an eschatological one. There are levels of meaning that emerge in different eras of Israelite life. And ultimately for later readers, whether Jewish or Christian, the open-ended character of certain proverbs may suggest a fuller meaning. **3** The usual view of retribution is expressed here. The Lord will intervene to provide physical needs, sustaining the just with food, in contrast to the wicked. See also 13:25; YHWH is the protector of those who are pious and devout, e.g., 10:29; 12:2. It is obvious that this is an ideal, not a real, event since the just do go hungry. But the saying expresses the usual Israelite understanding of divine justice. No proverb says it all. **4–5** The antithesis between the diligent and the lazy is fairly common, but most of the sayings deal explicitly with the lazy. In v 4 the corresponding results of their conduct are indicated. See also 12:24, 27; 21:5. In v 5 the type of work specified is the harvest where active hands would surely be necessary. As for the ultimate implications of poverty and riches, one must beware of drawing conclusions too quickly; poverty is not always brought on by laziness. A thorough treatment of this question can be found in R. N. Whybray, *Wealth and Poverty*, esp. 60–74. See also the *Excursus on Wealth and Poverty*.

6–7 These verses are connected by the repetition of just/wicked, and the catch word "blessing" (cf. also v 22). *Note* 6.a. indicates that there is probably some confusion in the text (v 6b = v 11b), which has never been solved. V 7 reflects the notion of the immortality of the name (cf. Prov 22:1; Eccl 7:1), the blessed memory that the virtuous leave after them; the just remain "forever" (10:25, 30).

8–11 One may perhaps associate these verses on the basis of wise/fool. True wisdom makes a person docile to teaching, and ensures their way for them. The fool is garrulous (literally "foolish of lips," vv 8b, 10b) and presumably not disposed to listen. The repetitions (vv 6b, 11b and vv 8b, 10b) make this section uncertain, although others, e.g., T. Krüger, "Komposition," 422–24, regard them as signs of unity. **8** The contrast between wise/fool and heart/lips is a sign that this verse is intact, even if "fall" is an uncertain meaning of the verb in v 8b. Almost by definition the wise is open to correction and eager to learn; cf. 9:8–9. **9** The alliteration in v 9a is striking: הולך בתם ילך בטח, "whoever walks honestly walks securely." Implied in the proverb is the teaching about the two ways (cf. 4:11–14). It is not stated how the crooked person will be "found out." Perhaps the meaning is that the perversity of such an individual is bound to assert itself; it will be both revealed and avoided. The obvious integrity of the wise enables them to go securely. **10** The precise implication of winking the eyes is not clear; cf. 6:13. It can be understood as a hostile gesture, perhaps like the magical spell of the "evil eye." For v 10b, see *Note* 10.a. The translation contrasts the disparate effects of the eye and the open reprimand. Paradoxically, the rebuke leads to peace. **11** The repetition of "mouth" is unusual; "lip" or "tongue" would be normal for the parallelism. "Fountain of life" means first of all flowing fresh water, but it is used symbolically, and is associated with the life-giving qualities of wisdom; cf. 13:14; 14:27; 16:22. Thus the mouth of the just would be a source of wisdom—wisdom as teaching, and wisdom as praxis. V 11b (see *Note* 11.a.) repeats v 6b, but yields the necessary parallelism. In contrast to the words of the just, the speech of the wicked, ever deceitful, produces destruction (חמס, a particularly strong term).

12 The translation attempts to convey the chiasm of the original. The contrast between love and hatred explains why quarrels can be quickly stopped or else prolonged. The meaning of "covering" is "pardoning," overlooking what may be a personal insult or harm—quite different from the "covering" (= concealing) in v 11. On v 12b see also 17:9a. The "covering of all (multitude of) sins" is taken up in Jas 5:20 (cf. 1 Pet 4:8), where it refers to divine forgiveness; interestingly, saving from death also occurs there; cf. Prov 10:2b; 11:4b.

13–14 These two verses can be grouped together in view of the terms lips/ mouth and wise/wisdom. **13** Cf. v 11a. The words of the wise display discernment, are uttered at the right time, and provide good advice. Such utterance is contrasted with the only language that a fool can understand—physical force. Even at that it is not clear whether they can learn. V 13b is a variant of 26:3b; physical means of enforcement seems to have been popular. **14** The knowledge accumulated (rather than "hidden" as some interpret the verb) by the wise is shared with others; they know how to use their wisdom, for this knowledge is a "fountain of life" (v 11). The juxtaposition of terms in v 14b has a striking effect.

15 The only connection with the preceding verse is the repetition of "ruin," but it is a distinctive proverb for both its content and its style; the translation above tries to bring out the chiastic juxtaposition of terms. The point seems so simple: Riches are a source of strength; poverty is ruinous. There is no intention of communicating here a moral lesson. This is simply a reflection upon reality; that is the way things are. But these sayings have a way of prompting new perspectives. Prov 18:11 points out the possibility that the rich can overrate their "strong city," especially when it is stated in the context (18:10) that the name of the Lord is a "strong tower." As is the case with so many proverbs, one must learn to balance them against each other.

16–17 The catch word is "life," a central notion for wisdom. **16** The style, as also in the next verse, is juxtapositional and striking. The opposition of "life" and "sin" instead of "death," or something similar, is unusual. Nothing is said about how the earning/income was attained, but there is an implication concerning the acquisition and use of such possessions. This is true of 11:28, where the opposite of the just is one who trusts in riches. The law of retribution calls for some differentiation: the efforts of the just will prosper, in contrast to the wicked who continue on their sinful ways without profit, v 2a. Perhaps sin stands here for punishment for sin, even death. A similar idea is found in 11:18–19. **17** See *Note* 17.a. The juxtaposition in v 17a is chiastic and very succinct. The translation above understands the terms as subject and predicate: the person who follows wisdom is a path to life for others (rather than "walks the path of life" for himself). Openness to both meanings may be intended. A familiar note is sounded: the need to put instruction into practice and to be docile. Only thus can one continue in the right "way."

18 The characteristic antithetical parallelism is lacking (see *Note* 18.a.), and the text is suspect. If this is synonymous parallelism, perhaps the sense is that the one who hides hatred is a liar (= "lying lips")—a natural liar, as it were, and one who slanders is a fool. But the two verbs are in contrast to each other: concealing and spreading (slander). Although the term "just" is not used, there is a clear moral implication in the description of the action of the "fool." The repetitions ("hatred," "hide" in vv 12 and 18) should be noted.

19–21 More clearly than the previous verse, the topic of speech is given attention. **19** The insistence on cautious and careful choice of words is typically sapiential. The sages were particularly alert to the danger of wordiness and to the value of silence; cf. Eccl 9:12–14a; Sir 20:1–6. Loquacity simply exposes one to making statements that are hasty (cf. 29:20!), or simply ill-considered, or downright iniquitous. In Jewish tradition, the Sayings of the Fathers (ʾAbot, 1, 17) recognizes the wrong that results from many words. It is true, silence is ambiguous, as Prov 17:27–28 indicates, but it is less likely to cause trouble. **20** The contrast between the tongue of the just and the heart of the wicked is not frequent. While heart is often properly translated by "sense" (for "lacking in heart," 10:13), or by "mind," it also indicates a basic orientation of the whole person (cf. 4:23). Choice silver is tested by fire; hence the metaphor implies a strong affirmation of trust in whatever the just person says. **21** The just person is pictured here as a shepherd who nourishes others; the metaphor of shepherd is applied to God and to king in the Bible, but only here to the just. The implication is that the just is to be identified with the wise person who provides sound teaching for others. Such a task is impossible for the fools, who are not even able to sustain themselves; they are dying while they "live."

22 The translation given above is the correct one. V 22b does not mean that the Lord does not add sorrow to the wealth (so Toy). Rather, it affirms emphatically the activity of the Lord in the achievement of prosperity; the Lord is responsible, not human effort. See Ps 127:1–2. This has the characteristic exaggeration of many proverbs; it does not mean that one gives up all personal activity. That would be contrary to the diligence inculcated in 10:4. Rather, it indicates the need to recognize human limitations, and to consider the major role played by the Lord. Proverbs have to be balanced off each other.

23–25 These sayings can be conveniently grouped together as describing various aspects of the just and the wicked. **23** Although the contrast is between the wise and the foolish, immoral action is specified; "sinful activity" (זמה) designates serious wrongdoing. The point is the moral bankruptcy of the fool, who takes his wrongdoing as lightly as a joke. This hardened cynicism is contrasted with the attitude of the intelligent person, for whom wisdom is the joy and delight; one may recall here the "playing" of Woman Wisdom to be with humankind, 8:30–31. What is true joy for the wise? According to Prov 21:15, it is doing what is right (משפט). **24** The question arises: just what do the wicked fear? The text does not make this explicit. One may imagine that they fear the possible loss by some evil turn of their goods and happiness. Or perhaps people they have injured will try to exact revenge. Or perhaps the doctrine of retribution might get to them after all—can they escape punishment? The "fear" is to be understood in an objective sense; these are not qualms of conscience on the part of the wicked. In any case, in the view of the collector of these sayings some unnamed fear will overtake the wicked;

they cannot escape. In contrast the just will experience the assurance already expressed in Ps 37:4, "Take delight in the Lord, and he will give you the desires of your heart." The last word in the verse can be interpreted passively, or also actively: (the Lord) will give. **25** The vivid portrayal of the effects of a violent storm is used to distinguish between the fate of the wicked and the just. The wicked simply disappear in the hurricane, but the just, thanks to a strong foundation, go on indefinitely; cf. Matt 7:24–27. **26** The pungency of the comparisons is striking; cf. also vv 4–5. The acidic effect of vinegar would seem to be the point of v 16a. The term "sluggard" (עצל) occurs almost only in this book, and it is featured in 26:13–16. The attention given to messengers is an indication of their importance; only a reliable person could serve to travel long distances and in a sense be responsible for the one who sent him; cf. 13:17; 25:13; 26:6.

27–32 The contrast between the just and wicked dominates these sayings, giving a strong moral tone to the ending of the chapter. **27** The "fear of the Lord" occurs for the first time in this collection, but will appear frequently: 14:26–27; 15:16, 33; 16:6; 19:23; 22:4. See 1:7 and the *Excursus on Fear of the Lord.* The abstract is equivalent to the concrete, the God-fearer, since it is parallel to the wicked. The wise are preeminently those who fear God, and hence they are closely aligned with the just. Prolongation of life is one of the blessings associated with wisdom; cf. 3:2, 16; 19:23. It is to be understood both qualitatively and quantitatively, a full and a long life. **28** V 28 picks up on v 24, and provides a very positive and fulfilling note to expectation; it is a hope that gives direction and meaning to life. Expectation and hope are used again in 11:7, which expands on v 28b, the hopelessness of the wicked. On the contrary, the hope of the just will never be cut off (23:18; 24:14). Without any eschatological props, hope is a vibrant reality in Israel. **29** See *Note* 29.a. God is the refuge (מעוז) in Ps 27:1, and it is unusual to find here instead "the way of the Lord." This "way" is not easy to define; it is in the singular, as opposed to "ways" found in Exod 33:13 and also at the end of Hosea (14:10). In the context of the verse it could be a reference to God's general way of acting, protecting the just. Perhaps it is better to relate it to the way of wisdom in 4:11 (cf. 3:17). Thus the doctrine of the two ways (cf. chaps. 1–9) is reflected here. V 19b is identical with 21:15b; in neither place is the parallelism perfect. **30** The thought of v 30 is not unlike that of v 25, but it is expressed in language familiar to the reader from the psalms, e.g., Pss 15:5; 21:8. Living in, or "inheriting" the land is a dominant idea in Ps 37. See also the metaphor of the land in Prov 2:21–22. The land may not only be the familiar "vine and fig tree" of the ancient Israelite, but also may suggest being among the living, as opposed to the shades who inhabit the depths. This is obviously a very important metaphor. **31–32** These proverbs deal with right speech, and also with perversity; תהפכות, literally "a turning upside down," is a catch word, along with "just." They are along traditional lines about the importance of words, and both employ the physical organs, mouth, lips, tongue. The subject of both is the just person, and once again justice and wisdom are associated, as in v 31. **31** The image is that of a fruit tree: the just yield wisdom as the fruit; the perverse, because of their yield, will be cut off. Bühlmann (*Vom rechten Reden,* 303–306) interprets v 31a as meaning "flourishes with wisdom"; in other words, wisdom is what makes the just succeed. He also points out three more proverbs that associate speech with a tree: 12:14; 13:2; 18:20. **32** "Favor" can refer to the favor of God or, more likely, to human approval. The just person knows what to say, and is met with acceptance.

Strict parallelism with v 32b would suggest that favor is the product of the lips, just as perversity flows from the mouth of the wicked.

Explanation

Plöger wisely remarks that this chapter cannot be summarized because of the many themes that are treated. But he is partial to the topics of poverty/riches along with laziness and diligence; these subjects will emerge often in the rest of the book. Alonso Schökel has pointed out the preoccupation with speech, enumerating twelve verses in which "mouth," "lips," "tongue," and "words" occur: 6, 8, 11–14, 18–21, 31–32.

However, there is one overarching topic that will be constantly appearing especially in the next four or five chapters, and that is the just/wicked contrast. It is roughly as frequent as the contrast between the wise and the foolish. What *is* the connection between wisdom and righteousness? Moreover, why is there such an abundance of the just/wicked contrasts in these opening chapters of the collection? A short answer would be a simple identification of just/wise and wicked/fool. If this is not an oversimplification, it at least conceals the kind of thinking that leads to the equation of these terms, which are not exactly identical. Perhaps the frequent reference to the just/wicked reinforced the teaching concerning the teaching about the wise/foolish within the family and the tribe. Some kind of retribution came to be seen as necessary. Whether this is interpreted as operating within the sphere of deed-consequence or directly by the intervention of the Lord makes little difference; see the *Excursus on Retribution*. Motivation and discipline were important features in teaching the right way to live. To rely, even if silently and implicitly, on the ethical standards of the people as they continued to grow since the days of Sinai gave authority to the sages. This authority might even seem greater, in a practical way, than the authority of the prophets, to judge from the failures of Israel to respond to the threats the prophets laid out. In a sense, the approach of the sage was more covert. It was unmistakable, for it raised questions of character, but it was not as confrontational.

Claus Westermann has strict criteria for wisdom sayings as opposed to wisdom teaching. The former originate in oral tradition, whereas the latter does not. It is a more reflective statement that inculcates virtue. For example, "The wage of the righteous (is) life, but the reward of the wicked (is) sin" (Prov 10:16). He comments that "in each of the sayings of this nature the same subject is expressed: the antithesis of the righteous and the wicked in action and in fate. . . . The possibility of this schematic having arisen from oral proverbs is out of the question, since a calculated thesis is developed within each statement. At the root of this model is a perceived observation, a conceptualization that has been thought out" (*Roots of Wisdom*, 76). Hence he concludes in a later essay that these "proverbs" are really a systematic teaching, but put in the form of a saying ("Grenzen der Weisheit," in *Das mündliche Wort*, AzT 82 [Stuttgart: Calwer, 1996] 141). To put it sharply, "Wisdom can of its nature not lead to a teaching; Wisdom and teaching are opposites" (*Das mündliche Wort*, 142). If one grants the narrow definition of a proverb, this conclusion may follow. But precisely there is the issue. Is there any evidence that the biblical writers made a distinction, even if they were aware of it, between oral/written, or observation/teaching? Instead, when the collections were finally put together, both observations and teachings were included without anything being made of the distinction and all in the name of wisdom. It would be a mistake to eliminate teaching from wisdom. Even if a proverb registers a sheer experience, telling it "the way it is," it was preserved and transmitted to "teach," at least to "challenge."

Hence several issues arise from this discussion: (1) the origins of Israelite wisdom in an oral culture. I think this is established; but I would not eliminate the development of the wisdom saying in written form at a later period. (2) The reflexive type of wisdom, such as is found in Prov 1–9 and in the just/wicked contrast, is no less wisdom, even if its roots in observation are less obvious. (3) This is both a question and an answer: Why did such a strong moral hue become associated with wisdom conduct? Because wisdom was seen as a source and even as a "tree" of life, dealing with moral formation, the just/wicked antithesis would have been a natural continuation and complement to the sayings.

Proverbs 11:1–31

Bibliography

Hermisson, H.-J. *Studien.* 171–83 (for Prov 10–15). **Plöger, O.** "Zur Auslegung der Sentenzensammlungen des Proverbienbuches." In *Probleme biblischer Theologie.* FS G. von Rad, ed. H. W. Wolff. Munich: Kaiser, 1971. 402–16. **Scoralick, R.** *Einzelspruch.* 164–79. **Whybray, R. N.** *Composition.* 96–97.

Translation

11:1 False scales, an abomination to the Lord,
        but a full weight, his pleasure.

2   When pride comes, then comes shame;
        but with the humble, wisdom.

3   The integrity of the upright guides them,
        but deceit destroys [a] the faithless.

4   Wealth is of no profit on the day of wrath,
        but justice delivers from death.

5   The justice of the upright keeps their way straight,
        but the wicked fall because of their wickedness.

6   The justice of the honest delivers them,
        but the faithless are caught by their desire.[a]

7   With the death of the wicked, hope vanishes;
        what strength can expect vanishes.[a]

8   The just are freed from distress,
        and the wicked take their place!

9   By mouth the impious destroy their neighbor,
        but by knowledge the just are saved.[a]

10   When the just prosper, a city is glad,
        and when the wicked perish, rejoicing.

11   *By the blessing of the upright a city is exalted,*
        but by the mouth of the wicked it is destroyed.

12   *One who despises his neighbor, lacking in sense;*
        but a man of intelligence keeps quiet.

13   *Whoever slanders, a revealer of confidences;*
        but the trustworthy, a keeper of secrets.

14   *No guidance, a people falls;*
        but in many counselors, safety.

15   *Whoever goes surety for a stranger suffers,*[a]
        but whoever hates giving pledges, secure.

16   *A graceful woman holds to honor,*
        but strong men hold on to riches.[a]

17   *The kind person benefits himself,*
        but the cruel one harms himself.

18   *The wicked: making empty profits,*
        but one sowing justice: sure wages.

19   *Justice is directed* [a] *to life,*
        but whoever pursues evil, to death.

20   *An abomination to the Lord, those crooked at heart;*
        but his pleasure, those upright in their path.

21   *Be assured, the evil person will not go unpunished,*
        but the descendants of the just will go free.

22   *A golden ring in the snout of a pig—*
        a woman beautiful but without sense.

23   *The desire of the just, only good;*
        the hope of the wicked, wrath.

24   *There is one scattering, and still the richer,*
        and one too sparing, only the poorer.

25   *Those who are a blessing to others will prosper,*
        and those who refresh others will themselves be refreshed.[a]

26   *Whoever holds back grain, the people will curse him,*
        but blessings on the head of the one who sells it.

27   *Whoever is intent on good, seeks favor,*
        but the one on the watch for evil—it will fall on him.

28   *Whoever trusts in their riches, that one will fall,*
        but the just shall bloom like foliage.

29   *Whoever disturbs his household will inherit the wind;*
        and a fool—servant to the wise of heart.

30   *The fruit of the just, a tree of life;*
        but violence [a] *takes away souls.*

31   *The just is recompensed on earth;*
        how much more the wicked and the sinner!

Notes

3.a. Read the Qere יְשַׁדֵּם, "destroys them."

6.a. The ancient versions reflect the reading וּבְהַוֹתָם, "and by their (desire)." The MT seems to be from הַוָּה, "desire" (or "disaster").

7.a. The Hebrew is difficult; line *a* seems to be overloaded (רָשָׁע אָדָם), but there is no agreement on which word is extra. The meaning of אונים is uncertain ("strength"? "riches"?). The sequence of imperfect and perfect for the *same* verb, אבד, "vanish," is unusual. The ancient versions are of no help; the LXX actually indicates that hope does not perish at the death of the just person. Finally, the synonymous parallelism is singular here. See the extensive discussion in Scoralick, *Einzelspruch*, 164–68, who decides in favor of the MT and translates: "at the death of the wicked, hope perishes and the expectation of riches/strength perishes." She points out that v 7 picks up on 10:28, and constitutes a framework; cf. also 10:2 and 11:4.

9.a. The second line is ambiguous; one can also translate: "by the knowledge of the just is one saved." Cf. GKC §144f for the use of the indefinite subject of the verb. It is not advisable to adopt the suggestions of *BHS*. The antithesis in this verse is not clear. Bühlmann (*Vom rechten Reden*, 295–98) claims the opposition is between the impious who destroy their neighbor and the just who are saved by knowledge or insight. Other translations recognize a contrast between mouth and knowledge. See the *Comment*.

15.a. רע, "suffering," is to be vocalized as the infinitive absolute; cf. *BHS*.

16.a. Attention may be called here to the LXX additions, and to the proposal signaled in *BHS*: "a disgraceful throne is a woman who hates just things"; so v 16b, and this is followed by: "possessions will be lacking to the lazy one." There is no solid reason for adopting these readings, *pace* B. Gemser and H. Ringgren.

19.a. There is no easy explanation of the first word, כן, and it seems best to emend it to חכן (haplography), indicated in *BHS*.

25.a. There is a play on the verb רוה. The second occurrence is the hophal; cf. GKC §69w.

30.a. Read חמס instead of חכם. The LXX reads for line *b*, "the souls of the lawless will be cut down before their time." But this could be a free rendering of a difficult text; cf. the *Comment* below.

Form/Structure/Setting

Chap. 11 is dominated by antithetic parallelism, especially between the just/wicked (vv 4–11, 18–21, 30–31), much more than the contrast of wise/fool. Exceptions to the antithesis are perhaps vv 7, 16, 25, 29. As to be expected, there is no clear principle of organization. But there are signs that sayings have been grouped together: Vv 9–12 all begin with the letter *beth,* and they are characterized by catch words ("freed/saved," vv 8–9; "city," vv 10–11). The viewpoint is the broader society, e.g., vv 9–16, 25–26. Catch words appear also in vv 23–24 ("only"), vv 25–26 ("blessing"), vv 30–31 ("just"); cf. Krispenz, *Spruchkomposition,* 166. Scoralick (*Einzelspruch,* 192–97) recognizes a unit in 11:18–12:13 in which 11:18–21 and 12:2–3 provide a framework for the intervening proverbs in 11:22–12:1. The final "framework" is to be seen in a certain correspondence between 11:8–17 and 12: 4–13. All these features indicate, however slightly, a broad sense of unity between groups of sayings that seem to us quite disparate. However, the arguments are fragile and not all will agree; see the summary of divisions among four scholars in Whybray, *Composition,* 96.

Comment

1 This opening verse is joined to 10:32 by the catch word "favor/pleasure." Deceitful practice in business is forbidden all through the Old Testament, both in the Torah (Lev 19:35; Deut 25:13–16, with "abomination") and often in the prophets (e.g., Amos 8:5), and it is recalled in Prov 16:11; 20:10, 23. This suggests that the practice must have been widespread, and was probably never wiped out. Dishonest weights are forbidden also in the teaching of Amenemope (chap. 16; *ANET,* 423): "Do not *lean on* the scales nor falsify the weights, Nor damage the fractions of the measure." Merchants could employ either false weights, or crooked scales. The condemnation ("abomination," תועבה) is quite strong.

2 The assonance and rhyme of v 2a is striking: בא זדון ויבא קלון, rendered by REB, "when pride comes in, in comes contempt." The saying is popular among many peoples: pride comes before a fall; cf. 15:33b; 16:18; 18:12. Following on this is a line that gives the appearance of just limping along. "Humble" is hapax legomenon, and it is considered to have the sense of modesty, a proper regard for oneself. Line *b* doesn't quite catch the contrast in line *a;* there is an antithesis between proud and humble, but that is all.

3–6 These verses exemplify the power of righteousness and the failure of its opposite (vv 3, 5, 6). **3** "Integrity" is a key term in the book of Job (can he keep to it, and why?). The saying reflects the confident optimism of the sages. The guidance that virtue provides is taken up in vv 5–6. **4** V 4b is repeated in 10:2b; see the *Comment* there. In v 4a "the day of wrath" refers to some disaster, or to death seen as some kind of punishment, or to financial ruin, etc. Implicitly, this is the Lord's wrath, and it cannot be bought off. Ps 49 echoes the same teaching: "you can't take it with you." The riches of v 4a are not the just desserts of the pious; there is the insinuation, especially in the context of v 1a, that the riches have been preferred to "justice," and something to be trusted in; cf. v 28. But they are ultimately vain. Significantly, v 4b repeats 10:2; see the detailed *Comment* there. The context emphasizes that the just person will be delivered from troubles; cf. vv 6 and 8. **5** Each word in v 5a is a key term in virtuous conduct: "justice," "integrity," "straight," and "way"; see also v 3. The image is that of going along a path without stumbling or falling. **6** See *Note* 6.a. This is almost a repetition of v 5; in both verses the just prevail, but the wicked fall because of their own wrongdoing. V 6b suggests that the evil deed causes the downfall; hence there is a connection between deed and result; cf. the *Excursus on Retribution.*

7 Translations differ (see *Note* 7.a.). The absence of antithesis in the saying raises suspicion. But v 7a is sound wisdom doctrine if it indicates the hopeless state of the wicked at death, as in the MT. All that the wicked put their hopes in, such as riches, will disappear. The same verb ("perish") is used in both lines. The ambiguous subject of v 7b ("strength" = "riches") will be of no help at death.

8 This is a classical example of the inevitability of retribution. The wicked cannot be allowed to profit; cf. 10:2a. The just will be delivered, only to be replaced by one who deserves to be punished, the wicked. It is not said that they have tried to do injury to the just. The precise manner of the replacement is not spelled out. The proverb is usually interpreted in the light of the deed-consequence view: concretely the wicked fall into the pit that the evil person has dug for the good (Prov 26:27; Ps 7:16, etc.). In view of the obvious exceptions to this view of reality, one may ask if the sages really set great store by it—was it more of a fond hope?

9 See *Note* 9.a. The meaning is problematical because the contrast between the two lines is not clear. The verse is joined to v 8 by a catch word, "freed/saved." It is not surprising that an impious person destroys by harmful speech. But how deliverance for the just is accomplished by "knowledge" is not clear. Perhaps it means an awareness of the deviousness and ploys of the wicked. But the combination of a mouth that destroys people, and knowledge that saves oneself (or perhaps others), is unusual. The mouth of the just is a "fountain of life" (10:9), so perhaps here the reference is to general knowledge or wisdom. The meaning is further complicated by the change from the singular in line *a* to the plural in line *b.*

10–11 These verses obviously belong together, and commentators generally point out that v 11 is the basis for v 10.   **10** The social accomplishments of the just are implied. Their standards and influence bring about the common good and happiness. No wonder there is rejoicing on the part of the city, since they have replaced the wicked. The spirit of the saying is reflected also in Prov 29:2.   **11** The antithesis is unusual, blessing and mouth; cf. the unusual antithesis in v 9. The mouth of the wicked would indicate the harm that the wicked wreak by their advice to government; the "blessing" signifies the advantages that the upright achieve for the city.

12–13 Control of one's speech, manifested by not speaking (vv 12b, 13b) is the issue. See also the *Explanation* below.   **12** Here one who disdains the neighbor is understood as unjust; cf. v 9a above, and also the characterization in 14:21a ("a sinner"). Such a person is judged by wisdom standards: lacking in sense (heart). The particular cause of the disdain is not stated, but one can imagine that poor or sick neighbors might be the object of harmful gossip. In 14:21b the meaning of silence is indicated: it is a measure of sympathy for the poor.   **13** This saying strikes out at any who would break a confidence, whether in a malicious, harmful way or in a light-headed manner. A warning about such a person is given in Prov 20:19. The confidences (Hebrew סוד, a word used of divine as well as human deliberations) are the "secret" that must be honored; cf. Prov 25:9. By contrast, the trustworthy, or literally "firm of spirit," is one who can keep a secret. The gossiper is literally "one goes about talking/chattering." There is only a very fine line between gossip and calumny.

14 For v 14b see 24:6. The need for several advisors is part of the wisdom tradition. Literally, guidance is "steerings"; cf. 1:5. The sages recognized the possibility of individual self-deception; hence the need of correction and advice. Although the king was recognized as being directed by God (Prov 21:1), he also needed advisors. The saying is all the more necessary when there is a question of community policy. See also 15:22.

15 See the *Comment* on Prov 6:1–5. The warning against going surety is frequent in the book, e.g., 17:18. It is framed in a general saying here with alliteration a striking feature of line *a*: רע ירוע כי ערב זר, literally "suffering he will suffer if he goes surety for a stranger." Line *b* consists of two participles, "hater" of pledges and "one who trusts," in the sense of one who is confident and secure; the Targum makes it explicit—trust in God. The disadvantages of such transactions are obvious, and the situation is sharpened if the "stranger" is a foreigner.

16 The text is unique in Proverbs in that men ("strong men") are contrasted with a woman. In both lines the same verb appears, תמך, "take hold of," but the objects are unusual: honor and riches. Thus, the antithesis is weak, but perhaps the saying could mean that the graceful, beautiful woman wins honor because of her grace, whereas the male relies on strength for the acquisition of riches. Or possibly, honor is innate, a "given" for the woman, whereas riches have to be acquired, usually on the part of the male, by expending oneself. Plöger remarks that the *tertium comparationis* lies in the public esteem accorded to both, though being attained by different means. Alonso Schökel adopts the LXX reading, also favored by Oesterley, Vaccari, and others, which presents a contrast between a gracious woman and a woman who is not just. The Greek also adds another couplet which has basically the same meaning as 10:4 and 13:4, but there is not sufficient reason to depart from the Hebrew text; cf. A. Barucq, 110.

17 Two terms are in opposition: the נֶפֶשׁ or "soul" and the שְׁאֵר or "flesh." Both stand for the self. The contrast is between kindness and cruelty. Do the good/bad results in this instance reflect the deed-consequence mentality? Probably so; no further detail about the actions is given. One might presuppose that the kind person will not be ruthless in pursuing his ends, and hence will benefit—as opposed to the cruel person who, lacking good judgment, will employ any means to attain a goal, only to hurt himself. Plöger sees the key to this saying in self-regard. The one does not exaggerate personal ability; the other, because of deficient judgment, hurts himself. Whybray interprets the whole saying in a social sense: "The point of the proverb is that one's behaviour towards others, whether good or bad, has unintended or unexpected consequences for oneself." He considers vv 18–21 as a development of this verse.

18–21 The just/wicked contrast governs this group of sayings. **18** There is a play on "empty profits" and "sure wages" (שֶׁקֶר/שֶׂכֶר) that brings out the intended contrast between compensations for the wicked and just. For the thought see also 11:4; 10:16. The image of "sowing" justice occurs in Hos 10:12; but one can also sow iniquity (Prov 22:8), and perhaps a lifetime of activity is implied. **19** See also 10:16; 12:28; 21:21. Life and death are probably to be understood metaphorically, or qualitatively, here. They are appropriate opposites for the characters mentioned; the saying continues the thought of the previous verse. **20** The description of the divine revulsion is strong; see also 11:1. The heart means more than mere "mind"; here it is the basic attitude of a person; cf. 17:20. **21** The precise nuance of "hand to hand" remains unknown; Alonso Schökel understands it to mean "sooner or later." Some kind of inevitability of proper retribution from the Lord is implied. Van Leeuwen points out that the phrase "will not go unpunished" occurs seven times in Proverbs, and also in the central text of Exod 34:7; the implication is that God will be involved. The mention of the descendants, literally "seed," of the just is surprising in this context, but it does indicate that the retribution for the just goes down to several generations; presumably the evil will have been punished and are without progeny; cf. Exod 34:7.

22 The saying is grotesque in that an ornamental ring should not be in the snout of an animal. The sarcasm is obvious since the women of the Bible wore such rings; Gen 24:47; Isa 3:21. Rings also adorned the ear: Prov 25:12. "Good sense" translates "taste," for which the wise Abigail is praised in 2 Sam 25:33. The comparison is not between a beautiful woman and swine, but between one who lacks good sense and the decorated swine. Beauty without wisdom is the height of incongruity; see also Prov 31:30.

23 The fate of the just and the wicked is evaluated in typical wisdom fashion: prosperity for one but wrath for the other. The question is: Whose wrath? This could be a calamity inflicted by God; cf. 11:4. It could also refer to the wrath that the wicked will incur at the hands of others. In light of the LXX reading many prefer the verb "perish" (a small emendation changing a *d* to an *r*), or "pass away" (a revocalization) instead of "wrath," but the MT provides a better parallelism with v 23a. The meaning is not affected. The phraseology recalls 10:24, 28; cf. also v 7.

24 A formula of fact, "there is" (יֵשׁ), begins the saying, and participles introduce the agents. The proverb has been interpreted on more than one level. First, it could merely point out a paradox: the big spender somehow gets richer; his opposite, carefully sparing, becomes poorer. No explanation is given and no moral edge is intended; the saying registers a fact, observable if not frequent. This could be conceived as an application of a saying that originally referred to the sowing of seed: the sower is generous with the seed and is enriched by the harvest. But if he does not sow the due amount of seed, he suffers a lack of produce. Second, one *can* apply it to the moral realm: the generous person thrives, whereas the one who is stingy (toward others) does not. In other words, generosity can bring a blessing. The first interpretation seems preferable, but there is a division of opinion, and even translations differ. See also the *Explanation* below.

25   See also v 17 for the general idea. Here the meaning is more specific. The subject is, literally, "a soul of blessing," i.e., one who brings blessings to others, or in v 25b, "one who waters." The parallelism is synonymous, and this is rare in the opening chapters of the collection, but cf. v 29. The saying can be associated especially with v 24a; blessing (others) leads to prosperity.

26   The catch word "blessing" ties this verse to the previous verse, and an example from real life is provided. Those who refuse to sell, because of a famine or any other reason, are profiting from a future rise in value—and the hardship they cause merits a curse. In contrast, the generous who will forego profit for the sake of the common good will receive a "blessing" that will be more tangible than popularity or fond memory (10:7), presumably from God.

27   This proverb seems to say that you get what you look for, whether for good or for evil. An oddity in the expression is that three synonyms for "seek" occur. The "favor" sought could be that of God or of humans or of both. "Evil" is used in two senses: wickedness, and also the punishment for the evil; cf. 10:24.

28   Although wealth is desirable from the point of view of the sages, e.g., 10:15, it becomes a snare if one trusts in it to the exclusion of God; cf. v 4, and also 28:25; 29:25; 1 Tim 6:17. The comparison of the just to the greening of a tree is frequent, e.g., Ps 1:3. Jer 17:7–8 contains the same sequence as here: trust and a flourishing tree. However this does not justify reading "wither" (so NRSV) instead of "fall" in v 28a, since there is no textual support for the emendation.

29   The parallelism is perhaps synonymous: the one who destroys the "house" (household; cf. 15:27) will inherit the "wind" (= nothing). It is not clear just what kind of action on the part of the master of the house is meant; perhaps tyrannical rule or incompetence in management. V 29a spells out the result: that fool will turn out to be servant to a smarter and new master. Incompetency of any kind leads to slavery.

30   The translation is uncertain (see *Note* 30.a.). The metaphors in v 30a are not clear: How can the "fruit" (good deeds?) of the just person be a "tree of life"? How can a fruit become a tree? A. Meinhold interprets this to mean that both words and actions of the just are instructive and helpful to others, and thus a source of life. He refers to 13:14, where the teaching of the wise is said to be a "tree of life." Read in that context, v 30a is intelligible. The MT of v 30b says literally that "the wise person takes souls." Meinhold interprets this to mean that the wise person wins over others to wisdom; this would agree with his interpretation of v 30a. But it is doubtful that the Hebrew can mean this (see "take my soul" in the sense of destroy life in Ps 31:14). It seems better to adopt a slight textual change. Then perhaps the verse is a contrast between the benevolent effects of the just person and the destructive efforts of the violent.

31   The verse has the appearance of an ending, following all the proverbs in this chapter which treat of the just/wicked. The judgment, presumably from God, is emphatically placed "on earth." This is an a fortiori statement. Both classes will get what comes to them, and the chapter has been at great pains to fill in details about this, but all the more so will the wicked be recompensed. This seems to be affirming judgment on the wicked, despite appearances to the contrary. But is the saying that clear? Is there an implication that the just one never sins, and therefore receives no punishment? Whybray quotes Eccl 7:20 against this. Or will the just receive only a certain amount of punishment? Since this verse is an a fortiori statement, why should the treatment of the wicked be more necessary than the treatment (presumably a reward?) of the just? There may be a hidden assumption that even the just person has weaknesses and is treated accordingly, but this is simply not comparable to what awaits "the wicked and the sinner." The author of 1 Pet 4:18 quotes the free rendering of the LXX here, but in the sense of an a fortiori with Christian presuppositions.

Explanation

The large number of just/wicked contrasts is striking, and the affinity of just/wicked with wise/fool calls attention to the discussion found in the *Explanation* for chap. 10. The general wisdom thesis is that the wise act virtuously. This identification can be documented, even if we are uncertain how the association came about. Perhaps one can assume that the Psalter, which has been described as the prayers of the just, played a role in this identification. The fact remains: just and wise are in one class, as opposed to the wicked and fool. This seems to go against the common separation of wisdom from Yahwism that has characterized biblical research in this century; see R. E. Murphy, "Wisdom and Yahwism," in *No Famine in the Land*, FS J. L. McKenzie, ed. J. Flanagan (Missoula, MT: Scholars, 1975) 117–26.

The book of Proverbs, and wisdom writings in general, place great emphasis on speech; see the *Excursus on Speech.* The modest saying in 11:12 calls attention to another perspective that is equally important: silence, knowing when to keep quiet. It was recognized that speech had a creative as well as a destructive power. Hence silence could be the most appropriate reaction. There was an insight into the ambiguity of silence; see the *Comment* on 17:27–28 and also on 26:4–5. But silence had many purposes. Especially, it could keep one out of trouble. One appreciates it by observing its opposite—garrulousness; as Prov 10:19 indicates, the more words spoken, the greater the possibility of error, even of wrongdoing. Silence is dictated by discretion, by caution, and by a clever weighing of circumstances. Much depends on the nature and situation of the person before whom one is silent. In 11:12, the silence is suggested out of kindness for another. In 30:32–33 one should have hand to mouth, i.e., to be silent after a mistake. It is necessary to be silent about the confidences of another: 25:9; cf. 11:13. The well-known figure of the "heated man" in the Teaching of Amenemope (e.g., chap. 9; Lichtheim, *AEL,* 2:153) is reflected in 22:24. There silence is assured by the command not to associate with such angry people.

Although the text of 11:7 is somewhat problematical, it is clear that hope and expectation (תקוה and תוחלת) are the issue. These same terms appear also in 10:28. How did the sages view hope? The things that are hoped for tell us something. The most common goal is to have a level of economic independence, riches of some kind. This is presupposed, and it is a reason for stressing a work ethic. At the same time, however, people must beware of allowing this laudable goal to usurp other values in life, such as social obligations. The very practical reason is given: riches disappear; they grow wings and fly to the heavens like an eagle (23:5). In addition to this slippery character of possessions, death was a distinctive limiting factor, because one had to relinquish everything, as so firmly stated in Ps 49. This affected the just and the wise as well. It would seem as though they had no advantage over the foolish and wicked. But the particulars of the human situation appear. There is a difference between the death of one whose desires have been fixed on acquiring things and the death of the one who did not make this the substance of his efforts. More grief awaits everyone, but especially so for the evil, who will lose by death their whole *raison d'être*. This cannot be said of the wise/ just since they had limited objectives: prosperity, yes, but within the limits imposed by the moral standards of wisdom and ethical teaching. There was a certain acceptance of the inevitability of death, although this comes to be questioned by Qoheleth (Eccl 2:15–16; 9:4–6). Underlying the hope that was centered in this life and its blessings is hope in the sense of relying upon the Lord. Thus 22:19 advises one to trust in God. Trust is found explicitly in 3:5–6. Hope in the Lord was such a common religious value that it is more or less presupposed.

The meaning of the terse saying in v 24 has been commented on above, but it deserves greater attention. It is a very profound and paradoxical proverb and has implications for modern living. It is pertinent to perspectives to which the author does not refer, but which are pointed out by Jean B. Elshtain in *W&W* 17 (1997) 353–57. She distinguishes between a "cash economy," which characterizes our society, and a "gift economy," and she describes the situation: "We cannot offer the gift of self to one another if we ourselves are entirely consumed by consumption; wholly given over to a relentless fast-paced life in which the more we earn, the more we spend, the more we need to earn—on and on without any apparent oasis in sight. The Christian gift economy holds that in giving we are enriched" (p. 356). See also Prov 11:24a.

Proverbs 12:1–28

Bibliography

Bühlmann, W. *Vom rechten Reden.* passim. **Scoralick, R.** *Einzelspruch.* 189–215. **Vawter, B.** "Intimations of Immortality and the Old Testament." *JBL* 91 (1972) 158–71. **Whybray, R. N.** *Composition.* 86–87, 96–97.

Translation

12:1	*A lover of instruction, a lover of knowledge;*
	but a hater of reproof, stupid!
2	*The good obtain favor from the Lord;*
	but the schemer, he condemns.

3   *No one can find a solid support in wickedness,*
        but the root of the just shall never be moved.

4   *A resourceful woman, the crown of her husband,*
        but like rot in his bones, a shameful one.

5   *The plans of the just, right!*
        the guidance of the wicked, deceit!

6   *The words of the wicked, a deadly ambush,*
        but the mouth of the upright delivers them.

7   *Overthrow the wicked, and they disappear,*
        but the house of the just will stand.

8   *A person is praised according to intelligence;*
        but the twisted of heart will be despised.

9   *Better the lightly regarded if he has a servant,*[a]
        than the one who puts on airs, but lacks sense.

10   *The just know the temperament of their livestock,*
        but the compassion of the wicked, cruel!

11   *The tiller of the soil will have enough food,*
        but whoever pursues empty nothings lacks sense.

12   *The wicked desire the snare of the evil,*[a]
        but the root of the just puts forth.[b]

13   *In the transgression of the lips, an evil trap,*[a]
        but the just person gets out of trouble.

14   *A person is filled with good from the fruit of his mouth,*
        and the work of his hands returns upon him.[a]

15   *The way of a fool, right in his own eyes,*
        but whoever listens to advice, a wise person!

16   *The anger of a fool is known immediately,*
        but whoever conceals insult, a clever one!

17   *The one who tells the truth, proves trustworthy,*
        but a lying witness, deceit!

18   *There is one who talks on and on, like sword thrusts,*
        but the tongue of the wise, healing!

19   *Truthful lips endure forever,*
        but a mere moment, the lying tongue.

20   *In the hearts of those who plan evil, deceit;*
        but for those who counsel peace, joy.

21   *No disaster befalls the just,*
        but the wicked get their fill of evil.

22   *An abomination to the Lord, lying lips,*
        but those who act truthfully, his pleasure.

23   *A clever person conceals his knowledge,*
        but the heart of fools proclaims folly.

24   *The hand of the diligent rules,*
        but slackness subjects one to labor.

25   *Anxiety in heart weighs a person down,*
        but a good word gives him joy.[a]

26   *The just person shows the way to his neighbor,*[a]
        but the way of the wicked leads them astray.

27   *Slackness will not have a roast to cook,*[a]
          but the wealth of a diligent person is precious.[b]
28   *In the path of justice, life;*
          the way of abomination, to death.[a]

Notes

9.a. So the MT, but it is also possible to vocalize thus: לוֹ וְעֹבֵד, and obtain the meaning "and works for himself," i.e., "is self-supporting." So the LXX, followed by the Vg; either interpretation makes sense with line *b*.

12.a. An attempt to translate the MT is given here, but it demonstrates that the present text cannot be translated successfully. It is corrupt, and there is no likely, much less accepted, solution. See the conjectural remedies proposed in *BHS* and various commentaries.

12.b. The Hebrew clearly has "the root of the just." On the basis of the LXX ("in strongholds") in place of "gives," בָּאיתָן has been conjectured, apparently meaning "endures." The NJV renders the entire verse: "The wicked covet the catch of evil men; the root of the righteous yields [fruit]," with the remark "meaning of Heb. uncertain."

13.a. "Evil trap," or "trap of an evil person"; both translations of the MT are possible. The LXX rendered freely "falls into traps."

14.a. The Qere would understand the Lord as the subject of the verb "cause to return."

25.a. There are unusual grammatical irregularities: a feminine subject of a verb in masculine gender in line *a*, and both verbs have feminine suffixes although these refer to a male. Whatever the reason for these inconcinnities, there is no doubt about the translation.

26.a. The Hebrew of this verse is hardly translatable. The translation follows Barucq who interprets יתר as the hiphil of תור, meaning "to make explore," and then, "to show the way." This solution seems to be adopted by the NJV: "A righteous man gives his friend direction," where it is marked with acknowledgment that the meaning of the Hebrew is uncertain. Many other solutions have been proposed, dealing with the vocalization and meaning of מרעהו ("neighbor," "pasture," "evil"). The difficulties are explored by J. Emerton in *ZAW* 76 (1964) 191–93, who translates "The righteous man is delivered (hophal of נתר) from harm (*mera'a*), but the way of the wicked leads them astray." Plöger and others adopt the conjecture in *BHS*, but the text remains problematic.

27.a. חרך is hapax and the meaning is not known ("roast"?). The context (lazy/diligent) suggests that the lazy person does not get his prey.

27.b. The second line is difficult due to the order of the words in the MT; literally, perhaps, it is: "the precious possession of a man, diligent"? Various changes in the word order have been proposed. Our translation transposes חרוץ, "diligent," with יקר, "be precious." The LXX translated: "a precious possession—a good (καθαρός) man." F. Delitzsch and A. Cohen keep the order of the MT and borrow from Rashi in order to translate: "a precious possession of a man is (to be) diligent."

28.a. The anomalies in line *b* are twofold: there are two words for "path," and the "not" is vocalized as the particle used with verbs. But "not-death," or "immortality," as some translations have, is not justified; see B. Vawter in *JBL* 91 (1971) 158–71. One should read אֶל, "to," for אַל, "not," as the ancient versions seem to have understood it as a preposition. One of the words for "path" should be emended to a term that contrasts with צְדָקָה, "righteousness," in line *a*. Although there is no consensus, the above translation presupposes תּוֹעֵבָה, "abomination." LXX has: "the paths of the malicious (lead) unto death."

Form/Structure/Setting

In keeping with this part of the collection, antithetic parallelism prevails except in vv 9 and 14. The contrast between just and wicked is more frequent than that of wise and foolish: vv 3, 5–7, 10, 12–13, 17, 20–21, 26, 28, as compared to vv 15–16, 23, 27. As already indicated, there is almost an identity between these classes. The series of sayings in vv 13–23 (although hardly v 21) has been singled out by commentators, for its emphasis on various aspects of speech. Krispenz, *Spruchkomposition*, 167, separates out vv 13–14, but demonstrates the catch words.

A. Meinhold gives a title to vv 13–23 indicating "true and false speech." Scoralick (*Einzelspruch,* 182–96, 198–215) included part of this chapter in a section extending from 11:8–12:13. Her next section is 12:14–13:2, which she considers the "nodal point" of chaps. 10–15; it creates a kind of central unity because the sayings reach backward to previous proverbs, but also forward (pp. 208–15). The framework is established by the close similarity between the beginning and end, 12:14a and 13:2a. Her arguments rely on the observation of chiasms and parallel repetitions within this section. These details may not be enough to determine structure, but they do indicate a careful assembling of the proverbs. Catch words are also evident: רשע, "wicked" (vv 2–3); "fool" (vv 15–16); "tongue" (vv 18–19); "evil" (vv 20–21).

Comment

1–3 Wisdom and justice permeate these sayings. **1** The love/hate relationship is without the emotional impact these words carry with us; it is a question of firm choice, of either/or; cf. 1:22; 9:8. The construction in v 1a juxtaposes two participles, either one of which could be the subject and the other the predicate. "Instruction" (*musar*) also denotes the discipline that is necessary. "Knowledge" is, as usual, practically oriented, but it also involves heeding the teachings of the sages. By definition the wise are docile, and open to reprimand; if not, one is as stupid as a brute animal; cf. Ps 32:9. **2** For v 2a see 8:35b, where the Lord's "favor" follows upon finding Wisdom. Virtue and wisdom come together in this manifestation of the Lord's differentiation between the good person and the schemer. The catch word linking up with v 3 is "condemn" (wickedness). **3** The permanence of the just and the evanescence or rootlessness of the wicked is a common thought; cf. v 7 and also 10:7, 25, 30. See also J. Hausmann, *Menschenbild,* 47–50. As O. Plöger remarks, while one does not learn anything new, there is a certain charm in the constant variation of the same old truth; repetition the mother of wisdom?

4 This verse has no relation to the context, but the importance of the אשת חיל, "resourceful woman"? "valorous wife"? is indicated by the poem dedicated to her in 31:10–31; cf. Ruth 3:11. It is typical of the culture that her value is calculated in relationship to the male. "Crown" serves as a symbol of the honor she brings to husband and home, just the contrary to the inner canker that an unworthy wife inflicts upon him.

5–7 The verses are bound by the obvious catch words. **5** The opposing characteristics of the just and wicked can hardly be expressed more clearly, and this difference is heightened in the next verse. "Guidance" is used in a favorable sense in 1:4. **6** See also 12:13. The Hebrew is more graphic: "deadly ambush" is literally "ambush for blood." The speech of the wicked is murderous. But they are answered by the just who escape from such attack. The situation is not specified, but it could be a judicial setting, and the upright are able to mount arguments that secure justice for "them," probably themselves rather than others. So W. Bühlmann, *Vom rechten Reden,* 301–2. **7** See the *Comment* on v 3 and cf. 10:25. Some catastrophe will wipe out the wicked, and that is the end of them. In contrast, the "house" of the just will remain, no matter the difficulties. The modern must recognize the full import of the metaphor of the "house." It stands for the household and everything precious to the individual, making it possible for him to truly live. Thus, in 14:11, the house of the wicked is destroyed, but the "tent" of the upright flourishes. Perhaps a modern counterpart would be the appreciation of what the "house" has meant to the many people in the United States whose homes and possessions have been devastated by floodwaters.

8 "Intelligence" (שכל) is to be understood in a practical sense, and the only praise that is genuine is to come from another (Prov 27:2), not from oneself. In fact, praise is the test of a person, 27:21b. The point of the saying is that personal wisdom wins the attention and approval of neighbors; cf. 13:15a. In contrast, there will be only contempt for whoever lacks the wisdom to cope with life ("twisted of heart/mind").

9 As indicated in *Note* 9.a., two translations of this "better" saying are possible. In either case the contrast is between a person of modest but independent means, whether working for oneself or able to have a servant, and a pretentious individual who lives beyond his means. The proverb sounds the note of sincerity about oneself and the implications for social status. Cf. Sir 10:27.

10–11 These two proverbs deal with farm life: care of animals and tilling the soil. **10** Concern for the נפש of the animals, their needs and desires and quirks, is a matter not merely of profit (cf. 27:23, 29), but of virtue, and the wicked lack this ability. The KJV translated "compassion" from the root רחם, with the expressive phrase "tender mercies," a kind of oxymoron when joined with the cruel wicked. **11** See the variant in 28:19. The saying underscores the application and diligence of a farmer, as opposed to the person who is a dilettante about the task of living. The "empty" things are not further defined, but presumably they are out of order with farm life—either laziness or incompetence. Similar advice is found in the Teaching of Amenemope (6:8, 17–18; *AEL,* 2:152), but one cannot suppose that such an obvious recommendation needed to be borrowed from a foreign source.

12 *Notes* 12.a. and 12.b. indicate the uncertainty of this proverb. Commentators end up explaining a text they have restored with the help of the versions and some ingenuity. The above translation of v 12a is intended as a literal rendering of the Hebrew, and in v 12b the text certainly reads "the root of the just." As translated, there is a contrast between the just and wicked that is along the usual lines. We can apply here what O. Plöger says of his own conjectural rendition of the verse: "a chase after wind"; cf. Eccl 1:14.

13–23 Commentators generally place these proverbs under the heading of speech; only v 21 is the exception. This topic was a favorite for the sages. Speech, silence, and self-control are all bound up together. Moreover, speech is viewed from more than one aspect; e.g., there is correct speech and deceitful speech. Another point of emphasis is the Hebrew manner of expressing speech by means of the parts of the body: lips, tongue, mouth, and even the palate. Every effort is made in the above translation to convey literally that use of the bodily organs. **13** See *Note* 13.a.; the "evil trap" can be a snare set by the evil in which they themselves are caught, or the trap by which the evil intend to catch others. In any case, the just cannot be ensnared by any wiles. **14** As indicated above, Scoralick regards 12:14–13:2 as a unit. V 14 extends the meaning of v 13. The parallelism is not antithetic; the second line specifies or adds to the first line. V 14a has a variant in 13:2 and 18:20. The image in line *a* is that a person's good words bring good fruit or result, whether for self or for others. Line *b* continues the good results; the image shifts to "hands" so that actions are meant. Thus the idea is that one reaps what one sows. The effects correspond to the nature of the cause, in line with the well-known "deed-consequence" theory advocated by K. Koch. See the *Comment* on 10:2. There is no denying the existence of a deed-consequence mentality, but it is difficult to gauge the amount of adherence to it; was it more expectation than fact? And did it lead to disappointment by its frequent default? Moreover, it should be noted that the Qere reading in this verse suggests that the subject ("he") is the Lord.   **15**   The sages distrusted merely personal opinion, and this is shown in many sayings about being "wise in one's own eyes": Prov 3:7; 26:12. Any conclusion that relies on "one's own eyes" can easily be a case of self-deception. Hence the wise listen to the advice of others; cf. 13:10b.   **16**   The attitude described in v 15 may be reflected in v 16, where the wise person exercises self-control in contrast to the fool whose emotions are immediately displayed when he is challenged. The saying envisages some sparring with others. If they attack, the wise course is to stay cool and conceal the insult. Anger will only lead one to play into the hands of an opponent.   **17**   The vocabulary indicates a judicial setting, and there are several variants of this insistence on true witness; cf. 6:19; 14:5, 25; 19:5, 9; 21:28. V 17b is particularly emphatic; such a witness is, as it were, deceit incarnate. Wisdom's concern is with the inner nature of the individual, the honesty and sincerity that must be displayed in critical cases. The verb "tells" is literally "breathes"; truth is to be something as natural as breathing. It is not surprising then that he "proves trustworthy," literally "proclaims justice."   **18**   The "there is" (שׁ) formula is frequent in Proverbs for the purpose of stating a fact. The speaker is one who is thoughtless and rambles on. But this is compared to sword thrusts; it is deadly. This drastic comparison indicates how seriously loquaciousness is condemned. The contrast is the healing brought about by the tongue of the wise.   **19**   "Tongue" is a catch word with v 18, but it is here associated with deceit. The chiasm heightens the contrast between the enduring truth and the lie of the moment. The translation attempts to bring out the clever chiasm of the Hebrew. The "mere moment" is literally the "blink of an eye." One can interpret this momentary life of a lie as meaning that it will be overcome by truth and hence will not prevail. This is the conclusion of the famous story of the bodyguards of Darius in 1 Esdr 3:1–4:4: "Great is truth and strongest of all!" But v 19b is rather overoptimistic, especially in view of v 18, where speech, and in this case lies, is compared to the deadly sword.   **20**   The contrast between deceit and joy is unusual. By deceit is meant probably not only the self-deception that afflicts the evil, but the intrigue they practice with others. The joy that comes to those who bring peace to the community derives from the inner satisfaction they experience at the well-being or shalom that they create.   **21**   This proverb falls outside the group, vv 13–24, and is a very general statement of the law of retribution that undergirds the book: no harm for the just; the wicked will experience evil, in the sense of lasting, penetrating trouble. Especially in view of later wisdom reflection, as in Job and Ecclesiastes, the limitations of this principle must be recalled. Thus, it is not adequate to comment, with Meinhold (p. 212), that v 21a can never be realized on earth, but only in the kingdom of God. He adds, "if the sage claims this for the present time, then he can mean it only in a spiritual metaphorical sense: that everything (including the hard things) turns out best for the just person." This certainly goes beyond the perspective of this verse. It is a theological view that is supplied from some other source; some might share that view, but it is not in the text.   **22**   The theme of truth in speech returns, and the phrase in v 22 is literally "do (the) truth"; cf. John 3:21. The opposition between abomination and favor (of God) was already used in 11:20; cf. also 12:2. This verse has a parallel in Amenemope, chap. 10, "Do not speak falsely to a man, The God abhors it" (13:15–16; Lichtheim, *AEL*, 2:154). The saying adds little to vv 17 or 19, except that the attitude of God is made explicit.   **23**   The contrast is between the one who speaks in due measure, and the fool whose talk betrays his incompetence. Silence at the proper time is the issue here; one must know when to speak and when to keep silent. The idea was already expressed in v 16; see also 10:14; 17:27 and the clever saying in Sir 21:26, "In the mouth of fools, their heart / in the heart of the wise, their mouth."

24   Laziness has been contrasted with diligence several times before (10:4–5). The sharpness of this saying is that it raises the issue of the independence of a person. The specter of forced labor, or corvée (cf. 1 Kgs 5:28), confronts the sluggard. In contrast, the diligent will be master of his own fate. Cf. also v 27.

25   The topic of speech returns; the proverb is a psychological observation without an explicit command. The "good word" (literally, in line *b*) is spoken by one who brings some comfort to the afflicted. The trouble is not specified, but there is no question that the "word" transforms the situation. There is perhaps an implicit recommendation to be cheerful oneself, and even to communicate that to others. The importance of cultivating cheerfulness in oneself is developed by Sirach, Sir 30:21–24.

26   See *Note* 26.a. Not much can be said in explanation of a text that is so uncertain as this. The meaning of line *b* (going astray) suggests that line *a* deals with direction. If so, the sense of the proverb is that the just provides proper direction, whereas the wicked leads himself and others into trouble.

27   Again, the text of the MT is uncertain; see *Notes* 27.a. and 27.b. There is a contrast between the diligent and the slack; the same word, literally "slackness," occurs also in v 24b. The details are not clear. As translated, line *a* indicates that the lazy person will not acquire food for sustenance, in contrast to the diligent person who will attain possessions that are described as "precious."

28   See *Note* 28.a. The oddity about this uncertain text is that its general meaning is clear: life is associated with the path to justice, and, less clearly, death is associated with another "way." In any case, one is not to seek for immortality in this verse. That justice delivers from death (and the meaning of this) has already been indicated; see the *Comment* on 10:2b and 11:4b.

Explanation

The concentration on speech in this chapter (vv 6, 13–23) underscores the importance of the word in the wisdom tradition. See the discussion of Prov 11:12 in the *Explanation* for chap. 11. Also, there is a reappearance of that compatible identification of wisdom and justice that has also been noted earlier in the book; see also the *Explanation* in chap. 11. While some would question this identification, there are two considerations to be weighed. First, how did such a large number of just/wicked sayings come to be bunched in with the wise/foolish proverbs? The positioning is obvious, and it strongly indicates at least that the mutuality between these classifications was recognized by the editor. Second, the fate of the wicked bears remarkable similarity to the fate of the foolish. For both the fateful choice is between life and death. Moreover, the "fear of the Lord/God"— which is the beginning of wisdom—involves decisions that are in the moral realm. Thus, in 14:2 the one who fears the Lord is the one who walks in his integrity. Fear of the Lord means trust in God, who becomes a refuge (14:26) and a shield (30:5). In 15:33 fear of the Lord is a bridge to wisdom, and in 16:6 it means turning from moral evil. Such connections bind wisdom and justice ever more tightly. See the *Excursus on Fear of the Lord.*

Proverbs 13:1–25

Bibliography

Bühlmann, W. *Vom rechten Reden,* passim. **Krispenz, J.** *Spruchkomposition.* 63–70. **Scoralick, R.** *Einzelspruch.* 215–22. **Whybray, R. N.** *Composition.* 99–100.

Translation

13:1   A wise son—discipline by a father,
          but a scoffer does not heed a scolding.[a]

2   A person eats good things from the fruit of the mouth,
          but the desire of the greedy, violence.

3   Whoever guards his mouth, one who preserves his life;
          whoever opens wide the lips, ruin for him.

4   A lazy person has great craving, but nothing else![a]
          but the desire of the diligent is fulfilled.

5   The just person hates a deceitful word,
          but the wicked causes shame[a] and disgrace.

6   Justice preserves the blameless in his path,
          but wickedness misleads the sinner.[a]

7   There is a person who pretends to riches, but with not a thing;
          who pretends to be poor, but with great wealth!

8   Ransom for the life of a man: his riches,
          but a poor person hears no threat.[a]

9   The light of the just rejoices,[a]
          but the lamp of the wicked goes out.

10   Arrogance yields only[a] quarreling,
          but with those who take advice, wisdom.

11   Wealth in haste[a] counts for little,
          but one who gathers by hand will have much.[b]

12   Hope deferred, sickness of heart;
          but a tree of life, desire fulfilled.

13   One who despises a word, it will go badly[a] for him,
          but one who reveres a command, he will be rewarded.

14　　　*The teaching of the wise, a fountain of life,*
　　　　　　for turning from deadly snares.
15　　　*Good insight brings favor,*
　　　　　　but the way of the faithless is their ruin.[a]
16　　　*Every clever person acts with knowledge,*
　　　　　　but a fool spouts folly.
17　　　*A wicked messenger falls into evil,*[a]
　　　　　　but a trustworthy envoy, healing!
18　　　*Poverty and shame: whoever rejects instruction!*
　　　　　　But whoever heeds reproof will be honored.
19　　　*A desire realized is sweet to a person,*
　　　　　　and an abomination to fools: turning from evil.
20　　　*Walk with the wise and be wise!*[a]
　　　　　　But the companion of fools fares badly.
21　　　*Evil pursues sinners,*
　　　　　　but as for the just, there is a good reward.[a]
22　　　*A good person leaves an inheritance to grandchildren,*
　　　　　　but stored up for the just: the wealth of a sinner.
23　　　*An abundance of food, the tillage of the poor,*
　　　　　　but property is swept away unjustly.[a]
24　　　*Whoever spares the rod, a hater of his son,*
　　　　　　but whoever loves him disciplines him early on.
25　　　*A just person, one who eats and satisfies hunger,*
　　　　　　but the belly of the wicked is empty.

Notes

1.a. The MT in line *a* provides a striking example of juxtaposition; literally, "a wise son—discipline (by) a father." Various conjectures have been proposed, the most common being to insert אהב, "love," on the basis of 12:1. Or one might claim that שמע, "heed," has been understood as doing double duty, although it is in the second and not the first line. The LXX reads "docile to the father," perhaps an interpretation, or else presupposing שמע. There is no need for changes if the juxtapositional character of these proverbial sayings is recognized.

4.a. נפשו, "his desire," can be explained as showing the (Aramaic) anticipatory suffix, or perhaps the survival of an archaic nominative (Joüon §93ab); a literal translation is "the desire (not the soul) of the lazy one craves, but nothing!"

5.a. The Hebrew verb derives from the word "stench," and hence can be interpreted as "odious" or "shameful." However, a slight emendation, preferred by *BHS,* yields the normal word for shame (בוש) which appears in Prov 19:26, parallel to the verb חפר, "cause disgrace," as here.

6.a. Both lines begin with personification; the objects are abstract, but are interpreted here as concrete, "one whose path is upright," "the sinner"; cf. also *Note* 10:29.a.

8.a. Although the last three words of the verse are identical with v 1, there is no reason to change the text, as some propose; see the *Comment.*

9.a. The antithesis between rejoice and be extinguished is suspect, but the evidence from the Greek διὰ παντός, "through everything" or "always," is too vague to be helpful. If "rejoice" is vocalized in the piel to mean "give joy," the parallelism would be better, but there could be personification here; see the *Comment.*

10.a. The revocalization of רך, "only," to רך yields "lightheaded" in many translations; this does not seem necessary. Some would suggest רע, "an evil one," on the basis of the Greek κακός, "a bad one."

11.a. Read מבהל, indicating "haste," for the questionable מהבל, "from nothing (?)," in the MT, as suggested in *BHS*; cf. LXX, Vg, also 20:21.

11.b. "By hand" indicates a slow, even gradual, process of gathering (is the image taken from farming?); it is closer to the Hebrew (literally, "on the hand") than the usual paraphrase.

13.a. There is no reason to revocalize the verb; לֹו, "for him," is the ethical dative, with the niphal. The Greek has an additional verse, a not infrequent phenomenon; see also 13:9.

15.a. The meaning of אֵיתָן, "permanent?" is uncertain; it is better to read אֵידָם, "their ruin," on the basis of the Greek ἀπωλεία, "destruction."

17.a. The MT makes sense, so there is no pressing need for a vocalization in the hiphil (יַפֵּל), for the sake of a stricter parallelism.

20.a. The translation follows the Ketib; the Qere ("one who walks" and "becomes wise") gives stricter parallelism, but there is hardly a change in meaning. The alliteration in v 20b is striking: *wrʿh ksylym yruʿ*.

21.a. Literally, line *b* has "he (God?) rewards the just with good"; or possible also is "good (i.e., good fortune) rewards the just."

23.a. Literally, line *a* has "an abundance of food, the tillage of chiefs." It is better to interpret רָאשִׁים as the plural participle from רוּשׁ, "poor." Line *b* is difficult, and the Greek had a different *Vorlage*. The above translation is possible (literally, "property is swept away with no right" [or "there is a sweeping away …"]). There does not seem to be a connection between the two lines, unless there is simply an indication that despite the abundance of food the poor are treated unjustly. The text may be corrupt.

Form/Structure/Setting

It is very difficult to find any structure for this chapter. The most significant sign is the appearance of catch words. Translation conceals the threefold repetition of the catch word נֶפֶשׁ, "desire, life," in vv 2–4, but the repetition of "preserve" in vv 3, 7 is clear. Forms of just/wicked unite both sayings in vv 5–6 (as in 10:2–3); cf. also vv 9, 25. The psychological observation in v 12 has a partial echo in v 19. V 14 has a remarkable variant in 14:27, and this becomes a sign for a particular unit (13:14–14:27) in the analysis of Scoralick; see the *Explanation* below. The usual antitheses appear, except in v 14, and perhaps v 22; v 23 is problematical. Certain topics are repeated, such as family instruction and discipline in vv 1, 18, 24. A. Meinhold attempts to unite vv 12–19 under the theme of desire, and vv 20–25 are entitled "the future of the wise son," but the unity is not clear. For Whybray (p. 99) "this chapter is dominated by the need to accept instruction and discipline"; see *Explanation* below. Krispenz, pp. 63–70, unites vv 15–25 (cf. the table on p. 168) but sees vv 15–21 given over to the question of how wisdom and ethics relate to each other, with the clarification in v 21.

Comment

1 See *Note* 1.a. The antithesis suggests that מוּסָר has the nuance of discipline as well as "instruction." "Scolding" was part of the educative process, but disregarded by the unruly; see also v 24. As happens so often in wisdom teaching, "hear" and "obey" are practically synonymous.

2–3 Both of these sayings deal with speech. **2** The "fruit of the mouth" is idiomatic for "words," and the phrase is found in 12:14 and again in 18:20 (all three passages analyzed in W. Bühlmann, *Vom rechten Reden*, 306–15). L. Alonso Schökel explains the image: "the mouth eats the fruits of a tree or the earth; but also the mouth is a tree that produces fruits that it has to eat. Language is not neutral, not sterile; it initiates a process that will come back to its origin, as a strict result." Although "good things" are specified here, the image can be applied to good or evil without distinction, as 18:21 (see the *Comment* there) makes clear: the tongue produces life and death. Line *b* (with נֶפֶשׁ, "desire," the catch word for vv 2–4) intensifies line *a* by describing both the food and the yield from the greedy or treacherous: violence. It is not simply the words, but the "desire," or שֶׁפֶנ, that issues in violence. **3** The ideal of the sage is the person who exercises self-control, especially as regards speech, e.g., 10:19, 21 and cf. 21:23. The contrast in this verse is between the silent type who chooses words well, and the fool whose open mouth is full of mere chatter (cf. Eccl 10:12–14a) that turns out to be ruinous to himself; cf. 18:7. See the *Explanation* in chap. 11.

4 Literally, the Hebrew says that the שֶׁפֶנ, "desire," of the diligent is "fattened." The point is that mere desire is utterly futile; industry is what counts. Lazy people are victims of the desires (literally שַׁפְנוּ) that consume them, and they simply have nothing to show for themselves.

5–6 These verses are united by the catch words just/wicked. **5** The "word of deceit" is simply plain lies, whatever might be the particular situation. V 5a could refer either to the harm caused to a community by the wicked person, presumably through lies or even calumny, or it may be simply descriptive of his character. In any case, a high premium is placed on honest speech. **6** See *Note* 6.a. The personification of vice and virtue is relatively rare in this book (but cf. 11:4–6), and of course virtue is the clear victor. The just/wicked contrast continues in v 9.

7–8 Both sayings have a common subject, riches; cf. also 15:6. ⟨**7** This proverb, which should be compared to 11:24, proclaims a paradox, but at the same time is ambiguous. The paradox is the contrast between the appearance and reality, being rich and having nothing, and being poor yet also rich. On the one hand, this could be merely an observation, an assessment of fact; appearances are deceiving. No moral issue need be involved; no motives are given. The nuance of "pretend," i.e., act differently, is not necessarily to deceive anyone. On the other hand, one can apply moral considerations by questioning the motives of individuals: Does the wealth of the poor person consist in another order of values, such as dependence upon God, or else in being satisfied with his lot? Is the "pretense" in either person a reprehensible act? Such questions are legitimate, and lead to other interpretations, but these seem to go beyond the literal sense and bring in extrinsic circumstances that lose sight of the irony implicit in the literal sense. **8** Money creates differences. There are the rich and the poor, but it is not said that one is better off than the other. True, the rich person is able to offer a ransom for life when threatened; perhaps the situation envisioned is that of ransom for census enrollment; cf. Exod 30:13. But the deeper question is: What led to such a saying as this? It is because they are wealthy that the rich have reason to fear for possible losses, e.g., that some would try to deprive them of their wealth, etc. Then they get entangled trying to extricate themselves, although they have the means for this. But the poor, precisely because they are poor, do not even merit a threat; they are safe because they have nothing to pay with. So although their financial condition cannot compare to that of the rich person, they are in a sense free of the worries of the wealthy. They have nothing and, ironically, have nothing to lose. The two examples seem to balance each other, without implying that one is better than the other. The final three words are striking because they repeat the final three words of v 1, but the context in both cases determines the meaning.

9 "Light" is one of the key symbols in the Bible, e.g., Prov 4:8–9; Eccl 11:7–8; Job 29:3, representing life with all its several levels of meaning. The rejoicing of the lamp has been questioned because of the unusual personification. See *Note* 9.a. For the association of "light" with "lamp," see Prov 6:23, but now in v 9 there is opposition: the lamp, whose light is artificial, is here a symbol of a flickering life, of darkness, and of gloom for the wicked.

10 See *Note* 10.a. If the translation can stand, there is a clear opposition between the arrogant and those who take advice. The latter are, by definition, the wise; cf. 19:20. The proud are not open to change; they know it all. Listening to others, on the contrary, brings about more options, and ultimately the opportunity to reach agreement, and thus wisdom.

11 See *Note* 11.a. "Wealth" picks up on v 7b. Whatever is associated with haste always seems suspect to the sage. This view is particularly applicable to riches; haste might imply a lack of appreciation for wealth, or more likely it suggests some kind of disreputable action, perhaps at the expense of others; cf. 20:21; 28:20b, 22a.

12 Of this verse Alonso Schökel remarks that it sounds like a kind of objection to the preceding, along with an answer. Collecting little by little may lead to abundance, but it takes time, and one's expectation may seem to be deferred (v 12a). However, the saying in itself merely registers a psychological observation. There is no moral judgment such as to be found in the related proverb, v 19. Rather, the verse registers the discouragement that comes from having one's hopes thwarted or unrealized, and the joy that comes from attaining what one desires. For the tree of life, see the *Comment* on 3:18.

13–14 "Word," "command," and "teaching of the wise" give a certain unity to these verses. The word and command refer, at least in the first instance, to the teaching of the sage, not to the Decalogue. The Hebrew style is very succinct. While the precise meaning of the verb in v 13a is not clear (see *Note* 13.a.), the antithetic parallelism indicates adversity for the one who despises the word. **14** This saying is almost identical with 14:27. The string of proverbs with antithetic parallelism is broken at this point, but there are some noteworthy associations with previous proverbs. The "fountain of life" is a high evaluation of wisdom teaching; cf. 10:11; 16:22. It also hearkens back to the "tree of life" in v 12. Again, life is to be understood in its total meaning: not just being spared from imminent or unexpected death, but also embracing a high quality of life. Thus one may regard v 14b as specifying the assurance in v 14a.

15–16 The advantages of wisdom are further described in these sayings. **15** See *Note* 15.a. The phrase translated as "good insight," demanded by the context, is the same as for "good esteem" in Prov 3:4. The typical law of retribution is at work here, and it is implied in the next verse. **16** The proverb contrasts the thoughtfulness that characterizes the actions of the clever with the impetuousness of the fool who blurts out folly. This stark contrast between the wise and the fool is merely a variation on the general theme of the superiority of wisdom. The frequency of such proverbs (see 12:23 and 5:2) would suggest that the sages needed to constantly emphasize the theme for the sake of their audience.

17 See *Note* 17.a. In the absence of other means of communication, the role of the messenger was very important; see 10:26 (laziness condemned); 22:21 (reliability stressed); 25:13; 26:6. Here the emphasis is upon the wicked character of the messenger who can distort the message, or even work deliberately against the will of the one who is trying to communicate with another. The "healing" achieved by the faithful messenger is not further described; it might even be the relief he brings to the one who sent him. The antithetic parallelism is vague.

18 A reprise of the theme in v 1 (cf. 12:1) points out the social results of acceptance or rejection of instruction. In all likelihood, one should not view instruction (מוסר) apart from discipline; they seem to be inseparable in practice. מוסר and תוכחת, "reproof," are a common word pair; cf. 10:17; 15:5, 32. The consequences, poverty and shame, are emphasized by their positioning in the juxtaposition of subject and predicate in v 18a.

19 There does not seem to be any connection between the two lines of the saying; they are reflected in different contexts in 13:12 and in 29:27 ("abomination"); line *a* is a psychological observation, and line *b* associates evil conduct with fools. In contrast to v 12 (see the *Comment* there), this proverb takes an ethical turn. The "abomination" phrase is unusual. Normally it is associated with the Lord, describing the divine reaction to unsatisfactory conduct, but here it designates the attitude of fools (כסיל) who feel a revulsion at the idea of turning from evil. Note the strong effect produced by the juxtaposition in v 19b; again the association of folly and evil is maintained.

20 See *Note* 20.a. Training in wisdom picks up v 1, and is continued in v 24; see also vv 10, 14. There is only a slight difference between the Qere reading and the Ketib. The former indicates that association with the wise produces a wise person. The latter is a command to associate with the wise in order to attain wisdom. In any case, the instruction of the sages, it was felt, needed support from people who lived wisely and were living examples of wisdom. A modern analogy would be the school teacher who judges that the home situation of a student must be of such quality as to reinforce education.

21–22 "Good" (טוב) is a catch word, although it stands for both person and thing in these verses; another is "sinner" (חטא).   **21** See *Note* 21.a. Here "evil" is personified as pursuing the evildoer who brings it into existence. It can include any misfortune that typically afflicts the sinner. A specific evil is mentioned in v 22b: the wicked will eventually lose their wealth. Although "sinner" can mean merely one who misses the mark, it seems to have an unmistakable moral nuance in these verses (*contra* Hausmann, *Menschenbild*, 54). In v 21b "good" might possibly be a personification, but more likely the Lord is the presumed subject of the verb "reward." In any case, there is a contrast between the just and sinners.   **22** It is important that death will not catch the "good" person napping; no matter the manner of his death, he will leave a goodly inheritance for his progeny. Thus should goodness be served. On the contrary, there can be no corresponding profit for the sinner. Even if he acquires wealth, he is not to enjoy it, according to the law of retribution. Indeed he merely stores it up for the just person; cf. 28:8; Job 27:16–17, and the *Comment* on Eccl 2:27 in R. E. Murphy, *Ecclesiastes*, WBC 23A (Dallas: Word Books, 1992).

23 For this uncertain verse, see *Note* 23.a. As translated above, it indicates that the labors of the poor are favored by a successful harvest, or whatever business that would bring them food. In contrast to this, line *b* asserts that unjust measures can deprive people, presumably the poor of v 23a, of their substance or property (יש).

24 Corporal punishment for unruly children was simply taken for granted in ancient Israel and Egypt, and it is mentioned frequently in Proverbs, e.g., 19:18;

23:13–14; cf. Sir 30:1–13. The paradox of the action is mirrored in the love/hate contrast: a beating is a sign of love. O. Plöger would place this verse at the end of the chapter after v 25 because of a "thematic connection" with v 1, providing a kind of framework to the chapter. L. Alonso Schökel grants that this move has didactic value, but it is without relevance for establishing the original text.

25 The contrast between the just/wicked is manifested here by underscoring the hunger/satisfaction that will spell the difference in the fate of these classes; cf. also 10:3.

Explanation

Within this chapter there are several instances of reprise, in varying forms, as indicated in the comment above. But there is no overarching unity. The comment has tried as much as possible to associate proverbs according to their sequence, based on the catch-word principle as well as on meaning. R. N. Whybray observes that the emphasis on the theme of instruction/discipline is to be found in vv 1, 13, 14, 18, 20, and 24, and is also echoed in vv 10, 15, and 16. But this hardly justifies his conclusion that "the chapter now constitutes a single instruction though of a fairly loose kind. Verses 1 and 24 with their specific references to the education of children mark its beginning and end" (*Composition*, 99). The observations are more helpful than the conclusion that we have here a "single instruction." The true "instruction" is exemplified in chaps. 1–9, which are obviously quite different.

The view of R. Scoralick is guided by catch words and variations. This leads her to recognize a unit in 13:14–14:27, framed by two remarkable variants on the fountain of life. As far as chap. 13 is concerned, she proposes, with some reservation, a continuity in 13:14–19 and in 13:20–14:2–14:7. The catch words for vv 14–19 are "turn from" (evil/deadly snares) and the use of "go" (הלך) in 13:20, 14:1, and 14:7. The advantage of such divisions is that one does not have to strain to recognize similarity of content; it is the catch words that speak for themselves and which can embrace disparate material.

Van Leeuwen in his commentary (NIB, 5:135) remarks about 13:24 that the "deeper issue in this proverb is the paradox of 'tough love,' both in the family and in society." He points out the obvious cases of disciplining young children, and he raises the question of the dehumanization of incarceration. One should honor the principle that "when legitimate authority fails to punish, we treat wrongdoers as less than human," but at the same time the situation is mightily affected by rehabilitation possibilities and impossible prison conditions.

Proverbs 14:1–35

Bibliography

Krispenz, J. *Spruchkomposition.* 68–70. **Scoralick, R.** *Einzelspruch.* 218–25. **Vattioni, F.** "La casa della sagezza (Prov 9:1; 14:1)." *Augustinianum* 7 (1967) 349–51. **Whybray, R. N.** *Composition.* 100–103.

Translation

14:1   *Wisdom*[a] *has built her house,*
     but Folly tears hers down by her own hands.

2   *Whoever walks uprightly: one who fears the Lord,*
     but whoever is devious in his ways: one who despises him.

3   *In the mouth of a fool, a shoot of pride,*[a]
     but the lips of the wise preserve them.[b]

4   *In the absence of oxen, the crib is empty,*
     but abundant produce, by the strength of an ox.[a]

5   *A trustworthy witness will not lie,*
     but a false witness spreads lies.

6   *The scoffer seeks wisdom, in vain!*
     but knowledge is easy for the intelligent.

7   *Stay away from a foolish person,*
     for you do not find knowledge on those lips![a]

8   *The wisdom of the clever: the understanding of their way,*
     but the folly of fools: deception.

9   *Fools scoff at a guilt offering,*
     but among the upright, favor.[a]

10   *The heart knows its bitterness of spirit,*
     and in its joy another[a] *cannot share.*

11   *The house of the wicked will be destroyed,*
     but the tent of the upright shall flourish.

12   *There is a way that seems right to a person,*
     but its end, ways to death.

13   *Even in laughter the heart may be sad,*
     and the end of joy, grief.[a]

14   *The unsteady of heart get their fill of their ways,*
     and good people, of their deeds.[a]

15   *The simple person believes everything,*
     but the clever one watches his step.

16   *The wise person: fearing and turning from evil,*
     but the fool: reckless and overconfident.

17   *The quick-tempered commit folly,*
     and the schemer is hated.[a]

18   *The simple inherit folly,*
     but the clever are crowned with knowledge.[a]

19   *The evil bow before the good,*
     and the wicked, at the gates of the just.

20   *The poor are hated even by their neighbor,*
     but those who love the rich, many!

21   *Whoever despises his neighbor, a sinner,*
     but happy, whoever is kind to the poor![a]

22   *Do not those who plan evil go astray?*
     But those who plan good, kindness and fidelity.

23   *In all work there will be profit,*
     but the talk of the lips—only to deprivation!

24   *The crown of the wise, their riches;*
       the folly of fools, folly! [a]

25   *A trusty witness, one who delivers souls,*
       but whoever spreads lies, deceit.

26   *The fear of the Lord, strength to trust in,*
       and one's children [a] *will have a refuge.*

27   *The fear of the Lord, a fountain of life,*
       to turn from the snares of death.

28   *A large population, a king's glory,*
       but without people, a leader's ruin.

29   *Slow to anger, great intelligence,*
       but the quick-tempered exalts [a] *folly.*

30   *The life of the body, a calm* [a] *heart,*
       but rot in the bones, envy.

31   *Whoever oppresses the needy blasphemes his maker,*
       but whoever is kind to the poor honors him.

32   *The wicked is overthrown by his evil,*
       but the just, one who relies on his integrity. [a]

33   *Wisdom nestles in the heart of the intelligent,*
       but among fools can it come to be known? [a]

34   *Justice exalts a nation,*
       but sin, a reproach [a] *for a people.*

35   *The favor of a king, for a clever servant,*
       but his wrath is for a shameful one. [a]

Notes

1.a. The MT has literally, "wisdom of women," which JPS translates as "the wisest of women." נשׁים, "women," overloads the line, and if it is deleted, as suggested in *BHS,* the text is identical with 9:1. Also with 9:1, חכמות can be revocalized to read חָכְמוֹת; refer to *Note* 1:20.a.

3.a. So the MT; חטר (often translated as "rod") is a rare word, elsewhere only in Isa 11:1, meaning "shoot." The ancient versions support the meaning "rod," a cudgel of some kind, but the image is odd: how is the mouth a rod for pride? A common correction is גוה for גאוה ("his back" for "pride"), but it has no basis in the ancient versions. The role of the "mouth" still remains unclear; if it speaks proud things, perhaps they are a rod for the back of the speaker? W. Bühlmann (*Vom rechten Reden,* 127–29) translates the MT reasonably: "In the mouth of a fool is a shoot of pride." That is to say, the mouth shoots forth arrogant words.

3.b. With the versions read תשׁמרום, "preserves them," as indicated in *BHS;* see Joüon §44c, for a comment on the abnormal form. The plural suffix is to be understood as referring back to the wise (*contra* Bühlmann).

4.a. A pure/clean (so the interpretation of בר = καθαραί in LXX) crib is an empty crib. The meaning "grain" (so W. McKane, "a crib of grain") is also possible. There is no need to adopt the conjectural emendation proposed in *BHS.*

7.a. The Hebrew is difficult, especially in v 7b. The LXX reads "all is contrary to the foolish person, but wise lips are weapons of perception." This is either highly interpretative or based on a different *Vorlage.* The MT can be translated "you (will have) known no lips of knowledge"; hence, you find no knowledge on those lips.

9.a. Any translation of this verse is quite uncertain. In v 9a it is not clear if the subject is "guilt offering" (if this is the meaning of אשׁם) or "fools"; if "fools," the verb should be normally in the plural. The LXX speaks of the houses of the impious and just, and this has triggered various doubtful emendations. There is no consensus on the reading of this verse, as the tortured explanations of commentators demonstrate; cf. also A. Bonora, "L'enigmatico proverbio di Pr 14,9," *RivB* 36 (1988) 61–66.

10.a. The reading of the Greek, "pride" for "a stranger" (or "another"), indicated in *BHS* can be safely disregarded.

13.a. As *BHS* suggests, one should attach the final *he* (read as definite article) to the following word; thus: אחרית השׂמחה, "the end of joy."

14.a. V 14b reads literally "and the good man from (upon) himself." This is not at all clear; it is better to read וממעלליו, "and from his deeds," as indicated in *BHS*.

17.a. There is no antithesis in this verse, and changes have been suggested; the LXX provides the antithesis (reading ישׂא, "lifts," for ישׂנא, "hates"): "the thoughtful man endures much." But the MT can be retained. The phrase translated as "schemer" occurs in that sense in Prov 12:2.

18.a. The MT has "inherit folly" in line *a*, but in light of Prov 25:12 *BHS* conjectures a noun, "ornament"; others impute the meaning "adorn" as if the verb were denominative from חלי, "ornament." This improves the parallelism, but it is on shaky semantic ground, and has no support from the ancient versions. יכתרו, "crowned," is the hiphil of a rare denominative verb; cf. GKC §53g.

21.a. It is better to read the Ketib, in contrast to the Qere "the humble."

24.a. The verse looks suspicious to many scholars. Hence there is the conjectural emendation from "riches" to "wisdom" (reading ערמתם [πανοῦργος in Greek]; cf. v 8 of LXX), but riches and prosperity are associated elsewhere (3:16; 8:18) with wisdom. In an effort to avoid the apparent tautology in line *b*, another change is suggested, ולוית, "garland," since this word is a fine parallel to "crown," and they both occur in Prov 4:19. The verse would express a vivid contrast between the respective adornment: crowns, riches, and folly. However, the tautology has its own virtue (see the *Comment* below).

26.a. There is no clear antecedent to the suffix in לבניו, "to his children," unless it is understood to refer to the Lord, or preferably to the father (implied in v 26a) who possesses the fear of the Lord.

29.a. If "exalt" is taken in the sense of "lift up, display," there is no need to go to another reading ("increase," מרבה); cf. also 3:35.

30.a. "Calm" comes from understanding the root of מרפא as רפה, "slack, loose."

32.a. The Hebrew has "in his death," presumably his own and not that of the wicked. But it is not clear how death can be something to rely on. Such a reading runs contrary to the perspectives on death in this book. Hence, with a metathesis of the consonants, and the support of the Greek and Syriac, read "in his integrity" (בתמו).

33.a. The MT says that "wisdom is known," or possibly "must make itself known." This is not in harmony with the antithesis that is expected. The accepted view of the sages was the opposition between wisdom and folly; so how can wisdom be known by "fools"? On the strength of the negative particle that appears in the Greek version, many translations insert "not." Another alternative is to understand line *b* as a question (expecting a negative answer): "will it come to be known?" This seems to be a preferable solution.

34.a. Retain חסר in the rare meaning of "reproach"; cf. 25:10.

35.a. The preposition *lamed* in v 35a is to be understood as also functioning in v 35b.

Form/Setting/Structure

There is very little agreement on the structure and division of chap. 14; cf. the data in Whybray, *Composition,* 100. But there is no reason to regard 14:1 as an introduction to an instruction (*contra* Whybray). Rather, there is the usual succession, if somewhat irregular, of proverbial sayings. Among them one can find signs of editing: catch words and repetitions. Scoralick (*Einzelspruch,* 223) points to the variant sayings in vv 8a and 15b and to the repetition of "folly" in vv 18 and 24. However, it remains difficult to find genuine structural elements here. There is simply no consensus on how to break down the units, because the criteria change so quickly—at one time, catch words, but at another time, themes. Krispenz presents a table of catch words for 14:2–9, 10–14, 15–18, 19–22, but the course of thought is rocky.

Comment

1–3 F. Delitzsch sees in this group a "beautiful *trifolium*" that speaks to wise management of a house, conduct according to fear of God, and the wisdom of silence—along with their contraries. **1** See *Note* 1.a. The interpretation depends closely on the translation, especially the recognition of personified Wisdom and Folly. The implication of this verse is that both of these figures have houses, and a key question is the meaning of "house." Obviously it must mean more than a material building, or the contrast between Wisdom and Folly would have little import. This very contrast points to Prov 9:1, 14, where the respective "houses" symbolize intimate associations with the one or the other, i.e., dining. The verbs contrast the positive and negative effects, building up and tearing down, or life and death. There is no deliberate reference to the superb care for the "house" (31:15, 21, 27) shown by the woman of valor in chap. 31. But this final poem, 31:10–31, is a concrete illustration of Prov 24:3–4, building a "house" with wisdom. Many commentators (e.g., Plöger, Meinhold, Hausmann, *Menschenbild*, 151) deny any reference to the personification of Wisdom/Folly in 14:1. They understand the verse as a positive evaluation of the role of women in establishing a home and household. Perhaps one can recognize a twofold meaning: the literal sense (house/household), but also a symbolic meaning in view of 9:1. While F. Delitzsch (pp. 34, 288) understands the verse in such a literal sense, he thinks it "suggested" the symbolic statement of 9:1, which he terms an "allegorical conclusion." For further comment, see the *Explanation*. **2** The juxtapositional character of both lines in this verse should be noted; it is not easy to distinguish the subject and predicate. The above translation recognizes a chiastic sequence here: predicate/subject, subject/predicate. J. Hausmann (*Menschenbild*, 268) sees subject and predicate permeating each other: fear of the Lord is the basis for upright conduct, and from such conduct one can conclude to fear of the Lord; cf. also 16:6. O. Plöger regards this verse as a continuation, a "suitable complement" to v 1, even though originally it was not so intended. It is a very general axiom, relating ethical conduct to wisdom by way of "fear of the Lord," a topic taken up again in vv 26–27. While one cannot regard wise/just and fool/wicked as simple synonyms in terms of semantic usage (Scoralick, *Einzelspruch*, 75), sayings such as this one support the equation of wisdom ("fear of the Lord") and virtuous conduct; cf. also Prov 15:33; 16:6; 22:4. There is an important and emphatic emphasis on *life*, wisdom's kerygma, as the result of fear of the Lord, when v 2a is compared with 19:23a. **3** See *Note* 3.a. Although many translations understand line *a* as indicating physical punishment, it should be taken as a vivid expression of the proud speech uttered by the fool, which is then contrasted with the speech of the wise. The wise are "preserved," presumably by their humble and honest words.

4 An empty crib indicates that there are no oxen to feed, and hence one is free of the trouble of cleaning and caring for the animals, and expenses would be less. But this "advantage" is offset in v 4b: without the use of oxen, it is implied, the harvest will not be great. See *Note* 4.a. Concerning McKane's interpretation, which is also possible, the crib may be full of grain because there are no oxen, but this may turn out ultimately to be a heavy price to pay because the use of oxen should lead to greater crops. The role of animals in agricultural work was all important, and it made the difference between meager and abundant harvests.

5 See v 25. This saying looks somewhat banal, as if it were merely tautological. But it is either emphasizing reality, or it is speaking to a serious situation: judicial witnesses who cannot be relied on because they are liars. Line *b* repeats 6:19a; see also 12:17; 19:5. The connection with the "false witness" of the Decalogue (Exod

20:16) is obvious, and leads one to ponder the influence of practical wisdom on the legal traditions.

6–8 The theme of wisdom/folly dominates these verses which contain several terms that are characteristic of the wisdom vocabulary. **6** By definition, the "scoffer" (לץ)—a difficult term in this book—cannot attain wisdom. Such a person is cynical and arrogant, lacking the necessary humility; cf. Prov 11:2b. It is even surprising that the scoffer should be described as seeking wisdom. Hence Meinhold translated v 6a as conditional: should the scoffer really seek after wisdom . . . . The failure is described succinctly: literally "and nothing." According to 17:26 the fool could not buy wisdom even if he had the money. The emphasis in line *b* is not on native intelligence, but on practical *savoir-faire*, which involves docility. **7** See *Note* 7.a. The admonition interrupts the series of antitheses, perhaps a sign that in this context the command is all the more serious. The basis for the admonition is experience: you have not found knowledge among fools, and you will not! Avoidance of fools means avoidance of folly; cf. 13:20; 17:12. "Knowledge" (*da'at*) is the catch word for vv 6–7. **8** Wisdom means the ability to see one's way, since it calls for foresight and prudence; cf. v 15b. But knowing one's way has its limitation, as v 12 will indicate. Even with such uncertainty (v 12), it is better than the "folly of fools." Here folly is described as, even identified with, deception. Although this is not a clear opposite to knowing the way, it can refer to deceiving oneself, and by the same token, perhaps others; cf. also vv 24–25.

9 An obscure verse; see *Note* 9.a. There is no unanimity concerning the subject of line *a*: if "fools," then the singular form of the verb should be changed; if "guilt" is the subject, how does it scoff at fools? The meaning of אשם, "guilt offering?" is unexpected and uncertain in the context; it is a cultic term. In line *b* "favor" can be that of God, or of human beings among themselves. The above translation contrasts the scoffing attitude of fools toward sacrifice with the favor or acceptance from God that exists among the upright.

10 This psychological observation recognizes that ultimately there are certain feelings, both joyous and sorrowful, that cannot be communicated, no matter how much sympathy and understanding may be present. It does not deny that one can identify to some extent with another's sorrows and joys, but it does imply that such sensitivity has its limits. The observation is all the more important in view of 15:11, which affirms that it is the Lord who knows the human heart; cf. also Ps 44:22. Indeed, the Lord knows humans better than they do themselves. As St. Augustine put it, God is "intimior intimo meo," closer to me than I am to myself. The proverb itself can be compared to the famous dictum of Blaise Pascal (quoted in J. G. Williams, "The Power of Form," 38, 49): *Le coeur a ses raisons que la raison ne connaît point*, "the heart has its reasons that reason does not know."

11 It is not clear if a contrast is intended between a solid house and a comparatively fragile tent; this distinction may be just a modern impression, for the ancients were also comfortable with tents, even if these were more characteristic of nomadic existence. Oddly, the tent is said to "bloom," an unusual metaphor that suggests that house/tent is to be taken for the occupants. The contrast between the lot of the just and the wicked is clearly stated: prosperity as opposed to destruction; cf. 12:7.

12–13 "End" is a significant catch word for this group of realistic observations. **12** The verse is repeated in 16:25. The Hebrew plays with "before," i.e., the way in front of a person, and with "after," or the final result. The way (cf. v 8) that seems so secure by human judgment *may* turn out to be not only erroneous, but unwise and leading to death! By death is meant a broad range of unhappy experiences, from simple adversity to one's (premature?) departure from this world. This saying makes room for the possibility of self-deception, and then the "way" chosen in wisdom can turn out to be folly. The sages were aware of incalculables in human existence, even if they did not sharpen them in the style of Qoheleth. Their aim was more modest: state problems and point out ambiguities, but trust in wisdom to solve most, though not all, of them. **13** This is another psychological observation; cf. v 10. As in v 12, the end may be quite different from the beginning, and one knows that joys must come to an end. The saying also has an element of the unexpected. Laughter does not usually hide sorrow, but it can, as more than one operatic aria ("ride, pagliacci") remind us. The verb in v 13a should be given a modal nuance; it is not an apodictic, declarative statement. That mood reflects the uncertainty about personal feelings. What sense does it make to muffle personal sorrow? The question is not answered, but the ambiguity behind emotional displays is indicated. V 13b (see *Note* 13.a.) is juxtapositional, but the tentativeness of v 13a carries over. Appearances can be deceptive.

14 See *Note* 14.a. The neat ambiguity of the verb ("get one's fill") is that it can apply to both the good and the bad. The traditional law of retribution is described at work here; cf. also v 11. It is all the more instructive that such an apparently dogmatic affirmation follows upon the very realistic observations of vv 12–13, which belie dogmatic conclusions.

15–18 O. Plöger combines these verses "in a loose context" under the heading of cleverness and folly. **15** V 15b is a reprise of v 8a. The whole purpose of the wisdom enterprise is to make the naive aware of reality and its complications, to enable them to make the right judgment and follow the right path. The caution of the prudent or clever (cf. 13:16) will preserve them from missteps. **16** The "fear" (so, literally, the Hebrew) of the wise means their natural caution (cf. v 15), not necessarily the "fear of the Lord," unless rather remotely. There is an ethical quality to the description; they turn from evil. But the fool simply plunges ahead, trusting in his own inadequate self. **17** See *Note* 17.a. Despite the uncertainty of the text, one can accept synonymous parallelism between those who lack self-control and those who scheme. There is a certain intensification between lines *a* and *b*, from foolish action to being hated; in each case, the results of their conduct are appropriate. **18** The contrast between the naive and the clever was already drawn sharply in v 15. See *Note* 18.a.; "inherit" is used in an active sense, meaning to get or acquire. Uninstructed, or failing to heed wisdom's call, the naive meet up with folly as their portion. The clever have knowledge (= wisdom) as their crown.

19 Although the verse is one of the rare examples of synonymous parallelism in the chapter, it enunciates the traditional principle that the just will finally prevail over the wicked. The "gates" in v 19b suggest not a judicial scene, but rather a splendid house where the just receive homage. There the wicked "bow"—an indication that they are beggars or slaves.

20–24 These verses can find a certain unity in the theme of riches and poverty. **20** The proverb makes a statement of fact: riches create differences in social life. This phenomenon is frequently mentioned; cf. 10:15; 19:4–7. It has

always been easy for those who are better off to take on a superior attitude toward
the poor; "hate," as so often, is without emotional nuance—it indicates rejection.
The "love," again unemotional, toward the rich is an easy choice; all are tempted
to curry favor with them; cf. 19:4, 6. The theme is typically sapiential; cf. Sir 6:10–
12; 13:21–24.   **21**   But should this truism in v 20 about human conduct be
allowed to dictate attitudes toward others, especially the poor? The verdict in v
21 is quite unequivocal; an inner disposition, as well as its outer expression, of
disdain is considered a sin, and a blessing is pronounced upon those who show
kindness to the poor. See also 14:31; 17:5; 19:17.   **22**   Those who "plan evil"
would, in this context, include also those who have no regard for the poor. The
question form in v 22a suggests a possible connection with the previous verses. In
itself, the saying probably is to be understood more generally. In both lines the
"planning" is singled out; the reward for the good can be understood as hendiadys:
faithful love, and this from the divine as well as the human point of view.   **23**   At
first this seems ill-suited to the context. But the context does deal with rich and
poor, and the verse repeats a common theme: only by diligent labor, and not by
mere talk, does one achieve an adequate level of decent living. Hence it serves as
a kind of corrective to the poor who might be tempted to be satisfied with
indolence over industry.   **24**   See *Note* 24.a. Despite the changes suggested for
the text, this saying stays within the bounds of wisdom thought. The metaphor of
"crown" to indicate the riches of the wise is unusual, but the instruction of the
father is compared to an adornment in 1:9; cf. 8:18. Wisdom leads to riches and
prosperity. The duplication of the word "folly" in line *b* is an unexpected tautology,
but it is also striking in its effect: fools do not change, and folly remains folly.

25   See the *Comment* on v 5 where there is a similar contrast, and also on 19:5,
9 where some of this terminology is repeated. The abstract "deceit" can be taken
to indicate the concrete "a deceiver." The assurance of honest witnesses in judicial
cases was an utter necessity, even to save lives; cf. the story of Naboth in 1 Kgs 25.

26–27   "Fear of the Lord" is the catch word; cf. also v 2 and the *Comment* there.
The sayings seem to affirm only general truisms, until one reflects on the
importance of this phrase, the motto of the book (1:7).   **26**   The key wisdom
virtue provides a source of trust because the Lord is the object of such confidence.
Thus protected, one need not fear another human being (cf. 29:25). Moreover,
the progeny of the god-fearer will benefit. How did the sages conceive this
extension to future descendants? Perhaps as the beneficent effects of good
example. At any rate, the children of the just are declared blessed in
20:7b.   **27**   This is almost identical with 13:14, except that "the teaching of the
wise" is now explicitly identified with the fear of the Lord. Does a comparison of
14:27 with 13:14 authorize the conclusion that we have an example here of a
"reinterpretation of wisdom in specifically Yahwistic terms" (so Whybray)? That
would be very difficult to prove; it presupposes that the use of the sacred name
implies of itself a reinterpretation, and also that the notion of "fear of the Lord,"
which is so highly touted in Prov 1:7, can be dated to a later period. Moreover,
the separation of Yahwism from wisdom is an academic, theoretical, separation.
Did it exist in reality or only in our logic? Wisdom and Yahwism are a blend, not
two entities one imposed on the other. Until hard evidence is submitted, "fear of
the Lord" is not to be divorced from genuine wisdom; cf. 15:33. See also the
Excursus on Fear of the Lord.

28 This is the first of two "king" sayings; cf. also v 35. Plöger thinks the two verses form the framework for the sayings in vv 28–35, but there seems to be little unity to the intervening verses. At first sight v 28 may seem banal, but it is a basic observation. The king must ultimately have subjects to rule over, and where they are few, where is the kingdom? There is no reason to imply any deep philosophical view about the nature of monarchy deriving its power from the people; it is simply a matter of numbers. In a somewhat mischievous way J. Hausmann (*Menschenbild*, 141) associates this by contrast with 30:27, which speaks of the locusts being without a king but proceeding in an orderly manner; kings are also expendable.

29–30 There is no reason to associate these verses with royalty, as Whybray does. They apply equally well to commoners; they make sense in terms of human nature.   **29** See *Note* 29.a. Constant emphasis is placed on the need of the wise to exercise self-control—an idea that was shared by Israel, e.g., Prov 19:11, and also by Egypt; cf. M. Lichtheim, *AEL*, 2:147, on the contrast between the "silent man" and the "heated man." The ideal is too universal in application to be restricted to royalty.   **30** This verse is allied with the previous idea; there is a certain correspondence between calmness and control of anger, and an opposition between intelligence ("heart") and envy. The "heart" is the centerpiece of human beings, and when that is sound, one truly lives. The association of envy with the metaphor of rottenness is expressive; envy eats away at the person. See also the psychosomatic observations in vv 10 and 13.

31 The motivation for care of the poor is clearly stated. Line *a* finds a resounding echo in 17:5a; see also 22:2; line *b* is reflected in 19:17a. The religious and ethical basis for one's relationship to the poor is undeniable, and it is developed at length in Deut 15:1–11. The "his" in "his maker" can refer to both the oppressor as well as to the oppressed; after all, God made them both (22:2).

32 See *Note* 32.a. The Hebrew text is difficult: It is not clear how the just can "find security in his death" (whether his own or the death of the wicked). One can rule out any notion of immortality here (cf. B. Vawter, *JBL* 91 [1972] 158–71). Trusting in one's "integrity" does not connote pride; it simply indicates the only human basis for assurance available to the sages—loyalty to God, such as Job manifested by clinging to his integrity. This trust in integrity presupposes divine aid, but it also assumes that God will respond.

33 See *Note* 33.a. for the justification of the translation, and thus the meaning of this verse. Instead of straining to make some sense of the MT, one is obliged to adopt either of the solutions proposed in the note. The JPS translation renders v 33b: "But among dullards it makes itself known." A. Vaccari agrees and adds in a note that the voice of wisdom is heard by the *wicked* in the remorse that strikes their conscience. But this assumption of remorse is gratuitous, and the opposition is between the intelligent or wise, and *fools*. Others (such as NIV) supply the word "even": "even among fools she lets herself be known." But the whole thrust of the book is against the association of wisdom with fools.

34 See *Note* 34.a. While the sages were preoccupied more with the individual, the relationship of the just person to the community is also a concern. The community to which the just belonged was primary, but one cannot rule out a more generalized meaning for all peoples; cf. the claim of personified Wisdom in Prov 8:15–16. The saying is a complement to v 28; not only numbers are necessary for the prosperity of a people; justice is required as well. (cf. also 16:12b).

35 See *Note* 35.a. The contrasting actions of the members of the royal court produce corresponding reactions from the king. The issues could be merely incompetence, but this is not easily distinguished from intrigue and corrupt activity. The king had an obligation to ensure a just reign; hence he had to exercise prudence in his choice of ministers; cf. 16:13–15; 22:11. Ps 101 displays a similar preoccupation.

Explanation

There are some noteworthy features to this chapter. Ringgren (p. 60) remarks that the emphasis on wisdom (more than on justice) continues, because twelve of the thirty-five verses deal with wisdom/folly. Here also "king" sayings make their first appearance. There are several psychological observations: vv 10, 13, 30.

The truth claim of the sayings deserves attention. In view of 14:11, 14, the lot of the just and the wicked would seem to be pretty much a foregone conclusion. Yet, 14:12 explodes any certainty. Human judgment—a way that is right for a person—can turn out to be dead wrong, in more ways than one. This human judgment includes all the wisdom that the sages collected for this book! Once more the reader becomes aware of the limitations that the sages themselves recognized. We are not to be deceived by their dogmatic style into thinking that they had a simplistic view of life. They had definite notions about the direction they wanted to impart. But this was not at the expense of the realization of the complexity of human beings and of the complex reality in which they live and move. Despite the frequent appearance of firm, unyielding conclusions, there is a kind of dialectic going on. By "dialectic" I mean that even their most dogmatic statements are in some respects conditional. There is enough disparity between the statements to prevent easy categorization. There had to be such movement for the sake of credibility, so that they could escape the rigidity of the three friends whose doctrine is parodied in the book of Job.

Three proverbial sayings deal with fear of the Lord; see also the *Excursus on Fear of the Lord*. The ambiguity in the translation of 14:2 does not conceal the fact of the ethical component to this basic attitude. The one who fears the Lord is described as walking in uprightness (יֹשֶׁר), and the connection of wisdom and virtue (or just = wise) is simply assumed. In v 26 it should not be surprising to see fear and trust put together without any misgiving. This reflects the Deuteronomic use of "fear" (e.g., Deut 10:12, 20), even with the meaning of love and obedience. The similarity between 14:27 and 13:14 is particularly striking, indicating the high regard for the teaching of the wise, which seems at times so modest and unimposing. But it involves life and death issues. See the *Excursus on Fear of the Lord*.

Finally, there is the problematic character of the meaning of 14:1. Van Leeuwen distinguishes between the earlier version and the later (in which נָשִׁים is added). The original saying had Wisdom building her (cosmic) house, but Folly tears it down, reducing Wisdom's house to chaos. The addition of "of women" is a later editorial expansion, but it "creates a distinction between human wisdom and cosmic wisdom as personified in 8:1 and 9:1" (NIB, 5:138). A difference between an earlier and later version can surely be admitted, and the comment is true as far as it goes. But the distinction, which already exists between cosmic wisdom in chaps. 1–9 and human wisdom in the later chapters, e.g., 24:3–4, is precisely the problem. They can certainly be distinguished conceptually, but is that not rather a modern analysis? Wisdom has many faces (as they appear to us) in this book, but ultimately there is only one Wisdom.

Proverbs 15:1–33

Bibliography

Bühlmann, W. *Vom rechten Reden*, passim. **Krispenz, J.** *Spruchkomposition*. 71–79, 170–71. **Scoralick, R.** *Einzelspruch*. 226–37. **Van Leeuwen, R.** "Wealth and Poverty: System and Contradiction in Proverbs." *HS* 33 (1992) 25–36. **Vanoni, G.** "Volkssprichwort und YHWH-Ethos. Beobachtungen zu Spr 15,16." *BN* 35 (1986) 73–108. **Whybray, R. N.** *Composition*. 103–6.

Translation

15:1	*A soft answer turns back wrath,*
	but a sharp word stirs up anger.
2	*The tongue of the wise advances* [a] *knowledge,*
	but the mouth of fools pours out folly.
3	*In every place, the eyes of the Lord,*
	watching the evil and the good.
4	*A healing* [a] *tongue, a tree of life,*
	but when perverse, a broken spirit.
5	*A fool despises the instruction of his father,*
	but whoever heeds reproof is smart.
6	*The house of the just, much treasure,*
	but in the revenue of the wicked, trouble. [a]
7	*The lips of the wise spread* [a] *knowledge,*
	but the heart of fools, not so. [b]
8	*The sacrifice of the wicked, an abomination to the Lord,*
	but the prayer of the just, his delight.
9	*An abomination to the Lord, the way of the wicked,*
	but whoever pursues justice, he loves.
10	*Discipline is an evil for one who abandons the way;*
	whoever hates reproof will die.
11	*Sheol and Abaddon before the Lord—*
	how much more, human hearts!
12	*The scoffer does not like being reproved;*
	to the wise he will not go.
13	*A joyful heart lights up the face,*
	but in a troubled heart, a crushed spirit.
14	*An understanding heart seeks out knowledge,*
	but the mouth [a] *of fools feeds on folly.*
15	*Every day of the afflicted, evil!*

> But the contented in heart, a continual feast.

16 Better a little with fear of the Lord,
>   than great treasure and with it trouble.

17 Better a dish of herbs, but with love,
>   than a well-fed ox, but with hatred.

18 An angry person stirs up strife,
>   but the patient man quiets disputes.

19 The way of the lazy, like a thorn hedge,
>   but the path of the upright,[a] a highway.

20 A wise son gives joy to the father,
>   but a fool of a man despises his mother.

21 Folly, joy to the one who lacks sense,
>   but one who has understanding goes straight ahead.

22 Plans are thwarted in the absence of counsel,
>   but with many counselors they will hold.

23 Joy to a man from the answer of his mouth,
>   and a timely word, how good!

24 For the prudent, a path of life upward,
>   in order to turn from Sheol below.

25 The Lord tears down the house of the proud,
>   but he makes firm the widow's landmark.

26 An abomination to the Lord, evil plans,
>   but gracious words, pure.[a]

27 A disturber of his own house, one who is greedy for gain,
>   but whoever hates a bribe will have life.

28 The heart of the just plans how to answer,
>   but the mouth of the wicked pours forth evil.

29 The Lord, far from the wicked,
>   but the prayer of the just he hears.

30 The light of the eyes give joy to the heart;
>   good news refreshes the bones.

31 The ear that listens to an enlivening reproof
>   lodges among the wise.

32 Whoever spurns instruction, one who loathes himself,
>   but whoever heeds reproof, one who acquires sense.

33 Fear of the Lord, instruction in wisdom;
>   and before glory, humility.

Notes

2.a. The verb in the MT means literally "makes good." This can be interpreted as promoting, making pleasant. There is no need to adopt the conjecture in BHS, תטיף, "drip." Perhaps the MT can be understood to indicate that the art of good speech, promoted by wisdom, adds an edge to understanding.

4.a. As in 14:30 (refer to Note 14:30.a.), the meaning of the word מרפה depends on which root it is associated with.

6.a. נעכרת is the niphal feminine participle, understood as a substantive and meaning "disorder, trouble." The antithetic parallelism is not clear; there seems to be opposition between the treasure and the trouble. There is no need to adopt the emendations suggested in BHS.

7.a. The verb is difficult; it means "scatter" (in a negative sense), and the piel form here is taken metaphorically to mean spread or disperse. Bühlmann (*Vom rechten Reden*, 129–31) understands it in the sense of "winnow," so that the wise eliminate any folly, and solid knowledge results.

7.b. It is also possible to translate "not right (firm)," referring to the unsteady heart (mind) of the fools.

14.a. One should read the Qere with the ancient versions. However, it may be questioned whether "feed" is to be taken in the sense of "feed on," or to "feed, pasture"; see the *Comment*.

19.a. The parallelism is rather loose, and many adopt "diligent," supposedly on the basis of the Greek, but ἀνδρείων means "strong."

26.a. נעם אמרי are the antithesis to the "evil plans" that have been mentioned. The usual opposition to "abomination" is favor or delight (cf. v 8), but here it is טהרים, "pure."

Form/Structure/Setting

Chap. 15 is conspicuous in the collections we have been examining. First, the antithetical parallelism that has been so predominant begins to fade (absent in vv 3, 10–11, 12, 23–24, 30–31, 33). Second, speech is a very frequent topic (1, 2, 4, 7, 23, 26, 28). Third, there is what Whybray calls its "theological tone" because nine of the thirty-three proverbs are YHWH sayings. He goes on to find an "instruction" beginning with v 7. Less felicitously, Whybray argues that vv 20–33 (and probably even vv 5–33) constitute a "complete instruction" because "there is more than a slight similarity here to the structure of the instructions in chs. 1–9" (p. 106). Instruction is not a fitting genre term to describe this chapter. It remains a collection of sayings, with catch words in vv 2–3, 8–9, 13–16, 29–32 ("hear!"). The divisions of this chapter vary considerably among commentators, but some agree on the unity of vv 25–33; see the *Comment* below. Krispenz agrees that these verses can be singled out for their paronomasia, but again it is not easy to recognize sequence of thought. The same observation can be made for vv 11–17, where she calls attention to the repetition of "heart" (לב) in vv 11, 13, 14, 15.

Comment

1–2 Speech is the topic in these verses. **1** How is one to deal with an angry person? The sages had learned the paradoxical fact that a soft tongue could break a bone (Prov 25:15b). Therefore one must handle such people carefully, even gently. This was all the more important in dealing with those of a higher class, such as kings, who had the power to hurt (16:14; 25:15). A tough response will only lead to greater problems. **2** See *Note* 2.a. and a possible explanation of the Hebrew text; cf. also 16:19, 21. As translated above, v 2a resembles v 7a, and v 2b is reflected in v 14b. See also vv 21 and 28; there seems to be an affinity between all these verses.

3 This saying appears suddenly, and its only connection with v 2 is verbal, the use of "good" (not apparent in the English version of v 2a). The all-seeing eyes of the Lord imply that he is everywhere; even Sheol is not out of range (v 11). This idea is clearly expressed also in 5:21, and the eye of God appears in Amenemope (15:10–14; 19:1–4; *AEL*, 2:156–157) in a threatening context. The statement in this verse is somewhat neutral, but the very fact that the "evil" ones are mentioned is already an indirect warning. Other expressions of divine omniscience are more threatening, in that the Lord "tests" and "requites" (e.g., 16:2; 24:12). The eyes of the Lord are featured again in 22:12 and 24:18.

4–7 Again, the subject of most of this group is speech. **4** See *Note* 4.a. The power of words to heal and enliven, or to overturn and break the spirit—whether of the speaker or, more probably, of others—is highlighted. Speech is double-edged; it can be beneficent or malicious. See 3:18 for the tree of life; the healing effect of words is brought up again in 16:24. **5** Before any words can be a source of life, there has to be docility. Readiness to be corrected is an important characteristic that distinguishes the wise from the foolish; cf. 12:1; 13:1, and, in this chapter, v 10. **6** See *Note* 6.a. This verse has little connection with the context. It reflects the idea of retribution for the just/wicked as conceived by the sages. The antithesis is not very sharp: treasure and trouble, but the trouble is difficult to specify. **7** See *Note* 7.a. No matter how this is translated, there is a contrast between the wise and the foolish. It is unusual to have the lips contrasted with the heart (understood in the sense of mind). It is presupposed that the lips of the wise express what has been well thought out, whereas the fool simply blurts out what is in his heart, namely folly; see also v 2.

8–9 The phrase "abomination to the Lord" serves to unite these two proverbs that join sincere liturgical worship with honorable conduct. **8** This is a commonplace with the prophets, e.g., Isa 1:10–20; external worship means nothing if it is not accompanied by conduct that pleases God. The saying should be understood in the light of the fuller context that is provided by v 29 and also 21:3, 27. The contrast is not between the relative values of sacrifice and prayer, but between the reaction of God and the contradictory actions of human beings. It is the sacrificer, not the sacrifice, that is the issue. The divine displeasure corresponds to the behavior of human beings. God's love, it will be remembered, does not exclude discipline (Prov 3:11), and the importance of discipline will be emphasized in the next verse. The divine love is not often explicitly mentioned in Proverbs.

10–12 Perhaps these three sayings can be grouped together because of catch words and the emphasis on reproof. **10** The need for discipline is described in unusually strong terms: it is an evil for those who will not accept it, for their fate will be "death," which is left unspecified. **11** The mention of death in v 10 may be the reason for placing this proverb here. It deals expressly with the Lord's unlimited knowledge of the human heart; cf. v 3. If such mysterious places as Sheol, the realm of Death, and the resting place of the shades are not beyond God's ken, certainly humans are no puzzle. "Abaddon" is formed from the word אבד, "perish," and is a synonym for Sheol; cf. Job 26:6. **12** Again the theme of reproof is taken up; cf. vv 5, 10. The "scoffer" is on the fringe, so to speak, and seems to represent the most hopeless case. In general, fools can not tolerate correction (12:1), and hence will avoid the company of the wise, although they are the ones who could possibly be of help; cf. v 31.

13–15 Two psychological observations are wrapped around a wisdom saying, with "heart" as the catch word in all three verses. **13** For the association of inner disposition and outward expression see also Prov 17:22 and Eccl 7:3. The meaning of v 13a is close to Sir 13:25: inner joy has an affect on one's appearance. The movement in v 13b is different: it remains interior, and it proceeds from heart to spirit. If spirit, or רוה, is to be understood as breath, there would be more obvious parallelism with v 13a; the trouble is manifested in the physical breathing of a person. The translation indicates that the heart that is troubled will betray a crushed, downtrodden, attitude, comparable to the "broken spirit" mentioned in v 4. **14** See *Note* 14.a. In v 7 the lips and heart were contrasted; here so also are the heart and the mouth—all in favor of the wise. W. Bühlmann (pp. 190–93) underscores the intensity of the verbs: the *search* or preoccupation of the intelligent heart and the "shepherding" (not just "feeding on") or cultivation of folly by the fools. Both lines of this proverb find an echo elsewhere: line *a* in 14:33 and line *b* in 15:2b. **15** At first sight the two lines seem to describe separate groups: the afflicted will have evil days all their lives, but others, not troubled by adversity, who are literally "good of heart," have a continual feast. These can hardly be two totally separate and unrelated observations. But is v 15a to be understood in an absolute manner, as though there could be no change in the plight of the afflicted? Perhaps in their affliction there can be no escape from suffering. Or perhaps the generalization of v 15b modifies the desperate situation found in v 15a, in the sense that the afflicted can and must cultivate a happy heart. Their lot is hard, but their interior attitude can help them attain some joy in life. Plöger and McKane are of this opinion. Whybray regards the verse as an "apparently contradictory proverb."

16–17 These two "better" sayings illustrate the kind of judgment that true wisdom exercises. They both modify conventional wisdom by pointing up paradox. See the *Comment* on 16:8. Both proverbs are similar to sayings in the Instruction of Amenemope, 9:5–8 (*AEL*, 2:152): "Better is poverty in the hand of the God, / Than wealth in the storehouse; / Better is bread with a happy heart / Than wealth with vexation." **16** Fear of the Lord is the beginning of wisdom, but it is no guarantee of prosperity and riches, even if these are the benefits promised to the wise. Wealth is preferable to poverty, but not at any price; it does not guarantee happiness. In themselves riches can create problems, as Qoheleth pointed out, Eccl 5:9–19. The "little" may not necessarily mean abject poverty—perhaps modest means; however, the force of the comparison should not be lost. The emphasis is placed on what is true value, despite life's problems. Prov 16:8 provides a close parallel. For further comment, see the *Explanation*. **17** The criterion for judgment is not specified, but it is clear that the imponderable and immaterial weighs more than the material. The spirit in which a meal is shared is far more important than the kind of food that is eaten; cf. 17:1. Alonso Schökel describes the "good" (טוֹב) that unites vv 15–17: a contented heart, fear of the Lord, and harmony with companions; thus, peace with self, God, and neighbor.

18 Another connection with an Egyptian ideal, the contrast between the heated and the silent man, is displayed in this saying about the angry (literally, "a man of heat") and the cool (literally, "stretched out, long," with regard to anger) person. The "hot-headed" person appears frequently; cf. Prov 28:25a; 29:22a; Sir 28:8–11. See the *Comment* on 14:29.

19 The antithesis between the lazy and the upright is not sharp enough for some commentators (e.g., C. Toy), who prefer to interpret the Greek version as indicating "the diligent" (see *Note* 19.a.). But the MT makes sense: the path of the "upright." The word for "upright" (יָשָׁר) itself is also used in the sense of straight, as the verb in v 21 indicates. The comparison to the thorn hedge is not spelled out, but it obviously represents obstacles, whether painful or simply hindrances, in the way. See also 16:17.

20 This first line is a repetition of 10:1a, and obedience to parental authority is common in Proverbs (e.g., 13:1; 29:3, 15). Does its somewhat sudden appearance here indicate the beginning of a new section? Hardly. One could argue just as well that this forms an inclusio to 10:1. There is every reason to think that the parental role deserves repetition. "Joy" serves as a catch word with vv 21, 23.

21   After the mention of true joy comes the false: the senselessness of the fool, paradoxically, gives him joy. There he finds his *raison d'être*. The contrast between the two lines is not obvious; perhaps foolish joy is fixed on its goal, folly, and goes nowhere—as opposed to the moral progress of the one who has understanding. If the fool moves, it is in the direction of death with which he flirts, and to which his "way" (cf. vv 9, 24) leads.

22   In contrast to 11:14, where the national interest is to the fore, consultation is advised here for more personal matters. Failure to seek advice is associated with pride in 13:10. However, lest it be thought that advice solves everything, 19:21 reminds the sage that the counsel of the Lord is uppermost, in fact mysterious. This saying interrupts the "joy" proverbs (vv 20, 21, 23).

23   The second line adds something to the first. Not only the content, but the timing is also important. Obviously good advice and good timing do not always coincide, especially in the delicate cases of human existence. One of the ideals of the sage was to have the right word at the right time, as this verse indicates; see 10:11a and also 15:1. The element of timing is expressed in the teaching of Ankhsheshonq: "Do not say something when it is not the time for it" (12:24; Lichtheim, *AEL*, 3:169).

24   The idea of the way or path, which is so central to wisdom teaching, e.g., 10:17, and especially chaps. 1–9, is taken up from v 19. "Upward" and "down" have nothing to do with a life beyond death, although they could be so understood by a later generation that nourished such a belief. Rather they indicate where the way of wisdom leads a person—upwards into life, avoiding a premature or unhappy death, as opposed to downwards to Sheol, which can be understood literally as death or metaphorically as adversity.

25–33   Because of the frequent appearance of YHWH in these sayings, they are grouped together by some authors (Plöger, Whybray, Meinhold). Scoralick (*Einzelspruch*, 233–37) limits the group to vv 28–32, within which the verb/noun "hear" is the catch word, appearing four times, when the term appears only seven times in all in chaps. 10–15. She deliberately excludes 15:33, on the fear of the Lord, but she is uncertain how it functions in the book: possibly connecting with the next collection or simply as an overall characterization, using the motto of 1:7 and 9:10 (p. 84). The repetition of מוּסָר, "instruction," and תוֹכַחַת, "reproof," in vv 31–33 should be noted.   **25**   The widow was particularly vulnerable in Israelite society, since she had none but herself to mount a defense against encroachments and oppression, as the prophets frequently indicate, e.g., Isa 1:23; Jer 7:6. And the guilty party would be precisely the powerful and arrogant. Appropriately in a kind of talion law, it is YHWH who will overturn *their* houses. The "landmark" of the widow indicates that the issue is ownership of property; cf. also 23:10.   **26**   See *Note* 26.a. The saying interiorizes the actions of the wicked: not only their "way" (v 9) but their very thoughts are an abomination. The usual antithesis is abomination/favor, but here "pure" appears in place of "favor," and it has both a ritual and ethical connotation. The "gracious words" are not sweet nothings; they are the opposite of the "evil plans" of v 26a, and thus express the virtuous designs of the just. These affect not only others, but also oneself, as they act in a healing manner, according to 16:24. **27** The parallelism indicates that the "gifts" are not innocent; they are bribes. The issue of gifts/bribes will reappear in 17:8; 18:16. The saying strikes out at excessive attachment to wealth which creates an atmosphere for bribery. Disturbance of a "house(hold?)" must mean to destroy it somehow; cf. 11:29. Instead, life is in store for the honest who refuse to engage in bribery. **28** This proverb is much like v 2, except that the just/wicked contrast has replaced the wise/fool; cf. also v 14. The thoughtful discourse of the just is the opposite of the rash, actually "evil" speech of the wicked. **29** The Lord hears the prayer of the just, presumably because of closeness to them; their prayer gives delight to God, according to v 8b. The distance of God from humans is a symbol of his not hearing their prayers; e.g., Ps 10:1. It is implied that the wicked also address "prayers" to God, but they are an abomination, according to v 8a. **30** This is another psychological observation; cf. v 13. The expressiveness of the eyes betrays an inner joy which others can recognize and be affected by. Line *b* continues the same idea, changing from the sense of sight to the sense of hearing: good news renews strength, whether of oneself or another; cf. 25:25 and also 29:13. **31** Line *b* continues the description of the listening ear; it is to be found among the wise. The saying is in opposition to the "scoffer" of v 12 and to anyone who will not listen to reproof. **32** Cf. vv 5 and 10. Whybray rightly remarks that v 32 "echoes in antithetical parallelism what v 31 states in a single sentence." In v 32b, "acquire heart" means to increase in understanding or wisdom; see also 19:8a. **33** This broad generalization takes up the theme of "fear of the Lord" from 1:7 and 9:10. V 33b repeats a familiar idea, found in 18:12, but it seems only loosely connected with line *a;* perhaps humility is presupposed in order that one may hear a reproof and increase in wisdom.

Explanation

This chapter raises questions never quite envisioned in previous chapters. The same apparently monotonous sequence of proverbs appears. But when they are carefully examined, several new aspects can be seen to surface. There is a mixture of *nova et vetera*, the new and the old.

The new is the extraordinary number of YHWH sayings, already pointed out above, and the old is the continuing reference to instruction and reproof, to the "way," and to the role of the "heart" and other organs of the body. We can consider the YHWH sayings in more detail. These should not be viewed as editorial revisions or editorial additions destined to make the sayings "orthodox," either explicitly or by association. The divinity that is implied in so many sayings is "Elohim" or YHWH, the only God that Israel professed, although one must allow for lapses into idolatry. Hence we do not have a group of "profane" sayings that were given a "religious" tone as a means to elevate them from the ordinary. Having said this, we must also admit that the pronounced bunching of YHWH sayings in this chapter is unusual. Of the nine such sayings four occur in vv 25–33, and this rate even increases in chap. 16. Whybray (*Composition*, 88) has numbered twenty in chaps. 15–16, and this is twenty out of the total number of fifty-eight in the alleged "Solomonic" collections (10:1–22:16 and 25:1–29:27). As we shall see, 16:1–11 contains nine YHWH sayings. Why are they all bunched together so conspicuously? Some have sought theological reasons (e.g., Whybray); others have thought only of a deliberate editorial move to connect chaps. 10–15 with 16:22. R. Scoralick has summarized the history of research on this question in *Einzelspruch,* 15–32, 91–159, and has pointed out the failure of scholarly efforts to offer convincing arguments to explain the structure; there have been many varying conclusions. She proposes her own understanding of chaps. 10–15, to which we already have alluded several times. Her survey remains valuable because it puts before the readers of Proverbs new insights into "instructional" sayings, especially paronomasia in its various forms, ranging from catch words to plays on words. While they do not settle the structural questions, they display the lively imagination of scholars in theorizing about possible combinations. Unanimity is hard to achieve in this kind of analysis. But let the reader judge the significance of 10:1–5 as the beginning and 15:32(33?) as the ending of these chapters. The final result is that almost everyone accepts a division between chaps. 10–15 and 16:1–22:16, whatever be the differences in their arguments.

The instructional teaching that was so characteristic of chaps. 1–9 should be seen as continuing, in a *different* form, in chaps. 10–15. There are many indications in chap. 15, although these are not instructions. They remain proverbial sayings, intended to form character. The "better" saying is a common literary form in wisdom literature. It appears here in vv 16–17 in the form, "better is A with B than C with D." This is made to order to express a paradox, to overturn what would normally be considered a plus, e.g., riches, into a minus. The theological importance of this kind of saying has been well described by R. Van Leeuwen in *HS* 33 (1992) 25–36. By examining only the proverbs dealing with wealth/poverty in relation to justice/wickedness, he shows that they contradict the so-called deed (or character)-consequence viewpoint of retribution. The parade examples are 16:8 ("Better a little with justice / than great income with injustice"); 16:16, 19; 17:1; 28:6. While the sages were optimistic about the rewards of virtue, they realized that nothing was guaranteed, as these exceptions show. But they insisted upon basic rules first; then one could learn the exceptions. They firmly believed that when necessary there would be a reversal of fortunes worked out by the God of justice (cf. Prov 2:21–22; 10:30; 24:20), even if this was shrouded in mystery. The "dogmatic" attitude attributed to the sages should be seen in the light of the paradoxes that they recognized. See also the *Excursus on Retribution.*

Proverbs 16:1–33

Bibliography

Brunner, H. "Gerechtigkeit als Fundament des Thrones." *VT* 8 (1958) 420–28. **Bühlmann, W.** *Vom rechten Reden,* passim. **Krispenz, J.** *Spruchkomposition.* 80–88. **Miles, J.** *God. A Biography.* New York: Random Vintage, 1995. 290–302. **Scoralick, R.** *Einzelspruch.* 85–108. **Whybray, R. N.** *Composition.* 87–90, 106–10.

Translation

16:1   *The designs of the heart, for human beings,*

    but from the Lord the response of the tongue.

2   *All the ways of a person, pure in his own eyes,*
      but the one who weighs the spirits, the Lord.

3   *Commit* [a] *your works to the Lord,*
      and your plans will be firm.

4   *The Lord has made everything for a purpose,*[a]
      even the wicked for the evil day.

5   *An abomination to the Lord, every proud heart;*
      be assured, they shall not go unpunished.[a]

6   *By kindness and fidelity iniquity is atoned for,*
      and by fear of the Lord, a turning from evil.[a]

7   *When a person's ways please the Lord,*
      he makes even his enemies peaceful toward him.

8   *Better a little with justice*
      than great income with injustice.

9   *The heart of a man plans his way,*
      but the Lord directs his steps.

10   *An oracle on the lips of a king:*
      justice from his mouth never fails.

11   *Honest balances and scales—the Lord's;*
      his concern, all the weights in the bag.

12   *Wicked actions, an abomination to kings,*
      for a throne is made firm by justice.

13   *Justice from lips, the delight of kings,*
      and they love the one who speaks honestly.[a]

14   *The wrath of a king, messengers of death;*
      but a wise person can pacify it.

15   *In the light of the king's face, life;*
      and his favor, like the cloud of rain in spring.

16   *How much* [a] *better to get* [b] *wisdom than gold,*
      preferable to silver, to get understanding.

17   *The highway of the upright, turning from evil;*
      whoever watches his way saves his life.

18   *Before a collapse, pride,*
      and before stumbling, haughtiness of spirit.

19   *Better humble in spirit with the poor,*[a]
      than dividing booty with the proud.

20   *Whoever ponders a word will find good,*
      but whoever trusts in the Lord, happiness!

21   *The wise of heart will be called intelligent,*
      and sweetness of lips increases learning.

22   *A fountain of life, a possessor of insight,*
      but folly, the discipline of fools.

23   *A wise heart makes a smart mouth,*
      and increases learning on the lips.

24   *A honeycomb, pleasant words!*
      Sweet to taste, and healing for bones.

25   *There is a way, straight for a person,*

        but its end, ways of death.
26   *The desire of a toiler toils for him,*
        for his mouth urges [a] *him on.*
27   *A villain,* [a] *a digger* [b] *of evil,*
        and upon his lips, like a burning fire.
28   *A perverse man initiates discord,*
        and a gossiper separates friends.
29   *A violent person seduces his neighbor,*
        and leads him in a way that is not good.
30   *Whoever winks* [a] *the eye, for planning upsets;*
        whoever purses the lips accomplishes evil.
31   *A crown of glory, gray hair;*
        it is found in the way of justice.
32   *Better one slow to anger, than a warrior,*
        whoever controls his spirit, than one who conquers a city.
33   *Into the lap the lot is cast,* [a]
        but from the Lord, its entire decision.

Notes

3.a. The verb is גלל, "roll, cast," not גלה, "uncover, remove"; cf. Ps 22:9. V 3 is lacking in the Greek text, which is shaky in these opening verses.

4.a. למענהו, "for a purpose," presents a puzzle; the word has both a suffix and a definite article, contrary to Masoretic vocalization. The above translation deliberately leaves open the antecedent of the suffix, which could be "everything" or the Lord ("its" or "his" purpose). Literally, מענה means "answer," but it is understood by most to indicate purpose here; cf. the *Comment* below.

5.a. The LXX adds two extra couplets here (vv 7–8 in Rahlfs) which can be associated with 16:6 and 28:5.

6.a. *BHS* notes how in the LXX vv 6–8 have been inserted at 15:27–29, but no explanation can be offered. Vv 1–9 in the LXX show great differences from the MT.

13.a. The verb "love" reflects the singular, although the presumed subject is plural "kings" (which is rendered as singular in the Greek). The consonantal text could be vocalized as in the MT, translated above, or as "honest speech" (cf. *BHS*). There is no real difference.

16.a. There is no compelling reason to eliminate מה, "what? how?" as a dittography from the preceding חכמה, "wisdom."

16.b. This form of the verb קנה is irregular; one would expect the form that appears in line *b;* cf. Joüon §79p.

19.a. On the basis of the Greek, the Qere reading is preferable to the Ketib; cf. *BHS*.

26.a. The verb is hapax, and seems to mean "press"; cf. Sir 46:5. Hunger, indicated by "mouth," is a weight that pressures a person.

27.a. For איש בליעל, "a man of belial, a villain," see the *Comment* on 6:12.

27.b. Some (e.g., Scott) prefer to read כור, "a furnace of evil," but the change is not necessary. On the MT see the *Comment* on v 27.

30.a. עצה, "winks?" is hapax, and the meaning doubtful; perhaps "shut." Elsewhere קרץ, "purse," (occurring in line *b* with "lips") is used, as in Prov 6:13.

33.a. The passive voice is used with the object in the accusative; cf. Joüon §128b.

Form/Structure/Setting

This chapter is remarkable in form and theme. It was discussed above (p. 68) in the context of the setting of proverbs in a book, as opposed to a setting in life. Vv 1 and 33 can be taken as an inclusio, in that both are YHWH sayings. The "Lord" dominates vv 1–9; v 8 is the exception. These are followed by "king" sayings in vv

10–15; v 11 is the exception. Whybray even claims that "the intention of the editor was to link the two topics [YHWH and king] together," and he sees this marked by the juxtaposition of vv 9–10, so that the "joining of these two groups together serves a double purpose: it teaches, on the one hand, that kings rule by divine permission and are Yahweh's representatives on earth, but, on the other, that as human beings they have this authority only if they acknowledge their subordinate status and rule righteously" (*Composition*, 88–89). His basic principle is that the "Yahweh" proverbs give a particular theological character to the collections. However, the presence of the divine name is being overworked. The "intention" of which Whybray speaks would be the editor or redactor, who placed these proverbs in the present sequence. However, the sequence in vv 1–9 of the LXX makes it difficult to speak of the work of the redactor. Thus after v 5 there are two couplets (vv 7–8 in Rahlfs edition) that resemble 16:6 and 28:5. V 6 in the MT appears after 15:27 (numbered v 27a in Rahlfs), and v 7 appears after 15:28 (numbered v 28a in Rahlfs); both are YHWH or Kyrios sayings. One might wonder if the view of overarching unity is more a modern than an ancient concern. Alonso Schökel also thinks that the two themes, Lord and king, are deliberately connected. He points to the use of מִשְׁפָּט, "justice, decision," for the king (v 9) and the Lord (v 33). Moreover, God and king are united in Prov 24:21 (fear the Lord and the king), and wickedness is an "abomination" to both, Prov 16:12; 15:9. Finally, the decisions of the king are superhuman: an "oracle" is in his mouth (v 10), so that he can judge his people rightly. For the rest of the chapter there is nothing unusual about the grouping. It may be noted that the Masora marks 16:17 as the center of the book. It should also be observed that the occurrences of antithetic parallelism diminish.

The flow of vv 1–9 has been well described by Whybray in his commentary (p. 239): "Vv. 2–4 further elaborate the thought of v. 1: Yahweh has complete knowledge of human motives (v. 2); he will give success to those who commit their plans to him (v. 3); all created things answer to his purpose, including the punishment of the wicked (v. 4). Vv. 5–7 speak in more detail of his dealings with mankind . . . ." The division between vv 1–9 and 10–15 seems to be ascertained by all, though Krispenz would include v 16. Meinhold considers v 16 to be redactional, exalting the value of wisdom, and deliberately placed before v 17, which is the middle verse of the book, as counted by the Masoretes.

Comment

1 This saying is often glossed by "man proposes, but God disposes." That is in general agreement with biblical thought, but it does not fully express the determinism that is intrinsic to this saying. The key to the meaning is in the "response of the tongue"; does it belong to a human being, or is it the Lord's answer? In the first case it is the human ability to express one's ideas, presumably in a worthy fashion (cf. v 2a). The "answer of the mouth" in 15:23 is similar; it is a word in good time, the goal of wisdom. This is not done without divine help, which v 1b indicates; as in Prov 2:6, wisdom is a gift of God. This is a bland interpretation; God is present somewhere in the background of human activity. However, in the second case the "answer" is totally the doing of the Lord, who has determined it. According to 15:11 the Lord knows the human heart, but here God works through the answer. The response of human beings cannot escape divine dominion. Human beings are totally dependent upon him, even though they are at the same time morally responsible agents. The Old Testament thinkers did not attempt to solve that conundrum, which later theologians explored under the theme of freedom of will. The ancients expressed the dilemma, that they must have seen (*pace* Whybray), but they lived with it. They affirmed the (free) choice between life and death; cf. Deut 30:15–19. Barucq translates "response" by "decision," and this captures the right emphasis. He also notes that the verse is lacking in the LXX, but is marked with an obelus in Origen's recension. There are similar sayings in the wisdom of the ancient Near East; e.g., Amenemope, 19:16–17, *AEL,* 2:157: "The words men say are one thing, / The deeds of the god are another." See also *ANET,* 423, and the treatment in Bühlmann, *Vom rechten Reden,* 322–24. The saying appears in the Instruction of Anchsheshonq, "The plans of the god are one thing, / the thoughts of [men] are another" (26:24; *AEL,* 3:179).

2 See especially 14:12 and 21:2; the slight variations in the vocabulary in this verse do not affect the meaning. Human judgment is fallible, despite good intentions. It is the Lord who sees straight, and evaluates human motives. Even those who fear the Lord need to be reminded of the possibility of self-deception. Their judgment is necessarily subjective; the Lord's is objective. Alonso Schökel offers a more tentative mood. He questions the word "all" in v 2a since 14:12 speaks only of the singular "way." He would take v 2a as concessive: even though everything seems right, who can be sure? The ultimate judgment is the Lord's. The weighing of the heart (see also 24:12) is reminiscent of the representation of the Egyptian god of the scribes, Thoth, weighing the heart of the dead person against the balance of *Ma'at,* "justice"; cf. *ANEP,* 210. For the Lord testing and trying the heart, cf. 17:3; 24:12; Pss 7:10; 17:3; Jer 11:21; 17:10; 20:12.

3 Trust in the Lord is a frequent topic in this book; here it is expressed in a command, while in v 20 it is in a saying. The sequence in this verse is arresting— from deeds to thoughts. Are these deeds still in the future, or have they been already performed? Probably the former. If they have already been done, the firming up of the plans is hard to fit in. The emphasis of the verse is on the initial act of entrusting self to God; this will secure the plans; cf. Ps 127:1–2. The literal meaning of v 3a is "roll" to the Lord your actions; see *Note* 3.a. and Pss 22:9; 37:5 for this use of the verb. The realization of "plans" is reflected in 4:26 and 20:18.

4 See *Note* 4.a. The meaning depends on the interpretation of "his/its answer/ purpose." The word "answer" can mean a reaction to God, and in the context of v 4b, it is the reaction of human beings, even the wicked, that is meant. Hence "its answer" would refer particularly to the reaction of the wicked; they do not escape. If God's "purpose" is meant, there is the same practical effect: even the punishment of the wicked is included in the divine plan. They will not escape; they will meet with the evil day. The distinction between a direct and indirect (one that is imprinted on creation by the creator) purpose of God is overly subtle and should not be applied to this verse. In either case, nothing, and especially not the wicked, escapes God's domination. In v 4b the "evil day" means any day of disaster, during life or at the moment of death. Ben Sira goes his own way in developing the "works of the Most High"; cf. Sir 33:7–15; 39:12–31. For further comment, see the *Explanation.*

5 See *Note* 5.a. The idiom "hand to hand" occurs also in 11:21; see the *Comment* there. This verse repeats phrases from 11:20–21. The emphasis is concrete in contrast to the abstract formulations in vv 18–19 below. It aims at those who are literally "proud of heart." They are an "abomination" to the Lord; the same strong term is used of those who have "haughty eyes" in 6:16–17.

6 Hope for forgiveness is based on the practice of "kindness and fidelity"—often mentioned as characteristics of the Lord, e.g., Exod 34:6, but here referring to relationships with others; cf. Prov 3:3. There is a love that covers or forgives the wrongdoings of others, 10:12. The saying is not anticult (*pace* McKane); it underscores that human חסד, "kindness," can be met by divine forgiveness. Line *a* is strengthened by the mention of fear of the Lord in line *b;* the "evil" is moral evil, as well as any physical harm.

7 In contrast to the "abomination" of v 5a is what "pleases" the Lord—the right "ways" of a person. These have been already examined in v 2. If they are genuine, the Lord will see to it that there is a reconciliation with one's enemies. "He," subject of the verb in line *b*, refers to the Lord rather than to a human being. Enemies have now become friends; it is not stated how this transformation will be effected.

8 This "better" saying appears suddenly, and is similar to 15:16–17; see the *Comment* there and also the *Explanation*. The paradoxical character of these sayings should be kept in mind. Poverty is not seen as a good in itself nor are the benefits of riches denied. The issue is whether or not a person has justice or, as 15:16 puts it, the fear of the Lord.

9 This verse is usually associated with vv 1–3, especially v 1, in virtue of the catch words "heart" and "man" (אדם), and similarity of thought. But the point is not exactly the same. This saying distinguishes between the human plan and the divine direction; it has a whole process in mind: the way through life. The journey involves many decisions, but there is consolation in the belief that the Lord's direction will bring success along the way. This interpretation is not negated by translating "and" in v 9b as "but." It presupposes harmony between human decisions and the guidance of God toward ultimate success. However, this is not always so. Sayings like 19:21 and 20:24 are warnings that one must be open to the uncertainties along the way. The final result is the Lord's doing, over which humans have no real control, and it may not be the "success" that is yearned for. The poignant confession of Jer 10:23 is appropriate here: "I know, O Lord, that man's road is not his [to choose], that man, as he walks, cannot direct his own steps." Human helplessness before God!

10–15 The following proverbs deal mainly with the king, presenting an ideal portrait of this figure. The whole Davidic tradition ennobled the status of the king, even if prophets could and did face them down. Several later "king" sayings will tone down vv 10–15. **10** It is unusual to find a term (*qesem*, "oracle") that has an unfavorable sense elsewhere, designating divination in Deut 18:10, applied here to the king in an honorable way. There seems to be no limit to exaggeration of royal prerogatives; e.g., the wisdom of David is likened to that of an angel of God in 2 Sam 14:20. In particular, "justice" (משפט) is a royal, as well as a divine, prerogative, and necessary for the king's reign. **11** Although this is not a "king" saying, "justice" is the catch word with the previous verse. The involvement of the Lord with business transactions that is portrayed here is striking: the weights are literally his work, or doing (translated above as "concern"); they reflect divine justice. This emphasis resembles the "abomination" statements concerning false weights in 11:1 or 20:23. Manipulation in balancing scales was apparently a well-known practice. For details on weights see any Bible dictionary, e.g., W. G. Dever, in *HBD,* 1126–31. **12** The use of "abomination," which is most often used of the Lord, indicates how far from the king must be any hint of injustice. In fact, justice is what secures his throne; the idea is repeated in 20:8; 25:5; 29:14. Such an ideal was also cultivated in Mesopotamia, but the most striking parallel is the Egyptian portrayal of the foundation of the royal throne, marked by the hieroglyph *ma'at,* or truth/justice. This representation is reflected also in Pss 89:15 and 97:2; cf. H. Brunner, *VT* 8 [1928] 420–28. **13** See *Note* 13.a. Justice is the catch word with v 12. Whose "justice" is being hailed, that of kings or courtiers? Perhaps both, and the king is expected to be a good example to his courtiers. The honest speech of courtiers would be indicated by Prov 22:11 and Ps 101. **14–15** There is another aspect to royalty: power over life and death. For royal wrath, cf. 19:12 and 20:2, and the objects of the king's wrath are mentioned in 14:35. But wisdom will prevail if it is put to work; cf. Prov 15:1, 4. The wise can turn aside wrath, 29:8b. In contrast to wrath is the favor of a king. The good effects of "the light of the eyes" were underlined in 15:9. Now the light of the king's face means life itself. This is high praise in view of the Aaronic blessing in Num 6:25, "Let the Lord's face shine . . ." In v 15b royal favor is compared to the cloud of the late rain. This rainy season comes in March-April, preparing the ground for sowing of summer crops.

16 Meinhold regards this as a redactional verse which recalls Prov 3:14–15 and 8:10–11. At the very middle of the book, the reader's attention is directed to what is central. There is the attractive suggestion that the saying grew out of two questions and answers: What is better than gold? Wisdom! What is better than silver? Understanding. Wisdom and understanding are frequently in parallelism. The superiority of wisdom to precious metals is a commonplace.

17 As already noted, this is the central verse of the book by the Masoretic count. The familiar theme of the way reappears; cf. 4:9–19 and the *Comment.* The stakes for staying on the right way are high; according to v 17b it is a question of saving one's life; cf. 13:3a. The "evil" in v 17a is better understood in a moral sense, although physical cannot be excluded. One preserves life by many different actions; cf. 19:16a; 21:23; 22:5.

18–19 These sayings are related by a theme that is found frequently in Proverbs: pride/humility; cf. 11:2a; 15:33b; 29:23. In addition, "stumbling" in v 18 continues the image of the "way." **18** Another form of this proverb appears in 18:12. Already in v 5 pride was singled out as an "abomination" to the Lord. **19** This "better" saying insinuates that the humble may be more often found among the poor. It is not according to the expectations of the sages, who consistently rate prosperity as a blessing that comes to the wise. But when riches are associated with the proud, the usual scale of values is turned upside down. See the extended comment in the *Excursus on Retribution* and the *Excursus on Wealth and Poverty.* The metaphor of "dividing the spoil" derives ultimately from the practice of victors in warfare, and is used pejoratively in the context of "the proud."

20–24 These verses have a certain unity because they deal with word and wisdom. **20** Normally the "word" would be the teaching of the sage, e.g., 4:4, and to "find good" is associated with wisdom in 19:8. But perhaps there is a certain nuance given by the blessing pronounced in the parallel line: it could be the word of the Lord in whom one trusts; this may indicate more than the word of the sage; see the *Comment* on 13:13. In any case, the emphasis on trust in the Lord carries this verse, and the notion will reappear in 28:25 and 29:25. **21** There seems to be no contrast between the two lines. If one translates "but," perhaps line *b* is insisting on the need for "sweetness of lips" for wisdom to succeed. However, the second line can be taken merely as a specification of the first. The phrase about sweetness is a unique characterization of wisdom language, but cf. v 24a; 27:9b. It does not mean "sugary"; it is a positive complement as to both manner and content. The right word contributes to the learning effort for oneself and others. Wisdom is measured by the words in which it is conveyed. The "learning" that it increases is the general teaching of the sages found in this book. **22** Literally, the Hebrew has "the insight of its possessor" as the subject of the 22a; for the "fountain of life," see 10:11; 13:14; 14:27. The idea is traditional: the beneficent effects of wisdom. Line *b* is very terse and hence ambiguous. Folly itself is the מוּסַר, "discipline," of fools; they will pay dearly. This understanding indicates that discipline is understood in the active sense of chastising fools. Or perhaps the meaning is that to administer discipline is folly, since the fools cannot and will not be taught; any attempt to instruct them is useless. **23** The meaning is similar to that of v 21. Intelligence and wisdom are requisite for wise speech. The term לְקַח, literally, "taking," can mean the learning or teaching that is taken in; it occurred already in v 21 with the verb "increase." Some would think that it includes persuasiveness; both mouth and lips are parallel, and they indicate the outward expression of an inner wisdom. This point is perhaps present in the next verse. **24** The "sweetness" of v 21 appears in another guise: the power of "pleasant words"; see the same phrase in 15:26. Such words affect the "soul," or נֶפֶשׁ (translated here as [sweet to] "the taste"), and the body; cf. also 15:30.

25 The saying is identical with 14:12; see the *Comment* there. This is a perceptive and telling proverb, although it appears somewhat isolated here and in chap. 14. Meinhold argues that it introduces vv 27–30 because, as he notes, the word אִישׁ, "man," of v 25a is repeated at the beginning of each verse. Indeed, vv 27–30 are united by this catch word, but they have no real connection with v 25.

26 Life is presented here as a struggle in which bodily appetite is seen as a powerful moving force. "Appetite" (נֶפֶשׁ) is paralleled by "mouth," which here is not the organ of speech, but serves as a synonym for desire or appetite. "Toil" (עָמָל) is a key word in Qoheleth, and Whybray interprets line *a* in the light of Eccl 4:7–8 (a rich person toiling out of greed) and 3:9 (toil seen as futile). However, such a context is forcing this proverb which is content to merely register an observation. A better analogy would be Eccl 6:7: "All human toil is for the mouth, but the appetite is never satisfied." Here mouth and appetite are in parallelism. Although the dissatisfaction of Qoheleth is apparent, his comment recognizes that the appetite for food is a basic fact that moves humankind to toil.

27–30 The repetition of אִישׁ, "man," with each one representing an unpleasant character, at the beginning of vv 27–29 (cf. also 29:8–10) unites the verses, and there is a thematic connection with v 30. **27** See *Notes* 27.a. and 27.b. The imagery is bold: digging or raking up the past, and firing out. The destructive effect of the speech of the "man of Belial" is aptly conveyed by the metaphor of fire, which seems to be pictured as issuing from the mouth; cf. Jas 3:6; elsewhere the mouth produces sword thrusts. **28** See 2:12 and 6:19 for the phraseology.

The perverse person is literally the one who turns things upside down; see v 30, "upsets." Although "friends" is in the singular, it is to be understood as a collective noun.   **29**   The description of the evil type of person is continued with the notion of "seduction," the term that is developed in Prov 1:10–16. It is an understatement to say that the way of the wicked is "not good"; cf. 4:14–17.   **30**   This is a kind of summary description of the wicked person of vv 27–29 with which it shares catch words (lips, evil, upsets). It is based on exterior characteristics that supposedly betray the evil designs of the inner spirit; cf. 6:12–14. Judgment from appearances is countenanced here.

31   Gray hair implies a wise, virtuous person, since it usually accompanies age, a long life that is considered a blessing from God; cf. 3:16. The second line makes this explicit by pointing out the just way (cf. v 17) that such a person has traversed; see also 20:29. The wicked die young—supposedly! A quite different twist is given to this saying in Wis 4:9, where one reads that understanding is the hoary crown and that an unsullied life replaces long life as a value.

32   A "better" saying that exploits military metaphors to exalt the ideal of self-control, which is better than strength or victory; cf. 24:5–6. Self-control is frequently and highly praised by the sages; see 14:29; 15:18. It is celebrated also in Egyptian wisdom, and it continued to be held high in Jewish tradition: "Better is the long-suffering than the mighty, and he that rules his spirit than he that takes a city" (*Pirqe 'Abot* 4, 1; *APOT,* 2:703).

33   The final saying reaches back and ties in with vv 1 and 9, but it is more definite. The use of lots is attested in many places in the Bible, e.g., 18:18; 1 Sam 14:40–42, etc. Their purpose varied, but was usually to find a proper course of action in accord with the will of God. The underlying belief is that the Lord, who determines all things, also determines the way the lots turn out. The precise physical appearance of lots (dice?) and the procedure to be followed are difficult to specify. Here they are said to be thrown into the "lap," i.e., the fold of a person's garment; this is not necessarily the breastplate of the priest where the Urim and Thummim were to be placed, Exod 28:30. Thus the divine will was ascertained. The practice appears in Acts 1:26 in the choice of Mathias to succeed Judas.

Explanation

Chap. 16 marks a turn in the book. Chaps. 10–15 were long considered (and still are; cf. Scoralick, *Einzelspruch*) to be a separate collection. The difference in chap. 16 is not only in style, e.g., less antithetical sayings, but also in theological content. It is not that the book previously lacked significant theology, but rather that the sovereign action of the Lord was not emphasized as much as here. And the very beginning is impressive: eight of the first nine verses are YHWH sayings. The dispute among scholars (e.g., D. Snell, R. N. Whybray) centers around chaps. 14–16. Is there a suture contained somewhere in these chapters that indicates that two collections have been joined? There is no sufficient consensus, but the reader can be advised that somewhere in this area there has probably been a juxtaposition of two collections.

The striking emphasis on divine activity within the heart/mind of human beings deserves a word of comment. It is a well-established fact that in the Old Testament view YHWH is the agent or cause of all that happens, even in the mysterious area of human activity. But it is equally clear that human beings cannot evade responsibility for their actions. They cannot, as it were, blame the divine activity. The entire thrust of the prophets, the condemnation of the people collectively and individually, rules this out. The Bible does not speak of free will, but that idea is presupposed. Interestingly enough, it appears explicitly first in the writing of Ben Sira: "Do not say, 'it was God's doing that I fell away' . . . When he created humankind, he made them subject to their own free choice"; Sir 15:11–14. This is not surprising. It is another way of putting the challenge of Deuteronomy: "Today I set before you life and death, blessing and curse. Choose life!" (30:19). But the interesting fact is that Israel never really struggled with the problem of human freedom and divine determination. This was an issue for later theologians, both Jewish and Christian, and it still remains without an adequate "explanation." Both sides of the question are affirmed equally in the Bible, almost without awareness of a problem. A parallel case would be the view of what happens to a human being after death. The individual goes to Sheol, as is asserted many times over. This is that murky place/condition, located in the belly of the earth, where one's condition is best described as "nonlife." Such individuals are called "shades" (*rĕphā'îm*). Words fail, and imagination takes over, in the description of this "existence" in the books of Job and Ezekiel especially. No attempt is made to define "who" one is. No one ever returned from the "land of no return." Indeed, Qoheleth gives the dimmest view of Sheol in Eccl 9:10, and his words in 12:7 are astounding: "the dust returns to the earth as it was, and the life-breath returns to God who gave it." "Who" is in Sheol?

In a quirky "biographical" interpretation of God according to the Tanach, J. Miles understands Prov 16:4 as a new and untraditional answer to the customary plea that the wicked receive their due. According to him (*God*, 291), the Lord is "here imagined to respond, 'I have my purpose for them, and [by clear implication] you must endure them.'" This interpretation does not do justice to either part of the verse. V 4a is not intended to be "comforting" (p. 292); it simply asserts the common overall conviction that the Lord controls everything. But the question arises, on many sides, as the Psalms illustrate, what is the relationship of God to the wicked? Don't they escape? V 4b says, no, not even the wicked can escape the evil day in store for them, whatever shape it may take (early death, losing one's fortune, impending disaster); it is inevitable and inescapable. Ultimately there is no timetable for divine intervention. This is traditional retribution, affirmed in the face of obvious difficulties. Miles also claims (pp. 304–5) that the solution to the problem of innocent suffering, manifested poignantly in Ps 49:18–20 and in the book of Job, does not go beyond Prov 16:4. There is allegedly a crucial correction already in the key statement, " 'The beginning of wisdom is the fear of the Lord,' namely reward/punishment occurs, *except when the Lord, for mysterious reasons of his own, decrees otherwise*" (p. 205, his emphasis). Miles presses the meaning of the proverb beyond reason. God has his purposes, but they are beyond human ken. The mystery of their God was a "given" for the Israelites, and the book of Proverbs as well, as clearly expressed in Prov 21:30, to the effect that there is no wisdom that counts in view of the Lord.

Proverbs 17:1–28

Bibliography

Bühlmann, W. *Vom rechten Reden*, passim. **Krispenz, J.** *Spruchkomposition*. 173. **Whybray, R. N.** *Composition*. 110–11.

Translation

17:1   *Better a dry crust, with quiet,*
    than a house full of feasting, with quarrels.

2   *A clever servant will rule a shameful son,*
    and will inherit along with the heirs.

3   *The crucible for silver, the furnace for gold—*
    but the tester of hearts: the Lord.

4   *An evildoer, one who listens to wicked lips;*
    a liar,[a] one with an ear[b] for a destructive tongue.

5   *Whoever mocks the poor blasphemes the Maker;*
    whoever rejoices at a disaster[a] will not go unpunished.

6   *The crown of old men, grandchildren,*
    and the glory of children, their fathers.

7   *Unbefitting a fool, honest[a] lips;*
    the more so, deceitful lips in a noble.

8   *A bribe, a charm in the eyes of the one who gives it;*
    everywhere he turns he succeeds.

9   *One who disregards a fault, one who seeks friendship;*
    one who insists on it,[a] one who loses a companion.

10   *A rebuke gets[a] to an intelligent person*
    better than a hundred lashes on a fool.

11   *The evil person seeks out only rebellion,[a]*
    but a cruel messenger will be sent to him.

12   *Encounter a bear deprived of her cubs—*
    but not a fool in his folly!

13   *Whoever returns evil for good—*
    evil will never depart[a] from that house.

14   *Whoever unleashes water, the beginning of strife;*
    so before the burst, stop quarreling!

15   *One who justifies the wicked or one who condemns the just—*
    an abomination to the Lord, both of them.

16   *For what purpose the price in the hand of a fool*
    to buy wisdom when there is no heart for it?

17   *A neighbor, loving at all times—*
    and a brother is born for adversity.

18   *A person lacking sense, one who pledges his hand,*
    going surety in the presence of his neighbor.

19   *One who loves iniquity, one who loves strife;*
    one who makes his gate high, one who seeks destruction.

20	*The crooked of heart cannot find good,*
	and one perverse of tongue[a] *falls into evil.*
21	*Whoever begets a fool, his the grief,*
	and the father of a stupid person can have no joy.
22	*A joyful heart makes for good health,*[a]
	but a crushed spirit dries up the bones.
23	*The wicked draw upon a pocketed bribe*
	to pervert the ways of justice.
24	*In front of the perceptive: wisdom,*
	but the eyes of a fool: on the ends of the earth.
25	*A vexation to his father, a foolish son,*
	and bitterness to the woman who bore him.
26	*Punishment of the just, surely not good;*
	striking honorable people, against justice.[a]
27	*Whoever moderates his words, a knowing person,*
	and the cool[a] *of spirit, an understanding person.*
28	*Even a fool, keeping silent, can be taken to be wise;*
	a tight-lipped person, intelligent.

Notes

4.a. "Liar" translates "lie"; an abstract is used for the concrete.

4.b. It is not unusual for the *aleph* to be elided with this type of verb; cf. Joüon §73f,h; GKC §68i.

5.a. The Greek seems to have read "the one who perishes" (cf. *BHS*); but perhaps the abstract is simply rendered as concrete.

7.a. The meaning of יתר, "honest," is not clear; ordinarily it indicates what is left over, and this is interpreted as "(a lip of) excellence" (cf. RSV). Some kind of antithesis to "deceitful lips" is needed, and the Greek provides πιστά, "faithful," which suggests reading ישׁר, "upright," as the above translation presupposes; but this is far from certain.

9.a. This phrase is literally "one who repeats a thing." Four participles are juxtaposed, as also elsewhere in this chapter (cf. vv 15a, 19, 28b).

10.a. The verb is to be derived from נחת, "go down," although the LXX seems to have derived it from חתת, "shatter," cf. *BHS*.

11.a. Translations of v 11 vary in that it is possible to take "evil" as the object and "rebel" as the subject: the rebel seeks out only evil. So for example, the NJV, Alonso Schökel, and Barucq.

13.a. There is no real difference between the Qere and Ketib; the issue is identity of the middle vowel: *waw* or *yod*.

20.a. It is also possible, although rather less probable, to render 20b: "one overturned by his tongue" and understand the "his" as referring to the "crooked of heart" in v 20a.

22.a. גהה, "healing, cure," is hapax, and the meaning uncertain; but on the basis of Hos 5:13 ("and he did not heal you of your sore") one can argue with F. Delitzsch for "healing," instead of adopting an emendation.

26.a. על־ישׁר means "against what is right"; other translations prefer to read על־יתר, "excessive, abundantly."

27.a. The Ketib, "cool," is to be preferred to the Qere ("precious" of spirit).

Form/Structure/Setting

This chapter resembles a hodgepodge of sayings. It presents a remarkable contrast to the previous chapter which in comparison appears as a finely chiseled whole. Alonso Schökel suggests some thematic undercurrents. Thus he groups vv

1, 3, 9, 14, 15, 19, 23, and 26 under the broad theme of dispute (litigation, judgment), and notes that it is interconnected with a "domestic" theme (house, brother, friends, father, son) that appears in vv 1, 2, 6, 9, 13, 17, 18, 19, 21, 25. The tenuous connection of these verses remains, and the suggestion of catch words does not achieve unity here. For example, לֵב ("heart") occurs in vv 3, 16, 18 ("sense"), 20, and 22. But this term is such a favorite of the sages that its frequent appearance does not signal unity unless other signs also can be detected. Antithetical sayings, as noted previously, are on the decrease. The use of participles, especially in juxtaposition, as the above translation has tried to bring out, is noteworthy; cf. vv 4, 9, 15, 19, 27. Meinhold makes a brave effort to unite chap. 17 under the heading of "training that fails," in so far as many sayings point to actions that are foolish. He finds the theme sketched in vv 1–6. Vv 7–15 present mostly examples of perverse speech and conduct, and this is continued in vv 16–20, while vv 21–28 are construed as a summary. Whybray finds "no sign of a comprehensive structure" (*Composition,* 110) and rejects the linking of 17:26–18:8 (so Krispenz, *Spruchkomposition*).

Comment

1 "Better" sayings have appeared before; see especially 15:16–17 and the *Explanation* for chap. 15, and also cf. 16:8. There has been some discussion about the cultic nuance in "sacrifices of strife" (translated as "feasting with quarrels"). Plöger simply dismisses this aspect. He is correct, but Alonso Schökel is more subtle; he recognizes here an ironic contrast to the "peace sacrifices," commonly mentioned in the liturgy. There is a stark contrast between the practically useless dry bread and the rich meal, making the preference all the more striking. As it is, v 1 displays the depth of this type of "better" saying. See also Amenemope, "Better is bread with a happy heart / Than wealth with vexation" (9:7–8; Lichtheim, *AEL,* 2:152).

2 The inheritance was divided among the sons; cf. Deut 21:17, according to which the oldest received two-thirds, the "double" portion. The likelihood of a slave receiving the inheritance was not great, although slaves were usually treated well; they were an important investment. This extreme example is used to strengthen the warning to those who might be tempted to shirk their duties; even the house servant may replace them by dint of his application; cf. 10:5 and 12:24.

3 The effect of the crucible and furnace would be to test these metals and remove the impurities. Similar work is also to be applied to human beings. They are to be tested not only by human praise, as in 27:21, but by the Lord no less, whose specialty is the human heart, which is notoriously tortuous (Jer 17:9–10; 20:10). The Lord knows the mysteries of the depths of Sheol, and therefore also the human heart; cf. 15:11. See also the image of the Lord's "weighing" hearts in 21:2; 24:12.

4 "Liar" is literally "lie," or "deceit," parallel to "evildoer." It is possible, but unnecessary, to switch the subject and predicate in v 4a. The pertinent parts of the body are, as usual, in evidence: lips and tongue are the means by which harmful effects are produced; cf. 16:27. The saying emphasizes the readiness, even the eagerness, of the wicked to listen to scurrilous talk.

5 In contrast to the actual oppression of the poor in 14:31, the *attitude* toward them is underscored here, and line *b* further emphasizes the evil of such callous conduct. Although the parallelism between the two lines leaves something to be desired, it is clear that the "disaster" refers to some calamity affecting the poor. One's treatment of others, especially the poor, is an index of one's treatment of God; one who is kind to the poor is making a loan to the Lord; cf. 19:17. See also 22:2; 29:13; Sir 11:4.

6 The relationship between three generations is described ("sons" occurs three times) in an ideal fashion: grandparents to grandchildren, and children to fathers. The grandparents are honored in that they have lived a long life and are able to behold their descendants who are a prolongation of themselves, their immortality, as it were. The children find a reflection of themselves in their worthy fathers; the honor of a son lies in the honor of his father, according to Sir 3:11a. The typical values of longevity and fertility are implied. This ideal description is to be balanced against the observations in vv 21 and 25, which portray more realistic situations—the grief that foolish children cause the parents.

7 The saying is made up of four juxtaposed participles, and the second line reinforces the first. For the translation, see *Note* 7.a.; this is contrary to the NRSV ("fine speech"), which is defended also by W. Buhlmann (*Vom rechten Reden*, 142–46). Whatever be the precise meaning of line *a*, the denial of what is proper is specified and heightened in the second line. The noble should have no shadow of deceit about them; *noblesse oblige*.

8 This proverb describes reality: the way a bribe works. It is a "stone of favor," whether for the giver (more likely), or the receiver. It is a kind of amulet or charm that ensures success "in the eyes of its owner"—at least, so it appears. Despite 18:16 (see the *Comment* there), it is difficult to establish that the sages made a distinction between a sheer gift and a gift that was meant to obligate another. V 23 clearly has bribery in mind and condemns it; perhaps the setting is judicial. In 21:14, the distorting effect of a "gift" seems to be meant; see the *Comment*. Meinhold thinks that v 8 is ambiguous; it can be merely an observation about bribery, or it can be also an ironic, even sarcastic, way of characterizing the effects of a "gift."

9 See *Note* 9.a. The purpose of the saying is to preserve friendship; this means "covering," as the first participle literally reads (cf. 10:12b, 18a), i.e., effectively forgiving, and even forgetting, the fault of another. The amicable relationship would be destroyed by harping on the fault, or all the more so, by repeating it to others, as some interpret line *b*. Such tolerance is in the spirit of Lev 19:18; cf. Sir 19:16.

10 The sages consistently urge openness to correction and to reprimand. Here the term is not the usual one (תוֹכַחַת), but a gruff rebuke (גְּעָרָה). Although corporal punishment was part of the "discipline," it could be avoided if one listened to reprimand. Since the fool seems incorrigible by definition, the beating is exaggerated: a hundred blows, an amount more than twice what is prescribed in Deut 12:3 for a guilty party. What was a normal practice for children is envisioned here for adults; the exaggeration suggests that it was hardly used. The point of the saying is to indicate that the wise person must stay open to the improvement that comes from correction by others (13:18b).

11 See *Note* 11.a. for an alternative translation. F. Delitzsch remarks that a series of sayings about "dangerous men" begins here. It is difficult to specify the nature of the rebellion—against God, king, or society? Correspondingly, the identity of the cruel messenger and also of the one who sent him is left open; perhaps that is all the more effective. In any case, the evil or the rebellious will pay for their actions. The parallelism is loose; v 11b specifies what will happen to the subject of v 11a.

12 This vivid exaggeration is not lacking in humor. The fools are considered here to be as dangerous and aggressive as bears, at least in the sense that their folly is exceedingly harmful. There is frequent mention of the need to steer clear of fools (14:7) and to associate with the wise (13:20a). This is because both folly and wisdom are contagious. However, one gets the impression that folly is more contagious, since it is described in such extreme language. It is ironic that the power of folly for harm is portrayed in graphic terms that are not used for the power of wisdom for good. Does this reveal a touch of pessimism about human nature? Rather, it is easier to threaten disaster and harder to motivate good. Moreover, one should recall that chaps. 1–9, as indeed the whole book, are written to set off the excellence of wisdom as a goal. Basically, the metaphors of life and death are always at work. The existence of bears is attested many times, e.g., David in 2 Sam 17:8. The Lord is compared to a bear in Hos 13:8; cf. also Prov 28:15.

13 There is a play on the word "evil" (רעה). Evil, in one form or another, never leaves, even though it be inflicted on another. When ingratitude is heightened not merely by indifference but by an evil return for a good deed, it is doubly reprehensible. The retribution is seen as collective, affecting the entire household of the evil person. It is not clear if retribution is directly the work of God, or is to be conceived here as exemplifying the deed-consequence mentality; "evil" has settled in that house(hold).

14 The picturesque metaphor of water bursting out from a hole is used to present the pent-up strife that can result from a small beginning but then gather power, developing into a full-scale dispute. The metaphor is well chosen to indicate the reality of argumentation over nothing.

15 The terminology suggests judicial background, and this downright abuse of justice is an "abomination" to the Lord. See the legislation in Deut 25:1. Likewise, the prophets were concerned especially with social justice; cf. Isa 5:23.

16 The point of this ironic proverb is to emphasize the hopeless situation of the fool. Even should he possess the means to become wise, he will not employ them. There is probably a sarcastic implication: the fool is dumb enough to think that the acquisition of wisdom is merely a matter of a monetary transaction. The reference to money does not necessarily mean that one had to pay for lessons in wisdom. Nowhere is there any indication that wisdom can be bought. The price for acquiring wisdom is only metaphorical; the fool does not have the "heart," i.e., the sense or desire to pursue the goal. See also v 24. According to 26:7, the fool is not able to implement a proverb, even though he "mouths" it.

17 This proverb is ambiguous, and interpreters differ among each other. It is not clear if the parallelism is synonymous or antithetical; the connective translated "and" can also frequently mean "but"; it is deliberately omitted in the translation above. If synonymous, then line *b* specifies the particular reliability of the friend; in a difficulty he becomes, as it were, a blood brother; cf. 24:10b and 27:10. This is a metaphorical use of "brother." See also 18:24, but the proverb in 27:10 goes in the other direction. If, however, a contrast is intended, there is a heightening: a brother is better than an ever-loyal neighbor. In a crisis one can always be sure, even more certain, of the help from a brother. A brother is made for that kind of trial; the crisis makes evident his loyalty. As we say, blood is thicker than water.

18 On going surety for another, see 6:1–5 with the *Comment*. Whoever does this is lacking "heart" (literally). "In the presence of his neighbor" in v 18b is not clear; some take it to mean "on behalf of"; others think it designates the neighbor as a third party and witness to the transaction. It would seem to point to an aggravating circumstance.

19 Again, the grammatical construction is the juxtaposition of four participles. But the verse is difficult. In v 19a, it is not clear which is the subject and which the predicate: the lover of strife is the lover of iniquity, or vice versa? The above translation agrees with the NRSV against the NIV. However, the real problem is v 19b; in the Greek this is added to v 16! No one really knows the meaning of "to make his opening high." One thinks of an elaborate entrance, either as a sign of stupid architecture, or of pride, or even as a way of keeping people out. Others have understood "opening" (or emended the text) as referring to "mouth," hence proud speech. In any case, the verse indicates a self-destructive move, since synonymous parallelism is clearly intended.

20 The "crooked at heart" appear in the plural in 11:20, and this type is characterized as abomination to the Lord; here they are hopelessly astray, unreliable, and unable to locate what is good. Their counterpart is specified as one who literally turns things upside down by means of the tongue, i.e., lies and deceit. Neither group in this saying comes out well; failure to "find good" is to fall into "evil," i.e., adversity of some kind.

21 This verse finds an echo in v 25, leading Whybray to suggest that along with the intervening verses, this was "once a distinct group." One may grant that v 24 fits in, but even Whybray admits this is "less obviously so" for vv 22 and 23. Meinhold also recognizes a unity in vv 21–25 and even extends it to v 27; he describes the entire passage as a summary concerning a failed training program. It is doubtful that one can read the mind of a redactor so precisely. V 21 takes up thoughts expressed in 10:1; 15:20; 19:13a, and elsewhere. The topos of the foolish and disgraceful son is quite common; in a sense it needs no comment, but its very frequency is a sign of the close tie between family training and family pride.

22 See *Note* 22.a. The first line is similar to 15:13 except that the uncertain "health" replaces "face." In both cases there is a recognition of what we would call a psychosomatic unity. Inner dispositions affect the body in terms of well-being or its opposite. For similar observations, see 14:13, 30.

23 It is clear that the issue is outright bribery, which is condemned. The setting seems to be a judicial one. The "pocketed bribe" is literally "a bribe from the bosom"—probably the bosom of the briber. It suggests the guilty secretiveness that appears also in 21:14. See the *Comment* on v 8. Different words are used to indicate bribe or gift, but the terms themselves do not settle the issue. One has to look to the possible context; cf. 18:16, which does not suggest any blame for a "gift."

24 Spatial images are used here to designate concentration or the lack of it. An understanding person has wisdom as the goal, directly in front. The fool is distracted and unfocused, looking everywhere, without ever fixing on the one thing that is necessary. In v 24a wisdom seems to be aggressive: literally, "in the face of the understanding person." In any case, she cannot be seen by the fool, who would not buy wisdom even if he saw her; cf. v 16.

25   See the *Comment* on v 21.

26   See *Note* 26.a. The heightening between the two lines is reminiscent of the same characteristic in v 7. The setting is judicial, but the type of punishment is not specified. If it is some kind of fine, then the heightening in the second line ("striking") would imply that probably flogging is meant; cf. Deut 25:1–2. An unjust decision is indicated, and it is all the more deplorable if noble people are involved. Apparently the "noble" person (cf. v 7) is also presumed to be just. McKane regards these as "two random samples of bad penal practice." In that case, they are to be associated with v 15.

27–28   These verses are united by the topic of speech/silence and by the clever antithesis between them. On the one hand, whoever speaks little can be seen as careful and thoughtful in expression (v 27). On the other hand, silence can be a sign of having nothing worth saying, as in the case of a silent fool (v 28). The "cool of spirit" (see *Note* 27.a.) is the opposite of what the Egyptian wisdom writings describe as the "heated man." He resembles the patient person, calm and slow to anger; see the *Comment* on 14:29. It is precisely because the fool usually cannot control his mouth and consistently utters stupidities (cf. Eccl 10:12–14; Sir 20:5–8; Job 13:5) that silence is the only salvation for him. But of course his silence is an ambiguous sign. There is an old Latin proverb to the effect that if one had kept silent one would have been taken to be a philosopher.

Explanation

The variegated character of this chapter makes it difficult to focus on any single emphasis. The lack of a dominant theme suggests that it is better to single out the most significant sayings. On this score, chap. 17 has great promise for the reader. The "better" sayings, in general, are telling, and this is true of v 1. V 3 on the testing of hearts is important from both a psychological and theological point of view. The attitude to the poor is to be based on the doctrine of creation, v 5. Bribery (vv 7 and 23) is important enough to have attracted attention to itself in many other sayings of this book. The danger of folly is caught by a picturesque description of meeting up with an irate bear in v 12, and the hopelessness of the fool is indicated by the witty saying in v 16. The contrast between the two sayings at the end of the chapter is perceptive and true. The ambiguity of silence is a good example of the high regard the sages had for the right word at the right time; see also Sir 20:5–7.

Proverbs 18:1–24

Bibliography

Bühlmann, W. *Vom rechten Reden,* passim. **Meinhold, A.** "Zur strukturellen Eingebundenheit der JHWH-Sprüche in Prov 18." In *Von Gott Reden.* FS S. Wagner, ed. D. Vieweger. BJEAT.

Neukirchen: Neukirchener, 1995. 247–54. **Whybray, R. N.** *Composition.* 112–13. **Williams, J. G.** "The Power of Form: A Study of Biblical Proverbs." In *Gnomic Wisdom.* Ed. J. D. Crossan. Chico: Scholars Press, 1980. 35–58.

Translation

18:1	*An alienated person seeks out his own desire;* *he quarrels with any success.*[a]
2	*A fool takes no pleasure in understanding,* *but rather in revealing what is in his heart.*
3	*Comes the wicked, comes scorn also,* *and with disgrace, reproach.*
4	*Deep waters, words from one's mouth;* *a flowing stream, a fountain of wisdom.*[a]
5	*Not good: showing favor to the wicked* *so as to oppress the just in a judgment.*
6	*The lips of a fool lead to strife;* *his mouth calls for blows.*
7	*The mouth of a fool, his destruction,* *and his lips, a snare for his life.*
8	*The words of a gossiper, like dainty morsels,*[a] *and they go down to one's inmost being.*
9	*Whoever is slack in his work,* *a brother to the destroyer.*
10	*The name of the Lord, a strong tower;* *the just run to it and are set on high.*
11	*The wealth of the rich, a strong city,* *and like a high wall, so he imagines.*[a]
12	*Before a collapse the heart is proud,* *but before honor, humility.*
13	*One who answers before listening,* *his the folly and shame.*
14	*The spirit of a person sustains him when ill,* *but a crushed spirit, who can bear?*
15	*An understanding heart acquires knowledge,* *and the ears of the wise seek out knowledge.*
16	*A man's gift*[a] *creates room for him,* *giving access to important people.*
17	*The first to plead a case—right!* *then comes*[a] *his opponent and examines him.*
18	*The lot settles quarrels,* *and is decisive among the powerful.*
19	*A brother offended, stronger than a city,* *and disputes, like the bars of a castle.*[a]
20	*By the fruit of one's mouth the belly is sated;* *by the product of the lips is one sated.*
21	*Death and life, in the power of the tongue;* *those*[a] *who love it will eat its fruit.*

22   *He who finds a wife finds good,*
          and obtains favor from the Lord.
23   *The poor utters entreaties,*
          but the rich reply roughly.
24   *Friends* [a]*—for one to associate with,*[b]
          but there is one more loving and closer than a brother.

Notes

1.a. The translation is uncertain. "Alienated" is literally "one who is separated"; the Hebrew has only the word "desire" (without "his own"). For this the LXX read προφάσεις, "pretexts," and this meaning is adopted by some who adduce an alleged parallel in Judg 14:4, where it is a hapax (reading תֹאֲנָה as in *BHS*). "Success" is a possible meaning of the Hebrew, but the LXX has καιρός, "time"—thus: "at all times."

4.a. The LXX reads "life" for "wisdom," perhaps influenced by the frequent phrase "fountain of life" (cf. *BHS*). There is no need to change the text, and there is little difference in meaning since the "fountain of life" is closely associated with wisdom.

8.a. מִתְלַהֲמִים, "dainty morsels," is hapax, and it is rendered by μαλακοί, "soft," in the LXX at 26:22. There is no certain solution for the word; little progress has been made since the discussions in F. Delitzsch and in C. Toy.

11.a. The LXX reads ἐπισκιάζει, "overshadow, protect," and from this has been inferred the conjecture in *BHS*, בְּמְשֻׂכָתוֹ, "in its hedge, protection"; cf. Prov 15:19. The MT is to be preferred; בְּמַשְׂכִּיתוֹ is literally "in his/its image," and the term is understood metaphorically to indicate "imagination." A sharper contrast with the previous verse is also achieved.

16.a. מַתֶּן, "gift," is to be considered as construct, despite the vocalization; cf. GKC §92g.

17.a. The Qere וּבָא, "he comes," is reflected in the versions, and is to be preferred; cf. *BHS*.

19.a. The Hebrew is difficult and probably corrupt. "Offended" is a dubious translation of the niphal participle of פָּשַׁע; hence *BHS* מוֹשִׁיעַ following the LXX βοηθούμενος suggests "a helping brother." The comparative *min* before "strong city" is obscure; perhaps it should be changed to "like" with the LXX ὡς. Line *b* translates the MT, but the meaning is uncertain.

21.a. For the disagreement in number between verb and subject, see GKC §145l.

24.a. A literal translation of the MT is "a man of friends," but most prefer to emend "man" to "there are" as suggested in some versional evidence: יֵשׁ for אִישׁ; the difference in translation is negligible.

24.b. The root of the verb can be רָעַע in the sense of "inflict harm," or רָעָה with the sense "associate with."

Form/Structure/Setting

The structure, or better the lack of it, characterizes this chapter as well as the previous one. There is no significant large group of sayings. In his commentary (p. 296), A. Meinhold recognizes "brother" in vv 9, 19, and 24 as an indication of a threefold division: vv 1–9 on perverse speech; vv 10–19 on the strengths that accrue to the wise; vv 20–24, on speech and friendship. But it is difficult to find true thematic unity here. Plays on words associate some verses (vv 1 and 2; 6 and 8; obvious only in the Hebrew text) that otherwise have little in common. However, Alonso Schökel observes that speaking and listening receive considerable attention: vv 2, 4, 6, 7, 8, 13, 15, 20, 21, 23. Strife and quarreling, probably in judicial cases, are featured in vv 5, 17–19, and the usual attention is given to the fool (vv 1–2, 6–7, 13).

Comment

1 See *Note* 1.a. The sense of the translation is that those who have alienated themselves from the community, whatever this be, family or larger group, go their own way. This individualism is quite contrary to the sense of collective identity shared by the ancient Israelite. Line *b* illustrates the effect of such antisocial activity; there is no acceptance of the general values of the community. The Septuagint rendering emphasizes the unwillingness, and hence the culpability, of the alienated ever to conform.

2 See also Prov 12:16, 23; 13:16. A fool by nature simply blurts out and reveals a lack of understanding. Again, heart and understanding are word pairs, but there is irony in v 2b: revealing what is in one's heart, i.e., nothing. As always in the wisdom tradition, speech is the index of a person. The fool is the total opposite of the wise person described in v 15.

3 The MT contrasts a concrete with an abstract, but there is no reason to change the vocalization in line *a* to read the abstract "wickedness." "Disgrace" is literally "lightness" (קָלוֹן), the opposite of "heavy/glory" (כָּבוֹד).

4 The meaning of the text depends upon the interpretation of "deep waters." On the one hand, the phrase can indicate what is deep and out of reach—thus stagnant or incomprehensible or perhaps even chaotic. In that case there is a contrast between such words and wisdom, which is described as a free-flowing fountain in v 4b. "Fountain of life" is a frequent symbol for wisdom: 10:11; 13:14; 14:27; 16:22. On the other hand, if deep waters is meant in a positive sense of something profound, as is suggested by the use of the phrase in Prov 20:5, then the metaphors in line *b* can be taken as continuous with the first line, specifying and heightening the "words." They would then symbolize positive qualities, such as would be expected from the mouth of the wise. This view seems more likely. See the lengthy discussion in W. Bühlmann, *Vom rechten Reden*, 275–79.

5 Another "not good" saying; cf. 16:29; 17:26. To show favor or partiality is literally "to lift up the face" of the one who is favored. It reflects a situation in which a superior instructs an inferior, who has bowed down, to stand up, and thus he lifts up the face. Here it describes the action of a judge who blatantly issues an unjust decision; cf. 17:23.

6–7 Both of these verses deal with the organs of speech (lips/mouth used chiastically), as employed by a fool, and hence they point out the bad effects of his talk. **6** It is not clear if the "blows" in line *b* are to be understood as a punishment that the fool receives (therefore, in a judicial case), or merely as a violent dispute that is brought about by his heedless speech. **7** This verse is a drastic and dramatic description of the price the fool will have to pay for his unbridled speech: it is a deadly trap; see also vv 20–21.

8 This verse appears also in 26:22, where it is perhaps more suitable to the context. See *Note* 8.a. "Dainty morsels" is a common, if uncertain, translation. Experience bears out the attraction that gossip exerts over human beings; it enters deeply into a person; the second line suggests this penetration and perhaps the hearer's relishing, if the translation of v 8a is correct. For harmful effects of gossip, cf. 16:28.

9 As far as results are concerned, the one who is only slack in work differs little from one who is downright lazy; both are reprehensible. The comparison to a destroyer or wrecker leaves uncertainty as to what has been destroyed; perhaps it is simply the assigned work. This seems to be a deliberate exaggeration; see 28:24b where the same term is used in connection with the brutal treatment of parents.

10–11   These verses are united by catch words ("strong," "high"), by theme, and by contrast. The just are contrasted with the rich; the theme is the source of one's trust (cf. Ps 52:9).   **10**   Reliance on the name of God is explicit in Pss 20:8; 124:8, and the Lord is described as a "tower" in Ps 61:8. Just as a besieged town might take refuge in a fortified tower, so also the just who are threatened by some adversity will be lifted "high" to safety; cf. Prov 29:25b; 28:25b.   **11**   The first line of the proverb deliberately picks up Prov 10:15, which expresses an obvious fact: riches are a protection. Even v 11b can be taken in a somewhat neutral sense, and seen as being in synonymous parallelism to line *a*. So the rich person thinks. This need not be an unreasonable or wicked viewpoint; it echoes Prov 10:15. However, the saying has more bite if "so he imagines" indicates only an *apparent*, but ultimately false, high point of safety. Thus it is in tension with the "high," or the name of the Lord, mentioned in v 10. Hence the situation has to be carefully weighed: in what or in whom do the rich really trust? This verse sounds a warning with regard to 10:15. Strictly, no judgment is passed on the rich; hence this proverb does not change the meaning of Prov 10:15, which is true as far as it goes. But a timely caution is sounded; the rich of v 11 must also keep v 10 in mind for the Lord provides strength that cannot fail. It is no wonder that Ben Sira sang the praises of the rich person who is found without fault, Sir 31:8–11. For further discussion, see R. E. Murphy, "Proverbs 22:1–9," *Int* 41 (1987) 398–402.

12   There is a *déja vu* about this verse; line *a* is similar to 16:18a, and line *b* repeats 15:33b. The idea that pride goes before a fall and humility before honor is a favorite with the sages; cf. Prov 11:2; 29:23; and 17:19b. "Proud" is literally "high," and hence this catch word associates the verse with vv 10–11, and provides another caution in addition to what is expressed there.

13   W. Bühlmann (*Vom rechten Reden,* 197–98) rightly argues that this verse is not to be limited specifically to a judicial hearing. It is much more general, and it is in line with the talkativeness of a fool; see v 7. Typically the fool does not listen to others and hence is not in real dialogue; he insists only on personal views. This saying is very closely matched by Sir 11:8, "Before hearing, do not answer, and do not interrupt anyone while they are talking." See also *Pirqe 'Abot,* 5:7. As always, effective speech is an ideal of the sage, and it depends upon hearing what the other says. Otherwise no communication is possible.

14   It is unusual that the word "spirit" appears twice. In v 14a it stands for the strength and determination of a person that can deal with physical sickness. In v 14b it is a "crushed spirit" that is so far depressed and shaken that it simply destroys a person. The phrase "crushed spirit" occurs in 15:13 and 17:22, where the contrast is with a joyful heart. Here the contrast is with the normal drive for life that anyone would usually have in confronting illness or adversity; the situation may be difficult, but one can recover; cf. Prov 12:25. However, the effect of the rhetorical question in line *b* is to throw doubt on the possibility of recovery, when one's courage fails.

15   Meinhold cleverly terms the heart and ear the "inner and outer" organs of reception, and refers to vv 12a, 13a. The learning process is heightened in the second line. The wise are open and even anxious to learn more—the ideal sage; cf. also 1:5; 15:14a. Again, there is a repetition, as in the previous verse with "spirit"; "knowledge" is found twice here.

16   Is the "gift" merely that, or is it an outright bribe to secure a favorable decision? See also 15:27; 17:8, 23 with the *Comments.* The various Hebrew terms

(מתן; שֹחד) are not sufficiently distinct to settle the issue. It is rather naive to think that the "gift" in this verse is disinterested; access to the great is made possible. While this is not necessarily a bribe that perverts a judgment, neither is it without influence on the formation of opinion. It is open to abuse, as the "lobbying" in current affairs in almost every modern country demonstrates. It can be said that the proverb is not an encouragement, but merely an observation, a recognition that this is reality. Many commentators (Whybray, Plöger, Meinhold) refer vv 16–19 to legal situations. They can be so applied, but one may also question if that was the original setting for all of the verses. And even if the original setting is a legal case, the proverb could be *applied* beyond that situation.

17 The implication is that the one who has the first word may seem to be in the right, but one should listen to the story of the other side—a second opinion, so to speak. Literally the Hebrew has "the just one, first in his contention." The terms "just," or more suggestively "innocent," and "contention" may indicate a court of justice in which two litigants will have different versions of the issue; cf. Deut 1:16. However, the proverb is grounded in a universal experience; one must hear out both sides on any issue—in the family, for example, and not only in court.

18 The role of casting lots was important in Israelite society; see 16:33, where it is understood to be an ultimate expression of the divine will. But most of the biblical contexts are religious; there is little evidence of its widespread use in society, and there is no evidence that it was used to settle a juridical dispute. Perhaps it could have served as a court of last instance, as it were. It is not clear just why the process should be mentioned in the case of the "powerful." This may be a heightening: "even" among the important people. Where they were involved, the casting of lots may have been perceived as safer and more equitable.

19 The translation of this verse is uncertain; see *Note* 19.a. There is a beautiful statement in Deut 1:16–17 of equity among the community, describing how disputes are to be resolved. This saying deals with a difficult case. It envisions the hard feelings that ensue after a serious dispute, whether or not it has gone to court. The "offended brother" may feel mistreated and continue to harbor resentment; cf. v 1. Especially among close relatives and friends can this be true. The comparison of the strife to the bars of a castle or fortress is not clear. Perhaps the reference is to the difficulty of penetrating any well protected and barred building. Similarly, the "brother" is not going to be won over easily. In any case, the wisdom of Prov 17:14 is applicable: squelch a dispute before it begins.

20–21 The catch word "fruit" unites these verses, which deal with the effects of speech. See the *Comments* on 12:14 and especially 13:2, and the treatment by W. Bühlmann, *Vom rechten Reden*, 303–15, 318–21. **20** Broadly interpreted, this proverb might appear to be neutral: one must bear the responsibility for whatever one says. But it is more likely that to be "sated" (the word occurs twice) indicates that the "fruit" is good; if it were not, would one eat so much of it? Whybray points out the oxymoron, which Alonso Schökel calls a paradox, in v 20a: How can one be sated by what comes out, instead of what goes into it? This figure is settled in the next line which makes the first line explicit; the "fruit" is speech, and presumably good, not bad, speech. Satiety to the belly is merely following out the metaphor which began with the consumption of fruit; the point is the happiness brought about by good words. **21** The significance of speech is intensified by the reference to death and life. Since these are particularly the domain of the Lord, there is a strong affirmation of "the power (literally 'hand') of the tongue." Does this refer to the speaker or those he addresses? Perhaps both. There is a similar proverb in Sir 37:18 concerning the power of the tongue over life and death. It is not clear what "it" in "love it" refers to. It seems to be the tongue and so would refer to the possibility of talking foolishly or wisely. This would seem to include the alternative of life/death. See also the *Comment* on 13:2.

22 Whybray agrees with Toy and Plöger that vv 22–24 "deal with different but important aspects of ordinary life: marriage, wealth, friendship." This is true, but hardly a sufficient reason to lump these sayings together; wisdom proverbs are nearly always dealing with human events, without necessarily seeking a common line between them. V 22, along with 19:14 (see the *Comment* there), takes a very favorable attitude to woman as wife. Admittedly, the judgment is from the male point of view. But it is also indicated that the husband has little to do acquiring such a prize. She is a gift from God; cf. 12:2a. The alliteration in v 22a seems of itself to be an added point of emphasis. Line *b* sounds like an echo of Prov 8:35b where it describes the "finding" (very often a key word in the passages in which it is used) of personified Wisdom. The LXX needlessly adds "good" to "woman," and also gives another couplet concerning an adulteress. The Greek text is problematic at this point, omitting vv 23–24 and the first two verses of the next chapter.

23 This proverb can be viewed as a declaratory statement about the privilege that the rich enjoy over the poor. They can afford to speak their mind in opposition, so confident are they; money talks; cf. v 11. But the poor have to watch their tongues lest they be rebuffed. Speech will betray the respective social classes. But is the saying merely declaratory, or is it issued here as a challenge to side with the poor against the rich? Previous contrasts between the rich and poor, e.g., 10:15; 14:20, would suggest that this saying is not entirely neutral—the Lord is the Maker of them both; cf. 14:31; 17:5; 22:2.

24 See *Note* 24.b.; different nuances are possible. As translated above, there is a contrast between casual friends and friends who are closer to one than even a brother. Thus the first line is considerably heightened in the second. If the verb in line *a* connotes harm, as *Note* 24.b. allows, then the saying refers to friends that somehow inflict harm or bring ruin. This reading is less likely, and other meanings have been sought to improve upon the above translation, but without much success.

Explanation

The general characteristics of this chapter have been noted above in the remarks on *Form*. Here we might point out a tendency to allow proverbs to be passed over, to lose their individuality, because they are smothered as it were by being associated with so many sayings. Thus, the sayings about bribery (v 5) and gifts (v 16) leave open an area of decision that challenges the reader; is there any difference between the two? Should they not provoke thought? Foolish talk is a common enough topic among the wisdom writers. That is the difficulty for us; do we appreciate the truth and intensity of vv 6–7? The contrast between the rich and the poor is not only widespread in society; it was bound to be picked up in proverbial sayings. A particularly clever instance is to be found in vv 10–11, joined to their subtle interplay with Prov 10:15. The frequency with which even today we answer before listening (v 13), or simply fail to listen, tells us how incorrigible human beings can be; is there a more universal trait? And how often are we impressed by someone's version of an incident before we hear the report of the other party (v 17).

V 22 sounds almost naive, until we meditate upon it. Delitzsch rehearses an interesting story from the Babylonian Talmud (*b. Yebam.* 63b; *b. Ber.* 8a) that can be used to fix this proverb in memory. The Jewish sages played on the verb in Prov 18:22 and its occurrence in Qoheleth. The verb is מצא, "find," and the saying in 18:22 is a happy one, but in Eccl 7:26, Qoheleth says: I found (מוצא) more bitter than death the woman . . . etc. Hence it came to be asked about marriage in Jewish tradition: מָצָא *māṣāʾ* or מוֹצֵא *môseʾ*? That is, was a person married happily or unhappily?

At first sight vv 20–21 seem clear enough. The mention of mouth and lips in v 20 refers to words or speech, but not without subtleties, as the *Comment* above indicates. V 21 has received various translations, pointed out by J. G. Williams (*Semeia* 17 [1980] 53–55). He emphasizes that death and life are in the "hand" (power) of the tongue; those who love her will eat of her fruit. What is the fruit in her hand that she offers to those who love her? Here Williams makes a bold "semiotic" move, illustrative of the intertextuality that is so cultivated in our times, and interprets the verse in the light of Gen 3. "The image of the tongue-as-speech, represented as a figure holding fruit is that of the woman in the garden of Eden. She is the unspoken comparison, the one who transmits knowledge of good and evil" (p. 54). This picture suggests that the offering is an open one: life instead of death? Or life and death? When this saying is framed in the story of Eve, new vistas are opened up that go beyond the literal meaning of the saying, and forge a theological interpretation in the light of another biblical work. But as it stands, the "life and death" in v 21, against the background of the statements about speech in the book of Proverbs, seems simply to underline the power of the tongue; it can go either way.

Proverbs 19:1–29

Bibliography

Hausmann, J. *Menschenbild*, passim, and cf. "Freund" in Index, p. 413. Whybray, R. N. *Composition.* 113–14.

Translation

19:1   Better the poor person, walking in integrity,
            than one with perverted lips, and a fool besides![a]

2   Not good: desire without knowledge;
            one who is hasty in step misses the goal.[a]

3   *Folly leads one astray,*
        but his heart rages against the Lord.

4   *Wealth makes many friends,*
        but the poor man—he is deserted by his friends.[a]

5   *A false witness will not go unpunished,*
        and one who tells lies will not escape.

6   *Many curry favor with a noble,*
        and all are friends of a giver of gifts.

7   *All the relatives of the poor hate them;*
        all the more do friends desert them.
    Whoever pursues words, they are not (fruitful?) [a]

8   *A keeper of heart, a lover of self;*
        a preserver of understanding—for finding [a] *happiness.*

9   *A false witness will not go unpunished,*
        and one who tells lies will perish.

10   *Unbefitting a fool: luxury;*
        all the more so, the rule of a slave over princes.

11   *It is the intelligent person who contains anger,*
        and it is an honor to overlook an offense.

12   *Like a lion's growling, anger of a king,*
        but like dew on the grass, his favor.

13   *A disaster to his father, a foolish son,*
        and a quarrelsome wife, a continual downpour.

14   *House and wealth, an inheritance from forebears,*
        but a prudent wife, from the Lord.

15   *Laziness brings on deep sleep,*
        and a slacker's appetite stays hungry.

16   *A keeper of a command, a keeper of life;*
        a despiser of his ways [a] *will die.*[b]

17   *Showing kindness to the poor: making a loan to the Lord,*
        and a reward will be given for it.

18   *Discipline your son while there is hope,*
        but no death! Don't get overwrought! [a]

19   *One of great wrath, a receiver of punishment—*
        for if you get (him) free, you must do it again.[a]

20   *Listen to advice and take instruction,*
        so that finally you become wise.

21   *Many are the intentions in one's heart,*
        but the plan of the Lord—that will prevail.

22   *One's desire, one's disgrace;* [a]
        so better poor than a liar.

23   *The fear of the Lord—for life,*
        and one spends the night satisfied and without harm.[a]

24   *A sluggard puts hand into the dish*
        without ever lifting it to the mouth.

25   *If you beat a scoffer, the naive will be wiser;*
        if you reprove the intelligent, they gain in knowledge.

26   *Whoever mistreats father, drives mother away,*

> *a shameful and disgraceful son.*
> 27 *Cease, my son, to listen to instruction—*
> *a wandering from words of knowledge!* [a]
> 28 *A malicious witness scoffs at what is right,*
> *and the mouth of the wicked swallows iniquity.*
> 29 *Judgments* [a] *are directed to scoffers,*
> *and blows for the backs of fools.*

Notes

1.a. Although the MT makes sense, many scholars have adopted readings supported by 28:6 and the versions; cf. *BHS*. Thus 28:6 reads "ways" (dual) instead of "his lips" (שְׂפָתָיו); see also 11:20 and 17:20, which speak of the (perverted) heart; 28:6 also reads עָשִׁיר, "rich," which gives better antithesis to רָשׁ, "poor person," than "fool" (כְּסִיל). The LXX lacks this and the following verse.

2.a. גַּם seems to be asseverative "surely," but need not be translated.

4.a. מֵרֵעֵהוּ, "by his friends," can also be vocalized to mean "his friends," and be the subject of the verb in v 4b.

7.a. This line is corrupt; it has no connection with the previous couplet, and it lacks a parallel line. A literal translation: "One who pursues words, not (so the Ketib) they." The Qere would be rendered, "they (are) his." *BHS* translates the extra couplet of the Greek into Hebrew, but this does not remedy the situation. It also proposes, on the basis of the Greek, the verb missing at the end of v 7b: "will not be saved." But this remains uncertain; see the discussion by F. Delitzsch in his commentary (VI, 15 and VII, 25). There is no reliable reconstruction.

8.a. The versions have a finite form "will find," but this can be merely an interpretation of the infinitive form of the current MT.

16.a. Many change "his ways" to "his words" for the sake of parallelism; in that case, the "his" would refer to God. Without the change, "his" can be referred to the sage who gives the command, or to the course of action taken by the youth. See the *Comment*. There is not sufficient reason to emend the text.

16.b. The Qere יָמוּת, "will die," is to be preferred to the Ketib יוּמַת, "shall be put to death," which is a customary form in a legal decision, but is not appropriate here.

18.a. Literally, line *b* reads: "and to kill him, do not lift up your soul." The last phrase is obscure: desire, set one's heart on? The Greek interprets "excessively" (εἰς δὲ ὕβριν). The translation above is guided by two negatives, אַל . . . אַל. See also 23:13; it should be recalled that Deut 18:18–21 set boundaries for such cases.

19.a. Literally, line *b* has "if you deliver (him), you will still add (or repeat)." This is taken to mean that if one saves a person (very wrathful, according to the Qere in v 19a), that individual will only cause the same trouble in the future. There is no reason to connect this with the preceding verse. Toy remarks that text and translation are doubtful, and he offers several interpretations that have been advanced. See the *Comment* below.

22.a. The translation understands "desire" in the sense of "greed," and חֶסֶד in the (rare) sense of "disgrace" (cf. 14:34). Other versions are possible: "the desire (or desirable) in/of/for a man is his goodness (loyalty)." The LXX (καρπὸς, "fruit"; cf. *BHS*) suggests that it read תְּבוּאָה instead of תַּאֲוַת, "income," instead of "desire," and this is adopted by A. Vaccari, W. McKane, and others, but it is hardly an improvement.

23.a. A verb like "leads" is understood in line *a*; cf. 14:27; 22:4. V 23b is literally "one who is satisfied spends the night; he is not visited by evil." The LXX goes in a different direction. The first part of the line, at least, seems to be corrupt.

27.a. The translation is doubtful; it seems so contradictory to v 20. The LXX rendered it in a safe manner, avoiding the command in v 17a. Meinhold points out Rashi's solution, which is reflected in the NJV and NRSV; the sense would be: cease straying and follow discipline—thus changing the sequence of lines. Perhaps one can interpret line *a* conditionally (so implicitly the NIV), "if you cease to listen," and line *b* "(it is) to stray . . . ." The translation above attempts to keep the irony, and interprets the infinitive in v 27b as a gerund construction (cf. GKC §114o) so that it continues the irony of v 27a. See the *Comment* on this verse.

29.a. The MT can stand since "judgment" is used here in the sense of punishment (so A. Barucq and NJV), but many would follow the emendation proposed in *BHS* for the sake of stricter parallelism on the basis of Greek μάστιγες, "blows."

Form/Structure/Setting

There is no obvious structure to this chapter, and only somewhat strained connections can be made. Whybray (*Composition,* 113) thinks that there has been a deliberate collection of sayings concerning "the importance of knowledge and instruction and/or the behaviour of children (vv. 2, 8, 13, 16, 18, 20, 25, 26, 27)." It is difficult to ascribe this to deliberate intention. There are several catch words, such as "good" in vv 1–2. Vv 4–7 also have catch words ("friend," "poor") and deal with the poor/rich difference. There are four YHWH proverbs (vv 3, 14, 17, 21, and "fear of the Lord" appears in v 23). Synonymous parallelism is more common than antithetic in this chapter, and there are more admonitions than usual; the appearance of "my son" in v 27 is singular in these chapters.

Comment

1 See *Note* 1.a. Despite the doubts cast on the Hebrew text, the opposition between a just poor person and a foolish liar is adequate. Meinhold does not see this verse influenced by 28:6, despite the obvious similarity. Rather, it fits in with the lying condemned in v 5, and he asks the meaning of the contrast. The liar "is either rich and considers himself wise (28:11)—and then resembles a fool (26:5, 12), or he is still poor, but by evil means (in this case, by words; cf. v 22b) he becomes rich. In both cases, he cannot truly succeed (17:20) and he thereby shows himself to be a fool . . . . But the situation of the poor man is different. For the sages, worse than poverty is to fail to be human. Poverty is neither idealized nor equal to piety, because in addition integrity is mentioned." It seems unnecessary to envision a complex background, as Meinhold has done. It is better here to recognize a simple comparison. V 1a refers to someone, poor but virtuous, who refuses to better his material situation by wrong means, such as lies. He is better off than the person in v 1b who has lied his way into success and probably riches; he may think he is well off, but he is a fool!

2 See *Note* 2.a. Hebrew נֶפֶשׁ, a word that can mean "person," "life," etc., can also mean "desire"; it suggests an impulsive action, and, since this is not sufficiently pondered, it will fail. There is an inevitable comparison with the mistakes committed by a person who is too hasty in pursuing a goal (line *b*). Mere activism will not achieve anything. Haste is regularly condemned by the sages; 21:5; 29:20. Meinhold understands נֶפֶשׁ to mean "life," and hence line *a* indicates a failure to direct one's life with knowledge, i.e., with wisdom. The NJV understands נֶפֶשׁ as "person," one who lacks knowledge and so is not good.

3 The foolish person blames the Lord instead of recognizing personal responsibility, the folly that has brought about losing the "way." The failure of the fool is not specified; it could be small or great, but the rage against God clearly indicates that the folly has damaged any personal relationship to God. Sir 15:11–20 explicitly forbids trying to transfer to God one's own responsibility. However, see the *Explanation* below.

4 This is a realistic observation about the difference that wealth creates. Although the verse stops short of questioning the value of such friends (cf. v 6!), it does describe social inequity and the hardship of the poor. This unhappy situation made an impression on the sages; cf. v 7 and also the *Comment* on 14:20, as well as the *Excursus on Wealth and Poverty*.

5   This is practically identical with v 9, and it reflects phrases used elsewhere; cf. 12:17; 14:5, 25; 21:28. Needless to say, perjury was judged to be a serious social crime.

6   This proverb is a wry observation on a certain level of society, where the "noble" attracts so much attention, and generosity draws a following. When this is joined with v 4a, the value of friendship by means of sharing one's affluence is put in question. Who can be trusted? "Curry favor" is literally "to stroke the face." While this phrase is used of the relationship of humans to God (Moses in Exod 32:11), it seems to have an accent of flattery here, where it is used of humans to each other. Such conduct can easily elicit a gift. Meinhold is overly subtle in finding ambiguity here, as though the "man of gifts" in v 6b refers to the noble (v 6a) who is anxious to receive gifts and thus attracts others to give them to him.

7   The first two lines recall 14:20a. There may be some irony in placing this proverb in the shadow of v 6. The poor have no one they can trust; typically their trust is in the Lord. But also their situation is aggravated because their "friends," and even their relatives, desert them. As often (11:5; 25:17), "hate" has no emotional overtones; it simply indicates the choice that is opposed to another. The meaning of the Hebrew of v 7c remains unknown, and the absence of a parallel line complicates it further; the versions are of no help. See *Note* 7.a.

8   The succinctness of the Hebrew underscores the primacy of understanding and wisdom. Its placement here contrasts with the folly manifested by the actors in the previous verses. "Heart" stands here for intelligence. In v 8b, "find good" is a pregnant phrase to indicate a high degree of value, joy, or whatever the context suggests; cf. 18:22a.

9   This verse is a variant of v 5. Alonso Schökel contrasts the perfect rhythm of v 5 with the 4/3 beat of this verse, but can see no great advantage. Delitzsch considers vv 9–16 as a frame for the proverbs within it.

10   "Not fitting" (cf. 17:7) sounds like an understatement, but the implication is clear; the fool who attains riches might conclude that it is an approval of his (false) way of life. Moreover, the example in v 10b indicates how seriously it is meant because the same concern about the reign of fools is expressed very strongly in 30:21–22. See the *Comment* there. The argument is *a minore ad majus*, "from less to greater." It is bad enough that any fool should prosper, but it is a disaster whenever an incompetent rules; how can a mere servant give orders to governors? The implication is that the servant's acquisition of power will confirm him in a show of power. For a realistic attitude toward slaves/servants, see Sir 33:25–33.

11   The need to be "slow to anger" has already been singled out; see the *Comment* on 14:29. After all, this is also a characteristic of the Lord, as in Exod 34:6 and often elsewhere. It enables one to deal more equitably with what is perceived as a hurt; cf. 15:18b. If the verse is associated with v 12, it points to the need of self-control in rulers. However, that limits the true breadth of the psychological and moral implication of the saying. It is based on the insight that time is needed for a perceived hurt to wear off, and ultimately forgiveness is godlike; cf. also 10:12b; 17:9a.

12   Rulers are obviously subject to observation and are a matter of concern. In contrast to v 11, the extremes are noted here: the wrath and the favor of royalty. Royal wrath is particularly to be feared; cf. 16:14 and especially 20:2. The saying is made especially expressive by the contrast between life-giving dew and the lion's roar. This is not the roar that is perceived in Ps 104:27 as a prayer to God for food!

13 V 13a recalls 10:1; 17:21, 25; v 13b echoes 21:9, 19; 25:24, and it is developed more in 27:15–16. It is not clear why a foolish son and a nagging wife should be joined together, except that the father/husband is the loser. A house with a roof that leaked, and this could easily happen in the average construction, was simply uninhabitable.

14 The "prudent wife" is quite a change from the picture in the previous verse, and v 14b receives strong confirmation from 18:22; see the *Comment* there. What such a wife could mean in reality is presented in the description of the woman in 31:10–31. An heir could count on receiving the inheritance, all things being equal, but it was another thing to acquire a wise wife. That is the supreme gift. However, it is the father who disposes of the inheritance (v 14a), and one is left wondering which would be considered the more important direction for the youth—to please the father and ensure the inheritance, or to trust in the Lord for a future companion? If the inheritance is almost automatic, specified by practice or law, the choice of a life-partner seems more of a gamble. It is presumed that in the Old Testament marriage in general was arranged between families or fathers; was Samson an exception? Cf. Judg 14. What recourse did a youth have, if he listened to this proverb? Would it justify his relying on the Lord, even if it meant disobedience to the father/family, and perhaps being disinherited? These questions may go beyond the reach of this proverb, but they are prompted by the heightening between the two lines: what the father *must give* by law, and what the Lord *gives as a gift*. See Sir 26:3, and also 26:23b, 26cd (NRSV). The saying should not be viewed as calling for a decision, but it does raise questions for a youth to ponder. If the previous verse, 19:13, was the result of an unhappy choice on someone's part, v 14 opens up the mystery of a man with a maiden which is mentioned in Prov 30:18–19 (see the *Comment* there). An enterprising sage might appreciate the certainty of an inheritance, but he would realize that a happy marriage was not on the same level. Another interesting aspect to this saying: granted that the Lord controls all that happens even down to the casting of lots, 16:33, are there some areas that are totally reserved to his control, such as the choice of a good wife?

15 The sleep that is meant is not casual, but a "deep sleep," as in Gen 2:21. It will not refresh, but rather enervate the sluggard. In fact, sloth leads to death as Prov 21:25 states, with some exaggeration. Not even hunger will stir the lazybones to activity, as 19:24 exemplifies. For a proper evaluation of sleep, cf. 20:13b.

16 See *Note* 16.a. The saying probably refers to the sage's command, not the Decalogue, and it places the youth before the typical sapiential life and death choice. In some historical period, the "command" could have been understood as referring to the Torah. For the phraseology, see 4:4; 7:2; 13:3, 13. Obedience and "hearing" (v 20) are at the heart of wisdom, and they bring life, just as folly is associated with death; cf. 10:21; 15:10. The antecedent of "his" is not explicit; it is either the Lord or the teacher whose command governs the course of action of the youth.

17 If the plight of the poor in vv 4, 6 did not hold out much hope for them, this proverb certainly encourages the Israelite to give them aid, as prescribed in Deut 15:1–11. The image in v 17a is quite strong: what is given to the poor is really a loan to the Lord. The implication is that God will repay the loan—with interest! See 14:31; 17:5, and also Sir 29:8–13.

18–20 These verses are admonitions that are best understood in a family context. **18** See *Note* 18.a. Corporal punishment was clearly practiced; cf. 13:24; 23:13–14. The meaning of the "hope" is that such discipline will preserve the son for the future, or at least bring about change, "because" (or more tentatively "if, while," כִּי) there will be hope for the future. If the chastisement is done at the right time, there will be hope. The prohibition not to cause death is startling, even in view of 23:13, which is a rather dry assurance that death will not occur. Physical death is meant, not just a premature death or spiritual insensitivity. But death was without doubt rare, if it happened at all. The legislation in Deut 21:18–21 sets definite limits to any lethal treatment of rebellious sons.

19 See *Note* 19.a. V 19a raises expectations: the wrathful person will be punished. But v 19b is not clear. Plöger, Meinhold, and also Oesterley connect this verse with the previous one. A wrathful person, perhaps the father, should not try to settle a drastic situation. Wrath never pays. Indeed it brings more trouble for oneself. The meaning of v 19b would be that even if one succeeds in changing the son, the same situation will only reappear. Meinhold regards v 19b as addressed directly by the father to the son. It seems better to treat v 19 separately from v 18; then the wrathful person will have to pay for his outburst and be punished, presumably for some wrongdoing. Furthermore, v 19b is a prohibition: do not try to free such a hothead, for he will be in trouble again, and you will be in the same situation again. V 11 is a clearer proverb concerning the containing of one's temper.

20 The command to listen to instruction is familiar; cf. 12:15, and it will be repeated again in 23:12; the sages never tire of insisting on it. "Finally" translates "in your end." This "end" probably refers to the end of the training; then one will be completely formed and wise. It is not that one becomes wise "in your own eyes," for that would be disastrous, as 26:12 points out. But one is to stay continually alert to growing in true wisdom. The sages never envision a state of "perfect wisdom" for anyone; there is always exhortation to make progress.

21 "Advice" ("plan," עֵצָה) is a catch word uniting this YHWH saying with the previous verse. The human heart is subject to many different impulses, but it is the "plan" of the Lord that will eventually win out. There seems to be a deliberate contrast also between the multitude of human intentions, probably many of them ill-conceived, and the single "plan" of YHWH. Cf. Prov 16:1, 9 with the *Comment*.

22 See *Note* 22.a.; the translation and meaning are uncertain. It is difficult to determine the relationship between the two lines. "Disgrace" is also rendered by many as "kindness," the normal meaning of Hebrew חֶסֶד. If so, then the meaning seems to be that a person's desire, or what is desired in a person, is loyalty/goodness, and the parallel line would indicate that the poor, who fulfill such an ideal, are therefore better than the wicked who are productive, but deceitful in their display of goodness. Thus, loyalty is better than deceit. However, as translated above, "desire" is taken as evil, as in the sense of greed, and the proverb is a saying in favor of the poor. For them there is no disgrace, but there is for those whose wealth is built on deceit. Yet it is to be admitted that there is little connection between the two lines, and in any interpretation there are certain assumptions that go beyond the text.

23 See *Note* 23.a. This is an echo of 14:27a about "fear of the Lord." It underlines once more the goal of wisdom/fear of the Lord: life. The connection with v 23b is unclear; v 23b is perhaps a kind of specification of the first line. Even against the dangers of the night, whoever fears the Lord is protected.

24 This is a variant of 26:15. In a sense the proverb is intended to be humorous or ironic—there is no extreme of which the lazy person is not capable, even if it is a question to preserve life by eating. Joined with v 15, the verse might justify the inference that such a one would even fall asleep at the meal.

25 A distinction is drawn between the incorrigible scoffer (לץ; cf. 1:22) and the simple or naive (פתי; cf. 1:4), who need instruction in order to keep on the right path. The attitude of the scoffer reflects what was said about him in 13:1 and 15:12. Apparently the naive learn from the scoffer's fate. The subject of v 25b ("they") can possibly refer to the naive (so Plöger), who see that even the intelligent need correction, and become more open ("gain in knowledge"). More probably the subject is the "intelligent," who learn from reprimands. The sages never tire of affirming that it is part of wisdom to be open to correction. Oesterley emphasizes that the sages affirm the possibility of "conversion" or learning. However, the "scoffer" (לץ) seems to be utterly incorrigible. See also 21:11.

26 The wicked son was already scored in v 13a. His conduct here may possibly consist in taking over the inheritance and driving out both of the parents; at least the flight of the mother is explicitly mentioned. The situation could be that of getting rid of elderly parents, whose only proper care and protection would reside within the family. The condemnation of any such conduct, already prohibited in the Decalogue, Deut 5:15, is expressed strongly in line *b*. See also 20:20; 28:24; 30:11.

27 See *Note* 27.a. for the various translations and interpretations of this verse. If one accepts the translation above, the address is filled with bitter irony, as many commentators suggest. Plöger defends this by joining it with the disgraceful conduct of the son mentioned in the previous verse, so that in context it is a kind of threat. However, he changes the form of the verb in v 23b. The above translation attempts to convey the irony. The form of the verse is unusual. This is the only direct address to "my son" in this collection, and in its imperative form it directly contradicts v 20a. There is no certain translation of this verse.

28–29 These verses can be taken together, as the catch word "scoff" suggests. **28** A judicial setting is presupposed by the first proverb. 1 Kgs 21:10 also describes the perjury perpetrated by "malicious witnesses" as done by "sons of Belial." The second line is vivid; they take in iniquity like they take in food. Alonso Schökel points to the paradox: they swallow what they say. **29** See *Note* 29.a. There can be no *remedial* punishment for such as are described, but they will be surely punished. Blows may well fail to change the fool (cf. 17:10; 26:3), who is in parallelism here with the scoffer. There is no escaping retribution.

Explanation

V 3 invites further comment. As a proverb, it calls out for context, and even for the company of proverbs that go in a different direction. Not all rage against God is to be considered simply the reaction of a fool. It is true that many are thwarted when they do not get their own way, when their own plans are not succeeding. Moreover, the fool, by definition, is at fault in the eyes of the sages. So his rage is considered blameworthy. But caution is desirable; this proverb would fit very well on the lips of the friends of Job. They considered him more than a fool, a truly obstinate and wicked man, and he has certainly raged against God. But the three friends were dead wrong; they did not speak rightly about God (cf. Job 42: 7–8).

One can instance many psalmists that "rage" against God because of some mysterious, inexplicable adversity in their lives. It is true that the laments sometimes express as much trust and praise as rage, but not all of them (cf. Ps 88). It is strange that the sages could contemplate disaster and evil with sangfroid, and even attempt to relieve YHWH of responsibility by means of their wise/just and foolish/unjust dichotomy. One would have expected a more explicit confrontation with the mystery of suffering. Or was this not considered as part of instruction in the early wisdom corpus? Since it involved mystery and was ultimately unanswerable, was it to be left to experiences in later life, the lessons of adulthood? Did those who handed down the sayings adhere deliberately to orthodox teaching about divine justice? It is difficult to be satisfied with the neatness of the view of Proverbs when one reads the Psalms and Job. At least, the relative silence on this point in the book of Proverbs is better than the platitudes, however reasonable in a given context, uttered by the three friends who "comforted" Job. The question of retribution (see the *Excursus on Retribution*) has to be seen in the light of the entire Bible.

Friendship is treated in several sayings, directly in vv 4, 6, 7, and implicitly in many others. There is no section of Proverbs that deals as explicitly and at length with this topic as in Sirach. See F. V. Reiterer, ed., *Freundschaft bei Ben Sira*, BZAW 244 (Berlin: de Gruyter, 1996). Friendship forms a specific topic for treatment in Sir 6:5–17; 11:29–12:18; 22:19–26; 37:1–6, and it is treated obliquely at other points. On the contrary, there are only occasional statements on this topic, almost in passing as it were, in Proverbs. Thus, in this chapter the concern is money and friendship (19:4, 7; cf. 14:20), i.e., the difficulty the poor have in acquiring any friends—but also the caution that the rich must exert concerning their friends. In other words, what does true friendship consist in? The sages described it by pointing out false as well as true criteria, awakening everyone to the fragility of close relationships. Cf. J. Hausmann, *Menschenbild*, 81–82.

Proverbs 20:1–30

Bibliography

Krispenz, J. *Spruchkomposition.* 95–97. **Meinhold, A.** *Die Sprüche.* 2:328–30. **Whybray, R. N.** *Composition.* 114–16.

Translation

20:1   *Wine, a scoffer; strong drink, stormy!*
       And whoever gets drunk on them is not wise.

² *The wrath ^a of a king, the roar of a lion;*
   whoever angers him, a gambler ^b with life.

³ *Ceasing ^a from strife, an honor to a person;*
   but any fool gets into a quarrel.^b

⁴ *In winter the sluggard does not plow;*
   at harvest he will look—but not a thing!

⁵ *Counsel in the human heart—deep waters;*
   but the understanding person draws it up.

⁶ *Many people—each one proclaiming personal loyalty,^a*
   but who can find the one to be trusted?

⁷ *Whoever walks in integrity—a just person;*
   happy the descendants after him.

⁸ *A king sitting on his judgment seat,*
   one who winnows any evil with his eyes.

⁹ *Who can say, "My heart is pure;*
   I am cleansed of my sin?"

¹⁰ *Alternate stones, alternate measures;^a*
   an abomination to the Lord—all of them!

¹¹ *Even by his acts a child is known,*
   whether his conduct will be pure and upright.^a

¹² *A listening ear, a seeing eye—*
   the Lord made them both.

¹³ *Do not love sleep lest you lose your inheritance;*
   keep your eyes open, have bread enough!

¹⁴ *"Bad, bad," says the buyer,*
   but he goes off and then boasts!

¹⁵ *There is gold, also a mass of rubies,*
   but a precious jewel—lips of knowledge.

¹⁶ *Take his garment for he has provided surety for a stranger,*
   and if for foreigners,^a hold him in pledge!

¹⁷ *Sweet to a person, the bread of deceit,*
   but afterward the mouth is filled with gravel.

¹⁸ *Plans are made firm by advice;*
   wage war with wise directions! ^a

¹⁹ *Whoever slanders, a revealer of secrets;*
   so have nothing to do with the open-mouthed.^a

²⁰ *Whoever curses father or mother—*
   his lamp will go out in deep darkness.^a

²¹ *An inheritance at first acquired in haste ^a*
   in the end will not be blessed.

²² *Do not say: "I will repay evil."*
   Wait for the Lord, and he will save you.

²³ *An abomination to the Lord, alternate stones; ^a*
   deceitful weights, not good!

²⁴ *From the Lord the steps of a person—*
   how can anyone understand the way to go?

²⁵ *A trap for a man who claims ^a "holy!"*
   and only after vows investigates.

26   *A winnower of the wicked, a wise king,*
          and he rolls the wheel over them.

27   *The lamp of the Lord, the human life-breath,*[a]
          searching all the inmost parts!

28   *Loyalty and fidelity preserve a king;*
          he supports his throne by loyalty.

29   *The glory of youth, their strength;*
          the adornment of elders, white hair.

30   *Wounds and bruises clean* [a] *away evil,*
          and blows, the inmost being.

Notes

2.a. The suggestion in *BHS* should be disregarded; there is no reason to conform to 19:12.

2.b. The word translated "gambler" is חטא, which means "miss the mark," and hence "to sin." The first meaning occurs fairly often (e.g., Prov 8:36). Emendation to חמס, "do wrong," is unnecessary.

3.a. שבת can be derived from ישב, "sit, remain," or from שבת, "cease," with little change of meaning.

3.b. גלע has occurred in 17:14 and 18:1 in the general sense of quarrel.

6.a. Several translations have been given for line *a*. Alonso Schökel presents no less than five, with slight differences in meaning; the real point is in line *b*. Note that the root קרא (here, "call" or possibly "be called") can be interpreted also as קרה, "meet"; cf. *BHS*. The above translation retains the MT, interpreting איש, "a person," as distributive.

10.a. Literally MT reads "stone and stone, ephah and ephah." These terms refer to the weights and measures in mercantile transactions, using balances. See also v 23 and 11:1.

11.a. The interpretation of יתנכר, "is known," varies; it can mean "disguise" or "dissemble," and this is seen in the Tanakh version: "A child may be dissembling in his behavior even though his actions are blameless and proper."

16.a. Cf. 27:13, which reads "strange woman" (נכריה), in contrast to the masculine plural, which is preferable here, with the Ketib.

18.a. MT has the imperative; in the light of 24:6 a finite form of the verb (תעשה, "wage, make") is preferred by many; cf. *BHS*. There is no need to vocalize the verb in v 18a as an infinitive; cf. GKC §145k.

19.a. This verb seems to have two meanings: "open" and "simple/foolish." In either case, irresponsible speech is meant.

20.a. Refer to *Note* 7:9.a.

21.a. The Qere is to be preferred to the Ketib, whose meaning is not certain; cf. 13:11.

23.a. See *Note* 10.a.

25.a. The meaning of ילע, "claims" (לעע root), is uncertain, but the context indicates some kind of rashly uttered vow.

27.a. There is a simple juxtaposition in v 27a, and the subject and predicate can be interchanged.

30.a. The translation is uncertain. The Ketib (a verb) is preferable to the Qere (a noun), even if the subjects are plural, and although the verb means "rub," rather than "cleanse."

Form/Structure/Setting

R. N. Whybray agrees with J. Krispenz (she includes v 13; cf. *Spruchkomposition,* 95–97, 175) in linking together vv 5–12: "every verse is concerned—though in a variety of ways—with the human mind and with the question how it may be possible to penetrate its secrets and discern human character. The unity of the group is strengthened by the particular links between consecutive verses" (*Composition,* 114). But this is a tenuous linkage to attribute to an editor. Rather, there is a potpourri of various types of sayings: six YHWH sayings (vv 10, 12, 22–24, 27) and four king sayings (vv 2, 8, 26, 28). The forms differ considerably, as well. There are only a few antithetic sayings, and there are more imperatives than usual. Noteworthy are the flat statements in the first colon, which call for and are supplied with a concluding statement in the second colon, as in vv 10 and 12. One need not here do more than mention the rather extravagant claim of A. Meinhold that 20:2–22:16, even allowing for individual differences, can be thematically grouped. For example, can one say that chap. 20 "is characterized by YHWH-piety that views human beings in total dependence on God" (p. 329)? Flashes of this YHWH-piety (which is fast becoming in certain quarters a kind of code word for postexilic piety) appear in the YHWH sayings, but they do not dominate the chapter.

Comment

1 The alcoholic drinks are personified and then characterized by being juxtaposed with predicates that describe the effects of excessive drinking. The condemnation of overindulgence is clear also from Prov 23:29–35. The same disapproval occurs in other contexts, e.g., as conducive to poverty (21:17; 23:21). It is not to be forgotten that Woman Wisdom serves wine (9:5). But inebriation is not for the wise person.

2 The comparison to the lion's roar recalls 19:12. Whether it is justified or not, the king's wrath can be lethal. See further 20:8, 28 and *Note* 2.b.

3 The attitude of the wise person is to avoid strife or at least (as "ceasing" might suggest), if it has erupted, to bring it to an end. Of course, the fool is only too ready to engage in dispute; elsewhere he has been characterized as proud and lacking in self-control. If there is no strife, he will create it.

4 Like the fool, the lazy person looks for any opportunity to do what he does best, even in the critical period of the plowing for the future harvest. After the early rain of October-November, one would sow the seed for the next harvest. Were he really expecting anything at harvest time (perhaps he is stupid enough), he might have sown without plowing and thus properly preparing the ground. But the saying is more interested in a condemnation of laziness than in details. The lazybones simply did not plow. See also 10:5.

5 The ambiguity of "deep waters" was discussed in the *Comment* on 18:4. Here it is a symbol of true wisdom buried in the human heart, which needs the insight of the wise to draw it out. It is not said whether this ability is directed toward oneself, where the wisdom could lie buried, or toward another; it is applicable to both. The observation, which in itself is a commendation of insight and wisdom, suggests more than it says; how expert is a person in knowing "the heart" of self or others? But other proverbs warn against self-deception and too ready a judgment; e.g., see vv 9, 24.

6 More than one translation of line *a* is possible, as indicated in *Note* 6.a. The point seems to be a contrast between those who are said to be loyal and trustworthy, and their true worth. The question form "who can find" is used successfully in the wisdom literature to indicate either rarity, as here, or even impossibility of occurrence.

7 The integrity of the just person is to be understood in the light of the question in v 9. It is not the result of examination of conscience, but rather the good reputation that accrued to the just person, as well as their own sense of themselves. There is a strong sense of collectivity; hence the descendants are said to be blessed. The solidarity is spiritual (cf. 10:7, where a happy memory is a blessing) as well as practical (cf. 13:22, where good people leave an inheritance to their progeny). As a principle of retribution it comes to be severely questioned, as shown by the objections voiced at the time of the exile in Jer 31:29 and Ezek 18:2.

8 See also v 26 for regal "winnowing." The king is a judge (cf. 16:10), but there must have been many deputies to carry out practical affairs. Ultimately, the royal power was responsible, and was held to this, as is clear from the ideal expressed in Ps 101.

9 The fragility and weakness of human nature is a "given," both in the Bible (e.g., Ps 51:7) and the ancient Fertile Crescent. It is made all the more striking here by the question form, which suggests the answer "No one." There is in the wisdom tradition a lively sense of human uncertainty especially in judging one's own actions (cf. Prov 16:2 = 21:2). However, human sinfulness is not seen as a reason for despair; there are other options for the Israelite. Moreover, a saying like this should be balanced against many other proverbs—indeed the whole wisdom teaching—which hold up justice as a practical and attainable ideal.

10 See *Note* 10.a. Switches in weights and measures were apparently a common practice; at least they are frequently condemned; cf. 11:1 and 16:11, as well as Deut 25:13–16; Lev 19:35. The seriousness with which cheating others was viewed is indicated by the strong phrase "abomination to the Lord."

11 For another possible interpretation of the Hebrew text, see *Note* 11.a. This verse is usually interpreted as indicating that the early training of a child will, all things considered, be a sign of the character of the adult that will emerge (so also 22:6). "Even" seems to refer to the actions, and it is not said whether these are good or bad. But presumably for the educator there has to be an early start in training. The second colon may expect a happy future, but that depends on early, persistent, and successful nurture.

12 This apparently simple proverb is rather far-reaching. At first it appears to register merely the fact of the creation by the Lord of the organs of eyes and ear, and their functions. If one coordinates the emphasis on the participles, there is an obvious sapiential thrust. It is through the ready hearing of the right teaching, and through the observant eye, that one becomes wise. But wisdom rates hearing over seeing, for the eyes have to be properly focused; cf. 17:24. This is consistently emphasized in the wisdom teaching of Prov 1–9, where the symbolism of the path, which must be seen and traversed, is highlighted, and "hearing" is practically the equivalent of obeying; cf. also 15:31; Sir 17:6; and Ps. 94:9.

13 "Eyes" seems to be the obvious catch word uniting this with the previous verse. Here the physical use of the eye comes into play: Keep those eyes open! Alas, the sluggard "loves" sleep: hence the threat of losing one's property—so unnecessary if one will only stay alert and busy. Other proverbs (11:29; 12:24) have already raised the possibility of losing one's family inheritance to another, even to a household slave. The imperatives (cf. also vv 16, 19, 22) are particularly effective—more so than the irony and humor of 26:14.

14 This is obviously a description of a lively scene rather than a proverb. The first colon raises expectations; what will happen? The reader follows the buyer, after the vivid haggling over the value of what is being purchased, to the moment of the victory concerning the bargain that the buyer, at least according to his conviction, has achieved. This is a striking description of a fact of life; therefore one should be alert in bartering—don't be fooled. This kind of "game" has not disappeared in any corner of the world. Boasting in a situation like this is very often a telltale sign of questionable achievement; cf. 25:14; 27:1–2. It is not a convincing sign of victory!

15 This implicit comparison between words of wisdom and valuables, such as gold and silver, is frequent enough; cf. Prov 10:20; 25:11–12. The comparisons are meant to be taken seriously. The proverb rates knowing lips, i.e., wise speech, as the most precious possession of all. There is a heightening in the second line of the saying.

16 See *Note* 16.a.; the verse is practically the same as 27:13. The saying strikes a different note because it is in the imperative. The warning about going surety is frequent enough (6:1–2; 11:15; 17:18). Here the case is specific: anyone who furnishes a guarantee for a creditor should realize the risk involved, and hold the garment (security for a loan; cf. Deut 24:10–13) that the creditor offers as the guarantee. This harsh measure is meant to teach the creditor a lesson; so do not spare him. The situation is particularly aggravated because there may be a default on the part of the person who was to be helped, a foreigner. So the Ketib; the Qere is influenced by 27:13 where "foreign/strange woman" does occur, perhaps due to the large role of this figure in the book. See also 22:27.

17 There is more than one meaning to the root ערב; it means "sweet" here, and in v 19 "deal with," after appearing in its common meaning of "go surety" in v 16. It does not occur in v 18, but it has obviously served as a catch word for this group. A question can be raised whether the bread of deceit stands for ill-gotten sustenance (cf. 9:17), or is rather a symbol for evildoing in general. In any case, the contrast is striking; instead of sweet food in the mouth, there is gravel, a vivid metaphor for the emptiness of the expected profit, or of any kind of statement (suggested by "mouth") that was made concerning it.

18 See *Note* 18.a. The sequence of thought shows a heightening in the second line: from counsel to actual battle. Emphasis on wise planning is a regular wisdom topos (cf. 11:14; 15:22), and in 24:6 it is associated with war, as here. Plöger and others (e.g., Whybray) understand the reference to war as *merely* an example of the need of planning if there is to be success. The thrust of the proverb is not to be limited to war; that is merely one application of v 18a. The imperative form of the verb is somewhat softened by the emendation to the passive voice (see *Note* 18.a.). The proverb can be broadened by the application to the struggle to survive in this life.

19 The first line is very similar to 11:3a. The slanderer is one who goes about talking, although the etymology of the word רכיל is difficult. Naturally, such a person is to be avoided. The parallel with the "open mouthed" (see *Note* 19.a.) would seem to indicate a character that we would term "loose-lipped."

20 Refer to *Note* 7:9.a. Cursing was not taken lightly in the ancient world (and recall "la maledizione" in the opera *Rigoletto*). Cursing of one's parents was punishable by death: Exod 21:17; Lev 20:9; cf. Prov 30:11. The metaphor of the lamp stands for the fate of the one who curses. The lamp of life will be extinguished. As Alonso Schökel puts it, "the son who turns against her who brought him to light, will himself remain without light."

21 See *Note* 21.a. As has been already remarked, haste is generally a sign of folly, or worse, flat-out wrongdoing (cf. 13:11; 28:20). The inheritance figured also in v 13; cf. Ben Sira about the regularization of inheritance (Sir 33:20–24).

The temporal indication ("beginning," "end") adds a threatening note for anyone who would not observe the saying.

22   The form of this saying ("do not say . . .") catches attention and occurs elsewhere: 3:28; 24:29; see also Eccl 5:5; Sir 5:3–4. There is a certain risk to be faced by one who obeys the proverb. One may give up one's judicial right and rely exclusively on the Lord, or one may go ahead and even violently achieve justice for oneself. The former course appears to be much riskier and, in view of the evidence of judicial proceedings (e.g., Lev 24:19–22), much rarer. But many felt that the Lord would not permit injustice to prevail (cf. Ps 37:5–7). See the sermonette by Sirach in 38:2–7, and the words of Amenemope, 22:1–8 (*ANET*, 424). It is difficult to measure the reception of proverbs like these; to what extent was this ideal realized in judicial or in daily life?

23   See v 11 and the *Comment;* also 11:1. It has been inferred that business methods in Israel must have been very devious, since there are so any pertinent proverbs that regulate honest measurement. But there is more than human knavery implied here. According to 16:11, scales and weights are the Lord's work; they are, literally, his. It is astonishing to see this kind of responsibility so closely tied to the Lord; it shows how highly regarded was honesty.

24   This is one of the most profound insights in the Bible, and there are several variants, notably Jer 10:23; Ps 37:23; cf. Prov 16:1, 9. On the one hand, there is human responsibility for one's actions, one's course of life; in fact, the whole thrust of the wisdom literature is to make one assume this responsibility in a serious way; cf. Prov 14:8a. And this is despite the difficulty that lies in recognizing the way (16:2; 21:2), and conforming to it. The human condition would be described by Sirach as endowed with free will: Sir 15:11–20. On the other hand, God is the agent behind everything that occurs. These two large "theological" truths have never been reconciled in Jewish or Christian theology. This proverb emphasizes the mystery of it all by the addition of line *b*, a question that sounds as if it comes from the brink of despair, but it is really pointing out the limitations, and mystery, of wisdom. The mystery of God's "work" is at the heart of Qoheleth's theology; it is totally unintelligible; cf. Eccl 3:11; 7:13; 8:17; 11:5. The sages realized that such ignorance, too, is wisdom.

25   See *Note* 25.a. The sages took vows seriously (cf. also Eccl 5:4), and vows played a prominent role in Israelite life. Saying "holy" (comparable to the Qorban of Matt 15:5) means that something, usually from one's possessions, has been consecrated to the Lord, for whatever reason, and it is therefore a very weighty matter. The point of the proverb is to exercise extreme care about making such a claim. The situation that prompted the vow is left undefined, but the precipitate vow is called a trap. This is another instance of the sapiential emphasis on the need to think before acting.

26   The winnowing of the king was already mentioned in v 8, highlighting his ability to ferret out and deal with wrongdoers. The mention of the "wheel" in line *b* has given rise to differing interpretations. The most dire is that of the wheels of a threshing sledge, and the image is that of torture or physical punishment of some kind. Cf. D. Snell, "The Wheel in Proverbs XX:26," *VT* 39 (1989) 503–7. But if the threshing sledge is merely the machine to press down the grain, separating the kernel from the chaff, then the winnowing takes place as the wind blows the chaff away from the grain (cf. Ps 1:4). This seems to agree with the process described in Isa 28:27–28.

27　See *Note* 27.a. The translation and interpretation of this verse varies. The "life-breath" (נשמה) is breathed into the man by God in Gen 2:7 and a living being results. Here it is called a "lamp of the Lord." Does this mean that it is God's way of knowing humans completely and utterly (cf. Prov 15:11), since it permeates the interior of a human being? In this understanding it could be either a consolation or also a warning. Or is it a human light, a God-given consciousness, or even conscience, by which we become aware of the most secret things in ourselves? In Job 32:8 we read that it is the נשמה of Shaddai that enables humans to understand. Perhaps both interpretations are valid; in the view of R. Van Leeuwen: "The proverb thus suggests both God's knowledge of humans and human self-knowledge as a gift of God, not either one or the other." For other opinions, see J. Hausmann, *Menschenbild,* 260.

28　The general truth of v 28a is specified by the addition of 28b, itself a variant of 16:2b. We know from Ps 89:25 that the Lord's "loyalty and fidelity" are with the king. According to Prov 25:5, the royal throne is established by righteousness. In v 28b it is expected that the king is to act accordingly; he solidifies his own throne by his actions.

29　There is an implicit contrast between the two lines of this proverb; white hair is a sign of having lived a long life (cf. 16:31)—thus virtuously and probably wisely as well. While the strength of a youth is not to be disdained, he has a future to face, and it is there that a true judgment of a person lies.

30　See *Note* 30.a. As the text is translated, it indicates the purificatory nature of suffering; exterior physical blows affect one's "inmost being" (just how is not said). This idea is not at all frequent in Proverbs, although there is a tantalizing suggestion in 3:11–12. But most of the time, physical beating is seen as a needed discipline to keep youths in line; cf. 13:24; 22:15.

Explanation

The discerning reader will have noticed the many references to the grouping of the disparate sayings within the collections of the book. Sometimes plays on words, repetitions, and themes combine to provide a certain unity to a group of sayings. We have argued that this does not change the interpretation of a given proverb, but it is of real value because it gives a fuller picture especially of themes that would perhaps be absolutized by a reader were it not for the realization that proverbs can be in some kind of conflict with each other. Besides, the deliberate grouping of proverbs is a sign certainly indicating that portions of the collections were not haphazardly formed. In line with recent trends, many commentators have adopted this approach with enthusiasm. One may single out Whybray, Plöger, and Meinhold especially. They have taken the lead as far as the book of Proverbs is concerned. The recognition of a context within a chapter on the basis of catch words, and the relationship of one saying to another, and so forth, makes the reading of the book more exciting. At the same time, one must beware of creating false unities within a chapter. It is a delicate operation to read the mind of the collector. Moreover, how much is gained? For example, the *Comment* has pointed out the clever use of the root ערב in vv 16, 17, 19. This is a demonstration of literary finesse, and a corresponding recognition by the author. But all things considered, it is a modest gain. Or one may consider the statement that Whybray makes concerning v 22: "This verse makes an appropriate comment on vv 20 and 21, both of which give assurances that sin and crime will in the end receive due punishment." That is true enough, but the idea of appropriate punishment is one of the pillars of thought in the entire book and hardly seems to be of immediate significance in this context. Another example: Whybray comments on vv 7–9 that "it is possible that these three verses have been placed here as commenting in various ways on the pessimism about human nature expressed in v 6." One may question the major premise: Is v 6 to be characterized properly as pessimistic—or realistic? One must also be fair to Whybray; he describes this as a possibility. That is one way of making the reader think more seriously about these proverbs.

The *Comment* has pointed out the theological aspects of some of these sayings in the chapter, especially vv 22, 24, and 27. These call for more emphasis, lest they simply be overlooked in the plethora of proverbs. In the *Comment* on v 22 the deed-consequence theory (see the *Excursus on Retribution*) was not even mentioned. The saying goes beyond it, urging one to give up personal avenging, no matter how justified, and to put the case in the hands of the Lord. This type of proverb calls for remarkable forbearance, or, better, it might call for supreme virtue. A cynic might remark how it presupposes that the Lord will exercise more adequate vengeance than a human can. But that prospect is supplied; it is not part of the proverb. The saying simply calls for a high degree of spiritual simplicity. Indeed, what moderns call the "spiritual life" is not usually associated with the book of Proverbs, which is supposed to deal with hardheaded and no-nonsense observations about life. But proverbs like v 22 have a depth that is not to be passed over lightly.

An even deeper insight into the human condition is contained in v 24. The proverb is superficially similar to Prov 16:1, 9; 19:21, and other passages. But the depth of all these sayings is not easy to sound. Of course there is the usual understanding of the connective "and" in these sayings as "but," thus contrasting the divine and the human (the "man proposes but God disposes" type of dictum). But the modern generalization covers over the mystery of human and divine action; we can deceive ourselves into thinking we know what the biblical writer was describing in such succinct proverbs. These seem to express the truth in harmless ways in which most human activities are played out. But in reality it is sayings like these that find their greatest echo in the excruciating experiences of life. One example is that of the prophet Jeremiah, "I know, O Lord, that the way of human beings is not in their control, that mortals as they walk cannot direct their steps" (NRSV, Jer 23:10). How helpless are human beings? How much are they without direction, despite the efforts of the sages to provide the path, the light, and the inspiration they claimed for their teachings?

The ambiguity of the beautiful proverb in v 27 was pointed out in the *Comment*. Perhaps there is truth in both interpretations offered there. But overriding all is the thorough knowledge that the Lord has of the human heart and its mysteries (see also Prov 15:11; 16:2; 21:2, and often). Seldom better, if at all, has this aspect of the divine human relationship been explored in the Torah and prophets. There is nothing more intimate to life than the life-breath, so also the "lamp" of the Lord, searching humans whether threatening or consoling them.

Proverbs 21:1–31

Bibliography

Bühlmann, W. *Vom rechten Reden,* passim. **Krispenz, J.** *Spruchkomposition.* 98–102, 176. **Whybray, R. N.** *Composition.* 117–19.

Translation

21:1	*Waterchannels, the heart of a king in the hand of the Lord;* *wherever he wishes, he turns it.*
2	*Every way, upright in a person's eyes,* *but the one who weighs hearts, the Lord.*
3	*The practice of justice and right—* *more preferable to the Lord than sacrifice.*
4	*Haughty eyes and arrogant heart—* *the tillage of the wicked, sin.*[a]
5	*The plans of the diligent—only for plenty,* *but everyone in haste—only for penury.*
6	*Acquiring*[a] *treasures by a lying tongue—* *driven vapor, snares*[b] *of death.*
7	*The violence of the wicked sweeps them off,* *for they refuse to act rightly.*
8	*Devious the way of a person, and strange,*[a] *but the pure, upright in conduct.*
9	*Better to dwell in a corner of a roof* *than with a quarrelsome woman and a shared house.*[a]
10	*The intent of the wicked craves evil;* *no neighbor experiences mercy in his eyes.*
11	*At the punishment of the scoffer, the naive become wise;* *at the instruction of the wise, they gain knowledge.*[a]
12	*The Just One attends to the house of the wicked,* *bringing the wicked to disaster.*[a]
13	*One stopping his ears at the cry of the poor—* *he too will cry, and not be heard.*
14	*A gift in secret assuages anger,* *and a pocketed present, vehement wrath.*
15	*Joy for the just, acting rightly;* *but ruin, for evildoers.*
16	*A person wandering from the way of insight* *will rest in the assembly of the shades.*
17	*A person in financial straits—a lover of pleasure;* *a lover of wine and oil shall never get rich.*
18	*The wicked, a ransom for the just,* *and replacing the upright, the faithless.*
19	*Better to live in a desert land* *than with a quarrelsome woman and strife.*

20 *Desirable treasure and oil in the house of the wise,*
    but a fool of a man will swallow them up.

21 *One pursuing justice and kindness*
    will find life [a] *and honor.*

22 *A wise man scales the city of warriors*
    and brings down the stronghold they trusted in.

23 *One guarding mouth and tongue—*
    one keeping self from troubles.

24 *Proud, arrogant—scoffer the name,*
    acting with excessive pride.

25 *The desire of the sluggard kills him,*
    for he refuses to work with his hands.

26 *All day one craves and craves,* [a]
    but the just person gives without stint.

27 *The sacrifice of the wicked, an abomination;*
    all the more so when offered with cunning!

28 *A lying witness will perish,*
    but one who listens will have the last word.

29 *The wicked person presses on,* [a]
    but the just, he discerns his course.

30 *No wisdom, and no understanding,*
    and no counsel against the Lord.

31 *The horse prepared for the day of battle—*
    but victory, the Lord's!

Notes

4.a. The meaning of נר is uncertain here, no matter how it is vocalized; it can mean lamp or tillage (i.e., ground newly broken), but it is difficult to associate the lines together. If v 4a is taken as a description of the pride of the wicked, then perhaps his very enterprise (the tillage—a symbol of whatever he undertakes) is bound to be sinful; so Plöger and apparently McKane understand. NRSV and NIV prefer "lamp" and regard it as in apposition to v 4a. After rehearsing several proposed emendations, Whybray comments that "the line remains obscure, and the text may be corrupt."

6.a. There is no need to read the participle with LXX; the MT makes sense.

6.b. MT has "seekers after death" for the last phrase. A slight emendation, with support from the ancient versions, gives better sense and is adopted here: ומוקשי, "snares," instead of מבקשי, "seekers."

8.a. The meaning of the word זור, despite countless attempts to explain it, remains unknown; this translation takes it as a joining of "and" with the common word "strange."

9.a. Various explanations of ובית חבר have been proposed; "shared house" is a guess based on the ἐν οἴκῳ κοινῷ of the Greek. Many other "solutions" have been offered on the basis of Ugaritic parallels (themselves obscure) and other evidence; cf. McKane, pp. 553–55. The sense of the verse is not affected.

11.a. Authors differ on the subject of the verb in line *b*: either "the naïve" or "the wise"; there is no denying the ambiguity. The above translation understands "they" to refer to the naive in the first line. BHS suggests a dittography that produced the preposition ל before חכם, "wise," but the MT can be translated as above.

12.a. The problem is the identity of צדיק, "a just one." The capitalization in line *a* indicates that God is the subject, although this is never used as an epithet for God elsewhere. But in line *b* God seems to be the one to cause disaster.

21.a. The repetition of "justice" in the second line is suspicious; omit it with the Greek.

26.a. The grammatical construction is that of a cognate accusative (or internal object): literally, "he desires a desire." It is not likely that the subject refers back to v 25. Rather, there is an indefinite personal subject (GKC §144d).

29.a. The Hebrew is difficult; it is similar to the construction in 7:13, where the woman is said to harden her face, but here the preposition בְּ is used before "face," and a different meaning seems to emerge, indicating direction: "the wicked man resolves in going ahead" (בְּפָנָיו). The brash decision of the wicked then contrasts with the discernment shown by the just person in line *b*. The Qere ("way" in the singular) is to be read in the second line.

Form/Structure/Setting

After somewhat of a hiatus, antithetical parallelism makes an assertive appearance in about one-third of the sayings. This is perhaps due in part to the contrasts between rich and poor, and just and unjust. Plöger (p. 243) points out that the chapter itself has five YHWH sayings as a kind of framework, vv 1–3, 30–31. The meaning of "framework" can be elusive. But Whybray bolsters the perspective of Plöger: "at some point in the editorial process the whole chapter may have been invested with a kind of loose unity. This is suggested by the fact that it is framed by two proverbs which are strikingly similar in their theme. Both are concerned with kings; and they stress the fact that royal plans and activities are subject to the control of Yahweh" (*Composition*, 117). He admits that the word "king" does not occur in v 31, and that rather militates against an "editorial" framework. But the observation itself is worth noting. For the rest, there is the customary variety of proverbs, many of them connected by theme (e.g., riches, vv 5–6) and catchwords (e.g., desire, crave, vv 25–26). Whybray is correct in criticizing Krispenz's effort to tie vv 1–8 together; only vv 1–4 have verbal links, but there is none in vv 5–6.

Comment

1 This proverb is a strong affirmation of an idea affirmed many times in the book. The Lord is the dominant actor in all that happens, and specifically is the one who weighs the hearts of all, commoner and king (cf. v 2 and also 16:2). Even kings, supposedly the highest and greatest of mortals in wisdom and might, can be said to be mere watercourses that the Lord directs at will. This is so, even if there is great emphasis in the book on listening to wise counsel. The metaphor of water (in the desert) is used in Isa 32:2, where king and ministers are singled out as a beneficent influence. Watercourses were small irrigation channels, in Mesopotamia and Egypt as well as in Palestine, that contributed toward the fertility of the difficult soil. The proverb has an added piquancy in view of the boldness with which prophets and even ordinary people, like Naboth, resisted royalty. Many commentators (e.g., Alonso Schökel, Hausmann, *Menschenbild*, 138) understand the saying as favorable to kingship. Whybray comments that since the king "is guided by Yahweh one may be confident of his good will and his justice." But the saying aims at glorifying the Lord, not the king.
2 We have remarked before that the context does not change the specific meaning of a proverb. But when two conflicting sayings, of which there are many, come together, more thought is generated. V 2 adds another dimension to the human condition since it is applicable to all human beings, including kings. This verse, and its sister saying in 16:2, has already been indicated in the *Comment* on v 1. It reflects an ever-present caution of the sages: the danger of self-deception. At

the same time, this is not intended in a *threatening* way. As Plöger sagely remarks, "admonition and encouragement lie side by side in this verse."

3 A reader of the Bible recognizes a *déja vu* in this proverb, which reflects Prov 15:8; 21:27, the famous scene of Saul's disobedience (1 Sam 15:22), and many other biblical verses. In v 27 it is said that the sacrifice by the wicked is an abomination; in other words, sacrifice must be accompanied by the proper interior devotion.

4 See *Note* 4.a. Whether "tillage" or "lamp" is the correct translation, the connection between the two lines is unclear. In this context, "broad of heart" means pride; cf. Ps 101:5. Whatever the wicked undertake (the "tillage") is bound to be sinful.

5–6 Both of these proverbs have to do with the acquisition of wealth. **5** The literary expression is stark and succinct. To succeed, one must make plans and not act hastily. Absent here is the frequent association of haste with wrongdoing, as is implied in many proverbs. **6.** This is a strong condemnation of any deceit employed in enriching oneself. What does one acquire? *Hebel* (הבל) or vanity, vapor; the implication of this metaphor is that no true value is attained. The second metaphor in v 6b is even more drastic. The necessary emendation suggested in *Note* 6.b. indicates that ill-gotten goods lead to death, as in Prov 10:2.

7 The very "violence" practiced by the wicked is personified as a power that carries them off like fish in a net (following the metaphor of this rare verb in Hab 1:15). A reason is given, even if hardly needed, in the second line: they fail to do משפט, "right," with its social and judicial implications—the very thing which brings joy to the just man to practice, v 15.

8 See *Note* 8.a. Despite the uncertainty in v 8a the general sense is clear; there is a contrast between the openness and honesty of the just and the devious style of the opposite type. The choice of terms is typically sapiential: the way and the conduct (literally, "work").

9 See *Note* 9.a. on this "better" saying, which is practically repeated in 25:24, and is similar to v 19; for the general topic see also 19:13b and 27:15. Even though the meaning of the final phrase is uncertain, the meaning of the saying is clear: to get as far away from the presumed "cause" of the trouble; dwelling in the corner of an open roof would not be comfortable, and is a bitter choice to make. The "woman" in question is not identified as a wife or another relative. Apparently there was a tendency to seek ever more drastic comparisons; cf. Sir 25:16. One wonders why the sexual roles are never reversed; such sayings are just as applicable to an autocratic and "quarrelsome" male.

10 Neither "desire" nor "intent" capture the intensity of נפש in describing the way the wicked is truly absorbed in evildoing. Having no sense of divine mercy they can show none to other human beings. Such a character is illustrated also by the sayings in vv 13 and 26.

11 See *Note* 11.a. Commentators point to a parallel in 19:25, but all depends on the translation of v 11. A basic belief of the wisdom tradition is to convert the simple or naive to wisdom. This could be achieved by the negative example of the punishment of the scoffer when he is punished, and by the good example of the wise person. That is the preferable meaning of the proverb. But it is also possible to understand v 11b as referring to the wise; they will increase in knowledge because they do not need to be spurred on by the punishment of the wicked; learning from instruction is, as it were, connatural to them.

12 See *Note* 12.a. Further difficulty in understanding is created by the duplication of the typical sapiential word, מַשְׂכִּיל (v 11b, "instruction"; v 12a, "attends to"). The above translation understands the Lord as punishing the wicked. The saying is rather flat, but the alternative translation is worse: the just person causes the disaster in v 12b (in contrast to a relatively passive stance in 29:16). It is not easy to imagine just how that is to be.

13 This verse was already mentioned in the *Comment* on v 10. The first line contains a striking metaphor for the malice of one who is pitiless. The talion law will work itself out for such a person. The verbs "cry" and "answer" are susceptible of further meaning: not simply neglect from a neighbor who will not listen, but from God as well. The setting could very well be a judicial one, and the saying can be illustrated from many parts of the Bible, e.g., Matt 18:23–35.

14 Sayings about gifts/bribery have occurred before: 17:8, 23; 18:16. Because of the stealth described (e.g., "secret," "a gift in the bosom"), this is a clear instance of bribery. Instead of being an explicit condemnation, it registers a fact that the naive person should be aware of: bribery works, even if it is not to be imitated. The setting is left vague: judicial? Who is bribing whom?

15 "Right conduct" is understood here as the subject and not as a circumstantial clause ("when justice is done"). The practice of מִשְׁפָּט is actually a joy (cf. v 3), whereas for evildoers the opposite is true; their wickedness brings about their ruin (cf. v 7). The placement of this proverb immediately after the noncommittal saying about bribery is probably significant.

16 One must walk the way "of understanding" (in the Greek, "of justice") in order to escape the death that is the lot of those who stray. Of course, everyone dies, so this must refer to an early or unhappy death—unhappy because one had an unworthy goal in this life; it is the end of a life that has somehow missed the mark. The aura of death that was prominent for fools in chaps. 1–9, e.g., 7:17; 9:18, reappears here; there is a certain ironic tone to "resting" with the shades.

17 This proverb comments on one reason for poverty—an extravagant indulgence, symbolized by "wine and oil" in the second line. "In financial straits" is perhaps too wordy for the succinctness of the Hebrew, "a person of want."

18 This proverb is often bracketed with 11:8, but they are not saying the same thing. In 11:8 there is an emphasis on punishment falling on the wicked who deserve it, while the just are delivered; the customary law of retribution is at work. But in v 18 it is implied that the just have done wrong, and need to provide ransom (כֹּפֶר) for themselves. Ransom is some kind of monetary compensation (Exod 21:30). By definition, however, the just should have no need of a ransom. Besides, there is no indication that the just person has been wrongly accused or mistreated; hence one cannot envision the wicked person as getting only what he deserves by paying a penalty in place of the just person. There is nothing in the text to suggest this. It is more reasonable to *apply* the proverb to collective retribution, as A. Vaccari (p. 61, n. 16) does. That is to say, the divine punishment destined for a group will affect only the wicked, who thus serve as "ransom" (a metaphorical use of the term) for the just who are spared. However, this appears to be an application, but not the original point of the proverb, which remains an enigma. Certain interpretations can be ruled out, if not admitted as ironic and bitter observations, such as that of W. Oesterley, "The words are an exaggerated utterance such as would be cried out by one in bitterness of spirit; they are meant to say that the righteous man suffers in order that the wicked may be in prosperity; he is, as it were, a ransom for the wicked; he takes his place."

19 See the *Comment* on v 9.

20 The teaching of the sages provides for prosperity as the lot of the wise person, although the concrete mention of oil (which has given rise to various conjectures) is surprising in the first line; it may be sign of opulence as in v 17. The antithesis is the action of the fool who lacks the sense to allow any possessions he might acquire ever to accumulate.

21 See *Note* 21.a. This is a model statement of the reward that accrues to those who pursue the path of justice and kindness. See Wisdom's boast about herself in the speech of 8:18.

22 The point is that strategy can overcome strength (David and Goliath?); cf. 16:32b; 24:5–6; Eccl 9:16.

23 The compactness and alliteration of the Hebrew expression is impressive, and it befits the sapiential emphasis on control of one's speech. Experience teaches how manifold are the troubles that unguarded speech can cause. See also 10:19; 13:3; 18:21, and the discussion in Bühlmann, *Vom rechten Reden*, 206–11. Careful speech is a common topos in ancient Near Eastern literature; see the *Excursus on Speech*.

24 The troublesome scoffer (לץ) is given a definition here, but it is clear that there is no simple English term that can adequately describe this character. The most obvious trait is pride (repeated here), but many other verses fill in to give a complicated picture: 1:22; 3:34; 9:7–8; 13:1; 14:6; 15:12; 19:25, 29; 20:1; 22:10; 24:9. See also M. V. Fox, *ZfA* 10 (1997) 4–15, esp. 7–8.

25 There is a certain paradox and exaggeration in the idea that the desire of the lazy person kills him; does he have *any* desire? If he does, his own laziness thwarts him. Ultimately, because he refuses to work (v 25b; recall such earlier sayings as 19:24 and cf. 26:15), he should come logically to an early death.

26 See *Note* 26.a. There is a contrast between the desperately greedy person whose desires will never be fulfilled, due to his nature, and the generosity of the just who, without concern, shares with others.

27 V 27a appeared already in 15:8 (which adds "to the Lord" after "abomination"). The meaning of זמה, "cunning," determines why the wicked bothered to sacrifice. Was it to win divine favor in a *do ut des* ("I give in order that you should give") attitude? Or possibly to cover up for some wrongdoing that will be continued anyway? Or just plain hypocrisy?

28 The meaning of the first line seems clear, and it might echo what has been said before about punishment for the false witness, e.g., 19:5a, 9a. But when joined with line *b* a different nuance appears; it is not so much the false witness as his words that are meant. Against lying testimony will be the words of the "one who listens." This would be a careful observer whose words in reply will stand permanently and convincingly because they have been well thought out, and they are honest. Literally line *b* has: "The listening man speaks definitively" (לנצח). The phraseology of Alonso Schökel and also R. Van Leeuwen expresses this neatly: "will have the last word."

29 See *Note* 29.a. The translation above ("presses on") suggests the determination, even obstinacy, of the wicked in plunging forward, in contrast to the care with which the just person discerns the right way. Other translations differ, especially in the first line where it is thought that the wicked "hardens his face." But the meaning of this is not clear (determination?); Whybray thinks he puts on a bold face, i.e., deviously hides true character behind a mask.

30 The verse underscores the superiority of the Lord to human wisdom, despite its cleverness, even its good intentions (such as "fear of the Lord"). Whybray objects to the translation "against" (לנגד) and insists on "face to face," but this is not necessary. The real point is that human wisdom, though it be a gift of God (Prov 2:6), comes up short. The idea is not unrelated to Prov 3:5 and 15:33; see the *Explanation* below.

31 This verse is related to v 30 in that it provides a concrete example of a face-off between humans and God. Even wars, which seem to be humanly accountable and which humans only too readily prepare for, do not escape the overarching causality of the Lord, without whom victory cannot be achieved.

Explanation

One of the most important theological statements in the book is to be found in v 30 concerning the inadequacy of any form of human wisdom when one has to count the Lord into the situation. And is this not *always?* Wisdom, or concretely the doctrine of the sages, has been taken to task in the past for eudaimonism, for materialism, and for many other supposed failings. One of the most stubborn objections against the sages is the belief that they had figured out reality and God in a neat formula. God rewards the wise/good and punishes the fools/wicked. One can easily document this, as we have seen, in the book of Proverbs, as well as in most other books of the Bible. But everything depends on how this was understood, and upon unspoken qualifications. Also, the passage of time gave rise to different understandings. In 21:30, which should be accounted as "early" wisdom, there is a clear affirmation of the mystery of God, against which human wisdom hurtles itself. Qoheleth discovered this painful fact, but he had the wisdom and courage to register his struggle. There are several reactions to this mystery in the book of Job. Sirach slides too easily perhaps into a theodicy that we would judge inadequate, but we may rightly question if he understood "theodicy" in our terms. It is totally inadequate for the modern theologian to take early wisdom to task as though it were a banal understanding of God and the world. G. von Rad commented thus on Prov 21:30–31: "In this astonishing sentence, the awareness of the limit round which earlier sentences were already circling is expressed in extremely radical terms and is even surpassed. The astonishing element in it is clearly seen when one realizes that its aim is certainly not to warn man against acquiring and using wisdom or even to prevent him from 'making ready' the horse before the battle. If one were to remove it from its context one could even perceive in it the expression of a radical, theological agnosticism. But this would be to misunderstand it completely. Its aim is, rather, to put a stop to the erroneous concept that a guarantee of success was to be found simply in practicing human wisdom and in making preparations. Man must always keep himself open to the activity of God, an activity which completely escapes all calculation, for between the putting into practice of the most reliable wisdom and that which then actually takes place, there always lies a great unknown" (*Wisdom*, 101).

Proverbs 22:1–16

Bibliography

Bühlmann, W. *Vom rechten Reden.* 59–64. **Murphy, R. E.** "Proverbs 22:1–9." *Int* 41 (1987) 398–402. **Whybray, R. N.** *Composition.* 119–20.

Translation

22:1	*A name is preferable to great wealth,*
	and graciousness better than silver and gold.
2	*The rich and the poor meet;*
	the Lord the maker of them all.
3	*The prudent person perceives an evil and disappears;* [a]
	the naive plunge forward and pay for it.
4	*The result of humility—the fear of the Lord:* [a]
	riches, honor, and life.
5	*Thorns,* [a] *snares, in the path of the perverse;*
	one who preserves his life stays distant from them.
6	*Train* [a] *a youth in the way he should go;*
	even in old age, he will not turn from it.
7	*The rich have power over the poor;*
	and one who borrows, a slave to one who lends.
8	*One who sows iniquity reaps calamity,*
	and the rod of his pride [a] *will fail.*
9	*The generous one, he will be blessed,*
	for he shares bread with the poor.
10	*Get rid of the scoffer and strife disappears,*
	and quarreling and insult cease.
11	*One who loves purity of heart—*
	gracious his lips, his friend a king. [a]
12	*The eyes of the Lord preserve the knowledgeable,*
	but he overturns the words of the renegade.
13	*The sluggard says: "A lion outside!*
	I'll be killed in the streets!"
14	*A deep pit, the mouth of women who are strangers;*
	one who incurs the Lord's anger will fall into it.
15	*Folly is bound up in the heart of a youth;*
	the rod of discipline will drive it far from him.
16	*One oppressing the poor—for his enrichment;*
	one giving to the rich—only for impoverishment! [a]

Notes

3.a. Read the niphal imperfect with the Ketib; the Qere is influenced by Prov 27:12.

4.a. The absence of the connective "and" after עֲנָוָה, "humility," can be explained grammatically as a case of asyndesis; so Plöger who understands it as a humility based on fear of the Lord. The second line then contains the predicate nominatives of the sentence.

5.a. There has been much discussion about "thorns" as the meaning of צִנִּים, but there is no certain solution. The Greek supplies the connective "and" with the next word, but this could be case of hendiadys.

6.a. חֲנֹךְ means to "dedicate" and, in this verse, "train." The "way he should go" is the usual translation of the idiomatic "according to the mouth of his way."

8.a. The Hebrew is difficult. The link between the two lines is unclear, due especially to the vagueness of עֶבְרָתוֹ, "his pride." It can be construed as "anger," "excess," or "pride." The LXX reads "his works" for it (cf. BHS), but this is not helpful. One can also question whether the suffix refers to God (divine anger) or, perhaps more likely, the wicked person. Moreover, it is not clear how the final verb ("fail") relates to the subject "rod"; hence various emendations have been proposed, none of them successful.

11.a. This translation attempts to render the MT literally, but it is uncertain. It reads the Qere for "pure" (of heart), and finds predicate nominatives in v 11b. See the Comment, and especially W. Bühlmann, Vom rechten Reden, 59–63, for detailed discussions.

16.a. This translation of a very succinct text is as literal as possible, but the text is ambiguous. In v 16a לוֹ, "to him, his," could refer to the poor (less likely) and not to the rich. In v 16b it is not clear how giving to the rich results in impoverishment, whether of the rich or of the poor. See the Comment.

Form/Structure/Setting

The cutoff after v 16 is due to the title (emended text), and the clear beginning in v 17 of a series of admonitions, in contrast to the style of the sayings which have dominated since 10:1. It should also be recalled that it has long been known that 10:1–22:16 contains 375 single-line proverbs, and this number is the numerical value of the letters of the Hebrew name "Solomon" given in the title at 10:1. This can hardly be a coincidence, and hence it is with certainty we can say that we have come to the end of the main collection, 10:1–22:16. Whybray has summarized the themes of this section: "four Yahweh proverbs (2, 4, 12, 14), six proverbs concerned with wealth and/or poverty (vv. 1, 2, 4, 7, 9, 16) and two on the training of children (vv. 6, 15), with a further verse on the importance of 'knowledge' (v. 12)" (Composition, 119). The forms of the sayings vary. V 3 is clearly antithetical; two sayings are imperatives (vv 6, 10), and one is a "better" saying (v 1). Others are synthetic. Still others are so uncertain in meaning that they cannot be characterized with certainty (vv 8, 11, 16).

Comment

1 The importance of a (good) name or reputation is a genuinely biblical concern, e.g., Eccl 7:1; Sir 41:11–13; hence the evaluation of riches is not surprising. But the parallel, charm, or graciousness (חֵן), while welcome, is somewhat unexpected until we recall that it is a trait that accompanies wisdom (Prov 3:3–4; 13:15a), and it is far from being a superficial air. As always (cf. 8:10; 16:16, etc.), no riches can be compared with the deeper values recognized by the sages; their sense of values is sound.

2 This verse anticipates 29:13 (and see also 14:31; 17:5), where the same verb

for the "meeting" of poor and rich occurs, and the implication of creation is also expressed. The "meeting" is not casual: a common life bestowed upon them by the Lord is meant. There is an implicit admonition here, suggesting how serious is the condition of any society in which there is a sharp cleft between rich and poor, as in Israel. Inequality is not only a matter of social concern, but of human dignity, in that the Lord is the creator of both classes. And both, but especially the rich for whom it is harder, should take to heart this basic human equality and cooperate with each other. The topic of riches creates a bond between the first two verses.

3 This verse is practically identical with 27:12; cf. also 14:15, 18. The "evil" seen by the wise is presumably some sort of disaster, or bad turn, and he takes pains to avoid it; literally, "he hides himself"; he is, as it were, an "artful dodger." This foresight is contrasted with the stupidity (perhaps curiosity?) of the naive who goes forward, blithely ignoring the danger signals that the clever person recognized, and who must pay the penalty (unspecified) for such carelessness.

4 See *Note* 4.a., which indicates that line *b* is to be understood as the fruit or result of line *a*. See also 21:21b for similar rewards, especially life and honor.

5 Cf. also 15:19. The difficulties that beset the path of the wicked will not threaten the wise person who is intent on preserving נפֶשׁ, "life" (cf. 13:3). Such terminology indicates that these are serious difficulties, but they can be avoided.

6 The verse is absent from the Greek, but admirably suits the optimism of the wisdom ideal: the earlier the better. As *Note* 6.a. indicates, the verb is "dedicate," as used of a temple. Thus one can hope that early training will perdure in later life. "The way he should go" is a common translation of the obscure Hebrew (literally, "according to the mouth of his way") and seems confirmed by the meaning of line *b*.

7 The first line is borne out in many other sayings where the advantages and power of riches are recorded without praise or blame. When this is joined to the second line, it might be a warning to the rich about hoarding their possessions. But it has more bite if it is directed to the poor, or to the ordinary person, since it warns them that they must strive to be independent, or they will lose their freedom to their creditors. There is a neat play in the Hebrew: לוה, "borrow"/מלוה, "lend."

8 The metaphor of sowing/reaping derives from farm life (cf. Ps 126:5–6; Gal 6:7) and is quite intelligible in itself as a statement of retribution for wickedness. But the translation of line *b* is uncertain; see *Note* 8.a. If it is taken as a specification of v 8a, it means that the pride (wielded like a rod) has come to an end. The final result is that the wicked person will be punished: the rod on which he relied will fail him; so also Plöger and Meinhold. *Alii aliter.*

9 The "generous one" is literally "the good of eye," just as "the evil of eye" is the opposite; cf. 23:6; 28:22. He is "blessed," not only by God, but probably also by the poor as well, with whom he shares.

10 The nature of the scoffer is illustrated in many of the proverbs. See the *Comment* on 21:24. Here he is seen as a troublemaker, provoking disputes in the community. The imperative in v 10a can be given its full weight, although it often has the value of a conditional clause.

11 See *Note* 11.a. The translation understands the second line as indicating the results achieved by the subject of the first line. Such a good person possesses winning speech, as indicated by "lips of grace"—a wisdom trait. And his influence extends to high places: "a king for a friend." It is also possible to divide the verse differently, so that the high quality of the heart and speech describe the one who is the friend of the king.

12 The translation understands the abstract for the concrete: "knowledge" stands for "the one who knows." The Lord has a favorable eye for such a person, in contrast to undoing the words of the godless. If "knowledge" is understood abstractly, it can be referred to the divine knowledge which subverts the speech of the godless.

13 This excuse for laziness is repeated in 26:13 (see also 26:14–15), and the same rough brand of humor and ridicule appears in 19:24. Any excuse, however improbable or unlikely, will be invoked by the sluggard.

14 The "stranger" (זרות, feminine plural in this verse) is conspicuous in chaps. 1–9; see the discussion at the end of chap. 9, and also the *Excursus on Woman Wisdom and Woman Folly*. The plural form appears only here in this collection. But a new twist is given to her familiar role as one who seduces by her speech. She is seen here as a deep pit (cf. 23:27) and thus a trap into which falls the man with whom the Lord is angry. The precise identity of the "strangers" in this verse is not easy to determine: a foreigner, another's wife, a prostitute?

15 The need for discipline or instruction (מוסר) in the training of youth is a common theme throughout the book, e.g., 1:7b; 13:24. However, the emphasis here is on a kind of innate folly which only discipline can eradicate. Normally not much hope is held out for the conversion of a fool (cf. e.g., 27:22), but if the young are trained early on, there is hope for them, as v 6 also suggests. The training is inescapable if there is to be any change.

16 See *Note* 16.a. The construction of the verse seems to intend some paradox, but the details are not clear. The problem is to determine who becomes rich in v 16a, and who becomes poor in v 16b. The translation given above stays open to the ambiguity, even if the following interpretation is favored. V 16a states a *fact*: The oppressor profits from oppression of the poor. One has to go to extremes to imagine how the oppression can profit the poor! A paradoxical turn is described in v 16b: whoever gives to the rich (e.g., by way of bribery?) will not profit. The giver is losing his money because the rich do not need that "gift," and thus it turns out to be unnecessary, a loss. There are many other interpretations. For example, A. Meinhold and the translation of JPS seem to agree: the final phrase, "only for loss," is taken to refer to *both* of the previous actions in v 16ab. JPS makes this clearer by paraphrasing: "To profit by withholding what is due to the poor / is like making gifts to the rich—pure loss." But the paradox that is indicated by the parallel structure of the two lines is dulled. Besides, there is no particle here to indicate a comparison.

Explanation

It may be no more than a coincidence that so many sayings relative to the rich and poor occur at the end of this collection: vv 2, 4, 7, 9, 16. Alonso Schökel notes the lack of reference to the sapiential area in particular. Instead, there are many references to the theme of the consequences of one's conduct: vv 3–12, 14, 16. The reader is referred to the *Excursus on Wealth and Poverty* for a more complete picture. Here it is worth noting some striking aspects on this topic that chap. 16

affords. Thus v 1 presents a significant turnabout. Riches are normally considered part of wisdom's achievement, although wisdom itself is praised for a value far beyond precious jewels; e.g., 3:14; 8:10–11. Now, a good name and personal grace are rated higher than riches. According to v 2 the rich and the poor are to be viewed in still another perspective: riches do not entitle one to establish class distinctions since God created all, both rich and poor. One cannot deny the differentiation between each of these classes. V 7 recognizes their existence— while it also hints at an apparently frequent reason: the practice of borrowing and lending, which may lead to virtual enslavement (at this point one should recall v 2!). Even more, according to v 9 generosity must be practiced, since it leads to blessing all around. V 16, despite the admitted ambiguity, seems to be a saying against the rich in favor of the poor. None of these provide any excuse for a blameworthy poverty, i.e., one born of laziness, as the ridicule poured upon the sluggard in v 13 clearly shows. This *Explanation* indicates how disparate sayings can be put together and enable one to draw further conclusions. The point is not that the collector intended all this—such an intention would be difficult to prove. Rather, the interpreter can discover new implications by balancing proverbs against each other.

The Words of The Wise   (22:17–24:22)

Proverbs 22:17–29

Bibliography

(For works pertaining to the Egyptian sage, Amenemope, and this portion of Proverbs see the *Excursus on the Book of Proverbs and Amenemope.*) **Bright, J.** "The Apodictic Prohibition: Some Observations." *JBL* 92 (1973) 185–204. **Bühlmann, W.** *Vom rechten Reden*, passim. **Cody, A.** "Notes on Proverbs 22,21 and 22,23b." *Bib* 61 (1980) 418–24. **Nel, P. J.** *The Structure and Ethos of the Wisdom Admonitions in Proverbs.* BZAW 158. Berlin: de Gruyter, 1982. **Römheld, D.** *Wege der Weisheit.* BZAW 184. Berlin: de Gruyter, 1989. 13–59. **Steiert, F.** *Fremdkörper.* 191–209. **Whybray, R. N.** *Composition.* 132–41.

Translation

22:17
Words of the Wise.[a]
Bend your ear and listen to my words,[b]
and apply your heart to my knowledge.

18
For it is well that you keep them in your belly;
let them settle together[a] on your lips.

19
That your trust may be in the Lord,
I make them known to you today—even you.[a]

20
Have I not written to you "Thirty"[a]
of counsels and knowledge?

21
To let you know truth,[a] words that are reliable,
to bring back reliable words to the one who sent you?

22
Do not rob the poor, because they are poor,
and do not crush the needy at the gate.

23
For the Lord will defend their cause,
and despoil[a] those who despoil them of life.

24
Do not be friendly with an irascible person,
and do not associate with the wrathful,

25
Lest you learn his ways
and get yourself ensnared.

26
Do not be one of those who pledge hands with another,
those who go surety for debts.

27
When you have nothing to pay,
why should he take your bed from under you?

28
Do not remove the ancient boundary mark
that your ancestors have fixed.

29   *Have you seen a person skilled in his work?*
          He shall serve kings;
          it will not be shadows [a] *that he serves!*

Notes

17.a. This title appears at the beginning of the LXX which incorporates it into v 17a: Λόγοις σοφῶν παράβαλλε σὸν οὖς καὶ ἄκουε ἐμὸν λόγον. "To the words of the wise, lend your ear and hear my word." The MT reads literally: "Bend your ear and hear the words of the wise." The title needs little justification since a new collection clearly begins here.

17.b. The reading "my words" is an insertion based on the Greek reading (in the singular) that is indicated in *Note* 17.a.

18.a. The MT should be retained here despite the temptation (cf. *BHS*) to emend it in the light of Amenemope ("like a tent-peg").

19.a. The ending of the verse is sudden and suspicious, but there is no compelling evidence for an emendation. On the basis of the Greek evidence *BHS* proposes "his/your path" as the object of the verb. But אף אתה, "even you," can be in apposition to the object "you."

20.a. Perhaps the most famous interpretation in the book deals with MT שלשום (Ketib), שלישים (Qere). The Ketib means "the day before yesterday"; the Qere suggests "officers" (or metaphorically "excellent things"?). The Greek has τρισσῶς, "three times." The evidence favors a number, and the "thirty" (sayings) of Amenemope serves as a confirmation of the meaning "thirty" in the judgment of very many scholars. NJV has "a threefold lore," marked as meaning of Hebrew uncertain.

21.a. קשט, "truth," seems to be an Aramaic word, occurring elsewhere in Dan 2:47 and 4:34, perhaps a gloss on the following words. A. Cody (*Bib* 61 [1980] 418–26) argues that it means probity. For the grammar of "reliable words" in the second line, see GKC §131c (a case of apposition).

23.a. The meaning of the verb is uncertain; Cody (*Bib* 61 [1980] 418–26) argues that it means "oppress."

29.a. Literally, חשכים means "darknesses, or dark things," hence "obscurities, unknowns."

Form/Structure/Setting

There is practically a unanimous agreement that a new collection begins here for the following reasons: the (emended) title, support by the Greek translation, the renewed invitation to the addressee to listen to the words of the teacher, and finally a change from the sayings of the previous collection to a different style. Now there appear couplets, usually containing an admonition and the reason for the admonition. This style continues down to 23:11, 19, in which "my son," so familiar from chaps. 1–9, reappears. From that point on, the forms vary; there are sayings, example stories, and admonitions which continue to 24:23 where a new superscription is provided for the next collection. The number of admonitions is seventeen, compared to the two that appeared in the previous collection (20:13, 22). Comparison with the work of Amenemope (see the *Excursus on the Book of Proverbs and Amenemope*) has led some scholars, such as R. Scott and W. McKane, to identify thirty sayings (note the emended reading "thirty" in 22:20) in 22:17–24:22. The NIV is printed in such a way as to yield that number, and several commentaries based upon it agree with that specific enumeration. This is a mistake; there is simply no consensus in identifying the units that make up the "thirty." Moreover, the relationship of the Hebrew text to Amenemope comes to an end at 23:11, although it is theoretically possible that an Israelite author/editor could have continued on, filling out from various sources the number "thirty." A threefold division, with slight variations in detail, has been proposed by several scholars. For example, Plöger divides the material thus: An introduction (22:17–21) is followed by (1) 22:22–23:14; (2) 23:15–18; (3) 24:1–22. Römheld (*Wege*, 58–59) holds stoutly to identifying thirty sayings, with divisions at 23:12 and 23:29. However, Whybray (*Composition*, 133) even denies the validity of the textual change to "thirty" in 22:20. His division of this section is 22:17–23:11 (which he compares to chaps. 1–9; cf. *Composition*, 135–36), followed by two appendixes, 23:12–24:22 and 24:23–34.

Comment

(In order to concentrate on the Hebrew text, discussion of the relationship of the text to Amenemope will be found in the *Excursus on the Book of Proverbs and Amenemope*).

22:17–21 This has the appearance of an introduction to the admonitions which are going to follow. **17** For the justification of the superscription and the changes, see *Notes* 17.a. and 17.b. This opening invitation, with its emphasis on "ear" and "heart," is certainly reminiscent of 2:1–2; 5:1, and would be typical of any teacher, just as it also opens the first chapter of Amenemope. **18** The words of the teacher are to permeate the student, from the inmost parts to the lips that are such an important organ for wise practice. "Inmost parts" is literally "belly," and thus resembles "in the casket of your belly" in Amenemope. **19** See *Note* 19.a. The striking affirmation in v 19a gives the purpose—trust in the Lord—of the teaching to follow. It is conspicuous in view of the fact that it is not present in Amenemope, while all around it there are echoes of the Egyptian sage. **20** As indicated in *Note* 20.a., "thirty" is a very widely accepted interpretation of the Hebrew text, and obviously this view is due to Amenemope, who speaks of his thirty chapters only at the very end, interestingly enough (chap. 30). **21** Bühlmann correctly points out the double task of the messenger. In v 21a he is to learn correctly what his master wishes to communicate, and in v 21b, he must faithfully bring back the reply. There is no apparent reason why the task of being a truthful messenger should be mentioned at this point. There has been a suitable emphasis on reliable messengers already in 10:26; 13:17, but why does it appear in this introduction? The topic is not a high priority in wisdom teaching. Perhaps because in the prologue to Amenemope (1:5–6), the same concern is expressed about a messenger replying to the one who sends him.

22–23 This prohibition is in line with the general biblical concern for the poor, expressed in the law codes (e.g., Exod 22:20–26), and elsewhere in Proverbs; cf. 14:31, 17:5, and see the *Excursus on Wealth and Poverty*. **22** The mention of the "gate" would indicate that a judicial case is meant. There is a certain ambiguity in the reason (line *b*), but probably it is because the poor has no one to defend him, and not merely because he is disdained by the oppressor. **23** A divine defense of the poor is reflected again in 23:1. They are truly helpless, but the Lord will make those robbers pay, perhaps with their very lives (cf. Prov 1:19b).

24–25 The prohibition is familiar, but the motivation is new. **24** The angry and ill-tempered people are mentioned often enough in Proverbs; see 15:18 and the *Comment* there; the "heated man" (in contrast to the "silent man") is also a frequent topic with Amenemope. The basic failure of such characters is their lack of self-control. **25** The motivation associates the command with an old wisdom symbol: the way (so the Ketib; the Qere has the plural, but either reading suffices for the symbol), and the wrong way would be a snare.

26–27 This warning deals with an old favorite of the sages—going surety—and provides a vivid motivation. **26** The hand pledge is specifically mentioned in Prov 6:1; see also 11:15; 17:8. It would seem that this form of social aid created more problems than it solved. **27** The vivid and ironic question sounds like a gibe at the person involved; as American slang has it, "why lose your shirt?" The pledge is not condemned outright, but the implication is that the risk (of going bail, or whatever the situation) is not worth it. The "bed" is a sign of luxury that not all enjoyed. Many slept on the floor with a cloak as the outer covering, and the Law (Exod 22:25–26; Deut 24:10–13) specified that a cloak that had been pawned should be returned before nightfall.

28 The general law covering such prohibitions as this can be found in Deut 19:14 (cf. Deut 27:17). There is no explanation as to why this is repeated in 23:10 (where it finds a motive clause, lacking here, in 23:11). The prohibition itself goes against a thirst for power and land-grabbing, which the upper class might indulge in, particularly to the disadvantage of the unprotected (cf. Prov 15:25b).

29 The question breaks the monotony of the prohibitions at the same time that it urges an ideal. The talent of the alert or skillful (מהיר) worker will not go unnoticed, but will be duly recognized. There may be a deliberate exaggeration in the idea of serving kings, who are contrasted with "dark ones" (see *Note* 29.a.) whose work itself is unimportant. Such talent should be, has to be, recognized. There is no objective evidence that a line is missing.

Explanation

The transition from the previous collection is obvious due to the lengthy invitation in vv 17–21. This also alerts the reader to adjust to a different kind of wisdom saying, the admonition, which has seldom appeared since chaps. 1–9 (see 3:1–12, 25–34, especially). The material is not particularly new or striking; it is even familiar, except for the glowing prospects of the skilled worker. This introduction is to be compared with the pertinent section of Amenemope; see the *Excursus on the Book of Proverbs and Amenemope.*

Proverbs 23:1–35

Bibliography

Bühlmann, W. *Vom rechten Reden*, passim. **Watson, W. G. E.** *Classical Hebrew Poetry: A Guide to Its Techniques.* Sheffield: JSOT, 1984. 20–30. **Whybray, R. N.** *Composition.* 141–43.

Translation

23:1   *When you sit down to eat with a ruler,*
          consider carefully the one before you,[a]

2   *And put a knife to your throat* [a]
         if you have a big appetite.
3   *Do not desire his dainties,*
         for they are a deceptive food.

4   *Do not wear yourself out to acquire wealth;*
         have enough sense to stop. [a]
5   *Will you let your eyes fix* [a] *on it?—It is gone!*
         For it [b] *grows wings for itself*
         and flies [a] *to the sky like an eagle.*

6   *Do not eat food with an avaricious person,*
         and do not desire his dainties,
7   *For it is like a hair in the throat!* [a]
         "Eat and drink," he says to you,
         but his heart is not with you.
8   *The little you have eaten you will vomit up,*
         and waste your pleasant words.

9   *Do not speak to the ears of a fool,*
         for he will despise the wisdom of your words.

10   *Do not move the ancient boundary mark,*
         and do not enter the fields of orphans.
11   *For their vindicator is strong;*
         he will fight for their cause against you.

12   *Apply your heart to instruction,*
         and your ears to words of knowledge.
13   *Do not hold back from disciplining a youth*
         because the blows of your rod will not kill him—
14   *If you beat him with a rod,*
         you will deliver him from Sheol.
15   *My son, if your heart is wise,*
         my heart, too, will be happy.
16   *My kidneys will rejoice*
         when your lips speak rightly.
17   *Let not your heart have envy for sinners—*
         rather, for the fear of the Lord, the whole day!
18   *For then* [a] *there is a future,*
         and your hope will not be cut off.
19   *You, my son, listen and be wise,*
         and walk the way of your heart.
20   *Do not be with those who soak up wine,*
         who glut themselves on meat,
21   *For wine addicts and gluttons will be impoverished,*
         and stupor clothes with rags.

22   *Listen to your father who begot you,*
        and do not disdain your mother because she is old.

23   *Get truth, but not for selling it:*
        Wisdom and instruction and understanding!

24   *The father of the just will greatly exult;*
        whoever begets a wise person will rejoice in him.[a]

25   *Your father and your mother will rejoice,*
        and she who bore you will exult.

26   *My son, give me your heart,*
        and let your eyes observe my ways,

27   *For a deep pit, the harlot,*
        and the woman who is a stranger, a narrow well,

28   *For like a robber she lies in wait,*
        and adds to faithless men.

29   *To whom "woes"? To whom "groans"?*[a]
        Whose the strife? Whose the troubles?
    To whom wounds for no reason?
        To whom glazed eyes?

30   *Those last to finish off the wine,*
        who gather to taste mixed wine.

31   *Do not look at wine when it is red,*
        when its eye shines in the cup,
        when it goes down smoothly.

32   *Its aftereffect: like a snake it bites,*
        and like an adder it stings.

33   *Your eyes see strange things,*
        and your heart utters incoherencies.

34   *And you are like one who lies down in the heart of the sea,*
        and like one who lies down at the top of a mast.[a]

35   *"They have struck me—I have no pain.*
        They have beaten me—I did not know it.
        When shall I wake again?—I'll keep looking for it."

Notes

1.a. It is also possible to construe the object in line *b* as "what is before you," namely, how you eat the food (so the LXX). Another possible meaning is "look to the situation that confronts you."

2.a. שכין, "knife," and לע, "throat," are hapax (Aramaisms?), but the translation is fairly certain.

4.a. Literally the line reads "cease from your understanding." This can be taken to mean "stop considering the proposal to get rich," or "cease because of [Hebrew מן] your intelligence."

5.a. "Fix" and "fly" translate the Ketib and then the Qere of the same verb, meaning "fly" (עוף).

5.b. There is no clear antecedent for the pronoun "it." It must refer to the wealth which was expressed in the verb form of v 4a.

7.a. The Hebrew is difficult, and no translation is certain. The above version reads שער as "hair" (so the Greek τρίχα) and also reads בנפש, "throat." The Hebrew seems to say, "like one who calculates in himself," but the verb is hapax (cf. NJV, "he is like one keeping accounts").

18.a. The repetition of כי אם after v 17b is disturbing; it must mean something like "surely" or "then" (cf. Joüon §164c). Some commentators follow the Greek, ἐὰν γὰρ τηρήσῃς αὐτά (cf. *BHS*), "if you keep them"; see the similar construction in 24:14, "find (them)."

24.a. Read the Ketib גּוֹל יָגוֹל, "exulting will exult" or "will greatly exult," for the first two instances, and the Qere יִשְׂמַח (no *waw*), "will rejoice," for the final verb.

29.a. אֲבוֹי is hapax, and the meaning is a guess based on the parallel אוֹי.

34.a. חִבֵּל, "mast," is hapax, and the meaning has to be derived, uncertainly, from the context. The LXX (cf. *BHS*) rendered this "as a sailor in a great wave."

Form/Structure/Setting

The admonitory style characteristic of this section continues in chap. 23, and deals with many different topics: eating with a ruler and with the avaricious, desire for riches, and the sacredness of the ancient boundary mark. As has often been noticed, the pronounced similarity to the Teaching of Amenemope comes to an end at 23:11. The admonitory style continues, but rather in the fashion of chaps. 1–9. It is not clear how many units can be separated out in 23:12–35. D. Römheld (*Wege*, 46) entitles vv 12–28 "the obedient son." There are certain clearly defined topics: the disciplining of youth (vv 12–16); the problem of envy of wrongdoers (vv 17–18); an exhortation concerning gluttony and intoxication (vv 19–21); the relationship of a youth to father and mother (vv 22–25); a warning about harlotry (vv 26–28); an admonition concerning intoxication and its dangers (vv 29–32). Authors divide the material differently, especially if they are intent on finding thirty units. The above suggestions merely try to follow the change of topics. In contrast, Whybray (*Composition*, 141–42) recognizes five introductions to admonitions that follow: 23:12–16; 23:19; 23:22–26 (and in chap. 24, vv 3–4 and 13–14). There is little to be gained by formal distinctions such as "my son," which occurs irregularly here, and not always in its usual initial position. The lively passage in 23:29–35 stands out because it departs from the admonitory style (except v 31). It has been diagnosed as a riddle (Whybray, McKane) consisting of six questions, with the answer in v 30: the drunkard. There follows an admonition and warning in vv 31–32, followed by a somewhat humorous description of the confused reactions of the drunkard.

Comment

1–3 Echoes of the Teaching of Amenemope continue up through v 11. For the admonition concerning table manners with important figures, see the Instruction to Kagemni (1.1–10; *AEL*, 1:59–60), the Instruction of Ptahhotep (119ff., *AEL*, 1:65), that of Amenemope (23, 13–20; *AEL*, 2:160), and the elaborate directions in Sir 31:12–32:13. This was obviously a well-known topos in the wisdom tradition. The conclusions to be drawn concerning the social status of the diner (as done by Whybray, *Composition*, 92–93) are quite speculative. **1** See *Note* 1.a.; it makes little difference whether the command is to consider the food or the host. Perhaps both are included in the caution. The host may be seen as testing the guest (cf. v 3). **2** The metaphor of the knife to the throat in v 2a has been interpreted in at least two ways: curb the appetite, or endanger one's life (by demonstrating a large appetite). The first interpretation is more reasonable. **3** "Deceptive food" is ambiguous; it could be the unpleasant effects of eating too much, or a sign that the food is not conducive to good health. But more likely, it points to the wily character of the host, who is testing the character of the guest. Hence the food can be considered deceptive because it does not serve the purpose of health or taste, but is "used" for private intent by the host.

4–5 There are many sayings about riches in the book, but this one is unique in that it warns directly *against* them, and on the basis of wisdom! They can become an all-consuming purpose in life, and also frustrating because they can disappear so easily. Cf. the drawbacks to riches described in Eccl 5:9–16. **4** See *Note* 4.a. The unbridled pursuit of riches is senseless. Wisdom should have a guiding role in this matter. **5** See *Note* 5.a. It should not seem unusual that the disappearance of wealth be compared to the speedy flight of birds. The comparison is similar to the flight of geese in the Teaching of Amenemope (9:15–10:5; *AEL*, 2:152) concerning riches that have been stolen.

6–8 This admonition is not unlike vv 1–3, but the emphasis is clearly on the character of the host. **6** For the phrase "evil of eye," meaning stingy, avaricious, see the *Comment* on 22:9. **7** As *Note* 7.a. indicates, the translation of v 7a is uncertain; the idea of the translation above is that the hair in the throat would provoke vomiting. In a different context Amenemope speaks of a block in the throat and ensuing vomit that comes from coveting the possessions of a poor person (14,5–7, 15–19; *AEL*, 2:154–55). The hypocrisy of the host is obvious from the contrast between his words and his "heart." **8** Whatever the pleasant or praiseworthy words (in honor of the host?) might have been, they have been canceled by the vomiting. Both proceed from the same mouth. The vomiting can be taken as metaphorical; the guest is disgusted at his own words because they have been proven untrue, or unworthy of the occasion.

9 This saying illustrates an aspect of Prov 26:4 about not speaking to a fool, but the motivation is different: Do not waste words on such a person who has no ear for what is said. See also Sir 22:9–10, 13. Fools may not be failing in real intelligence, but they just will not "listen" or take to heart any advice. Bühlmann (*Vom rechten Reden*, 220) points out that "speak into the ears of" denotes urgency; cf. Gen 44:18; 1 Sam 25:24.

10–11 See the *Comment* on 22:28, where respect for the boundary markers set by the ancients is underscored. Here the motive is given: concern for the defenseless, such as orphans; for the widow, see 15:15b. The implication is that God is the גֹּאֵל, "next of kin, redeemer," rather than some human relative. The same concern is recognized by Amenemope (8:9–15; *AEL*, 152). The general parallels to the text of Amenemope are not continued in what follows.

12 The absolute necessity of being docile and open to instruction is affirmed many times e.g., 19:20. This very general admonition has no motivating verse, but stands on its own. It may be associated with the following verse because of the word מוּסָר, "instruction, discipline."

13–14 In contrast to the general character of the previous verse, these lines are specifically addressed to the parent/teacher on the subject of disciplining youth. The notion of physical beating is certainly not new (cf. 13:24; 19:18), but the casual way in which the perspective of death emerges in the context is somewhat jarring (cf. also Ahiqar, 81–82; Charlesworth, *OTP*, 2:498). The meaning of the whole is to be derived from v 14, which provides the motivation and obviously shades the meaning: The youth will be delivered from death, i.e., from Sheol, which is understood here as the adversity or nonlife that awaits the fool and the wicked here and now, or, perhaps more concretely, an early and unexpected death, but not at the hands of the parent.

15–16 The repetition of "heart" (לב) is very effective, since it is often the organ of understanding. But it also spills over into the meaning of the entire person, indicated by the "kidneys" (or, more euphemistically, "inmost being"—although heart and kidneys occur in Psalms and especially Jeremiah, Jer 11:20). The lips, of course, will speak from the wise heart, uttering what is just and right. The sayings are almost naive in that the motive for being wise lies in the simple joy that it gives to the teacher. This attitude serves to offset the apparently harsh words in v 13.

17–18 Envy of sinners because of their apparent good fortune is well known from Pss 37 and 73. **17** There is a clever play on the verb "envy." In a sense there are two kinds: the selfish and perhaps sinful envy concerning the prosperity of the wicked, which is contrasted with the true envy for the fear of God; perhaps the abstract should be taken for the concrete, those who fear the Lord. **18** See *Note* 18.a. Many commentators regard this verse as paired with v 17, and in a sense it provides a motive: look to the future. However, the verse is a repetition of the ending of 24:14, where it is wisdom that provides a future. In both cases, there is a statement of a very general idea: a good end to life. This of course has nothing to do with the next life; rather, it is a life well lived in the here and now and celebrated by an honorable death which is not foreshortened, or marked by adversity. The absence of an "eschatological" hope should not delude the reader into underrating the intensity and the reality of this hope for the Israelite; it burned brightly.

19 The appeal of the teacher/parent to the youth could appear anywhere in the admonitions characteristic of chaps. 1–9 as well as here. For that reason it is best to interpret the "way" (a significant symbol in chaps. 1–9) as the way of wisdom, thus implementing the imperative of v 19a. The "ways of your heart" in Eccl 11:9 has a different nuance in its context, and it gave trouble to the rabbis of old.

20–21 This admonition against excessive drinking and even overeating is direct, as compared to the indirect style of vv 29–35 concerning intoxication. The motivation is the threat of poverty, surely a reasonable prospect for such conduct in any culture. The two classes are described in Deut 21:20, where such wayward youths are also threatened with death by the community. Cf. also Prov 21:17.

22–25 There is a clear inclusion in these verses, with the mention of parents at the beginning and end. **22** The appeal to listen to the father is traditional (e.g., 1:8), and the prohibition in favor of the aged mother seems designed to have an emotional pull on the youth. **23** This verse is not found in the Greek, and it falls outside of the parent/teacher theme. The absence is one among other reasons that move Whybray and also Plöger to disregard these verses as forming an original unit of instruction. But it picks up the urgent theme of 4:5, 7; see the *Comment* there. The acquisition of "truth" is not a mercantile purchase (how could it be bought?); it means being founded and steadied in fidelity, not in abstract "truth," which is further defined in v 23b. **24–25** It is not surprising that joy is in store for the parents whose children will listen to them; cf. v 15. The mention of the "just" in v 24 indicates once more the equation of justice or righteousness and wisdom. The mention of the mother twice in v 25 is unusual.

26–28 Most commentators understand v 26 as a kind of introduction to the description of the harlot in vv 27–28. **26** As in v 19b, "heart" and "way" are repeated. Alonso Schökel makes the interesting observation that Israelite wisdom lacks any "response" to the exhortations of the parent/teacher, such as one finds in Egypt where Khonsuhotep answers his father Any, and with strong objections (cf. *AEL*, 2:144–45). **27** "Deep pit," which was used to describe the strangers (זרות) in 22:14, appears here as a metaphor for a harlot (זונה), who is paired with the "stranger" (נכריה). One need not belabor the metaphors to understand their sexual references. The old question rises again: Just what group of women is intended? A true foreigner, a sacred prostitute, the wife of another? See the *Excursus on Woman Wisdom and Woman Folly.* In any case, she is "off-limits," and consorting with her has the same result as dealing with the woman of chap. 7; cf. 7:27. **28** This is the only time that such a woman is likened to a *robber* lurking for a victim. The meaning of v 28b seems to be that her action increases the number of unfaithful among men.

29–35 This is one of the most remarkable literary passages in the book: questions, observations, answers, warning, a description of the attractions as well as of the effects of wine, a description of the condition of the drunkard, and the drunkard's own befuddled statements. **29** See *Note* 29.a. All the questions, even if the nuances of some escape us, vividly portray the various actions and moods of a drunkard. **30** The answer as to the identity raised in the questions of v 29 is now given. The whole may be considered a riddle and answer, as suggested above, although the answer seems too obvious to justify the term "riddle." **31** The admonition is remarkably imaginative. Wine, too, has an "eye"; it is the "sparkle" of wine which looks up, almost appealing, to the eyes of the beholder. The fetching attraction of wine is increased by the memory of its smooth run in the mouth of the individual; cf. Cant 7:9 for its smooth course. Hence, the only safe course is: Do not even *look* at wine! **32** Then comes the reality check, made all the stronger by the comparison to the bite of poisonous animals; cf. Deut 32:33. **33** The addressee (doubtless the youth is intended) is given a personalized description of the results: "your eyes" and "your heart" experience the befuddling effects of too much alcoholic drink. And obviously this is bound to be evident to any onlooker. **34** The precise comparison is not clear. One can understand the "heart of the sea" as the trough in the roll of the water, in contrast to being at the "top" of something (translated doubtfully as "mast"; see *Note* 34.a.). As a general description of the chaos in which the drunkard finds himself, this is an adequate understanding. Barucq points out that Ps 107:27 provides a contrary comparison: a passenger on a boat is compared to a drunkard, as regards the effects of seasickness. **35** The ending is dire: the words are the bluster and bravado of a "macho" drinker who regards his "hangover" as somehow victorious: he has taken all the hard knocks, and he is ready for the next round of drinks.

Explanation

It is tempting to expand on the striking description of intoxication and its effects. The verses themselves are just right. Why spoil them with a heavy-handed expatiation on the evils of "rum"? The poem itself does not "instruct." It invites the reader to consider what one must pay for excessive drinking. Much can be learned from the clever pedagogical ploys of the writer. Particularly noteworthy is the indirect approach: the startling opening that calls attention to the problem, while it lists some of the effects that will be described in later verses, and the obviously knowledgeable appraisal of wine (its "eye") and its pleasure. Hence the clever exaggeration not even to *look* at it—rather astounding when one recalls that wine was part of the staple diet. Then this is suddenly and climactically followed by wine's "sting." Outside of the gentle remonstrance about looking at wine (v 31), the only direct words to the youth are not for blame or blind prohibition; they simply describe the undesirable effects that excessive drinking can bring on.

But this interesting ending does not conceal the strangeness of a chapter that continues the echoes of Amenemope, and then suddenly changes (v 12) to a quite different direction, less interesting perhaps, and more traditional: discipline, exhortations to wisdom, consideration for the training given by parents, respect for the boundary stone, and the dangers represented by harlotry and by inebriation.

Proverbs 24:1–22

Bibliography

Bühlmann, W. *Vom rechten Reden*, passim. **Meinhold, A.** *Die Sprüche*. 2:374, 400–401. **Whybray, R. N.** *Composition*. 142–45.

Translation

24:1   *Do not envy the evil,*
             and have no desire to be with them,

2   *Because their heart plans violence,*
             and their lips speak troubles.

3   *By wisdom is a house built,*
             and by understanding it is established,

4   *For by knowledge are the chambers filled*
             with all precious and pleasant wealth.

5   *A wise person: in strength;*
             and one who has knowledge grows in power,[a]

6   *Because by cleverness you win battles,*
             and with many counselors, victory.

7   *Wisdom is too high* [a] *for a fool;*
             he cannot open his mouth in the gate.

8   *To whoever plans to do evil*
             the name "crafty one" is given.

9   *Foolish plans: sin;*[a]
             an abomination to a man: the scoffer.

10   *If you give up on a day of pressure,*
             depressed: your strength.[a]

11   *Deliver those dragged off to death!*
        Do not [a] *hold back from those stumbling to slaughter;*
12   *If you say, "Well, we did not know this."*
        The one who weighs the hearts—does he not understand?
        The one who guards your life—does he not know?
        And will he not render to all according to their deeds?

13   *Eat honey, my son, for it is good,*
        and the honeycomb sweet to your palate;
14   *Know that wisdom is such for you;*
        If you find it, then there is a future,
        and your hope will not be cut off. [a]

15   *Do not lie in wait* [a] *at the dwelling of the just;*
        do not destroy his home.
16   *For the just may fall seven times, but he will rise;*
        while the wicked stumble about in misfortune.

17   *Do not be happy over the fall of your enemy,*
        and let not your heart rejoice when he stumbles,
18   *Lest the Lord see it, and it be evil in his eyes;*
        then he will turn aside his wrath from him.

19   *Do not be angry at evildoers;*
        do not envy the wicked;
20   *For the evildoer has no future;*
        the lamp of the wicked goes out.

21   *My son, fear the Lord and the king;*
        do not associate with those who rebel against them. [a]
22   *For destruction from them will rise suddenly,*
        and the ruin from both—who can know?

Notes

5.a. The translation follows the MT; the preposition in v 5a may be the *beth essentiae*. The Greek, with the help of the ancient versions (cf. *BHS*), supports an easier reading: "The wise man is better than the strong man, and the knowledgeable person than one who is mighty in power." The necessary emendations are adopted, in whole or in part, by many modern versions. The principal change is the recognition of the comparative *min* in both colons.

7.a. ראמות probably means "corals" (Ezek 27:16), a precious stone. It is better to understand the word as an unusual spelling for רמות, "high."

9.a. This can also be rendered by the concrete for the abstract: "the plans of the fool: sinful," and the parallelism with v 9b is clearer.

10.a. The Hebrew text may be defective. The translation attempts to bring out the repetition of צך ("depressed, pressure"). The verse is conditional: if the individual fails under some unspecified pressure to act as he should, then . . . (v 11).

11.a. If the text is not corrupt, אם, "if," in v 11b can be taken as equivalent to an oath formula (GKC §149; Joüon §165), and thus equivalent to a prohibition; cf. Greek and Vulgate (*BHS*).

14.a. The verse has three lines and seems to be disturbed, but the emendation proposed in *BHS* is guess work. See the *Comment*.

15.a. The phrase "O wicked man" is suspicious since the sayings are directed to the youth, as v 13 indicates, and it seems to overload the line; hence it is omitted, although there is no textual support for this. If the MT is retained, רשע can be in apposition (NRSV, "like an outlaw").

21.a. The translation is possible, but there are uncertainties, e.g., "rebel" is an interpretation of "those who change" (שונים). Various emendations have been proposed, as *BHS*, suggesting on the basis of LXX, "do not disobey either of them." Note also that the Greek has five extra verses (vv 22a–e in Rahlfs) that are mainly a warning about the wrath of a king.

Form/Structure/Setting

The couplet style continues, but at times for more than two verses. There is a variety of moods: admonitions (vv 1–2, 10–12), sayings (vv 3–9), imperatives with motivation (vv 13–20). The chapter thus presents a kind of miscellany, reaching back to the "my son" address of the previous chapter, which is especially characteristic of chaps. 1–9. The neat, if complicated, division of these verses by Meinhold will not stand. As mentioned before, those who are intent on finding the "thirty" sayings of 20:20 complete their search with the thirtieth in vv 21–22. There is no apparent explanation why the theme of (not) envying sinners occurs so frequently: 24:1–2, 19–20; cf. 23:17–18. Similarly, a house that is built by wisdom (24:3–4) takes up a previous theme (9:1; 14:1).

Comment

1–2 This well-known admonition (Ps 37:1; cf. 73:3) takes up Prov 3:31 and 23:17, and will appear again in 24:19–20. The motivation lays more stress on what the wicked intend ("plan," "speak") than on what they will yet do. See further comment in the *Explanation*.

3–4 Just as the Lord "founded" the earth by wisdom (Prov 3:19), so humans need the same for building their "house." But this building requires also the cooperation of those who will live in it in order that there be appropriate material subsistence. The saying moves from the material building, for which technical ability or practical wisdom is required, to the less tangible quality of knowledge that truly makes the house livable. As an example, see Prov 31:15, 21, 27. Although the form of v 3 is a saying, the couplet provides the motivation in v 4, making it urgent to carry out the implication of the saying.

5–6 For a different understanding of v 5, see *Note* 5.a. Again, the style is a saying followed by the motive. "Strength" and "power" are predicated of the wise person because their strength is increased by their strategy and the wisdom of the advice they follow (cf. 11:14; 20:18).

7 See *Note* 7.a. It makes little difference whether "high" or "corals" is adopted. The point is that wisdom is simply out of reach for the fool, by any comparison. Hence in any public discussion (the "gate" would suggest an occasion of juridical nature), his opinion would be disregarded. More than that, the reason is that he really has no opinion: "he cannot open his mouth" for people know that he has nothing worthwhile to say; cf. the ambiguities of silence, esp. Prov 17:28b. His loquaciousness has already revealed how shallow he is, and hence his inability to judge.

8–9 "Plans" (root זמם) is the catch word for these two verses; it can be found in a favorable, but also, as here, in an unfavorable sense. **8** "Crafty one" is literally a master/possessor of plans. **9** "Plans of folly" are to be taken in a concrete sense: the fool plans sin. He is equated with the scoffer, and deserves the name (v 8) that he gets. The emphasis is on the interior attitude; here the "sin" begins. "Abomination" is used most often in Proverbs concerning something displeasing to God; here humans are concerned.

10–12 Several questions have to be answered in order to reach even a partial understanding of these difficult verses: Who is being addressed in the singular in v 10, and is this verse connected with the following? Are those destined for death in v 11 justly or unjustly condemned? What is the validity of the excuse offered in v 12, in view of the Lord's omniscience and check for accountability? **10** See *Note* 10.a. Although the opening verse is phrased as a conditional, it amounts to an accusation of some kind of faintheartedness or cowardice, of a failure to meet a responsibility. The person who is pressured/depressed (note the play on the word צר) has authority to act in the case that is brought up in v 11. However, not all agree that v 10 introduces v 11, e.g., McKane. **11** See *Note* 11.a. The situation described in these verses remains vague, and interpreters envision several possible circumstances (e.g., cf. Whybray, NCBC, *Proverbs*). The substantial question is the innocence or guilt of those being led to death. If they were justly condemned, no interference would be tolerated, and neither could the lack of it be blamed, contrary to the implication of vv 10 and 12. Therefore the condemnation must be an unjust one, and the command to "deliver" in v 11 is meant seriously. **12** A plea of ignorance, whether feigned or innocent, is dismissed. Because the omniscient and just God (cf. 16:2; 21:2) knows! Cowardice in the face of injustice is reprehensible.

13–14 This imperative is delivered with the address "my son," as also v 21, a familiar phrase from chaps. 1–9. The comparison of wisdom and honey (cf. 16:24) may seem ordinary; this is because the "you" in v 14 is נפש, here to be understood as desire or appetite. Wisdom, symbolized here by honey, will appeal to the one who has the appetite for it. The same comparison is made in Sir 24:20. The "honeycomb" would contain the best and sweetest honey. Many authors, e.g., Plöger, suppose probably correctly that there is some kind of omission in v 14, such as a second line, since the present second and third lines are a repetition of 23:18 (see the *Comment* there), with the exception of the first two words ("if you find . . ."). These last two lines have the appearance of hanging in the air; they simply repeat a promise for a future.

15–16 Plöger (pp. 282–83) rightly remarks of the rest of the chapter (vv 15–22) that it contains admonitions dealing with various aspects of one theme: the antithesis between the just and the wicked. He also goes on to say that this "allows one to recognize a closer relationship to Yahwistic faith." **15** See *Note* 15.a. The "wicked man" of the MT is either in apposition to the subject, or is the vocative; but it is better omitted since nowhere else in the book is the wicked ever addressed directly. The admonition recalls the enticement by the wicked in Prov 1:11–18, where also the verb to "lie in wait" is used twice; see also the description of the woman in 7:12; 23:28. **16** This verse provides the motive. Even if the machinations against the dwelling of the just (v 15) should succeed, these reversals will be only temporary, for no matter how many times (the proverbial seven) the just one falls, he will rise again, in contrast to the stumbling of the wicked. Qoheleth, however, spoke of the sinner doing evil a hundred times without paying for it. The "optimism" of the book of Proverbs should not be exaggerated. It is presumed that the just will not be without troubles, but there is also the belief that in the long run shalom will be restored.

17–18 The positioning of these verses is probably due to the catch words "fall" and "stumble" (v 16). **17** *Schadenfreude,* or rejoicing over an enemy's downfall, seems both tolerated and even yearned for; cf. Ps 58:11; but in Ps 35:13–15 it is characteristic of the wicked, and in Job 31:29 it is condemned. Here it is ruled out. **18** The motive is not clear. Does it mean that the Lord judges such vengeful feelings in a human being as "evil," and will therefore put an end to the divine wrath that caused the enemy to fall? Or is one to relinquish such joy in the secure hope that the Lord's wrath will persist and bring about the fall of the enemy? It is also possible that the Lord is so displeased with such an attitude (cf. also 25:21) that he may turn the divine anger upon the one who was originally happy over the fall of the enemy. One wonders if this saying is deliberately ambiguous.

19–20 The prohibition not to be vexed or angry (as in Ps 37:1, 7) over the seeming prosperity of the wicked returns to the similar attitude of envying the wicked in v 1 (see *Comment* there). **20** The reason given is that the wicked have no future; this is the opposite of v 14 and 23:18. There is a repetition of 13:9b: the "lamp"—a metaphor for life—and the "values" of the wicked shall disappear.

21–22 Respect for God and king is the point of this curious admonition. The address "my son" reflects v 13. It is surprising to see fear of the Lord bracketed (it occurs only here) with the king. Hausmann (*Menschenbild,* 137) comments: "King and YHWH are characterized here rather as 'Greats' to whom one must pay equal attention because one never knows exactly when they will allow a misfortune to overtake the one who is not acting properly toward them. Herein alone, according to this text, is the commonality (viewed negatively in the eyes of the author) between YHWH and the king." These words explain the fear that comes to the average person in dealing with the great in this life; to get caught on the side of rebels means certain death or imprisonment. This reaction is understandable as regards a king, but it is astonishing as regards the Lord, Hausmann thinks. However, one should look closely at the point of comparison: neither the Lord nor the king can be held accountable to their constituents for their actions. The comparison is not surprising; both can freely change their course of action, especially in the face of rebellion (see *Note* 21.a.). There are plenty of proverbs to show that the Lord is regarded as superior to the king (cf. especially Prov 21:1; 25:2). In v 22, "them" refers to God and king.

Explanation

There are several interesting theological issues raised in a chapter that seems to be merely the tail end of a collection. One is the theological tensions that exist not only in this book, but within the entire Old Testament. Perhaps the greatest of these concerns retribution (see the *Excursus on Retribution*). Anger and then the envy of the wicked are scored twice (vv 1, 19). The good fortune of the wicked understandably was a severe trial for the just. Their obvious short-term theodicy had no ready answer. So the battle is mounted at the beginning: repress those feelings of anger and envy. At the same time there is the apparently sovereign assurance that the wicked will meet with misfortune, that their "lamp" will go out: vv 16, 20. Elsewhere other motivations are suggested. Obviously a benign and traditional interpretation of divine providence and justice had its difficulties. But the strength of the affirmation remained fairly steady. Often it was fortified by a description contrasting the assurance of hope and a future for the wise, as opposed to what faced the evildoer, as here in vv 14b, 20a. It is surprising that within this truncated chapter of Proverbs the problem should be so vividly illustrated. It is given lengthy treatment in Pss 37 and 73. Vv 17–18 are intriguing; do they mean only that the Lord will stop the punishment of the enemy who "stumbles" (used also of the wicked in v 16) simply because the presumably innocent person has rejoiced to see their downfall (*Schadenfreude*)? Or is there an implied threat that the divine wrath will then be directed toward the one who rejoiced (see the *Comment* above)? There is also an interesting example of what moderns call the "sin of omission" in vv 10–12. The failure to act in a just cause is no excuse in the sight of God. Finally, the juxtaposition of God and king is not to be misunderstood. In the ancient world the king was a channel of blessing, but especially in Israel was his human dimension recognized. In the case of these verses his power enables him to be rated with the Lord in the sense that it is unquestionable in the human sphere. There is no court of appeal.

The Words of the Wise

Proverbs 24:23–34

Bibliography

Bühlmann, W. *Vom rechten Reden.* 104–9. **Whybray, R. N.** *Composition.* 145–47.

Translation

24:23	*These also by the wise.*[a]
24	*Showing partiality in judgment, not good;* *whoever says to the wicked: "Just one!"* [a] *peoples shall curse him, nations condemn him.*
25	*But it will go well for those who make the accusations;* *upon them will come generous blessing.*
26	*He kisses the lips,* *whoever replies with honest words.*

27	*Arrange your outside work,*
	    and get your things ready in the field;
	    afterwards build [a] *your house.*

28	*Do not testify against your neighbor without cause,*[a] *or would you deceive with your lips?*
29	*Do not say, "As he did to me, so I will do to him;* *I will render to him according to his deed."*
30	*I passed by the field of a sluggard,* *by the vineyard of one who lacks heart.*

31	*And—all of it overgrown with thistles!*
	    Nettles covered its surface,
	    and the stone wall was broken down.

32	*And I gazed—taking it to heart;* *I took a lesson from what I saw.*
33	*"A little sleep, a little slumber,* *a little folding of the arms to rest* [a]—*
34	*Then your poverty will come like a robber,* *and destitution like an armed man."*

Notes

23.a. This is the title for the small section: more "words of the wise," which is separated in the LXX from 24:22 by five extra verses and by the insertion of 30:1–14. There is no conclusive explanation available for the variations from the order of the MT. In v 23 the Greek has a full sentence: "I speak to you, sages, that you may know this . . . ," thus forming a couplet with line *b*. Instead, v 23b (cf. 28:21) should be taken as the first of five lines (vv 24–25) dealing with honest (legal) judgment.

24.a. Literally, the text reads: "just (are) you"—perhaps a set formula.

27.a. The grammatical construction of the verb is the perfect consecutive; see GKC §112oo; Joüon §119l.

28.a. The MT should be kept; see the *Comment* for the nature of the witness; the "false witness" of the LXX seems to be interpretive; at any rate, disregard the suggestion in *BHS*.

33.a. Refer to *Notes* 6:11.a. and 6:11b.

Form/Structure/Setting

The differences between the MT and the Greek have been indicated above in *Note* 23.a. The spacing in the translation indicates a rather loose structure of various topics: title; condemnation of partiality; the beauty of honesty; an order of priority in work; prohibitions concerning relationship to a neighbor; a lesson gained from observation of a sluggard's field. There is no convincing explanation of the position of this section, or even of the importance of its contents. The conclusion of Whybray is merely impressionistic: "Prov. 24:23–34 originated in part in quite separate circles from the earlier instructional material in the book. It has a single comprehensive heading, and may once have existed as a separate short collection despite its very miscellaneous character" (*Composition*, 147). Meinhold describes the section shortly and sharply: "Two basic areas of life—judicial law and work—twice form a framework . . . Thus we have an expression of what is of particular importance for human life" (p. 410). His outline of the structure summarizes the whole:

Conduct in court:	(Judges: vv 24–25)	(Witnesses: v 28)
Speaking, thinking:	(Honest speech: v 26)	(Harmful speech: v 29)
Attitude to work:	(Positive: v 27)	(Negative: vv 30–34)

Comment

23a See *Note* 23.a.

23b–25 A judgment is followed by two couplets that are antithetical in nature and demonstrate the corresponding results that ensue from its observance or neglect. **23b.** This ideal judgment is a familiar one; it is repeated in 28:21, and found in the Law, e.g., Deut 16:19. The Hebrew idiom for showing partiality is either "lifting the face" (cf. 18:5) or, as here, "recognizing the face." **24** The implication of this verse is that the judgment is universally recognized; the cursing, which invokes the exertion of divine justice upon the villain, is justifiable. The singular would suggest that one judge is meant; this is in contrast to the plural in the next verse. This judge can be seen as a type for all those who exercise their office dishonestly. **25** The "generous blessing" is to be understood in the usual biblical sense of prosperity and honor.

26 The physical sign of intimacy underlines the great importance of honest speech, which is also effected by lips. This seems to be a broad, universal, saying that has no necessary connection with the previous verses. Of itself, it could refer to the reliability of a messenger, to simple honesty between friends, or to many other social situations. For further discussion of "kiss" in the ancient Near East, cf. W. Bühlmann, *Vom rechten Reden,* 105–7; he interprets it in this verse as a sign of trusting affection.

27 The imperatival saying indicates a certain priority of values for a young man. Preparation for the material needs involved in marriage and establishing a family should be attended to first. The sages were practical; see also 27:23–27.

28–29 Perhaps these two admonitions can be taken together, dealing with judicial witness and thus reflecting back on vv 23–25. **28** The implication of "without cause" is that the person concerned has no reason to give witness. Whatever be his intentions, they are suspect since he is not properly involved. Any witness should have a good reason, and not simply yield to pressure or casually take up the responsibility. The Greek tradition interpreted the case as involving "false witness." V 28b is an intensification, and again (v 26) the lips are in play. **29** The prohibition seems to reject the well-known *jus talionis* (eye for an eye . . .). A desire for revenge cannot justify retaliation. See Prov 20:22; even the last line of v 29 repeats the words uttered concerning the Lord in 24:12d.

30–34 The verses constitute an "example story," or the report of an observation made by the sage. It is beside the point to ask whether the situation is real or made up for pedagogical purposes. The exaggeration suggests that it is a type; cf. Prov 6:9–11. **30–31** The vineyard and field of the sluggard are in dreadful condition, and open to the depredations of wild animals; see Isa 28:24–29 for the care of the land that a conscientious farmer should exercise. **32** The reaction of the observer is profound. "Heart" takes up the word "heart" in v 30; there is more than mere "intelligence" at stake here. **33–34** It is rather surprising to see a repetition of 6:10–11; see the *Comment* there. Plöger recognizes here a kind of proverbial reference to the sluggard and his uselessness for the community. That is perhaps all that can be said in view of the text itself, but one might have expected more from a story that started out rather imaginatively; it retains its irony and sharpness, but why the repetition? Alonso Schökel remarks that 6:10–11 are a simple proverb, but they appear in 24:33–34 as an "epiphenomenon, as the final reflection of an observation. This is the sapiential style: to observe in turn life, note its significant details, offer them to others as teaching and admonition" (p. 445).

Explanation

Not much can be added to the above description of the structure and comment on this very brief unit. As a whole, it remains a curious mixture of instruction, statements, and the "lesson" of vv 30–34. McKane makes the interesting observation that the poem with which the chapter ends "is a new way of accepting *mūsār*—not by paying attention to the authoritative instruction of a teacher and acting on his advice, but by direct observation, followed by reflection, then conviction" (p. 572). However, one may question whether the authority of the storyteller can be so sharply divided from the point of the story.

The Proverbs of Solomon   (25:1–29:27)

Proverbs 25:1–28

Bibliography

Bryce, G. E. "Another Wisdom-'Book' in Proverbs." *JBL* 91 (1972) 145–57. ———. *A Legacy of Wisdom.* Lewisburg: Bucknell University, 1979. **Bühlmann, W.** *Vom rechten Reden,* passim. **Meinhold, A.** "Der Umgang mit dem Feind nach Spr 25,21f. als Masstab für das Menschsein." In *Alttestamentlicher Glaube und Biblische Theologie.* FS H. D. Preuss, ed. J. Hausmann et al. Stuttgart: Kohlhammer, 1992. 244–52. **Van Leeuwen, R. C.** *Context and Meaning in Proverbs 25–27.* SBLDS 96. Atlanta: Scholars, 1988. **Whybray, R. N.** *Composition.* 120–23. For older bibliography, see Plöger, 294.

Translation

25:1   *The Proverbs of Solomon, which the men of King Hezekiah of Judah copied*
    out.[a]

2   *The glory of God, to conceal a matter,*
    and the glory of kings, to search out a matter.

3   *The heaven for height, the earth for depth,*
    the hearts of kings: unsearchable.

4   *Remove*[a] *dross from silver,*
    and a vessel emerges for a refiner.[b]

5   *Remove the wicked from before the king,*
    and his throne is made firm by justice.

6   *Do not claim honor in the presence of a king,*
    and do not take over the place of the great,

7   *For it is better to be told "Go up ahead,"*
    than to be humiliated before a nobleman.
    Whatever your eyes see,[a]

8   *do not be quick to argue for;*
    Lest[a] *. . . what will you do afterwards*
    when your neighbor makes a shame of you?

9   *Argue your own case with your neighbor,*
    but do not reveal the secret of another,

10   *Lest the one who hears it reviles*[a] *you,*
    and your bad reputation never ceases.

11   *Apples of gold in silver settings,*[a]
    a word spoken at the right time.[b]

12   *A gold earring, an ornament of fine gold—*
    the sage who reproves a listening ear.

13   *Like the cold of snow on a harvest day,*
    a faithful messenger for the one[a] *who sent him,*

>¹⁴ *for he restores the spirit of his master.*^a
> *Clouds and wind, but no rain:*
> *one who boasts of a gift never given.*

>¹⁵ *By patience a ruler can be persuaded,*
> *and a soft tongue can break a bone.*

>¹⁶ *If you find honey,*^a *eat only what you need,*
> *lest you have your fill of it and vomit it up.*

>¹⁷ *Let your foot be seldom in your neighbor's house,*
> *lest he have his fill of you and hate you.*

>¹⁸ *A club,*^a *sword, and sharp arrow:*
> *one bearing false witness against a neighbor.*

>¹⁹ *A bad tooth and an unsteady* ^a *foot:*
> *trusting a faithless person in time of trouble.*

>²⁰ *One who takes off*^a *clothes on a cold day—*
> *vinegar on a wound* ^b—
> *one who sings songs to a sad heart.*

>²¹ *If your enemy is hungry, give him food to eat;*
> *or if thirsty, water to drink;*

>²² *For you will heap coals on his head,*
> *and the Lord will reward you.*

>²³ *The north wind brings rain,*
> *and a backbiting tongue, angry faces.*

>²⁴ *Better to dwell in a corner of a roof*
> *than with a quarrelsome woman and a shared house.*^a

>²⁵ *Cold water for a dry throat:*
> *good news from a far country.*

>²⁶ *A trampled spring, or a polluted fountain—*
> *a just person who gives way before the wicked.*

>²⁷ *Eating much honey, not good;*
> *nor to seek honor after honor.*^a

>²⁸ *A city breached, without a wall—*
> *a man without self-control.*

Notes

1.a. The meaning of the verb (הֶעְתִּיקוּ) is uncertain, but it is generally rendered as "copy" or "transmit."

4.a. The infinitive absolute functions here (and in v 5) as an imperative, giving the effect of a conditional clause; cf. Joüon §123u.

4.b. Changes have been suggested in the light of the Greek ("and it will be cleansed, all clean"; cf. *BHS*), but the above version is justifiable and observes the parallelism with v 5b. On this verse see R. Van Leeuwen, *ZAW* 98 (1986) 112–13.

7.a. This line is included in v 7 by the Masoretes, but it belongs to the following verse, as the above translation indicates; so also the jps. For the grammatical construction of the relative clause, see Joüon §158l.

8.a. פֶּן, "lest," is grammatically difficult here and is paraphrased in various translations as "otherwise" or "for," etc. LXX rendered ἵνα μή, "so that not." It is probably better to recognize here an anacolouthon: "lest . . . what will you do?" So F. Delitzsch, R. Van Leeuwen, *Context*, 57.

10.a. יְחַסֶּדְךָ, "reviles you," is a difficult verb; see also Prov 14:34 and the lengthy discussion in Van Leeuwen, *Context*, 58, n. 3, who takes it as a denominative verb (חֶסֶד) in the sense of "condemn." Others render it as a privative piel, "revile."

11.a. The precise meaning of מַשְׂכִּית is uncertain; it indicates some kind of image, especially idolatrous (cf. Lev 26:1), or even imagination (Prov 18:11). LXX rendered "on a necklace of cornelian."

11.b. The translation is doubtful. Literally the text has "on its two wheels." Obviously the first line is a positive appraisal of the "word" spoken in the second line, but the meaning of עַל־אָפְנָיו, "at the right time," is uncertain. The translation understands it on the analogy of בְּעִתּוֹ as in 15:23. Another common interpretation is "well turned" (phrase); see a rather complete discussion by W. Bühlmann, *Vom rechten Reden*, 45–53.

13.a. To justify the rendering of the singular, see GKC §1124k.

16.a. The declarative clause is equivalent to a condition; cf. Joüon §167a.

18.a. The parallelism of terms in v 18a suggests the emendation of מֵפִיץ (hiphil participle from פּוּץ, "be dispersed, scattered"), meaning "scatterer, disperser," to מֵפֵץ, "club, hammer," with the LXX (cf. *BHS*).

19.a. The root is probably מָעַד, "unsteady," which some would vocalize as qal participle; the form in the MT can be explained as pual participle without preformative *mem*.

20.a. The form is considered to be the hiphil participle of עָדָה, "one who takes off," if the text has not been corrupted.

20.b. The meaning "wound" is found in the Greek ἕλκει, and this is followed by many. Others (e.g., JPS) interpret the word as "natron," a sodium mineral.

24.a. Refer to *Note* 21:9.a.

27.a. The translation of the Hebrew is literally "the search of their glory is glory." The LXX is not helpful: "it is right to honor glorious words" (cf. *BHS*). Various emendations have been proposed and surveyed by R. C. Van Leeuwen ("Proverbs xxv 27 Once Again," *VT* 36 [1986] 105–14) and by W. Bühlmann (*Vom rechten Reden*, 179–83); see the *Comment* on this verse below. The latter proposes a translation of the MT: "and the search for one's own honor is a burden." Van Leeuwen advocates the following: "To seek difficult things is (no) glory." JPS gives, with a note that the meaning of the Hebrew is uncertain: "Nor is it honorable to search for honor." Barucq and NAB have a very simple emendation: כָּבוֹד מִכָּבוֹד, "honor after honor." This is adopted in the above translation.

Form/Structure/Setting

There is widespread agreement that there are at least two different collections within these chapters: chaps. 25–27 and chaps. 28–29. The first three chapters are quite vivid in metaphors and similes; there is relatively little antithetical parallelism, but admonitions are many. Chap. 25 has been subjected to detailed treatment by G. Bryce (*Legacy*, 135–62; see also *JBL* 91 [1972] 145–57). His view was taken up and considerably expanded by R. C. Van Leeuwen (*Context*, 57–86). Both detect an overall unity in 25:2–27, so much so that Van Leeuwen can term this a "proverb poem," while Bryce describes it as a "small wisdom book" reminiscent of the wisdom (or *Sebayit*) of the Egyptian Sehetepibre, and also the *Kemyt* (this word means "complete," and designates the training for a court scribe). What evidence have these scholars produced to show the unity of the chapter? Only the highpoints of their exposition can be indicated here. Van Leeuwen has discussed both surface and "deep" structure, but we will point out only the relevant aspects of the surface structure.

We can prescind from v 1, the superscription, which will be dealt with in the *Comment;* besides, it is a heading that counts for the next four chapters, and not merely for chap. 25. The basic contention is the unity of 25:2–27, suggested by the obvious connection between the first and last verses, dealing with glory; searching/concealing; God and humans (kings). Within this range can be found several meaningful connections, e.g., the chiastic patterns of word pairs: כָּבֹד - דְּבַשׁ, "glory-honey" (vv 2, 16, 17); כָּבֹד - חֵקֶר, "glory-search" (vv 2, 27b); דְּבַשׁ - אָכַל, "honey-eat" (vv 16, 27a). Van Leeuwen points to רָשָׁע - צַדִּיק, "wicked-righteous," in vv 5, 26 and

שׂנֵא אכל - שֹנְאֶךָ, "eat-hate you," in vv 16–17, 21–22. Thus there is not only the major inclusion for the poem (vv 2–27), but others, such as vv 16–17, which are linked to vv 21–22. These devices suggest a unified poem. The themes also contribute to this; at least for the first seven verses a courtly setting is appropriate, even if, as Van Leeuwen himself states, "these sayings have a wide applicability beyond the court" (*Context*, 73). That precise "applicability" is also apparent in most of the following verses. Thus, vv 11–15 seem to be quite independent in themselves, as he admits (p. 82), but he accommodates them to the life setting of the court; the alleged inclusion of the first part of the poem (vv 2–3 and 15), however, is not convincing.

The forms can be thus classified: sayings, vv 2–3, 4–5; admonitions, vv 6–7, 7c–10; sayings, vv 11–12, 13–14, 15. Admonitions open the second part, vv 16–17, linked by catch words (פֶּן, "lest"; שָׂבַע, "have enough"). These are followed by sayings, vv 18–20, again marked by clear catch words; an admonition in vv 21–22; sayings in 23-24. Three sayings end the chapter: v 26 echoes terms found in v 5, and the final verse reflects both v 16 (v 27a, "honey") and vv 2–3 (v 27b, "search," "glory"). V 28 is not included in the poem, but Van Leeuwen questions if it may have been added to reach the 140 lines suggested by Skehan for chaps. 25–29 on the basis of the numerical equivalent in the name of Hezekiah (spelled יְחִזְקִיָּה; cf. Skehan, *Studies*, 17, 22, 44).

There is more to the analysis than is described above, and the reader has to digest Van Leeuwen's arguments to be convinced. But as it stands, it is certainly the most striking example so far of the careful matching of proverbs by the editor. Later commentaries have taken little notice of it, with the exception of R. N. Whybray, whose comment deals more with Bryce than with the detailed analysis of Van Leeuwen; he finds "their thesis as a whole is unconvincing" (NCBC, *Proverbs*, 358). In his *Composition*, 120–121, he lists the divisions of Plöger, Krispenz, and Meinhold, which all differ from each other. Whybray grants the "striking" verbal link between vv 2–3 and v 27b, but 27b is "probably corrupt." In general, most commentators have simply remarked on the couplet style, the catch words, and the mixture of admonitions and sayings, thus recognizing small groups, but no overarching unity.

Comment

1 The superscription has provoked much questioning. Are these "men" of Hezekiah professional court scribes? So thought R. B. Y. Scott, who ascribes considerable activity to Hezekiah in assembling wisdom from both the north and the south (pp. xxxiv–xxxv; p. 21; see also his article in VTSup 3 [1955] 262–79). M. Carasik ("Who Were the 'Men of Hezekiah' [Proverbs XXV 1]?" *VT* 44 [1994] 289–300) thinks that the historical situation described in 2 Kgs 18–19 (the siege of Jerusalem) provided the occasion for the ascription of this role to Hezekiah's counselors. But we really are ignorant of their relationship to the collection called "the proverbs of Solomon." As *Note* 1.a. indicates, even their role (copy, transmit?) is not clear.

2–3 These two verses are deliberately placed together, with "king" and "search" as catch words. 2 Plöger insists that "God," and not YHWH, is used in the comparison, because of Prov 21:1: the heart of the king is totally subject to the action of YHWH. Perhaps he is right, but was the distinction between YHWH and *Elohim* felt that deeply? The real point of v 2 is to exalt the superiority of God.

The king is a powerful figure whose actions may not need to be explained to his subjects (v 2), but his success and achievement is measured by what he has searched out, as v 3 indicates. God's secret, or unsearchability, is proof of divine power—these are secrets that humans cannot even guess. What God does not reveal demonstrates who God really is. In contrast, the king is transparent, obvious. He must also ultimately be able to explain ("search out a matter"), and Solomon is praised for his wisdom, a wisdom of Elohim (1 Kgs 3:28). The Hebrew of this verse is very clever, and there must be some connection with the words of Raphael in Tob 12:7. **3** Lest the royal power seem like nothing, these implicit comparisons are made; there is a certain similarity to 24:21–22 (see *Comment*), and cf. also Deut 29:28. Van Leeuwen devotes several pages to comment on vv 2–3 (*Context*, 73–77).

4–5 See *Notes* 4.a. and 4.b. **4** The text describes some kind of purification of precious metal, silver. This image forms the basis for the analogy (the removal of scoundrels from the court) that follows. **5** The need for a king to surround himself with honest servants is frequently emphasized, e.g., Ps 101. This is in agreement with the idea that justice is the foundation of his throne; see the *Comment* on Prov 16:12, and cf. 20:28; 29:14. Although the imperatives can be translated as conditional clauses, there is no doubt about the seriousness of this ideal, which is both a warning to royalty and a hope for the subjects.

6–7a The two verses go together; the command is motivated by the better saying that follows it. Self-praise is suspicious; the verdict of others is more objective. **6** This negative admonition needs to be balanced by 22:29, which recognizes that talent will be noticed and rewarded by a king, but of course it must be honest and sincere. **7a** The "better" saying recognizes that modesty can have its rewards also in a similar situation. There is a decent middle way between being a braggart and "pushy," and simply groveling; one has to have the prudence to know one's ability, one's place. Such prudence, it is implied, will be observed and rewarded accordingly. Note also the similarity to Sir 13:9–10 and Luke 14:7–11.

7b–8 See *Note* 7.a. concerning binding these four lines together. The interpretation depends on the nature of the conflict: Is it private or is it public, in a judicial setting? Either situation is possible. The prohibition argues against a quick judgment based on visual evidence, and against any readiness to enter into a dispute with a neighbor. In the end he can catch you up and exploit your shame for such rashness. Don't take action merely on the basis of what you see. Some commentators interpret the verse as an admonition against making the affair public by judicial litigation.

9–10 The same question arises here as for vv 7b–8: is this a judicial contention with a neighbor, or merely a private dispute? Several commentators regard vv 7b–10 as a unit, a quatrain. There is no objection to this if the topic in these verses is the same, namely, a judicial contention with a neighbor. **9** The imperatival saying recognizes the right to argue, whether in private or in public. But no secrets are to be revealed. The care for confidentiality might be caused by evidence in a judicial procedure. This could draw in a third party who is privy to special knowledge; then the issue of revealing secrets would arise. So Bühlmann (*Vom rechten Reden*, 247) understands it; the result of breaking confidence would then be described in v 10. If the dispute is a private one between two people, then the "secrets" must refer to the confidentiality that the two disputants once enjoyed with each other. They are not to be divulged, at the price of being reviled. **10** The "one who hears" can have the technical sense of "judging" (in a legal dispute).

11 See *Note* 11.a. Speech is a key topic in the wisdom writings (see the *Excursus on Speech*), and here it is praised with a metaphor that is not clear (v 11a); we do not know whether we are dealing with fruit (translated very uncertainly as "apple") or some kind of handmade artistry. In v 11b the description of the "word" in the second line is uncertain. The above translation is influenced by Prov 15:23. The Hebrew words have also been interpreted to mean "a phrase well turned" (cf. JPS), and even to refer specifically to the parallelism of poetic lines (cf. Sir 50:27).

12 The extravagant metaphor of v 11a is continued here ("gold"), and with good reason. There is nothing more essential to the wisdom enterprise than a willingness to learn, "a listening ear." And the sage teacher, more literally the "sage who reproves," is indeed as invaluable as gold. The wordplay between the two lines is well done: The נזם, "ring" or "earring," is coordinated with the (listening) אזן, "ear," in sound and in function.

13 The first two lines underscore the relief that a trusty messenger brings to those who make use of him (cf. 13:25b). The comparison seems rather extreme since there could not really be snow during the harvest heat (cf. 26:1), and the "cold water" metaphor of 25:12 is probably closer to the reality. But the choice of snow may be a deliberate exaggeration. There is a striking play in קציר/ציר, "harvest/ messenger," in these lines. Because the three-line style interrupts the pattern of two lines, many regard v 13c as a gloss (Alonso Schökel; cf. Bühlmann, *Vom rechten Reden,* 157). However, it might refer to the relief of the one who responds (in v 13c, the "master") to know that the answer will also be faithfully returned.

14 The comparison of the unproductive clouds in v 14a to a "giver" who does not give is quite picturesque, and perfectly clear. Van Leeuwen (*Context,* 83) unites vv 13–14 "as bound together by weather imagery," but he fits this into the "courtly" situation which he claims for this chapter. Plöger points to an antithesis between the two verses: the contrast between the reliable and unreliable. That would seem to be the broadest meaning of the saying, which can then be applied to many different situations.

15 The paradox (or, oxymoron; cf. Bühlmann, *Vom rechten Reden,* 78) of v 15b is striking, but it is nonetheless meant seriously because it is quite true. It is possible to influence others, even those of high station (and perhaps these are deliberately mentioned), by persistence; but at the same time the effect is secured by a certain "softness" in verbal approach. This saying flows from wisdom ideals concerning those who are slow to anger (14:29 and especially 16:32) and patient (15:18), but it also pays tribute to the power of the word itself, a wisdom emphasis. For the alleged parallels in Ahiqar (vii, 105–6; *ANET,* 429) and Sir 28:17, see the analysis of McKane (pp. 584–85), who effectively shows that the similarities are merely verbal.

16–17 Although these may have been originally independent, they are neatly joined to yield a flowing sense; excess in indulging good things is to be avoided. **16** In the form of an admonition one is warned against excess in eating honey. The honey is of course a symbol of something good and attractive. That is precisely the reason why the prohibition is in order: avoidance of any and all kinds of excess. A similar warning is found in Sir 37:27–31. **17** Excess, in frequency or in length of time, is also the issue in nourishing a friendship. Literally, the admonition is picturesque: "make your foot precious"—do not overdo your visiting, or overstay it. One's presence to another can become oppressive, since everyone is entitled to a certain amount of solitude or privacy. The ending of v 17b is obviously modeled on that of v 16b (catch word "have one's fill").

18 See *Note* 18.a. False witness is condemned in the Decalogue (Exod 20:16). Its frightful effects are brought out by the implicit comparison to lethal weapons contained in v 18a.

19 As in the previous verse, the implicit comparisons, rather striking, are placed first in v 19a. Here biting leads to pain and walking can lead to a fall. They are more than adequate to express the disappointment and confusion begotten by the betrayal of trust at a critical time.

20 See *Notes* 20.a. and 20.b. One should also note that the Greek has an extra verse (v 20a in Rahlfs). The text and also the translation are uncertain; there seems to be a contamination of the words of v 19b with v 20a, but there is no compelling emendation of the Hebrew text. As it stands there are two implicit comparisons: (1) removing clothing on a cold day is unreasonable; is one to look for a paradox here? (2) Vinegar on a wound is irritating, not soothing as ointment would be. This is another foolish action. If the correct translation is that vinegar is poured on natron, the implication is that the soda is rendered ineffective. The main assertion of v 20 is to underscore the folly of singing, presumably a cheerful song, to a sad heart; cf. Sir 22:6a.

21–22 This quatrain, made famous also by Rom 12:17–21, has given rise to many studies and differing interpretations. **21** The command is so clear that it loses its quality of shock, and perhaps it has become domesticated by long use. But in itself it is paradoxical: Feed your enemy! Instead of seeking revenge, one is to give an enemy the means to live; a similar idea can be found in Amenemope 5:1–9 (cf. *AEL*, 2:150). It is the explanation of the motivation in the next verse that raises questions. **22** What does it mean to "heap coals on the head" of a person? One answer was found in an Egyptian rite in which a person expiated wrongdoing by bearing coals on the head (proposed by S. Morenz, "Feurige Kohlen auf dem Haupt," *TLZ* 78 [1953] 187–92). By analogy, it is inferred that such a phrase would indicate bringing about the conversion of one's enemy. Despite the verbal similarity, this Egyptian background has not been generally accepted; there is no evidence for such a rite in the Old Testament, nor is it clear how this rite would have found its way into Israel. Several other meanings have been proposed. The action is interpreted as producing punishment, or a burning shame, or remorse and conversion. Of these, the best understanding is that a change of heart on the part of the enemy is produced. Moreover, there is the assurance that the Lord will reward the person who acts with such magnanimity toward an enemy. See also the *Explanation* below.

23 There is a similarity to v 14, not merely in the mention of rain, but in the implicit comparison between a phenomenon in physical nature and a characteristic human trait. The "problem" in v 23a is that the north wind does not bring rain. At least four explanations are given by Whybray in an effort to keep the obvious meaning of "north" (צָפוֹן). The best of these is given by H. Ringgren and also by J. van der Ploeg (*VT* 3 [1953] 189–91): the recognition of the meaning of "hidden" in the root צפן, which corresponds to סתר, "hidden," or backbiting tongue in v 23b.

In other words, there is a play on צפון, "north" wind/hidden. This is captured neatly in the translation of Van Leeuwen (*Context*, 60): "A north [hidden] wind produces a downpour, and a 'hidden' tongue (produces) angry faces."

24 See 21:9 with the *Comment* there and *Note* 21:9.a.

25 There is a certain similarity to v 13. There it was question of a reliable messenger who "restores the spirit of his master." Here it is the message itself, the "good news" (cf. 15:30b), which is the analogue to the cold water for a dry throat (literally, a tired נפש). There is also a heightening of the effect in that the message arrives from a considerable distance.

26 The contrast between the just and the wicked, so familiar from chaps. 10–15, appears here with the striking metaphors that characterize chap. 25. See Prov 12:3 and Ps 55:23—the just are those who should never be moved or shaken. Should they give way, the Israelite idea of retribution is jarred (e.g., the book of Job). Hence drastic metaphors are used: spring water is corrupted and rendered undrinkable, a lifeline is cut off for inhabitants.

27 See *Note* 27.a. V 27a is in agreement with v 16a; if anything, it may heighten that saying. The problem is with v 27b, which yields no sense in the Hebrew, as *Note* 27.a. indicates. One must recover a line parallel to v 27a: just as one must moderate an appetite for a good thing, such as honey (an understatement), so must one moderate an appetite for a good thing, honor. For various attempts to correct the text in order to arrive at other suitable translations, see the references in *Note* 27.a. Van Leeuwen (*Context*, 86, n. 77) notes that "*every* word in v 27b is derived from vv 2–3." With regard to the various and valiant efforts of commentators in struggling with v 27b, Alonso Schökel remarks that perhaps it would be better for a commentator to practice humility and not "each much honey."

28 A typical emphasis on moderation (cf. 14:29; 16:32) lies behind this final proverb. One must keep within bounds the appetites and passions, which are expressed by the word רוח, "spirit." Otherwise one is exposed naked to the attack of an enemy, as the metaphors in v 28a indicate. As the Ketib of Prov 17:27 puts it, one should be "cool of spirit."

Explanation

The first thing to be noticed is the variety and the richness of the metaphors that are used in this chapter and also in chaps. 26–27—another suggestion that these three are in some sense separate from chaps. 28–29. Perhaps the most outstanding metaphors are in chap. 25, and several of them have some connection with each other: vv 11 and 12, 13 and 25, 14 and 15, 16 and 28.

The chapter is far from being just plays on words, although these several "apples of gold" (v 11) should be duly appreciated. As indicated in the *Comment*, perhaps the most famous verses are vv 21–22 about the feeding of one's enemy, coals on the head, and reward from the Lord. The enigma of coals on the head is not the issue (if it can even be understood) that calls for discussion here. Rather, it is the sharp commands: feed, give drink to the one who *hates* you, literally—not merely a vague "enemy." The concrete situation is not known, but the application has a universal impact; who does not have enemies? The saying, along with Prov 24:17 (cf. 20:22), is contrary to the *Schadenfreude*, the joy in the downfall of an enemy, that is not uncommon in the Old

Testament. It belongs with the strong command of love of neighbor expressed in Lev 19:17–18, even if the perspective is that of the Israelite community. A. Meinhold ("Der Umgang," 248–50) divides the chapter into three sections (vv 1–10, 11–22, 23–28) and characterizes each unit by the leading idea: reserve (*Zurückhaltung*), moderation (*Mässigung*), and self-control (*Selbstbeherrschung*). Within the second unit ("moderation") he claims that vv 21–22 are the primary saying, or goal. This kind of global characterization is helpful in assessing a chapter, but at the same time it tends to gloss over sharp contours of individual proverbs.

The reference to the Lord's "rewarding" in v 22 suggests a perspective other than the mechanical deed-consequence view of retribution; see the *Excursus on Retribution*. J. Hausmann (*Menschenbild*, 236, 240) points to v 22 and several other proverbs in which the Lord is portrayed as actively helping the just and opposing the interests of the wicked: 10:3, 29; 12:2; 15:29; 16:7. In sayings of this nature the Lord protects, and is obviously pleased with the conduct of the just, in contrast to the attitude displayed toward the wicked. The issue becomes acute when the possibility of reconciliation is brought up (16:7, but especially here, 25:21–22). In this area there is no certainty of success. In 16:7 reconciliation depends on the Lord's intervention, not on a mechanical law. Indeed, one is not to seek revenge (Prov 20:22), but rather hope that the Lord will take over. Vv 21–22 forbid revenge implicitly by commanding charity. The aim is reconciliation. Coupled with Prov 24:17–18, which forbids rejoicing over the fall of an enemy, vv 21–22 contravene the automatic correspondence between deed and consequence. It may be easier to claim (but on what grounds?) this kind of correspondence in the case of generalizations; particular cases seem to call for the intervention of the Lord in a special way.

Pertinent to the discussion is reference to trusting in the Lord (16:20 [see the *Comment* there]; 28:25; 29:25–26). True judgment (משפט) comes not from humans, but from the Lord (29:26). One should also recall the explicit mention of trust in the Lord which occurs in the midst of lines related to the teaching of Amenemope (Prov 22:19). Hausmann's view is expressed in these words: "It is thus clear that Proverbs 10ff. is in no way involved in a dogmatizing of the deed/consequence mentality. Rather, this is already broken through by the fact that in the concrete case of a conflict between two people the solution is not simply left to the deed/consequence view, but YHWH is consciously introduced and named as a third party" (*Menschenbild*, 242). With regard to the wide discussion of this issue in scholarly writings, she thinks (p. 243) that it is clear that one cannot speak of exclusivity, namely eliminating the direct intervention of the Lord, in favor of the deed-consequence view. See also R. E. Murphy, *The Tree of Life*, 117, 224.

Proverbs 26:1–28

Bibliography

Hoglund, K. G. "The Fool and the Wise in Dialogue." In *The Listening Heart*. Ed. K. Hoglund et al. JSOTSup 58. Sheffield: JSOT, 1987. 161–80. **Van Leeuwen, R. C.** *Context*. 87–122. **Whybray, R. N.** *Composition*. 123–25.

Translation

26:1 *Like snow in summer, and like rain at harvest,*
      so honor is not fitting for a fool.

2   *Like a bird for flitting, like a swallow for flying,*
      so a curse without reason never [a] *arrives.*

3   *A whip for the horse, a bridle for the donkey:*
      and a rod for the back of fools.

4   *Do not answer a fool according to his folly,*
      lest you too become like him.

5   *Answer a fool according to his folly,*
      lest he be wise in his own eyes.

6   *Cutting off feet, drinking down violence:* [a]
      one who sends a message by a fool.

7   *Legs dangle* [a] *from a cripple:*
      and a proverb in the mouth of fools.

8   *Like tying* [a] *a stone in a sling,* [b]
      so the one who gives honor to a fool.

9   *A thorn goes up into the hand of a drunkard:* [a]
      and a proverb in the mouth of fools.

10   *An archer wounding all who pass by:*
      one who hires a fool and drunkard. [a]

11   *Like a dog that returns to its vomit,*
      a fool repeating his folly.

12   *If you see a man wise in his own eyes,*
      there is more hope for a fool than for him.

13   *The sluggard says: "A lion in the street!*
      A lion in the squares!"

14   *The door turns on its hinge,*
      and the sluggard on his bed.

15   *The sluggard buries his hand in the dish,*
      too lazy to lift it to his mouth.

16   *The sluggard, wiser in his own eyes*
      than seven who answer smartly.

17   *Whoever grabs a passing* [a] *dog by the ears:*
      one who meddles [b] *in another's quarrel.*

18   *Like a madman* [a] *slinging firebrands,*
      arrows and death,

19   *So the one who deceives his neighbor*
      and says, "I was only joking."

20   *Without wood, a fire goes out,*
      and without a gossiper, a quarrel comes to an end.

21   *Charcoal* [a] *for coals, and wood for fire,*
      and a quarrelsome person for enkindling strife.

22   *The words of a gossiper, like dainty morsels,*
      and they go down to one's inmost being.

23 *Silver dross*[a] *laid upon earthenware:*
burning[b] *lips and an evil heart.*
24 *One who hates dissembles with his lips,*
and he keeps deceit within.
25 *When his speech is kind, do not believe him,*
for in his heart, seven abominations.
26 *Hatred is covered over*[a] *by deceit;*
his evil[b] *is revealed in the assembly.*
27 *Whoever digs a pit may fall into it;*
and whoever rolls a stone—it can come back upon him.[a]
28 *A deceitful tongue hates those it crushes,*[a]
and a smooth mouth works ruin.

Notes

2.a. Obviously the Qere ("not") is to be followed.

6.a. This strange image reflects the MT, and there have been no successful emendations. It should be noticed that the proverb is formed by juxtaposition of three participles.

7.a. The Masoretic vocalization of the verb is peculiar and has not been satisfactorily explained (see the effort of Delitzsch and McKane). The consonants should be revocalized as the perfect third person qal, either from דלה (preferable) or דלל. The meaning is "dangle, hang."

8.a. The translation of v 8a is uncertain. The verb is interpreted as the infinitive construct qal of צרר, "bind, tie," although some prefer to change it to the participle, "like one who ties." Cf. *BHS*.

8.b. מרגמה is hapax. It is usually taken to mean "sling" (preferable). If it is interpreted as "stone heap," then the stone placed therein is presumed to be a precious stone; this is not likely.

9.a. The translation preserves the ambiguity of the Hebrew, at least partially. "Thorn" can mean a thornbush or thorn stick, and the verb does not make clear whether this wounds the drunkard, or is wielded by him as a kind of weapon. See the *Comment* below.

10.a. This verse is corrupt. A literal rendering of the MT might be "An archer wounding all, one who hires a fool and who hires passersby." Several words have differing meanings; e.g., רב can mean "much," "master," and "archer." See the commentary of C. Toy for a summary of various translations, from the LXX up to modern commentators. The translation above moves the last word of line *b* to the end of line *a*, and in line *b* a neat play (see also v 9a) is achieved by reading the second שֹׂכֵר, "hire," as שִׁכֹּר, "drunkard." See the *Comment* below.

17.a. Transfer the *athnach* to the next word in order to read "passing dog," instead of "a passerby" in the next line. The LXX has "tail" instead of "ear."

17.b. The Hebrew has "get angry," but a metathesis yields מתעבר, "meddles."

18.a. This word is hapax, and its nuance is uncertain.

21.a. Although the word for "charcoal" (פחם) is uncertain here, it should not be changed to מפח, "bellows" (so *BHS*), on the basis of the Greek rendering ἐσχάρα, "hearth."

23.a. What is apparently meant by the Hebrew words is the leftover of the process of purifying silver. "Like glaze" (כספסגים), a conjectural emendation based on Ugaritic, is widely adopted despite being controverted.

23.b. דלקים, "burning," should be retained, although it is an unusual description of lips; LXX reads λεῖα, "smooth" (urged by *BHS* חלקים), which is so obvious it is suspicious.

26.a. The first word is parsed as hithpael, with assimilation of the *t*, as noted in GKC §54c.

26.b. The suffix on "evil" would suggest reading the piel participle, as *BHS* suggests, but the suffix can be explained as referring to the subject of v 25, or even to one who personifies the hatred.

27.a. Both verbs can be translated as modal, rather than indicative; cf. Joüon §114h-j.

28.a. The meaning of דכיו is "his/its oppressed ones," but this does not fit easily with a tongue that hates. For various attempts to improve the text, see Toy and McKane, and a defense of the MT by Van Leeuwen, *Context*, 112, n. 5, who derives the word from דכא, "crush," used metaphorically in a juridical context. In line *b* מדחה, "ruin," is hapax, probably derived from דחה, "push."

Form/Structure/Setting

It is obvious that a thematic structure is fixed by the discussion of the fool, vv 1–12, and the sluggard, vv 13–16. Van Leeuwen argues that "Prov 26:1–12 is a proverb poem or 'treatise' on the 'hermeneutics' of wisdom . . . exegesis of Prov 26:1–12 will show it to be carefully constructed to force the reader to confront perennial problems which are properly labelled hermeneutic. That is, how are the proverbs to be used and applied in various, even contradictory life settings?" (*Context*, 99). The theme of the remaining verses is not so clear; in the broadest sense they are all concerned with wicked, foolish behavior (deceit, slander, hatred). Moreover, there are several catch words within these verses: quarrel and fire, vv 20–21; gossip, vv 20, 22; lips, vv 23–24; hate, vv 26, 28. This phenomenon suggests the following units for these verses: 17–19, 20–22, 23–25, 26–28, each with its own unity. Surely this chapter helps belie the claim that the collecting of proverbs was simply random. However, it is difficult to agree with Krispenz (pp. 113–16, 178) that there is a concentric circle in vv 17–22; it is too much to accept vv 18–19 as being left in "structural indefiniteness" to challenge the reader to look more closely at structural phenomena (p. 114).

Comment

1–3   As indicated above, "fool" (כסיל) unites the first several verses. Van Leeuwen has added an important qualification. In vv 1–12 the subject is the fool "*in his various relations*" (his emphasis). In vv 1 and 3 it is indicated that "honor" is not fitting for a fool, but rather is a "rod" for the back.   **1**   The regularity of the seasons is presupposed. Any serious reversal is not merely catastrophic for the farmer; it simply would not occur—the irregularity in 1 Sam 12:17–18 is called a "sign." The same necessity governs one's relationship to a fool: to honor such a person would be destructive of society. Nature and society have certain laws that are to be observed.   **2**   Only v 2 lacks the word "fool," but it deals with something that is unsuitable, like vv 1, 3; hence there is no need to separate v 2 from the first threesome, as Plöger does. The comparisons to the flight of birds are modeled on the "as . . . so" of v 1. The aimlessness symbolizes the failure of the curse, which is presumed to be an unjust curse. This too is not fitting because the curse is directed against an innocent person. A curse is a word of power, and it will have its effect, except in the case of the innocent; then it is neutralized. Meinhold sees a kind of personification here: the curse is smarter than the curser. Like a bird it flits in the air without alighting at its would-be destination.   **3**   Now we see what is fitting for a fool: physical beating (see 10:13b), such as one would use with dumb animals. This seems to be heavier than the blows, or discipline, that are meant for the training of youth, e.g., 23:13–14. Rather, the comparisons imply a sound physical beating, administered to the incorrigible fool, the one who refuses to listen. A certain note of despair is sounded; one has given up hope of teaching and persuading by word. However, we cannot but question how neat was the division between the wise and the fools. The dichotomy between them is perhaps part of an educational ploy, an exaggeration, for the sake of emphasis; it is not a philosophical conclusion about humankind.

4–5   One of the more famous and more interesting "contradictions" in the Bible is found here. It caught the attention of the rabbis (*b. Šabb.* 30b; *t. Šabb.*

30b), who agreed that one should not answer the fool (v 5) except where it was question of an error concerning the Torah. Implicit in this view is the question: What kind of statement on the part of the fool is presupposed? Although this is not answered, and perhaps cannot be answered, it lurks behind any interpretation of the verses. It is well to recall that every proverb retains its own meaning, however partial and imperfect, independent of the literary context which may affect its application. In other words, no proverb can be absolutized; such is the nature of the partial view of reality implicit in a proverb. We may assume that these two sayings were originally separate and had their own independent meanings, at least in conception. But then, what does the juxtaposition of the two imply? Finally, what is the bearing of 26:12 (to be wise in one's own eyes) on the understanding of 26:5b? For a discussion of various interpretations of these verses, see the *Explanation* below. **4** This clear prohibition is intended to keep the listener, who is presumed to have some wisdom at least, from the danger of becoming a fool by engaging in conversation with a fool—not even a reply! This is not surprising in view of many sayings which warn against associating with fools. The most drastic is 17:12: confrontation with a bereaved she-bear is better, i.e., safer, than meeting with a fool. In the context of vv 1–12, one may also say that deigning to give an answer is to give honor to one who does not deserve it, 26:1. The prohibition in 26:4 is a possible application of v 1, but certainly not the only one. The immediate sense of v 4 is that one should not even speak with fools, so dangerous and deleterious is their influence. Nothing explicit is said about the nature of the utterance of the fool that precipitates this prohibition. It is presumed that they speak only folly, e.g., 10:14, 21, which is dangerous. Hence there is the general impression that a reply will lead to harm, indeed, even to becoming a fool. **5** This clear command orders a reply to a fool apparently for the sake of the fool, "lest he be wise in his own eyes." Is this meant positively or negatively? To keep the fool from greater folly, or to keep the fool from putting on airs for having reduced the wise person to silence? The first purpose could arise from a genuine concern for the fool (even that he would somehow be converted?). The second is hostile: Do not give any opening to a fool, for he will try to turn it to his own advantage. There is a certain ambiguity in the proverb that should probably be left open. However, in view of the context of vv 1–12, it is hardly likely that a genuine concern for the fool is meant here. Rather, the fool must be kept in place, lest folly win out over wisdom. What light does v 12 shed on "being wise in one's own eyes?" To be in such a condition is to be *worse* than a fool, to be without any hope of change or improvement. One remains, utterly and irreparably, a fool par excellence. "More hope for a fool" occurs again in 29:12b, a less drastic context that warns against speaking thoughtlessly. There it serves as a threat, an exaggeration. That nuance is absent from 26:5, 12. But in light of 26:12 it can be said that there is a greater danger for the wise than replying to fools, namely that they think they are wise ("wise in their own eyes"). This seems to be the greatest "sin," as it were. Theoretically, one might argue that one should answer a fool to keep him from becoming a greater fool! This can hardly be the true intention of the saying. There is irony here. The reply in v 5a is described as being "according to his folly." That can mean that the answer is on the same level as the fool's statement that provoked the reply. Here, too, the indication is that the reply is not really helpful to the fool; it merely underscores the folly.

We have analyzed vv 4–5 separately, and partially in context, but we have not addressed the question of why the two proverbs are brought together in an obviously challenging way. For the moment, let us say it is to encourage discernment on the part of the wise. Other answers will be considered in the *Explanation*.

6 See *Note* 1.a. Reliance upon messengers was a priority in the ancient world, and there is frequent reference to them in this book, 10:26; 13:17; 25:13. The image of cutting off the feet is apt, although rather extreme and sarcastic, since the sender has in effect cut off the line of communication by employing a messenger that cannot be trusted. But "drinking down violence" is obscure; apparently it affects adversely the sender, being the result of his making use of an incompetent messenger. "Violence" (חמס) is a very strong word, indicating injustice and violence, but what does this have to do with the sender? It is better to acknowledge the uncertainty here than to adopt any of the emendations, which are not worth listing.

7 Like v 9, this saying weighs the value of a proverb for a fool. Since the fool by definition is unwise and unwilling, no profit can be drawn from the proverb. Hence the comparison to the legs of a crippled person: these cannot support the weight of the body; neither can the proverb serve the fool. The latter may know the wisdom teaching theoretically, but he knows neither the right application nor the right time; neither does he have the will.

8 See *Note* 8.b. Although the word for "sling" is hapax, the LXX understood it so. The folly of the action is to fix a stone in a sling in such manner that it can not be ejected. The point is that one is not acting in one's own best interest. V 8b puts this in the context supplied by v 1; it is another example of the futility of giving honor to a fool—which is not fitting. Some have interpreted the "stone" as precious, and understand this as a foolish squandering of something valuable; this is not likely.

9 The two parts of the sayings of v 7 and v 9 are simply joined by a connective "and." The second line is the same in both verses. However, the implicit comparison in v 9a is obscure; see *Note* 9.a. If the thorn (bush?) turns out to be a wound for the inebriated person, who is too unsteady to watch out for his own good, then the knowledge of the proverb may be even harmful for its possessor. But if the image is that of a thorn stick wielded by the inebriate, the proverb can do harm to someone else because of the fool who offers it. Yet also possible is that the image of a drunkard spouting off a proverb is enough of a contradiction to render the proverb ineffective.

10 See *Note* 10.a. The text is quite uncertain, and so translations differ widely. The commentaries of Toy and Delitzsch discuss various emendations and solutions, none of them compelling. The above translation condemns, by an implicit comparison, the person who employs irresponsible people, fools or drunkards. He is himself as irresponsible as an archer shooting randomly at passersby.

11 The comparison to the dog's action underlines the continuousness and sameness of the actions of fools; they never get out of the rut they are in, and they keep on making the same gaffes.

12 This is an astounding proverb. Are there degrees of folly? And is there a degree of folly that is simply off the graph? And can this folly be that of the sage who would lay claim to wisdom? These questions would seem to be justified, even implied, by v 12. The verse refers to the normal individual who thinks he has acquired some wisdom, and seemingly also to all who might have a deserved reputation for their wisdom. As soon as the wise person can say that he is wise, he turns out to be *worse* than a fool. So tenuous is the grasp of the wise upon wisdom! Qoheleth admitted that the wisdom he strove after was beyond his reach, Eccl 7:23–24. In view of Prov 26:12 he cannot be accused of folly! He knew well the human limitations, even if they irked him. Nowhere else is the "danger" of wisdom explored, although there are frequent warnings against self-deception; cf. 16:25. This is not the same as pride. A form of super-wisdom is meant, and it turns out to be blindness; one cannot any longer evaluate one's self. To be wise in one's own eyes is a threat; it is not described and no warning signs are given. Although wisdom is praised in Proverbs, it has its own dangers which are left unexplored. There is more pedagogical value to be found in warning against folly and its dangers. J. Hausmann is so impressed by this verse that she raises the question whether it is not a "later correction," inserted by someone who could not endure the negative proverbs of this chapter, and "possibly in an ironic mood tempered the sayings of 26:1–11 that appear to be so arrogant in appearance" (*Menschenbild*, 32). That is not the answer. See Prov 3:7; 3:5. Van Leeuwen neatly describes the impact of this verse (*Context*, 105): "Prov 26:12 is thus a dangerous Saying, in the same way that Nathan's parable to David after the death of Uriah is dangerous (2 Sam 12:1–4). Even as 'you' look down upon the fool whose self-perception is awry, you yourself may be 'wise in your own eyes' (cf. vv 4b, 5b)." See the *Comment* on vv 4–5 for the bearing of this verse on answering a fool and further comment in the *Explanation*.

13–16 The sluggard has received dishonorable mention in the narrative form in 24:30–34 (cf. also 6:9–11), and in many individual proverbs. In chap. 16 four proverbs outdo each other in describing the sad situation of the עָצֵל, "sluggard." **13** See the variant in 22:13. This ridiculous excuse "justifies" the sluggard in staying inside, probably at rest; cf. v 14. **14** Alonso Schökel regards this "as one of the best proverbs in the whole book . . . Moving in order not to move appears to be the height of laziness." It is a neat picture: the door merely swings on its hinge, and goes nowhere; just so the sluggard in his bed. **15** This is almost the same as 29:24. The exaggeration and irony continue. The sluggard just cannot work up the energy to feed himself in order to live. **16** One should not think the sluggard is without his own rationale for his actions. He is supremely confident in his own brand of wisdom, more perspicacious "in his own eyes" than "seven" (an arbitrary but significant number throughout the Bible) wise people. Irony is the high point of this description of the sluggard; for subtle nuances in the Hebrew, see Van Leeuwen, *Context*, 109–10, who comments on the imagery, remarking on the continuity of place: "Having made his excuse not to go out of the house (v 13), the sluggard doesn't even get out of bed (v 14). He turns on his bed like a door, but won't open the door—for fear of a cat. Vv 15 and 16 find him still at home, stuck to his table, and feeling complacently wise" (p. 110).

17–19 As remarked above, the rest of the chapter consists of four units, three verses to each. **17** See *Notes* 17.a. and 17.b. Despite the uncertainty, the image of seizing a dog by the ears is an indication of an irresponsible and dangerous action. This would be a suitable image to warn against getting embroiled in the quarrels of one's neighbors. Mind your own business?—is that what the proverb is intended to convey? Or is it just a warning to be careful and prudent in judging the quarrels of others? The answer will depend upon the prudence exercised by the wise person, who has herewith received sufficient warning. **18–19** See *Note* 18.a. A trigger-happy madman, who deals out death indiscriminately by his actions, serves as the comparison for the one who recklessly deceives a neighbor, and tries to pass it off as a joke. Such an "excuse" is totally inadequate, for there is question of doing harm by deception. But many excuses border on improbability and cynicism. In any case, irresponsible behavior is not to be allowed to go unrecognized for what it is.

20–22 The subject of these verses is the quarreling that is occasioned by gossip and calumny. **20–21** Fire, whether kindled or doused, is an appropriate image for quarrel and strife. The trouble caused by a gossiper was signaled in 16:28. V 21 sharpens the general comparison of the previous verse by its juxtaposition of phrases and mention of coal/wood. **22** This repeats 18:8. See the *Comment* there.

23–25 These proverbs deal with deceitful speech, and seem to follow naturally the previous verses on slander and quarreling. They are united by the contrast between the evil inner disposition ("heart," "within") and the deceitful outer expression ("lips" that speak falsely). **23** See *Note* 23.a. There can be little doubt that the "silver" image has to do with a cover-up for an earthen pot. The image is one of hypocrisy as far as the application to human beings is concerned: speech can hide an evil disposition. The image of "burning lips" is not immediately obvious, and many change "burning" to "smooth," which is often used of deceitful speech, and it may be suggested here by the LXX. But Van Leeuwen rightly points out that Prov 16:27 associates burning fire with the lips of a scoundrel. Hence these lips cannot be considered as burning with affection; they burn with the hatred that springs from the evil heart. **24–25** These verses reinforce the interpretation given to v 23. Hatred and hypocritical, flattering speech can go together, so one must be alert to discern the real character of the speaker, in whose heart may be found "seven abominations"—a figure for a hatred that is well nigh "perfect." Hence the admonition in v 25 is to be taken seriously.

26–28 These verses can be treated as a unit, although v 26 seems to be thematically tied to the condemnation of deceit in vv 23–25. Van Leeuwen unites the verses mainly on the basis of the act-consequence pattern, which is clear at least for v 27. **26** See *Notes* 26.a. and 26.b. Hatred may be personified here. What was difficult to discern in the hypocrite of vv 23–25 will be revealed to the public in an assembly. Just how this revelation is to be envisioned (judicial?) is not specified. **27** See *Note* 27.a. When this verse, found equivalently in Ps 7:16, Eccl 10:8, and many other places, is translated in the indicative mood as a matter of fact, it tends to become a hard and fast rule of retribution; see the *Excursus on Retribution*. The presumption is that the one who digs the pit is evil, and tries to entrap someone else; instead, he falls into the pit. By analogy, the one who rolls the stone will be struck by the stone in a boomerang effect. The uncertainties of life made this kind of "poetic justice" an ideal, a hope more often than a fact. Hence, there is no need to *assume* that the pit-digger or stone-roller will be automatically "hoist with his own petard" and so penalized for attempting to hurt an innocent person. Of themselves, these actions merely point out possibilities: one *can* fall into the pit, and one *can* be struck by a stone that rolls back. To apply these to a person of evil intent is a second move. **28** See *Note* 28.a. The uncertainty of the text further clouds the meaning of this verse. Hatred and lying can be seen to belong together (v 28a; cf. vv 24, 26), but it is not clear who suffers the "ruin"—the one who hates, or others. Plöger thinks the MT makes sufficient sense: hatred triggers the lying and deceptive actions, and it has no sympathy for whoever is hated.

Explanation

The "contradiction" in 26:4–5 continues to fascinate scholars. We have given an exegesis above, but without indicating other interpretations that have been advanced. K. Hoglund interpreted the verses in the light of the context of vv 1–12 and concluded that "the juxtaposition of contrasting admonitions at verses 4–5 delineates the crux of the dilemma as the clash between the sage's didactic responsibilities and the potential risk in fulfilling these same responsibilities. To enter into dialogue with the fool is both an obligation and a threat for the wise" ("Dialogue," 169). Thus, a certain ambivalence is inherent in the function of the sage, and even inescapable: to maintain or to cut off the dialogue with the fool—this, despite many proverbs that insist on avoiding fools. The editor who put these together did not take a position, but he indicated the need for the wise person to make a clear, enlightened decision. Thus, the attitude of the editor, or the brunt of the juxtaposition, does not suggest to adopt one of the proverbs at one time, and the opposing proverb at another time. It is to educate the reader to the ambiguities of life and to be careful in speech. Whybray proposes another solution, which comes down to what is essentially a true observation: "no human wisdom can encompass the whole truth; in particular . . . a short proverb can express only one aspect of it" (NCBC, *Proverbs*, 372). True—but it is not the intention of the juxtaposition of vv 4–5 to teach that. Bühlmann settles the issue too easily by interpreting "answer" in v 5 to mean "humble," "rebuke." The "contradiction" disappears. Hausmann (*Menschenbild*, 22) sees in the combination of the verses an intention to make more evident the fool's folly and to avoid contamination; no communication is possible. Plöger treats the verses independently, without attempting to analyze the juxtaposition: "in both cases, there is question of the reaction of a wise person to the conduct of a fool." Meinhold points out that the "contradiction" disappears since v 4 deals with the addressee, and v 5 with the fool, and "according to" has correspondingly different meanings. The implication of v 4 is that "you" might become as arrogant as the fool; the implication of v 5 is that folly must be answered, and only the wise can do this in a constructive manner. He does not think that v 12 offers anything hopeful for the future of a fool. Vv 4–5 seem to have many applications.

Because of its frequency and importance, a brief note is in order on the idiom *X b'yny P* ("X in the eyes of P"), as Van Leeuwen calls it (*Context*, 104, n. 43). The X stands for an evaluation, e.g., "wise," and P refers to the one making a judgment, self or another. It occurs in Judg 17:6; 21:25, but it is especially current in Proverbs, e.g., 12:15; 28:11. In this chapter, as Van Leeuwen points out, vv 5, 12 are to be interpreted against the background of reliance upon self instead of trust in the Lord; cf. Prov 3:5, 7; 28:25–26.

Proverbs 27:1–27

Bibliography

Malchow, B. "A Manual for Future Monarchs." *CBQ* 47 (1985) 238–45. **Van Leeuwen, R. C.** *Context.* 123–43. **Whybray, R. N.** *Composition.* 125–26.

Translation

27:1   *Do not boast about tomorrow,*
          for you do not know what a day can bring forth.
2   *Let another praise you, and not your own mouth;*
          a stranger, and not your own lips.

3   *Heavy stone and weighty sand—*
          but vexation from a fool is heavier than both.
4   *Cruel wrath and raging anger—*
          but who can stand before jealousy?

5   *Better an open rebuke*
          than a love that is hidden.
6   *Reliable the wounds from one who loves,*
          unwelcome[a] *the kisses from one who hates.*

7   *A person who is full tramples on honey,*
          but the hungry person—anything bitter, sweet.
8   *Like a bird wandering from its nest,*
          so one who wanders from his place.

9   *Oil and incense make the heart joyful,*
          and the sweetness of a friend, more than one's own counsel.[a]
10   *Do not abandon your friend and the friend of your father,*
          and do not enter your brother's house on the day of your misfortune—
          better a near neighbor than a distant brother.

11   *Be wise, my son, and give joy to my heart,*
          that I may give answer to the one who taunts me.
12   *The prudent person perceives an evil—he disappears;*
          the naive plunge forward—they pay for it.
13   *Take his garment for he has provided surety for a stranger,*
          and if for a woman who is a stranger, hold him in pledge!
14   *Whoever greets a neighbor with a loud voice in early morning—*
          to him it will be counted a curse.

15   *A continual downpour on a rainy day*
          and a quarrelsome woman are alike.[a]
16   *Whoever hides her, hides the wind;*
          and his right hand meets oil.[a]

17   *Iron is sharpened* [a] *by iron,*
        and a man sharpens [a] *the face* [b] *of his friend.*

18   *Whoever tends a fig tree eats its fruit,*
        and whoever cares for his master shall receive honor.

19   *Like water—face to face;*
        so the heart of a man to a man.[a]

20   *Sheol and Abaddon* [a] *are never satisfied,*
        nor the eyes of human beings ever satisfied.

21   *Crucible for silver and furnace for gold,*
        and a human being—according to the praise.[a]

22   *If you crush a fool in a mortar*
        with a pestle among the grains,[a]
        his folly will not depart from him.

23   *Know well the state of your flock;*
        pay attention to your herds.

24   *Because not forever, riches;*
        nor a crown,[a] *for all generations.*

25   *The hay is removed, and the new growth appears,*
        and the greens from the mountains are gathered in:[a]

26   *Lambs for your clothes,*
        and goats, the price of a field;

27   *Enough goats' milk for your food,*
        food for your household,[a]
        and sustenance for your maidens.

Notes

6.a. The MT has the feminine plural niphal participle of עתר, "plead" (here "prayed against," hence "no violence"), but the parallelism suggests a meaning like the proposed emendations in *BHS,* "deceitful" or "twisted." No satisfactory emendation has thus far been accepted. "Profuse," in the sense of "insincere," is a common, but doubtful, translation. See the discussion of N. Waldmann, *JQR* 67 (1967–68) 142–45.

9.a. The Hebrew is difficult, reading literally "and the sweetness of his friend from the counsel of soul." Perhaps this can be construed to mean that the friend's advice produces sweetness; cf. NIV. Or, if the *min* is comparative, the sweetness of a friend is better than one's own counsel; cf. NJV and A. Barucq. There are no compelling emendations; cf. McKane, pp. 612–13, for various "solutions."

15.a. For an explanation of this niphal form, cf. GKC §75x.

16.a. The translation presupposes v 15, and the verb of the MT, יִקְרָא, "he calls," is to be read as יִקְרֶא, "meet," with שֶׁמֶן, "oil," as the grammatical object. See the *Comment* below.

17.a. The vocalization of the word יַחַד should be יֻחַד (hophal), and the second time, יְחַד (hiphil); cf. *BHS.* Others would understand the second verb to be jussive piel of חדה, "give joy to" (so Meinhold).

17.b. "Face" is the literal translation, and various paraphrases have been proposed: "wit," "perception," "conduct," etc.

19.a. The translation keeps the succinctness of the Hebrew. One can paraphrase the first line: "corresponds to" or "shows" or "is reflected"; thus the water acts like a mirror. The repetition of אָדָם, "man," in the next line raises the question of whether one or two persons are involved; see the *Comment.*

20.a. However the spelling of the Qere and the Ketib is to be explained, the normal spelling is to be found in Prov 15:11. The v 20a in Rahlfs' LXX (cf. *BHS*) can be disregarded.

21.a. The expression reads literally "to the mouth of his praise" (cf. 12:8a, לְפִי), and hence means with respect to the praise the person receives. "Praise" is a hapax, but it is not necessary to read with the

LXX (cf. *BHS*) the participle. The notion of testing in line *a* continues into the next line. Again, the LXX has an extra verse (v 21a) concerning the wicked and upright heart; cf. *BHS*.

22.a. The verse seems too long, and "in a mortar among the grains" has been judged to be a gloss; it does not add to the sense; yet, there seems to be no reason for a gloss.

24.a. "Crown" is what the Hebrew has, but many object to a sign of royalty in this context, and various emendations are offered simply on the basis of the parallelism, e.g., "wealth." The word is introduced by אִם, "and if," indicating a question, but the Greek has οὐδέ (= וְאִין, "and no"). GKC §150g, n. 1 urges this reading. In any case, the sense is negative; neither riches nor crown lasts forever.

25.a. This verse has the effect of a temporal clause: when the work is done, then . . . (v 26).

27.a. The verse looks overloaded, and this phrase is lacking in the LXX; however, the Greek has the appearance of a free paraphrase.

Form/Structure/Setting

The "atmosphere" of this chapter is notably different from the previous chapters in the Hezekian collection. The sparkling comparisons have almost disappeared, and the proverbs, with some notable exceptions, seem more pedestrian. The format of the above translation attempts to call attention to a tendency in this chapter to unite the proverbs in couplets. Not all would agree with Van Leeuwen that these are to be found *throughout* vv 1–22; some of the pairs seem forced. But there is a visible effort to connect verses by means of catch words which will be mentioned in the *Comment*. Van Leeuwen singles out friendship as garnering the most verses: vv 5–6, 9(?)–10, 17, 19, and there are several doublets: v 12 (22:3), v 13 (20:16), v 15 (19:13). Quite different is the ending, 27:23–27, which forms a separate unit and is a recommendation concerning care for the flocks. In general, the forms are many: sayings, commands and prohibitions. B. Malchow (*CBQ* 47 [1985] 238–45) sees an added meaning intended by the editor, who placed it just before a manual for future rulers, e.g., chaps. 28–29, as interpreted by Malchow. Independently, Van Leeuwen argues that these verses are to be interpreted as addressed to the king as "shepherd" of the people. "In parabolic fashion it urges the king to execute his task wisely by caring for his flock" (*Context*, 142). Neither of these views is compelling.

Comment

1–2 These sayings have as a catch word הלל, "boast, praise," and both reflect the cautious approach of the wise. **1** The uncertainty of the future, over which humans have no control, is at the basis of this admonition. If anything is certain, it is human ignorance of what will happen—this is a sphere that belongs to God. The attitude is simply realism, more than the virtue of humility. The present is more than enough to deal with. The idea is reflected in Egyptian wisdom, as in Amenemope (19:13; *ANET*, 423: "Man knows not what the morrow is like"), and in many other sources: Sir 11:19; Jas 4:14. Qoheleth emphasizes our ignorance of what God is doing in the present, e.g., Eccl 8:16–18. **2** No one is a judge in his own case. Such judgment is bound to be biased, whereas the judgment of a stranger does not labor under that difficulty; cf. Prov 16:2; 21:2. See also v 21. Again, the realism of these sayings is admirable; one cuts a ridiculous figure by singling oneself out for praise.

3–4 These verses are linked by a similar pattern of implicit comparisons, with the key statement coming in the second line; the argument is *a minore ad majus*, from the less to the greater. **3** The physical fatigue caused by bearing heavy burdens is obvious, but worse is the mental and spiritual pain that a fool provokes;

see Sir 22:14–15.   **4**   This verse singles out the devastating effects, including both physical and mental, that anger can inflict upon another. But worse than that is envy, "rot in the bones" (Prov 14:30b), of both the envious and the envied. Anger is out in the open, but envy is so often hidden (as exemplified by Iago in Shakespeare's *Othello*). And if it be public, it still wreaks insidious damage; cf. 6:34–35. The rhetorical question makes this saying most effective.

5–6   The root אהב, "love," is the catch word for these verses, which are also related thematically. Both take on the air of paradoxes: Can a rebuke be a sign of true love? Can kisses hide betrayal?   **5**   This "better" saying has been prepared for by proverbs that stress the need of the wise person to be open to reprimand and correction; cf. 3:11–12; 13:14. Hence one who truly loves will not be afraid to offer, or receive, needed correction. To remain silent is not a sign of love, whatever be the reason, whether weakness or fear of losing a "friend."   **6**   Indeed, the correction can seem like a "wound"! This calls for bravery and honesty on both sides, or the alleged friendship is simply not worth cultivating. Now it can be seen to be reliable. Despite the uncertainty of the description of the "kisses" (see *Note* 6.a.), they are said to come from "one who hates." That makes the point obvious; the signs of love are clearly not genuine. Both proverbs challenge the reader to look sharply into personal relationships, their strengths and weaknesses.

7–8   Both verses find an inner repetition: נפש, "person," and נדד, "wander." "Sweet" (v 7) is taken up again in v 9, and "friend" (v 9) finds echoes in v 10. There is a kind of concatenation of verses, perhaps coincidental. Paradox is present again; how can anything bitter be sweet (v 7b)?   **7**   Although the proverb deals with honey—a food that finds frequent mention in Prov 5:3; 16:24; 24:13; 25:16, 27—this can easily be taken as a symbol of anything *good* with which one becomes surfeited. One wonders what exceptions were made to this proverb—perhaps money or power. One also loses appetite or zest for certain things precisely because they are so easily attainable. Alonso Schökel points out a remarkable exception—Wisdom herself: "Whoever eats of me will hunger more; whoever drinks of me will thirst for more" (Sir 24:21). That bitter can become sweet because of hunger seems to have been a well-known theme; cf. the sayings of Ahiqar (line 188; cf. *ANET*, 430). Again, circumstances can make things relative.   **8**   What is the nature of the wandering, whether of birds (cf. Isa 16:2) or humans? It hardly refers to occasional leaving and returning; rather it has to do with uprooting, moving away from one's origins and having no permanent dwelling. Sir 29:21–28 serves as appropriate comment on such a mode of existence. Our modern culture does not resonate in the same way to the realities assumed in the proverb, perhaps because movement and at least temporary settlement has simply become an accepted part of life. Some nations are highly conscious of their "turf," and this feeling appears to have been much stronger in Israelite life. It is also possible to interpret the wandering of the bird as a symbol of the fluctuations and inconsistencies in human existence.

9–10   The theme common to these verses is friendship; the catch word is friend.   **9**   See *Note* 9.a. The connection between the two lines is not obvious due to the uncertainty of the meaning of line *b*. Oil and incense are to be understood as desirable possessions in themselves, but they may also have a symbolic value, anticipating the "sweetness of a friend." So Plöger understands v 9b; he emends and translates, with many others, "the sweetness of a friend strengthens the spirit."   **10**   This verse does not help much to clarify the relationship of friends. There are three recommendations that do not really hang together: an admonition to be faithful in friendship, especially an established family friendship; a second admonition not to have recourse to a brother when in trouble (this apparently contradicts 17:17); finally, a "better" saying in favor of a nearby neighbor. These recommendations seem to go in several directions. Each one can be understood independently, but the general aim is not clear. In 18:24b the friend-brother relationship also appeared; see the *Comment* there. One can understand that distance is an important factor in seeking help, and the nearby neighbor is a better risk than a distant brother, but it is not clear why all of these differing situations are mentioned here (*pace* Alonso Schökel, who regards the third line as a motive or justification for the counsel in the first two lines).

11–14 The couplet form seems to be abandoned in this section, which begins as an instruction to "my son," so frequent in this book. Two previous sayings are repeated. **11** In words similar to 23:15, the sage encourages the son to progress in wisdom. This will not only be a personal achievement, but give particular joy to the sage, for he can justify his teaching to those who raise questions or make accusation, for whatever reason, against him. **12** This is a variant of 22:3; see the *Comment* there. **13** See the *Comment* on 20:16, which is repeated here, although the Ketib of 20:16 had "strangers," not a woman stranger. **14** The loud greeting is interpreted as exaggerated, even insincere, and perhaps as harmful since it is to be accounted as a curse. This greeting raises more questions than answers. The "early morning" clause looks suspicious since it overloads the line; in any case, the significance of the time of the day is not clear, unless it is a sign of intensity and perhaps exaggeration. It must mean more than merely arousing another at an early time. The "him" to whom the curse is referred is ambiguous: the greeter or the one greeted? Probably the boisterous greeter, but Meinhold thinks this ambiguity may be deliberate: the greeted one sees it as a curse; the greeter will discover that his false affability will be judged for what it is.

15–16 This couplet deals with the "quarrelsome woman." **15** An echo of 19:13b is found here; cf. also 21:9, 19; 25:24. The metaphor is interpreted graphically by Alonso Schökel as a "cosmic force," and "drop by drop the husband is subjected to a refined torture." J. Hausmann (*Menschenbild*, 154–55) comments on the unusual "emotional involvement" of commentators with this topic; she cites only males. In any case, she points out that this quality is not seen as a universal or essential quality of women. She quotes (p. 155) a pertinent statement of J. Goldingay ("The Bible and Sexuality," *SJT* 39 [1986] 175–88): a "woman who is loved is unlikely to nag. But a woman who nags is not loved. It is a vicious circle" (p. 182). **16** This verse is grammatically tied to v 15 by the pronominal suffix ("her"). Controlling (literally "hiding") her is to control the wind, an impossible task. The translation of the second line is uncertain (literally "the oil of his right hand calls"; JPS, "or to declare one's right hand to be oil"). See *Note* 16.a. The above translation of line *b* supplies another metaphor for something slippery; oil will run through the fingers, and like the wind is not something that one can reach or control.

17 See *Note* 17.b. The first part is clear: iron sharpens iron, but line *b* is obscure because of the many meanings of "face" in Hebrew. It is widely interpreted by commentators as intelligence, personality, etc. At the very least, the saying points to the beneficent personal effects that individuals can or do have upon each other; no man is an island. This is an optimistic view of social intercourse.

18 This proverb has no connection with the preceding. Care of one's fig tree, thereby being able to maintain oneself, is the metaphor for the rewarding service tendered to one's lord. There is an intensification in v 18b: fruit, and then honor.

19–20 The verses have a catch word, אָדָם, "man, human," and the constructions have some similarity in so far as the second line heightens the first. **19** The translation above is literal. In that way, one can appreciate the succinctness of the proverb. The meaning of line *a* is that water reflects the face that peers into it. Similarly the heart serves as a mirror, and when you look honestly and directly into it, you attain greater knowledge. The question is: Whose heart is being looked into? Your own or that of another? Both are possible, and both are productive in generating knowledge of self. The ambiguity here is important, for there is a reciprocal relationship. As Alonso Schökel puts it, "we need the other to know ourselves; we know the other by (knowing) ourselves." In this way, v 19 seems to be a prolongation of the "sharpening" in v 17. Cf. Sir 37:7–15, where one is to seek out and discern good advice, but also to heed the counsel of one's heart (as well as pray!). **20** Sheol and Abaddon are paired as in 15:11; see the *Comment* there. They serve not as symbols of mystery, but as dynamic powers that engulf their victims. Sheol is insatiable (Prov 30:16), and is paired with Death in the Psalms especially as in pursuit of humankind. In Cant 8:6 they serve as compliments to human love, which is as strong as Sheol. In this saying they are topped by the insatiable eyes of human beings. While this can be interpreted as registering a fact, it has a further echo. This would include the desire for riches, like the "eyes" in Eccl 4:8, but also in a more general way it points to the insatiability of human desires in general; see 1 John 2:16.

21–22 The idea of testing and refining unites these verses. **21** See *Note* 21.a. The favorite subjects for refining are silver and gold, as in 17:3, but here a new and very human point is made. The test comes not from the Lord, but from the praise that one receives. This is a profound psychological observation. In what sense is praise a "test" for a person? If it is understood as genuine praise from others that is ennobling and encouraging, all is fine. But praise of oneself is always suspect; cf. v 2. If v 21b is compared with the almost identical turn in Prov 12:8a ("according to his intelligence"), it can indicate a well-earned reputation, because such a person has shown true mettle. If a genuine public reputation is reached, especially among the company of the wise, the testing has produced a truly wise person, who has withstood a rigorous scrutiny of fellow human beings. However, the praise of others is a two-edged sword. Even if merited, it can have an adverse effect such as undue self-confidence or pride. If unmerited, it can lead to self-deception. Alonso Schökel is right in pushing this testing further: Is the praise of others adequate? No, it has to be verified in one's life by the person's real worth, which is perceived by all. It is worth recalling that a crucible not only purges but purifies. **22** However, the testing and purification of a fool is an impossible task. It is compared to the vivid work of pulverizing, of pounding with a pestle in a mortar; see *Note* 22.a. Such a metaphor, one would think, indicates that something would have to be accomplished. But no matter what is done to a fool, even by way of physical discipline, his folly is inherent and cannot be separated out. See the *Explanation* below.

23–27 The unit seems to be straightforward advice concerning the life of a farmer, with emphasis upon care for flocks and cattle; but see the *Explanation* for another view.   **23**   The passage begins with an emphatic imperative to watch for the well-being of sheep and goats, animals that played a large role in the life of the Israelite peasant.   **24**   The motivation for v 23 and what follows is realistic: riches do not last. However, the parallelism of riches and (royal) crown seems odd. Whybray suggests that this may be a royal proverb, a contrast between the ordinary person and the king: "Since even a royal dynasty may not last for ever, a private fortune is even more precarious; nothing is certain in this world." But this explanation seems strained.   **25**   The verse describes the growths that will be necessary for the feeding of the livestock and in so doing it indicates the time, namely when nature has made the necessary preparations, that feeding and animal husbandry can proceed.   **26–27**   The important results are indicated: clothing, acquisition of land, and enough food to sustain the entire household. Woolen clothing was the gift of the lambs, and goats were sold to extend land holdings; cf. 31:16, and note the industry of the diligent wife as applied to needed clothing, 31:13, 21–25. Although v 27 is long, the meaning comes across clearly; there is again another common feature with chap. 31: the reference to the maidens; cf. 31:15.

Explanation

The incorrigibility of a fool is expressed in a quite vivid metaphor (v 22). Of course, it reflects the usual attitude of the sage. This kind of exaggeration has its purpose: to strengthen all that has been said about the hopeless situation of the fool. See the *Comment* on 26:4–5 and also the *Explanation* for 9:7–10 for a more subtle analysis of the situation.

As indicated above, R. Van Leeuwen interpreted chaps. 25–26 as proverb poems, but he had to admit that this chapter reverts to the style of the proverb collections. However, he offers a creative and imaginative approach to the ending, vv 23–27. "My thesis is that Prov 27:23–27 is not only susceptible to a metaphorical reading, but that its *Sitz im Buch* and internal details are best accounted for when the text is so read, as addressed to the king (and his court) as 'shepherd' of his people" (*Context*, 136–37). The ideology of kingship in Israel, and even more clearly throughout the ancient Near East, recognized the king as shepherd of the people. Van Leeuwen does not deny that on one level of meaning the passage can refer to farming. Yet this topic is only tangentially referred to elsewhere. Why does it get such attention here? Moreover, the reference to the kingly crown (v 24, נֵזֶר) is difficult to explain unless some kind of royal activity is being described. In this view, then, the command in v 23 is motivated negatively by the warning in v 24, and positively by the statements in vv 25–27: "The kingdom, as it were, rests ultimately upon the reliability of the fruitful earth. In vv 26–27 the poem returns to its beginning concern with flocks and herds. Here they are particularized and become the basis for the entire economy of the 'house,' providing clothing, capital for real estate, enough food and provisions for the 'house' and its 'maidens'" (*Context*, 140). He also points to the similarities with chap. 31, which itself can be understood to make a connection between the advice for kings (Lemuel, in chap. 30), and the work of the valiant woman for her household; see the cross-references in the *Comment* above: "Prov 27:23–27 has a similar relation to kingship. In a parabolic fashion, it urges the king to execute his task wisely by caring for his flock. Positively, such wisdom produces prosperity (cf. 8:18; 31:10, 31) and continuity of the dynasty" (*Context*, p. 142). This approach is ingenious but hardly convincing.

A similar understanding of these verses was suggested, but not really developed, by B. Malchow in *CBQ* 47 (1985) 238–45. His contention is that chaps. 28–29 are the "manual," but he regards 27:23–27 as an introduction which "addresses royal readers and admonishes them to pay attention to the situation of their people lest they lose their riches and crown through neglect of their duties" (p. 245). But there is difficulty in accepting the arguments for his claim that chaps. 28–29 are really a manual for monarchs. Hence his suggestion for an "introduction" in 27:23–27 has never caught on.

Whatever decision a reader may come to in the interpretation of the last five verses of the chapter, an important hermeneutical point is illustrated by Van Leeuwen's study. Even though he goes beyond it, he allows that the obvious meaning "makes sense." Indeed, it is the sense that I prefer. But then he makes a telling comment: "just as 'Strike while the iron is hot' makes sense in the smithy. But this latter saying is commonly used metaphorically to refer to situations outside the smithy" (*Context*, 136). That observation should be kept in mind when interpreting all the proverbs in the book.

Proverbs 28:1–28

Bibliography

Malchow, B. "A Manual for Future Monarchs." *CBQ* 47 (1985) 238–45. **Whybray, R. N.** *Composition.* 126–27.

Translation

28:1   The wicked flees,[a] without anyone pursuing,
        but the just [a] has the confidence of a lion.

2   Because of transgression of the land—many its princes;
        but with a person intelligent, knowing—stability will endure.[a]

3   A man poor,[a] but oppressing the lowly—
        a torrential rain and no food.

4   Those who abandon the law [a] praise the wicked,
        but those who observe the law oppose them.

5   Evil people do not understand what is right,
        but those who seek the Lord understand everything.

6   Better the poor, walking in integrity,
        than one with twisted ways,[a] though rich.

7   One who keeps to the teaching, a wise son,
        but a companion of the riotous shames his father.

8   Whoever acquires wealth by interest and overcharging [a]
        gathers it for those who are kind to the poor.

9   Whoever turns aside his ear from hearing the law [a]—
        his very prayer is an abomination.

10   Whoever seduces the upright to an evil way
        will fall into his own pit,[a]

but the blameless will inherit good.

11   A rich man: wise in his own eyes;
          though poor, an understanding person sees through him.

12   When the just rejoice,[a] great glory;
          but when the wicked arise, people hide.[b]

13   Whoever conceals his transgressions will not prosper,
          but whoever confesses and desists will receive mercy.

14   Happy the person who is ever cautious,
          but the one who hardens his heart falls into evil.

15   A roaring lion or rampant bear—
          a wicked ruler over a poor people.

16   A prince, lacking in revenues, increases oppressions [a]—
          whoever hates unjust gain will prolong his days.

17   A man oppressed by the blood of a person [a]
          is in flight to a pit—let no one support him.[b]

18   Whoever walks blamelessly will be safe,
          but one with twisted ways [a] will fall quickly.[b]

19   Whoever works the soil will get plenty of food,
          but whoever pursues empty goals will get plenty of poverty.

20   A faithful person—greatly blessed;
          but one in haste for riches does not go unpunished.

21   Showing partiality, not good;
          even for a piece of bread people do wrong.

22   An avaricious person is in a hurry to get rich,
          but unaware that loss is coming to him.

23   Whoever rebukes a person finds favor afterwards,[a]
          more than the one who is smooth-tongued.

24   Whoever robs father or mother and then says: "nothing wrong"—
          a companion to a destroyer, he.

25   The greedy person stirs up strife,
          but whoever trusts in the Lord will be refreshed.

26   Whoever trusts in his own heart—a fool!
          but one who walks in wisdom—he will be delivered.

27   Whoever gives to the poor—nothing lacking;
          whoever closes his eyes—many a curse.

28   When the wicked arise, people hide;
          but when they perish, the just are many.

Notes

1.a. Dittography accounts for the plural verb in the MT; read the singular with LXX and Vg.

1.b. Parallelism would suggest the singular צדיק, "the just," again with the support of the versions.

2.a. The Hebrew is difficult and obscure. Hence many differing versions have been offered, some with emendations based on the LXX (cf. BHS). Our translation of line a is fairly literal; it understands "land" as personified and guilty of sin. The wrongdoing perhaps begets revolts and results in many rulers, probably one after another. Line b is problematical. כן in the sense of stability is doubtful, and it is the subject of a verb that is usually used in the idiom for prolonging one's days. Hence another translation is possible: "prolongs order" (כן); so the NIV and NRSV. The asyndetic relationship of מבין ידע can be rendered, "by an intelligent (person) who knows what is right." The LXX reads "Because of the sins of the wicked disputes arise, but an intelligent person will extinguish them." This reflects a different *Vorlage,* and presents no solid basis for emendations.

3.a. The unusual idea of the poor afflicting the poor has led to changes in the text, either replacing רָשׁ, "poor," by another word, such as "wicked," or revocalizing it as "chief" (cf. *BHS*). It seems better to retain the MT.

4.a. The translation of תּוֹרָה, "law, instruction," in this book has usually been "teaching," interpreted as the instruction of the parent/teacher. In 28:4, 9 it is more likely that the "law" of the Lord is meant, since the usual context of the teacher's command is absent. V 7 has such a context.

6.a. As in v 18, "ways" is vocalized as the dual in the MT; hence perhaps the reference is to a twisting of the well-known doctrine of the "two ways"—the good way is bad and vice versa. Alonso Schökel retains the MT, arguing that "two" is a sign of division and even duplicity, a "double heart," as it were. The translation "ways" avoids these subtleties; cf. also JPS.

8.a. "Overcharging" translates the Qere "increase" (תַּרְבִּית), but the precise nuance is not clear; cf. also Lev 25:36.

9.a. See *Note* 4.a.

10.a. שַׁחַת, "pit," is hapax, but there is no doubt about the meaning; cf. 26:27. This verse appears overloaded, with v 10b being perhaps an addition. Yet it appears in garbled form in the LXX, along with a fourth line.

12.a. Although textual changes have been suggested, especially in the light of v 28, the MT can stand. There is no textual basis for changing "rejoice" to "arise" (despite *BHS*).

12.b. As for the pual of חָפַשׂ, "hide," perhaps the hithpael would be more in accord with "grammar," but there is no doubt about the general meaning.

16.a. The MT has literally "a prince, lacking in understanding(s) (or intelligence), and great (רַב) in oppressions." Perhaps this can be understood as a pure exclamation. The translation above follows the LXX "revenues" (cf. *BHS*), instead of "intelligence," and reads רָב, "increases." However, there is no clear correlation with v 16b.

17.a. The rendering of v 17a is doubtful, reading literally "a man oppressed by life blood." The blood is personified as oppressing (a unique meaning for עָשַׁק) the one who shed it. To be oppressed by the blood of another is understood by many as indicating a bad conscience, presumably that of a murderer who is in flight.

17.b. "Pit" is generally understood to refer to Sheol or its entrance (cf. Prov 1:12), and not to a cistern. The command "do not lay hold of him" can mean: "do not interfere," since he will be punished; also possible: "do not support him."

18.a. See *Note* 6.a. on "ways."

18.b. בְּאֶחָת means "in one," interpreted somewhat uncertainly in an adverbial sense as "suddenly" or "at once."

23.a. The MT has "after me," which can hardly be intended. What is wanted is a form of אַחַר meaning "afterwards" or "in the end"; so the Vg *postea.* There is no reason to read "paths" or "conduct" on the basis of LXX.

Form/Structure/Setting

It is generally recognized that chap. 27 has brought about a relative closure, and that a somewhat new section begins with this chapter. It differs from previous chapters in that the parallelism is largely antithetic. The material draws mainly on ethical considerations, and the just/wicked contrast is frequent. There is perhaps a reference to the Law in vv 4 (twice), 9; the word torah occurs only thirteen times in the book, but usually in reference to the teaching of the wise. However, A. Meinhold (p. 464) offers a structure for 28:1–29:27, based on key sayings in 28:1, 12, 28 and 29:16, 27. This would create four divisions: (1) the Torah as a measure for rule, especially of the rich over the poor, 28:2–11; (2) a relationship to God as the measure for rule and acquisition of gains, 28:13–27; (3) training and rule with reference to dealing with the poor and lowly, 29:1–15; (4) training and relationship to God, 29:17–26.

Independently of Meinhold, B. Malchow had already underscored the

importance of most of the verses singled out above: just and wicked in 28:1 and
29:27, with four proverbs at 28:12, 28; 29:2 (not 29:1) and 29:16. "These four
proverbs as a unity point out the responsibility of a sovereign to reign righteously.
Since this whole collection is structured around these four, this seems to be its
primary exhortation to its reader, the future ruler" (*CBQ* 47 [1985] 239). He also
points out the assonances and catch words peculiar to each of these four groups.
Even if the royal "manual" be rejected as an explanation of this chapter, structure
is another matter. The relatively close agreement of Meinhold and Malchow on
the structure, whatever differences may appear between them, is striking. It is
difficult to deny some kind of structure, recognized by two different scholars, of
a collection of sayings that at first sight seems so fragmented. It is all the more
remarkable in view of the reasonable statement of R. N. Whybray that both
chapters lack a "comprehensive structure" (*Composition,* 126). The form remains
that of proverb. The setting is a separate problem, and is difficult to determine.
More will be said in the *Explanation.* The setting would seem to depend on the
purpose of the editor, or the one responsible for the collocation of these sayings.

Comment

1   The contrast is a familiar one, between the just and the wicked. The saying
would seem to have a broad application. The wicked may be hounded by a bad
conscience, by legal authority, or whatever. At any rate, they have their fears. In
contrast is the confidence which buoys up the just. In virtue of vv 25–26, it is clear
that the lionlike confidence is due to the Lord. For a remarkable description of
fears besetting human beings, see Wis 17.

2   See *Note* 2.a. The wrongdoing in the country can be interpreted as leading
to a multiplication of controlling officials. If the situation is serious enough, there
may be a series of revolts, and this means new leaders; some commentators think
of the rapid change of dynasties in the northern kingdom. Hence this is a picture
of political chaos. In contrast, one truly wise person is considered to be sufficient
to secure peace.

3   See *Note* 3.a. The textual modifications seem to be prompted by the
supposedly unusual description of a poor man oppressing other unfortunate
people. But this could very well happen on the supposition that the poor came
into some riches and power. One is reminded of the topsy-turvy conditions of
30:21–23, when a slave becomes the ruler. The *nouveau riche* could very well be
self-centered and grasping. Then the image in v 3b closes off any hope of sympathy
for former friends who shared his poverty. The rain, a good thing in itself, turns
out to be a devastating torrent.

4   Meinhold regards vv 4–11 as dealing with the understanding of Torah: vv
4–5 in a general way and the remaining verses concretely. Not all would agree
that תורה here should be translated as "law," at least in a technical sense, but the
issue does seem to involve obedience to the divine will; more is at stake than the
advice of the parent. The lines are drawn clearly: one's attitude to the Law is also
one's attitude to the "wicked" (רשע), understood here as a collective noun.

5   This verse continues the idea of v 4 from a different point of view. Just as
"law" occurs twice in v 4, so here "understand," in its usual sapiential sense,
connoting a practical, effective activity, is repeated. Justice or right simply does

not belong to the world of evil people. The meaning of understanding "everything" (v 5b) is left undefined; in context it seems to refer to "what is right." But there is a strong religious emphasis in the phrase "seek the Lord." Many relate it to the knowledge of "good and evil" in Gen 2:9, 17; 3:5, but Plöger is correct in claiming that this is not exclusively moral. It also refers to what is valuable for living; perhaps one should understand it as "valuable before God."

G. von Rad has an intriguing comment on 28:5: He correlates the understanding/knowledge with fear of the Lord: "Thus it could, for example, be said that evil men do not know what is right but that those who seek Yahweh understand all things (Prov. 28,5). The opinion is evidently that turning to Yahweh facilitates the difficult distinction between right and wrong. But this was surely not true only of the narrower sphere of moral behaviour. Faith does not—as is popularly believed today—hinder knowledge; on the contrary it is what liberates knowledge, enables it really to come to the point and indicates to it its proper place in the sphere of varied, human activity. In Israel, the intellect never freed itself from or became independent of the foundation of its whole existence, that is its commitment to Yahweh" (*Wisdom*, 68).

6 The first line of this "better" saying repeats 19:1a. Again we should note the concealed paradox: whoever walks in integrity is not supposed to be poor according to ideal wisdom—but reality cannot be denied. Then what can be said? Despite everything, such a person is better than the rich one who is wicked. This is a faith statement, in the wisdom tradition, reminiscent of the robust affirmations in Ps 37; cf. also 15:16. The Masoretic vocalization has "two ways" as also v 18; see the suggestion in *Note* 6.a. There is no substantial change in meaning. For another contrast between rich and poor, see v 11, which Meinhold regards as creating a "frame" for vv 6–11.

7 The "torah" of v 7a, unlike v 4, must be the teaching of the father and not the Law. This is also suggested by the contrast with riotous companions, who are also included in the wisdom context of 23:19–20. Youths are constantly urged to bring joy to parents, e.g., 23:24–25.

8 See *Note* 8.a. Transactions involving interest were forbidden in the Law (Exod 22:24; Deut 23:20), but apparently this did not apply to foreigners (Deut 23:21). The unspoken motivation is that the Lord will act, and will prevent the unjust dealer from enjoying his ill-gotten profits. Instead they will be turned to the advantage of a generous person; cf. Prov 14:31; 19:17. V 8b repeats the idea of 13:22b; see the *Comment* there.

9 Alonso Schökel finds a kind of talion law at work here: whoever will not listen will not be listened to. "Hearing" is equivalent to obeying. Whoever fails to observe the Law will be an "abomination" to the Lord; such a person is a hypocrite and has no basis for uttering a prayer; see Prov 15:8, 29.

10 The first two lines are a typical example of mechanical retribution; cf. 27:26, and also the *Excursus on Retribution*. But one should not consider the deed-consequence view as simply unchangeable. The final line, which looks like a fragment of a verse, is an assurance that the good person ultimately prevails. See *Note* 10.a.

11 See v 6. Riches bring prestige and power, but this is not proof of true wisdom. Even worse than folly is to think that one is wise ("wise in his own eyes"; cf. Prov 26:12). One thinks of the rich Nabal, who lived up to his name "fool" (1

Sam 25). Paradoxically, the poor person can be wiser than the rich; according to v 5 those who seek the Lord know everything and hence will see through such a fraud.

12 See *Note* 12.a. Because of the similarity of this verse to v 28, Meinhold is inclined to recognize a frame here, vv 12–28. The saying contrasts the social situations under the control of the just and the wicked. Although the Hebrew of v 12a is very succinct, the implication is that the reign of the just person is beneficial to all, for it ensures the "glory" of the populace. In contrast, v 12b claims that the rule of the wicked has the effect of driving people into hiding to get out of the way of injustice; cf. v 28, which helps in the interpretation of the Hebrew verb; also see 29:2b.

13–14 Meinhold is correct in uniting these two sayings because of their form, and also the implication that the Lord is involved (mercy and also blessing). **13** The verse stands out as being the only one in Proverbs to indicate the need of public confession, and also the divine offer of mercy that this entails. The need for such confession is registered in striking fashion in Ps 32; see also Job 31:33–34. One can "cover" the faults of another (Prov 10:12), but not one's own sins. **14** The blessing, indicated by "happy," is for those who avoid sin. They are "cautious," that is, literally, they "fear." They fear their own weakness, or perhaps even the fear of God is not absent from this verb. In contrast is the hard-hearted, who are sure of themselves and who will end up with trouble. The verse should be compared with 14:16.

15–16 These verses can be taken together as dealing with unjust rule. **15** The comparison to these predatory animals is extreme, but fitting. Rulers have supreme power; their wrath, compared to that of a lion in 19:12; 20:2, is surely to be feared; it is no wonder that people want to make themselves scarce; cf. v 12. **16** The Hebrew is difficult, and various translations have been offered; see *Note* 16.a. V 16a is to be understood as a cynical comment about an unjust "prince" (נגיד); he lacks what is needed (whether it be prudence or revenues) and abounds in wrongdoing. No matter how it is translated, v 16a does not combine easily with v 16b. Length of life (cf. 15:27b) is commonly attributed to the wise and the just; this is not surprising in itself, but its appearance is quite sudden here.

17 See *Notes* 17.a. and 17.b. The translation posits the case of a murderer who is in flight until the end of his life, whether pursued by an avenger or driven by a bad conscience. The advice that is given in this situation is: Do not interfere; let justice be done.

18–19 The verses are characterized by participles, and they describe the results of certain actions. **18** The one who walks blamelessly (cf. Ps 15:2) will be safe from the evil results that can be expected to come upon the wicked. See *Note* 6.a. "Ways" is vocalized in the dual form; hence the MT could be understood to mean "will fall into one (of the two ways)," in the sense that his double-dealing will catch up with him and bring about downfall. **19** This is a variant of 12:11 about the rewards of diligence in pursuing the life of farming. The "plenty," twice deliberately repeated, depends on the seriousness with which one pursues one's goals; "empty," literally "vanities," is not defined, but what is meant is any distraction from serious farming.

20 The nuance of "faithful" is not clear: honesty? Or fidelity and steadiness in personal application? Both meanings are possible in view of the contrast with the hasty person. Any one who gets rich quick is suspect. "Haste" is looked upon askance, and is even suggestive of wrongdoing in some cases; cf. v 19, and also 19:2; 20:21. The blessing for the faithful individual would be preeminently the blessing of God; cf. Prov 10:22.

21 V 21a is a "not good" saying; cf. 16:29 and 18:5. This is not a weak negative. See also 24:23, of which this verse seems to be a variant, but v 21a is more general, whereas 24:23 envisions a judicial case. The "piece of bread" is a deliberate exaggeration, and probably chosen to indicate how paltry and despicable may be even the smallest "gift/bribe," but it creates unforeseen and undue pressures and obligations.

22 "Avaricious" is literally "evil of eye"; see the *Comment* on 23:6 and 22:9. Again (cf. v 20) a haste for riches suggests something that involves evildoing. Appropriately the greedy person is threatened here with a loss. No matter the cautions he takes, he will lose in the end because that is the way retribution works.

23 Rebuke or reprimand is highly appreciated by the wise; cf. 19:25; 25:12; 27:5. But it may happen that the value and truth of this advice is at first not recognized and appreciated. Hence the importance of the adverb "afterwards," or "in the end"; see *Note* 23.a. The comparison with a smooth talker seems almost too easy in view of what is said about "smooth" talk in the rest of the book, e.g., 7:5. But that is why the saying is important; it is always preferable to listen to flattery and to words that feed one's ego.

24 The details of the "robbery" are not given, but perhaps it would include manipulating so as to obtain the property or other belongings of the parents. When the evil of such despicable action is furthermore blandly denied, no words of condemnation are strong enough: the robber is a destroyer, in a sense, a murderer. The command of the Decalogue is supported by various concrete sayings: 19:26; 20:20; 28:24; 30:11, 17.

25–26 "Trust" is the catch word uniting these two verses: trust in the Lord as opposed to trust in oneself. **25** "Greedy" is literally "broad of soul/appetite." Elsewhere hatred (10:12) and anger (15:18; 29:22) are scored as causing strife (15:18; 29:22), but it is easy to see how a desire for more possessions will bring about dissension. The contrast with trust in the Lord implies that the essential evil of greed is trust in riches. Again there is a paradoxical quality to the possession of riches; can they overwhelm a person and engender greed? **26** This is a sapiential form of the previous saying, which made the religious dimension more prominent (trust in YHWH). But wisdom brings about association with God (Prov 2:5) and includes trust in the Lord (3:5).

27 In contrast to the greedy (v 25) is one who is generous to the poor. He is "good of eye" (22:9) and in fact "lends to the Lord" (19:17). Paradoxically he will not suffer lack, however great his sharing with the poor. To ignore the cry of the poor brings curses, in contrast to the blessings mentioned in v 20. The curses can come from the Lord (3:33) and from the poor; see especially Sir 4:1–6.

28 See v 12 and also 29:2. The saying refers to an unjust social situation which is eventually reversed. One goes into hiding to avoid harm from wicked authorities. But with the downfall of the wicked, the just come into the open: they are "many"; i.e., they emerge and prosper; they are now in positions of some power.

Explanation

The discussion of the structure of this chapter indicated something of its contents and themes. Although the form and content seem relatively conservative, one cannot but be impressed by the way certain ideas weave in and out of the twenty-eight verses. Alonso Schökel has claimed that all but three deal with ethical considerations. Recall the references to the wicked, to the law/instruction, to prayer and repentance, vv 9, 13. But some nine sayings are sapiential; recall the difference between the emphases in vv 25–26. In addition he points to an abundance of sayings that fall under the rubric of economics: vv 3, 6, 8, 11, 16 19–22, 24?, 27. He remarks that perhaps the unifying theme of this chapter is the political: "The greater part of the verses deal with the correct exercise, or abuse, of power, either political or economical. It is as if the instruction were directed expressly to youths destined for positions of power and influence in society" (p. 482). He singles out vv 2, 12, 18 for political power; vv 8, 19–22, 24–25 for riches. In other cases, one can recognize the possession and exercise of power in vv 3, 5, 15, 16, 21, or the possession of riches in vv 6, 11, 15, 17. There is also the fascinating insight that comes from his pairing of different stichs that turn out to be similar; see vv 20a/27b; vv 21a/16b; vv 20b/21b; vv 20b/27b; vv 22a/27a; vv 26a/25b; vv 18a/26b.

This view of the chapter is more intriguing than a "manual" for future monarchs. Were the latter intended, the proverbs should betray more of a focus on rulers. Hence the "setting" for the proverbs in this chapter is the same as for most of the sayings in chaps. 10–29: the teaching of the sages. However, the collocation of the sayings should be seen in the light of the observations in the above paragraph.

Proverbs 29:1–27

Bibliography

Malchow, B. "A Manual for Future Monarchs." *CBQ* 47 (1938) 238–45. **Whybray, R. N.** *Composition.* 127–129.

Translation

29:1   *Stiff-necked, a person*[a] *reprimanded*
        will be broken suddenly and without remedy.

2   *When the just are many,*[a] *the people rejoice,*
        but when the wicked[b] *rules, people groan.*

3   *A lover of wisdom gives joy to his father,*
        but a companion of harlots squanders possessions.

4   *By justice a king maintains a country,*
        but one who makes demands[a] *tears it down.*

5   *One who deceives*[a] *his neighbor*
        spreads a net for his steps.

6   *In the wrongdoing* [a] *of an evil person, a snare,*
     but the just person sings [b] *and rejoices.*

7   *A just person acknowledges the rights of the poor,*
     but the wicked does not understand acknowledgment.

8   *Scoffers fire up a city,*
     but the wise turn away anger.

9   *A wise person disputing with a fool—*
     anger or laughter, but no peace.

10 *Those who shed blood hate the blameless,*
     but the upright seeks him out. [a]

11 *A fool expresses all his wrath,*
     but a wise person keeps it still within. [a]

12 *A ruler listening to lies—*
     all his ministers, wicked.

13 *Poor and oppressor meet—*
     the Lord gives light to the eyes of both.

14 *A king judging the poor with honesty—*
     the throne is forever firm.

15 *Rod and reprimand yield wisdom,*
     but a youth unrestrained shames the mother.

16 *The more wicked, the more wrongdoing,*
     but the just shall see their downfall.

17 *Discipline your son and he will be a comfort to you,*
     and bring delight to your life.

18 *Without vision, people have no restraint;*
     whoever observes the law, happy!

19 *With words a servant is not to be corrected;*
     though he understands, no response!

20 *You see someone hasty with words?*
     There is more hope for a fool than for him.

21 *Whoever pampers a servant from childhood—*
     the final result is trouble. [a]

22 *An angry person stirs up strife;*
     a wrathful person—much wrongdoing.

23 *Human pride brings one low,*
     but a lowly spirit obtains honor.

24 *Whoever goes with a thief, a hater of self;*
     he hears a curse, but says nothing.

25 *Fear of someone* [a] *provides a snare,*
     but one trusting in the Lord is set on high.

26 *Many seek the presence of a ruler,*
     but from the Lord: judgment of a person.

27 *An abomination to the just: an evildoer;*
     and an abomination to the wicked: one whose way is upright.

Notes

1.a. Literally, "a man of reproofs"; cf. v 4, "a man of exactions." Because of what follows, the phrase seems pejorative; such a person does not listen. The similarity to 12:1, 15:10 ("a hater of reproofs") is not enough to justify the emendation suggested in *BHS*. The line can possibly be translated: "A person reprimanded: stiff-necked," as though reproving produced hardness of heart; cf. Prov 28:14b. The self-destruction described in the second line is a repetition of 6:15b.

2.a. The LXX perhaps reads "in the blessings" (proposed in *BHS*), but this is unnecessary.

2.b. "Wicked" is singular in the MT, but it could be taken as a collective; cf. 11:10.

4.a. This is literally "a man of things lifted up," i.e., of contributions in cultic worship. That is the ordinary meaning of תרומה. It is not clear how the meaning of gift or offering was transformed into "exactions, taxes," as it is often translated.

5.a. "Deceives" is literally "smooths," with either "tongue" or "words" understood, since those terms occur frequently in Proverbs with this verb, especially describing the enticement of the "outsider" woman, e.g., 5:3. Colloquially, one speaks of a "smooth-talker," i.e., one who flatters, deceives, etc.

6.a. A change in a diacritical point, from *shin* to *sin*, yields פשע with the meaning "in the step/path of," but the MT can stand.

6.b. The exceptional vocalization is noted by Joüon §82l, as due to a contamination with *'ayin/waw* verbs.

10.a. Normally, "to seek the soul" is a hostile action (= kill), which is not suitable here. Emendations of both the subject and the verb have been proposed (cf. *BHS*), but it is better to stay with the literal translation of the MT, although the meaning of the key phrase is uncertain and even doubtful.

11.a. "Within" is literally "in the back," whether temporally or spatially.

21.a. מנון, "trouble?" is hapax and the meaning unknown. As Whybray comments on it: "Emendations which have been proposed are based simply on guessing what kind of meaning seems most appropriate" (NCBC, 404). "Trouble" suggests an original יגון; Vg has "refractory" (cf. *BHS*).

25.a. See the *Comment* below for the meaning of "fear of someone."

Form/Structure/Setting

Antithetic parallelism predominates in a chapter that shows little of the color and comparisons found in chaps. 25–27. A large number of continuous sentences is also to be noted: vv 1, 5, 9, 12–14, 19–21, 24. Despite Malchow's claim that a manual for kings is to be found here, this can hardly square with bulk of the material. It is worthy of note that the topic of kings forms a bond with the previous chapter; cf. 28:2, 15, 16 and 29:4, 12, 14, 16. Moreover the attitude to royal power is somewhat judgmental: 29:4b, 14, 26. There are hardly any signs of coordinating the sayings. Vv 15 and 17 deal with the training of youth, but v 16 seems interruptive. Thematic units, even were they deliberate, are not striking. It is not helpful to force connections, as Meinhold does when he points to "man" as the catch word for vv 1–7 and 8–10, claiming that the sayings in vv 8–10 are examples of what is stated in v 7. The occurrence of the word "man" (איש) throughout the chapter is striking: vv 1, 3, 4, 6, 9–10, 13, 20, 22, 26–27. It is rather bewildering to think that there is a deliberate connection between vv 3 and 15 (raising children) and vv 4 and 14 (a just king). These are simply common topics. It is better to acknowledge a wide range of topics, some of them broadly related to each other. Alonso Schökel recognizes two groups of sapiential values: vv 3, 7, 8, 9, 11, 20 are general, but 1, 5, 15, 17, 19, 21 deal with matters of correction; thus vv 1 and 5 indicate the danger of neglecting reproof and listening to flattery. In addition to the political realm is the domestic (son, father, mother) that governs vv 3, 15, 19, 21. Van Leeuwen develops the pattern first pointed out by F. Delitzsch, the alternating of subject dealing with family and people in vv 15–18. He points out that this "leapfrog" pattern reaches v 21, for v 15 can be linked up with 29:17, 19, 21, which deal with the discipline of sons or servants.

Comment

1 See *Note* 1.a. Reproof or reprimand is favorably regarded in the wisdom tradition, for it should lead to correction and improvement. However, this verse recognizes that there are obstinate individuals who will not accept reproof. "Stiff-necked" is the adjective used frequently of the people; cf. Deut 31:27; Exod 32:9. That kind of person will suffer the consequences, described in v 1b (= 6:15b). See the *Comment* on v 5.

2 This antithetical proverb is akin to the ideas expressed in v 16 and in 28:12, 28; see the *Comment* on these verses. The lack of the definite article before "people" in line *b* is not necessarily for the sake of indicating individuals as opposed to the collectivity in line *a*, *pace* Meinhold. However, the contrast between the just community and the single unjust ruler should be noted. See also 11:10.

3 "A lover of wisdom" is, in the Greek sense, a philosopher (φιλος/σοφος). The contrast with one who squanders his possessions on harlots is rather unexpected, but perhaps due to the mention of the father in line *a* who can take no joy in seeing the inheritance wasted. Cf. Luke 15:30. There is no intimation of the Wisdom/Folly (harlot) opposition of chaps. 1–9, *pace* Alonso Schökel.

4 The ideal of the just king and the corresponding security of the throne existed in Israel and in the ancient Near East; see Prov 16:10–13; 20:28, etc. Although "demands" (see *Note* 4.a.) is an uncertain translation, some kind of contrast is dictated by the antithetic parallelism.

5 See *Note* 5.a. In 28:23 a smooth tongue is contrasted with a reproof. V 5 can be seen as a kind of comment on v 1 above; whoever is insensitive to reproof is undone. The warnings about the dangers of "smooth" talk/tongue, whether or not an evil intent is presupposed, indicate how seriously the sages looked upon the task of alerting the naive. It is possible to refer "his steps" back to the deceiver (his own steps), and the ambiguity may be deliberate.

6 See *Notes* 6.a. and 6.b. The first line of Prov 12:13 is similar to v 6a; the implication of the "snare" (compare the "net" in v 5) may be that the perpetrator is ensnared by his own evil act. The precise activity of the just person in v 6b is not clear. If he "sings" (and not "runs," as some claim, emending the text), he obviously escapes any possible snares, and goes on his way happy and victorious; cf. v 16b.

7 The setting is a judicial case, and the sensitivity of the just to the rights of the poor is indicated. "Acknowledgment" is literally "knowledge," and in the context there is a contrast between the just "knowing" or acknowledging what is right and the failure of the wicked to have such caring and practical "knowledge." This is not a failure to understand and carry through abstract justice (cf. 28:5a); the issue is concrete: cases involving the poor.

8 The "scoffers" are literally "men of the tongue" as in Isa 28:14 where they appear to be arrogant politicians; here the term may be conceived more broadly as those who are causing social unrest, setting things afire; cf. 26:21. It requires no little wisdom to deal with angry emotions. Meinhold instances the example of the wise woman who confronted Joab at Beth-maacah, 2 Sam 20:14–22.

9 The situation may be judicial, but the proverb is reminiscent of the dilemma of 26:4–5: when to answer a fool. There is a (deliberate?) ambiguity in line *b*: Who is the subject? Is it the wise person or the fool? If the wise, as the Vulgate has it, the dispute will lead to emotional highs and lows, but without any result. If the fool, he goes from anger to ridicule, without understanding. Or perhaps both? The wise person rages, and the fool just laughs? Perhaps this is a situation for which 26:4 is truly pertinent.

10 See *Note* 10.a. The translation, however uncertain, contrasts the reaction of the wicked, literally "men of bloods," and the upright to those who are blameless.

11 Doubt is raised whether the wise person controls his own wrath or the anger of the fool. Probably the former is meant, since self-control is a common emphasis in the wisdom teaching; e.g., 14:17. Then the contrast with v 11a (the fool cannot hold back) stands out more sharply; cf. 12:16 and 14:29 for similar ideas.

12 See the *Comment* on 25:5. The values and conduct of the ruler will be reflected in his ministers also; cf. Ps 101; Sir 10:1–3.

13 See the variant, with the *Comment,* in 22:2. The situation is sharply indicated by the two classes that meet; there can be little doubt that the poverty of one is due to the oppression by the other. To "give light to the eyes" has the same meaning as to give life. The Lord has created them both. The tone is somewhat low key, but it is clearly a threat to the oppressor, in view of the justice that the Lord calls for.

14 Cf. v 4 and *Comment.* A duty of the king is care for the poor, but no impartiality is to be permitted on this level. There is no official "option for the poor," but the juxtaposition of vv 13–14 is significant. It is the responsibility of the king to ensure justice for those who are least likely to be heard. The stability of the throne is made dependent upon this royal conduct; line *b* is a variant of 16:12b and 20:28b; cf. also Pss 45:7–8; 72:4, 12.

15 The emphasis on physical discipline has already appeared more than once; cf. 13:24; 19:18; 22:15; 23:13–14. The way to wisdom is not an easy one; one cannot allow children to "grow wild," as it were; they have to be cared for. Worthy of note is the concern about "shame"; cf. 10:5; 12:4. It is generally accepted that shame plays a large role in Israelite culture. If the father alone was referred to in v 3, here the mother only is mentioned; cf. 17:25 and also v 17.

16 This verse recalls 28:12, 28, and 29:2. The just and the wicked are contrasted, and the increase of either group leads to greater power and influence. Here an increase in wrongdoing will be reversed; it is not said how, but the victory of the just is signaled by the witnessing of the downfall of the wicked—a frequent topos in the Psalms; e.g., Pss 37:34–36; 54:9.

17 The satisfaction and joy that parents should find in their children is echoed elsewhere, e.g., 10:1, and this verse insists upon the need for discipline, as in v 15; cf. 19:18; 23:13. The word "delight," used elsewhere for culinary delicacies (Gen 49:20; Lam 4:8), is a metaphor for the joy a responsible son brings; care for aging parents would be a consideration.

18 Two of the words have distinct theological relevance: "vision" and "law." Whether they retain this nuance in the book of Proverbs is a matter of debate. In prophetic literature especially, *ḥāzôn* designates the vision of the prophet, but it occurs only here in Proverbs. Still, it could be a reflection on the social situation in which prophets are disregarded, or are lacking; cf. the famine for the word of the Lord in Amos 8:11–12. The parallel term תורה, "law," occurs elsewhere, especially in Prov 28:7, for the command of the sage, or possibly the priests. If it is strictly parallel to the prophetic "vision," it may refer to the greater "law" of the

Pentateuch. In a broad sense the terms indicate at least the teaching and instruction of the sage, but usually their words are directed to an individual or a class. Here, the "people" are involved. Moreover, it is less common to use the beatitude formula of a "people"; it is more frequent with an individual.

19 A strict discipline is meted out to servants and slaves, as well as to children, although bodily injury is punishable by law, Exod 21:20–21, 26–27. This proverb singles out silent resistance ("no response"). Commentators point to Papyrus Insinger, 14:11 (*AEL*, 3:196): "if the stick is far from the master, the servant does not listen to him." The relationship between owner and servants is a common topos.

20 Since דבר means deed as well as word, the proverb has a wide application. Hastiness, as used in Proverbs, is usually a bad sign, e.g., 13:11; 28:20. In speech it would point to a lack of self-control, inability to utter the right word at the right time, etc. The sapiential ideal is not served. In addition, hasty action shares in the same weakness manifested in hasty words. There is no implication in v 20b (cf. 26:12) that there is hope for a better life, etc., for a fool. This is a case of deliberate exaggeration to bring out the seriousness of v 20a. Cf. W. Bühlmann, *Vom rechten Reden*, 187–90. See Sir 9:18; Jas 1:19.

21 See *Note* 21.a. Although "pamper" and "trouble" are hapax, there is little doubt about the general meaning of the proverb. Pampering a slave will not achieve anything, either for the owner or for the slave. Probably a slave born into a slave family is meant (Exod 21:4), since it is question of educating and training the individual. Vv 19 and 21 have to be balanced against each other.

22 An angry person is described in a similar way in 15:18a; cf. also 28:25. The parallel line indicates a person who afflicts himself as well as others.

23 For the idea, see 11:2; 16:18; Sir 10:6–18. V 23 features a chiasm and also a play on the word "low." Undergirding the proverb is a revulsion for egoism, but respect for true honor (כבוד). The implication is that this is a sinful pride, a boasting, that is far from truth.

24 V 24a is clear, but v 24b presumes a specific judicial situation. Consorting with a thief implies sharing in unlawful deeds and their fruits, and it is self-destructive. The "curse" in v 24b is to be understood in the light of the legislation of Lev 5:1–5. The law required that those who know of a crime must give witness; an oath is laid upon such to do so. If they keep silent, despite "hearing" the oath invoked upon them, they are as guilty as the thief. It is not often that a proverbial saying "interprets," as it were, a specific law, although an exception should be made for the fourth commandment to honor parents.

25 "Someone" can be either a subjective or objective genitive. The fear (חרד is the root) does not refer to the common "fear of the Lord"; it designates trembling, and it could be anxiety about one's own person (self-paralysis) or fear of another. It points to uncertainty and a susceptibility to be easy prey to the desires of oneself or of another. In contrast stands v 25b; at first sight, the "high" post might seem like indomitable self-confidence, but it is rooted in trust in the Lord; cf. 18:10b; 28:25b.

26 This verse provides a lively comment on the timorous person of v 25. Such people seek the "presence" of the great; that is, they curry favor (cf. 19:6) with a ruler, whatever that may involve. They little realize that ultimately what counts is the judgment of the Lord. Trust in God is more reliable than the decisions of the great and powerful in this world. Plöger observes astutely, "Verse 26 blames the attempt to compensate for a deficient trust in the Lord by seeking the favor of humans."

27 Alonso Schökel remarks that the collection of chaps. 25–29 has ended, and v 27 is the colophon, beginning with the final letter of the alphabet, *taw* (תועבה, "abomination"). Fittingly, too, the ending contrasts the just and the wicked, which has been a steady topic in the book and also in this collection. "Abomination" has been used frequently, e.g., 11:20, and although the Lord is not explicitly mentioned, the divine presence may be carried over from vv 25–26, and be felt in the contrast itself. However, the twofold mention of "abomination" suggests that it refers to the reaction of human beings.

Explanation

Compared to the more picturesque sayings earlier in chaps. 25–26, the collection of chaps. 25–29 seems to end in a whisper. But several valuable points are made in this humble literary dress. We may single out here the proverbs dealing with parental authority and obligations. To be sure, this general topic is frequent enough in the book, but at this point a summary view is in order. The verses in question are only a few: v 3, joy to the father; v 15, shame to the mother; v 17, directed to the father, discipline is advised. This is not new teaching, but the emphasis on shame should be noted here. Shame or dishonor comes to parents if their children are "fools" or worse. With the "shame" of the mother can be compared the "taunting" that a father might receive, indicated in 27:11, where the speaker seems to be the father. The saying in 27:11 is unusual in that it is more concerned with the father than the son, so sharply does the conduct of children reflect upon parents. The joy/sorrow of parents in this matter is underscored several times: 17:25; 23:24–25; 28:7. However, if one were to judge from the frequency of the sayings that indicate mistreatment of parents, the insensitivity of children was a very real factor in society: 19:26; 20:20 (even cursing parents! cf. 30:11); 28:24 (stealing from parents). Probably the most severe judgment passed on this kind of conduct is 30:17: the exposure of the eye/corpse to birds of prey. The frequency and the quality of these proverbs suggest abuses in familial relationships, although we know very little of the concrete historical situations. We may also infer that the commandment in the Decalogue to honor the parents was not otiose; it was necessary, and it may owe its exalted position to the persistence of the wisdom teaching in Israel. Indeed, when one stands back to assess the book of Proverbs, there is no other office ascribed to parents than that of education of children. Even if one interprets the parent/son relationship in a broad sense outside of family, such as teacher/pupil, one cannot escape the implications for the Israelite family. Cf. R. E. Murphy, "Israelite Wisdom and the Home," *Où demeures-tu: La maison depuis le monde biblique.* FS G. Couturier, ed. J.-C. Petit et al. (Montreal: Fides, 1994) 199–212.

The Words of Agur

Proverbs 30:1–14

Bibliography

Alt, A. "Die Weisheit Salomos." *TLZ* 76 (1951) 139–44. ET: "Solomonic Wisdom." In *Studies in Ancient Israelite Wisdom.* Ed. J. L. Crenshaw. New York: Ktav, 1976. 102–12. **Crenshaw, J. L.** "Clanging Symbols." In *Justice and the Holy.* Ed. D. Knight. Philadelphia: Fortess, 1989. 51–64. **Franklyn, P.** "The Sayings of Agur in Proverbs 30: Piety or Scepticism?" *ZAW* 95 (1983) 238–52. **Gunneweg, A. H. J.** "Weisheit, Prophetie und Kanonformel: Erwägungen zu Proverbia 30,1–9." In *Alttestamentlicher Glaube und Biblische Theologie.* FS H. D. Preuss, ed. J. Hausmann et al. Stuttgart: Kohlhammer, 1992. 253–59. **Moore, R. D.** "A Home for the Alien: Worldly Wisdom and Covenantal Confession." *ZAW* 106 (1994) 96–107. **Sauer, G.** *Die Sprüche Agurs.* BWANT 84. Stuttgart: Kohlhammer, 1963. **Skehan, P.** *Studies.* 15, n. 2; 41–43. **Torrey, C. C.** "Proverbs, Chapter 30." *JBL* 73 (1954) 93–96. **Van Leeuwen, R. C.** "The Background to Proverbs 30:4aα." In *My Sister.* Ed. M. Barré. CBQMS 29. Washington: Catholic Biblical Association, 1997. 102–221. **Whybray, R. N.** *Composition.* 148–50. ———. *The Book of Proverbs.* 86–91.

Translation

30:1   *The words of Agur, son of Jakeh, the Massaite.*[a]
  The oracle[b] *of the man: I am not God,*[c]
   I am not God, that I should prevail.[d]

2   *More brute than human, I;*
  not mine, human intelligence.

3   *I have not learned wisdom,*
  nor do I have knowledge of the Holy One.[a]

4   *Who went up to heaven and came down?*
  Who gathered the wind in open hands?
  Who tied up the waters in a cloak?
  Who set up all the ends of the earth?
  What is his name, and the name of his son,
   if you know?

5   *Tested: every word of Eloah,*[a]
  a shield to those who trust in him.

6   *Add nothing to his words,*
  lest he reprove you and you be proved a liar.

7   *Two things I ask of you;*
  do not deny them to me before I die:

8   *Put falsehood and lying far from me;*
  give me neither poverty nor riches;

9
    feed me with my ration of food,
  Lest, being full, I become a renegade,
    and say: The Lord—who?
  Or lest, being poor, I steal,
    and blaspheme the name of my God.

10
  Do not speak [a] *about a servant to his master,*
    lest he curse you, and you be held guilty.

11
  A generation: they curse their father,
    and their mother they do not bless.

12
  A generation: pure in their own eyes,
    but not washed of their filth.

13
  A generation: how haughty their eyes;
    how lofty their orbs!

14
  A generation: swords their teeth,
    and knives their jaws,
  Devouring the needy from the earth
    and the poor from the people. [a]

Notes

1.a. הַמַּשָּׂא means (1) burden; (2) pronouncement or oracle (the "burden" of a message); (3) the designation of a people or tribe from north Arabia, Gen 25:14; 1 Chr 1:30, related to Ishmael. Since נְאֻם, "oracle," also occurs here, "Massaite" is the better translation, although it is conjectural (הַמַּשָּׂאִי; see *BHS*). Cf. also 31:1. The reading of the LXX goes back to a different *Vorlage:* "fear my words, O son, and receiving them, repent."

1.b. "Oracle" is frequent in prophetic literature. "Oracle of the man," as here, occurs in Num 24:3, 15, indicating Balaam's pronouncement (cf. also 2 Sam 23:1).

1.c. The traditional translation "to Ithiel, to Ithiel and Ucal," referring presumably to persons, is incorrect, but no translation has achieved a consensus; see the representative list in Whybray, *Proverbs,* 88. These conjectural emendations, for example, range from "there is no god" to "I am not god." Our translation follows the NAB, which depends on the Aramaizing interpretation of C. C. Torrey (*JBL* 73 [1954] 93–96): *la' 'itay 'el la' 'itay 'el.* This is a palindrome, reading the same backwards as forwards: לֹא־אִיתִיאֵל.

1.d. וָאֻכָל, "that I should prevail," has been emended and derived from כלה (cf. *BHS*), but it can be understood as the imperfect consecutive of יכל, "that I am able."

3.a. The "Holy One" is the plural of excellence, as in Prov 9:10; cf. Joüon §136d. In this sentence it is an objective genitive, i.e., knowledge about God. The negative particle of v 3a affects v 3b; hence one should not translate "I have knowledge of the Holy One."

5.a. As a form for the more common Elohim, Eloah also occurs elsewhere, especially in Job, but in Proverbs it is found only here.

10.a. The form of the verb is the hiphil with denominative function (cf. Waltke-O'Connor, §27.4), meaning to "use the tongue on." The action can be interpreted as neutral or hostile (slander).

14.a. The Hebrew is אָדָם, "man," in the sense of human beings. For the sake of parallelism others emend or understand it as אֲדָמָה, "ground or earth."

Form/Structure/Setting

This section, vv 1–14, is found after 24:22 in the LXX. The words of Agur present many problems beside the famous crux in v 1. How many verses are they? Vv 2–4? 2–9? 2–14? or even the whole chapter? After an initial profession of animal-like ignorance, vv 1b–3, appears a series of questions that have a kind of riddling quality, v 4. Then comes a saying about the word of God with an admonition not to add to it, vv 5–6. Vv 7–9 are a prayer in the form of a numerical saying. V 10 is an admonition concerning speech. Vv 11–14 have a numerical quality: four classes of people are described. The various literary forms that have just been indicated have provided reasons for scholars to cut off the words of Agur at vv 4, 9, or 14. No consensus can be arrived at by this means. Since there is no prolonged continuity within the general collections of proverbs, there is no reason to be surprised at the discontinuities in chap. 30. Therefore, no cutoff point is certain. There is no special title to indicate a separate collection at v 15, as there is in 24:23 (for vv 23–34). V 15a (the leech and two daughters) might be an independent saying, unrelated to the numerical proverbs which constitute a certain "unity" for vv 16–33. Indeed, it is to be admitted that one cannot demonstrate that vv 16–33 must be separated from the words of Agur. G. Sauer argued that they did belong to Agur. The LXX tradition, in a sense, favored v 14 as a cutoff point because it inserted the "words of the wise" between 30:14 and 30:15. Our presentation follows this hint given by the LXX, also because it is practical to treat 30:15(16)–33 as a group of numerical proverbs. The commentary of Alonso Schökel distinguishes between various units, but seems to attribute them all to the Agur of v 1. In his commentary (NIB, 5:151), R. Van Leeuwen regards vv 1–3, 4, 5–6, 7–9 as an "editorial 'anthological' poem," deliberately formed by references to other parts of Scripture having a "deliberate and theological function."

Comment

1–4 See *Notes* 1.a.-1.d. **1** The identity of Agur is a mystery, but since he is more likely from Massa, he would seem not to be an Israelite; likewise, the name of his father is unknown. It is also possible that Agur is not historical, but a fiction invented for the occasion, whose oracle in v 1 defies interpretation. See the *Explanation* for an interpretation of the proper names. Agur is the "man" who pronounces the enigmatic oracle. The translation understands it to mean an avowal of his weakness and impotence, in short, his human condition. But as indicated in *Notes* 1.a.-1.d., there is no sure translation of the verse. It is worth noting that the LXX tradition did not find the names of persons in v 1. Instead, it offers a very different understanding. The "man" speaks to "(my) son," and urges *metanoia*. The LXX continues, describing Agur as admitting human ignorance, in line with general Old Testament thought. And in v 3 Agur claims that God has taught him wisdom and that he has a knowledge of the Holy One, a revelation from God! The Hebrew is quite different. **2** The "oracle" continues, elaborating on the lack of understanding in an exaggerated (Pss 73:22; 92:7) but honest manner, based on the drastic admission of human frailty in v 1. It is quite improbable that this is a sarcastic avowal of ignorance that is not really meant by Agur, as though to say, "I am not stupid like others." Neither is this admission to be denied by interpreting v 3b as an affirmation of knowing the Holy One. **3** This verse is to be understood in the same vein as vv 1–2. The connection between wisdom and the knowledge of God ("the Holy One"; cf. 9:10) should be noted. But Agur, like Job and Qoheleth, has not been successful in his quest for wisdom. As background to vv 3–4, one should read Job 28 about the inaccessibility of wisdom. The same theme is sounded in Bar 3:9–37, and Qoheleth lamented that he never attained wisdom, which remained distant from him, Eccl 7:23–24. **4** Five rhetorical questions follow which seem to underline the point that has been made about the great divide between the divine and the human. The speaker is not identified; it could be Agur himself who exalts God by these questions, or an imagined interlocutor. A. Barucq claims that v 4 is spoken by God. In any case, it seems obvious that the *answer* to the first four queries is: God. The questions are reminiscent of those that God directs to Job in Job 38–41. The only suggestion of sarcasm occurs at the end of the fifth question, "if you know"; cf. Job 38:18. This final question of v 4 is really a double question, and the obvious answer (God) to the first seems to be canceled by the nature of the second question: What is the name of the son? Are the questions as simple as they seem, or is some sort of riddle involved? The first four questions are straightforward: (1) God moves between heaven and earth. The idea of a human making such a move to flee from God is entertained by the psalmist in Ps 139:8, only to be recognized as impossible. What is odd is the question itself, since God is already in heaven by definition. But perhaps the question, even unconsciously, recalls the question about the torah in Deut 30:12, "who of us can go up to the heavens and get it?" Another even more pointed biblical echo is found in Bar 3:29, "who has gone up to heaven and taken her (wisdom!)." For a thorough investigation of the topos of heavenly ascent and descent in the ancient Near East, see the study by R. C. Van Leeuwen, who concludes ("Background," 121): "The main purpose of the topos is to reaffirm the great gulf that separates humans from the divine realm and the prerogatives of deity, such as immortality, superhuman knowledge, wisdom, and power." (2) This question is picturesque—holding the wind in the hollow of the hand. According to Amos 4:13, God created the wind, which he contains in vaults; cf. Ps 135:7. (3) The third query deals with the rainwater that is described as in Job 26:8; the "cloak" is the clouds that contain the rain. (4) Finally, it is God who has established the ends of the earth, i.e., the furthest confines; cf. Ps 22:28; see also Prov 8:27–29. (5) But the fifth question is totally different from the previous ones. It concerns identity, and it begins with "what" and not "who." It is not easy to answer. Many commentators see it as sarcastic and ironic, as the last two words may suggest. But it is not clear why the name of the son is included with the question. Whybray remarks in his commentary that "this is not an enquiry after the nature of the identity of the creator-god; rather, Agur is asked ironically to name a human being able to do these things." But why should a third party, "a human being," be introduced here? Whybray is correct in pointing out that the reference cannot be to the "sons" in the heavenly court, since they are never identified by name in the Old Testament.

Irony, then, does not really explain the mention of the son or the query about the son's name. This final question has the characteristics of a riddle. If so, the most challenging explanation has been offered by P. Skehan, who finds an answer in the data of the heading (v 1, Agur, son of Jakeh [יקה]). Translated, Agur means "I am a sojourner," and this correlates with Gen 47:9, where Jacob describes himself to Pharaoh, "the number of the years of my sojournings (מגורי) is 130 years." And the psalmist, Ps 39:13, describes himself as a גר, a תושב, "a transient." By his very name then, Agur suggests that he is a mere mortal inhabiting this earth. In addition, his denial of having knowledge of the Holy One (v 3) is reminiscent of the γνῶσιν ἁγίων, "knowledge of holy ones," attributed to Jacob in Wis 10:10. The allusions in this passage become more striking. The initial question about going up to heaven and coming down can be associated with Gen 28:12–13 where Jacob's dream is described: he sees "angels of God" going up and down a ladder that reaches to the "heavens," and the Lord is standing beside Jacob. Agur is a *Doppelgänger* for Jacob, and Jacob/Israel is the Lord's son according to Exod 4:22, "Israel is my son, my firstborn." Agur/Jacob, then, is the son of יקה (spelled in English as Jakeh in v 1). But who is יקה? He is the Lord. The name יקה is "an abbreviation of *Yhwh qādōš hūʾ*, an antecedent to the well-known *haqqādōš, bārûk hūʾ* of later times" (Skehan, *Studies*, 43). According to this explanation, the answer to the riddle in the fifth question is: Agur (= Jacob/Israel), the son of the Lord. One should recall the mention of riddles in the prologue to the book of Proverbs, 1:6. The final question of v 4 has created a riddle out of vv 1–4. Van Leeuwen (NIB, 5:251) disagrees with the riddle interpretation because everyone knew the name YHWH. But the point of the riddle is to lead the reader to the acknowledgment of the Lord's creative power and (covenant) relationship to Agur-Israel, not to reveal the sacred name. It may be objected that the answer to the first four questions is too obvious to form a riddle, but the riddle is not really there; it is in the final double question. The very obviousness of the first four questions sets the reader up, as it were, for the last mysterious question.

5–6 V 1 opened with the "words of Agur." Now these verses describe the words of God. While it is debatable whether they are originally a continuation of the "words of Agur," they provide a convenient "reply" to the lament of Agur in vv 2–3 about his stupidity. He, and every one, is to rely on the tested word of God. **5** This verse is practically a quotation from Ps 18:31 (= 2 Sam 22:31), stressing "every" word. The revelation of Eloah, presumably in the torah that is described as pure and tested (cf. Ps 19:8–10; 119:140), is clearly asserted, despite vv 2–3. God is a shield, as in Prov 2:7, that gives protection to those who trust in him; cf. 16:20b. **6** The sudden warning is a reminiscence of Deut 4:2 and 13:1 to the effect that nothing is to be added to these words; subtraction is not mentioned. See also Sir 18:5–6a. The threat implies that any addition would be a falsification, and hence subject to divine reproof.

7–9 The prayer is unique in the book of Proverbs. Its relationship to the context is the catch word "lying" (כזב, vv 6–7). As Alonso Schökel points out, the ideal is to stay always *in medio*, in the middle, neither adding (v 6) nor taking away. Although the prayer is a petition (v 7) with motives provided (v 8), it is cast in the form of a numerical saying. The content indicates a significant degree of reflection about one's personal situation. **7** The number two is explicitly indicated, but the prayer asks for three things: no falsehood, no poverty/riches, sufficient food. The phrase "before I die" means "as long as I live." **8** By "falsehood" is meant more than a casual lie; it designates deceit and pretense, whether before God as in the Decalogue, Exod 20:7, or before humans. On the one hand, it is striking that "riches" are not per se desirable, in view of the typical understanding of riches as a normal indication of divine blessing. Of course, there are several "better" sayings that also point in an opposite direction; cf. Prov 15:16–17. On the other hand, the problems attendant on poverty, which have been illustrated often in the book, should be eliminated. It is God who makes rich and makes poor (1 Sam 2:7), so the petitioner is apparently asking, one may infer, to continue on the present course—that there be enough to subsist on, a kind of *via media*, or balanced pattern in life. The Hebrew "bread of my portion" is often translated as daily bread; it indicates a proper ration, the food one needs.   **9**   The dangers inherent in both riches and poverty are recognized, but most important is the standard of fidelity to the Lord. Satiety can lead to the denial of God ("who is YHWH?"), and poverty is a temptation to thievery. Theft is seen as leading to the final danger—injury to the name of God. The precise nuance of "seizing" or "handling" (so the meaning of the word rendered as "blaspheme") the name of God escapes us.

10   See *Note* 10.a. This admonition has no inherent connection to the context. The servant has little or no defense against anything that is reported to the owner, whether it be true or slanderous. He can only invoke God and utter a curse against anyone who would give a slanderous report; such a person would be "held guilty" before God. Deut 23:16 prohibits returning a slave who seeks refuge from an unjust master. Whybray prefers to recognize that the subject of "curse" in v 10b is the master, who reacts strongly against the one who brings the report. In any case, the general sense of the admonition is: mind your own business, and do not get embroiled in the affairs of others.

11–14   "Curse" is possibly a catch word in vv 10–11, but it is more important to observe that this unit constitutes a numerical proverb, even though an introduction that might have contained the number to be expected, four, is absent. Each verse begins with the word דּוֹר, literally "generation," "class," or "breed" (NJV).   **11**   See also the *Comment* on 30:17, and the *Explanation* for chap. 29 concerning parents. The death penalty is prescribed in Exod 21:15, 17 for this kind of treatment of parents. Perhaps that is why v 11 has no explicit condemnation, in lively contrast to 20:20. There is also an implicit condemnation because this class is grouped in the following verses with evil people. It is guilt by association.   **12**   This is an explicit condemnation of those who are satisfied with themselves, but fail to recognize their folly and filth; see 16:2; 20:9.   **13**   The style changes to exclamation, condemning the proud and arrogant who betray themselves by exterior behavior. As in 6:17a and 21:4, the action of the "eyes" symbolizes the behavior.   **14**   Just as there were two words for "eyes" in v 13, there are two words for the "teeth" that consume the poor, i.e., the greed and cruelty that destroy the unfortunate.

Explanation˙

This chapter contains some challenging ideas, no matter the extent of Agur's words. The reader is invited to weigh the riddle proposed for vv 1–4. But also one must measure the description of the "word of Eloah" as revelation, vv 5–6. Does the revelation consist in the promise of God, the presence of God to those who trust in him? What is meant by the "word of God" here? Is it referring to a written word in the Torah? It is more likely that it stands for the total experience of hope and security that was promised to the people of God. In the past it has not been rare that the sages were accused of eudaimonism, a calculated personal ethic of reward. Such a view fails to recognize the depth of the prayer in vv 7–10. It is impossible to grasp the identity of Agur the Massaite, but the above solution to the riddle would indicate that he knew Israelite tradition. Finally, there is the numerical saying in vv 11–14. It is all the more powerful for not being tailored in the graded fashion, x and x + 1. There is no introduction like "there are" or "woe," such as various scholars have conjectured for it. Instead there is the constant repetition of דור דור, "a generation, a generation!" The effect is almost mesmerizing: the sharp indictment of those who dishonor their parents, a condemnation of hypocrisy and arrogance, and a fierce indictment of those who eat up the poor.

Numerical Sayings

Proverbs 30:15–33

Bibliography

See also the bibliography for the Words of Agur. **Haran, M.** "The Graded Numerical Sequence and the Phenomenon of 'Automatism' in Biblical Poetry." In *Congress Volume Uppsala.* VTSup 22. Leiden: Brill, 1972. 238–67. **Roth, W. M.** *Numerical Sayings in the Old Testament. A Form-Critical Study.* VTSup 13. Leiden: Brill, 1963. **Van Leeuwen, R.** "Proverbs 30:21–23 and the Biblical World Upside Down." *JBL* 105 (1986) 599–610. **Whybray, R. N.** *Composition.* 150–53. ———. *Proverbs.* 91–98.

Translation

30:15
> To the leech:[a] two[b] daughters,
>> "Give," "Give."[c]

> Three things are never satisfied;
>> Four never say, "Enough!":

16
> Sheol and a barren womb,
>> the earth, ever thirsting for water,
>> and fire, never saying, "Enough!"

17
> The eye that mocks a father,
>> and despises obedience[a] due a mother—
> Let the vultures of the valley pluck it out,
>> let the brood of eagles consume it.

18
> Three things are too wonderful for me,
>> and four I cannot understand:
19
> The way of an eagle in the sky,
>> the way of a serpent on a rock,
> The way of a ship on the high seas,
>> and the way of a man with a woman.
20
> Such is the way of an adulteress:
>> she eats and wipes her mouth,
>> and says, "I have done no wrong."

21
> Under three things the earth trembles,
>> under four it cannot carry on:
22
> A slave when he becomes king,
>> a fool when he has enough to eat,
23
> A hateful woman when she is married,
>> a maidservant when she displaces[a] her mistress.

24   *Four things—smallest on earth,*
     but wiser than the wisest ᵃ—

25   *Ants, a group not strong,*
     but they prepare their food in the summer.

26   *Badgers, a group not powerful,*
     but have their home in rocky crags.

27   *Locusts, without a king,*
     *but they all go forth in order.*ᵃ

28   *Lizards* ᵃ*—you catch them by hand,*
     but, in royal palaces!

29   *Three things, stately in stride;*
     four, stately in carriage:

30   *The lion, champion among beasts,*
     and never retreating before anything.

31   *The strutting cock,*ᵃ *the he-goat,*
     and the king leading ᵇ *his people.*

32   *If you have acted foolishly in your pride,*
     *or if you have been plotting,*ᵃ
     hand on mouth!

33   *For pressure* ᵃ *on milk yields curds;*
     pressure on the nose yields blood;
     pressure on anger yields strife.

Notes

15.a. "Leech" is the probable meaning of the Hebrew hapax legomenon, for which various other meanings have been suggested, such as "Aluqah" (a proper name, so Ringgren).

15.b. The LXX reads "three" beloved daughters, and joins the line with the 3/4 numerical saying that follows, attributing three daughters to the leech. This should be disregarded.

15.c. The two imperatives are hapax, and presumably derived from a root, יהב, "give," which does not otherwise occur in biblical Hebrew; cf. Joüon §75k.

17.a. Despite the unusual vocalization of the noun, it is the construct form of יקהה, "obedience," which occurs elsewhere only in Gen 49:10, with this probable meaning; the Greek reads "old age" (γῆρας).

23.a. MT has "inherit" (ירש), which may also mean "dispossess"). The LXX has ἐκβάλη, which conveys the sense "drive out."

24.a. MT מְחֻכָּמִים, a hophal participle meaning "made wise"; probably one should read with LXX and Vg τῶν σοφῶν = מֵחֲכָמִים, "from the wise."

27.a. The meaning of the infrequent verb seems to be "cut," "divide"; hence the locusts are lined up in marching order (LXX, εὐτάκτως, "well ordered").

28.a. This is the common translation, but the precise identity is uncertain; JPS and NRSV indicate "spider" in the notes.

31.a. The LXX has an expanded reading concerning the animals mentioned in v 31. The translation of זרזיר (hapax legomenon) as "cock" is based on the ancient versions, but the translation of the line is very uncertain ("girt[?] at the loins or the he-goat"—so perhaps the MT).

31.b. The אלקום of the MT is not translatable, but the corrupt text is not easily solved. The context suggests a reading that would describe the king at the head of his people (קָם אֶל עַמּוֹ, "he stood before his people," or אֶל קֶדֶם עַמּוֹ, "to the front of his people"?).

32.a. זמם, "plotting," is rendered here in an evil sense, but it can also mean simply "plan" (as in 31:16).

33.a. מִצּ is hapax, and is generally rendered as "pressure," although the nuance is different in each of the three occurrences in this verse.

Form/Structure/Setting

It will be recalled that this section is separated from vv 1–14 in the LXX by the placement of 24:23–34, and that it follows the Hebrew 24:34. Although the title given for 30:15–33 is "numerical proverbs," this does not derive from the text itself. Rather, it characterizes the type of saying found here in contrast to what goes before; notice, however, that 30:11–14 enumerated four "generations." Numerical saying is the broadest description of a literary device which is found elsewhere in the Bible, e.g., Amos, 1:3–2:6; Mic 5:4; Eccl 11:2, etc. According to W. Roth (*VT* 12 [1962] 300–11), the formula occurs thirty-eight times in the Old Testament and Sirach. It appeared already in Prov 6:16–19 in the form of the "graded" numerical saying x and x + 1, and this form occurs here in vv 15b–16, 18–19, 21–23, and 29–31. The other "numerical" sayings are so called in a loose sense; there may be merely an enumeration of things, as in 30:11–14, which have no introductory formula. Similarly, in vv 24–28 a given number, four, is simply mentioned. V 15a has the number two, but this saying may be merely a fragment. "Two" is also mentioned in the words of Lemuel, 30:7–9. Vv 17, 20 (clearly an observation attached to vv 18–19) and the admonition in vv 32–33 are not numerical sayings. Thus this collection seems to be somewhat of a mixed bag, and unified only by the dominant form of the numerical saying. The function of this kind of proverb is not easy to determine. Does it merely designate a number, sometimes left indefinite? Is it a device for emphasis? Is it a riddle for entertainment? Finally, are these sayings "parables" commenting on the human condition (so Meinhold, 506)? No sure answer has been given to these questions that have in fact been answered affirmatively by one scholar or another. Whybray groups the various views about the function and meaning of the numerical sayings under four heads: entertainment, simple observation, education, and reflection (*Proverbs*, 97–98). The form itself is attractive. However, it did not suffer from overuse. See also the discussion of the numerical saying in the *Introduction:* Literary Forms.

Comment

15a Despite the truncated look of these words, they can be explained as a commentary on the action of the leech. See *Note* 15.a. The leech has two suckers at each end of its body with which it draws blood until bloated. These are the "daughters," just as branches are construed as "daughters" of a tree in the difficult text of Gen 49:22. They are further personified by the twofold imperative, asking for more blood until satisfaction is reached. In itself, this saying simply registers an observation. Its application could be varied, but in the context of vv 15b–16, these bloodsuckers are an appropriate introduction to the insatiability of the four things that are to be enumerated.

15b–16 This is a typical graded (3/4) numerical saying that is in itself independent of v 15a. Of the four items mentioned, only Sheol is left without a description, perhaps because of the well-known understanding of Sheol as a dynamic, and not merely static, *power* that pursues every living thing, e.g., Cant 8:6; Pss 49:16; 89:49. If the others had been left without any qualification, they might have been understood just by using imagination: the womb—yearning to be fertilized, cf. Gen 30:1; land—yearning for rain (or for growth?); fire—yearning for something to consume so that it can continue to burn. Insatiability is, of course, the point. The observations are based on life experiences, and they can have many applications, such as greed. "Enough" is the commonly accepted translation of הוֹן, which is so understood also in the LXX.

17 See *Note* 17.a. This verse has no connection with what precedes or follows, but it does recall the observation of 30:11. Here the violence wished upon the offending "eye" is striking. The organ would seem to stand for a whole combination of actions, especially pride; cf. 30:12–13. The implication is that the person dies out in the open, only to have the cadaver consumed by vultures; cf. 1 Kgs 14:11 and Rizpah in 2 Sam 21:10. There was a true fear of dying without burial; hence v 17cd could hardly be more vivid and threatening.

18–19 These verses are another graded (3/4) numerical saying. The understanding of this proverb is not as easy as it appears to be at first sight. Many different solutions have been proposed to explain the wonder occasioned by the four examples. **18** The introductory formula notes that there are four wonderful things in all, with the fourth carrying the main emphasis. These are not objects of investigation, but rather of admiration because they surpass human understanding. The choice of the examples seems to be dictated by what the author felt were truly worthy of wonder. But note that it is not the eagle, serpent, ship, or man that is the real target; it is the "way" (דרך), repeated in each of the examples. Commentators have proposed various solutions to the "wonder." One is "how"—how does the eagle stay up; how does the serpent move without legs—in other words the mystery of movement. Others have seen something marvelous in that supposedly no trace is left by these objects. This solution resembles superficially the words in Wis 5:10–12, which deals with human transience. That understanding, the absence of any trace, seems to be reflected also in the following v 20. However, one must evaluate better the fourfold repetition of the "way." The saying underscores the course of an action—that is "the way." It is not that these objects—eagle, serpent, ship—leave no trace. Rather, their course is not *recoverable*. At any given point one cannot describe the path of the eagle to where it is, or that of the serpent, or the course of the ship in its traversing the water. But the way has not been without its goal. If we follow this lead to contemplating the way of a man with a woman, there is marvel and astonishment at the *course* of the attachment that has made the two one, the mystery of how this was accomplished. After many encounters and years, they are to become one. This refers not only to the "yearning" of the woman for the man (Gen 3:16), or of the man for the woman (Cant 7:10), but to the whole mystery of their relationship: how it came to be and what brought them together finally. An observation like this is singular in the book of Proverbs. One wishes that more of the numerical sayings would have been handed down. In view of the not uncommon charge that the sages were simplistic in their observations and teachings, this openness to wonder and the contemplation of one of the deepest mysteries in human relationship is not to be forgotten.

20 However valid in itself the observation in this verse may be, it is not a harmonious sequence to vv 18–19. It goes beyond the numerical saying which closed with the fourth item in v 19d. Moreover, it betrays no wonder, which was a key to the previous verses, and it also seizes upon the misleading issue of no trace being left by the eagle in the air, etc. It is better to translate "so" at the beginning as "such," introducing a new theme independent of vv 19–20. The theme is familiar from chap. 7: the "way" of an adulteress. She regards her wrongdoing so lightly that it can be compared to wiping away any fragment of food from her mouth. The symbolism of eating to indicate a sexual encounter appeared already in the invitation issued by Woman Folly in 9:16–17.

21–23 The graded numerical proverb is a vivid description of "the world upside down." This is a topos of the ancient Near East, as well as of modern culture, as shown and illustrated by R. Van Leeuwen (*Context*, 36, 38; *JBL* 105 [1986] 599–610). The issue is the portrayal of inverted social relations, even if some of the examples may strike the modern reader as humorous. Whether or not the verses are to be understood "from a royal perspective," the context recognized by Van Leeuwen, they clearly illustrate the theme, and are rightly compared to the psalm of Hannah in 1 Sam 2:1–10, in which God and the anointed will invert Hannah's upside-down world. **21** The trembling of the earth is only an apparent exaggeration, if the theme is recognized. The Bible associates social cataclysm with physical disturbance, e.g., Amos 7:10; cf. "the pillars of the earth are the Lord's" in 1 Sam 2:10. **22** The first example, however, is truly earthshaking since it is a concrete example of a revolution that replaces the royal line with one who can only be regarded as an upstart. The example of slave/king is also found in Eccl 10:5–7. The second example, the fool's appetite being sated, is less obvious. But one should recognize here, too, an inversion. Van Leeuwen points appropriately to Prov 19:10: luxury does not befit a fool, and still less should "a servant rule over princes." There is the same social inversion: slaves and fools. Moreover, having "enough to eat" depends on responsible action and diligence, Prov 28:19; 20:13. Hence there is an inversion in v 22b: the fool, by definition, should not have enough to eat. **23** "Hateful" is literally "hated," and the term is ambiguous. It is difficult to determine the precise situation: a woman who was at first spurned, but eventually married? Or if already married, she was not at first favored (cf. Deut 21:14–15)? Or a woman divorced and taken back (but cf. Deut 24:3)? In any case, there is a clear contrast between her former and later statuses. There existed also the possibility for a maidservant to gain the inheritance by displacing her mistress. The means are not indicated, but it might be the favor of the husband, or the birth of a child; cf. the story of Sarah and Hagar.

24–28 This numerical saying lacks the introductory formula of a graded saying; cf. vv 18, 21. It deals with the animal world, in contrast to the previous saying about human beings. The animals are small and unimportant, but they are praised for a wisdom that enables them to achieve unexpected success. Thus they seem to be deliberately chosen to challenge the "superior" wisdom of human beings. **24** The ant was already singled out for its diligence and wise foresight in 6:6–8. Here they are noted as a group, insignificant but very practical in providing for food. **25** The rock badgers, if that is the correct identification of the animal (cf. Ps 104:18), inhabit rocky crevices, and this small "group," literally "people," is thus inaccessible to the average enemy. **27** See *Note* 27.a. The locusts seem to have no need of a king, for they are a mighty army—as it must have seemed to the Israelite farmer who had to suffer from the scourge; cf. Joel 2:7–9; Amos 7:1–2. **28** See *Note* 28.a. This seems to be a humorous gibe at human beings who might dearly love to have access to the palace of the king. Yet, even lizards can find a place there!

29–31 Another, and final, graded numerical saying features examples from the animal world, but climaxes with a king. **29** "Stately" is a contextual translation of a verb meaning "to do or make well." **30** The lion, as "king" (literally "warrior") of beasts, is a natural choice for the list. **31** See *Notes* 31.a. and 31.b. The interpretation of this verse is totally uncertain; only the identities of the he-goat and the king are sure. The mention of the stately stride in v 29, exemplified in the lion, has governed various guesses and emendations for this verse. In place of comment, a translation of the LXX is provided: "the cock marches bravely among the hens; the he-goat, who leads the flock; a king who harangues the people."

32–33 An admonition with motivation follows the numerical sayings, and there seems to be a deliberate threefold repetition of "pressure" in v 33. **32** The word for fool here is *nbl*, the same consonants which appear in the name of Nabal in 2 Sam 25, whose conduct exemplified "pride" as well. It is not clear what "plans" (see *Note* 32.a.) are meant, but in an admonition such as this against foolish pride they are probably foolish. The gesture of hand to mouth is broad enough to indicate various reactions. In Job 21:5 it appears to designate being appalled, but here it is a clear command: Silence! This reaction is suggested by the motivation described in the next verse. **33** The warning is against taking any action that would only lead to further embroilment. The translation repeats the literal "pressure" three times, so that the reader can follow the play on the word. In the first case, it indicates the churning of milk (therefore, a symbol for some sort of change); in the second instance it indicates a blow that produces nosebleed; and in the third it is said to create anger (a play on אַף/אַפַּיִם, "nose/anger") that in turn produces strife.

Explanation

The title given to 31:14–33, "numerical proverbs," is well deserved. There can be no doubt that the editor has deliberately brought these sayings together, governed by a numerical formula. Indeed, one may ask if the numerical aspect does not already appear in 30:7–9 (the number two) and in 30:12–14 ("four" generations). The interest of the sages in numbers has been noted before. Perhaps the most striking is the number of 375 single-line verses in Prov 10:1–22:16, which corresponds to the numerical value of the Hebrew name "Solomon" in the title "Proverbs of Solomon" (10:1). There has been some textual corruption in those chapters, but also there is a substantial integrity in the number of sayings, and this suggests that we are dealing with more than mere coincidence. Then in 22:17 "thirty" is mentioned, even though there is no unanimity in identifying the thirty sayings in 22:17–24:22. The variations in the style of the numerical sayings, i.e., either a plain list or a graded list, would indicate that there was a certain freedom in the production of these proverbs. The particular selection of numerical sayings in this section illustrates a wide range of interests: insatiable realities, marvels in nature and in human relationship that stir admiration and avowal of incomprehension, examples of "the world upside down," small being wise (if not beautiful). The fairly lengthy comments needed to explain vv 18–19 and vv 21–

23 indicate that these verses were meant to be intriguing. They do not always yield up a meaning until after careful consideration.

The Words of Lemuel

Proverbs 31:1–9

Bibliography

Crenshaw, J. L. "A Mother's Instruction to Her Son (Proverbs 31:1–9)." In *Perspectives on the Hebrew Bible*. Ed. J. Crenshaw. Macon, GA: Mercer University Press, 1988. 9–22. **Lichtenstein, M.** "Chiasm and Symmetry in Proverbs 31." *CBQ* 44 (1982) 202–11. **Whybray, R. N.** *Composition*. 153. ———. *Proverbs*. 98–100.

Translation

31:1 *The words of*[a] *Lemuel,*[b] *king of Massa,*[c] *with which his mother instructed him.*

2 *What,*[a] *my son?*
      What, son of my womb?
      What, son of my vows?[b]

3 *Do not give your strength to women*
      or your power to those who destroy kings.[a]

4 *Not for kings, Lemuel,*
      not for kings to drink[a] *wine,*
      or[b] *strong drink for princes,*

5 *Lest they*[a] *drink and forget the decrees*
      and violate the rights of all the afflicted.

6 *Give strong drink to whoever is perishing,*
      and wine to the bitter in spirit.

7 *Let them drink and forget their poverty;*
      then they will no longer recall their troubles.

8 *Open your mouth for the mute,*
      in defense of all the dispossessed.[a]

9 *Open your mouth, give a just sentence,*
      and defend the afflicted and the poor.

Notes

1.a. The *lamed* before Lemuel can be interpreted either as possessive ("of"), or as the indirect object of the teaching of the queen mother.

1.b. Lemuel is vocalized differently in v 4 (Lemoel); the LXX has no proper names, and seems to have understood the name Lemuel as (words) "from God," למו אל‎.

1.c. Massa, as in 30:1, is understood here as an area in North Arabia, over which Lemuel is king; this interpretation disregards the *athnach* under מלך‎ in the MT. Some follow a literal interpretation of the MT: "the burden (or, instruction) with which his mother instructed him."

2.a. There are varying interpretations of מה‎, e.g., "hear," on the basis of Arabic; so Plöger following Ben Yehuda. It has also been interpreted as a negative particle "no"; so Barucq, citing Joüon §144h. But the MT can be rendered literally as "what?" with a verb of some kind such as "say" being understood. The word for "son" is the Aramaic form בר‎.

2.b. The expanded reading of the LXX, urged in *BHS*, is not to be adopted; cf. Barucq, 228, note 2c.

3.a. The three words in v 3b need comment: דרכיך would normally mean "your ways," and one could arrive at a translation: (do not) direct your ways to destroy kings. This makes sense, but it is at odds with the parallelism. It is better to render the word as "strength" on the basis of the meaning of Ugaritic *drk*, as the parallelism also suggests. The vocalization of the MT, "to destroy," should be changed to the feminine plural participle of מחה, "those who destroy." This preserves the parallelism with נשׁים, "women." The last word "kings" appears in its Aramaic form, *nun* for *mem;* cf. the word for "son" in v 2.

4.a. שׁתו, "to drink," seems to be an infinitive construct, instead of the infinitive absolute, which is needed here; see GKC §75n.

4.b. The translation follows the Ketib. The Qere reads "where?" This would require supplying some words for the sense, such as "not for princes to say, 'Where is the strong drink'?" There is no need to change the word to the infinitive construct piel of אוה (cf. *BHS*).

5.a. There is a change from plural to singular verb forms, but the plural appears in the imperative in v 6; "kings" may be taken as a collective here. The verbs appear in the plural in the LXX.

8.a. The meaning of חלוף, "one passed on or over or away," is difficult to determine (ὑγιῶς, "soundly"; "judge all things soundly" in LXX). The root of this word means change, disappear, etc. Various translations have been proposed, but ultimately it is the context that suggests something like weak, abandoned, unfortunate, etc. The dittography of ף suggested in *BHS* yields חלי, "sickness" or "suffering."

Form/Structure/Setting

This section is clearly defined by a superscription and by an acrostic poem at the end (vv 10–31). In the LXX, chaps. 25–29 follow v 9. As for form, these verses are compared to the royal testaments known from Egyptian literature, such as Merikare and Amenemhet (cf. *ANET*, 414–20) and the Babylonian "Advice to a Prince" (cf. W. Lambert, *BWL*, 110–15). This precedent suggests to many scholars that the unit is a borrowing from some foreign wisdom source, as the Aramaisms in vv 2–3 (see *Notes* 2.a. and 3.a.) may also indicate. But elsewhere there is no example of an instruction given by the mother of a king, as here. After the initial address to the king, she addresses two issues: "women and wine." She gives him a direct command concerning his relationship to the harem (v 3). There follows a clever chiastic schema in vv 4–7, described by M. Lichtenstein (*CBQ* 44 [1982] 204): "A. A prohibition against *yayin* and *sekar,* 'wine and beer,' followed by the justification that the king's drinking (*yisteh*) might lead to forgetting (*yiskah*) his judicial duties to the detriment of the poor. B. An injunction to provide *sekar* and *yayin,* 'beer and wine,' to the distraught, followed by the justification that drinking (*yisteh*) and so forgetfulness (*yiskah*) provide merciful relief to the wretched." Lichtenstein observes further that in the coda (vv 7–9) two commands are given to the king, each using the phrase "open your mouth" and the legal term דין. He goes on to find an analogous chiastic structure in the alphabetic poem that follows, vv 10–31, thus indicating a reason for the juxtaposition of two independent poems in this final chapter. This also suggests to me that these are Hebrew compositions, despite the mention of Lemuel, king of Massa.

Comment

1 See *Notes* 1.a.-1.c. on this superscription. "Words" are used, as in 30:1, to designate the following wisdom admonitions, and the term also appears in 22:17. Lemuel is otherwise unknown, and efforts to associate him with Edom are guesswork.

2 It is obvious that the mother of the king is speaking, although it is not clear if she is the queen mother, or the mother of one of the palace heirs who rose to the kingship. The nuance of her statements is not clear; see *Note* 2.a. But she is certainly calling attention to the advice she is about to give. And she emphasizes her authority by referring to her maternal privilege; she has not only borne him, but apparently dedicated him as well ("son of my vows"; cf. Hannah in 1 Sam 1:11, 28).

3 Her advice is to be understood broadly as a warning against the intrigues that are often associated with a harem ("those who destroy kings"; see *Note* 3.a.) but especially sexual promiscuity. She might also be referring to other details of royal rule if the alternative translation is adopted ("your ways"; cf. *Note* 3.a.).

4–5 See *Form/Structure/Setting* above for vv 4–7. Inebriation is singled out as an enemy to royal justice. **4** See *Notes* 4.a. and 4.b. Concerning the danger of intoxication, cf. Prov 20:1; Isa 28:7. **5** See *Note* 5.a. The singular verb forms can be understood as emphasizing each and every individual ruler. The danger is that drunkenness can lead to a neglect of duty, especially the judicial obligations (Hebrew דין, picked up again in vv 8–9). The "afflicted" are the little people, who are most likely to be neglected by careless judges.

6–7 The emphasis on royal justice is followed by a rather bold and singular recommendation. Instead of enjoying personal consumption of the royal cellar, the king is to provide a supply of drink for the unfortunate people who need it as a kind of comfort (?) for their misery. This strange command has provoked several hypotheses. On the one hand, it has been considered to be "cynical" and perhaps a later addition; as noted in *Note* 5.a., the command is in the plural. On the other hand, it has been interpreted as providing some relief for the unfortunate. What is to be, as it were, doled out to kings is to be provided generously for afflicted members of the realm, whose comforts are little enough. Even though this can be only a temporary measure, a kind of ancient opium (as well as modern?), it is nonetheless recommended. But it is also clear that this does not excuse the king from positive action in favor of lesser people.

8–9 After the apparent digression in vv 6–7, the queenly advice returns to urging just ideals, especially for those who do not have much of a voice. The "mute" are not so much physically as they are socially weak, without a voice among those who administer justice. Here the king is to enter in favor of the "dispossessed"; see *Note* 8.a. The Hebrew phrase for this class has been interpreted to refer to orphans, or particularly unfortunate people in society. Despite the vagueness, it is clear that those who need help to establish their rights are meant.

Explanation

The tone of this chapter is unusual. From the lips of the mother of the king come demands that go beyond the more carefully phrased sayings about royal justice in other parts of the book. There is an undercurrent of criticism in such sayings as 28:16 and 29:12. The royal wrath is recognized (cf. 16:14; 19:12; 20:2), but there is also much talk of the ideal king, e.g., 16:10–15. The advice given to Lemuel emphasizes the social responsibilities of the monarch. In view of the attention given to the role of the king and the court in Egyptian and Mesopotamian literature, it is noteworthy that the topic of kingship does not loom large in the book of Proverbs. That is why 30:1–9 is all the more striking. The background of the royal court, or even school, is frequently affirmed in discussions concerning the proverbs in chaps. 10–29, and the mention of the men of King Hezekiah in 25:1 is surely significant. But on the whole, a royal flavor is absent from the various collections. The references to kingship and its exercise can be expected at every level of society; after all, "a cat can look at a king."

The Ideal Woman

Proverbs 31:10–31

Bibliography

Bonora, A. "La donna eccellente, la sapienza, il sapiente." *RivB* 36 (1988) 137–64. **Camp, C.** *Wisdom and the Feminine.* BLS 11. Sheffield: Almond/JSOT, 1985. 90–93, 251–52, 262–63. **Crook, M. B.** "The Marriageable Maiden of Proverbs 31:10–31." *JNES* 13 (1954) 137–40. **Hausmann, J.** "Beobachtungen zu Spr 31,10–31." In *Alttestamentlicher Glaube und Biblische Theologie.* FS H. D. Preuss, ed. J. Hausmann et al. Stuttgart: Kohlhammer, 1992. 261–67. **Jacob, E.** "Sagesse et alphabet. A propos de Proverbes 31.10–31." In *Hommages à André Dupont-Sommer.* Ed. A. Caquot et al. Paris: Adrien-Maisonneuve, 1971. 287–95. **Lichtenstein, M.** "Chiasm and Symmetry in Proverbs 31." *CBQ* 44 (1982) 202–11. **Lyons, E. L.** "A Note on Proverbs 31.10–31." In *The Listening Heart.* Ed. K. G. Hoglund et al. JSOTSup 58. FS R. E. Murphy. Sheffield: JSOT, 1987. 237–45. **McCreesh, T.** "Wisdom as Wife: Proverbs 31:10–31." *RB* 92 (1985) 25–46. **Wolters, A.** "*Ṣôpiyyâ* (Prov 31:27) as Hymnic Participle and Play on *Sophia.*" *JBL* 104 (1985) 577–87. ———. "Proverbs xxxi 10–31 as Heroic Hymn." *VT* 38 (1988) 446–57.

Translation

31:10   *A woman of valor, who can find?*
    Her value is beyond rubies.

11   *Her husband entrusts his heart to her,*
    and never lacks for profit.[a]

12   *She brings him good, not evil,*
    all the days of her life.

13   *She seeks out wool and flax,*
    and works with joyful hands.[a]

14   *She is like a merchant ship;*
    she brings her food from afar.

15   *She rises while it is still night*
    and provides food[a] for her household,
    a ration for her maidservants.[b]

16   *She surveys a field and takes it over;*
    from what her hands achieve, she plants[a] a vineyard.

17   *She girds herself with strength,*
    and makes her arms sturdy.[a]

18   *She senses that her profit is good;*
    her lamp never turns off at night.

19   *She puts her hand to the distaff;*
    her palms grasp the spindle.

20   *Her palms she extends to the poor;*
    her hands she reaches to the needy.

21 *If it snows, she has no fear for her household,*
   for they are all doubly^a *clothed.*

22 *She makes covers for herself;*
   fine linen and purple, her clothing.

23 *Her husband is well known at the gates,*
   presiding with the elders of the land.

24 *She makes garments*^a *and sells them,*
   and provides girdles for merchants.

25 *Strength and dignity, her clothing,*
   and she laughs at the days ahead.

26 *Her mouth she opens with wisdom,*
   and kind instruction on her tongue.

27 *She watches over*^a *the activity of her household,*
   and does not eat the bread of idleness.

28 *Her children rise up and call her "happy!";*
   her husband, he too praises her:

29 *"Many women act with valor,*
   but you are above them all."

30 *Deceptive, grace—and vain, beauty;*
   Fear of the Lord in a woman, that is to be praised.^a

31 *Celebrate*^a *what her hands achieve,*
   and let her deeds be her praise at the gates.

Notes

11.a. Although the Hebrew does not specify, the likely subject is the husband, contrary to the LXX (cf. *BHS*).

13.a. The meaning is not obvious; literally, she works with hands בְּחֵפֶץ, i.e., with purpose, or busily, or with pleasure.

15.a. טֶרֶף normally designates "prey"; it is also used for "food"; cf. Ps 111:5; Mal 3:10.

15.b. The extra line in this verse is suspicious, especially in view of its resemblance to 27:27.

16.a. Read the Qere.

17.a. The Greek adds "for work" (cf. *BHS*), but this seems merely redundant.

21.a. שָׁנִים (a rare plural, "scarlet") of the MT should be read as שְׁנָיִם, "double," with the LXX and Vg.

24.a. סָדִין, "garments," is a foreign term (Egyptian?) of uncertain meaning, perhaps an undergarment (Isa 3:23).

27.a. The Hebrew form of this feminine qal participle is a rare one (cf. GKC §75v), but not at all impossible (צוֹפָה would be the "normal" form). However, there may be a good reason, as A. Wolters pointed out in *JBL* 104 (1985) 577–87. The form צוֹפִיָּה resembles the Greek σοφία, and this seems to be a deliberate play on the word, as well as suggestive of a relationship between the woman and personified wisdom. It is the only participle to appear in the poem, which mainly employs verbs in the finite form.

30.a. V 30b is not as simple as it looks. יִרְאַת of the MT can be interpreted as a feminine adjective ("fearing YHWH") modifying "woman"; thus, "the woman who fears the Lord," although the normal vocalization would be יְרֵאָה. It is also possible to understand the consonantal text as יִרְאַת, construct of the noun meaning "fear." Then this could be seen as in apposition to "woman"; thus, "the woman, the fear of the Lord, she is to be praised." But it is also possible to construe "fear of the Lord" as the object of the verb; thus, "the woman, she is to glory in (i.e., find praise in) the fear of the Lord." For v 30b the LXX reads: "For a wise woman (cf. *BHS*) is praised; but the fear of the Lord let her praise." Cf. T. McCreesh, *RB* 92 (1985) 28–29, n. 11 with further references.

31.a. תנו, "celebrate," is to be vocalized as the piel imperative of the verb meaning "sing" or "celebrate." The MT derives it from the verb "to give." The difference in meaning is negligible.

Form/Structure/Setting

The Septuagint places this acrostic poem at the end of the book, but that means after chap. 29. Several different approaches to the figure of the "woman of valor" have emerged, especially in more recent years. They display a wide range of opinion on the form, structure, and setting. The structure has been minutely described by M. Lichtenstein in a manner analogous to his analysis of 31:1–9. He points to a verbal inclusion in vv 10, 29: חיל, "valor," and in vv 11, 28, בעלה, "her husband." Vv 10–18 and 21–29 are two units of nine verses each, which balance each other: Incomparability, vv 10, 29; the husband, vv 11, 23; moral qualities, vv 12, 26; expertise in handiwork, vv 13, 22, 24, and management of the household, vv 15, 21, 27, as well as broader commerce, vv 16, 24. Running through the whole is her industry, vv 15, 18, 27. Within these verses, no less than fourteen terms are shared by each unit; while some of these are run-of-the-mill terms and hence not surprising, others are unusual in this short compass: בעל, "husband"; חגר, "gird"; מכר, "price." It is the cumulative effect of the repetitions that is striking. In addition there is a very distinctive chiasm in vv 19–20 (see the translation above), dividing the two basic units, and the final coda of vv 30–31 repeats a key term, "praise." That praise is the goal or purpose of the poem. Coincidence cannot explain such minute symmetry in these various levels: verbal, structural, and thematic. One is confronted by a highly articulated poetic work. It is often said that an acrostic pattern infringes on poetic expression. Obviously it is not true in this case. Moreover, it is intriguing to note the similarities pointed out by Lichtenstein between the poem in vv 2–9 and the acrostic of vv 10–31. They suggest that the two poems have been deliberately juxtaposed. In any case, the structural analysis of Lichtenstein for each section is convincing.

A. Wolters (*VT* 38 [1988] 446–57) has presented a form-critical analysis of the poem, following the typical criteria of a song of praise. He characterizes the poem as a "heroic hymn" with the following structure: introduction in vv 10–12, the body of the praise in vv 13–27, and the conclusion urging praise of the woman. Among other things he notes a similarity to Ps 112; wisdom, wealth, and children are common to both. The hymn is in the tradition of heroic poetry, and it also contains a critique (cf. v 30) of the erotic praise of woman in the ancient Near East. Other characterizations have been offered. Less likely is the view of M. Crook (*JNES* 13 [1954] 137–40) who regarded the poem as an instruction for a young woman contemplating a future in marriage. In other words the woman is meant to be the ideal wife. But can one take the description so literally? See the *Comment* on the question in v 10a. Who could possibly achieve in many lifetimes what she achieves in these verses? Although A. Bonora interpreted the poem realistically, he also incorporated other dimensions. She is a symbol of Wisdom, the type of a truly wise person (*RivBib* 36 [1988] 160). C. Camp (*Wisdom and the Feminine*, 92) sees here "an idealized portrait of a wise wife in an ideal household in an ideal society." However, for her the idealistic description blends into the symbol of Woman Wisdom: the wise wife is "the mediator of Yahweh's blessings to the house: it is through her work and her 'fear of Yahweh' that shalom prevails" (pp. 263–64). T. McCreesh also goes in this direction: "This wife is primarily a symbol" (*RB* 92 [1985] 28). He concludes that the various features of the poem, especially the similarities between the "wife" and descriptions of Wisdom in the book of Proverbs, indicate that "chapter 31 is the book's final masterful portrait of Wisdom" (p. 46).

If the setting of this portrait is not a practical instruction given within the family or the school, perhaps a setting in the book can be more satisfying. Hence this final poem is paired with chaps. 1–9 and interpreted in view of the female imagery as a kind of inclusion. Camp (*Wisdom and the Feminine*, 179–208, especially 188–89, 192–93) has pointed out eight details that bind these two units together. For example, the torah of the mother (1:8) appears in the torah of kindness in 31:26. Wisdom is "more precious than corals (or rubies)" in 3:15; 8:11; so also the woman in 31:10. Just as Wisdom brings material gain in 3:14 and 8:21, so also the woman in 31:11. Moreover, there are allusions binding several sayings in the collections with the inclusion. Thus the finding of a wife in Prov 18:22 (cf. 8:35) can be aligned with the opening verse, 31:10. House-building by wisdom in 14:1 and 24:3 is echoed in the care for the "house" in 31:15, 21, 27. These and other details constitute rather delicate evidence, which cannot "prove" intentionality in the structure, but they do form a kind of cumulative argument that challenges the reader to beware of an atomistic approach. This unusual poem (which could originally have been an independent composition) should be envisioned in the total context of the book. J. Hausmann also argues that a one-sided interpretation of chap. 31 merely stays on the surface and fails to recognize the levels of understanding; see the *Explanation* below.

Comment

31:10 The question "who can find . . . ?" is somewhat ambiguous. It could indicate impossibility; cf. Job 28:12, where another form of the question implies the answer "no one"—wisdom cannot be found because wisdom is with God. In Prov 18:22 the possibility of "finding a wife" is affirmed, but only as a gift of God. The verb means more than a casual finding, and, significantly, it indicates acquiring Wisdom in 1:28; 8:35; cf. Job 28:12–13. In the context of the acrostic poem the question may be indicating a paradox. On the one hand, finding a (good) wife is not possible for merely human effort since it is God's doing, 18:22. But on the other, the present poem describes a wife who is married, and so was "found," and is deservedly the object of her husband's praise, vv 28–29. The value (מכר, literally "price," a commercial term) of the woman is beyond that of precious jewels, usually translated as "corals" or "rubies"; cf. 3:15; 8:11; 20:15.

11–12 The mention of the husband seems almost casual; he serves only to underscore her excellence. "Profit" is literally "booty" or "plunder," a strange use of the word even if it is intended as a metaphor for the following economic successes that are to be described. The husband's trust in her is manifested by the relative absence of any significant mention of him in the poem, except for his lounging at the city gates, v 23, and praising her, vv 28–29.

13 The mention of wool and flax anticipates the concern she has for the clothing of her household, vv 21–22. She does not wait for them to come to her.

Perhaps she sought out the materials from the animals of the home farm, or from traders. For the meaning of v 13b see *Note* 13.a.

14 Even if this verse indicates only that she engaged in a broad range of barter and transactions with locals, the comparison with "merchant ships" is unexpected and seems exaggerated. It refers to the contents of the ship, and the implication is that she acquired foreign, perhaps exotic, imports. Phoenician traders on the coast, not the Jews, managed the shipping commerce in the Mediterranean.

15 This woman does not spare herself in supplying provisions for the household. This is the only verse with three lines, and the final, v 15c, may be a gloss; cf. 27:27.

16 One might have expected that the husband would be mentioned, and thus be involved in the assessment and purchase of a field and the cultivation of a vineyard. The reference to her hands (literally "from the fruit of her hands"; cf. also v 31) may be an anticipation of her work with distaff and spindle, v 19, that could provide the means to hire laborers.

17 The description of this woman as girding her loins with strength indicates that she approaches her work with determination, with readiness, and with strength. This prepares for the work of v 19.

18 The profit from her work borrows phraseology from 3:14a about wisdom. The verse suggests that the woman is urged on by her own success, so that she continues to work beyond what might normally be expected; her "lamp" never goes out. She seems to enjoy her labors.

19–20 The distinctive chiasm in vv 19–20 (evident in the translation "hands/palms") was pointed out above in discussing structure. **19** Although the words for distaff and spindle are hapax, there is no doubt that the verse refers to spinning and weaving. **20** The catch words that described her home industry are now used to indicate her generosity to the poor.

21–22 The second half of the poem begins with the letter *lamed,* and the word "fear" will be repeated in the next to last verse (v 30). **21** See *Note* 21.a. The emendation to "double" covering seems warranted by the mention of snow. "Scarlet" would suggest rich clothing. **22** The "covers" seem to refer to her couch, or bed; cf. the same word in 7:16. V 22b indicates that her clothing is of expensive and classy material.

23 It was at the gates that business was transacted, affairs were settled, and the news of the community was circulated. This husband had a competent woman as wife, caring for things at home; cf. 12:4, the resourceful woman is the "crown of the husband." Hence he could afford to take a position among the prominent leaders at the gates. It is usually thought that the entire poem is written from a male point of view. In the sense that the woman is praised for activities that are usually associated with the male head of the house, this would seem to be accurate. But one may wonder if there is a sly subversion or irony here because the role of the male is so inconsequential. He is reduced to hanging out with the crowd at the gates, while she is the effective power in the household.

24 After the digression, as it were, about the husband, the description returns to the activity of the woman who is engaged in further production and commerce. The merchants are literally "Canaanites," a term that came to be understood of commercial traders. They may serve the same function as the "ships" in v 14.

25 The metaphor of being clothed with an abstraction is very biblical: justice, Ps 132:9; joy, Ps 30:11; cf. also Ps 104:1. This does not mean that "clothes make the man/woman"; rather, they speak a language that betrays the person. The woman's view of the future is quite optimistic, expressed in the exuberance of laughter; she has nothing to fear (v 21).

26 It should be noted that nothing has been said so far about her speech, although this would seem to be very much in demand in view of her activities around the home. It occurs now in typical sapiential fashion: speech is associated with wisdom. The parallel to wisdom is significant. It is the "torah of kindness," either the teaching about kindness or kindness with which she gives instruction. Unfortunately, we cannot determine exactly to whom she might give instruction, but it is probably to her children or her maidservants.

27 This verse seems anticlimactic in view of the detailing of the woman's accomplishments and industry throughout the poem. One might ask indeed: Just why is it here? Is it merely by chance or does this concern for her house provide the occasion to correlate her with Sophia, or Wisdom? See *Note* 27.a. for the play on the Hebrew word צוֹפִיָּה, translated as "watch over." "Bread of idleness" is bread that is not earned by the one who eats it; cf. "bread of wickedness" in 4:17. The two words do not really go together because idleness does not lead to food, and food should not tolerate idleness in the one who consumes it. This is an understatement when applied to this industrious woman. The line is a kind of motto endorsing her lifestyle: one who does not work cannot eat (2 Thess 3:10); no lazybones can be tolerated in that house.

28–29 It is about time that some reaction from the members of her family be expressed. Their praise is quoted in v 29, where the word חַיִל, as in woman of חַיִל or valor (v 10), serves as an inclusio for the poem.

30 This verse gives a didactic, some might say pedantic, twist to the acrostic poem, while it also serves acrostic purposes. It gives the impression of an observer passing judgment for others to abide by. Is the judgment in this verse to be taken at face value? The typical Hebrew polarity should be recognized here: not so much this, as that. Not so much the gifts of beauty and grace which will pass away with time, but the supreme value "fear of the Lord!" It would be well to recall that in Prov 5:15–19 the description of wifely attractiveness appeared as a motivation for fidelity. It appears from *Note* 30.a. that the meaning of v 30b was not always clearly understood, and it remains difficult to translate. Perhaps the most important question to be put to the text is, why does the "fear of the Lord" appear in this poem at all, and in a climactic place at the end? Wisdom and fear of the Lord are practically synonymous in this book. But what has this to do with a description of a superindustrious and supertalented woman? The only mention of wisdom is the passing reference in v 26, where her speech is characterized. It is also true that her concrete acts are to be classified as virtuous. Still, it is surprising that the poem should culminate on this note. Unless, perhaps, there is more than one level of meaning being suggested? The attentive reader will recall Prov 1:7, the motto of the book, identifying wisdom and fear of the Lord. But is there more here than a literary inclusio, so that the woman of valor is to be identified with Woman Wisdom? One is left with an eerie feeling of identity: both Woman Wisdom and the woman of valor are into house-building (cf. Prov 9:1; 14:1); both influence the public, and both are associated with fear of the Lord.

31 See *Note* 31.a. Like v 30, this verse also gives the impression of being an observation by the poet. It is a counterpart to the actual quotation of praise in v 29; both have to do with the reaction "in the gates." It does not add much to what has been said there. "What her hands achieve" (literally "fruit of her hands"), a phrase used in v 16, is a global reference to all the achievements portrayed in the poem, which are then neatly personified in the "deeds" (v 31b) that proclaim her praise.

Explanation

The intriguing characteristics of this poem have been indicated in the discussion of the structure and in the *Comment*. It is part of the tensions in the Bible that the Song of Songs extols the beauty of the woman and lingers over the attractiveness of her body, while in this poem all is businesslike. Arms, hands, and palms are mentioned, but only in a frenzy of activity. Presumably, this is what the husband sees as worthy of praise, vv 28–29, whereas the lover in the Song sang a different tune. The husband is hardly present in vv 10–31, and he is only a foil for the description of the wife. And she pays little enough attention to him. This is where her workaholic tendencies appear most vividly; her intimate feelings are never touched upon. She does not seem to have time for him, in contrast to the amatory interests of the woman in the Song of Songs. It may not be legitimate to insist so strongly on this contrast, but neither is it to be neglected. Some have interpreted the acrostic, which goes, so to speak, from a to z, as bespeaking totality and perfection. That perception of the meaning of an acrostic does not fit here.

It has already been suggested above that levels of interpretation can be detected within the poem; in other words, Woman Wisdom has cast a shadow here. How convincing are these indications? First, as J. Hausmann ("Beobachtungen," 262–63) has also pointed out, there is the playful ambiguity of the opening question. The description of the woman is not truly real; no one can perform all that she does. The answer to the tantalizing question defeats itself, and one begins to wonder, in the light of this superwoman, if this is not the Wisdom that cannot be found in Job 28 because it is with God; cf. also Prov 8:22–30. Second, Hausmann also points out that this ending to the book of Proverbs is strange if it is merely a matter of praising the industry and skill of a woman, when there is nothing in chaps. 10–29 to prepare for it, or resemble it, not even 19:14. Moreover, can one really expect that a woman would be the subject of praise at the "gates" (31:28–29)? Despite the indication in the book of Ruth, Ruth 3:11, we are ignorant of what transpired in such situations. Surely there was gossip. But was this post mainly for men? Is such praise realistic in this culture? It may be a deliberate exaggeration, just as in Cant 6:9, maidens, queens, and concubines are said (by the lover, whose own praise of the beloved can hardly be surpassed) to praise the beloved. Finally, while the textual evidence in 31:30 is not enough to prove that the woman is identified with "fear of the Lord," it is suggestive. A. Meinhold argues from the unusual instance of the participial form, "Yahweh-fearing," that this is an intentional allusion to Wisdom, since the woman can now just as well be called "fear of the Lord" (p. 530). Thus both at the beginning of the book as well as at the end, Wisdom and fear of the Lord have appeared as Woman.

T. McCreesh (*RB* 92 [1985] 46) relates the poem to the summons of Woman

Wisdom in 9:4–6. If Wisdom is inviting guests to her home in chap. 9, the portrait in chap. 31 symbolizes Wisdom finally settled down with her own. "She [Wisdom] was presented in chapter 9 as the young marriageable woman seeking lovers who would accept the gifts and life she could offer. Now that time of courtship, of learning, is over. In chapter 31 Wisdom is a faithful wife and a skilled mistress of her household, finally settled with her own. This ingenious symbolic framework of the book of *Proverbs* presents a consistent picture of Wisdom. She is not some lofty, remote ideal for those initiated into her mysteries, but a practical, ever-present, faithful guide and lifelong companion for all who choose her ways. Her origins are with God (8:22–30) and her teaching wins blessings from God (8:35). But her home is in this world. This is the way Wisdom herself wanted it. Even while she was beside the Creator, playing before him, she was also, in her own words from 8:31:

> rejoicing in his inhabited world
> and delighting in the sons of men.

Excursuses

Excursus on Translating Proverbs

Bibliography

Alter, R. "The Poetry of Wit." In *The Art of Biblical Poetry*. New York: Basic Books, 1985. 163–84. **Berlin, A.** *The Dynamics of Biblical Parallelism*. Indianapolis: Indiana UP, 1985/92. **Hermisson, H.-J.** "Redeformen der israelitischen Spruchweisheit als Formen weisheitlichen Denkens." In *Studien zur israelitischen Spruchweisheit*. WMANT 28. Neukirchen: Neukirchener, 1968. 136–72. **Schneider, Theo R.** *The Sharpening of Wisdom: Old Testament Proverbs in Translation*. OTSSA 1. Pretoria: Old Testament Society of South Africa, 1992. **Williams, J. G.** "The Power of Form: A Study of Biblical Proverbs." In *Gnomic Wisdom*. Ed. J. D. Crossan. Chico: Scholars Press, 1980. 35–58.

Everyone acknowledges that the proverbial sayings are poetic, if the typical biblical parallelism is a valid sign of poetry. Usually a line has an accentual meter of three to four beats, and normally the proverb consists of two lines or, at times, three. It is well-nigh impossible to capture the accents in translation, but the parallelism seems easy enough to express. Or is it? Nominal sentences, which consist of juxtaposed nouns or phrases without any verb, and sentences with verbs both occur, but translations do not distinguish between them. For example, Prov 11:1 has literally:

> *False scales, an abomination to the Lord,*
> *and a full weight, his pleasure.*

The normal translation is along the lines of the NRSV:

> *A false balance is an abomination to the Lord,*
> *and an accurate weight is his delight.*

The punch of the juxtaposition in the original disappears with the insertion of the copula, which creates the look of a prose sentence. What is lost by such a matter-of-fact approach to the Hebrew idiom? The rhythm and the deliberate density of the Hebrew is flattened out for the sake of clarity. That is too high a price to pay. The Hebrew style is far from impenetrable, and its flavor is desirable in a culture that has been permeated by the English Bible tradition. Moreover, the relationship of the subject and predicate, which may have been ambiguous in the original, is now determined by the insertion of the copula. For example, what in Prov 14:2a is the subject and what is the predicate: the one who walks uprightly, or the one who fears the Lord?

It may be rightly objected that in translations designed to be proclaimed in public, as in the liturgy, the more "prosy" style is desirable. One who is bombarded with one succinct proverb after another will feel overwhelmed and be unable to catch such proverbs on the wing. The message will suffer at the expense of poetic effect. Recently there has been a rash of more and more paraphrastic versions of the Bible. Good intentions lie behind explanatory translations, and in many individual instances some paraphrase is necessary. An example taken from Proverbs itself is the phrase "hand upon hand" (11:21; 16:5), which fails to convey any meaning. It is probably best rendered "my hand upon it!" or "assuredly."

Even the "literal" translation of 11:1 given above fails to convey the full flavor of the Hebrew, which can be expressed in this manner:

> Scales-of-lying, abomination-of-the-Lord
> and-a-full-weight, his-pleasure.

The example is instructive for Hebrew syntax in that it demonstrates how words and possessive pronouns, etc., can be related to each other. It is well for a reader to keep such a phenomenon in mind. But this example will not serve as a model for translation into English. Moreover, the translation of the connective "and" is left uninterpreted, honoring the paratactic nature of the original. It is by no means wrong to translate it by "but." Such a disjunctive term gives a hint to the reader that the two lines are in an antithetical relationship, although sometimes the antithesis is not clear in the original.

There are two basic reasons why a more literal style of translating Hebrew proverbs is desirable. The different idiom becomes a challenge to the reader— and this purpose is inherent to a proverbial saying, which often points out paradoxes and overturns preconceived ideas. Moreover, a more literal rendering does justice to the ambiguity of a saying that might be eliminated when it is translated in too bland a fashion. An example of challenge is Prov 10:15:

> The wealth of the rich, a strong city;
> the ruin of the poor, their poverty.

The abruptness of these four phrases challenges a reader to sift through the implications: To what extent can the rich rely upon their wealth? Is it a "strong city" that can withstand any adversity? Is poverty ruination? Is there no hope for the poor? This will call for an examination of other pertinent proverbial sayings (e.g., Prov 18:10–11). An example of a paradox appears in Prov 11:24:

> There is one scattering, and still the richer,
> and one too sparing, only the poorer.

The very succinctness warns the reader to think this through. Do we have an ethical command implied? Or is this simply a paradoxical observation about how misleading appearances can be?

This approach to the Hebrew text is not new. The most effective description of the aphoristic quality of the biblical proverb has been done briefly by such scholars as R. Alter, H-J. Hermisson, and J. G. Williams. But most translators feel bound to a smooth and perfectly clear rendering. The format of a detailed commentary, however, provides an opportunity to depart from the traditional style. A translation that is accompanied by a commentary is not destined for public recitation; it is designed for study, and it provides full opportunity to deal with the obscurity of the English translation (not to mention the obscurity of the Hebrew original!), which can and should be clarified by the commentator. Hence this seems to be an ideal vehicle for a translation that would attempt to convey the flavor of Hebrew idiom. No claim is being made that such would be a "better" translation—there are too many intangible factors to come to such a conclusion. Rather, it is a different translation for the purpose of enabling a reader to enter more fully into the pungency, and often the mystery, of a proverb. Sometimes limits have to be observed, since the receptor language forces a translator to draw back in order to avoid what might be seen as nonsense.

This mode of translation cannot escape the problem of gender inclusivity/ exclusivity that affects any attempt to translate the Bible. The fact is that biblical writers do refer to God as male, and this attribution appears in many grammatical indications ("he," "his," etc.). We are also constrained by the limitations of the patriarchalism that has molded our own English language. There are no satisfactory means as yet by which we can extricate ourselves from this bind. There can be no denial that Israelite culture (among others!) was patriarchal, and I thoroughly respect the demand that inclusivity be a mark of public and liturgical presentation of the biblical word. In the case of Proverbs, there is more than the difficulty inherent in translation. As R. J. Clifford, S.J., has put it, "its world is male" (*The Book of Proverbs and Our Search for Wisdom* [Pere Marquette lecture, Milwaukee, WI, 1995] 7–8). But he also points out that while the assumptions are patriarchal, the intentions (obvious in Prov 1:1–7) are not, and the intention overrides the implicit assumptions.

Not all biblical proverbs can be released from the apparently stodgy style of the English language in which they are currently imprisoned. Moreover, some of them are not all that gripping, and may even be classified as banal. But this is no reason to treat them all alike, or to fail to reflect the often staccato style they favor. If one were to write a commentary on the aphorisms of Montaigne or of an ancient classical writer, such as Ovid, one would keep the literal wording and refuse to bowdlerize for the sake of clarity. The biblical proverb deserves no less respect.

For those who are not convinced of the need of this manner of translation of sayings, it may be helpful to recall the succinctness of English proverbial sayings (which also are not to be rendered into a prose paraphrase). One may cite: "A penny saved, a penny earned." Usage and various associations have made the meaning clear to us, spontaneously, almost without thinking. We would not want to make a neat prose sentence as the equivalent lest we close off the openendedness of the saying.

Can a program such as is proposed here really be carried through the entire book of Proverbs? Perhaps at this point more examples of translation of biblical proverbs would be an effective way of establishing the claim (see also the examples selected by J. G. Williams in "The Power of Form," 41–42). There may be a need for readers to get accustomed to elliptical phraseology.

11:10   *When the just prosper, a city is glad,*
                  and (but) when the wicked perish, rejoicing.
11:14   *No guidance, a people falls;*
                  but in many counselors, safety.

11:18	*The wicked: making empty profits,* *but one sowing justice: sure wages.*
11:23	*The desire of the just, only good;* *the hope of the wicked, wrath.*
11:29	*Whoever disturbs his household will inherit the wind;* *and a fool—servant to the wise of heart.*
12:1	*A lover of instruction, a lover of knowledge;* *but a hater of reproof, stupid!*
25:14	*Clouds and wind, but no rain:* *one who boasts of a gift never given.*
25:19	*A bad tooth and an unsteady foot:* *trusting a faithless person in time of trouble.*
25:26	*A trampled spring, or a polluted fountain—* *a just person who gives way before the wicked.*
28:3	*A man poor, but oppressing the lowly—* *a torrential rain and no food.*
28:27	*Whoever gives to the poor—nothing lacking;* *whoever closes his eyes—many a curse.*
29:9	*A wise person disputing with a fool—* *anger or laughter, but no peace.*
30:5	*Tested: every word of Eloah,* *a shield to those who trust in him.*

Many other examples can be given, but these suffice to make the point. The discrete sayings in Prov 10–29 are not prose and are better appreciated if "prosaic" features are not inserted into them.

Excursus on Fear of the Lord

Bibliography

The literature on this topic is far too vast to record here. Rather, only the works that influenced the production of this excursus need be mentioned.

Barré, M. "'Fear of God' and the World of Wisdom." *BTB* 11 (1981) 41–43. **Becker, J.** *Gottesfurcht im Alten Testament.* AnBib 25. Rome: Biblical Institute, 1965. **Cox, D.** "Fear or Conscience?: *Yirʾat* YHWH in Proverbs 1–9." *Studia Hierosolymitana* 3 (1982) 83–90. **Derousseaux, L.** *La crainte de Dieu dans l'Ancien Testament.* Paris: du Cerf, 1970. **Fox, M. V.** "Ideas of Wisdom in Proverbs 1–9." *JBL* 116 (1997) 613–33. **Fuhs, H.** ירא *yareʾ.* *TDOT* 6:290–315. **Hausmann, J.** *Menschenbild.* 265–76. **Murphy, R. E.** "Religious Dimensions of Israelite Wisdom." In *Ancient Israelite Religion.* FS F. M. Cross, ed. P. Miller et al. Philadelphia: Fortress, 1987. 449–58. **Plath, S.** *Furcht Gottes.* Stuttgart: Calwer, 1962. **Preuss, H. D.** *Einführung in die alttestamentliche Weisheitsliteratur.* Stuttgart: Kohlhammer, 1987. 57–66, 174–86. **Rad, G. von.** *Wisdom in Israel.* Nashville: Abingdon, 1972. 53–73. **Schmid, H.-H.** "Timor Domini Initium Sapientiae." In *Ernten was man sät.* Ed. D. R. Daniels et al. Neukirchen: Neukirchener, 1991. 519–31. **Vanoni, G.** "Volkssprichwort und YHWH-Ethos. Beobachtungen zu Spr 15,16." *BN* 35 (1986) 73–108.

The fear of the Lord (יראת יהוה) is a concept that is central to the biblical wisdom literature, and especially to the book of Proverbs. Its position within the book calls attention to the idea: it is the motto at the beginning, 1:7, and this unites with 9:10 to form a frame for the collection in chaps. 1–9. A further frame for the entire book is the connection between 1:7 and 31:30. But the idea did not suddenly appear with this book or with wisdom literature. In one form or another fear of the Lord/God permeates the entire Bible. It must be seen in its biblical context if one is to understand it more clearly and especially its place within wisdom. It seems undeniable that fear of God is rooted in a basic attitude of mortal beings before the Numen. That is simply the fear that the Bible expresses so often and in so many ways. Only a few instances can be mentioned here. One of the prime examples is the Sinai revelation and the reaction of the people indicated in Exod 19:16; 20:15–18. The role of nature in the theophany intensifies the awfulness of these events. Another expression is the belief that to see the Lord means death—a belief attested all through the Bible. The divine utterance in Exod 33:20 is reflected in one episode after another where, paradoxically, the person concerned lives to tell the tale! The concept of the "holiness" of the Lord is another expression associated with fear of the Lord. It is a characterization of the divinity as totally other, as being in a sphere of its own that differs from the level in which mortals find themselves. Both the Numinous and the Holy beget certain standards if one is to be able to live in their proximity. This is exemplified in the experience of Isaiah in his confrontation with the Lord in Isa 6:1–7. The prophet recognizes his sinfulness in the face of this vision of God, but he is purified by the action of one of the seraphim.

Already the notion of the fear of God has acquired certain nuances, and that is the tantalizing aspect of the idea within the Bible. It comes to denote several things. Even if these are rooted in the basic stance of mortals before the numinous—and this should always be kept in mind—definite new meanings are acquired at different levels of biblical writings. J. Becker (*Gottesfurcht*, 75–84) describes three basic types of fear that develop from the numinous, which he describes as the cultic, moral, and nomistic.

The cultic expression is to be found in the Deuteronomic and Deuteronomistic writings. The dominant aspect is loyalty to the Lord as the God of the covenant, with the corresponding honor that is due to him. As Deut 10:12 puts it, "Now, Israel, what does the Lord your God ask of you? This: to fear the Lord your God, to walk only in his ways, to love him and to serve the Lord your God with all your heart and soul." Our common distinction between fear and love is obviously not applicable to this mentality; "fear of the Lord" also includes love. There is naturally a cultic (which includes the note of proper conduct) sense to be found in the Psalms, and here a communal aspect emerges; the one who fears God is one of the worshiping community. The moral aspect (but without any explicit reference to the obligations of Torah) is found in the book of Proverbs especially, and we shall return to this point. In the famous verse of Job 28:28, against the background of unattainable Wisdom, the fear of the Lord is allied with avoiding evil—hence a moral nuance. Qoheleth does not use the phrase, but he uses the verb "fear (God)" and is unique in his usage (cf. R. Murphy, *Ecclesiastes*, WBC 23A, lxiv–lxvi). Finally, the nomistic usage, with specific reference to the Law, is characteristic of Ben Sira.

We are concerned with the usage in Proverbs especially. This is strikingly presented in what has been called the "motto" of the book in Prov 1:7. The importance of this saying is indicated by its effective repetition in many other places: Prov 9:10; 15:33; Job 28:28; Ps 111:10. First of all, it is the "beginning" (not the "best part," although this is a possible meaning) of wisdom, that is, a training that leads to wisdom, a moral formation to which wisdom contributes while it is also dependent upon it. Second, within the book of Proverbs is a striking parallelism between "knowledge" (*da'at*) and fear of the Lord: 1:7, 29; 2:5; 9:10; 30:3. In addition to these texts Becker (*Gottesfurcht*, 222–41) has pointed out other ramifications of the phrase. Thus it is associated with retribution in 10:27; 14:26–27; 15:16; 16:6; 19:23 and 22:24. In 14:22 it describes one who walks uprightly, and in 15:33 it means training for wisdom. While the notion is considered characteristic of "later" wisdom (e.g., Prov 1–9), it is arbitrary to impose a limit since it appears also in chaps. 10–29. There is no way of limiting "fear of the Lord" to a given temporal pigeonhole. Neither can it be considered an infallible sign pointing towards prosperity. According to 15:16 it can tolerate (relative?) poverty, for that is preferable to being overpreoccupied about one's personal state and the problems it begets.

The merit of having explored the full meaning of the wisdom connection and fear of the Lord goes to G. von Rad: "The thesis that all human knowledge comes back to the question about commitment to God is a statement of penetrating perspicacity. It has, of course, been so worn by centuries of Christian teaching that it has to be seen anew in all its provocative pungency. In the most concise phraseology it encompasses a wide range of intellectual content and can itself be understood only as the result of a long process of thought. It contains in a nutshell the whole Israelite theory of knowledge. . . . The statement that the fear of the Lord was the beginning of wisdom was Israel's most special possession. But this does not mean that everything is now clear. In a word, her thinking had to operate within spheres of tension indicated by the prior gift of the knowledge of God" (*Wisdom*, 67–68). It might seem to be an overstatement to say that the "fear of the Lord" contains in a nutshell a theory of knowledge. Epistemology sounds too abstract to be linked up to such an attitude. Yet, von Rad's perception is basically correct. The oft-maligned wisdom literature is not simply secular or profane or self-centered. It is anthropological and creational, and the pertinence of the divine to these areas should be clearly evident.

This understanding of the fear of the Lord and wisdom is worlds apart from other views that have been expressed, and for which the late H. D. Preuss can be taken as spokesman. He argues (*Einführung*, 57) that the other religions likewise cultivate a fear of the deity, and that in this respect the older wisdom in Israel (specifically Prov 10–29) does not differ from ancient Near Eastern wisdom in its conception of the Lord. It would surely be wrong as well as foolish to consider the idea of "fear of God" as exclusive to Israel; it is a natural response to a Higher Being who cannot be fathomed. But neither is fear of God to be considered merely a common denominator or catchall in the religious understanding of the ancient Near East. Preuss and others have united the expressions of fear into a basic stance before an *Urhebergott*, or God of origins, a rather theoretical divinity (worthy, indeed, of fear!). This patterning is hypothetical and the product of a deductive method that goes beyond our control of the history and development of ancient texts, both those of the ancient Near East and of Israel. At the present time, a holistic approach, without obliterating historical indications, seems to be the safest way of evaluating "fear of God/Lord" in Israel's wisdom. Certainly it is a key concept in Israelite wisdom literature and even the rest of the Old Testament, when Israel's writings are compared to the other writings of the ancient Near East. Its treatment is too extensive, both in Proverbs and the rest of Israelite wisdom, and unique to be dismissed merely as a "parallel." One cannot be satisfied with a shortsighted historical approach to the concept and fail to evaluate its function within the *present* form of the literature. The historical approach merely yields questions, but a holistic approach, as can be exemplified in von Rad's exposition, interprets the literature as it stands.

It seems clear that the author/editor of the book regarded 1:7 ("The fear of the Lord: the beginning of knowledge; wisdom and instruction fools despise") as central to the work. "Fear of the Lord" is not opposed to "Fear of God." There is only one God for the editor: the Lord. The phrase certainly serves in 1:7 as a kind of motto, as many contemporary scholars hold. It is set off from the first six verses of chap. 1, and from the first appeal to hearken to the instruction of the parents (vv 8–9), and from the lengthy warning about evil company (vv 10–18). The parallel line within 1:7 is also important: "wisdom and instruction fools despise." Wisdom (חכמה) is what the book of Proverbs is about. Its companion is instruction or מוסר, whether in the sense of instruction or discipline, or both. As M. Fox puts it, "The wisdom that Wisdom speaks is מוסר (8:33), which refers to all admonitions bearing an ethical and religious message" (*JBL* 116 [1997] 632). It is clear from the warning against the evil way proposed in 1:10–18 that the way of wisdom involves a life of responsibility and virtue. A similar admonition is to be found in Prov 24:1–2, where one is urged to shun evil people. In 1:29 Woman Wisdom complains about those who do not choose "fear of the Lord" and who hate knowledge. In 2:5 fear of the Lord is paired with knowledge of God. What is this knowledge? It is the practical way of life indicated in 2:9 (cf. 1:3): "then you will understand justice and judgment and right." In this context the text of Isa 11:2 ("a spirit of wisdom and understanding . . . a spirit of knowledge and fear of the Lord") should be noted; it predicates of the shoot from Jesse's stump these "spirit" gifts; cf. also Isa 33:6. The saying of Prov 1:7 is given a slight refinement in 9:10; now the fear of the Lord is defined as "the beginning of wisdom." Paradoxically, "fear of the Lord" can be the antithesis of wisdom (Prov 3:7)—i.e., a certain kind of wisdom, the wisdom that derives from one's personal judgment ("wise in your own eyes;" cf. Prov 26:12).

According to Becker (*Gottesfurcht*, 221–28), "fear of the Lord" is usually associated with retribution in Prov 10–22: 10:27; 14:26, 27; 15:16; 16:6; 19:23; 22:4. He considers 15:33 to be an exception, for it is more in the spirit of chaps. 1–9 in that it is termed "wise instruction." I think that chap. 14 of Proverbs is also an exception; see the *Comment,* with the *Explanation,* on 14:2, 26, 27. The function of fear of the Lord in 16:6 is particularly important; it enables one to "avoid evil." The parallelism within the verse indicates that evil should be understood in a moral sense, and not merely in the meaning of a physical disaster. Both 16:6 and 3:7, examples of early and late texts, affirm this centrality of "fear of the Lord." In Prov 19:23, fear leads to "life," which is so often promised in Proverbs, e.g., 8:35. Although 8:13 has an interruptive character in Woman Wisdom's description of herself in the first person, it is certainly a valid statement about the way fear of the Lord is understood: the fear of the Lord—hatred of evil. Finally, there is the tantalizing appearance of "fear of the Lord" in the summary description of the "woman of valor" in 31:30. However this verse is to be translated (see the *Comment* and *Explanation*), it seems to be an inclusion with 1:8, and underlines the importance of fear of the Lord in this book.

Excursus on Speech

Bibliography

Alter, R. "The Poetry of Wit." *The Art of Biblical Poetry.* New York: Basic Books, 1985. 163–84. **Bühlmann, W.** *Vom rechten Reden: Studien zu Proverbien 10–31.* OBO 12. Freiburg: Universitätsverlag, 1976. **Hausmann, J.** *Studien zum Menschenbild der älteren Weisheit (Spr 10ff.)* FAT 7. Tübingen: Mohr (Siebeck), 1995. 186–213. **McCreesh, T.** *Biblical Sound and Sense: Poetic Sound Patterns in Proverbs 10–29.* JSOTSup 128. Sheffield: JSOT Press, 1991. **Scoralick, R.** "Paronomasien und Stichwörter." In *Einzelspruch und Sammlung.* BZAW 232. Berlin: de Gruyter, 1995. 111–30. **Shupak, N.** *Where Can Wisdom be Found? The Sage's Language in the Bible and in Ancient Egyptian Literature.* OBO 130. Frieburg: Universitätsverlag, 1933. Passim.

There are several reasons for calling attention to speech in discussing the book of Proverbs. First, speech or orality was the medium by which early wisdom was primarily communicated. Second, it becomes a very frequent topic in and for itself; perhaps about 20 percent of chaps. 10–29 deal with it. The frequency points to its importance in the eyes of the sages: when to speak and when to keep silent. Third, the wisdom ideal is to say a thing well, from several points of view: linguistic finesse, pungency, depth, etc. Such verbal excellence would include all kinds of tricks with words, syllables, consonants, assonance, alliteration, etc., and the book of Proverbs provides many examples of this; cf. T. McCreesh, *Biblical Sound and Sense*, passim. Fourth, it was believed that speech could exercise a certain power and influence; hence the sages wished to be masters of the word, for good purposes. In this they reflect a steady emphasis of Egyptian wisdom which also prized highly clever speech; cf. Shupak, *Where*, 334–36. Only a few proverbs explicitly propose what we may call the ideal of the sages. Prov 25:11 is not without problems as far as translation is concerned, but it seems to indicate an appreciation of phrases that are well-turned: (literally "a word spoken on wheels [?]"). A "timely word" was highly regarded, 15:23. Words were powerful. It was not merely that a soft answer could turn wrath aside (15:1), but that a soft tongue could break a bone! (25:15). The "pleasant" words attributed to Qoheleth were not sweet nothings, Eccl 12:10. They were carefully molded. He decried fools precisely because all the fool was capable of was sheer talk, Eccl 10:12–14. It would appear that the right word at the right time was an ideal; one had to know when to respond to a fool, and when to keep silent, Prov 26:4–5. While this goal is not often made explicit, the many proverbs dealing with speech seem to be formed with that purpose in mind. A proverb was really an art form about which no theory was written, but the practical results are obvious in the styles reflected in the book itself.

It is not only the highly expressive quality of the sayings themselves that illustrate the importance of speech. The *Excursus on Woman Wisdom and Woman Folly* points out the dangers of speech, the seductive power of the word. Evil people are dangerous and to be feared on account of their words, rather than for overt actions. Words can be "smooth," "honeyed," and put to evil purpose; they can seduce precisely because they are pleasing (cf. the warning in 26:23–25).

Many times in the commentary the use of the organs of the body to indicate speech, as well as other activities, have been pointed out: mouth, tongue, eyes, feet, etc. W. Bühlmann (*Von rechten Reden*, 12–13) shows that bodily organs are more frequent than the abstract nouns, such as "word" or "utterance." In the book of Proverbs "mouth" (פה) is used forty-one times. "Lips" (שפתים) occurs forty-eight times, exclusively for speech. "Tongue" (לשון) designates both good and false speech nineteen times. Elsewhere in the Bible the abstract terms are used for the utterances of the Lord, but in the case of Proverbs, as Bühlmann remarks, it is the human person that is in the foreground, for good or bad speech. Lies, deceit, false witness, calumny, flattery, gossip—all kinds of "bad" speech are condemned or warned against. The negative emphasis is designed to promote the right use of words.

N. Shupak has pointed out the profound agreement between Hebrew and Egyptian usage of the word "heart" (לב): "In Egyptian and in Hebrew the 'heart' signifies the innermost being, on which a man's life depends" (*Where*, 298). It is the "seat of understanding," "the residence of feelings," and ultimately the character and moral strength of a person. It is important in translating the Bible to render literally the parts of the body that are mentioned, as far as this is possible in the receptor language. An exception can be made for "heart," i.e., understanding, in a phrase like "lacking in heart" (חסר לב), which means "has no sense." This phrase occurs ten times, and only in Proverbs. Similarly, "a tongue of secret" (25:23) means secretive, harmful words. Despite the harm that the word can inflict, the benefit that flows from the good word is easily recognized: it brings healing (12:18) and joy (12:25), even a kiss on the lips (24:26). Even in the form of reprimand, it is better than a love that keeps silent, 27:5; cf. 28:23. If only one listens!

"No other corpus in the Old Testament offers such an extensive reflection concerning the possibilities and functions of language, as Proverbs," affirms J. Hausmann (*Menschenbild*, 186). She underlines this claim by pointing to the comparisons of proper speech to riches, such as gold and silver: 10:20; 20:15; 25:11–12. Proper talk is intrinsically associated with wisdom, 10:31; 15:2, 7. It is fraught with issues of life and death (13:2–3; 18:7; 21:23; cf. the discussion of 18:20–21 below), depending on whether it is wise or foolish. It heals, 12:25; 16:24, but it also harms, 16:27; 17:4.

Speech is perhaps the truest indication whether one is wise or foolish. It betrays who one is. Properly, speech is the province of the wise person, but fools pervert it, Prov 10:31–32; 15:2. Correct speech depends upon the "heart" or understanding, which the fool does not have, 15:28; 16:21, 23. The power of the tongue is, as we say, proverbial, and one of the most famous descriptions is contained in the epistle of James, Jas 3:1–12. This is in genuine continuity with Old Testament sapiential thought, "A fountain of life—the mouth of the just, but the mouth of the wicked conceals violence" (Prov 10:11). This view is reflected in those sayings that destroy community, 16:27; 17:4. Outright lying or deceit is of course condemned. There is a very idealistic view that the lip of truth will last, but the lying tongue will not, 12:19. Certain lies, however, are particularly despicable: those that are false witness against a neighbor: 12:17; 14:5, 25. This was already forbidden in the Decalogue. The situation was not only pertinent to the witness and his honesty, but to the entire operation of justice: Could witnesses be trusted? These liars will not escape punishment, 19:5, 9; they are an abomination to the Lord, 6:16, 19; cf. 12:22.

A particularly suggestive phrase is "the fruit of the mouth," which N. Shupak thinks may derive from an Egyptian phrase; cf. *Where*, 321–24. It occurs three times in Proverbs, and in each case the parallel line differs. In 12:14 it refers to a good, parallel to what the work of the hands achieves. In 13:2 the "good" is contrasted with the violence that comes from the treacherous. In 18:20 the fruit is associated with satiety, and is presumably "good." In every case, the tongue stands for speech. In this connection the ambiguity of 18:21 should be noted: "Death and life (are) in the power of the tongue; those who love it will eat its fruit." It seems to be a neutral saying; the tongue/speech is referred to in the second line, but it is not clear at first sight whether its fruit is death or life (see the *Comment* on this verse).

In a particular way, loquaciousness is to be avoided. The gift of speech has to be handled carefully. "In much talk, iniquity will not be lacking, but those who restrain their lips, sensible people" (10:19). One who just keeps on talking is likened to one who is making dangerous thrusts with a sword, 18:18. The mark of a fool is the failure to control speech: 18:2, 6, 7. This is at first sight a disarming observation, of only modest import. But the sages were on target. It is a very profound observation, constantly verified in experience. Therefore, whoever keeps a watch on words stays alive, 13:3; 21:23. The need to guard one's tongue is affirmed many times, e.g., 10:19b; 13:3a. However, the sages were not gullible. Silence is a sign of intelligence, 11:12b, of a person who has knowledge, 17:27. On the one hand, such an individual is presumed to be careful in thought and word. But on the other, it was also realized that silence could be a sign of a person who has nothing worthwhile to say. The wise are "clever" or "prudent," not in the sense of being crafty, but of appreciating the import of speech. They manifest true wisdom when they speak. In certain ways Qoheleth tilted with traditional wisdom, but he was at one with the sages in this respect: "Words from the mouth of the wise win favor, but the lips of a fool destroy him. The words of his mouth start with folly; his talk ends in dangerous nonsense—for the fool never stops talking" (Eccl 10:12–14a; cf. 5:1–6). One is tempted to say that speech is the all-important pivot in life. It can be the sign of evil, of everything that is contrary to wisdom. But were speech to be in every sense true, all else would fall into line. The sages were completely sensitive to the abuses to which the tongue was subject: lies, calumny, false witness, hypocrisy—there is hardly any wrongdoing in which the tongue was not involved; that is why they called for extreme care in speech. This emphasis is not to be dismissed as negative. It is aimed at producing speakers who know how to use their tongues wisely. As Wittgenstein put it, "Whereof one cannot speak, thereof one must be silent" (*Tractatus*, 7).

Excursus on Wealth and Poverty

Bibliography

Delkurt, H. *Ethische Einsichten.* 84–140. **Hausmann, J.** *Menschenbild.* 77–93, 331–44. **Murphy, R. E.** "Proverbs 22:1–9." *Int* 41 (1987) 398–402. **Pleins, J.** "Poverty in the Social World of the Wise." *JSOT* 37 (1987) 61–78. **Schwantes, M.** *Das Recht der Armen*. BET 4. Frankfurt: Lang, 1977. 260–279. **Van Leeuwen, R.** "Wealth and Poverty: System and Contradiction in Proverbs." *HS* 23 (1992) 25–36. **Washington, H. C.** *Wealth and Poverty in the Instruction of Amenemope and the Hebrew Proverbs*. SBLDS 142. Atlanta: Scholars, 1994. **Whybray, R. N.** *Wealth and Poverty in the Book of Proverbs*. JSOTSup 99. Sheffield: JSOT, 1990.

The purpose of this excursus is not to arrive at a harmonious view concerning riches/poverty in the book of Proverbs, but to put together the disparate opinions on the subject. One may hazard a guess that the abundant references to riches and poverty are due especially to the sapiential thesis that wisdom and prosperity go together. If that is so, how is one to understand the plight of the poor? It is suggestive that there are several words used in Proverbs to designate a poor person, where there is only one, עָשִׁיר, designating the rich. Can one simply say that the poor deserve their condition due to laziness, or because of their folly or wrongdoing? And how does all this shape up with "the rights of the poor" (Exod 23:6, 11) in the Law? As far as the book of Proverbs is concerned, there is no one answer to the problem of riches and poverty; several attitudes are portrayed and left in tension with each other. That is no surprise, due to the inherent limitations of a proverb, and also to the varied social settings that these sayings necessarily reflect. On the one hand, riches are a proper goal for the wise, and the poor may deserve their poverty, e.g., because of laziness. On the other, the questions arise: How did the rich acquire their possessions? (hastily? through bribery?), and how did the poor come to be afflicted? (through an inexplicable disaster? through oppression?). No ethical rules are laid out to cover all the situations, and there is no consistency in the observations, since different circumstances call for different observations. H. Delkurt (*Ethische Einsichten*, 84) counts more than fifty sayings that deal with the theme of rich and poor in Prov 10–29.

Poverty is taken for granted; the poor are a fact of life, and this is as great a problem for the ancients as for the moderns. It is significant that in Israelite wisdom literature they become a special object of care due to their relationship to the Lord. Such is the motive invoked in 14:31; 17:5; 22:2: both rich and poor were created by God, so that mockery of the poor is a blasphemy. It is misguided to take Proverbs to task for not decrying social abuses, such as one finds the prophets doing. That is not in the wisdom style; there is enough about bribery and other aspects of the rich/poor situation to lead to conversion those who will listen. An argument from silence is not an argument. There is a particularly striking expression in 19:17: "Showing kindness to the poor: making a loan to the Lord, and a reward will be given for it." G. von Rad (*Wisdom*, 94) remarks that among the instructions (the traditions of the past, present experiences) there are also "experiences which men have had directly of Yahweh, that he proves to be the defendant of those who are without legal rights, that he quite personally 'complements' a good deed with his blessing." The Lord will fight for the cause of the poor; in Prov 22:23 God is described as the גֹּאֵל, or champion, of the fatherless; cf. 23:11. In 14:21 one who despises a neighbor is called a sinner (חוֹטֵא), while a blessing comes to the one who is kind to the poor. Perhaps it is even more striking that curses are the lot of those who close their eyes to the poor (28:27).

The "better" saying provides a typically sapiential form for weighing the advantages of poverty and riches. The *Excursus on Retribution* points out how these sayings reversed the usual value of riches and poverty and thus pointed away from any deed-consequence theory. The classical expression is 16:8: Better is a little with justice than great income with injustice. This recognizes that life is not fair, that the just can be poor and the rich be unjust, contrary to a common idea held by perhaps the majority of the people. Was there a way out of this dilemma? There is the frequent hope that the future will change the situation. There is no future for the evil person, 11:28; 24:20, and "justice delivers from death," 10:2b; 11:4b. But mainly there is simply the dogged insistence that virtue will prevail, 28:6, 18. In such circumstances, the "better than" sayings are all the more remarkable; there are values that surpass riches (22:1; see the commentary on 22:1–9).

There is a hard-nosed realism about the advantages of wealth. It is probable that the sayings originated among the family circle, and not among an elite class. The vantage point of the proverbs, while they display a commendable caution, is that riches are indeed a good, a blessing from God, Prov 3:1–10; Ps 37. This is apparent in the realistic observations that in this world riches make a great difference. As it reads in 18:23, the poor man implores, but the rich get away with rough and harsh words. The rich rule over the poor, 22:7; they wield influence among the community. They acquire many "friends," in contrast to the poor (14:20; 19:4), who often enough will be looked down upon, 19:7. The poor have nothing to lose and nothing that others can profit from. Therefore, one must look hard at reality. Riches are a "strong city," a refuge for the rich man, whereas poverty spells ruin, 10:15. There is no moralizing about this fact of life. But that is not the last word. The "strong city" occurs in 18:11a, and here it receives an ironic twist in the parallel line: it is like a high wall, as the rich person imagines, or thinks. The point is made all the stronger by the previous verse, 18:10, where it is said that the "name of YHWH" (יהוה שֵׁם, the only time this phrase occurs in the book) is a strong tower for the just person. Thus a neat counterthrust is provided; the true refuge is the Lord. One cannot read 10:15 or 18:11a without considering the telling points that are made in 18:10 and 18:11b. In addition, 18:12 carries the warning that pride goes before a fall! It should not be inferred from these examples that there is after all a contextual approach to the interpretation of proverbs. Properly speaking, there is no context (outside of a common topic); there are only clashing viewpoints. If one considers that very many of these sayings were handed down by oral tradition, no true context is possible. And the collections are not dominated by interpretative concerns among the many sayings. Proverbs can be at war with each other. But they are at war precisely because they retain their own independence and meaning. Otherwise there would be no "war."

There is a further question: How was wealth obtained? Emphasis is placed upon human diligence, and also upon the reward of a virtuous life. The sages do not really examine the means, but they say enough to question the morality. If riches are acquired in haste, they seem to be suspect. They will not be appreciated, and thus they may be squandered, 13:11. Riches have a way of acquiring wings and flying off like birds, 23:4–5. Or at least there is the suspicion that some evildoing was involved: "but one in haste for riches does not go unpunished," 28:20b. And there is the verdict that "Treasures obtained by wickedness do not profit," 10:2a. Bribery was a fact of life. On the one hand, it was only too often successful. Prov 21:14 describes the effectiveness of a secret gift or bribe. But on the other hand, was every gift necessarily a bribe? There seems to be a fascination about the power of a gift in 17:8, and perhaps 18:6 refers to the benefits of well-placed gifts that were not, strictly speaking, outright bribes. In view of modern practice, we are inclined to suspect that kind of "lobbying," and perhaps the ancients did also.

Prayers are not cultivated by the collectors of Proverbs, but there is a remarkable prayer pertinent to the theme of wealth/poverty among the sayings of Agur (or of someone else? See the *Comment*). The individual asks for two things before death arrives—to be kept from falsehood and lying, and then: "Give me neither poverty nor riches; feed me with my ration of food, lest, being full, I become a renegade, and say: The Lord—who? Or lest, being poor, I steal, and blaspheme the name of my God," 10:8–9. This pious ideal is unique among the wisdom sayings. There is no effort here to evaluate riches or poverty, but the dangers attendant upon either extreme were known, and to be avoided. The caution typical of the Israelite sage comes to expression.

It is to be expected that the phenomenon of wealth/poverty would capture the attention of observers in many cultures before and after the heyday of Israelite wisdom. The study of H. C. Washington (*Wealth and Poverty*, 135–45, 185–204) recognizes the influence of international wisdom on the book of Proverbs, but he is properly cautious and proceeds soberly between the extreme positions that have been taken on this issue. For a discussion of the relationship between the Instruction of Amenemope and Prov 22:17–24:11 (23:13) see the commentary at 22:17 and also the *Excursus on the Book of Proverbs and Amenemope*. If the issues of wealth and poverty were not extensively treated throughout the book of Proverbs, Washington's arguments for the influence of the Egyptian work upon Israelite views might be more convincing. To take an example, Prov 22:28 (= 23:10) prohibits tampering with the landmark, the boundaries of a field that belong to a widow. This concern is also found in Amenemope (7:11–15; 8:9–12; *AEL*, 151–52). But it is hard to imagine that this concern about landmarks, which Washington notes is present in Hos 5:10; Deut 24:17 and Job 24:2, is to be considered as dependent upon the Egyptian work. It was very much a concern in Israel. Its appearance in this section of Proverbs, which indubitably betrays a dependence on Amenemope, is not unusual, for the idea itself was far from foreign to Israelite life. One may phrase the question from another angle: How much in Egyptian (and other) wisdom works did the Israelite writer(s) find in harmony with what they already knew, conclusions they had already arrived at from their national experience?

On the whole, the ambivalent attitude which Proverbs displays concerning riches is surprising. In Israelite society, as we have seen, wealth is a blessing. But Proverbs is very much concerned that riches be handled with caution, and that their inner effects on the possessor be considered. Nowhere else in the Bible do we find this investigation into the character of the one who is "blessed" with riches. The sages penetrated below the obvious level of pleasure or power. One cannot derive from the proverbs any neat laws about the ethics governing riches/poverty. R. Whybray (*Wealth and Poverty*, 60–61) lists nine conclusions that he draws from chaps. 10–22 and 25–29, and such a number indicates the qualifications necessary to present any general description of the position of the sages. Similarly, H. Delkurt (*Ethische Einsichten*, 129–40) is forced to go into details and so avoid the danger of generalizations. Many scholars have drawn conclusions about the social classes involved, both those who composed the proverbs, and those for whom the proverbs, in written form, were intended. For example, the socio-historical conditions that have been reconstructed point to the Persian period as the date of the final form of the book. Such conclusions have to be supported by other considerations; in themselves they are too hypothetical to win a consensus. But there can be no doubt about the wealth of observations and their wide-ranging scope. What a mistake it is to deem the sages simplistic!

Excursus on Retribution

Bibliography

Boström, L. *The God of the Sages.* CBOT 29. Stockholm: Almquist & Wiksell, 1990. 90–140. **Campbell, A. F.** *The Study Companion to Old Testament Literature.* Wilmington: Glazier, 1989. 414–36. **Fox, M. V.** "World Order and Ma'at: A Crooked Parallel." *JANESCU* 23 (1995) 37–48. **Gladson, J.** *Retributive Paradoxes in Proverbs 10–29.* Ann Arbor, MI: University Microfilms International, no. 7909275. **Hausmann, J.** *Menschenbild.* 37–66. **Huwiler, E.** *Control of Reality in Israelite Wisdom.* Duke University dissertation, 1988. **Janowski, B.** "Die Tat kehrt zum Täter zurück. Offene Frage im Umkreis des 'Tun-Ergehen-Zusammenhangs.'" *ZTK* 91 (1994) 247–71. **Koch, K.** "Gibt es ein Vergeltungsdogma im Alten Testament?" *ZTK* 51 (1955) 1–42 (ET in *Theodicy in the Old Testament.* Ed. J. L. Crenshaw. Philadelphia: Fortress, 1983. 57–87). **Murphy, R. E.** *The Tree of Life.* 2nd rev. ed. Grand Rapids, MI: Eerdmans, 1996. 111–31, 212, 224. **Scoralick, R.** *Einzelspruch und Sammlung.* 27–43, 62–75. **Skladny, U.** "Der Gerechte—der Frevler." In *Die ältesten Spruchsammlungen in Israel.* Göttingen: Vandenhoeck & Ruprecht, 1962. 7–13. **Towner, S.** "The Renewed Authority of Old Testament Wisdom for Contemporary Faith." In *Canon and Authority.* Ed. G. W. Coats et al. Philadelphia: Fortress, 1977. 132–47. **Van Leeuwen, R.** "Wealth and Poverty: System and Contradiction in Proverbs." *HS* 33 (1992) 25–36.

Retribution, or the treatment of saint and sinner by the Lord, is a complicated issue in the Bible. Too glibly do we mortals judge Divinity by our standards of justice, and even try vigorously to enforce these, and to question God when they are not observed. The fact of the matter is that there is no uniform and consistent biblical doctrine on this topic. It is commonly said that God rewards the good and punishes the evil, but such a global statement says more about us than it does about God. The mystery of divine retribution stands beyond all human formulation, even that of Israel.

Within the Old Testament itself there are conflicting treatments of the subject, and a simple sketch of historical development is not possible. One can recall here the most venerable and well-remembered passages. The most imposing, and most often quoted, is Exod 34:6–7, where the Lord passes before Moses and proclaims the holy Name: "a God compassionate and gracious, slow to anger, abounding in kindness and faithfulness, extending kindness to the thousandth generation, forgiving iniquity, transgression, and sin; yet he does not remit all punishment, but visits the iniquity of parents upon children and children's children, upon the third and fourth generation" (NJV). But one reads in Ps 103:8–10: "The Lord is compassionate and gracious, slow to anger, abounding in steadfast love. He will not contend forever, or nurse His anger for all time. He has not dealt with us according to our sins, nor has He requited us according to our iniquities" (NJV). While the psalm reflects a common motif, moving the Lord to pity, it nevertheless carries with it a different evaluation of the Exodus statement.

One of the central difficulties is the role of collective retribution. This was inherent in the culture of Israel, yet it also came to be felt as a problem. In Genesis there is that pathetic cry of Abraham, "Will you indeed sweep away the righteous with the wicked?" (18:23). There is also the well-known saying that the parents eat the sour grapes, but it is the children's teeth that are set on edge (Ezek 18:2). This does not mean that individual responsibility was dismissed. Justice seemed to be operative on both the individual and collective level. But by that very fact, it remained a difficult thing to understand. The collective guilt was magnified with the downfall of Jerusalem and the Exile, and it never really disappeared. It was accepted without too much objection. Habakkuk stands out as one who is questioning the way divine justice seems to be operating with the people. More pointedly, Ps 89 questions the promise to David—a promise that was given to the dynasty, and therefore collective.

On the national scale, divine retribution is never posed with the same acuity and anguish as it is on the individual level. And it is precisely here that the wisdom literature, and one should also include the Psalms, plays a large role. This is due to the books of Job and Qoheleth, in particular. What about the book of Proverbs? This is usually characterized as a work of optimism, of serenity, almost, of unreality. It seems utterly unaware of the inequities in life so vividly portrayed in the other two wisdom books. That is a superficial view. This excursus aims not at "defending" the views enunciated in the book, but at understanding them in a sympathetic manner. A recognition of their complexity is the desideratum.

Before examining the book itself, it is advisable to examine a very common interpretation of biblical retribution known as the *Tat-Ergehen Zusammenhang*, or deed-consequence nexus, first established by Klaus Koch and widely adopted, especially among European scholars. This view holds for a mechanical association between a good action (some insist on attitude or *Haltung*) and its good result, and between a bad action, or moral attitude, and its bad result. "As you sow, so you reap." Every act has built-in consequences for the actor. This is the "order" of things set up by God, who in the manner of a "midwife," to use the terminology of K. Koch, watches over this divinely established connection. In basic outline, this mentality seems to be reflected at several places in the Bible itself; it is a viewpoint of ancient Israel. The parade example is that of a person who digs a pit for another to fall into, but instead falls into it himself. A sort of poetic justice is at work: the quality of the action is met by a corresponding effect; cf. Ps 7:16–17; Prov 26:27; 28:10, etc. There seems to be no reason to deny this is an aspect of Israelite mentality with regard to both reward and punishment. However, equally and probably more frequently affirmed is the direct agency or causality of God, causing good as well as evil. This is expressed in a striking manner in such statements as Isa 45:7 and Amos 3:2, 6. It is hard to determine how seriously the ancients understood the working of deed-consequence. Was it merely an expectation, a hope? Was this the regularity that was supposed to work in view of the common belief in justice, and in a just God? How many holes did one have to dig for others before falling in oneself? It is a beautiful idea that evil corrupts, that good is somehow diffusive of itself. But does this reconstruction of Hebrew mentality square with the reality or is it itself askew? If events were frequently occurring contrary to this alleged order, what credence was given to it? Did people believe in an intermediate order supervised by the Lord, who was, as it were, an absentee landlord? Did the Lord have the freedom for personal intervention? Perhaps the retribution for the evil deed can be likened to the Shakespearean phrase "hoist with one's own petard." It is appropriate: evil begets corruption; this is the kind of retaliation that one would like to see at work. But this is ultimately inadequate because it is an incomplete understanding of biblical justice.

In this connection, it is quite common to speak of "order" intrinsic to the operations in this world, as though the object of the sages was to find an order that was established in nature and in human conduct. If we consider just a few aspects of wisdom teaching, there does not seem to be room for "order." The very fact that the wise person is constantly subject to reprimand, to discipline, to "hearing," and ultimately to a kind of conversion suggests an ongoing journey, and not the discovery of an order that simplified life. The wise are not seen as "safe"; they must always be open to correction. The exhortatory sayings in Prov 9:8–9 indicate movement, not a position or order that one can rest in: "Share with the wise and they become wiser; teach the just and they go on learning." There was always the reminder that the human heart could make plans, but the Lord directs the steps, Prov 16:9. "Order" cannot adequately explain such insights as "One who disregards a fault, one who seeks friendship" (Prov 17:9a). Love and mercy (10:12; 16:6) cannot be regulated. And who is bold enough to have trust (16:20; cf. Ps 118:8)?

The problem, as far as the Old Testament is concerned, is aggravated in that K. Koch's view has been interpreted as a blind, unyielding law. More importantly, it has been taken up as a kind of mechanism that was at the heart of the wisdom movement. According to the late H. D. Preuss (*Einführung*, 124, 137), this postulated world order was the basic dogma of wisdom. When it broke down, as seen in Job and Qoheleth, there was the famous "crisis" of wisdom that has attracted so much attention in scholarly writings. This view is a serious mistake because it has led in effect to the dismissal of wisdom (Preuss would have excluded wisdom from the pulpit). The system, as reconstructed, turned out to be stronger than God—no wonder it had to go! But this is shadow boxing or, at best, defeating a straw man. The historical development of the wisdom movement is not that simple. The authors of the books of Job and Ecclesiastes differ from the more optimistic views of traditional wisdom, but they stay in dialogue with it. The book of Proverbs was never rejected, for it was not without recognizing the limitations of wisdom. The book of Sirach, which reflects a great deal of the views of the earlier sages, continues in the traditional vein. There was no "scandal" taken at the books of Job and Ecclesiastes, or at the alleged "failure," which remains even to this day; who can make sense of divine justice?

Recent scholars (among others, Boström, Fox, Van Leeuwen, Janowski; see the view of J. Hausmann indicated in the *Explanation* of chap. 25) have taken issue with this mechanical view of retribution, for several reasons in addition to those just mentioned. The critique of R. Van Leeuwen (*HS* 33 [1992]) is particularly keen. It approaches the theory from the point of view of sayings about riches and poverty. It would appear that wealth is better than poverty as is many times affirmed, and the virtue of diligence is accordingly highlighted; this is the way to success (Prov 10:4–5). Yet, as Van Leeuwen affirms, "it is mistaken to apply the term 'dogmatism' to Proverbs or a class of sayings within the book . . . Proverbs are inherently *partial utterances*" (p. 29). Therefore one must attend to the sayings which affirm that fools de facto do succeed (19:10a), and the wicked do have treasures (10:2). There are reversals of form, especially in the "better than" sayings (e.g., poverty with justice better than wealth with wickedness). The sages do look to a reversal of fortunes. "The affirmation that in the future justice will be done seems to me a hallmark of Yahwistic faith, a hope in that which is yet invisible and intangible. It is belief in something that experience does not verify" (p. 34). The sages were far from naive about reality, but they were people of faith. Or in the words of M. Fox, the sayings that give evidence of deed and consequence "are just assertions of predictability" (*JANESCU* 23 [1995] 48). Like all things predictable, events can turn out differently.

We may conclude that the optimism of traditional wisdom reflects the faith of those who contributed to it. The sages were not blind, but the limitations and boundaries of experience could be transcended by faith. Life was not a matter of mathematical certainty. Their optimism is all the more remarkable for having come down relatively unscathed. The book of Proverbs was given its final form in the postexilic period, when one might not be expected to entertain such hope after the catastrophic events of 587 B.C. Certainly Qoheleth was defeated by the vagaries of retribution; his quest for wisdom, he tells us, did not succeed (Eccl 7:23). He could not make sense of the "work of God" (Eccl 3:11; 7:13; 8:17). But this did not destroy his faith. Qoheleth accepted God on God's mysterious terms. Neither did the wisdom tradition disappear. It was able to assert itself with the preservation of the old and new in Proverbs and find a stout echo of approval in the wisdom of Ben Sira. We may conclude then that this reconstruction of deed-consequence did not play the *critical* role envisioned for it by many scholars, and more importantly, that the book of Proverbs cannot be reduced to the ashes of mechanistic retribution, as implied by the evaluation of H. D. Preuss.

In a sense, this treatment of the deed-consequence theory is a distraction. The reconstruction of deed-consequence can be inferred from the Bible (from the prophets as well; cf. A. Campbell, *The Study Companion*, 427–36). However, it calls attention away from a more fundamental question about the just and the wicked (צדיק/רשע) that is certainly one of the prime concerns of Proverbs and other books, especially the Psalms. It will be recalled that we presuppose, with the majority of scholars, that chaps. 1–9 are probably postexilic, and that chaps. 10–29 are primarily preexilic. What is striking is the preponderance of sayings about the just/wicked in chaps. 10–29. It should be noticed that space does not allow an investigation of the significance of the difference between singular and plural forms of these terms. Scoralick (*Einzelspruch*, 63–64) points out that "just" is usually used in the singular, in contrast to "wicked" in the plural. She presents (pp. 63–65) the statistics for chaps. 10–22: "just" forty-nine times, and "wicked" fifty-four times. In chaps. 10–15 there is a concentration of these terms, each (!) appearing thirty-nine times; allowing for some problems, the numbers for the entire book appear to be sixty-six and seventy-eight, respectively. Perhaps most significant is the contrast between chaps. 10–12 (ninety-one sayings), and chaps. 13–15 (ninety-three sayings): chaps. 10–12 have almost three times the number of references to the just, and more than half the references to the wicked.

This unusual concentration calls for some comment. (1) Is it possibly due to the frequently affirmed equation of just = wise, wicked = fool? One can see such an equation in Prov 10:16–17,

The wage of the righteous leads to life,
  the gain of the wicked to sin.
Whoever heeds instruction is on the path to life,
  but one who rejects a rebuke goes astray. (NRSV)

Here the just (v 16) is the one who heeds instruction (v 17), that is, the wise one. The wicked (v 16) rejects a rebuke (v 17), by definition, therefore, a fool. There are also similar identifications available elsewhere (cf. 15:2 with 15:28). On the whole, Scoralick is opposed to the equation as being too glib, and hence inaccurate. From a semantic point of view, there is not strong evidence for the equation. But one must also realize that "just" is equivalently expressed by such synonyms as "upright" (יָשָׁר) and "integrity" (תָּם).

(2) Can the equation be affirmed by reason of the general moral teaching of the book in which wise and righteous conduct is contrasted with foolish and destructive conduct? I think so, even if a rigid semantic equivalence is not to be found. The bunching together of such "virtuous" sayings with "wisdom" sayings is surely deliberate. One should recall the opening preface (Prov 1:3); this wisdom book is concerned with "justice and judgment and right." Although many of the sayings do not have an obvious and immediate moral reference, moral concerns are uppermost.

It is important to recognize that "wisdom" insights, even though our culture might label many of them as profane, are distinctly moral in view of the goal that the wisdom teachers were trying to achieve. This goal was not foreign to those who wished to inculcate morality and the ideals of the covenant stipulations. The "fear of the Lord" is a steady compass for moral actions. Some may judge that the teachings are not always lofty ideals. Thus one is urged to be just/wise in order to live longer, to prosper, to succeed in coping with life, e.g., Prov 3:1–4. The motivation may not be as "pure" as some wish, but neither is it simply to be neglected, for it also involved a relationship to the Lord.

C. Westermann (*Roots of Wisdom,* 75–84) regards the just/wicked proverbs as artificial, schematic constructions. By his count there are 117 such sayings, the largest "group" in the book of Proverbs. They are not true wisdom sayings because they do not arise from an experience or observation. In fact, they can be all lumped together as so many variations on the one theme of the just and the wicked. While one can admire their "inventiveness," and be reminded of the style of Ps 119, one must recognize that they have a *literary,* as opposed to an oral, origin. Westermann's narrow viewpoint is supported only by his understanding of the primacy of oral sayings. There *is* a difference between the style of the just/wicked proverbs and the colorful sayings that reflect experience, but this should not dictate a definition of wisdom, or a division into experiential and didactic in which didactic is simply dismissed. One should beware of limiting wisdom to the world of oral and experiential sayings. The experiential can become didactic, and it does so by its very context of the traditional teaching. The wisdom literature is also concerned about the moral dimensions of the actions of the "fool." The plethora of just/wicked sayings throughout the book, but especially in chaps. 10–15, are not to be dismissed as a kind of secondhand wisdom. How did they come to be handed down, mixed with the experiential observations, unless they were seen in some kind of harmony with those wisdom values? The present text, with its mixture of oral and written proverbs, of sayings about the wise and the just, has to be explained as a whole.

J. Hausmann (*Menschenbild,* 65) has noted that the just/wicked contrast is scarcely found in Egyptian wisdom. Only in the late period, the period of Papyrus Insinger, is there something similar. M. Lichtheim comments: "In the teaching of P. Insinger morality and piety have been completely fused and they are exemplified in the character of the 'wise man' who is capable of enduring reversals of fortune and remains confident of vindication. His counterpart is the 'fool' or 'impious man' whose disregard of the divine commands makes him commit crimes which, inevitably, result in his punishment" (*AEL,* 3:185).

Some scholars remain convinced that the views of the sages on retribution, as expressed in the book of Proverbs, are too optimistic and simplistic. We have indicated above that such an interpretation does not adequately weigh the complexity of the sayings or the mentality of the sages. One final remark should be added here. Perhaps the rigidity of the friends of Job is partially to blame for this; they argued backward—from suffering to the existence of sin in the one who suffers. At the same time it should be evident that it was a sage who is responsible for the book of Job, a work that embraces a wide range of views concerning retribution: simple acceptance of whatever comes from the hand of God, the legitimacy of complaining to God (and hence the need for integrity), the inadequacy of arguing from suffering to sin as its "cause," the mystery of the Lord and the divine governance of creation, and even, "where is wisdom to be found?" (Job 28:12, 20). There is no "answer" to the question, no "solution" to the suffering of the just person. Similarly, Qoheleth admitted that he could not understand the "work of God" (Eccl 3:11; 7:13; 8:17). It is by contrast with these bold thinkers that the achievement of the earlier sages is accused of being simplistic. That this one-sided judgment is not the final one is evidenced by the wisdom of Sirach. He too struggles with the problem of theodicy as he understands it in wisdom terms, but he is unable to solve it. The view arrived at in the Wisdom of Solomon is not a solution. He does say that justice is undying or immortal (Wis 1:15). This plays Prov 10:2 (cf. 11:4) in a higher key, but it is still not a solution. Divine justice, and hence, human suffering, remains a mystery, and the struggling of the sages must be appreciated in that light.

Excursus on Theology

Bibliography

Albertz. R. *A History of Israelite Religion in the Old Testament Period.* OTL. Louisville: Westminster, 1994–95. 2 vols. **Barr, J.** *Biblical Faith and Natural Theology.* Oxford: Clarendon, 1993. **Brown, W. P.** *Character in Crisis.* Grand Rapids, MI: Eerdmans, 1966. **Clements, R. E.** *Wisdom in Theology.* Grand Rapids, MI: Eerdmans, 1992. **Collins, J. J.** "Proverbial Wisdom and the Yahwist Vision." In *Gnomic Wisdom.* Ed. J. D. Crossan. Chico: Scholars Press, 1980. 1–17. **Ernst, A. B.** *Weisheitliche Kultkritik: Zu Theologie und Ethik der Sprüchebuchs und der Prophetie des 8 Jahrhunderts.* BThSt 23. Neukirchen: Neukirchener, 1994. **Gese, H.** "Wisdom, Son of Man, and the Origins of Christology: The Consistent Development of Biblical Theology." *HBT* 3 (1981) 23–57. **Hausmann, J.** " 'Weisheit' im Kontext alttestamentlicher Theologie." In *Weisheit ausserhalb der kanonischen Weisheitsschriften.* Ed. B. Janowski. Gütersloh:

Gütersloher Verl.-Haus, 1996. 9–19. **Joncheray, J.** "Actualité de la Sagesse." In *La sagesse biblique*. LD 160. 503–17. **Murphy, R. E.** "Proverbs and Theological Exegesis." In *The Hermeneutical Quest*. FS J. L. Mays, ed. D. G. Miller. Allison Park, PA: Pickwick, 1986. 87–95. ———. "Wisdom and Yahwism Revisited." In FS J. Crenshaw, ed. D. Penchansky. Winona Lake, IN: Eisenbrauns, forthcoming. ———. "Wisdom Literature and Theology." In *The Tree of Life*. 2nd rev. ed. Grand Rapids: Eerdmans, 1996. 111–31, 223–27. **Perdue, L.** *Wisdom and Cult*. SBLDS 30. Missoula, MT: Scholars Press, 1977. **Preuss, H. D.** *Theologie des Alten Testaments*. 2 vols. Stuttgart: Kohlhammer, 1991. ET: *Old Testament Theology*. 2 vols. OTL. Louisville: Westminster/John Knox, 1995–96. **Reventlow, H. G.** *Problems in Old Testament Theology in the Twentieth Century*. Philadelphia: Fortress, 1985. **Westermann, C.** "Grenzen der Weisheit" and "Weisheit und Theologie." In *Das mündliche Wort*. AzT 82. Stuttgart: Calwer, 1996. 140–59, 160–75. **Whybray, R. N.** "Yahweh-sayings and their Contexts in Proverbs, 10,1–22,16." In *La Sagesse de l'Ancien Testament*. Ed. M. Gilbert. BETL 51. Leuven: University Press, 1979. 153–65. ———. "Ideas and Theology." In *The Book of Proverbs*. HIBS 1. Leiden: Brill, 1995. 112–49. **Zimmerli, W.** "The Place and the Limit of the Wisdom in the Framework of Old Testament Theology." *SJT* 17 (1964) 146–58, reprinted in *Studies in Ancient Israelite Wisdom*. Ed. J. L. Crenshaw. New York: Ktav, 1976. 314–26.

At best, biblical theology can be only selective. There is no all-comprehensive formula or umbrella that can embrace the biblical data about God and human beings. Just the relationship between the Testaments alone is a severe problem. No attempt to smooth over the differences between the Testaments by some overarching formula (e.g., promise-fulfillment) has been successful, as an abundance of studies have proved. Moreover, the Old Testament itself is such a varied composite of writings scattered over centuries and provoked by changing circumstances. It is unreasonable to expect a twentieth-century scholar to make a true synthesis of doctrine or beliefs of ancient Israel, when the Israelites did not do it for themselves. Or did they do that? Yes, they did, but in restricted ways. There is a kind of Torah theology that can more or less characterize the Pentateuch. The work of the Chronicler (if one can speak of an individual) is a theological synthesis of Israel's history for his day. The so-called Deuteronomistic History (from Joshua to Kings) is a modern reconstructed theological synthesis of Israel's history. In other words, what we have within the Old Testament are several *theologies*, written by Israelites, which cannot be adequately presented by the well-meant and truly valuable volumes of our day that attempt to synthesize what is called Old Testament theology.

Various scholars have organized their presentation of biblical theology around particular emphases. Well known are the attempts in favor of covenant (W. Eichrodt), or God's redemptive action in history (G. E. Wright), or "righteousness" (R. Knierim), or "canonical shape" (B. S. Childs). Hence it is not surprising to see the multiplicity of definitions and methodologies employed in modern studies. One result has been the troubling issue of the validity of biblical theology. How does it differ from a history-of-religions approach to the Bible? Can theology be separated, and should it be separated from the worldview of ancient Israel? It is not easy to draw the line in these matters. The recent study of Rainer Albertz argues vigorously that *Religionsgeschichte* is the "more meaningful comprehensive Old Testament discipline," as opposed to Old Testament theology (*A History*, 1:16–17). But one wonders if sociology is not replacing theology in this instance. As far as Old Testament wisdom is concerned, the treatment of it has ranged from benign neglect to opposition. Recently the question has been raised whether this is a suitable area for theological exploration (H. D. Preuss, *Einführung*, passim). More substantially, H. G. Reventlow looked to the future: "The incorporation of wisdom into Old Testament theology remains a still unresolved task for the future to deal with" (*Problems,* 184). The split between Yahwism and Wisdom is still cultivated in many quarters. Can one then expect that anything of a theological nature is to be found in so modest a book as Proverbs?

In the popular "biblical theology" movement of the middle of the nineteenth century, so much emphasis was placed on salvation history as the essence of the Old Testament that scholars were embarrassed by the wisdom literature; they did not know what to do with it. There were attempts to make it "respectable" by inserting it into the Torah. Thus wisdom theology was seen in the light of creation theology (W. Zimmerli) and understood as an extension of the command to humans in Gen 1:28 to fill the earth and have dominion over it. In a similar way, C. Westermann has attached wisdom to the divine blessing which figures so largely in the opening pages of Genesis (*Das mündliche Wort,* 140, 161–62). Without detailing just how the two were to be united, G. von Rad concluded that "the wisdom practised in Israel was a response made by a Yahwism confronted with specific experiences of the world" (*Wisdom,* 307). This solution seems to imply that Yahwism and wisdom, while theoretically and academically separable, are not to be separated in fact. The worshipers of YHWH counted the wise among them, and the wise faced the realities of experience from the point of view of the Yahwist faith that was theirs. Daily experiences were also the arena where Israel met the Lord. As von Rad put it, "the experiences of the world were for her [Israel] always divine experiences as well, and the experiences of God were for her experiences of the world" (*Wisdom,* 62). He is quite emphatic on this point (p. 61): "The conclusion has, for example, been drawn that this old proverbial wisdom was still scarcely touched by Yahwism, and that it was still only at the very beginning of a process of interpretation by Yahwism. Against this, it can be categorically stated that for Israel there was only one world of experience and that this was apperceived by means of a perceptive apparatus in which rational and religious perceptions were not differentiated. Nor was this any different in the case of the prophets."

Lurking at the corners of this problem of Yahwism and wisdom is the issue of revelation. J. Barr has raised it in connection with the discussion of the existence of examples of "natural theology" in the Bible. He poses the question, "If one believes that God was revealing himself in his creation and continues to do so, why is that 'natural' theology and not 'revealed'? . . . If one believes that God was revealing himself in ancient Israel, why is this not 'natural'? Perhaps all theology is both 'natural' and 'revealed'?" These are more than impish questions. Traditional Christian theology has consistently distinguished between natural theology (unrevealed or, if revealed in the Bible, "natural" because it does not deal with supernatural mysteries, e.g., the Trinity) and supernatural theology (revealed, and beyond human ken). This academic distinction has its truth and its usefulness, but it remains theoretical. Does it fit the concrete historical circumstances in which the revelation of the God of the Bible has taken place? A study of creation (not the origins of the world, but continuous creation) and of day-to-day living is a study of the de facto supernatural order in which all human beings live. O. H. Steck has described this correctly: "To be exposed to Yahweh in absolutely everything, to encounter him, to find meaningful existence solely in orientation toward him, in what he gives and what he takes away, in his reliably revealed activity and in the activity that is mysteriously unexplorable—this was the determining background against which Israel perceived the natural world and environment, perceived it in experience, knowledge, and formative activity" (*World and Environment*, BES [Nashville: Abingdon, 1980] 167–68). Part of this "natural world" is the experience with one's neighbors, as well as with events of nature, and the sages tried to frame this in their teaching. This has as much right to be regarded as revealing the divine, as the memory of Sinai has.

In other words, there is another model, biblical at that, for understanding divine revelation apart from the historical mode (in which salvation history also retains its validity). This is exemplified by biblical wisdom, in which a dialogue with Divinity takes place essentially through human experience and creation. The wisdom experience is an appropriation of the lessons that the Israelites drew from day-to-day living, from the realm of personal intercourse and the surprises of creation. The dialogue with the environment was also a dialogue with the God who was worshiped as creator and savior. This is the basis for a salvific faith. Such an understanding of biblical wisdom is important for nonbiblical religions, for trillions who have never heard of the name YHWH or Christ. It makes possible a faith response that is not explicitly related or limited to a particular mode, history, for the revelation of God. Israel learned of the Lord through the Exodus and the ensuing historical events, but also through experience and creation.

I have described the wisdom experience in the following words: "the experience which generated the insights into the world and human beings (from which in the Israelite view God is never absent), the משלים that resulted from the outlay of energy and enterprise with which Israel grappled with the mysteries of creation and daily existence. The wisdom experience consists in the encounter, which is encoded in the proverbs. Both sayings and admonitions reflect the experience and the attempt to communicate it. The experience itself is multifaceted. It can begin, as Aristotle (*Metaphysics*, I:ii, 9) remarked about philosophy, in wonder (θαυμάζειν). Thus an encounter with the mystery of the other in sexual attraction leads to a comparison with other 'ways' (דרך) in the world, such as the way of an eagle in the air (Prov 30:18–20). On the other hand, an event as modest as the summer storing of food by ants has something to say about wisdom and smallness. The emotional levels of human reactions do not go unnoticed. They are reflected in normal conditions (the effect of joy upon a person, Prov 13:12; 14:10; 17:22) as well as in conflicting feelings (sadness in laughter, Prov 14:13). An important emphasis is self-control, most sharply expressed in the many sayings relative to speech. If one can control this aspect of conduct, then the possibility of 'hearing,' or docility, presents itself" (R. E. Murphy, "Proverbs and Theological Exegesis," 89). It is appropriate to recall the claim of wisdom not merely to be at the side of God before creation, but to be "delight," and that her delights were to be with human beings, Prov 8:30–31. There is surely more than one way of utilizing the wisdom literature in the service of theology (see the *Excursus on Woman Wisdom and Woman Folly*). When one looks at the history of interpretation of Proverbs, it appears that only Prov 8:22–31 was appropriated by Christian theology. Much more remains to be done.

The foregoing remarks are particularly appropriate in view of the discussion of Yahwism and Wisdom in the last several decades (cf. R. Murphy, "Wisdom and Yahwism Revisited"). The mere distinction of these two areas is often taken as a sign that they are not compatible, and it frequently leads to the dismissal of wisdom as theologically irrelevant. The discussion has been warped by various presuppositions. Among them is the assumption that Yahwism, defined in terms of the Exodus, Sinai, Zion, and Davidic traditions, is orthodox belief. When this measuring rod is used, wisdom is in an adversarial position, and indeed seems "foreign." The relationship is, moreover, an academic, not a real one. I am tempted simply to turn the picture around and view wisdom as a basic attitude toward God and the world in which the people of Israel lived, and to it "Yahwism" has been added (and rightfully so). In this perspective, the bias disappears, and creator and deliverer are seen as one. In a sense the book of Job can be taken as an example of such union. Although the book does not feature any particular basic tenets of Yahwism as popularly understood (Exodus, Sinai, etc.), the God of Job is not an *Urhebergott*, or god of origins. He is not a stranger to the reader, even if he is a mystery; it is YHWH (יהוה) who appears in the whirlwind to argue with Job. Despite the non-Israelite identity of the main characters, Job and the three friends, the book is obviously written from an Israelite point of view, and it was received without any hesitation as being part of the broader revelation to the people of God. This is true also of Qoheleth, despite the claim of some that the God of Qoheleth is not the God of the patriarchs. Theological compartmentalization cannot be allowed to define living faith.

The most obvious area in which one might expect a theological contribution from Old Testament wisdom, and from Proverbs in particular, is that of ethics. The topics of several of our excursuses suggest fields for a varied theological exploration: fear of the Lord; a biblical attitude towards the created world; an evaluation of riches and poverty. The problem of methodology (as always, it seems) is particularly difficult. How does one best utilize a book of such distinctive characteristics? Can disparate sayings yield a satisfying conclusion? One has to deal with proverbs that by their very nature are incomplete views of reality, that are destined to be shaded and even contradicted by opposing proverbs. Perhaps the most difficult question is that of authority. The tendency is to dismiss the authority of Proverbs and the sages. This tendency is all the more strengthened by contrast with the authority of the Decalogue or the authority of a prophet speaking in the name of the Lord and denouncing some wrongdoing. But this manner of comparison is somewhat simplistic; the reality is more complicated. The description of the "just" and the "wicked" in Proverbs shares authority with the description of the same characters in Ps 1, as one can see from their respective "ways" in Ps 1:6. In Ps 15:2, it is the one who walks in integrity and does justice that will dwell in the Lord's tent. What is the authority of a psalm? Or even, the authority of a proverbial saying? One can point to other supposedly "more authoritative" books of the Bible for examples similar to the above.

Perhaps one can describe the situation this way: the book of Proverbs possesses the authority of biblical insights that those who honor the Bible as a foundational document can appropriate and utilize. The title of the work of H. Delkurt (*Ethische Einsichten in der alttestamentlichen Spruchweisheit*, BTS 21 [Neukirchen: Neukirchener, 1993]) is along that line. The title is modest: "ethical insights." First of all, he establishes that the "ethical" teaching of Proverbs is not in conflict with the teaching of the prophets. He goes on to summarize his treatment of parents and children, man and woman, diligence and laziness, poverty and riches in eight points, thus covering an area of practical ethical concerns that interlock with, but also expand, the Decalogue. Most importantly he successfully defends wisdom teaching against the charges of utilitarianism or eudaimonism, and recognizes that the trust of the wisdom teachers is in YHWH (יהוה), and not in any infallible order of deed-consequence. The theological insights in the wisdom tradition seem so modest as to be negligible, but that is not so. Here one may instance the many sayings that deal with the family and the teaching of children. This perspective is most marked in chaps. 1–9, but it is also sounded frequently in the later sayings: 10:1; 15:5, 20; 17:23, 25. Discipline, including corporal punishment, was a feature of raising children (13:14; 19:18; cf. 22:6). What is important for the modern reader is the concern manifested in the raising of children. There is no single command: have proper care for children. Instead, that is the brunt of *many* sayings. All things considered, Delkurt has provided a sound biblical basis for the "ethical insights" that are presented in the book of Proverbs.

Wisdom and cult are terms that sum up two important streams of biblical tradition. One might think there would be little occasion for overlap. But there are some important wisdom sayings that are indeed pertinent to cult, and even of a critical nature. Usually these have been considered as influenced by prophetic doctrine. W. McKane (see pp. 10–22 of his commentary) and, to a certain extent, R. Whybray ("Yahweh-sayings," 153–65) have fitted this phenomenon into their views on the theological development from profane to religious wisdom. Leo Perdue (*Wisdom and Cult*, 155–62, 265) located the compatibility of wisdom and cult in their sharing in a common notion of world order. Recently A. B. Ernst (*Weisheitliche Kultkritik*) has argued that the prophets of the eighth century (Amos and Hosea, and he includes Isaiah) took up insights from the older wisdom tradition. It is true; the prophets condemn abuse, as is made clear in Amos 5:21–17; 4:4–5; 5:4–7, 10; Hos 6:6; Isa 1:10–17. Such declarations serve to justify the coming intervention of God. They are not so much urging conversion as they are announcing the reason for the disaster to come. In what respect were they influenced by the wisdom tradition? Ernst analyzes certain key texts: Prov 15:8, 29; 17:1; 21:3, 27; 28:9. In a general way they can be described as indicating the ethos or inner attitude that should govern one's relationship to God. According to 15:8 efficacious sacrifice and prayer derive from integrity of character. If the זבח, "sacrifice," in the "better" saying of 17:1 is cultic, it has little worth when peace is lacking. The famous dictum of 1 Sam 15:22 is also found substantially in Prov 21:3 to the effect that obedience (righteousness) is better than sacrifice. Prov 21:27 is a strong condemnation of the זבח, "sacrifice," of the wicked; it is abomination, i.e., to the Lord. Finally, prayer itself is an "abomination" when one refuses to listen to the "law" (28:9), however the word torah is to be interpreted; see the *Comment* on this verse.

As a whole these texts, whose origin in the preexilic period is not to be denied, bear on a fundamental disposition that is a necessary prerequisite for sincerity in worship, and which must govern any material expression of honor for the divinity. They seem to be clear presuppositions to the traditional prophetic denunciation of formalism in worship. Their "origins" cannot be traced, but it can be surmised that they grew out of or along with convictions like those in Ps 51:18–19—a basic honesty rooted in fear of the Lord. When one compares the ethical attitudes demanded by the sages with the "gate liturgies" in Pss 15 and 24, it is clear that these liturgies lay down specific ideals for approaching God. But wisdom stresses the inner attitude.

Ernst's claim perhaps cannot be proved, but his inferences are not at all exaggerated; they deserve a hearing that in the past has not been granted to the views in Proverbs. This is not the place to defend or dispute his analysis of the passages from the prophetical books. The point here is to highlight the views of the sages on cultic worship. He has provided the wisdom background that needs to be supplied to fill out the prophetic complaints. He summarizes thus: "As Israel did not follow the wisdom admonition to seek the Lord in the right way, but threw out judgment and justice, so also the promise of life connected with seeking after the Lord was bound up or even changed to a proclamation of the destruction of holy places" (pp. 151–52).

The approach of W. P. Brown (*Character in Crisis*) is another successful investigation of the ethical thrust of the book. His perspective includes the books of Job and Qoheleth as well, and he sketches a journey through these wisdom books. He does not seek out rules. His object is more subtle and in conformity with the spirit of Proverbs. He is concerned with "moral formation." He interprets Prov 1–9 as laying out a program, the "way" of wisdom. In a sense it is a narrative that profiles the journey through life, with its ideals and its dangers, that a youth is to pursue. Righteousness, justice, and equity (Prov 1:3b; cf. 2:9), developed in the first nine chapters, "guide the reader in the act of reading, listening, and appropriating the myriad of proverbial sayings that begin in ch. 10" (p. 45). The youth who receives instruction hears competing voices in the introductory chapters, which even end with the siren song of Folly in 9:13–18. That is the way life is; one must expect to encounter folly. The rest of the book calls attention to the various ways that a youth can become a responsible and virtuous human being. Finally there is a portrayal of the woman of valor in chap. 31 (an extension of Woman Wisdom?) that the youth is to "find" and is to marry. He has traveled from home to the city gates (Prov 31:28) where he basks in the security provided by his mate.

The moral implications of the book of Proverbs have been well described by A. Barucq in his commentary (*Le livre*, 167): "The sages did not propose two ways in life toward perfection, one that would be for the laity—submission to wisdom considered as a sort of stoicism—and the other that would be the basis for religious submission to Yahweh. The fear of Yahweh and the teaching of the sage lead back to the one same reality in 15:33a, and their effects are presented as identical (13:14 = 14:27). The understanding of a wisdom morality that takes into account the frequently expressed concern to bind religion and the moral life (see also 13:14; 15:9; 16:6b) seems preferable to that which tends to separate human, worldly, values from religious values. The religion of the sages is the very same as that of their people and their spiritual leaders. It shows itself as fully Yahwist, and believes in the power of the words of the Law and its promises for human happiness."

The assessment of biblical ethics is a difficult one, and questions of methodology abound. In one of the latest studies (*Ethics and Politics in the Hebrew Bible*, ed. D. Knight [Atlanta: Scholars Press, 1994]) it is only tangentially that wisdom literature is mentioned. From the point of view of wisdom, how should "ethics" be understood? I would offer the following considerations. It is not just commands and condemnations, but rather the art of living honestly together with others before God. This is the program that the book of Proverbs promotes. And it promotes this more by indirection, more by persuasion than by threat. If the motivation is conditioned by the application of human standards of justice to the Lord, such is the inevitable position before the mystery of God. This "limitation" of the ethical views of Proverbs applies to the entire Bible. The confidence that the sages express in their teachings is generally judged very severely by modern readers, as though the teachers were living in a fools' paradise (see the *Excursus on Retribution*)! But already in Proverbs, not to mention Job and Qoheleth, there is a sense that humans should not and cannot overrate their understanding, that hubris is folly, and that ultimately the Lord is not to be contained by their insights: "No wisdom, and no understanding, and no counsel against the Lord" (Prov 21:30). The words of Prov 20:24, "From the Lord the steps of a person—how can anyone understand the way to go?" resonate with those of Jer 10:23, "I know, Lord, that the way of a human is not his to control; that humans, as they walk, cannot direct their own steps."

Three short observations are in order at this point. First, the sayings and exhortations, the general content of the wisdom books, derive from the basic material that is eventually codified in the law codes (exception being made for the cult). They are not to be eliminated from the biblical legacy as deficient in biblical authority, simply because they were not delivered by a prophet. Second, because the wisdom "teaching" is presented in a persuasive and experiential, rather than apodictic, manner, it is not any the less authoritative. The issues remain: life or death. Third, the goal of the teaching is formation of character, and this transcends the casuistry that forms a necessary part of ethical thought.

Finally, what about theological pluralism? Does the wisdom literature have anything to contribute to this question, which has been asked so vigorously in recent times? This is a staggering question, but perhaps it is profitable to pay attention to the modest contribution that wisdom can make. First of all, we may point to the Hebrew classification: "the Writings," within which three wisdom books are found along with many other literary types, and to which Ben Sira and the Wisdom of Solomon can be added. The diversity itself is an omen of the plurality in theology which is quickly illustrated by perusing the books themselves. This observation is all the stronger in view of the many instances of wisdom influence on other books of the Bible. Recent research has pointed to many areas of the Bible where wisdom has seeped in; cf. R. E. Murphy, *The Tree of Life*, 97–131, 221–27. Wisdom does not lie still; even in its "finished" form it leaves questions to ponder.

Second, there is the nature of the wisdom enterprise. No proverb says it all, as has been clear in this commentary. There are contrasts and contradictions, apodictic sayings, and ambiguities, paradoxes that tease further thought. Only the most general effort is made to bring these varied teachings under one umbrella. Indeed, the umbrella turns out to have several ribs. The sayings can be grouped under "fear of the Lord." They can be associated with moral criteria as exercised in Israel; they contribute to "moral formation." Within the limited purpose of the sages, the primary aim is to describe all the aspects of folly, so that wisdom can be attained. The popular characterization of wisdom as a search for order is an oversimplification. It turns out that it yields an attractive disorder, closer to reality than the theoretical analysis of scholars. This is vividly described in Ben Sira's theme about the works of God, all of them good though different, each in its time (Sir 39:16–35): "See all the works of the Most High: they come in pairs, the one the opposite of the other," Sir 33:15; cf. 42:24–25. But Sirach surely exaggerated the harmony, even while he recognized the oppositions.

Perhaps the problem should be posed more sharply. There is more than one kind of wisdom; contrast Prov 1–9 with 10–29. And there is a wisdom that moves a person to be "wise in his own eyes," 26:12. Can one just float in this sea of wisdom exhortations and observations? No, Wisdom herself challenges her children to make decisions. Sometimes the goals may be too broad for a secure decision to be reached. But that ambiguity, too, was not beyond the range of biblical Wisdom.

Third, the discussion of the personification of Wisdom as a woman has risen to a new height (see the *Excursus on Woman Wisdom and Woman Folly*). The testimony of the past indicates that the topic never disappeared from human consciousness, but there is a continual resurgence. Today this is particularly fortunate since Woman Wisdom points up a fundamental problem, the place of women in a society that has been dominated by patriarchal concerns. It is ironic that the traditional wisdom, which seems so steadily aimed at males, e.g., "my son" in Prov 1–9, and thus drenched with patriarchalism, should also provide an antidote in Woman Wisdom. This role of personified Wisdom up to now has never really been explored, as the studies of C. Camp, C. Maier, and G. Baumann, to mention only a few, abundantly testify. Is there a certain symbolism here, or better, a symbiosis between male and female, that will contribute to the current discussion?

Excursus on Woman Wisdom and Woman Folly

Bibliography

See the pertinent bibliography in the commentary on chaps. 1, 8 (especially), and 9. **Baumann, G.** *Die Weisheitsgestalt in Proverbien 1–9. Traditionsgeschichtliche und theologische Studien.* FAT 16. Tübingen: Mohr (Siebeck), 1996. **Bonnard, P.** "De la sagesse personifiée dans l'Ancien Testament à la sagesse en personne dans le Nouveau." In *La Sagesse de l'Ancien Testament.* Ed. M. Gilbert. Louvain: Duculot, 1979. 117–49. **Camp, C.** *Wisdom and the Feminine in the Book of Proverbs.* BLS 11. Sheffield: JSOT, 1985. ———. "Woman Wisdom as Root Metaphor: A Theological Consideration." In *The Listening Heart.* Ed. K. Hoglund et al. JSOTSup 58. Sheffield: JSOT, 1987. 45–76. **Clifford, R.** "Woman Wisdom in the Book of Proverbs." In *Biblische Theologie und gesellschaftlicher Wandel.* FS N. Lohfink, ed. G. Braulick et al. Freiburg:

Herder, 1993. **Fontaine, C. R.** "The Personification of Wisdom." In *HBC*. 501–3. **Fox, M. V.** "Ideas of Wisdom in Proverbs 1–9." *JBL* 116 (1997) 613–33. **Hadley, J.** "Wisdom and the Goddess." In *Wisdom in Ancient Israel: Essays in Honour of J. A. Emerton*. Ed. J. Day et al. Cambridge: Cambridge UP, 1995. 234–43. **Lang, B.** *Wisdom and the Book of Proverbs: An Israelite Goddess Redefined*. New York: Pilgrim, 1986 (revision of *Frau Weisheit*. Düsseldorf: Patmos, 1975). ———. "Figure ancienne, figure nouvelle de la Sagesse en Pr 1 à 9." In *La sagesse biblique de l'Ancien au Nouveau Testament*. Ed. J. Trublet. LD 160. Paris: Cerf, 1995. 61–97. **Maier, C.** *Die 'fremde Frau' in Proverbien 1–9*. OBO 144. Freiburg: Universitätsverlag, 1995. **Murphy, R. E.** "The Personification of Wisdom." In *Wisdom in Ancient Israel: Essays in Honour of J. A. Emerton*. Ed. J. Day et al. Cambridge: Cambridge UP, 1995. 222–33. ———. "The Faces of Wisdom in the Book of Proverbs." In AOAT 212. FS H. Cazelles. Neukirchen: Neukirchener, 1981. 337–45. **Schröer, S.** "Die göttliche Weisheit und der nachexilische Monotheismus." In *Der eine Gott und die Göttin*. Ed. M. T. Wacker and E. Zenger. QD 135 Freiburg: Herder, 1991. 151–82. This is reproduced in her *Die Weisheit hat ihr Haus gebaut. Studien zur Gestalt der Sophia in den biblischen Schriften*. Mainz: Grünewald, 1996. 27–62. **Terrien, S.** "The Play of Wisdom: Turning Point in Biblical Theology." *HBT* 3 (1981) 125–53.

Because the figure of the "stranger" or "outsider" woman is closely connected with Woman Wisdom, a special bibliography concerning that figure is in order. **Blenkinsopp, J.** "The Social Context of the 'Outsider Woman' in Proverbs 1–9." *Bib* 72 (1991) 457–73. **Boström, G.** *Proverbiastudien. Die Weisheit und das fremde Weib in Spr. 1–9*. LUÅ 30.3. Lund: Gleerup, 1935. **Cook, J.** אשה זרה (Proverbs 1–9 Septuagint): A Metaphor for Foreign Wisdom?" *ZAW* 106 (1994) 458–76. **Harrington, D. J.** *Wisdom Texts from Qumran*. London: Routledge, 1996. **Newsom, C. A.** "Woman and the Discourse of Patriarchal Wisdom: A Study of Proverbs 1–9." In *Gender and Difference in Ancient Israel*. Ed. P. L. Day. Minneapolis: Fortress, 1989. 142–60. **Vattioni, F.** "'La straniera' nel libro dei Proverbi." *Augustinianum* 7 (1967) 352–57. **Washington, H. C.** "The Strange Woman (אשה זרה נכריה) of Proverbs 1–9 and Post-exilic Judean Society." In *Second Temple Studies 2. Temple and Community in the Persian Period*. Ed. T. C. Eskenazi and K. Richards. JSOTSup 175. Sheffield: JSOT, 1994. 217–42. **Yee, G.** " 'I have perfumed my bed with myrrh': The Foreign Woman (*'iššâ zārâ*) in Proverbs 1–9." *JSOT* 43 (1989) 53–68.

There are four "women" in the book of Proverbs. Most conspicuous is Woman Wisdom (1:20–33; 3:13–20?; 4:5–9; 7:4; 8:1–36; 9:1–6); her opposite number is Woman Folly (9:13–18); further, there is the woman who is one's marriage partner (5:15–19); and finally, the "Stranger" (2:16–19; 5:1–14, 20; 6:24–32(35); 7:25–27). The primary purpose of this excursus is to explore the role of Woman Wisdom. Any reading of Proverbs would be deficient were there no enlargement of the perspectives in which this figure has been seen. The following provides a context for a reasonable understanding, even if many questions remain unanswered. Four aspects will be considered: origins; extent of personification; the three characters of Wisdom, Folly, and Stranger; and, finally, theological considerations. We presume that we are dealing with a literary personification; cf. righteousness and truth kissing in Ps 85:11–13, or wine and strong drink in Prov 20:1. Others insist on hypostasis, or person.

(1) *Origins.* We can begin with a straightforward assertion of ignorance. There are many theories, but there is no agreement as to the origins of the personification of Wisdom. B. Lang rightly calls her a "riddle," while at the same time he reviews the various theories concerning her identity (*Frau Weisheit*, 147–76). He rejects the idea that the personification of Wisdom has its origin in a foreign goddess (although in his later publication, he claims that she was originally an Israelite

goddess). Perhaps some borrowing from the mythology of goddesses in Israel's environment could have occurred. On this C. Fontaine has remarked that "it may be that by 'co-option' of surrounding goddesses to create the Yahwistically subordinated figure of Woman Wisdom, Israel met its own psychological need for female imagery of the divine without serious compromise of patriarchal monotheism" ("Personification," 502). Lang's arguments against a frequently quoted text from Ahiqar (94–95; cf. *ANET*, 427), in which wisdom is allegedly personified, are valid. The text itself is defective, and more is made of it than it deserves; there is no real context for it in the Mesopotamian realm. As for the Hellenistic Isis (see also J. Kloppenborg, "Isis and Sophia in the Book of Wisdom," *HTR* 75 [1982] 57–84), Lang correlates her with Sir 24, but not with Prov 8, although he correctly sees that the Proverbs personification is the model for Sir 24. Was there an *early* Jewish hypostasis theology? It is very difficult to arrive at one definition of hypostasis. Perhaps the later figure of the Shekinah, or presence of God in the world, would be an example. Much has been made of the "gnostic" myth of the descent and return (cf. 1 Enoch 42:1–3; Charlesworth, *OTP*, 1:33) of a heavenly figure of Wisdom. However, this does not fit the biblical description of Wisdom; the myth itself is a scholarly reconstruction. Lang's own view is that Woman Wisdom is so described because חכמה, "wisdom," is a feminine noun, and feminine personifications (e.g., "Daughter Zion") were agreeable to Israel, and also because her divine and royal attributes made her appealing to those who attended school. Finally, the erotic aspect, e.g., Prov 4:5–9; 7:4, made Wisdom appealing to students. In other words, Woman Wisdom is a pedagogical device. But those considerations (see also Camp, *Wisdom*, 21–70) are rather flat.

Scholarly research has been more successful in devising theories than in proposing a convincing explanation for the origin of the personification of Woman Wisdom. These remarks by no means exclude outside influence upon the figure of Wisdom, but it should be recognized that there is great uncertainty on this score. The point is that the biblical presentation itself is independent enough to be heard largely on its own as something new and unique. The meaning of the personification, as it stands within Proverbs, and especially within the context of the wisdom literature, has to be examined.

(2) *Extent of personification.* Although our primary subject is personification in Proverbs, the larger context must be considered: Job 28; Bar 3:9–44; Sir 1:1–10 and 24:1–33, and Wis 7:1–9:18. All of these texts associate Wisdom with God in an intimate way. Job 28:12 poses the question, "Where is wisdom to be found?" (cf. 28:20). In this magnificent poem we learn that precious minerals have been found and dug out from the earth, but no one above or below the earth knows where wisdom is. Only God knows the way to it, because of the tremendous range of divine vision, 28:24. God saw and measured wisdom, apparently putting it somewhere. But this chapter of Job is tantalizing for two reasons at least. First, it is not clear that wisdom is personified as a woman, although it can be considered so in the context of our discussion. Second, we are not told where God put wisdom. At a later period an answer is given to this question by Ben Sira. In 1:9–10 Sirach makes a clear reference to God's action in Job 28:27 when he says that God created and saw her, and then poured out wisdom upon every living thing, lavishing wisdom upon the "friends" of God (the chosen people).

The *pièce de résistance* is the description of Woman Wisdom in Proverbs. We will limit ourselves to chap. 8. Wisdom's speech contains no great surprises until she begins to describe her relationship to the Lord, 8:22–31. Here the following claims are clearly made: the birth of wisdom from the Lord, and her existence before creation; her witnessing of the creative acts where she plays an undetermined role (artisan or child?); the delight and "play" of Wisdom before God; and finally her delight to be with earthlings as well. This stunning passage is followed by Wisdom's appeal that her message be heard because the issue is one of life or death (8:32–36). These are almost incredible claims, not to be heard elsewhere in the Hebrew Bible. She seems to be divine, but subject to the Lord whose delight she is, and she is also involved with human beings. Her actual role in creation—a moot point—is not as important as her outreach to all the human race. Has she said enough to be identified? It has been commonly held that she is an attribute of God. This prerogative fails to do her justice. It is perhaps an adequate comment for Prov 3:19 (the Lord by wisdom created the world), but it does not do justice to her claims in chap. 8. In the commentary we noted that G. von Rad considered her to be the "self-revelation of creation." This is closer to the mark, but it leaves untouched her intimate relationship to the Deity. I would suggest that she is a surrogate for YHWH. She represents the Lord's orientation to creation, the divine presence in the world, a divine communication. She offers life to all who will "listen" (8:32–34). But who is she? Is she an aspect of Israel's God? Instead of speaking about "attribute," should one not recognize a gender designation, by analogy? Thus she would be the "feminine" in God, who created human beings in the divine image when he "created them male and female" (Gen 1:27b). This seems to be the implication of Prov 8. In the light of its postexilic composition, Prov 1–9 attributes to this incomparable figure a divine status, and she makes the same offer of life and death that the Lord gave to the people through Moses: Choose life! (Deut 30:15).

However, the versatility of the symbol of Woman Wisdom is not exhausted. In the books of Baruch and Sirach she is given a specific identity. She is explicitly identified by Ben Sira as the Torah or Law (Sir 24:23). While this identification can be understood in the light of Ben Sira's devotion to the Law as the true way of life, the qualities attributed to her in Prov 8 are not lost sight of. She rules the world and traverses all of it before she receives the command of the Lord to settle in Jerusalem (Sir 24:10–12). Baruch (3:15) repeats the questions of Job 28:12, 20 as to the location of wisdom, and gives a forthright answer, identical with Sirach: "She is the book of the commandments of God, the Torah that endures forever" (Bar 4:11). But her universal thrust is retained in 3:38(37): "Since then she has appeared on earth and moved among men." There is not sufficient reason to remove this verse as a Christian gloss; it is in line with Prov 8:31 and with Sir 24:7, 12, 18. Finally, the author of the Wisdom of Solomon proposes more than one identification. Wisdom is a spirit (Wis 1:6; 7:7), and her penetration of all things (12:1) makes her similar to the Stoic world-soul. At the same time, she is given a definite role, more specified than the ambiguous אָמוֹן of Prov 8:30: she is an artisan (τεχνῖτις, Wis 7:21; 8:6), working with God in creation. But the most startling claim is in 7:25–26, where she is described in metaphors that connote divine identity: she is the "breath" (ἀτμὶς) of God's power, an emanation (ἀπόρροια) of the divine glory. Now her intimacy with God seems to be the model of the intimacy that humans are to cultivate with Wisdom (7:9, 16). If Wisdom was inaccessible in Job, now she is available. She is a gift, but paradoxically one must pray to receive her. In the famous chap. 9 of Wisdom (only faintly echoing 1 Kgs 3) we are assured by pseudo-Solomon's prayer, "Who has learned your counsel, unless you have given Wisdom and sent your holy spirit from on high?" (9:17). The vision of Woman Wisdom in this book is simply breathtaking, while at the same time it rests upon the earlier descriptions for her person and activity.

We have given a kind of canonical perspective, in the sense that we have gone beyond the data of Proverbs in order to situate Woman Wisdom in the larger understanding that Israel achieved. It may also suggest that the identity of Wisdom cannot remain focused, or at least adequately defined, at any one point along this path from Proverbs to Sirach and beyond. This is important, because in the biblical perspective the meaning of Woman Wisdom is not exhausted by the striking chapters in Proverbs. In the broadest sense she is of God, and she is a communication from God to all creation as well as to Israel. In this light we may understand also the Christian development of this figure. I do not mean merely the role of Christ as sage, as the synoptic Gospels do depict him, but also the mysterious Wisdom of God that is reflected in the Pauline letters (cf. 1 Cor 1:24; Col 1:15–17; Heb 1:3).

(3) *Three Women: Woman Wisdom, Woman Folly, and the "Stranger" Woman.* It is helpful to distinguish three figures in order to determine if there are ultimately only two important ones. The "stranger" (זרה or נכריה) is explicitly mentioned in Prov 2:16; 5:3, 20; 6:24; 7:5. C. Maier has provided a summary of the various theories about the identity of this woman. The 1935 monograph of G. Boström proposed that she was a foreigner and a devotee of a goddess such as Astarte, whose cultic role (sex) is supposedly described in Prov 7. Others understood her to be only the (Israelite) wife of another person, and an adulteress, in view of chap. 7. For still others, she appeared to be simply an "outsider" who threatened the order of society. Others are more general and recognize her as a symbolic figure. After a thorough review of the available historical and sociological data, Maier offers the following description: "every woman outside one own's [*sic*] family is 'strange' if she breaks the socially accepted standards in gender relations. The speeches about the 'strange woman' warn against sexual intercourse with women outside regular marriage relations and announce dramatic consequences, such as loss of property and social disgrace, to any man who would not listen to their instructions. These instructions were produced among educated women and men belonging to the urban upper class of the Yehud province. Their teaching is conceived as an interpretation and an actualization of Torah commandments. They plead for the preservation of existing family ties within ancestral houses (*bāttê ʾābôt*) as a basic prerequisite for wealth and high social status" (author's summary on final, unnumbered page). This analysis is predicated on a reconstruction of the historical setting, and it may very well be historically accurate. But the setting in the book would suggest another, and fuller, conclusion, which Maier is aware of, but this is not the subject of her research. For example, her analysis of the scenes in Prov 9 presents two opposing portraits: Wisdom and the "stranger" woman, who acts like a professional prostitute. Wisdom invites to a

meal, but the "stranger" invites to illicit love (9:17, stolen water and hidden food).
Woman Folly receives here a demonic and destructive aspect. She stands for more
than sexual misconduct, and becomes transcendent because of her association
with death (9:18; cf. 2:18; 7:27). The contrast with Woman Wisdom is intended
to steer the youth in the right way to conformity with the Law, or to "life," and
the symbolism contributes towards this goal.

Thus there is a challenge to set some criteria for the symbolism of Woman
Wisdom and Woman Folly. The clearest indication of their opposition is the similar
invitations issued by each in 9:4 and 9:16 to "those who lack sense." Folly resembles
the Woman Stranger and her machinations. The smooth talk (2:16; 5:3; 6:24;
7:5, 21) of the Woman Stranger is exemplified in 9:17 by the clever symbolism of
"stolen water" (notable in that the youth is told to drink of his own water, 5:15;
cf. Cant 4:15). The "bread eaten in secret" is a symbol of the sexual seduction she
proposes. The honeyed words of the "stranger" are the opposite of the "honey"
that wisdom provides in Prov 24:13–14. A certain strategy is at work here: both
Women speak partly along the same lines. But the honeyed words of the Woman
Stranger are warned against. Hence Woman Wisdom must boast of the noble
purposes and truths which she will speak forth (8:6–7, to be contrasted with 5:3).
Indeed, death and life are in the power of the tongue (Prov 18:21)! Chap. 9
suggests a symbolic identification of Woman Stranger with Woman Folly, and this
figure is opposed to Wisdom. The previous chapters have prepared the ground
for this. Wisdom is the Daughter of YHWH (יהוה, 8:22–25), and she represents all
the virtues that the youth can assimilate. Woman Folly's origin is never given; she
is a woman of the streets, with a "house" (9:14; 16), but bent on the pursuit of
youths. Woman Stranger and Woman Folly are clearly etched as opposing figures.

A fragmentary but rather full manuscript from Qumran deals with Woman Folly,
and it has been known since its first faulty publication in 1970. We point it out here
merely to indicate the *Nachleben* of this doughty figure in the wisdom tradition. It is
known as 4Q184, and is clearly in the tradition of the Wisdom/Folly antithesis.
One of the editors of the definitive edition (DJD), D. J. Harrington (*Wisdom Texts
from Qumran*, 31–35), translates part of the text, and he comments on the significance
of a couplet concerning Folly (e.g., "in the foundations of gloom she sets up her
dwelling, and she inhabits the tents of silence. Amid everlasting fire is her
inheritance, not among all those who shine brightly"—lines 6–8 of the first section):
"In this respect—the theme of the eternal rewards for following Lady Wisdom and
the eternal punishment for following Lady Folly, the Qumran text goes beyond
what appears in its biblical model, Proverbs 1–9" (p. 33).

Nor did Qumran neglect Woman Wisdom. The Cave 11 Psalms Scroll was found
to contain the Hebrew text of Sir 51:13–19, 30. Whether or not it was a product
of the Qumran community may be debated, just as the intensity of the eroticism
in text is questioned. But there is no doubt that this poem is an original Hebrew
acrostic and describes the mutual search of a young man (the speaker) and
Woman Wisdom for each other. For translations, see the version of Sir 51:13–30
in the NRSV, where the text has been supplied in English translation, and also the
version in P. Skehan and A. Di Lella, *The Wisdom of Ben Sira*, AB 39 (New York:
Doubleday, 1997) 572–80. For further bibliography and discussion see D. J.
Harrington, *Wisdom Texts*, 28–30.

(4) *Theological Considerations.* The contrast between Woman Wisdom and Woman Folly has further implications. Wisdom offers life. This is a fairly common theme, implicit and explicit, running through chaps. 1–9. The perspective is general (3:18; 4:13); Wisdom sums it up in her proclamation that whoever "finds" her "finds" life (8:35). The virtues which she incorporates (8:6–14) and which she urges upon the youths are all positive and thus life-giving. On the contrary, the death knell is sounded frequently when the activity of Woman Folly/Stranger is described—most vividly in 2:18; 5:5; 6:32; 7:27. Finally, there is the devastating comment (9:18) of the author that the acceptance of her invitation means living with the shades, where the rest of her invitees have arrived: in the depths of Sheol. Although the perspective of the book is limited to this world, there are overtones to the life/death contrast. Acceptance of the invitation of Woman Folly does not lead simply to physical death (as the Qumran document cited above bears witness). Woman Folly in the person of the stranger is not just a casual acquaintance; she stalks her prey, as the stranger did in chap. 7. It is not necessary to fix upon a given aspect of Wisdom/Folly in such a way as to sift out the ideal from the real, the imaginative from the literal. These various details serve to indicate the subtlety of the figures—how open-ended they are. This is due to the art of the composer of these chapters.

The opposition between the two women is clear, but at the same time not easily absorbed in modern culture. As C. Newsom has put it, "One is the gate of Sheol, the other the gate of Heaven" ("Woman and the Discourse," 157). In the patriarchal culture in which we move and live, it is very hard, if not impossible, for male scholars and readers of the Bible to appreciate the difficulty which many women experience in trying to absorb the duality expressed in chaps. 1–9 (not to mention other similar difficulties within the Bible). The figure of the father overshadows the mother. He mediates all the teaching, including the image of Woman Wisdom herself, to the son. He demands that his תורה, "instruction," and his מצות, "commands," be heard (3:1)—and this carries an overtone of the demands that God has laid upon Israel. His authority is strengthened by the experience he has had with his own father who taught him (4:3–4). Everything is focused on the son, and the reality (and symbol) of woman is now used in two divergent directions. On the one hand, she is on a transcendent level as Woman Wisdom. On the other hand, she is the earthy "other" woman, the stranger, the adulteress, and finally Woman Folly, to be matched on a transcendent level with Woman Wisdom. Newsom's feminist analysis of chaps. 1–9 seems irrefutable: "for the reader who does not take up the subject position offered by the text, Proverbs 1–9 ceases to be a simple text of initiation and becomes a text about the problematic nature of discourse itself. . . . Israel's wisdom tradition never examined its patriarchal assumptions. But its commitment to the centrality of discourse as such and its fascination with the dissident voice in Job and Qohelet made it the locus within Israel for radical challenges to the complacency of the dominant symbolic order" ("Woman and the Discourse," 159). There remains the problem of the validity or appropriateness of reading the biblical text "against the grain," as it were, in order to create some new (and true) meaning—or to read it with all its human imperfections.

J. E. McKinlay has read "against the grain," or deconstructively, and issued an interesting theological challenge (*Gendering Wisdom,* 238–53). What is to be made of the convergence of Woman Wisdom with YHWH (יהוה, Prov 8), her identification with Torah (Sir 24) and exemplification in the male ancestors of Israel (Sir 44–50), and finally her being subsumed (Wisdom/Logos) in the male Jesus? Has something been lost along the way, or is something new yet to emerge? Indeed, where *is* Wisdom to be found? Thus far, this masculinizing of the Wisdom tradition has not been adequately explained. Or is it ultimately misleading to speak of this "masculinizing"? That is to say, the *gender* of biblical Wisdom cannot determine its theological meaning. Gender cannot be applied to the biblical God, even though the (revelatory) language of the Bible could not escape the limitations of the patriarchalism (hence the "masculinizing" of YHWH [יהוה]) that colors it. If, as I have claimed, Wisdom is best understood as a communication of God, manifested in the world, in the Torah, and (for the Christian) in Christ, all three levels are somehow to be affirmed. Wisdom is not to be sacrificed to either patriarchalism or to feminism.

From other vantage points, and despite the trappings of patriarchalism, has any progress been made in arriving at a more adequate understanding of Woman Wisdom? C. Camp ("Root Metaphor") has described her role as a surrogate for kingship in the postexilic period, and explores the idea that Wisdom can be an efficacious symbol in modern times. In the history of Christian thought biblical wisdom received a strong overlay of Greco-Roman ideas, and has remained largely theoretical in Christian theology. A closer reliance on biblical data seems in order. Camp proposes both an appreciation and a critique of "Woman Wisdom as a theological root metaphor which creates possibilities for a new kind of human experience in the world" (p. 51). C. R. Fontaine warns against trivializing Woman Wisdom: "By ignoring the human and divine antecedents of Woman Wisdom and Woman Stranger, some commentators on the text have preferred to deal minimally with the significance of this female imagery. In such treatments, Woman Wisdom and Woman Stranger become 'mere' literary devices whose symbolic meaning becomes relatively insignificant, despite its anomalous appearance in an androcentric literature. Woman Wisdom is seen as the embodiment of the sages' teachings (but why as *woman?*) or the voice of the world-order addressing men or as a sort of Teacher Temptress, urging male students to greater learning by use of sexually nuanced speech. Some note the way Woman Wisdom often incorporates prophetic modes of speech into her poems and, as a result, view her as prophet and preacher. However, it is unlikely that any ancient Israelite would have viewed a female figure lifting her voice in the streets in quite such positive terms. . . . Failure to explore seriously the significance of Woman Wisdom imagery is no longer an option" ("Personification," 503).

Theologians are struggling to evaluate this "imagery" or symbolism. The basic question is: Does it touch the ontological aspect of divinity or is it properly anthropomorphic? It cannot be truly ontological, if God, as rightly claimed, is beyond sex. Hence it must be anthropomorphic, describing God in human terms. (Of course, the obvious response to this is, "why is God represented always as he?") Or, one may ask, is this "either/or" the right way of putting the question? The discussion may be helped by the concept of analogy (cf. R. E. Murphy, *BTB* 24 [1994] 4–7). Theologians have learned to evaluate the biblical indications of divine "repentance" or change of mind. One cannot apply Greek philosophical ideas concerning act and potency, perfection and imperfection, in such a way as to "cage" the divine freedom. The biblical description of divine repentance points to the mysterious inner life of the deity. Does Woman Wisdom reflect something of the divine nature that goes beyond sexual gender?

G. Baumann (*Weisheitsgestalt*, 312–16) argues that the vagueness and difficulty of the terminology describing Woman Wisdom in Prov 8:22–31 is a sign that the relationship between YHWH (יהוה) and wisdom cannot be determined. What is said is that "Wisdom is a transcendent creature of YHWH" (p. 312). In Prov 1–9 she is a transcendent creature who, thanks to her knowledge of the Lord's plan, communicates a teaching or ethos to human beings that is similar to carrying out the Torah. There is no cult here, but "human beings are to love the figure of Wisdom as a 'personal goddess,' and to follow her" (p. 313). However, there is a mystery about her: Is she a kind of intermediary because the figure of the Lord has become remote, or has she been designed to render the Lord more transcendent, more clearly distinct from the creation? In all this speculation it is important to remember that the "only way of honoring her consists in following her way. That path agrees broadly with an indirect form of YHWH worship: the carrying out of the divine will" (p. 315).

Baumann attempts to steer a course between S. Schroer and C. Newsom. The former ("göttliche Weisheit," cf. 167–69) sees Wisdom as Israel's God in the form of a woman; the latter would see the figure of Wisdom as a legitimation of male dominance, and hence not useful theologically. Baumann insists on the validity of female "voices" that other feminist theologians hear reflected in the text. Moreover, it was not necessary for Wisdom to be pictured as a woman. This was not due to chance, and it must be given proper theological acknowledgment. For one thing, the voice of Woman Wisdom is stronger than the voice of the parent/teacher (whether father or mother) in chaps. 1–9. Baumann concludes, "In her the statement of Gen 1:17 is taken up again and filled out, that the picture of God is feminine as well as masculine" (p. 324).

Conclusion. What follows is by way of a conclusion, not a solution. These considerations may help to agree/disagree about certain presuppositions and affirmations in this prickly area. (1) As has been affirmed, the God of the Bible is beyond sex. That phrase does not mean simply "asexual"; it connotes the chasm that exists in the biblical understanding between the divine and the human. (2) At the same time, human beings, both female and male, are created in the divine image (Gen 1:27); the fact that they have the same "nature," or are "equal," is also indicated by the creation of the woman in Gen 2:23–24. The sexual aspect of their being is somehow rooted in the creator God (just as the flames of love are somehow the שלהבתיה, "flame of Yah"? Cant 8:6). (3) How is one to deal with the Bible from these two aspects: the misogynism that marks biblical culture, and the relative absence of the feminine in the portrayal both of God and of human beings? First, misogynism (such as exemplified in Ben Sira, for example) is to be recognized for what it is: a cultural limitation of the revelation made to the people of God; it is not a pattern backed by divine mandate and hence to be adopted. Moreover, this "limitation" is not peculiar to Israel; it pervades the thinking of the entire Fertile Crescent. Second, the absence of the feminine is due to the same cultural limitation. But the important issue here is to examine how it can be remedied, to see if there are possible avenues around the limitation. It is not helpful to say that there is no real absence, since the biblical message is meant for both male and female. That happens to be true, but when the female sees no sign of adequate recognition of herself in the biblical record, we are faced with the current impasse. One may say that God is beyond sex, but that remains terribly theoretical, when the Bible well-nigh exclusively presents God as male. While a vast improvement can be made in translating the Bible in a more inclusive manner, this move will ultimately not be sufficient. As far as the English language is concerned, we are locked into an exclusivity that cannot be cracked by such ruses as he/she or his/her or other linguistic atrocities. It belongs to the future to say whether "she" and "her" will come into usage in this area. Neither is it ultimately helpful to single out biblical passages (which will be few in number) that depict God acting like a woman. To adopt that strategy is to approve implicitly the male portrayal of God against which one is arguing. God is no more female than male.

(4) The use of a female metaphor, Woman Wisdom, in such close association with YHWH (יהוה) still calls for exploration—despite all the efforts that have been made. I am unwilling to accept the idea that this figure is irremediably patriarchal in its use and therefore theologically irrelevant as far as women are concerned. The patriarchal coloring to the pursuit of Woman Wisdom (how can the female be conceived of pursuing her?) is undeniable. But equally undeniable is Woman Wisdom's origin and place with YHWH (יהוה) on the one hand, and on the other, a figure whose delight is to be with human beings (Prov 8:30–31; Sir 1:10). The symbolic value and meaning of Life/Death associated with Wisdom and Folly transcend the gender identity. Legitimate feminist concerns hopefully will not deny that dimension. Moreover, the image of Woman Wisdom is not to be reduced to being an object of sexual pursuit. Her speeches, and her role in creation, and also her incarnation of the womanly roles of mother, counselor, etc., all deserve attention. The figure of Woman Wisdom can give a certain delight to being a woman in the world. (5) Finally, the inherent patriarchalism of the Bible should not be allowed to dominate its message. There is more than one limitation to the biblical message, e.g., the figure of God the Warrior, or the commonly alleged instances of revenge and violence. These are not enough to close off the Bible from those who accept it as the Word. So much depends on the way in which one hears the Word of God. Is the current Western emphasis on, and repudiation of, misogynism in the Bible, however justifiable a reaction, to be allowed to dictate theological relevance by the standards of sexual equality? Then what happens to a "redemption" of all, male and female, that is part of the biblical message? In terms of reader-response theory, the feminist movement is relatively recent, and relatively limited to a given level of modern culture. The ultimate achievements of the movement are still in the future and will doubtless be successful. But it would be shortsighted to make it the sole axis of interpretation. There are different levels of appropriation. Feminist liberation is not the approach taken by most women in the Third World. They are suffering from oppression, poverty, and simply the struggle to stay alive. Thus far, exclusive language in the Bible constitutes no hurdle for them; they hear liberation at the basic level of subsistence. At the same time, they must be awakened to a dignity that is fully human, and the feminist movement contributes to that end. This is not said by way of any put-

down. In fact, one should fervently hope that in the future, conscientization relative to female dignity will pervade that world more fully. But it is incumbent to put feminist interpretation of the Bible into perspective, precisely in order to recognize its validity.

Excursus on International Wisdom

Bibliography

See the brief orientation above in the *Introduction,* and also the bibliography in **Murphy, R. E.** *The Tree of Life.* 151–71. Secondary literature pertinent to Egypt will be found in the *Excursus on the Book of Proverbs and Amenemope.* There is no satisfactory overall summary of wisdom in Mesopotamia. The standard English translations are to be found in **Lambert, W. G.** *Babylonian Wisdom Literature.* Oxford: Clarendon, 1960, and, by the same author, "Some New Babylonian Wisdom Literature." In *Wisdom in Ancient Israel. Essays in Honour of J. A. Emerton.* Ed. J. Day et al. Cambridge: Cambridge UP, 1995. 30–42. See also the summary article by **Buccellati, G.** In *JAOS* 101/1 (1981) 35–47, and the brief study of Instructions and Proverbs in **McKane, W.** *Proverbs.* 151–208. For ancient Sumer, see **Gordon, E. J.** *Sumerian Proverbs.* Philadelphia: University of Pennsylvania Museum, 1959, and several publications of **Bendt Alster,** more recently, "Early Dynastic Proverbs and Other Contributions to the Study of Literary Texts from Abu Salabikh." *AfO* 38 (1991) 1–51.

MESOPOTAMIA

Scholars on the Mesopotamian scene are not happy with the term wisdom as applied to their discipline. Thus, G. Buccellati considers Wisdom as "an intellectual phenomenon in itself. It is the second degree reflective function as it begins to emerge in human culture; in Mesopotamia, it takes shape in a variety of realizations and institutions, from onomastics to literature, from religion to school" (p. 47). Be that as it may, it suffices for our purposes to restrict our concern to proverbs. The study of E. Gordon published many Sumerian proverbs (although a lot of problems in the translation of Sumerian literature remain to be solved), and these studies have been continued by Bendt Alster, but much more work must be done before any general picture emerges. The translation of Babylonian proverbs by W. Lambert are clearer, but all in all, one can hardly say more than the generalization that the ancients as well as the moderns also had their proverbs. The important comparisons between the Bible and Mesopotamian literature lie elsewhere, as in the *Enuma Elish,* or the Story of Gilgamesh, and the Atrahasis epic. For wisdom concerns, one looks to the famous poem, *Ludlul,* to the "Dialogue of Pessimism," and other works (see the summary in *The Tree of Life,* 155–58). But these illustrate only one facet of wisdom literature.

AHIKAR

Day, J. "Foreign Semitic Influence on the Wisdom of Israel and Its Appropriation in the Book of Proverbs." In *Wisdom in Ancient Israel. Essays in Honour of J. A. Emerton.* Ed. J. Day et al. Cambridge: Cambridge UP, 1995. 55–70, esp. 62–70. **Kottsieper, I.** "Die alttestamentliche Weisheit im Licht aramäischer Weisheitstraditionen." In *Weisheit ausserhalb der kanonischen*

Weisheitsschriften. Ed. B. Janowski. VWGTh 10. Gütersloh: Gütersloh Verlagshaus, 1996. 128–62. For the text, see *ANET,* 427–30; **Lindenberger, J. M.** *The Aramaic Proverbs of Ahiqar.* Baltimore: Johns Hopkins UP, 1983, and his translation in Charlesworth, *OTP,* 2:479–507.

The history of the transmission of the text of Ahiqar is most unusual, as it was reproduced in many ancient languages, from Armenian to Arabic. The Aramaic text was discovered on the island of Elephantine in the Nile, at the beginning of the twentieth century, and is dated to about the fifth century B.C. Although the story of Ahiqar has a Mesopotamian background (King Sennacherib), there is wide agreement that the Sayings were composed in Aramaic, and Kottsieper even speaks of "Aramaic wisdom traditions." At the present time, it is better to restrict oneself to Ahiqar, and here one can find some commonalities with the biblical proverbs. Kottsieper rightly points out that Israelite wisdom shares an interest in "Naturweisheit" with Ahiqar, and in fables (cf. 2 Kgs 14:9 and Judg 9:8–15). In the past, some commonplaces that Proverbs shares with the Sayings (e.g., Prov 22:13 and Ahiqar 81–82 on corporal punishment for a son; cf. *ANET,* 428) have been pointed out. Due to the frequency of this topos, a relationship of Proverbs to Ahiqar cannot be affirmed. Unfortunately, the text of lines 94–95, which seem to deal with personified wisdom is quite uncertain; cf. the translation of H. L. Ginzberg in *ANET,* 428.

EGYPT

The startling discovery and publication of the Teaching of Amenemope in the 1920s opened a torrent of scholarly analyses of the wisdom of Egypt and Israel. Many other "wisdom" writings (*Sebayit*) came to light, but the primary focus was on Amenemope, to which a special excursus is devoted. As is clear from the *Comment* on Prov 22:17ff., this commentary takes the position that there *is* an Egyptian connection, and the comparison of Prov 22:17–23:11 with the Teaching of Amenemope is the clearest example.

Here we wish to call attention to other pertinent Egyptian works. There are also similarities between some biblical proverbs and those found in the Instructions of other Egyptians, such as Ptahhotep and Any (or Ani). What does all this suggest? The similarities in many respects are about commonplaces in human experience, and to postulate derivation simply because there is an Egyptian counterpart, and because the Egyptian works are earlier, is not a conclusive argument. One can just as well postulate a common stock of sayings, drawn from various sources, that became current in the cultures in this part of the Fertile Crescent, and without any obvious parentage. It is generally granted, however, that the case of Amenemope differs from any other resemblance that Proverbs might have to extrabiblical sources. Yet even here, D. Römheld postulates a Canaanite intermediary before Amenemope entered into the Israelite world (*Wege,* 183–84), and he points out a paradox about the biblical teaching. It does not adopt the tone of "personal piety" so obvious in Amenemope, but rather reflects the mood of earlier Egyptian wisdom teaching. Hence he concludes that the development of Israelite wisdom followed its own inner-Israelite laws. He comments on Prov 10:22 that this proverb really means that human wisdom no longer reaches its goal. If God is the one who determines human fate, then it is the relationship to God that counts, not the (old) wisdom. God stands far off from the prayer of the wicked, but he hears the plea of the just (Prov 15:16). Römheld thinks that this religious attitude is distinct from early wisdom which was presumably profane. However, such hypothetical dating of the material is problematical.

While the relationship of Proverbs to Amenemope has occupied the limelight, the late Egyptian wisdom preserved in two demotic (an Egyptian cursive hand, arising as early as the seventh century) compositions deserves notice. The Instruction of Ankhsheshonq (Lichtheim, *AEL*, 3:159–84) derives perhaps from the Ptolemaic period, if not earlier. The plight of Ankhsheshonq is reminiscent of Ahiqar. He is imprisoned on a charge of conniving in a plot against the king, and he writes out his advice for his son. It does not reflect a royal court style or manners; it deals with the situation of ordinary people: wealth, 8:17–23 ("the wealth of a man is his speech"); advice on borrowing money, 16:9–12; human character, 11:11–14. These are largely short, epigrammatic sentences that are often expressed as imperatives and admonitions. Several of these catch one's attention: "He who is bitten of the bite of a snake is afraid of a coil of rope," 14:14; "The plans of the god are one thing, the thoughts of [men] are another," 26:14; cf. Prov 16:1, 9. The other Instruction is called the Papyrus Insinger, after the name of the man who purchased the work for the Leiden royal museum in 1895, and it dates from the Ptolemaic period. It is somewhat of a paradox that both of these late works have distinct similarities to the "earlier" Israelite wisdom contained in Prov 10–29. First, there is the style: single-sentence aphorisms consisting of one complete line. Second, the sayings reflect a more popular approach to life's realities than the class-conscious character of earlier Egyptian wisdom. A random example chosen from Ankhsheshonq: "Borrow money at interest and celebrate your birthday. Do not borrow money at interest in order to live well on it" (16:11–12; *AEL*, 111, 172). Miriam Lichtheim, the translator, has also called attention to the unusual ending of the several teachings in Papyrus Insinger: in paradoxes and conclusions about Fate and Fortune, a kind of refrain (*AEL*, 3:184–217, esp. 185). The vagaries of poverty and possessions are exemplified in 7:13–19 (*AEL*, 3:191); the importance of the "heart," in 12:14–22 (*AEL*, 3:195).

A less desirable result of the comparison of Egyptian with Israelite wisdom was the imposition of the Egyptian worldview upon Israelite wisdom, what I have called the "ma'atizing" of wisdom (cf. *The Tree of Life*, 115–18). Ma'at, which means truth and justice, is an important idea that pervades the whole Egyptian corpus of writings; cf. J. Assman, *Ma'at. Gerechtigkeit und Unsterblichkeit im Alten Ägypten* (Munich: Beck, 1990). This came to be summarized as world order, and in the influential studies of H. Gese, H. Schmid, H. D. Preuss, and others Israelite wisdom was interpreted early on as a search for order. Along with this went the idea that the wisdom divinity was seen as an *Urhebergott*, a god of origins, not the God of Israel. The bankruptcy of wisdom became a common theme, as the shortcomings of the book of Proverbs (traditional wisdom did not, of course, answer all questions) were pointed up by later wisdom literature such as Qoheleth. M. Fox (*JANESCU* 23 [1995] 37–48, esp. 37–44) effectively disposes of the alleged parallelism between the Egyptian concept and the idea of "world order": "The

Israelite sages could not have undertaken a survey of Egyptian texts of all genres and extracted a highly abstract, philosophical idea such as the world order and made that the basis of their own philosophy. The sages of Israel were not Egyptologists" (p. 48). More study remains to be done in comparing Egyptian and Israelite wisdom, but without the bias of a previous generation. This will serve to make the comparisons more pertinent. An example of this new direction is already seen in J. Assmann, "Die Wende der Weisheit im Alten Agypten," in *Weisheit ausserhalb der kanonischen Weisheitsschriften*, ed. B. Janowski, VWGTh 10 (Gütersloh: Gütersloh Verlagshaus, 1996) 20–39. He signals the personal turn that wisdom takes "in setting God in one's heart." The divine guidance of the heart transcends the norms of ma'at and yields to the divine will. When the Egyptian worldview is better appreciated, the biblical understanding of wisdom will also benefit.

MODERN "NONBIBLICAL" CULTURES

Naré, L. *Proverbes salomoniens et proverbes mossi: Etude comparative à partir d'une nouvelle analyse de Pr 25–29.* EHS.T 283. Frankfurt: Lang, 1986. **Nzambi, P. D.** *Proverbes bibliques et proverbes kongo.* Religionswissenschaft 5. Frankfurt: Lang, 1992. **Westermann, C.** "Weisheit im Sprichwort." In *Forschung am Alten Testament.* Vol. 2. Munich, 1974. 149–61 (originally in *Schalom* [FS A. Jepsen. 1971]).

Among modern Old Testament scholars, C. Westermann appears to have been the first to point out the relevance of proverbs from "primitive" cultures for Old Testament study. This has aided him in establishing his distinction between the *Weisheitsspruch,* or wisdom saying, such as found in Prov 10–29 and the *Lehrweisheit,* or more reflective wisdom represented by Prov 1–9. Later studies by native African scholars have exploited the aspect of "sayings" or "aphorisms." Indeed no counterpart to the reflective biblical wisdom has appeared in these cultures.

More work remains to be done by African scholars who can collect and publish the proverbial sayings in their native cultures. Among recent European scholars, publications in this area by F. Golka have been important; see, e.g., *The Leopard's Spots: Biblical and African Wisdom in Proverbs* (Edinburgh: T. & T. Clark, 1993).

Excursus on the Book of Proverbs and Amenemope

Bibliography

The study of **Whybray, R. N.** *Proverbs,* 6–18, 78–84, contains an extensive summary and a selective bibliography of books and articles on this topic that have appeared in the twentieth century. The following list indicates the works used most often for this excursus.

Brunner, H. "Zentralbegriffe ägyptischer und israelitischer Weisheitslehren." In *Das hörende Herz.* Ed. W. Rollig. OBO 80. Freiburg: Universitätsverlag, 1988. 402–16. **Bryce, G. E.** *A Legacy of Wisdom: The Egyptian Contribution to the Wisdom of Israel.* Lewisburg: Bucknell UP, 1979. **Kitchen, K. A.** "Proverbs and Wisdom Books of the Ancient Near East: The Factual History of Literary Form." *TynBul* 28 (1977–78) 69–114. **McKane, W.** "The Egyptian Instruction." In *Proverbs.* OTL. Philadelphia: Westminster, 1970. 51–150. **Römheld, D.** *Wege der Weisheit: Die Lehren Amenemopes und Proverbien 22,17–24,22.* BZAW 184. Berlin: de Gruyter, 1989; see also the discussion of this study in the *Excursus on International Wisdom.* **Ruffle, J.**

"The Teaching of Amenemope and Its Connection with the Book of Proverbs." *TynBul* 28 (1977) 29–68. **Shupak, N.** *Where Can Wisdom Be Found? The Sage's Language in the Bible and in Ancient Egyptian Literature.* OBO 130. Freiburg: Universitätsverlag, 1993. passim. **Steiert, F.-J.** *Die Weisheit Israels—ein Fremdkörper im Alten Testament? Eine Untersuchung zum Buch der Sprüche auf dem Hintergrund der ägyptischen Weisheitslehren.* FTS 143. Freiburg: Herder, 1990. **Washington, H. C.** *Wealth and Poverty in the Instruction of Amenemope and the Hebrew Proverbs.* SBLDS 142. Atlanta: Scholars, 1994. **Whybray, R. N.** *Proverbs: A Survey of Modern Study.* HBIS 1. Brill: Leiden, 1995.

As stated in the *Comment*, it was judged prudent to treat the relationship between Amenemope and the book of Proverbs separately because it constitutes a special case with a long history of scholarly discussion. This also facilitates more intense concentration on the biblical text for its own sake, without always raising the question of the relationship.

Most of the relevant history of the question from the time of the publication of the Egyptian work (1923) has been briefly summarized by R. N. Whybray in *Proverbs*, 6–14, 78–84. Thus there is no reason to go over old ground here, such as the disputes that have continued even up to recent times (e.g., the failure of the claims of E. Drioton). These are adequately covered by the summaries and bibliography provided in Whybray. As a basic observation it may be said that there is practically unanimous agreement that the work of Amenemope influenced the collection that begins in Prov 22:17. The manner and the extent of the influence, however, are moot points: oral or written sources, or both? Through the courts of the respective nations, or by some other channel? Does the dependence of the biblical text on Amenemope cease, in this collection, at Prov 23:11? If so, how does the rest of this section, 23:12–24:22, relate to the issue of dependence? Is there evidence of the influence of the teaching of Amenemope on other parts of the book of Proverbs? These different questions can be answered only with varying degrees of probability or even possibility.

In addition, several specific and difficult issues arise. To what extent can the Hebrew text be emended in the light of the text of Amenemope? What form of the text, if any, of Amenemope was available in Israel? Is there a prehistory to the text of Amenemope, as D. Römheld, among others, has argued, that might have a bearing on the whole question? These are issues that experts try to unravel, both Egyptologists and Hebrew scholars. Hence readers will be confronted with more than one solution to a problem, more than one answer to a textual question. This is an ongoing study, as its history during almost the entire twentieth century bears witness. The purpose of this excursus is modest: (1) to show as clearly as possible whatever influence may have been exercised by the Egyptian work, even if the precise details are in some respects debatable; (2) to enable the reader to form a general impression of the relationship on the basis of the evidence presented.

With or without discussion, many works contain cross-references to Proverbs and/or Amenemope. The English translation in *ANET*, 424, n. 26, contains references based on the parallels pointed out by D. C. Simpson. The study of H. Washington (*Wealth and Poverty*, 136) has a "list of parallels." F.-J. Steiert (*Fremdkörper*, 196–200) has a lengthy descriptive list of the parallels. D. Römheld (*Wege*, 58–59) gives a list of "thirty" sayings in Prov 22:22–24:22 (thus corresponding to the "thirty" of Amenemope, although there is little agreement about the precise division of units). Among the English translations of the difficult Egyptian text should be noted especially Miriam Lichtheim, *AEL*, 2:146–63, and also W. K. Simpson, ed., *The Literature of Ancient Egypt*, 2nd ed. (New Haven: Yale UP, 1973) 241–65.

The following observations are provided with appropriate, though not exhaustive, evidence relevant to the discussion:

(1) No one, it appears, would deny that a new unit, or collection of sayings, within the book of Proverbs begins at 22:17. There may be a small measure of disagreement on the adoption of a specific title for the unit, namely, "the Sayings of the Wise." See *Note* 17.a. and the *Comment* on 22:17.

(2) The end of this unit can be determined by the certain and indisputable appearance of a title at 24:23, "These also by the wise," which opens a small and fairly compact section, 24:23–34. The long and significant title in 25:1 indicates that still another collection begins.

(3) One is faced immediately with the difficult question of trying to determine the unity of 22:17–24:22. That is to say, is it to be conceived as a real unit in imitation of Amenemope's "thirty" units? There appears to be more than one break in this section; this is suggested by the address "my son" in 23:15, 19, 26, which is reminiscent of the frequent address in chaps. 1–9. This question will be discussed below under item 4b.

(4) What is the proper understanding of Prov 22:20 in the light of Amenemope's explicit mention of his own thirty chapters? There are two problems here: (a) Is the number "thirty" to be read in 22:20? (b) If it is the correct reading, as most scholars agree, does it imply that there are thirty sayings or units in Proverbs, extending to the next section, 24:23? These questions can be considered separately.

(a) The reading of 22:20 testifies to uncertainty within the Masoretic tradition. The Ketib has שִׁלְשׁוֹם, "the day before yesterday," or "formerly," and this obviously is suspect. The Qere suggests שָׁלִישִׁים, "officers," or some kind of metaphorical meaning, such as "excellent" things. Because Amenemope clearly speaks of thirty chapters (at the beginning of his chap. 30; cf. Lichtheim, *AEL*, 2:162), the majority of translations read "thirty" (שְׁלוֹשִׁים) at 22:20—despite the objections of some scholars, notably Whybray. For a detailed analysis, see Bryce, *Legacy*, 78–86.

(b) Assuming that "thirty" is the correct reading in 22:20, does this mean that one can or must identify thirty sayings in Prov 22:17–24:22? Many efforts have been made to mark out such an identification—the determination of thirty sayings in all—but no consensus has been reached, although the NIV distinguishes thirty sayings in its layout of the text. But perhaps the inability to delimit "thirty" sayings within the Hebrew text is not a major concern. The divisions proposed by scholars are in the general neighborhood of thirty, despite differences. Besides, it does not follow that the Israelite editor felt compelled to imitate the number "thirty." It could be understood as a reference to the work of Amenemope. Hence the reading of "thirty" in Prov 20:20 cannot be considered arbitrary.

Moreover, a much more enlightening fact has emerged from scholarly discussion: there is widespread agreement that the close resemblance to Amenemope ends at 23:11. This is very important. If one assumes that the Israelite author/editor was dependent upon the Egyptian work, he obviously displayed considerable independence in putting together his collection of proverbs. His dependence upon Amenemope was far from slavish. One may even express wonderment that there was not more imitation of the Egyptian original in the rest of this unit. Indeed, Washington has argued for "close affinities with a number of literary antecedents other than Amenemope" in 22:17–24:22 (*Wealth and Poverty*, 144). For example, 23:13–14 on the disciplining of children is also to be found in the proverbs of Ahiqar, 81–82 (Charlesworth, *OTP*, 2:498), where there are verbal similarities. It is to be admitted, however, that this is a very common theme throughout the ancient world. So common is it that it makes little sense to speak of dependency in any direction. Or another example: some verses (Prov 23:31–35) in the poem about drunkenness reflect, in Washington's view, common motifs and even the common order of a similar description in the Instruction of Any (text in Lichtheim, *AEL*, 2:137). These examples illustrate a common sharing of values about rearing children, and about inebriation, which would seem to be independently acceptable in almost any culture, and they serve as a caution not to conclude too easily to "dependence" of one source upon another.

(5) G. Bryce (*Legacy*, 101–2) has pointed to some telling details in the parallel between Prov 22:17–18 and the beginning of the first chapter of Amenemope. This consists in the occurrence of certain key phrases in which the Hebrew agrees with the sequence of these phrases as they appear in the Egyptian work (3:9–15; cf. *AEL*, 2:149): your ear(s)/your ear; hear/hear; words/sayings; your heart/your heart; it is pleasant/it profits; casket of your belly/your belly; your lips/your tongue. Yet, it is all the more remarkable that in the midst of this similarity the note of trust in the Lord appears in Prov 23:19, almost as a bolt out of the blue, and is noticeably absent from the beginning of Amenemope (which itself is marked by a religious spirit). Obviously, this reference to trust is due to the Israelite editor, who is working with his own premises, even on the supposition that he found certain lines of Amenemope agreeable to his purpose.

(6) Several other similarities have been pointed out. Not all are so remarkable as to call for discussion here. But it is interesting that the first admonition after the introduction in Prov 22:17–21, and also after the corresponding introduction in Amenemope, prohibits robbing the poor. The Hebrew text specifies the familiar "in the gates," i.e., in a judicial case, and also notes that the Lord will plead their cause. The Egyptian passage is in Amenemope 4:4–5; cf. *AEL*, 2:150. One of the principal themes in Amenemope is the "heated man," the irascible person (4:17; 6:21; cf. *AEL*, 2:150). Bryce remarks (*Legacy*, 90) that "of the seven proverbs dealing with the 'hot' and the 'silent' man in Proverbs, four verses provide almost exact equivalents: Prov. 15:18, 22:24, 29:22, and 17:27." Let Prov 22:24–25 serve as an example: "Do not be friendly with an irascible person, and do not associate with the wrathful, lest you learn his ways and get yourself ensnared."

Thus far, we have noted even the same sequence in both sources. But in 22:26–27 the advice against going surety for another is simply absent from the Egyptian work. The warning that one must respect the boundary mark of the lands (Prov 22:28) is matched by a similar prohibition, but repeated several times in Amenemope (7:11–15; 8:9; *AEL*, 2:151–52). The skill that merits service at the royal court (Prov 23:23) seems to reflect the reward of an Egyptian scribe: he is worthy of being a courtier (27:15–17; *AEL*, 2:162; this is found at the end of the Teaching of Amenemope). The caution concerning eating with a ruler (Prov 23:1–3) finds an echo (only a slight one) in Amenemope, 23:13–20, e.g., "Do not eat in the presence of an official . . . Look at the bowl that is before you, and let it serve your needs . . ." (*AEL*, 2:160). The biblical admonition concerning the pursuit of wealth (23:4–5) is very brief compared to the series of admonitions in Amenemope, 9:10–10:15; *AEL*, 2:152–53, which are indeed very edifying. There is an interesting point of comparison in the manner in which riches can disappear: in both works, the flight of riches to the sky is compared to winged animals, "eagle/geese." Other comparisons can be made between the two sources, but these can suffice to give the flavor of the relationship.

(7) Conclusion: the strongest elements of the evidence for dependence have been briefly indicated. What conclusions can be drawn? That the Egyptian source was known, in *some* form or other, and utilized in this section of Proverbs seems undeniable. But puzzles remain. Why did the Israelite source not make greater use of Amenemope? After all, 22:17–23:11 is a very brief portion. Another question: Why do the selections come from such disparate parts of the Egyptian source? This would seem to indicate the rather independent nature of the biblical writer. But there was a lot more in Amenemope that could easily and profitably have been used. And still another consideration: the similarities to Amenemope are not limited to Prov 22:17–23:11. Other chapters of Proverbs reveal connections with Amenemope, a kind of one-on-one correspondence, that would suggest some kind of dependence. One example: the "better" sayings in Amenemope 9:5–8 (*AEL*, 2:152, and repeated in 16:13–14; *AEL*, 2:156) are as follows: "Better is poverty in the hand of the god, / Than wealth in the storehouse; / Better is bread with a happy heart / Than wealth with vexation." This can be compared to Prov 15:16–17, "Better a little with fear of the Lord, / than great treasure and with it trouble. / Better a dish of herbs, but with love, / than a well-fed ox, but with hatred." And still another saying from Amenemope (8:19–20; *AEL*, 2:151) is comparable to those we have just instanced: "Better is a bushel given you by the god, / Than five thousand through wrongdoing." However, it is impossible to trace the direction of influences. These and similar proverbs could have been common property, as it were, throughout the ancient Near East, providing a store that anyone could choose from, and also shape to another end. The comparison with Amenemope does not exhaust the issue of "influences" on the book of Proverbs. We have mentioned above some similarities to the sayings of Ahiqar; see also the *Excursus on International Wisdom*.

295

Index of Authors Cited

Index of Biblical and Other Ancient Texts

The Old Testament

New Testament

Apocrypha

Other Ancient Texts

A Select Index of Principal Subjects